# Student, Parent, Teacher
# Internet Resources

Science Online   glencoe.com

Access your Student Edition on the Internet so you don't need to bring your textbook home every night. You can link to features and get additional practice with these Online Study Tools.

**Check out the following features on your Online Learning Center:**

## Study Tools

- Animated Illustrations
- Section Self-Check Quizzes
- Chapter Test Practice
- Intermediate-Level Science Examination Practice

- Vocabulary PuzzleMaker
- Interactive Tutor
- Multilingual Science Glossary
- Online Student Edition
- BrainPOP Movies

## Extensions

- Virtual Labs
- Microscopy Links
- Periodic Table Links
- Career Links

- Prescreened Web Links
- WebQuest Project
- Science Fair Ideas
- Internet Labs

## For Teachers

- Teacher Bulletin Board
- Teaching Today, and much more!

# SAFETY SYMBOLS

| SAFETY SYMBOLS | HAZARD | EXAMPLES | PRECAUTION | REMEDY |
|---|---|---|---|---|
| DISPOSAL | Special disposal procedures need to be followed. | certain chemicals, living organisms | Do not dispose of these materials in the sink or trash can. | Dispose of wastes as directed by your teacher. |
| BIOLOGICAL | Organisms or other biological materials that might be harmful to humans | bacteria, fungi, blood, unpreserved tissues, plant materials | Avoid skin contact with these materials. Wear mask or gloves. | Notify your teacher if you suspect contact with material. Wash hands thoroughly. |
| EXTREME TEMPERATURE | Objects that can burn skin by being too cold or too hot | boiling liquids, hot plates, dry ice, liquid nitrogen | Use proper protection when handling. | Go to your teacher for first aid. |
| SHARP OBJECT | Use of tools or glassware that can easily puncture or slice skin | razor blades, pins, scalpels, pointed tools, dissecting probes, broken glass | Practice common-sense behavior and follow guidelines for use of the tool. | Go to your teacher for first aid. |
| FUME | Possible danger to respiratory tract from fumes | ammonia, acetone, nail polish remover, heated sulfur, moth balls | Make sure there is good ventilation. Never smell fumes directly. Wear a mask. | Leave foul area and notify your teacher immediately. |
| ELECTRICAL | Possible danger from electrical shock or burn | improper grounding, liquid spills, short circuits, exposed wires | Double-check setup with teacher. Check condition of wires and apparatus. | Do not attempt to fix electrical problems. Notify your teacher immediately. |
| IRRITANT | Substances that can irritate the skin or mucous membranes of the respiratory tract | pollen, moth balls, steel wool, fiberglass, potassium permanganate | Wear dust mask and gloves. Practice extra care when handling these materials. | Go to your teacher for first aid. |
| CHEMICAL | Chemicals can react with and destroy tissue and other materials | bleaches such as hydrogen peroxide; acids such as sulfuric acid, hydrochloric acid; bases such as ammonia, sodium hydroxide | Wear goggles, gloves, and an apron. | Immediately flush the affected area with water and notify your teacher. |
| TOXIC | Substance may be poisonous if touched, inhaled, or swallowed. | mercury, many metal compounds, iodine, poinsettia plant parts | Follow your teacher's instructions. | Always wash hands thoroughly after use. Go to your teacher for first aid. |
| FLAMMABLE | Flammable chemicals may be ignited by open flame, spark, or exposed heat. | alcohol, kerosene, potassium permanganate | Avoid open flames and heat when using flammable chemicals. | Notify your teacher immediately. Use fire safety equipment if applicable. |
| OPEN FLAME | Open flame in use, may cause fire. | hair, clothing, paper, synthetic materials | Tie back hair and loose clothing. Follow teacher's instruction on lighting and extinguishing flames. | Notify your teacher immediately. Use fire safety equipment if applicable. |

 **Eye Safety** Proper eye protection should be worn at all times by anyone performing or observing science activities.

 **Clothing Protection** This symbol appears when substances could stain or burn clothing.

 **Animal Safety** This symbol appears when safety of animals and students must be ensured.

 **Handwashing** After the lab, wash hands with soap and water before removing goggles.

Glencoe Science

# New York Science

### Grade 7

glencoe.com

NATIONAL GEOGRAPHIC

Glencoe

New York, New York    Columbus, Ohio    Chicago, Illinois    Peoria, Illinois    Woodland Hills, California

# New York Grade 7

The Statue of Liberty's green color is caused by oxidation, a chemical reaction between its copper exterior and water vapor in the air. Although the Eastern Blue bird, the New York State bird, was once an endangered species, conservation efforts have resulted in the species' gradual recovery. Niagara Falls was formed from the erosion of rock layers by water draining from the Great Lakes following the last ice age.

 **Glencoe**

Send all inquiries to:
Glencoe/McGraw-Hill
8787 Orion Place
Columbus, OH 43240-4027

ISBN: 978-0-07-877864-3
MHID: 0-07-877864-6

4 5 6 7 8 9 10  071/055  12 11 10 09 08

# Contents In Brief

## Authors

**NATIONAL GEOGRAPHIC**
Education Division
Washington, D.C.

**Alton Biggs**
Retired Biology Teacher
Allen High School
Allen, TX

**Lucy Daniel, PhD**
Teacher/Consultant
Rutherford County Schools
Rutherfordton, NC

**Ralph M. Feather Jr., PhD**
Assistant Professor
Department of Educational Studies and
Secondary Education
Bloomsburg University
Bloomsburg, PA

**Edward Ortleb**
Science Consultant
St. Louis, MO

**Susan Leach Snyder**
Retired Teacher, Consultant
Jones Middle School
Upper Arlington, OH

**Dinah Zike**
Educational Consultant
Dinah-Might Activities, Inc.
San Antonio, TX

## Series Consultants

### CONTENT

**Alton J. Banks, PhD**
Director of the Faculty Center
for Teaching and Learning
North Carolina State University
Raleigh, NC

**Jack Cooper**
Ennis High School
Ennis, TX

**Sandra K. Enger, PhD**
Associate Director,
Associate Professor
UAH Institute for Science Education
Huntsville, AL

**David G. Haase, PhD**
North Carolina State University
Raleigh, NC

**Michael A. Hoggarth, PhD**
Department of Life and
Earth Sciences
Otterbein College
Westerville, OH

**Jerome A. Jackson, PhD**
Whitaker Eminent Scholar in Science
Program Director
Center for Science, Mathematics,
and Technology Education
Florida Gulf Coast University
Fort Meyers, FL

**William C. Keel, PhD**
Department of Physics
and Astronomy
University of Alabama
Tuscaloosa, AL

**Linda McGaw**
Science Program Coordinator
Advanced Placement Strategies, Inc.
Dallas, TX

**Madelaine Meek**
Physics Consultant Editor
Lebanon, OH

**Robert Nierste**
Science Department Head
Hendrick Middle School, Plano ISD
Plano, TX

**Connie Rizzo, MD, PhD**
Depatment of Science/Math
Marymount Manhattan College
New York, NY

**v**

## Teacher Advisory Board

## Student Advisory Board

The Glencoe middle school science Student Advisory Board taking a timeout at COSI, a science museum in Columbus, Ohio.

# Contents

# Geology—2

In each chapter, look for these opportunities for review and assessment:
- Reading Checks
- Caption Questions
- Section Review
- Chapter Study Guide
- Chapter Review
- Intermediate-Level Science Examination Practice
- Online practice at **glencoe.com**

# Contents

**chapter 4**

## Weathering and Erosion—92

**chapter 5**

## Clues to Earth's Past—118

**chapter 6**

## Plate Tectonics—148

In each chapter, look for these opportunities for review and assessment:
- Reading Checks
- Caption Questions
- Section Review
- Chapter Study Guide
- Chapter Review
- Intermediate-Level Science Examination Practice
- Online practice at glencoe.com

# Contents

**unit 2**

# Interactions Between Matter and Energy—208

# Contents

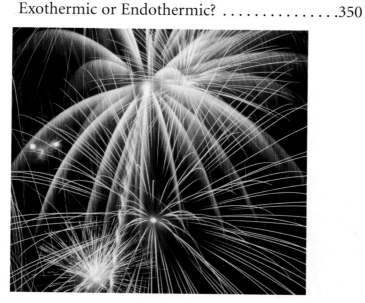

In each chapter, look for these opportunities for review and assessment:
- **Reading Checks**
- **Caption Questions**
- **Section Review**
- **Chapter Study Guide**
- **Chapter Review**
- **Intermediate-Level Science Examination Practice**
- **Online practice at glencoe.com**

# Contents

In each chapter, look for these opportunities for review and assessment:
- Reading Checks
- Caption Questions
- Section Review
- Chapter Study Guide
- Chapter Review
- Intermediate-Level Science Examination Practice
- Online practice at glencoe.com

# Contents

# Student Resources—630

# Cross-Curricular Readings

## NATIONAL GEOGRAPHIC Unit Openers

## NATIONAL GEOGRAPHIC VISUALIZING

Content Details

# Cross-Curricular Readings

available as a video lab on DVD

## Mini LAB

Mini **LAB** *Try at Home*

LABS

 available as a video lab on DVD

Content Details

## One-Page Labs

# LABS

Content Details

# Activities

## Applying Math

## Applying Science

**INTEGRATE**

**Science Online**

### Intermediate-Level Science Examination Practice

# The Glencoe Formula

for successfully mastering the New York Intermediate Level Science Core Curriculum.

## Learning + Practicing = *Success!*

**Learning**

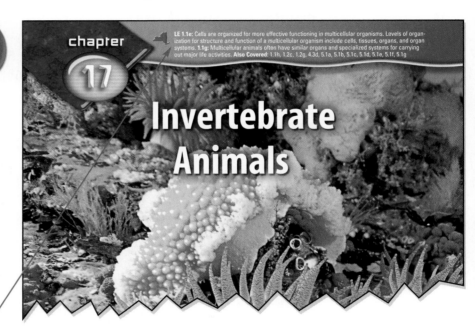

**chapter 17**

LE 1.1e: Cells are organized for more effective functioning in multicellular organisms. Levels of organization for structure and function of a multicellular organism include cells, tissues, organs, and organ systems. 1.1g: Multicellular animals often have similar organs and specialized systems for carrying out major life activities. **Also Covered:** 1.1h, 1.2c, 1.2g, 4.3d, 5.1a, 5.1b, 5.1c, 5.1d, 5.1e, 5.1f, 5.1g

## Invertebrate Animals

**Major Understandings**
- The beginning of each chapter lists the Major Understandings you'll learn in that chapter.

- The beginning of each section lists the Major Understandings you'll learn in that section.

**section 1**

LE 1.1h: Living things are classified by shared characteristics on the cellular and organism level. In classifying organisms, biologists consider details of internal and external structures. Biological classification systems are arranged from general (kingdom) to specific (species). **Also Covered:** LE 1.1e, 1.1g, 1.2c, 1.2g, 5.1a, 5.1c, 5.1d, 5.1e, 5.1f, 5.1g

## What is an animal?

**as you read**

*What* **You'll Learn**
- **Identify** the characteristics of animals.
- **Differentiate** between vertebrates and invertebrates.
- **Explain** how the symmetry of animals differs.

*Why* **It's Important**
All animals have characteristics in common.

**⨀ Review Vocabulary**
**organelle:** structure in the cytoplasm of a eukaryotic cell that act as storage site, process

### Animal Characteristics

If you asked ten people for a characteristic common to all animals, you might get ten different answers or a few repeated answers. Look at the animals in **Figure 1.** What are their common characteristics? What makes an animal an animal?

1. Animals are many-celled organisms that are made of different kinds of cells. These cells might digest food, get rid of wastes, help in reproduction, or be part of systems that have these functions.

2. Most animal cells have a nucleus and organelles. The nucleus and many organelles are surrounded by a membrane. This type of cell is called a eukaryotic (yew ker ee AH tihk) cell.

3. Animals cannot make their own food. Some animals eat plants to supply their energy needs. Some animals eat other animals, some eat both plants and animals.

# The Glencoe Formula

## Practicing

**Major Understanding Focus**
- Focuses on and assesses Major Understandings presented in that section

**Living Environment**

**1.1h: Summarize** how scientists classify living things.

**New York Intermediate Level Science Examination Practice**
Two pages created specifically for New York covering the New York Intermediate-Level Science Core Curriculum

Content Details

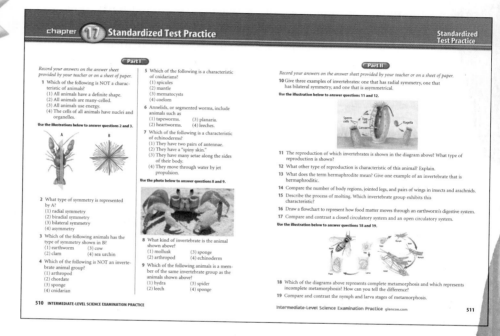

## Test–Taking Tips

✓ Go to bed early the night before the test. You will think more clearly after a good night's rest.

✓ Read each problem carefully, underline key words, and think about ways to solve the problem before answering the question.

✓ Relax. It's natural to be nervous when taking a test. Just do your best.

✓ Try to answer each question in order. If you are unsure of an answer, mark your best guess and then mark the question in your test booklet. This will be a reminder to come back to the question at the end of the test.

✓ Think positively. Some problems may seem hard to you, but you may be able to figure out what to do if you read each question carefully.

✓ If no figure is provided, draw one. If one is furnished, mark it up to help you solve the problem.

✓ When you have finished each problem, reread it to make sure your answer is complete and reasonable.

✓ Make sure that the number of the question on the answer sheet matches the number of the question on which you are working in your test booklet.

**XXV**

## The Intermediate-Level Science Core Curriculum

The New York State Intermediate Level Science Core Curriculum was written to guide instruction and assessment for Standards 1, 2, 4, 6, and 7 of the New York State Learning Standards for Mathematics, Science, and Technology. The standards have been organized into Key Ideas, Performance Indicators, and Major Understandings.

- **Key Ideas** are broad, unifying, general statements of what students need to know.
- **Performance Indicators** for each Key Idea are statements of what students should be able to do to provide evidence that they understand the Key Idea.
- **Major Understandings** provide specific detail about the concepts underlying each Performance Indicator.

## Interpreting Major Understanding Identifiers

Major Understanding identifiers appear at the beginning of each chapter and section and are organized into the following categories:

| | |
|---|---|
| **LE** | The Living Environment |
| **PS** | The Physical Setting |
| **AID** | Analysis Inquiry and Design |
| **IS** | Information Systems |
| **ICT** | Interconnectedness: Common Themes |
| **IPS** | Interdisciplinary Problem Solving |

Here is how to interpret the Major Understanding for **LE 1.1e.**

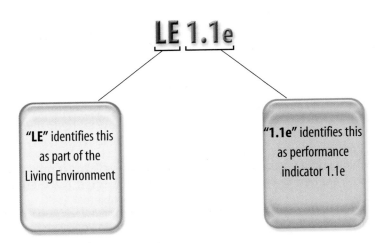

**LE 1.1e**

"**LE**" identifies this as part of the Living Environment

"**1.1e**" identifies this as performance indicator 1.1e

# STANDARDS 1, 2, 6, AND 7: EXPANDED PROCESS SKILLS

*Science process skills should be based on a series of discoveries. Students learn most effectively when they have a central role in the discovery process. To that end, Standards 1, 2, 6, and 7 incorporate in the Intermediate Core Curriculum a student centered, problem-solving approach to intermediate science. The following is an expanded version of the skills found in Standards 1, 2, 6, and 7 of the Learning Standards for Mathematics, Science, and Technology. This list is not intended to be an all-inclusive list of the content or skills that teachers are expected to incorporate into their curriculum. It should be a goal of the instructor to encourage science process skills that will provide students with background and curiosity sufficient to prompt investigation of important issues in the world around them.*

| Standards | Page Numbers |
|---|---|
| **STANDARD 1—Analysis, Inquiry, and Design** Students will use mathematical analysis, scientific inquiry, and engineering design, as appropriate, to pose questions, seek answers, and develop solutions. | |
| **MATHEMATICAL ANALYSIS:** *Key Idea 1:* Abstraction and symbolic representation are used to communicate mathematically. | |
| M1.1 Extend mathematical notation and symbolism to include variables and algebraic expressions in order to describe and compare quantities and express mathematical relationships. | 157, 198, 216, 338, 371, 396, 531, 587, 605 |
| M1.1a identify independent and dependent variables | 11, 110–111, 260–261, 350–351, 374-375, 408–409, 436-437, 504–505 |
| M1.1c apply mathematical equations to describe relationships among variables in the natural world | 157, 198, 216, 338, 371, 396, 531, 587, 605 |
| *Key Idea 2:* Deductive and inductive reasoning are used to reach mathematical conclusions. | |
| M2.1a interpolate and extrapolate from data | 61, 134, 157, 168–169, 200–201, 232–233, 290–291, 417 |
| M2.1b quantify patterns and trends | 157, 168–169, 232–233 |
| *Key Idea 3:* Critical thinking skills are used in the solution of mathematical problems. | |
| M3.1 Apply mathematical knowledge to solve real-world problems and problems that arise from the investigation of mathematical ideas, using representations such as pictures, charts, and tables. | 25, 291, 233 |
| M3.1a use appropriate scientific tools to solve problems about the natural world | 7, 8, 33, 84–85, 140–141, 157, 168–169, 200–201, 232–233, 290–291, 349, 368, 370, 534–535 |
| **SCIENTIFIC INQUIRY:** *Key Idea 1:* The central purpose of scientific inquiry is to develop explanations of natural phenomena in a continuing, creative process. | |
| S1.1a formulate questions about natural phenomena | 110–111, 260–261, 350–351, 374–375, 417, 504–505, 534–535, 566–567 |

| Standards | Page Numbers |
|---|---|
| S1.1b  identify appropriate references to investigate a question | 260–261 |
| S1.1c  refine and clarify questions so that they are subject to scientific investigation | 260–261 |
| S1.2  Construct explanations independently for natural phenomena, especially by proposing preliminary visual models of phenomena. | 622–623 |
| S1.2a  independently formulate a hypothesis | 7, 110–111, 134, 260–261, 350–351, 408–409, 436–437, 566–567 |
| S1.2b  propose a model of a natural phenomenon | 83, 110–111, 140–141, 149, 152, 366, 513, 534–535 |
| S1.2c  differentiate among observations, inferences, predictions, and explanations | 61, 566–567 |
| S1.3  Represent, present, and defend their proposed explanations of everyday observations so that they can be understood and assessed by others. | 5, 61, 83, 84–85, 200–201, 260–261, 284, 361, 388, 417, 513, 534–535, 566–567, 622–623 |
| S1.4  Seek to clarify, to assess critically, and to reconcile with their own thinking the ideas presented by others, including peers, teachers, authors, and scientists. | 5, 23, 140–141, 241, 260–261, 272, 284, 534–535, 566–567 |
| *Key Idea 2:*  Beyond the use of reasoning and consensus, scientific inquiry involves the testing of proposed explanations involving the use of conventional techniques and procedures and usually requiring considerable ingenuity. | |
| S2.1  Use conventional techniques and those of their own design to make further observations and refine their explanations, guided by a need for more information. | 110–111, 260–261, 350–351, 374–375, 408–409, 436–437, 504–505 |
| S2.1a  demonstrate appropriate safety techniques | 5, 11, 19, 23, 24, 33, 36, 41, 51, 52, 61, 67, 76, 83, 84, 93, 97, 98, 100, 110, 119, 121, 134, 136, 140, 149, 152, 158, 163, 168, 177, 179, 188, 193, 200, 211, 217, 224, 228, 232, 241, 245, 256, 259, 260, 269, 272, 284, 286, 290, 299, |

| Standards | Page Numbers |
|---|---|
| | 503, 524, 530, 534–535, 543, 566–567, 575, 579, 584, 588, 592–593, 601, 610, 614, 616 |
| S2.2a include appropriate safety procedures | 350–351, 374–375, 504–505 |
| S2.2b design scientific investigations (e.g., observing, describing, and comparing; collecting samples; seeking more information, conducting a controlled experiment; discovering new objects or phenomena; making models) | 8, 11, 110–111, 260–261, 322–323, 350–351, 374–375, 408–409, 436–437, 504–505 |
| S2.2c design a simple controlled experiment | 9, 11, 36, 260–261, 350–351, 374–375, 408–409, 436–437, 504–505 |
| S2.2d identify independent variables (manipulated), dependent variables (responding), and constants in a simple controlled experiment | 11, 24–25, 260–261, 350–351, 374–375, 408–409, 436–437, 470–471, 504–505 |
| S2.2e choose appropriate sample size and number of trials | 350–351 |
| S2.3 Carry out their research proposals, recording observations and measurements (e.g., lab notes, audiotape, computer disk, videotape) to help assess the explanation. | 110–111, 260–261, 350–351, 374–375, 408–409, 436–437, 504–505 |
| S2.3a use appropriate safety procedures | 193, 322–323, 350–351, 374–375, 388, 408–409, 436–437, 504–505 |
| S2.3b conduct a scientific investigation | 11, 193, 200–201, 245, 260–261, 322–323, 350–351, 374–375, 388, 408–409, 427, 436–437, 504–505, 566–567, 592–593 |
| S2.3c collect quantitative and qualitative data | 24–25, 200–201, 245, 260–261, 286, |

| Standards | Page Numbers |
|---|---|
| | 290–291, 322–323, 336, 350–351, 374–375, 388, 408–409, 427, 436–437, 461, 470–471, 503, 504–505, 566–567, 575, 579, 584, 592–593, 614 |
| *Key Idea 3:* The observations made while testing proposed explanations, when analyzed using conventional and invented methods, provide new insights into phenomena. | |
| S3.1 Design charts, tables, graphs, and other representations of observations in conventional and creative ways to help them address their research question or hypothesis. | 25, 111, 233, 261, 291, 351, 375, 417, 505, 535, 567 |
| S3.1a organize results, using appropriate graphs, diagrams, data tables, and other models to show relationships | 24–25, 51 52–53, 67, 84–85, 100, 110–111, 140–141, 152, 157, 163, 168–169, 177, 200–201, 224, 232–233, 256, 260–261, 290–291, 310, 322–323, 349, 350–351, 368, 370, 374–375, 408–409, 417, 427, 436–437, 457, 470–471, 481, 503, 504–505, 524, 534–535, 566–567, 584, 592–593, 614 |
| S3.1b generate and use scales, create legends, and appropriately label axes | 36, 51, 52–53, 93, 168–169, 366 |
| S3.2 Interpret the organized data to answer the research question or hypothesis and to gain insight into the problem. | 21, 49, 67, 107, 138, 160, 257, 287, 311, 432, 468, 494, 552 |
| S3.2a accurately describe the procedures used and the data gathered | 24–25, 67, 76, 83, 97, 98, 100, 110–111, 119, 136, 177, 179, 188, 193, 200–201, 211, 232–233, 241, 245, 256, 259, 260–261, |

| Standards | Page Numbers |
|---|---|
| | 269, 284, 290–291, 310, 313, 315, 322–323, 331, 336, 349, 374–375, 386, 408–409, 419, 427, 436–437, 453, 457, 470–471, 492, 504–505, 524, 534–535, 566–567, 592–593, 622–623 |
| S3.2b  identify sources of error and the limitations of data collected | 5, 24–25, 98, 140–141, 217, 260–261, 350–351, 388, 534–535, 566–567 |
| S3.2c  evaluate the original hypothesis in light of the data | 19, 23, 52–53, 93, 110–111, 260–261, 374–375 |
| S3.2d  formulate and defend explanations and conclusions as they relate to scientific phenomena | 18, 110–111, 163, 168–169, 177, 179, 188, 193, 200–201, 217, 224, 228, 232–233, 241, 256, 260–261, 269, 286, 290–291, 299, 310, 313, 315, 322–323, 331, 336, 346, 349, 350–351, 368, 374–375, 383, 386, 388, 405, 408–409, 419, 427, 430, 436–437, 445, 453, 457, 461, 470–471, 481, 492, 501, 503, 504–505, 524, 527, 530, 534–535, 557, 565, 566–567, 575, 579, 584, 588, 592–593, 601, 610, 614, 616, 622–623 |
| S3.2e  form and defend a logical argument about cause-and-effect relationships in an investigation | 110–111, 157, 260–261, 622–623 |

| Standards | Page Numbers |
|---|---|
| S3.2f  make predictions based on experimental data | 97, 121, 136, 259, 260–261, 272, 284, 290–291, 322–323, 374–375, 408–409, 436–437, 470–471 |
| S3.2g  suggest improvements and recommendations for further studying | 18, 366, 622–623 |
| S3.2h  use and interpret graphs and data tables | 24–25, 110–111, 260–261, 322–323 |
| S3.3  Modify their personal understanding of phenomena based on evaluation of their hypothesis. | 36, 52–53, 84–85, 110–111, 177, 260–261, 315, 322–323, 350–351, 370 |
| **ENGINEERING DESIGN:** *Key Idea 1:* Engineering design is an iterative process involving modeling and optimization (finding the best solution within given constraints); this process is used to develop technological solutions to problems within given constraints. | |
| T1.1a  identify a scientific or human need that is subject to a technological solution which applies scientific principles | 12 |
| T1.2  Locate and utilize a range of printed, electronic, and human information resources to obtain ideas. | 2–3, 208–209, 358–359, 478–479 |
| T1.2a  use all available information systems for a preliminary search that addresses the need | 23, 168–169 |
| T1.4a  design and construct a model of the product or process | 140–141, 534–535 |
| T1.4b  construct a model of the product or process | 140–141, 177, 534–535 |
| T1.5a  test a design | 140–141 |
| T1.5b  evaluate a design | 140–141 |

| Standards | Page Numbers |
|---|---|
| **STANDARD 2—Information Systems** Students will access, generate, process, and transfer information, using appropriate technologies. | |
| *Key Idea 1:* Information technology is used to retrieve, process, and communicate information as a tool to enhance learning. | |
| 1.2 Use spreadsheets and database software to collect, process, display, and analyze information. Students access needed information from electronic databases and on-line telecommunication services. | 534–535 |
| 1.3 Systematically obtain accurate and relevant information pertaining to a particular topic from a range of sources, including local and national media, libraries, museums, governmental agencies, industries, and individuals. | 23, 33 |
| 1.4a collect the data, using the appropriate, available tool | 36, 41 |
| 1.4b organize the data | 36 |
| 1.4c use the collected data to communicate a scientific concept | 36 |
| 1.5 Use simple modeling programs to make predictions. | 177, 200–201 |
| *Key Idea 3:* Information technology can have positive and negative impacts on society, depending upon how it is used. | |
| 3.2 Describe applications of information technology in mathematics, science, and other technologies that address needs and solve problems in the community. | 6–12, 14 |
| **STANDARD 6—Interconnectedness: Common Themes** Students will understand the relationships and common themes that connect mathematics, science, and technology and apply the themes to these and other areas of learning. | |
| **MODELS:** *Key Idea 2:* Models are simplified representations of objects, structures, or systems used in analysis, explanation, interpretation, or design. | |
| 2.1 Select an appropriate model to begin the search for answers or solutions to a question or problem. | 44–46, 48–50, 534–535 |
| 2.2 Use models to study processes that cannot be studied directly (e.g., when the real process is too slow, too fast, or too dangerous for direct observation). | 44–46, 48–50 |
| 2.3 Demonstrate the effectiveness of different models to represent the same thing and the same model to represent different things. | 44–46, 48–50 |

| Standards | Page Numbers |
|---|---|

**STANDARD 7—Interdisciplinary Problem Solving** Students will apply the knowledge and thinking skills of mathematics, science, and technology to address real-life problems and make informed decisions.

**CONNECTIONS:** *Key Idea 1:* The knowledge and skills of mathematics, science, and technology are used together to make informed decisions and solve problems, especially those relating to issues of science/technology/society, consumer decision making, design, and inquiry into phenomena.

| Standards | Page Numbers |
|---|---|
| 1.2 Make informed consumer decisions by seeking answers to appropriate questions about products, services, and systems; determining the cost/benefit and risk/benefit tradeoffs; and applying this knowledge to a potential purchase. | 566–567 |
| 1.3 Design solutions to real-world problems of general social interest related to home, school, or community using scientific experimentation to inform the solution and applying mathematical concepts and reasoning to assist in developing a solution. | 6–12, 14, 534–535 |
| 1.4 Describe and explain phenomena by designing and conducting investigations involving systematic observations, accurate measurements, and the identification and control of variables; by inquiring into relevant mathematical ideas; and by using mathematical and technological tools and procedures to assist in the investigation. | 110, 260, 350, 374, 408, 436, 504 |

**STRATEGIES:** *Key Idea 2:* Solving interdisciplinary problems involves a variety of skills and strategies, including effective work habits; gathering and processing information; generating and analyzing ideas; realizing ideas; making connections among the common themes of mathematics, science, and technology; and presenting results.

| Standards | Page Numbers |
|---|---|
| 2.1 Students participate in an extended, culminating mathematics, science, and technology project. The project would require students to:<br>• **Working Effectively:** Contributing to the work of a brainstorming group, laboratory partnership, cooperative learning group, or project team; planning procedures; identify and managing responsibilities of team members; and staying on task, whether working alone or as part of a group.<br>• **Gathering and Processing Information:** Accessing information from printed media, electronic data bases, and community resources and using the information to develop a definition of the problem and to research possible solutions.<br>• **Generating and Analyzing Ideas:** Developing ideas for proposed solutions, investigating ideas, collecting data, and showing relationships and patterns in the data.<br>• **Common Themes:** Observing examples of common unifying themes, applying them to the problem, and using them to better understand the dimensions of the problem.<br>• **Realizing Ideas:** Constructing components or models, arriving at a solution, and evaluating the result.<br>• **Presenting Results:** Using a variety of media to present the solution and to communicate the results. | 110–111, 260–261, 322–323, 350–351, 374–375, 408–409, 436–437 |

| Standards | Page Numbers |
|---|---|
| **PROCESS SKILLS BASED ON STANDARD 4** | |
| **General Skills** | |
| 1.  follow safety procedures in the classroom and laboratory | 5, 11, 19, 23, 24, 33, 36, 41, 51, 52, 61, 67, 76, 83, 84, 93, 97, 98, 100, 110, 119, 121, 134, 136, 140, 149, 152, 158, 163, 168, 177, 179, 188, 193, 200, 211, 217, 224, 228, 232, 241, 245, 256, 259, 260, 269, 272, 284, 286, 290, 299, 310, 313, 315, 322, 331, 336, 346, 349, 350, 361, 366, 368, 370, 374, 383, 386, 388, 405, 408, 417, 419, 427, 430, 436, 445, 453, 457, 461, 470, 481, 492, 501, 503, 504, 513, 524, 527, 530, 534, 543, 551, 557, 565, 566, 575, 579, 584, 588, 592, 601, 610, 614, 616, 622, 641–643, 644–654 |
| 2.  safely and accurately use the following measurement tools: | |
| • metric ruler | 5, 24–25, 51, 52–53, 157, 200–201, 388, 408–409 |
| • balance | 110, 349, 551, 457, 470–471 |
| • stopwatch | 110, 349, 350–351, 427, 445, 470–471 |
| • graduated cylinder | 193, 245, 156, 259, 349, 350–351, 436, 457, 551 |

| Standards | Page Numbers |
|---|---|
| 3. use appropriate units for measured or calculated values | 157, 198, 216, 338, 371, 396, 531, 587, 605 |
| 4. recognize and analyze patterns and trends | 5, 11, 19, 24–25, 83, 84–85, 93, 111, 134, 136, 152, 158, 163, 168–169, 177, 179, 193, 200–201, 211, 224, 232–233, 260–261, 284, 290–291, 299, 313, 349, 350–351, 408–409, 445, 453, 457, 470, 501, 503, 504–505, 527, 579, 592–593, 601, 644, 646, 648, 649, 651 |
| 5. classify objects according to an established scheme and a student-generated scheme | 284 |
| 7. sequence events | 134, 136 |
| 8. identify cause-and-effect relationships | 83, 97, 134, 163, 193, 217, 224, 232–233, 260–261, 299, 310, 313, 315, 322–323, 349, 350–351, 386, 427, 436–437, 445, 504–505, 579, 588, 592–593, 557, 614, 616, 623, 646, 648, 653 |
| 9. use indicators and interpret results | 290–291, 322–323, 457 |
| **Living Environment Skills** | |
| 1. manipulate a compound microscope to view microscopic objects | 361, 368, 584, 614, 679 |
| 3. prepare a wet mount slide | 368, 584, 614, 679 |
| 6. classify living things according to a student-generated scheme and an established scheme | 565, 639, 684–687 |
| 8. identify pulse points and pulse rates | 427 |
| 9. identify structure and function relationships in organisms | 366, 368, 374–375, 383, 419, 461, 492, 503, 524, 527, 530, 557, 614 |

| Standards | Page Numbers |
|---|---|
| **Physical Setting Skills** | |
| 1. given the latitude and longitude of a location, indicate its position on a map and determine the latitude and longitude of a given location on a map | 41 |
| 2. using identification tests and a flow chart, identify mineral samples | 84–85 |
| 4. plot the location of recent earthquake and volcanic activity on a map and identify patterns of distribution | 168–169 |
| 6. measure the angular elevation of an object, using appropriate instruments | 51, 52–53 |
| 7. generate and interpret field maps including topographic and weather maps | 51, 52–53, 644 |
| 8. predict the characteristics of an air mass based on the origin of the air mass | 678 |
| 9. measure weather variables such as wind speed and direction, relative humidity, barometric pressure, etc. | 678 |
| 10. determine the density of liquids, and regular- and irregular-shaped solids | 259 |
| 11. determine the volume of a regular- and an irregular-shaped solid, using water displacement | 245 |
| 12. using the periodic table, identify an element as a metal, nonmetal, or noble gas | 284 |
| 13. determine the identity of an unknown element, using physical and chemical properties | 284 |
| 14. using appropriate resources, separate the parts of a mixture | 290–291 |

**STANDARD 4—The Living Environment** Students will understand and apply scientific concepts, principles, and theories pertaining to the physical setting and living environment and recognize the historical development of ideas in science.

*Key Idea 1:* Living things are both similar to and different from each other and from nonliving things.

**PERFORMANCE INDICATOR 1.1** *Compare and contrast the parts of plants, animals, and one-celled organisms.*

| | |
|---|---|
| 1.1a  Living things are composed of cells. Cells provide structure and carry on major functions to sustain life. Cells are usually microscopic in size. | 362 |
| 1.1b  The way in which cells function is similar in all living things. Cells grow and divide, producing more cells. Cells take in nutrients, which they use to provide energy for the work that cells do and to make the materials that a cell or an organism needs. | 362–367 |
| 1.1c  Most cells have cell membranes, genetic material, and cytoplasm. Some cells have a cell wall and/or chloroplasts. Many cells have a nucleus. | 364, 362–367, 544–547, 549, 550–555, 556–564, 602–608, 615–621 |
| 1.1d  Some organisms are single cells; others, including humans, are multicellular. | 362–367, 602, 609–610, 612–613 |
| 1.1e  Cells are organized for more effective functioning in multicellular organisms. Levels of organization for structure and function of a multicellular organism include cells, tissues, organs, and organ systems. | 369, 482–484 |

| Standards | Page Numbers |
|---|---|
| 1.1f  Many plants have roots, stems, leaves, and reproductive structures. These organized groups of tissues are responsible for a plant's life activities. | 362–367, 544–547, 549 |
| 1.1g  Multicellular animals often have similar organs and specialized systems for carrying out major life activities. | 362–367, 482–484 |
| 1.1h  Living things are classified by shared characteristics on the cellular and organism level. In classifying organisms, biologists consider details of internal and external structures. Biological classification systems are arranged from general (kingdom) to specific (species). | 484, 485–489, 514–516, 518, 549 |

**PERFORMANCE INDICATOR 1.2** *Explain the functioning of the major human organ systems and their interactions.*

| Standards | Page Numbers |
|---|---|
| 1.2a  Each system is composed of organs and tissues which perform specific functions and interact with each other, e.g., digestion, gas exchange, excretion, circulation, locomotion, control, coordination, reproduction, and protection from disease. | 384, 389, 394, 399–407, 418–423, 425–426, 428–433, 434–435, 446–450, 458–461, 463–464, 465–469 |
| 1.2b  Tissues, organs, and organ systems help to provide all cells with nutrients, oxygen, and waste removal. | 384–387, 446–450 |
| 1.2c  The digestive system consists of organs that are responsible for the mechanical and chemical breakdown of food. The breakdown process results in molecules that can be absorbed and transported to cells. | 446, 482–484 |
| 1.2d  During respiration, cells use oxygen to release the energy stored in food. The respiratory system supplies oxygen and removes carbon dioxide (gas exchange). | 458 |
| 1.2e  The excretory system functions in the disposal of dissolved waste molecules, the elimination of liquid and gaseous wastes, and the removal of excess heat energy. | 465 |
| 1.2f  The circulatory system moves substances to and from cells, where they are needed or produced, responding to changing demands. | 418, 428, 434 |
| 1.2g  Locomotion, necessary to escape danger, obtain food and shelter, and reproduce, is accomplished by the interaction of the skeletal and muscular systems, and coordinated by the nervous system. | 390, 397, 482–484 |
| 1.2h  The nervous and endocrine systems interact to control and coordinate the body's responses to changes in the environment, and to regulate growth, development, and reproduction. Hormones are chemicals produced by the endocrine system; hormones regulate many body functions. | 399, 485–489 |
| 1.2j  Disease breaks down the structures or functions of an organism. Some diseases are the result of failures of the system. Other diseases are the result of damage by infection from other organisms (germ theory). Specialized cells protect the body from infectious disease. The chemicals they produce identify and destroy microbes that enter the body. | 418–423, 425–426, 428–433, 434–435, 458–461, 463–464, 602–608 |

| Standards | Page Numbers |
|---|---|

*Key Idea 3:* Individual organisms and species change over time.

**PERFORMANCE INDICATOR 3.1** *Describe sources of variation in organisms and their structures and relate the variations to survival.*

| | |
|---|---|
| 3.1b  Changes in environmental conditions can affect the survival of individual organisms with a particular trait. Small differences between parents and offspring can accumulate in successive generations so that descendants are very different from their ancestors. Individual organisms with certain traits are more likely to survive and have offspring than individuals without those traits. | 544–547, 549 |

**PERFORMANCE INDICATOR 3.2** *Describe factors responsible for competition within species and the significance of that competition.*

| | |
|---|---|
| 3.2a  In all environments, organisms with similar needs may compete with one another for resources. | 258 |
| 3.2b  Extinction of a species occurs when the environment changes and the adaptive characteristics of a species are insufficient to permit its survival. Extinction of species is common. Fossils are evidence that a great variety of species existed in the past. | 121 |
| 3.2c  Many thousands of layers of sedimentary rock provide evidence for the long history of Earth and for the long history of changing lifeforms whose remains are found in the rocks. Recently deposited rock layers are more likely to contain fossils resembling existing species. | 120–127, 128, 135 |

*Key Idea 4:*  The continuity of life is sustained through reproduction and development.

**PERFORMANCE INDICATOR 4.1** *Observe and describe the variations in reproductive patterns of organisms, including asexual and sexual reproduction.*

| | |
|---|---|
| 4.1a  Some organisms reproduce asexually. Other organisms reproduce sexually. Some organisms can reproduce both sexually and asexually. | 485–489, 544–547, 549, 609–610, 612–613, 615–621 |
| 4.1b  There are many methods of asexual reproduction, including division of a cell into two cells, or separation of part of an animal or plant from the parent, resulting in the growth of another individual. | 544–547, 549, 550–555 |
| 4.1d  Fertilization and/or development in organisms may be internal or external. | 529–533 |

**PERFORMANCE INDICATOR 4.3** *Observe and describe developmental patterns in selected plants and animals (e.g., insects, frogs, humans, seed-bearing plants).*

| | |
|---|---|
| 4.3d  Patterns of development vary among animals. In some species the young resemble the adult, while in others they do not. Some insects and amphibians undergo metamorphosis as they mature. | 497, 521 |
| 4.3e  Patterns of development vary among plants. In seed-bearing plants, seeds contain stored food for early development. Their later development into adulthood is characterized by varying patterns of growth from species to species. | 544–547, 549 |
| 4.3f  As an individual organism ages, various body structures and functions change. | 519–523 |

| Standards | Page Numbers |
|---|---|
| *Key Idea 5:* Organisms maintain a dynamic equilibrium that sustains life. | |

**PERFORMANCE INDICATOR 5.1** *Compare the way a variety of living specimens carry out basic life functions and maintain dynamic equilibrium.*

| Standards | Page Numbers |
|---|---|
| 5.1a  Animals and plants have a great variety of body plans and internal structures that contribute to their ability to maintain a balanced condition. | 384–387, 399–407, 482–484, 485–489, 490, 492, 496, 501, 514, 519–523, 525–528, 529–533, 544–547, 549, 585 |
| 5.1b  An organism's overall body plan and its environment determine the way that the organism carries out the life processes. | 485, 490–495, 496–497, 500–502, 514–516, 518, 519–523, 525, 529, 544, 556, 576–583, 585–591, 609, 615 |
| 5.1c  All organisms require energy to survive. The amount of energy needed and the method for obtaining this energy vary among cells. Some cells use oxygen to release the energy stored in food. | 581, 482–484 |
| 5.1d  The methods for obtaining nutrients vary among organisms. Producers, such as green plants, use light energy to make their food. Consumers, such as animals, take in energy-rich foods. | 602, 482–484, 485–489, 490–495, 496–497, 500–502, 514–516, 518, 525–528, 529–533, 544–547, 549, 550–555, 556–564, 609–610, 612–613 |
| 5.1e  Herbivores obtain energy from plants. Carnivores obtain energy from animals. Omnivores obtain energy from both plants and animals. Decomposers, such as bacteria and fungi, obtain energy by consuming wastes and/or dead organisms. | 602, 482–484, 485–489, 514–516, 518, 525–528, 609–610, 612–613, 615–621 |
| 5.1f  Regulation of an organism's internal environment involves sensing the internal environment and changing physiological activities to keep conditions within the range required for survival. Regulation includes a variety of nervous and hormonal feedback systems. | 482–484, 514–516, 518, 529–533 |
| 5.1g  The survival of an organism depends on its ability to sense and respond to its external environment. | 482–484, 490–495, 496–497, 500–502, 514–516, 518, 544–547, 549, 585–591 |

| Standards | Page Numbers |
|---|---|

**PERFORMANCE INDICATOR 5.2** *Describe the importance of major nutrients, vitamins, and minerals in maintaining health and promoting growth, and explain the need for a constant input of energy for living organisms.*

| | |
|---|---|
| 5.2a  Food provides molecules that serve as fuel and building material for all organisms. All living things, including plants, must release energy from their food, using it to carry on their life processes. | 451–456 |
| 5.2b  Foods contain a variety of substances, which include carbohydrates, fats, vitamins, proteins, minerals, and water. Each substance is vital to the survival of the organism. | 451 |
| 5.2e  In order to maintain a balanced state, all organisms have a minimum daily intake of each type of nutrient based on species, size, age, sex, activity, etc. An imbalance in any of the nutrients might result in weight gain, weight loss, or a diseased state. | 451, 544–547, 549 |
| 5.2f  Contraction of infectious disease, and personal behaviors such as use of toxic substances and some dietary habits, may interfere with one's dynamic equilibrium. During pregnancy these conditions may also affect the development of the child. Some effects of these conditions are immediate; others may not appear for many years. | 399–407 |

*Key Idea 6:*  Plants and animals depend on each other and their physical environment.

**PERFORMANCE INDICATOR 6.1** *Describe the flow of energy and matter through food chains and food webs.*

| | |
|---|---|
| 6.1a  Energy flows through ecosystems in one direction, usually from the Sun, through producers to consumers and then to decomposers. This process may be visualized with food chains or energy pyramids. | 602–608 |

**PERFORMANCE INDICATOR 6.2** *Provide evidence that green plants make food and explain the significance of this process to other organisms.*

| | |
|---|---|
| 6.2a  Photosynthesis is carried on by green plants and other organisms containing chlorophyll. In this process, the Sun's energy is converted into and stored as chemical energy in the form of a sugar. The quantity of sugar molecules increases in green plants during photosynthesis in the presence of sunlight. | 579 |
| 6.2b  The major source of atmospheric oxygen is photosynthesis. Carbon dioxide is removed from the atmosphere and oxygen is released during photosynthesis. | 576–583 |
| 6.2c  Green plants are the producers of food which is used directly or indirectly by consumers. | 544–547, 549, 576–583, 602–608 |

| Standards | Page Numbers |
|---|---|

**STANDARD 4—The Physical Setting** Students will understand and apply scientific concepts, principles, and theories pertaining to the physical setting and living environment and recognize the historical development of ideas in science.

*Key Idea 1:* The Earth and celestial phenomena can be described by principles of relative motion and perspective.

**PERFORMANCE INDICATOR 1.1** *Explain daily, monthly, and seasonal changes on Earth.*

| | |
|---|---|
| 1.1e  Most objects in the solar system have a regular and predictable motion. These motions explain such phenomena as a day, a year, phases of the Moon, eclipses, tides, meteor showers, and comets. | 40–43 |
| 1.1f  The latitude/longitude coordinate system and our system of time are based on celestial observations. | 40, 41, 44–46, 48–50 |
| 1.1h  The apparent motions of the Sun, Moon, planets, and stars across the sky can be explained by Earth's rotation and revolution. Earth's rotation causes the length of one day to be approximately 24 hours. This rotation also causes the Sun and Moon to appear to rise along the eastern horizon and to set along the western horizon. Earth's revolution around the Sun defines the length of the year as 365 1/4 days. | 41 |

*Key Idea 2:* Many of the phenomena that we observe on Earth involve interactions among components of air, water, and land.

**PERFORMANCE INDICATOR 2.1** *Explain how the atmosphere (air), hydrosphere (water), and lithosphere (land) interact, evolve, and change.*

| | |
|---|---|
| 2.1c  The rock at Earth's surface forms a nearly continuous shell around Earth called the lithosphere. | 158–160, 162–167 |
| 2.1e  Rocks are composed of minerals. Only a few rock-forming minerals make up most of the rocks of Earth. Minerals are identified on the basis of physical properties such as streak, hardness, and reaction to acid. | 62, 64, 65, 66 |
| 2.1f  Fossils are usually found in sedimentary rocks. Fossils can be used to study past climates and environments. | 121 |
| 2.1g  The dynamic processes that wear away Earth's surface include weathering and erosion. | 94, 101, 103–109 |
| 2.1h  The process of weathering breaks down rocks to form sediment. Soil consists of sediment, organic material, water, and air. | 78–82, 94, 98 |
| 2.1i  Erosion is the transport of sediment. Gravity is the driving force behind erosion. Gravity can act directly or through agents such as moving water, wind, and glaciers. | 101 |

**PERFORMANCE INDICATOR 2.2** *Describe volcano and earthquake patterns, the rock cycle, and weather and climate changes.*

| | |
|---|---|
| 2.2a  The interior of Earth is hot. Heat flow and movement of material within Earth cause sections of Earth's crust to move. This may result in earthquakes, volcanic eruption, and the creation of mountains and ocean basins. | 155, 178, 187, 194 |
| 2.2b  Analysis of earthquake wave data (vibrational disturbances) leads to the conclusion that there are layers within Earth. These layers—the crust, mantle, outer core, and inner core—have distinct properties. | 158–160, 162–167, 178–183, 185–186 |
| 2.2c  Folded, tilted, faulted, and displaced rock layers suggest past crustal movement. | 35, 128–130, 132–133, 158–160, 162–167, 179, 187–192 |

| Standards | Page Numbers |
|---|---|
| 2.2d  Continents fitting together like puzzle parts and fossil correlations provided initial evidence that continents were once together. | 150 |
| 2.2e  The Theory of Plate Tectonics explains how the "solid" lithosphere consists of a series of plates that "float" on the partially molten section of the mantle. Convection cells within the mantle may be the driving force for the movement of the plates. | 158, 194–199 |
| 2.2f  Plates may collide, move apart, or slide past one another. Most volcanic activity and mountain building occur at the boundaries of these plates, often resulting in earthquakes. | 37, 71–73, 75–77, 159, 178–183, 185–186, 187, 194–199 |
| 2.2g  Rocks are classified according to their method of formation. The three classes of rocks are sedimentary, metamorphic, and igneous. Most rocks show characteristics that give clues to their formation conditions. | 44–46, 48–50, 71, 75, 79 |
| 2.2h  The rock cycle model shows how types of rock or rock material may be transformed from one type of rock to another. | 71–73, 75–77, 81 |

*Key Idea 3:*  Matter is made up of particles whose properties determine the observable characteristics of matter and its reactivity.

**PERFORMANCE INDICATOR 3.1**  *Observe and describe properties of materials, such as density, conductivity, and solubility.*

| | |
|---|---|
| 3.1a  Substances have characteristic properties. Some of these properties include color, odor, phase at room temperature, density, solubility, heat and electrical conductivity, hardness, and boiling and freezing points. | 242–249, 251, 252, 300, 314, 318 |
| 3.1b  Solubility can be affected by the nature of the solute and solvent, temperature, and pressure. The rate of solution can be affected by the size of the particles, stirring, temperature, and the amount of solute already dissolved. | 309, 310 |
| 3.1c  The motion of particles helps to explain the phases (states) of matter as well as changes from one phase to another. The phase in which matter exists depends on the attractive forces among its particles. | 245 |
| 3.1d  Gases have neither a determined shape nor a definite volume. Gases assume the shape and volume of a closed container. | 242–249, 251 |
| 3.1e  A liquid has definite volume, but takes the shape of a container. | 242–249, 251 |
| 3.1f  A solid has definite shape and volume. Particles resist a change in position. | 242–249, 251 |
| 3.1g  Characteristic properties can be used to identify different materials, and separate a mixture of substances into its components. For example, iron can be removed from a mixture by means of a magnet. An insoluble substance can be separated from a soluble substance by such processes as filtration, settling, and evaporation. | 242, 252–258, 285–289, 300–305 |

**PERFORMANCE INDICATOR 3.2**  *Distinguish between chemical and physical changes.*

| | |
|---|---|
| 3.2a  During a physical change a substance keeps its chemical composition and properties. Examples of physical changes include freezing, melting, condensation, boiling, evaporation, tearing, and crushing. | 242–249, 251 |
| 3.2b  Mixtures are physical combinations of materials and can be separated by physical means. | 287 |

| Standards | Page Numbers |
|---|---|
| 3.2c  During a chemical change, substances react in characteristic ways to form new substances with different physical and chemical properties. Examples of chemical changes include burning of wood, cooking of an egg, rusting of iron, and souring of milk. | 150–153, 253, 332, 342 |
| 3.2d  Substances are often placed in categories if they react in similar ways. Examples include metals, nonmetals, and noble gases. | 278–279, 281–283 |
| 3.2e  The Law of Conservation of Mass states that during an ordinary chemical reaction matter cannot be created or destroyed. In chemical reactions, the total mass of the reactants equals the total mass of the products. | 257, 336 |

**PERFORMANCE INDICATOR 3.3**  *Develop mental models to explain common chemical reactions and changes in states of matter.*

| Standards | Page Numbers |
|---|---|
| 3.3a  All matter is made up of atoms. Atoms are far too small to see with a light microscope. | 135–139, 270, 273 |
| 3.3b  Atoms and molecules are perpetually in motion. The greater the temperature, the greater the motion. | 270–277 |
| 3.3c  Atoms may join together in well-defined molecules or may be arranged in regular geometric patterns. | 270–277, 64 |
| 3.3d  Interactions among atoms and/or molecules result in chemical reactions. | 332, 334–341, 342–348 |
| 3.3e  The atoms of any one element are different from the atoms of other elements. | 278–279, 281–283 |
| 3.3f  There are more than 100 elements. Elements combine in a multitude of ways to produce compounds that account for all living and nonliving substances. Few elements are found in their pure form. | 278, 285, 300–305 |
| 3.3g  The periodic table is one useful model for classifying elements. The periodic table can be used to predict properties of elements (metals, nonmetals, noble gases). | 279, 285–289 |

*Key Idea 4:*  Energy exists in many forms, and when these forms change energy is conserved.

**PERFORMANCE INDICATOR 4.2**  *Observe and describe heating and cooling events.*

| Standards | Page Numbers |
|---|---|
| 4.2e  Temperature affects the solubility of some substances in water. | 306–312 |

**PERFORMANCE INDICATOR 4.3**  *Observe and describe energy changes as related to chemical reactions.*

| Standards | Page Numbers |
|---|---|
| 4.3a  In chemical reactions, energy is transferred into or out of a system. Light, electricity, or mechanical motion may be involved in such transfers in addition to heat. | 332, 334–341, 342–348 |

**PERFORMANCE INDICATOR 4.4**  Observe and describe the properties of sound, light, magnetism, and electricity.

| Standards | Page Numbers |
|---|---|
| 4.4a  Different forms of electromagnetic energy have different wavelengths. Some examples of electromagnetic energy are microwaves, infrared light, visible light, ultraviolet light, X-rays, and gamma rays. | 212–218, 225, 226 |
| 4.4b  Light passes through some materials, sometimes refracting in the process. Materials absorb and reflect light, and may transmit light. To see an object, light from that object, emitted by or reflected from it, must enter the eye. | 212–218, 225–229, 231 |
| 4.4c  Vibrations in materials set up wave-like disturbances that spread away from the source. Sound waves are an example. Vibrational waves move at different speeds in different materials. Sound cannot travel in a vacuum. | 212, 213, 219 |

# HOW TO...

## Use Your Science Book

### Why do I need my science book?

Have you ever been in class and not understood all of what was presented? Or, you understood everything in class, but at home, got stuck on how to answer a question? Maybe you just wondered when you were ever going to use this stuff?

These next few pages are designed to help you understand everything your science book can be used for . . . besides a paperweight!

## Before You Read

- **Chapter Opener**  Science is occurring all around you, and the opening photo of each chapter will preview the science you will be learning about. The **Chapter Preview** will give you an idea of what you will be learning about, and you can try the **Launch Lab** to help get your brain headed in the right direction. The **Foldables** exercise is a fun way to keep you organized.

- **Section Opener**  Chapters are divided into two to four sections. The **As You Read** in the margin of the first page of each section will let you know what is most important in the section. It is divided into four parts. **What You'll Learn** will tell you the major topics you will be covering. **Why It's Important** will remind you why you are studying this in the first place! The **Review Vocabulary** word is a word you already know, either from your science studies or your prior knowledge. The **New Vocabulary** words are words that you need to learn to understand this section. These words will be in **boldfaced** print and highlighted in the section. Make a note to yourself to recognize these words as you are reading the section.

# As You Read

- **Headings** Each section has a title in large red letters, and is further divided into blue titles and small red titles at the beginnings of some paragraphs. To help you study, make an outline of the headings and subheadings.

- **Margins** In the margins of your text, you will find many helpful resources. The **Science Online** exercises and **Integrate** activities help you explore the topics you are studying. **MiniLabs** reinforce the science concepts you have learned.

- **Building Skills** You also will find an **Applying Math** or **Applying Science** activity in each chapter. This gives you extra practice using your new knowledge, and helps prepare you for standardized tests.

- **Student Resources** At the end of the book you will find **Student Resources** to help you throughout your studies. These include **Science, Technology,** and **Math Skill Handbooks,** an **English/Spanish Glossary,** and an **Index.** Also, use your **Foldables** as a resource. It will help you organize information, and review before a test.

- **In Class** Remember, you can always ask your teacher to explain anything you don't understand.

---

**FOLDABLES™**
**Study Organizer**

**Science Vocabulary** Make the following Foldable to help you understand the vocabulary terms in this chapter.

**STEP 1** Fold a vertical sheet of notebook paper from side to side.

**STEP 2** Cut along every third line of only the top layer to form tabs.

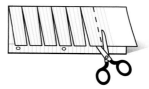

**STEP 3** Label each tab with a vocabulary word from the chapter.

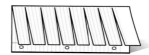

**Build Vocabulary** As you read the chapter, list the vocabulary words on the tabs. As you learn the definitions, write them under the tab for each vocabulary word.

---

Look For...

**FOLDABLES™**

At the beginning of every section.

# In Lab

Working in the laboratory is one of the best ways to understand the concepts you are studying. Your book will be your guide through your laboratory experiences, and help you begin to think like a scientist. In it, you not only will find the steps necessary to follow the investigations, but you also will find helpful tips to make the most of your time.

- Each lab provides you with a **Real-World Question** to remind you that science is something you use every day, not just in class. This may lead to many more questions about how things happen in your world.

- Remember, experiments do not always produce the result you expect. Scientists have made many discoveries based on investigations with unexpected results. You can try the experiment again to make sure your results were accurate, or perhaps form a new hypothesis to test.

- Keeping a **Science Journal** is how scientists keep accurate records of observations and data. In your journal, you also can write any questions that may arise during your investigation. This is a great method of reminding yourself to find the answers later.

Look For...
- **Launch Labs** start every chapter.
- **MiniLabs** in the margin of each chapter.
- **Two Full-Period Labs** in every chapter.
- **EXTRA Try at Home Labs** at the end of your book.
- the Web site with **laboratory demonstrations**.

# Before a Test

Admit it! You don't like to take tests! However, there *are* ways to review that make them less painful. Your book will help you be more successful taking tests if you use the resources provided to you.

- Review all of the **New Vocabulary** words and be sure you understand their definitions.

- Review the notes you've taken on your **Foldables,** in class, and in lab. Write down any question that you still need answered.

- Review the **Summaries** and **Self Check questions** at the end of each section.

- Study the concepts presented in the chapter by reading the **Study Guide** and answering the questions in the **Chapter Review.**

## Look For...

- **Reading Checks** and **caption questions** throughout the text.
- the **Summaries** and **Self Check questions** at the end of each section.
- the **Study Guide** and **Review** at the end of each chapter.
- the **Intermediate-Level Science Examination Practice** after each chapter.

# How Are Volcanoes & Fish Connected?

It's hard to know exactly what happened four and a half billion years ago, when Earth was very young. But it's likely that Earth was much more volcanically active than it is today. Along with lava and ash, volcanoes emit gases—including water vapor. Some scientists think that ancient volcanoes spewed tremendous amounts of water vapor into the early atmosphere. When the water vapor cooled, it would have condensed to form liquid water. Then the water would have fallen to the surface and collected in low areas, creating the oceans. Scientists hypothesize that roughly three and a half billion to four billion years ago, the first living things developed in the oceans. According to this hypothesis, these early life-forms gradually gave rise to more and more complex organisms—including the multitudes of fish that swim through the world's waters.

## unit ⚡ projects

Visit **glencoe.com** to find project ideas and resources.
Projects include:

- **History** Create a time line of volcano trivia with facts such as location, greatest magnitude, most destructive, and first volcano recorded. Can volcanoes be predicted?
- **Careers** Study the specialized skills of various careers as you design and prepare a city for a natural disaster.
- **Model** Research, design, construct, test, evaluate, and present your home seismograph in a 5-minute infomercial.

**WebQuest** *Volcanoes and the Ring of Fire* is an online study of plate tectonics. Design a chart of recent volcano activity, and use it to produce a map of the Ring of Fire with the names and ages of each volcano.

# chapter

## 1

**AID M3.1a:** Use appropriate scientific tools to solve problems about the natural world.
**S1.2a:** Independently formulate a hypothesis. **Also Covered:** S2.1c, S2.2b, S2.2c, S3.1a, S3.2b, S3.2d, S3.2g, IS 3.2, IPS 1.3

# The Nature of Science

## A 66-million-year-old heart?

Inside the chest of a small dinosaur nick-named Willo is something amazing—what appears to be a heart preserved as stone. Scientists still are debating whether this clump of stone is a preserved heart, and more research will be necessary. But that's the nature of science.

**Science Journal**  How do you think scientists could learn more about the clump of stone that could be a heart?

# Start-Up Activities

## Measure in SI

*Big* and *small* are words people use a lot. But, the meaning of these words depends on your experiences and what you are describing. Early in human history, people developed ways to measure things. In the following lab, try some of these measuring devices.

1. Using only your hands and fingers as measuring devices, measure the length and width of the cover of this book.

2. Compare your measurements with those of other students.

3. Using a metric ruler, repeat the measurement process.

4. Again, compare your measurements with the measurements of other students in the classroom.

5. **Think Critically** Infer and describe several advantages of using standardized measuring devices.

 Preview this chapter's content and activities at glencoe.com

 **Science Vocabulary** Make the following Foldable to help you understand the vocabulary terms in this chapter.

**STEP 1** Fold a vertical sheet of notebook paper from side to side.

**STEP 2** Cut along every third line of only the top layer to form tabs.

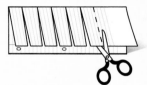

**STEP 3** Label each tab with a vocabulary word from the chapter.

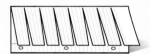

**Build Vocabulary** As you read the chapter, list the vocabulary words on the tabs. As you learn the definitions, write them under the tab for each vocabulary word. Exchange your Vocabulary Foldable with a classmate and quiz each other to see how many vocabulary words you can define without looking under the tabs.

# section 1

# Science All Around

## as you read

### *What* You'll Learn

■ **Describe** scientific methods.
■ **Define** science and Earth science.
■ **Distinguish** among independent variables, dependent variables, constants, and controls.

### *Why* It's Important

Scientific methods are used every day when you solve problems.

### 🔍 Review Vocabulary

**analyze:** to examine methodically

### New Vocabulary

● hypothesis
● scientific methods
● science
● Earth science
● variable
● independent variable
● constant
● dependent variable
● control
● technology

## Mysteries and Problems

Scientists are often much like detectives trying to solve a mystery. One such mystery occurred in 1996 when Japanese scientists were looking through historical records. They reported finding accounts of a tsunami that had smashed the coast of the island of Honshu on January 27, 1700. That led to the question: What had triggered these huge ocean waves?

**The Search for Answers** The scientists suspected that an earthquake along the coast of North America was to blame. From the coast of British Columbia to northern California is an area called the Cascadia subduction zone, shown in **Figure 1.** A subduction zone is where one section of Earth's outer, rigid layer, called a plate, is sinking beneath another plate. In areas like this, earthquakes are common. However, one problem remained. Based on the size of the tsunami, the earthquake had to have been an extremely powerful one, sending waves rolling all the way across the Pacific Ocean. That would be a much stronger earthquake than any known to have occurred in the area. Could evidence be found for such a large earthquake?

**Figure 1** Along the Cascadia subduction zone, the Juan de Fuca Plate is sinking under the North American Plate.

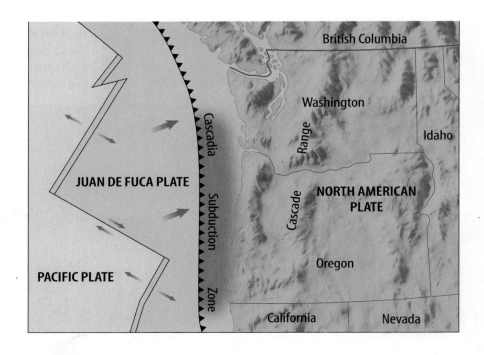

**Gathering Evidence** Evidence of a large earthquake in the distant past did seem to exist along the coasts of Washington and Oregon. Much of the coast in that area had sunk, submerging coastal forests and killing thousands of trees. However, dating the earthquake to a specific year would be difficult.

**A Possible Solution** One scientist, whose field of study was tree rings, thought he knew how the earthquake could be dated. He made an educated guess, called a **hypothesis,** that tree rings in the drowned trees could be used to determine when the earthquake occurred.

**Reading Check** *What is a hypothesis?*

The hypothesis was based on what scientists know about tree growth. Each year, a living tree makes a new ring of tissue in its trunk, called an annual growth ring. You can see the annual rings in the cross section of a tree trunk shown in **Figure 2.** Two groups of scientists analyzed the rings in drowned trees along the coast, like the remains of cedar trees shown in **Figure 3.** Their data showed that the trees had died or were damaged after August 1699 but before the spring growing season of 1700. That evidence put the date of the earthquake in the same time period as the tsunami on Honshu.

**Importance of Solving the Mystery** In addition to solving the mystery of what caused the tsunami, the tree rings also provided a warning for people living in the Pacific Northwest. Earthquakes much stronger than any that have occurred in modern times are possible. Scientists warn that it's only a matter of time until another huge quake occurs.

**Figure 2** You can see the growth rings in this tree trunk. **Determine** *How much time does each ring represent?*

**Analysis, Inquiry, and Design**

**M3.1a, S1.2a Describe** how a scientist might use natural phenomena to explain real-world problems. List three tools the scientist might use in scientific work.

**Figure 3** Growth rings from these and other trees linked a huge earthquake along the coast of Washington to a tsunami in Japan that occurred more than 300 years ago.

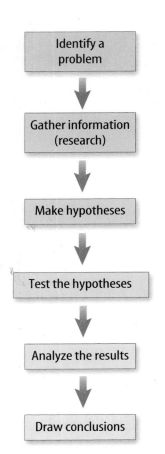

Identify a problem

↓

Gather information (research)

↓

Make hypotheses

↓

Test the hypotheses

↓

Analyze the results

↓

Draw conclusions

**Figure 4** By using scientific methods, you can solve many problems.

**Analysis, Inquiry, and Design**

**M3.1a, S2.2b** **Identify** a problem that might be solved using the scientific method. Discuss how the six steps of the scientific method could be applied to the problem.

**Figure 5** The columns in Devils Postpile rise between 12 m and 18 m from the valley floor. This unusual formation was created when hot lava cooled and cracked.

# Scientific Methods

When scientists try to solve a mystery like what caused the tsunami in Japan in 1700, they perform problem-solving procedures called **scientific methods.** As shown in **Figure 4,** some of the scientific methods they use include identifying a problem, gathering information (researching), developing hypotheses, testing the hypotheses, analyzing the results, and drawing conclusions. When you use methods like these, you are solving problems in a scientific way.

# Science

*Science* means "having knowledge." **Science** is a process of observing, studying, and thinking about things in your world to gain knowledge. Many observations can't be explained easily. When people can't explain things, they ask questions. For example, you might observe that the sky appears to be blue during the day but often appears to be red at sunset and sunrise. You might ask yourself why this happens. You might visit or see a picture of Devils Postpile in California, shown in **Figure 5,** and notice that the dark rock is divided into long, thin, six-sided columns. Many fallen columns lie at the base of this mass of rock. You might wonder how and when this strange-looking rock formed. You also might wonder why rocks can be smooth or rough, shiny or dull, and can be so many different colors. Science involves trying to answer questions and solve problems to better understand the world. Every time you attempt to find out how and why things look and behave the way they do, you are performing science.

**Reading Check** *What is science?*

**Earth Science** Science is divided into different areas of study. The kind of science you will learn about this year is Earth science. **Earth science** is the study of Earth and space. Some Earth science topics include rocks, minerals, soil, volcanoes, earthquakes, maps, fossils, mountains, climates, weather, ocean water, and objects in space. Some of these topics are represented in **Figure 6.** Much of the information you'll learn about has been discovered through the ages by people who conducted scientific tests or investigations. However, many unanswered questions remain and much more is waiting to be discovered.

**✔ Reading Check** *What topics do Earth scientists study?*

# Working in the Lab

Testing, or experimenting, is an important part of science, and if you really want to learn from an investigation, the experiment must be carefully designed. Suppose that after listening to advertisements for several dishwashing liquids, you want to know which brand of dishwashing liquid cleans dishes the best. To find the answer, you would need to do some library or Internet research on dishwashing liquids. After researching, several thoughts might go through your mind. For example, you might hypothesize that brand X will clean dishes better than any other brand. You also might consider that there might be no difference in how well the different liquids clean.

Next, you would design an experiment that tests the validity of your hypotheses. You would need to think about which dishwashing liquids you would test, the amount of each dishwashing liquid you would use, the temperature of the water, the number of dishes you would wash, the kind and amount of grease you would put on the dishes, and the brand of paper towels you would use. All these factors can affect the outcome.

**Science Online**

**Topic: Earth Science**
Visit glencoe.com for Web links to information about the different areas of Earth science.

**Activity** Prepare a collage that illustrates what you learn.

**Analysis, Inquiry, and Design**

**S2.2c Design** a simple, original controlled experiment.

**Figure 7** Wiping each dish in the same manner with a different paper towel is an important constant.
**Explain** *why it is necessary to have a constant in your experiment.*

**Soil Experiment** Suppose you wanted to design an experiment to find out what kind of soil is best for growing cactus plants. What would be your variables and constants in the experiment?

**Variables and Constants** The different factors that can change in an experiment are **variables.** However, you want to design your experiment so you test only one variable at a time. The variable you want to test is the brand of dishwashing liquid. This is called the **independent variable**—the variable that you change. **Constants** are the variables that do not change in an experiment. Constants in this experiment would be the amount of dishwashing liquid used, the amount of water, the water temperature, the number of dishes, the kind and amount of grease applied to each dish, the brand of paper towels that were used, and the manner in which each dish was wiped. For example, you might use 20 equally greasy dishes that are identical in size, soaked in 20 L of hot water (30°C) to which 10 mL of dishwashing liquid have been added. You might rub each dish with a different dry paper towel of the same brand after it has soaked for 20 min and air dried, as the student in **Figure 7** is doing. If grease does not appear on the towel, you would consider the dish to be clean. The amount of grease on the towel is a measure of how clean each dish is and is called the dependent variable. A **dependent variable** is the variable being measured.

**Controls** Many experiments also need a control. A **control** is a standard to which your results can be compared. The control in your experiment is the same number of greasy dishes, placed in 20 L of hot water except that no dishwashing liquid is added to the water. These dishes also are allowed to soak for 20 min and air dry. Then they are wiped with paper towels in the same manner as the other dishes were wiped.

 **Reading Check** *Why is a control used in an experiment?*

**Repeating Experiments** For your results to be valid or reliable, your tests should be repeated many times to see whether you can confirm your original results. For example, you might design your experiment so you repeat the procedures five times for each different dishwashing liquid and control. Also, the number of samples being tested should be large. That is why 20 plates would be chosen for each test of each dishwashing liquid. The control group also would have 20 plates. By repeating an experiment five times, you can be more confident that your conclusions are accurate because your total sample for each dishwashing liquid would be 100 plates. If something in an experiment occurs just once, you can't base a scientific conclusion on it. However, if you can show that brand X cleans best in 100 trials under the same conditions, then you have a conclusion you can feel confident about.

**Testing** After you have decided how you will conduct an experiment, you can begin testing. During the experiment, you should observe what happens and carefully record your data in a table, like the one shown in **Figure 8.** Your final step is to draw your conclusions. You analyze your results and try to understand what they mean.

When you are making and recording observations, be sure to include any unexpected results. Many discoveries have been made when experiments produced unexpected results.

## Mini LAB

### Designing an Experiment

**Procedure**
1. Design an experiment to test the question: *Which flashlight battery lasts the longest?*
2. In your design, be sure to include detailed steps of your experiment.
3. Identify the independent variable, constants, dependent variable, and control.

**Analysis**
1. List the equipment you would need to do your experiment.
2. Explain why you should repeat the experiment.

*Try at Home*

**Figure 8** Arranging your data in a table makes the information easier to understand and analyze.

# Technology

Science doesn't just add to the understanding of your natural surroundings, it also allows people to make discoveries that help others. Science makes the discoveries, and technology puts the discoveries to use. **Technology** is the use of scientific discoveries for practical purposes.

When people first picked up stones to use as tools or weapons, the age of technology had started. The discovery of fire and its ability to change clay into pottery or rocks into metals made the world you live in possible. Think back to the Launch Lab at the beginning of this chapter. Measuring devices like the metric ruler you used are examples of technology.

Everywhere you look, you can see ways that science and technology have shaped your world. Look at **Figure 9** to see how many examples of technology you can identify in each of the pictures. **Figure 10** shows a time line of some important examples of technology used in Earth science. Notice how different cultures have added to discoveries and inventions over the centuries.

**Analysis, Inquiry, and Design**

**T1.1a Identify** a scientific or human need that technology could help solve.

**Figure 9** Examples of technology are all around you.
**Identify** *What are some ways these examples affect your life?*

**Figure 10**

For thousands of years, discoveries made by people of many cultures have advanced the study of Earth. This time line shows milestones and inventions that have shaped the development of Earth science technology and led to a greater understanding of the planet and its place in the universe.

10,000 B.C.: First pottery (Japan)

7000 B.C.: Copper metalworking (Turkey)

A.D. 132 (CHINA) This early seismograph helped detect earthquakes.

3500 B.C.: Bronze tools and weapons (Mesopotamia)

900: Terraced field for soil conservation (Peru)

650: Windmill (Persia)

**1000 B.C.**

**A.D. 100**

80 B.C.: Astronomical calendar (Greece)

1943 (FRANCE) Breathing from tanks of compressed air lets divers move underwater without being tethered to an air source at the surface.

1814 (GERMANY) A spectroscope allowed scientists to determine which elements are present in an object or substance that is giving off light.

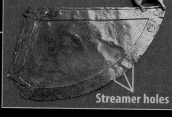

**Streamer holes**

1090: Magnetic compass (Arabia, China)

1000 (NORWAY) Streamers tied through holes in Viking wind vanes indicated wind direction and strength.

1880: Modern seismograph (England)

1538: Diving bell (Spain)

1592: Thermometer (Italy)

1957: Space satellite (former U.S.S.R.)

1998–2006: *INTERNATIONAL SPACE STATION* With participants from 16 countries, the *International Space Station* is helping scientists better understand Earth and beyond.

1926: Liquid-fuel rocket (United States)

**2000**

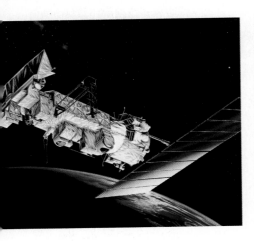

**Figure 11** Weather satellites help forecasters predict future storms.
**Predict** *How might this same technology be used to protect endangered species?*

**Using Technology** Most people immediately think of complex and exotic inventions when the word *technology* is mentioned. However, the use of scientific knowledge has resulted in such common yet important things as paper, can openers, buckets, aspirin, rubber boots, locks and keys, microfiber clothing, ironing boards, bandages, and scissors. It also has resulted in robots that check underwater oil rigs for leaks and others that manufacture cars. Technology also includes calculators and computers that process information.

**Transferable Technology** Technology is a natural outcome of using scientific knowledge to solve problems and make people's lives easier and better. The wonderful thing about technology is that it is transferable, which means that it can be applied to new situations. For example, many types of technology that are now common were originally developed for use in outer space.

Scientists developed robotic parts, new fibers, and micro-miniaturized instruments for spacecraft and satellites. After these materials were developed, many were modified for use here on Earth. Technology that once was developed by the military, such as radar and sonar, has applications in the study of space, weather, Earth's structures, and medicine.

Earth scientists rely on information from weather satellites like the one in **Figure 11** to gather weather data. But biologists also use satellites to track animals. A tiny radio transmitter attached to an animal sends signals up to a satellite. The satellite then sends data on the animal's location to a ground station. Some researchers use the data to track bird migration.

## section 1 review

### Summary

**Mysteries and Problems**
- Scientists develop and test hypotheses to explain phenomena they observe.

**Scientific Methods**
- Scientific methods consist of a series of problem-solving procedures.

**Working in the Lab**
- Scientists experiment with independent and dependent variables, constants, and controls.

**Technology**
- Technology uses scientific discoveries for practical purposes.

### Self Check

1. **Define** the term *hypothesis*. Why must it be testable?
2. **Define** the term *Earth science*.
3. **Explain** why it is important that scientists perform an experiment more than one time.
4. **Think Critically** Why is it important to use constants in an experiment?

#### Applying Skills

5. **Communicate** In your Science Journal, write a paragraph about how you would try to describe a modern device such as a TV, microwave oven, or computer to someone living in 1800.

**More Section Review** glencoe.com

**section**

**2**

# Scientific Enterprise

## A Work in Progress

Throughout time, people have been both frightened by and curious about their surroundings. Storms, erupting volcanoes, comets, seasonal changes, and other natural phenomena fascinated people thousands of years ago, and they fascinate people today. As shown in **Figure 12,** early people relied on mythology to explain what they observed. They believed that mythological gods were responsible for creating storms, causing volcanoes to erupt, causing earthquakes, bringing the seasons, and making comets appear in the sky.

**Recording Observations** Some early civilizations went so far as to record what they saw. They developed calendars that described natural recurring phenomena. Six thousand years ago, Egyptian farmers observed that the Nile River flooded their lands every summer. Their crops had to be planted at the right time in order to make use of this water. The farmers noticed that shortly before flood time, the brightest star in the sky, Sirius, appeared at dawn in the east. The Egyptians developed a calendar based on the appearance of this star, which occurred about every 365 days.

Later, civilizations created instruments to measure with. As you saw in the Launch Lab, instruments allow for precise measurements. As instruments became better, accuracy of observations improved. While observations were being made, people tried to reason why things happened the way they did. They made inferences, or conclusions, to help explain things. Some people developed hypotheses that they tested. Their experimental conclusions allowed them to learn even more.

**as you read**

*What* **You'll Learn**

■ **Explain** why science is always changing.
■ **Compare and contrast** scientific theories and scientific laws.
■ **Discuss** the limits of science.

*Why* **It's Important**

Science helps you understand the world around you.

🔍 **Review Vocabulary**
**observation:** act of using the senses to gather information

**New Vocabulary**
● scientific theory    ● ethics
● scientific law        ● bias

**Figure 12** Early Scandinavian and Germanic peoples believed that a god named Thor controlled the weather. In this drawing, Thor is creating a storm. Lightning flashed whenever he threw his heavy hammer.

# The History of Meteorology

Today, scientists know what they know because of all the knowledge that has been collected over time. The history of meteorology, which is the study of weather, illustrates how an understanding of one area of Earth science has developed over time.

**Weather Instruments** As you have read, ancient peoples believed that their gods controlled weather. However, even early civilizations observed and recorded some weather information. The rain gauge was probably the first weather instrument. The earliest reference to the use of a rain gauge to record the amount of rainfall appears in a book by the ruler of India from 321 B.C. to 296 B.C.

It wasn't until the 1600s that scientists in Italy began to use instruments extensively to study weather. These instruments included the barometer—to measure air pressure; the thermometer—to measure temperature, shown in **Figure 13;** the hygrometer—to measure water vapor in the air; and the anemometer—to measure wind speed. With these instruments, the scientists set up weather stations across Italy.

✔ **Reading Check** *What instruments were used extensively in Italy in the 1600s to study weather?*

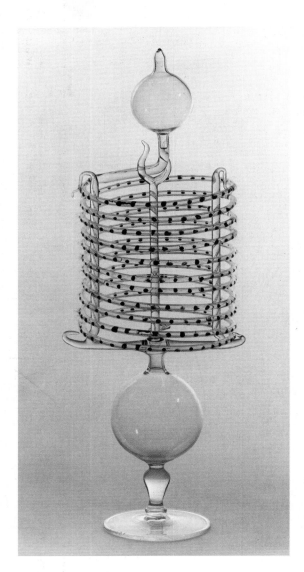

**Figure 13** This photo shows a replica of a 1660 Italian alcohol thermometer.

## Weather Prediction in the United States

Benjamin Franklin was the first American to suggest that weather could be predicted. Franklin read accounts of storms from newspapers across the country. From these articles, Franklin concluded that severe storms generally move across the country from west to east. He also concluded that observers could monitor a storm and notify those ahead of its path that it was coming. Franklin's ideas were put to practical use shortly after the telegraph was invented in 1837.

By 1849, an organized system of weather observation sites was set up and weather reports from volunteer weather observers were sent by telegraph to the Smithsonian Institution. In 1850, Joseph Henry, secretary of the Smithsonian Institution in the United States, began drawing maps from the weather data he received. A large weather map was displayed at the Smithsonian and a weather report was sent to the *Washington Evening Post* to be published in the newspaper.

**National Weather Service** By the late 1800s, the United States Weather Bureau was functioning with more than 350 observing sites across the country. By 1923, weather forecasts were being carried by 140 radio stations across the United States. In 1970, the bureau's name was changed to the National Weather Service and it became part of the National Oceanic and Atmospheric Administration (NOAA).

Today's weather is forecast using orbiting satellites, weather balloons, radar, and other sophisticated technology. Each day about 60,000 reports from weather stations, ships, aircraft, and radar transmitters are gathered and filed. **Figure 14** shows instruments used to gather data at a weather station. All the information gathered is compiled into a report that is distributed to radio stations, television networks, and other news media.

Today, if you want to know about the weather anywhere in the world—at any time of day or night—you could watch a television weather channel, listen to a radio news station, or check an internet site. If you live in an area that has tornadoes, hurricanes, or other severe weather conditions, you know it is important to have weather watches and warnings available to your community.

**Science** nline

**Topic: Weather Forecasting**
Visit glencoe.com for Web links to information about weather forecasting.

**Activity** Prepare a detailed forecast for an imaginary snowstorm using information based on the research you have conducted.

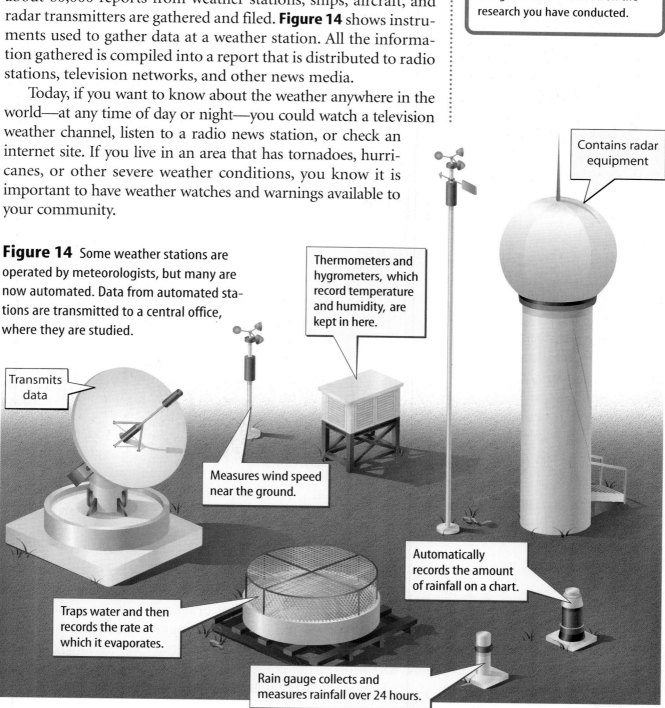

**Figure 14** Some weather stations are operated by meteorologists, but many are now automated. Data from automated stations are transmitted to a central office, where they are studied.

Contains radar equipment

Thermometers and hygrometers, which record temperature and humidity, are kept in here.

Transmits data

Measures wind speed near the ground.

Automatically records the amount of rainfall on a chart.

Traps water and then records the rate at which it evaporates.

Rain gauge collects and measures rainfall over 24 hours.

## Continuing Research

Scientific knowledge continues to change as scientists develop better instruments and testing procedures. As it changes, scientists have a greater understanding of nature. As you saw in **Figure 14,** scientists use a variety of technologies to study weather. Scientists have similar technologies to study Earth's interior, the oceans, environmental problems, and space. How could the technology shown in **Figure 15** be used by Earth scientists?

It is impossible to predict the types of instruments scientists will have in the future. But it is easy to predict that as research continues and instruments improve, knowledge will grow. Perhaps one day you will make a scientific breakthrough that changes people's understanding of the world.

**Scientific Theories** As you learned earlier, scientists test hypotheses. If data gathered over a long period of time support a hypothesis, scientists become convinced that the hypothesis is useful. They use results from many scientists' work to develop a scientific theory. A **scientific theory** is an explanation or model backed by results obtained from many tests or experiments.

**Figure 15** The Global Positioning System (GPS) can pinpoint a person's location on Earth. A radio receiver gets signals from several orbiting *Navstar* satellites like this one. By comparing how far the receiver is from each satellite, the receiver's position can be determined and displayed.

### Analysis, Inquiry, and Design

**S3.2g Discuss** how scientific knowledge can change as scientists develop better instruments and testing procedures.

✅ **Reading Check** *How can a scientific hypothesis become a scientific theory?*

Examine how one hypothesis became a theory. Comets once were believed to be the forecasters of disaster. People often were terrified yet fascinated by the ghostly balls appearing in the sky. Slowly over the years, comets lost much of their mystery. However, from the 1800s until 1949, most scientists hypothesized that comets were made of many particles of different kinds of materials swarming in a cluster. Based on this hypothesis, a comet was described as a swirling cloud of dust.

In 1949, American astronomer Fred L. Whipple proposed a hypothesis that a comet was more like a dirty snowball—that the nucleus of a comet contains practically all of a comet's mass and consists of ice and dust. If a comet's orbit brings it close to the Sun, the heat vaporizes some of the ice, releasing dust and gas, which form the comet's tail. Dr. Whipple's hypothesis was published in the March 1950 *Astrophysical Journal.*

**Hypothesis Supported** Before it became an accepted theory, Dr. Whipple's hypothesis was subjected to many years of tests and observations. Some of the most important were the 1986 observations of Halley's comet, shown in **Figure 16.** A group of astronomers from the University of Arizona, headed by Dr. Susan Wyckoff, studied the composition of the comet. Dr. Wyckoff observed the comet many times, using giant telescopes in Arizona and Chile in South America. At other times, she studied the observations of other astronomers, including those who studied data collected by the *Giotto* and other spacecrafts. All these observations and data supported Dr. Whipple's original hypothesis. With so much support, Dr. Whipple's hypothesis has become an accepted scientific theory.

**INTEGRATE Physics** **Scientific Laws** A **scientific law** is a rule that describes the behavior of something in nature. Usually, a scientific law describes what will happen in a given situation but doesn't explain why it happens. An example of a scientific law is Newton's first law of motion. According to this law, an object, such as a marble or a spacecraft, will continue in motion or remain at rest until it's acted upon by an outside force. According to Newton's second law of motion, when a force acts on an object, the object will change speed, direction, or both. Finally, according to Newton's third law, for every action, there is an equal and opposite reaction. This law explains how rockets that are used to launch space probes to study Halley's comet and other objects in space work. When a rocket forces burning gases out of its engines, the gases push back on the rocket with a force of equal strength and propel the rocket forward.

**Figure 16** The view of Halley's comet from the *Giotto* spacecraft allowed scientists to determine the size of the icy nucleus, and that the nucleus was covered by a black crust of dust. Jets of gas blasted out from holes in the crust to form the comet's tail.

**Figure 17** Ethical questions can't be solved by using scientific methods.

Disease-carrying mosquitoes can live in this swamp. **Debate** *Should swamps be drained, even if other species lose their habitat?*

These animals live on the African plains. **Form an Opinion** *Should they be hunted as trophies?*

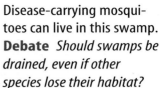

Helmets reduce serious head injuries. **Think Critically** *Should the government require motorcycle riders to wear helmets?*

**INTEGRATE**
**Career**

**Science Ethics** The question of whether or not to use humans in medical research studies is matter of ethics. As a class, discuss and list some pros and cons of using humans as test subjects. Explain why there is no right or wrong answer to this question.

## Limits of Science

Will science always provide answers to all your questions? No, science doesn't have answers to all the questions and problems in the universe. Science is limited in what it can explain. For a question or problem to be scientifically studied, there must be variables that can be observed, measured, and tested. Problems that deal with ethics and belief systems cannot be answered using these methods. **Ethics** deals with moral values about what is good or bad. Belief systems deal with religious and/or other beliefs. Examples of ethical and belief-system questions that science cannot answer are: Do humans have more value on Earth than other life-forms?, Should the federal government regulate car emissions?, and Should animals be used in medical experiments? Look at **Figure 17.** What's your opinion?

 **Reading Check** *Why can't science be used to answer ethical questions?*

## Doing Science Right

Although ethical questions cannot be answered by science, there are ethical ways of doing science. The correct approach to doing science is to perform experiments in a way that honestly tests hypotheses and draws conclusions in an unbiased way.

**Being Objective** When you do scientific experiments, be sure that you design your experiments in such a way that you objectively test your hypotheses. If you don't, your **bias,** or personal opinion, can affect your observations. For example, in the 1940s, Soviet scientist Trofim Lysenko believed that individuals of the same species would not compete with one another. His ideas were based on the political beliefs held in the Soviet Union at that time. Based on his personal opinion, Lysenko ordered 300,000 tree seedlings planted in groups in a reforestation project. He believed that the trees in each group would aid one another in competing against other plant species. However, the area where the trees were planted was extremely dry, and all of the trees were competing for water and nutrients. As a result, many trees died. Lysenko's personal opinion and lack of knowledge turned out to be a costly experiment for the Soviet government.

**Figure 18** These seedlings are crowded into a single pot.
**Predict** *How many do you think could survive?*

Suppose you wanted to grow as many plants as possible in a single flowerpot. Would you assume that all of the plants in the pot shown in **Figure 18** could survive, or would you set up an experiment to objectively test this hypothesis? Unless you test various numbers of plants in pots under the same conditions, you could not make a valid conclusion.

## Applying Science

### How can bias affect your observations?

Do you think bias can affect a person's observations? With the help of her classmates, Sharon performed an experiment to find out.

### Identifying the Problem

Sharon showed ten friends a photograph of an uncut amethyst and asked them to rank the quality of color from 1 to 10. She then wrote the words *Prize Amethyst* on top of the photo and asked ten more friends to rank the quality of color.

### Solving the Problem

1. Examine the tables. Do you think the hint affected the way Sharon's classmates

| Rankings Without Hint | | Rankings With Hint | |
|---|---|---|---|
| 5 | 7 | 7 | 8 |
| 4 | 5 | 8 | 9 |
| 6 | 4 | 9 | 8 |
| 5 | 6 | 10 | 8 |
| 5 | 3 | 7 | 9 |
| Average: 5.0 | | Average: 8.3 | |

rated the amethyst? What effect did the hint have on them?

2. Do you think bias could affect the results of a scientific experiment? Explain. How could this bias be prevented?

**Figure 19** Scientists take detailed notes of procedures and observations when they do science experiments.
**Explain** *why you should do the same thing.*

**Being Ethical and Open** People who perform science in ethical and unbiased ways keep detailed notes of their procedures, like the scientists shown in **Figure 19.** Their conclusions are based on precise measurements and tests. They communicate their discoveries by publishing their research in journals or presenting reports at scientific meetings. This allows other scientists to examine and evaluate their work. Scientific knowledge advances when people work together. Much of the science you know today has come about because of the collaboration of investigations done by many different people over many years.

The opposite of ethical behavior in science is fraud. Scientific fraud involves dishonest acts or statements. Fraud could include such things as making up data, changing the results of experiments, or taking credit for work done by others.

## section 2 review

### Summary

**A Work in Progress**
- Early people used mythology to explain what they observed.

**Continuing Research**
- After data are gathered over a long period of time to test a hypothesis, the information might be developed into a scientific theory.
- A scientific law is a rule that describes the behavior of something.

**Limits of Science**
- Science is limited to what it can explain.
- Scientists need to remain open and unbiased in their research.

### Self Check

1. **Explain** why science is always changing.
2. **List** ways a hypothesis can be supported.
3. **Compare and contrast** scientific theory and scientific law.
4. **Determine** What kinds of questions can't be answered by science?
5. **Think Critically** When reading science articles, why should you look for the authors' biases?

#### Applying Skills

6. **Draw Conclusions** Describe what would have happened if the 1986 observations of Halley's comet had not supported Dr. Whipple's original hypothesis.

# Understanding Science Articles

Scientists conduct investigations to learn things about our world. It is important for researchers to share what they learn so other researchers can repeat and expand upon their results. One important way that scientific results are shared is by publishing them in journals and magazines.

## ◉ *Real-World Question*

What information about Earth science and scientific methods can you learn by reading an appropriate magazine article?

### Goals
- Obtain a recent magazine article concerning a research topic in Earth science.
- Identify aspects of science and scientific methods in the article.

### Materials
magazine articles about Earth science topics

## ◉ *Procedure*

1. Locate a recent magazine article about a topic in Earth science research.

2. Read the article, paying attention to details that are related to science, research, and scientific methods.

3. What branch of Earth science does the article discuss?

4. **Describe** what the article is about. Does it describe a particular event or discuss more general research?

5. Are the names of any scientists mentioned? If so, what were their roles?

6. Are particular hypotheses being tested? If so, is the research project complete or is it still continuing?

7. **Describe** how the research is conducted. What is being measured? What observations are recorded?

## ◉ *Conclude and Apply*

1. **Explain** Are data available that do or do not support the hypotheses?

2. **Infer** What do other scientists think about the research?

3. Are references provided that tell you where you can find more information about this particular research or the more general topic? If not, what are some sources where you might locate more information?

### 𝒞ommunicating **Your Data**

Prepare an oral report on the article you read. Present your report to the class. **For more help, refer to the** Science Skill Handbook.

# Testing Variables of a Pendulum

## Real-World Question

A pendulum is an old, but accurate, timekeeping device. It works because of two natural phenomena—gravity and inertia—that are important in the study of Earth science. Gravity makes all objects fall toward Earth's surface. Inertia makes matter remain at rest or in motion unless acted upon by an external force. In the following lab, you will test some variables that might affect the swing of a pendulum. How do the length of a pendulum, the attached mass, and the angle of the release of the mass affect the swing of a pendulum?

### Goals

- **Manipulate** variables of a pendulum.
- **Draw** conclusions from experimentation with pendulums.

### Materials

string (60 cm)
metal washers (5)
watch with a second hand
metric ruler
paper clip
protractor

### Safety Precautions

## Procedure

1. Copy the three data tables into your Science Journal.
2. Bend the paper clip into an S shape and tie it to one end of the string.
3. Hang one washer from the paper clip.

| Table 1 Length of the Pendulum | | | |
|---|---|---|---|
| Length of String (cm) | Swings Per Minute | | |
| | Trial 1 | Trial 2 | Average |
| 10 | | | |
| 20 | | | |
| 30 | Do not write in this book. | | |
| 40 | | | |
| 50 | | | |

| Table 2 Amount of Mass on the Pendulum | | | |
|---|---|---|---|
| Units of Mass | Swings Per Minute | | |
| | Trial 1 | Trial 2 | Average |
| 1 | | | |
| 2 | | | |
| 3 | Do not write in this book. | | |
| 4 | | | |
| 5 | | | |

| Table 3 Angle of the Release of the Mass | | | |
|---|---|---|---|
| Angle of Release | Swings Per Minute | | |
| | Trial 1 | Trial 2 | Average |
| 90° | | | |
| 80° | | | |
| 70° | Do not write in this book. | | |
| 60° | | | |
| 50° | | | |

4. **Measure** 10 cm of string from the washer and hold the string at that distance with one hand.

5. Use your other hand to pull back the end of the pendulum with the washer so it is parallel with the ground. Let go of the washer.

6. Count the number of complete swings the pendulum makes in 1 min. Record this number in **Table 1.**

7. Repeat steps 5 and 6 and record the number of swings in **Table 1** under "Trial 2."

8. Average the results of steps 6 and 7 and record the average swings per minute in **Table 1.**

9. Repeat steps 4 through 8, using string lengths of 20 cm, 30 cm, 40 cm, and 50 cm. Record your data in **Table 1.**

10. Copy the data with the string length of 50 cm in **Table 2.**

11. Repeat steps 5 through 8 using a 50 cm length of string and two, three, four, and five washers. Record these data in **Table 2.**

12. Use 50 cm of string and one washer for the third set of tests.

13. Use the protractor to measure a 90° drop of the mass. Repeat this procedure, calculate the average, and record the data in **Table 3.**

14. Repeat procedures 12 and 13, using angles of 80°, 70°, 60°, and 50°.

## ▶ Conclude and Apply

1. **Explain** When you tested the effect of the angle of the drop of the pendulum on the swings per minute, which variables did you keep constant?

2. **Infer** which of the variables you tested affects the swing of a pendulum.

3. **Predict** Suppose you have a pendulum clock that indicates an earlier time than it really is. (This means it has too few swings per minute.) What could you do to the clock to make it keep better time?

### Communicating Your Data

**Graph** the data from your tables. Title and label the graphs. Use different colored pencils for each graph. **Compare** your graphs with the graphs of other members of your class.

# "The Microscope"

## by Maxine Kumin

**Maxine Kumin**

Anton Leeuwenhoek was Dutch.
He sold pincushions, cloth, and such.
The waiting townsfolk fumed and fussed
As Anton's dry goods gathered dust.

He worked, instead of tending store,
At grinding special lenses for
A microscope. Some of the things
He looked at were: mosquitoes' wings,
the hairs of sheep, the legs of lice,
the skin of people, dogs, and mice;
ox eyes, spiders' spinning gear,
fishes' scales, a little smear
of his own blood, and best of all,
the unknown, busy, very small
bugs that swim and bump and hop
inside a simple water drop.

Impossible! Most Dutchmen said.
This Anton's crazy in the head!
We ought to ship him off to Spain.
He says he's seen a housefly's brain.
He says the water that we drink
Is full of bugs. He's mad, we think!

They called him *dumkopf,* which means "dope."
That's how we got the microscope.

## Understanding Literature

**Rhyming Couplets** A couplet is a poetic convention in which every two lines rhyme. Some of the most famous poems that use rhyming couplets describe heroic deeds and often are epic tales. An epic tale is a long story that describes a journey of exploration. Why do you think the poet used rhyming couplets in the poem you just read?

## Respond to the Reading

1. Do you think Anton was a scientist by trade? Why or why not?
2. What did Anton find inside a water drop?
3. **Linking Science and Writing** Write a heroic verse or poem that rhymes. Pick a scientific method or discovery from your textbook.

Scientific instruments can increase scientific knowledge. For example, microscopes have changed the scale at which humans can make observations. Electron microscopes allow observers to obtain images at magnifications of $10,000\times$ to $1,000,000\times$. In a microscope with a magnification of $10,000\times$, a 0.001-mm object will appear as a 1-cm image. Microscopes are used in Earth science to observe the arrangement and composition of minerals in rocks. These give clues about the conditions that formed the rock.

## Reviewing Main Ideas

### Section 1 Science All Around

1. Scientific methods include identifying a problem or question, gathering information, developing hypotheses, designing an experiment to test the hypotheses, performing the experiment, collecting and analyzing data, and forming conclusions.

2. Science experiments should be repeated to see whether results are consistent.

3. In an experiment, the independent variable is the variable being tested. Constants are variables that do not change. The variable being measured is the dependent variable. A control is a standard to which things can be compared.

4. Technology is the use of scientific discoveries.

### Section 2 Scientific Enterprise

1. Today, everything known in science results from knowledge that has been collected over time. Science has changed and will continue to change because of continuing research and improvements in instruments and testing procedures.

2. Scientific theories are explanations or models that are supported by repeated experimentation.

3. Scientific laws are rules that describe the behavior of something in nature. They do not explain why something happens.

4. Problems that deal with ethics and belief systems cannot be answered using scientific methods.

## Visualizing Main Ideas

*Copy and complete the following concept map about variables and constants.*

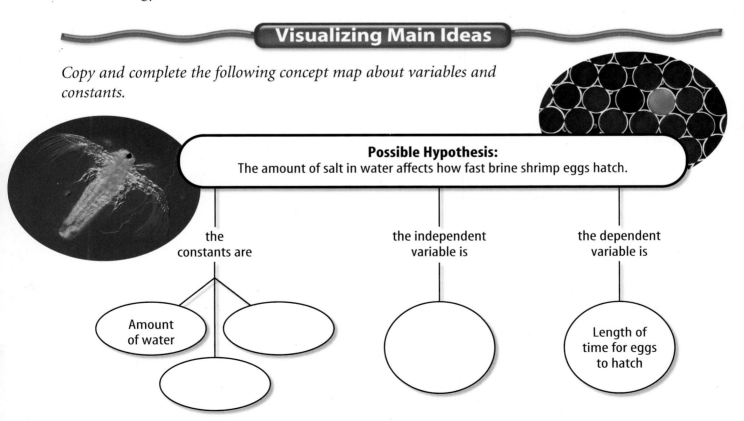

**Possible Hypothesis:**
The amount of salt in water affects how fast brine shrimp eggs hatch.

the constants are

the independent variable is

the dependent variable is

Amount of water

Length of time for eggs to hatch

## Using Vocabulary

| | |
|---|---|
| bias p.21 | independent variable p.10 |
| constant p.10 | science p.8 |
| control p.10 | scientific law p.19 |
| dependent variable p.10 | scientific methods p.8 |
| Earth science p.9 | scientific theory p.18 |
| ethics p.20 | technology p.12 |
| hypothesis p.7 | variable p.10 |

*Use what you know about the vocabulary words to explain the differences between the words in the following sets. Then explain how the words are related.*

1. constant—control

2. dependent variable—independent variable

3. scientific law—scientific theory

4. science—technology

5. hypothesis—scientific theory

6. science—Earth science

7. independent variable—constant

8. variable—control

9. Earth science—technology

10. ethics—bias

## Checking Concepts

*Choose the word or phrase that best answers the question.*

11. Which word means an educated guess?
    A) theory
    B) hypothesis
    C) variable
    D) law

12. The idea that a comet is like a dirty snowball is which of the following?
    A) hypothesis          C) law
    B) variable            D) theory

13. Which of the following is the first step in using scientific methods?
    A) develop hypotheses
    B) make conclusions
    C) test hypotheses
    D) identify a problem

14. The statement that an object at rest will remain at rest unless acted upon by a force is an example of which of the following?
    A) hypothesis          C) law
    B) variable            D) theory

15. Which of the following questions could NOT be answered using scientific methods?
    A) Should lying be illegal?
    B) Does sulfur affect the growth of grass?
    C) How do waves cause erosion?
    D) Does land heat up faster than water?

16. Which of the following describes variables that stay the same in an experiment?
    A) dependent variables
    B) independent variables
    C) constants
    D) controls

17. Which of the following is a variable that is being tested in a science experiment?
    A) dependent variable
    B) independent variable
    C) constant
    D) control

18. What should you do if your data are different from what you expected?
    A) Conclude that you made a mistake in the way you collected the data.
    B) Change your data to be consistent with your expectation.
    C) Conclude that you made a mistake when you recorded your data.
    D) Conclude that your expectation might have been wrong.

*Vocabulary Puzzlemaker* glencoe.com

## Thinking Critically

**19. Recognize Cause and Effect** Suppose you had two plants—a cactus and a palm. You planted them in soil and watered them daily. After two weeks, the cactus was dead. What scientific methods could you use to find out why the cactus died?

**20. Think Critically** How have advances in technology affected society?

**21. Explain** what is meant by the statement, *Technology is transferable.*

**22. Evaluate** Why don't all hypotheses become theories?

**23. Identify** some scientific methods you use every day to answer questions or solve problems?

**24. Identify and Manipulate Variables and Controls** How would you set up a simple experiment to test whether salt-crystal growth is affected by temperature?

**25. Form Hypotheses** You observe two beakers containing clear liquid and ice cubes. In the first beaker, the ice cubes are floating. In the second, the ice cubes are on the bottom of the beaker. Write a hypothesis to explain the difference in your observations about the two beakers.

**26. Recognize Cause and Effect** Explain why scientific methods cannot be used to answer ethical questions.

**27. Draw Conclusions** A laboratory tests a hypothesis through an experiment and publishes its findings that confirm the hypothesis is true. Ten other laboratories attempt to duplicate the findings, but none are able to prove the hypothesis true. Give a possible explanation why the labs' results did not agree.

## Performance Activities

**28. Poster** Research an example of Earth science technology that is not shown in Figure 10. Create a poster that explains the contribution this technology made to the understanding of Earth science.

*Hot Words Hot Topics*: Bk 2 (29) p. 194; (30) p. 303

## Applying Math

**Use the table below to answer questions 29–30.**

### Color and Heat Absorption

| Color | Beginning Temperature (°C) | Temperature (°C) after 10 minutes |
|-------|----------------------------|-----------------------------------|
| Red | 24° | 26° |
| Black | 24° | 28° |
| Blue | 24° | 27° |
| White | 24° | 25° |
| Green | 24° | 27° |

**29. A Color Experiment** A friend tells you that dark colors absorb more heat than light colors do. You conduct an experiment to determine which color of fabric absorbs the most heat. Analyze your data below. Was your friend correct? Explain.

**30. Variables** Identify the independent variables and the dependent variables of the experiment.

**Part I**

*Record your answers on the answer sheet provided by your teacher or on a sheet of paper.*

**Use the illustration below to answer question 1.**

20 mL water    20 mL water    20 mL water    20 mL water
0 mL chlorine  5 mL chlorine  10 mL chlorine 15 mL chlorine

1  The test tubes were left at room temperature for a week to see if algae would grow. Which variable is being investigated?
   (1) the volume of water used
   (2) the temperature of the test tube's contents
   (3) the amount of chlorine present
   (4) the amount of algae present

2  Which of the following is the study of Earth and space?
   (1) life science
   (2) Earth science
   (3) physical science
   (4) chemical science

3  Which of these is a factor to which experimental results can be compared?
   (1) independent variable
   (2) dependent variable
   (3) control
   (4) constant

4  What is the use of scientific discoveries for practical purposes?
   (1) bias
   (2) scientific methods
   (3) science
   (4) technology

5  Which of the following is an explanation or model that is supported by many experiments and observations?
   (1) hypothesis          (3) theory
   (2) law                 (4) estimate

6  Which is a rule that describes the behavior of something in nature?
   (1) hypothesis          (3) estimate
   (2) law                 (4) theory

**Use the illustrations below to answer questions 7–9.**

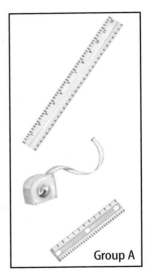
Group A

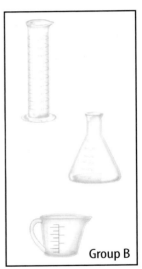
Group B

7  Which quality can be measured using the tools in group A?
   (1) distance            (3) volume
   (2) weight              (4) mass

8  Which quality can be measured using the tools in group B?
   (1) distance            (3) volume
   (2) weight              (4) mass

9  Which of the following belongs in group B above?
   (1) spring scale        (3) beaker
   (2) thermometer         (4) stopwatch

**Part II**

*Record your answers on the answer sheet provided by your teacher or on a sheet of paper.*

**10** What's the difference between an independent variable and a dependent variable?

**11** Why is it a good idea to repeat an experiment?

**12** Would a scientist be convinced that his or her results were accurate after one trial? Support your reasoning.

**Use the illustration below to answer questions 13–15.**

**13** Alicia taped the meterstick shown above to her bedroom wall and recorded her height on her birthday for five consecutive years. The bottom of the meterstick was 1 m above the floor. How many centimeters tall was Alicia when she was 10 years old?

**14** How many centimeters did she grow between her 10th birthday and her 14th birthday?

**15** What was the maximum amount that Alicia grew in any one year?

**16** Define the terms *scientific theory* and *scientific law*. Give an example of each.

**Use the graph below to answer questions 17 and 18.**

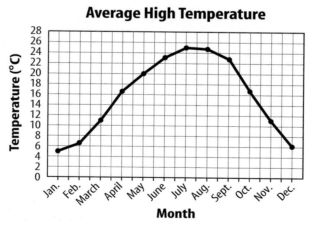

**17** Describe how the average high temperature changes through the year. Which month is warmest? Which is coldest? How much is the difference?

**18** How do you think the average temperature data were obtained? What measurements were recorded? What calculations were performed?

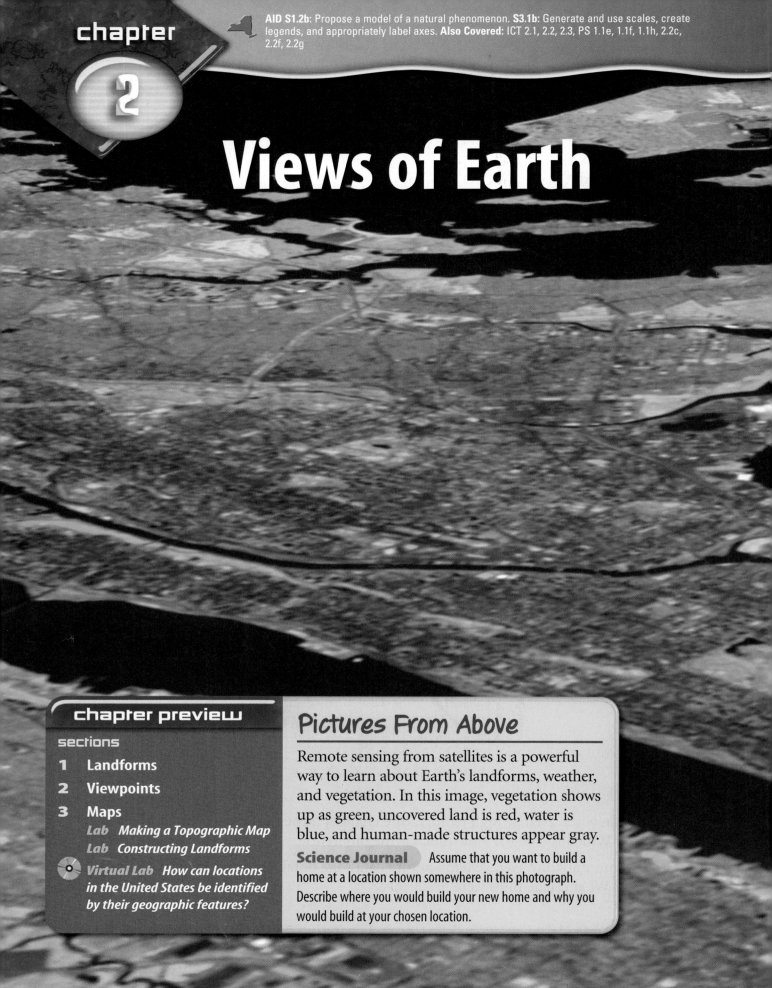

**AID S1.2b:** Propose a model of a natural phenomenon. **S3.1b:** Generate and use scales, create legends, and appropriately label axes. **Also Covered:** ICT 2.1, 2.2, 2.3, PS 1.1e, 1.1f, 1.1h, 2.2c, 2.2f, 2.2g

# Views of Earth

## chapter preview

## Pictures From Above

Remote sensing from satellites is a powerful way to learn about Earth's landforms, weather, and vegetation. In this image, vegetation shows up as green, uncovered land is red, water is blue, and human-made structures appear gray.

**Science Journal** Assume that you want to build a home at a location shown somewhere in this photograph. Describe where you would build your new home and why you would build at your chosen location.

# Start-Up Activities

## Describe Landforms

Pictures of Earth from space are acquired by instruments attached to satellites. Scientists use these images to make maps because they show features of Earth's surface, such as mountains and rivers.

1. Using a globe, atlas, or a world map, locate the following features and describe their positions on Earth relative to other major features.

   a. Andes mountains

   b. Amazon, Ganges, and Mississippi Rivers

   c. Indian Ocean, the Sea of Japan, and the Baltic Sea

   d. Australia, South America, and North America

2. Provide any other details that would help someone else find them.

3. **Think Critically** Choose one country on the globe or map and describe its major physical features in your Science Journal.

**Science Online** | Preview this chapter's content and activities at glencoe.com

**Views of Earth** Make the following Foldable to help identify what you already know, what you want to know, and what you learned about the views of Earth.

**STEP 1** Fold a vertical sheet of paper from side to side. Make the front edge about 1.25 cm shorter than the back edge.

**STEP 2** Turn lengthwise and **fold** into thirds.

**STEP 3** Unfold and cut only the top layer along both folds to make three tabs.

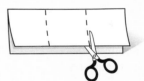

**STEP 4** Label each tab.

| Know? | Want to know? | Learned? |

**Identify Questions** Before you read the chapter, write what you already know about the views of Earth under the left tab of your Foldable, and write questions about what you want to know under the center tab. After you read the chapter, list what you learned under the right tab.

# section 1

# Landforms

## as you read

### *What* You'll Learn

- **Discuss** differences between plains and plateaus.
- **Describe** folded, upwarped, fault-block, and volcanic mountains.

### *Why* It's Important

Landforms influence how people can use land.

### ⊙ Review Vocabulary

**landform:** a natural feature of a land surface

### New Vocabulary

- plain
- plateau
- folded mountain
- upwarped mountain
- fault-block mountain
- volcanic mountain

## Plains

Earth offers abundant variety—from tropics to tundras, deserts to rain forests, and freshwater mountain streams to saltwater tidal marshes. Some of Earth's most stunning features are its landforms, which can provide beautiful vistas, such as vast, flat, fertile plains; deep gorges that cut through steep walls of rock; and towering, snowcapped peaks. **Figure 1** shows the three basic types of landforms—plains, plateaus, and mountains.

Even if you haven't ever visited mountains, you might have seen hundreds of pictures of them in your lifetime. Plains are more common than mountains, but they are more difficult to visualize. **Plains** are large, flat areas, often found in the interior regions of continents. The flat land of plains is ideal for agriculture. Plains often have thick, fertile soils and abundant, grassy meadows suitable for grazing animals. Plains also are home to a variety of wildlife, including foxes, ground squirrels, and snakes. When plains are found near the ocean, they're called coastal plains. Together, interior plains and coastal plains make up half of all the land in the United States.

**Figure 1** Three basic types of landforms are plains, plateaus, and mountains.

Plateau

Mountains

Plain

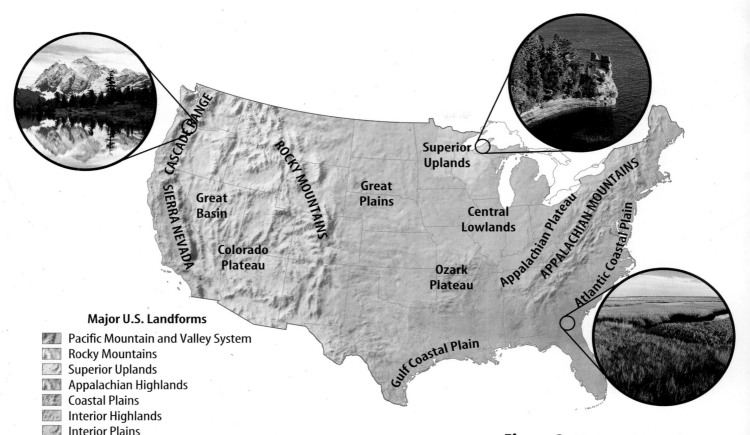

**Major U.S. Landforms**

- Pacific Mountain and Valley System
- Rocky Mountains
- Superior Uplands
- Appalachian Highlands
- Coastal Plains
- Interior Highlands
- Interior Plains
- Intermontane Plateaus and Basin

**Figure 2** The United States has eight major landform regions, which include plains, mountains, and plateaus.
**Describe** *the region that you live in.*

**Coastal Plains** A coastal plain often is called a lowland because it is lower in elevation, or distance above sea level, than the land around it. You can think of the coastal plains as being the exposed portion of a continental shelf. The continental shelf is the part of a continent that extends into the ocean. The Atlantic Coastal Plain is a good example of this type of landform. It stretches along the east coast of the United States from New Jersey to Florida. This area has low rolling hills, swamps, and marshes. A marsh is a grassy wetland that usually is flooded with water.

The Atlantic Coastal Plain, shown in **Figure 2,** began forming about 70 million years ago as sediment began accumulating on the ocean floor. Sea level eventually dropped, and the seafloor was exposed. As a result, the coastal plain was born. The size of the coastal plain varies over time. That's because sea level rises and falls. During the last ice age, the coastal plain was larger than it is now because so much of Earth's water was contained in glaciers.

The Gulf Coastal Plain includes the lowlands in the southern United States that surround the Gulf of Mexico. Much of this plain was formed from sediment deposited in deltas by the many rivers that enter the Gulf of Mexico.

**Analysis, Inquiry, and Design**

**S1.2b, ICT 2.1, 2.2, 2.3**
**Model** the three basic landforms in a sketch, clay model, paper structure, or other material.

**✓ Reading Check** *How are coastal plains formed?*

**Interior Plains** The central portion of the United States is comprised largely of interior plains. Shown in **Figure 3,** you'll find them between the Rocky Mountains, the Appalachian Mountains, and the Gulf Coastal Plain. They include the Central Lowlands around the Missouri and Mississippi Rivers and the rolling hills of the Great Lakes area.

A large part of the interior plains is known as the Great Plains. This area lies between the Mississippi River and the Rocky Mountains. It is a flat, grassy, dry area with few trees. The Great Plains also are referred to as the high plains because of their elevation, which ranges from 350 m above sea level at the eastern border to 1,500 m in the west. The Great Plains consist of nearly horizontal layers of sedimentary rocks.

## Plateaus

At somewhat higher elevations, you will find plateaus (pla TOHZ). **Plateaus** are flat, raised areas of land made up of nearly horizontal rocks that have been uplifted by forces within Earth. They are different from plains in that their edges rise steeply from the land around them. Because of this uplifting, it is common for plateaus, such as the Colorado Plateau, to be cut through by deep river valleys and canyons. The Colorado River, as shown in **Figure 3,** has cut deeply into the rock layers of the plateau, forming the Grand Canyon. Because the Colorado Plateau is located mostly in what is now a dry region, only a few rivers have developed on its surface. If you hiked around on this plateau, you would encounter a high, rugged environment.

**Figure 3** Plains and plateaus are fairly flat, but plateaus have higher elevation.

# Mountains

Mountains with snowcapped peaks often are shrouded in clouds and tower high above the surrounding land. If you climb them, the views are spectacular. The world's highest mountain peak is Mount Everest in the Himalaya—more than 8,800 m above sea level. By contrast, the highest mountain peaks in the United States reach just over 6,000 m. Mountains also vary in how they are formed. The four main types of mountains are folded, upwarped, fault-block, and volcanic.

**Reading Check** *What is the highest mountain peak on Earth?*

**Science Online**

**Topic: Landforms**
Visit glencoe.com for Web links to information about some ways landforms affect economic development.

**Activity** Create four colorful postcards with captions explaining how landforms have affected economic development in your area.

**Folded Mountains** The Appalachian Mountains and the Rocky Mountains in Canada, shown in **Figure 4,** are comprised of folded rock layers. In **folded mountains,** the rock layers are folded like a rug that has been pushed up against a wall.

**INTEGRATE Physics** To form folded mountains, tremendous forces inside Earth squeeze horizontal rock layers, causing them to fold. The Appalachian Mountains formed between 480 million and 250 million years ago and are among the oldest and longest mountain ranges in North America. The Appalachians once were higher than the Rocky Mountains, but weathering and erosion have worn them down. They now are less than 2,000 m above sea level. The Ouachita (WAH shuh tah) Mountains of Arkansas are extensions of the same mountain range.

**Figure 4** Folded mountains form when rock layers are squeezed from opposite sides. These mountains in Banff National Park, Canada, consist of folded rock layers.

**Figure 5** The southern Rocky Mountains are upwarped mountains that formed when crust was pushed up by forces inside Earth.

**Upwarped Mountains** The Adirondack Mountains in New York, the southern Rocky Mountains in Colorado and New Mexico, and the Black Hills in South Dakota are upwarped mountains. **Figure 5** shows a mountain range in Colorado. Notice the high peaks and sharp ridges that are common to this type of mountain. **Upwarped mountains** form when blocks of Earth's crust are pushed up by forces inside Earth. Over time, the soil and sedimentary rocks at the top of Earth's crust erode, exposing the hard, crystalline rock underneath. As these rocks erode, they form the peaks and ridges.

**Fault-Block Mountains** **Fault-block mountains** are made of huge, tilted blocks of rock that are separated from surrounding rock by faults. These faults are large fractures in rock along which mostly vertical movement has occurred. The Grand Tetons of Wyoming, shown in **Figure 6,** and the Sierra Nevada in California, are examples of fault-block mountains. As **Figure 6** shows, when these mountains formed, one block was pushed up, while the adjacent block dropped down. This mountain-building process produces majestic peaks and steep slopes.

**Figure 6** Fault-block mountains such as the Grand Tetons are formed when faults occur. Some rock blocks move up, and others move down. **Describe** *the difference between fault-block mountains and upwarped mountains.*

**Figure 7** Mount Shasta is a volcanic mountain made up of layers of lava flows and ash.

**Volcanic Mountains** **Volcanic mountains,** like the one shown in **Figure 7,** begin to form when molten material reaches the surface through a weak area of the crust. The deposited materials pile up, layer upon layer, until a cone-shaped structure forms. Two volcanic mountains in the United States are Mount St. Helens in Washington and Mount Shasta in California. The Hawaiian Islands are the peaks of huge volcanoes that sit on the ocean floor. Measured from the base, Mauna Loa in Hawaii would be higher than Mount Everest.

Plains, plateaus, and mountains offer different kinds of land-forms to explore. They range from low, coastal plains and high, desert plateaus to mountain ranges thousands of meters high.

## section 1 review

### Summary

**Plains and Plateaus**

- Plains are large, flat landforms that are usually found in the interior region of a continent.
- Plateaus are flat, raised landforms made of nearly horizontal, uplifted rocks.

**Mountains**

- Folded mountains form when horizontal rock layers are squeezed from opposite sides.
- Upwarped mountains form when blocks of Earth's crust are pushed up by forces inside Earth.
- Fault-block mountains form from huge, tilted blocks of rock that are separated by faults.
- Volcanic mountains form when molten rock forms cone-shaped structures at Earth's surface.

### Self Check

1. **Describe** the eight major landform regions in the United States that are mentioned in this chapter.
2. **Compare and contrast** volcanic mountains, folded mountains, and upwarped mountains using a three-circle Venn diagram.
3. **Think Critically** If you wanted to know whether a particular mountain was formed by movement along a fault, what would you look for? Support your reasoning.

**Applying Skills**

4. **Concept Map** Make an events-chain concept map to explain how interior plains and coastal plains form.

# Viewpoints

**as you read**

*What* **You'll Learn**

- **Define** latitude and longitude.
- **Explain** how latitude and longitude are used to identify locations on Earth.
- **Determine** the time and date in different time zones.

*Why* **It's Important**

Latitude and longitude allow you to locate places on Earth.

🔍 **Review Vocabulary**

**pole:** either end of an axis of a sphere

**New Vocabulary**

- ● equator
- ● latitude
- ● prime meridian
- ● longitude

## Latitude and Longitude

During hurricane season, meteorologists track storms as they form in the Atlantic Ocean. To identify the exact location of a storm, latitude and longitude lines are used. These lines form an imaginary grid system that allows people to locate any place on Earth accurately.

**Latitude** Look at **Figure 8.** The **equator** is an imaginary line around Earth exactly halfway between the north and south poles. It separates Earth into two equal halves called the northern hemisphere and the southern hemisphere. Lines running parallel to the equator are called lines of **latitude,** or parallels. Latitude is the distance, measured in degrees, either north or south of the equator. Because they are parallel, lines of latitude do not intersect, or cross, one another.

The equator is at 0° latitude, and the poles are each at 90° latitude. Locations north and south of the equator are referred to by degrees north latitude and degrees south latitude, respectively. Each degree is further divided into segments called minutes and seconds. There are 60 minutes in one degree and 60 seconds in one minute.

**Figure 8** Latitude and longitude are measurements that are used to indicate locations on Earth's surface.

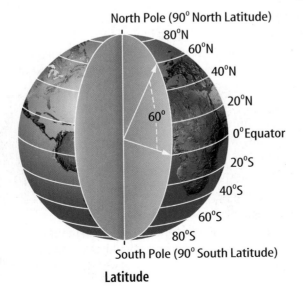

**Latitude**

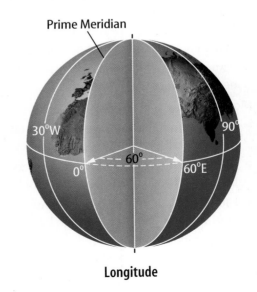

**Longitude**

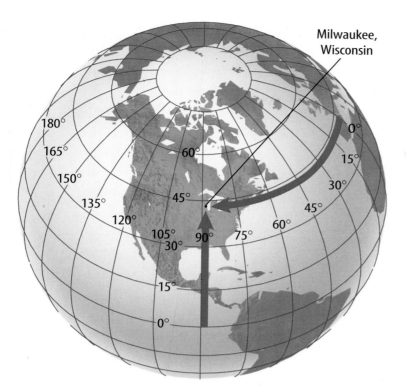

Milwaukee, Wisconsin

**Figure 9** The city of Milwaukee, Wisconsin is located at about 43°N, 88°W. **Explain** *the difference between latitude and longitude.*

**Physical Setting**

**1.1f** *Our system of time is based on celestial observations.* **Explain** the relationship of 24 hours in each day and Earth's 24 time zones.

**Longitude** The vertical lines, seen in **Figure 8,** have two names—meridians and lines of longitude. Longitude lines are different from latitude lines in many important ways. Just as the equator is used as a reference point for lines of latitude, there's a reference point for lines of longitude—the **prime meridian.** This imaginary line represents 0° longitude. In 1884, astronomers decided the prime meridian should go through the Greenwich (GREN ihtch) Observatory near London, England. The prime meridian had to be agreed upon, because no natural point of reference exists.

**Longitude** refers to distances in degrees east or west of the prime meridian. Points west of the prime meridian have west longitude measured from 0° to 180°, and points east of the prime meridian have east longitude, measured similarly.

**Prime Meridian** The prime meridian does not circle Earth as the equator does. Rather, it runs from the north pole through Greenwich, England, to the south pole. The line of longitude on the opposite side of Earth from the prime meridian is the 180° meridian. East lines of longitude meet west lines of longitude at the 180° meridian. You can locate places accurately using latitude and longitude as shown in **Figure 9.** Note that latitude position always comes first when a location is given.

 *What line of longitude is found opposite the prime meridian?*

## Mini LAB

**Interpreting Latitude and Longitude**

**Procedure**
1. Find the equator and prime meridian on a **world map.**
2. Move your finger to latitudes north of the equator, then south of the equator. Move your finger to longitudes west of the prime meridian, then east of the prime meridian.

**Analysis**
1. Identify the cities that have the following coordinates:
   a. 56°N, 38°E
   b. 34°S, 18°E
   c. 23°N, 82°W
2. Determine the latitude and longitude of the following cities:
   a. London, England
   b. Melbourne, Australia
   c. Buenos Aires, Argentina

**Figure 10** The United States has six time zones.

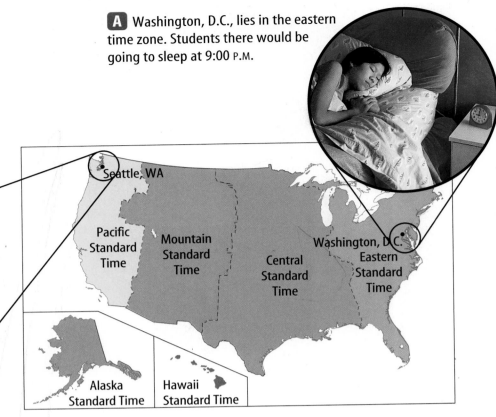

**A** Washington, D.C., lies in the eastern time zone. Students there would be going to sleep at 9:00 P.M.

**B** But students in Seattle, Washington, which lies in the Pacific time zone, are eating dinner. **Determine** *what time it would be in Seattle when the students in Washington, D.C., are sleeping at 9:00 P.M.*

Seattle, WA

Pacific Standard Time

Mountain Standard Time

Central Standard Time

Washington, D.C.

Eastern Standard Time

Alaska Standard Time

Hawaii Standard Time

**Physical Setting**

**1.1h** *The apparent motions of the Sun, Moon, planets, and stars across the sky can be explained by Earth's rotation and revolution.* **Discuss** Earth's rotation and revolution and how they affect day and night and the length of the year.

**INTEGRATE Social Studies**

**International Travel** If you travel east or west across three or more time zones, you could suffer from jet lag. Jet lag occurs when your internal time clock does not match the new time zone. Jet lag can disrupt the daily rhythms of sleeping and eating. Have you or any of your classmates ever traveled to a foreign country and suffered from jet lag?

# Time Zones

What time it is depends on where you are on Earth. Time is measured by tracking Earth's movement in relation to the Sun. Each day has 24 h, so Earth is divided into 24 time zones. Each time zone is about 15° of longitude wide and is 1 h different from the zones on each side of it. The United States has six different time zones. As you can see in **Figure 10,** people in different parts of the country don't experience dusk simultaneously. Because Earth rotates, the eastern states end a day while the western states are still in sunlight.

**Reading Check** *What is the basis for dividing Earth into 24 time zones?*

Time zones do not follow lines of longitude strictly. Time zone boundaries are adjusted in local areas. For example, if a city were split by a time zone boundary, the results would be confusing. In such a situation, the time zone boundary is moved outside the city.

# Calendar Dates

In each time zone, one day ends and the next day begins at midnight. If it is 11:59 P.M. Tuesday, then 2 min later it will be 12:01 A.M. Wednesday in that particular time zone.

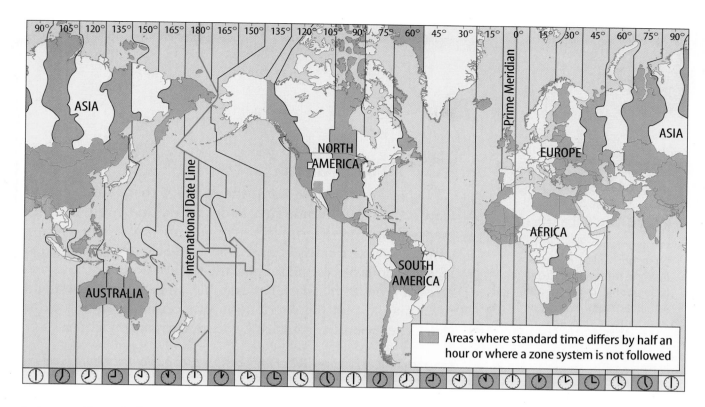

**International Date Line** You gain or lose time when you enter a new time zone. If you travel far enough, you can gain or lose a whole day. The International Date Line, shown on **Figure 11,** is the transition line for calendar days. If you were traveling west across the International Date Line, located near the 180° meridian, you would move your calendar forward one day. Traveling east, you would move your calendar back one day.

**Figure 11** Lines of longitude roughly determine the locations of time zone boundaries. These boundaries are adjusted locally to avoid splitting cities and other political subdivisions, such as counties, into different time zones.

## section 2 review

### Summary

**Latitude and Longitude**

- The equator is the imaginary line that wraps around Earth at 0° latitude.
- Latitude is the distance in degrees north or south of the equator.
- The prime meridian is the imaginary line that represents 0° longitude and runs north to south through Greenwich, England.
- Longitude is the distance in degrees east or west of the prime meridian.

**Time Zones and Calendar Dates**

- Earth is divided into 24 one-hour time zones.
- The International Date Line is the transition line for calendar days.

### Self Check

1. **Explain** how lines of latitude and longitude help people find locations on Earth.
2. **Determine** the latitude and longitude of New Orleans, Louisiana.
3. **Calculate** what time it would be in Los Angeles if it were 7:00 P.M. in New York City.
4. **Think Critically** How could you leave home on Monday to go sailing on the ocean, sail for 1 h on Sunday, and return home on Monday?

*Hot Words Hot Topics*: Bk 2 (5) p. 120

### Applying Math

5. **Use Fractions** If you started at the prime meridian and traveled east one-fourth of the way around Earth, what line of longitude would you reach?

# section 3

# Maps

## as you read

### *What* You'll Learn

- **Compare and contrast** map projections and their uses.
- **Analyze** information from topographic, geologic, and satellite maps.

### *Why* It's Important

Maps help people navigate and understand Earth.

### ⊙ Review Vocabulary
**globe:** a spherical representation of Earth

### New Vocabulary
- conic projection
- topographic map
- contour line
- map scale
- map legend

## Map Projections

Maps—road maps, world maps, maps that show physical features such as mountains and valleys, and even treasure maps—help you determine where you are and where you are going. They are models of Earth's surface. Scientists use maps to locate various places and to show the distribution of various features or types of material. For example, an Earth scientist might use a map to plot the distribution of a certain type of rock or soil. Other scientists could draw ocean currents on a map.

**✓ Reading Check** *What are possible uses a scientist would have for maps?*

Many maps are made as projections. A map projection is made when points and lines on a globe's surface are transferred onto paper, as shown in **Figure 12.** Map projections can be made in several different ways, but all types of projections distort the shapes of landmasses or their areas. Antarctica, for instance, might look smaller or larger than it is as a result of the projection that is used for a particular map.

**Figure 12** Lines of longitude are drawn parallel to one another in Mercator projections.
**Describe** *what happens near the poles in Mercator projections.*

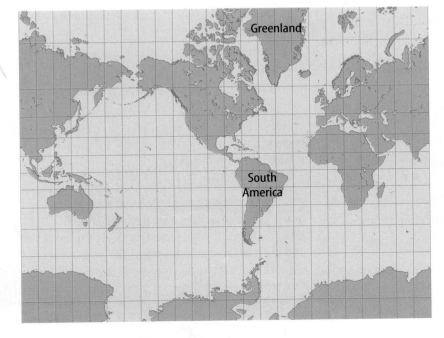

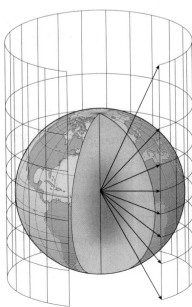

**Figure 13** Robinson projections show little distortion in continent shapes and sizes.

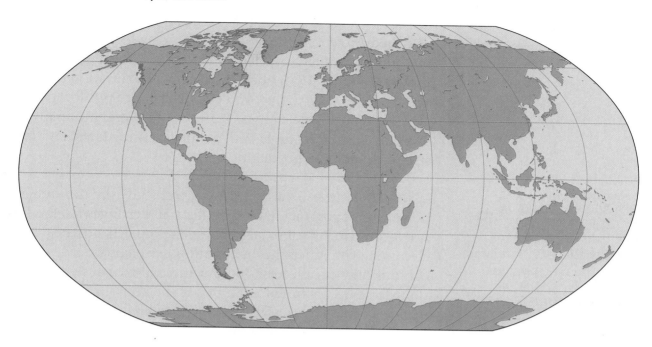

**Mercator Projection** Mercator (mer KAY ter) projections are used mainly on ships. They project correct shapes of continents, but the areas are distorted. Lines of longitude are projected onto the map parallel to each other. As you learned earlier, only latitude lines are parallel. Longitude lines meet at the poles. When longitude lines are projected as parallel, areas near the poles appear bigger than they are. Greenland, in the Mercator projection in **Figure 12,** appears to be larger than South America, but Greenland is actually smaller.

**Robinson Projection** A Robinson projection shows accurate continent shapes and more accurate land areas. As shown in **Figure 13,** lines of latitude remain parallel, and lines of longitude are curved as they are on a globe. This results in less distortion near the poles.

**Conic Projection** When you look at a road map or a weather map, you are using a conic (KAH nihk) projection. Conic projections, like the one shown in **Figure 14,** often are used to produce maps of small areas. These maps are well suited for middle latitude regions but are not as useful for mapping polar or equatorial regions. **Conic projections** are made by projecting points and lines from a globe onto a cone.

**Reading Check** *How are conic projections made?*

**Figure 14** Small areas are mapped accurately using conic projections.

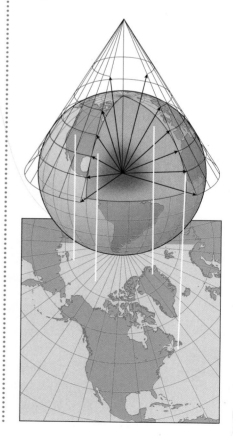

# Topographic Maps

For nature hiking, a conic map projection can be helpful by directing you to the location where you will start your hike. On your hike, however, you would need a detailed map identifying the hills and valleys of that specific area. A **topographic map,** shown in **Figure 15,** models the changes in elevation of Earth's surface. With such a map, you can determine your location relative to identifiable natural features. Topographic maps also indicate cultural features such as roads, cities, dams, and other structures built by people.

**Contour Lines** Before your hike, you study the contour lines on your topographic map to see the trail's changes in elevation. A **contour line** is a line on a map that connects points of equal elevation. The difference in elevation between two side-by-side contour lines is called the contour interval, which remains constant for each map. For example, if the contour interval on a map is 10 m and you walk between two lines anywhere on that map, you will have walked up or down 10 m.

In mountainous areas, the contour lines are close together. This situation models a steep slope. However, if the change in elevation is slight, the contour lines will be far apart. Often large contour intervals are used for mountainous terrain, and small contour intervals are used for fairly flat areas. Why? **Table 1** gives additional tips for examining contour lines.

**Index Contours** Some contour lines, called index contours, are marked with their elevation. If the contour interval is 5 m, you can determine the elevation of other lines around the index contour by adding or subtracting 5 m from the elevation shown on the index contour.

**INTEGRATE Physics**

**Mapping Planets** Satellites are used to map the surface of Earth and other planets. Space probes have made topographic maps of Venus and Mars. Satellites and probes send a radar beam or laser pulses to the surface and measure how long it takes for the beam or pulses to return to the space vehicle.

| Table 1  Contour Rules |
| --- |
| 1. **Contour lines close around hills and basins.** To decide whether you're looking at a hill or basin, you can read the elevation numbers or look for hachures (ha SHOORZ). These are short lines drawn at right angles to the contour line. They show depressions by pointing toward lower elevations. |
| 2. **Contour lines never cross.** If they did, it would mean that the spot where they cross would have two different elevations. |
| 3. **Contour lines form Vs that point upstream when they cross streams.** This is because streams flow in depressions that are beneath the elevation of the surrounding land surface. When the contour lines cross the depression, they appear as Vs pointing upstream on the map. |

## Figure 15

**P**lanning a hike? A topographic map will show you changes in elevation. With such a map, you can see at a glance how steep a mountain trail is, as well as its location relative to rivers, lakes, roads, and cities nearby. The steps in creating a topographic map are shown here.

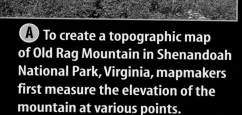

**A** To create a topographic map of Old Rag Mountain in Shenandoah National Park, Virginia, mapmakers first measure the elevation of the mountain at various points.

**B** These points are then projected onto paper. Points at the same elevation are connected, forming contour lines that encircle the mountain.

**C** Where contour lines on a topographic map are close together, elevation is changing rapidly—and the trail is very steep!

**Topic: Map Technology**
Visit glencoe.com for Web links to information about modern cartography and technology.

**Activity** Become a cartographer by developing a plan that uses map technology. For example, plan a traveling vacation or design a home or recreation area. Make a map of your trip or new environment.

**Figure 16** Geologists use block diagrams to understand Earth's subsurface. The different colors represent different rock layers.

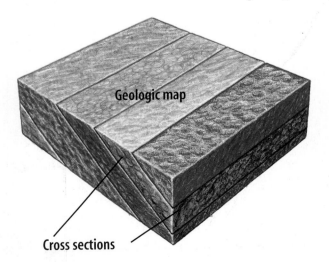

Geologic map

Cross sections

**Map Scale** When planning your hike, you'll want to determine the distance to your destination before you leave. Because maps are small models of Earth's surface, distances and sizes of things shown on a map are proportional to the real thing on Earth. Therefore, real distances can be found by using a scale.

The **map scale** is the relationship between the distances on the map and distances on Earth's surface. Scale often is represented as a ratio. For example, a topographic map of the Grand Canyon might have a scale that reads 1:80,000. This means that one unit on the map represents 80,000 units on land. If the unit you wanted to use was a centimeter, then 1 cm on the map would equal 80,000 cm on land. The unit of distance could be feet or millimeters or any other measure of distance. However, the units of measure on each side of the ratio must always be the same. A map scale also can be shown in the form of a small bar that is divided into sections and scaled down to match real distances on Earth.

**Map Legend** Topographic maps and most other maps have a legend. A **map legend** explains what the symbols used on the map mean. Some frequently used symbols for topographic maps are shown in the appendix at the back of the book.

**Map Series** Topographic maps are made to cover different amounts of Earth's surface. A map series includes maps that have the same dimensions of latitude and longitude. For example, one map series includes maps that are 7.5 minutes of latitude by 7.5 minutes of longitude. Other map series include maps covering larger areas of Earth's surface.

## Geologic Maps

One of the more important tools to Earth scientists is the geologic map. Geologic maps show the arrangement and types of rocks at Earth's surface. Using geologic maps and data collected from rock exposures, a geologist can infer how rock layers might look below Earth's surface. The block diagram in **Figure 16** is a 3-D model that illustrates a solid section of Earth. The top surface of the block is the geologic map. Side views of the block are called cross sections, which are derived from the surface map. Developing geologic maps and cross sections is extremely important for the exploration and extraction of natural resources. What can a scientist do to determine whether a cross section accurately represents the underground features?

**Three-Dimensional Maps** Topographic maps and geologic maps are two-dimensional models that are used to study features of Earth's surface. To visualize Earth three dimensionally, scientists often rely on computers. Using computers, information is digitized to create a three-dimensional view of features such as rock layers or river systems. Digitizing is a process by which points are plotted on a coordinate grid.

**Map Uses** As you have learned, Earth can be viewed in many different ways. Maps are chosen depending upon the situation. If you wanted to determine New Zealand's location relative to Canada and you didn't have a globe, you probably would examine a Mercator projection. In your search, you would use lines of latitude and longitude, and a map scale. If you wanted to travel across the country, you would rely on a road map, or conic projection. You also would use a map legend to help locate features along the way. To climb the highest peak in your region, you would take along a topographic map.

**Analysis, Inquiry, and Design**

**S1.2b, S3.1b, ICT 2.3** Briefly compare and contrast map projections, topographic maps, geologic maps, and a globe. Explain why a map scale is always necessary.

## Applying Science

### How can you create a cross section from a geologic map?

Earth scientists are interested in knowing the types of rocks and their configurations underground. To help them visualize this, they use geologic maps. Geologic maps offer a two-dimensional view of the three-dimensional situation found under Earth's surface. You don't have to be a professional geologist to understand a geologic map. Use your ability to create graphs to interpret this geologic map.

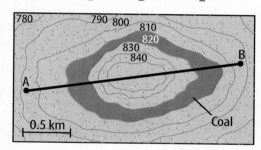

### Identifying the Problem

Above is a simple geologic map showing where a coal seam is found on Earth's surface. Place a straight edge of paper along the line marked A–B and mark the points where it meets a contour. Make a different color mark where it meets the exposure of coal. Make a graph on which the various elevations (in meters) are marked on the *y*-axis. Lay your marked edge of paper along the *x*-axis and transfer the points directly above onto the proper elevation line. Now connect the dots to draw in the land's surface and connect the marks you made for the coal seam separately.

### Solving the Problem

1. What type of topography does the map represent?
2. At what elevation is the coal seam?
3. Does this seam tilt, or is it horizontal? Explain how you know.

# Remote Sensing

Scientists use remote-sensing techniques to collect much of the data used for making maps. Remote sensing is a way of collecting information about Earth from a distance, often using satellites.

**Landsat** One way that Earth's surface has been studied is with data collected from Landsat satellites, as shown in **Figure 17.** These satellites take pictures of Earth's surface using different wavelengths of light. The images can be used to make maps of snow cover over the United States or to evaluate the impact of forest fires, such as those that occurred in the western United States during the summer of 2000. The newest Landsat satellite, *Landsat 7,* can acquire detailed images by detecting light reflected off landforms on Earth.

**Global Positioning System** The Global Positioning System, or GPS, is a satellite-based, radio-navigation system that allows users to determine their exact position anywhere on Earth. Twenty-four satellites orbit 20,200 km above the planet. Each satellite sends a position signal and a time signal. The satellites are arranged in their orbits so that signals from at least six can be picked up at any given moment by someone using a GPS receiver. By processing the signals, the receiver calculates the user's exact location. GPS technology is used to navigate, to create detailed maps, and to track wildlife.

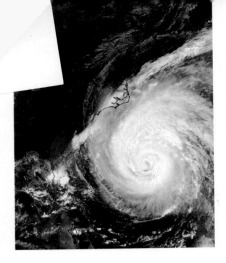

**Figure 17** Hurricane Isabel's wind lashed the North Carolina and Virginia coasts on September 18, 2003.
**Analyze** *this satellite photo of Hurricane Isabel approaching the North Carolina Outer Banks. How many states do you think might be affected by this weather system?*

## section 3 review

### Summary

**Map Projections**
- A map projection is the projection of points and lines of a globe's surface onto paper.

**Topographic Maps**
- Topographic maps show the changes in elevation of Earth's surface by using contour lines.

**Geologic Maps**
- Geologic maps show the arrangement and types of rocks at Earth's surface.

**Remote Sensing**
- Remote sensing is a way of collecting information about Earth from a distance, often by using satellites.
- Distant planets can be mapped using satellites.

### Self Check

1. **Compare and contrast** Mercator and conic projections.
2. **Explain** why Greenland appears larger on a Mercator projection than it does on a Robinson projection.
3. **Describe** why contour lines never cross.
4. **Explain** whether a topographic map or a geologic map would be most useful for drilling a water well.
5. **Think Critically** Review the satellite photograph at the beginning of this chapter. Is most of the city near or far from the water? Why is it located there?

#### Applying Skills

6. **Make Models** Architects make detailed maps called scale drawings to help them plan their work. Make a scale drawing of your classroom.

**More Section Review** glencoe.com

# Making a T⦿pographic Map

Have you ever wondered how topographic maps are made? Today, radar and remote-sensing devices aboard satellites collect data, and computers and graphic systems make the maps. In the past, surveyors and aerial photographers collected data. Then, maps were hand drawn by cartographers, or mapmakers. In this lab, you can practice cartography.

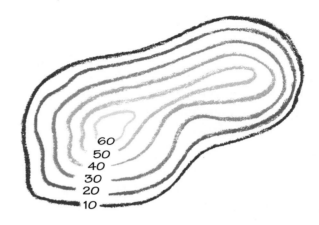

## ⊙ Real-World Question

How is a topographic map made?

### Goals
■ **Draw** a topographic map.
■ **Compare and contrast** contour intervals.

### Materials
plastic model of a landform
water tinted with food coloring
transparency
clear-plastic storage box with lid
beaker
metric ruler
tape
transparency marker

## ⊙ Procedure

1. Using the ruler and the transparency marker, make marks up the side of the storage box that are 2 cm apart.

2. Secure the transparency to the outside of the box lid with tape.

3. Place the plastic model in the box. The bottom of the box will be zero elevation.

4. Using the beaker, pour water into the box to a height of 2 cm. Place the lid on the box.

5. Use the transparency marker to trace the top of the water line on the transparency.

6. Using the scale 2 cm = 10 m, mark the elevation on the line.

7. Repeat the process of adding 2 cm of water and tracing until the landform is mapped.

8. Transfer the tracing of the landform onto a sheet of white paper.

## ⊙ Conclude and Apply

1. **Identify** the contour interval of this topographic map.

2. **Evaluate** how the distance between contour lines on the map shows the steepness of the slope on the landform model.

3. **Determine** the total elevation of the landform you have selected.

4. **Describe** how elevation was represented on your map.

5. **Explain** how elevations are shown on topographic maps.

6. Must all topographic maps have a contour line that represents 0 m of elevation? Explain.

# Model and Invent

## Constructing Landfors

### Goals

■ **Research** how contour lines show relief on a topographic map.

■ **Determine** what scale you can best use to model a landscape of your choice.

■ Working cooperatively with your classmates, model a landscape in three dimensions from the information given on a topographic map.

### Possible Materials

U.S. Geological Survey 7.5-minute quadrangle maps

sandbox sand

rolls of brown paper towels

spray bottle filled with water

ruler

### Real-World Question

Most maps perform well in helping you get from place to place. A road map, for example, will allow you to choose the shortest route from one place to another. If you are hiking, though, distance might not be so important. You might want to choose a route that avoids steep terrain. In this case you need a map that shows the highs and lows of Earth's surface, called relief. Topographic maps use contour lines to show the landscape in three dimensions. Among their many uses, such maps allow hikers to choose routes that maximize the scenery and minimize the physical exertion. What does a landscape depicted on a two-dimensional topographic map look like in three dimensions? How can you model a landscape?

### Make a Model

1. **Choose** a topographic map showing a landscape easily modeled using sand. Check to see what contour interval is used on the map. Use the index contours to find the difference between the lowest and the highest elevations shown on the landscape. Check the distance scale to determine how much area the landscape covers.

2. **Determine** the scale you will use to convert the elevations shown on your map to heights on your model. Make sure the scale is proportional to the distances on your map.

3. **Plan** a model of the landscape in sand by sketching the main features and their scaled heights onto paper. Note the degree of steepness found on all sides of the features.

4. **Prepare** a document that shows the scale you plan to use for your model and the calculations you used to derive that scale. Remember to use the same scale for distance as you use for height. If your landscape is fairly flat, you can exaggerate the vertical scale by a factor of two or three. Be sure your paper is neat, is easy to follow, and includes all units. Present the document to your teacher for approval.

## ◉ Test Your Model

1. Using the sand, spray bottle, and ruler, create a scale model of your landscape on the brown paper towels.
2. **Check** your topographic map to be sure your model includes the landscape features at their proper heights and proper degrees of steepness.

## ◉ Analyze Your Data

1. **Determine** if your model accurately represents the landscape depicted on your topographic map. Discuss the strengths and weaknesses of your model.
2. **Explain** why it was important to use the same scale for height and distance. If you exaggerated the height, why was it important to indicate the exaggeration on your model?

## ◉ Conclude and Apply

1. **Infer** why the mapmakers chose the contour interval used on your topographic map?
2. **Predict** the contour intervals mapmakers might choose for topographic maps of the world's tallest mountains—the Himalaya—and for topographic maps of Kansas, which is fairly flat.

### Communicating Your Data

Prepare a vacation getaway commercial to advertise the topographical features of your model landscape. Be sure to discuss the landscape elevation and features, scale, and similarities to actual landforms.

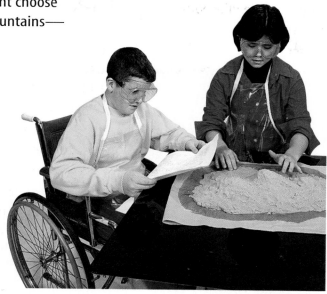

New York Harbor in 1849

Rich Midwest farmland

Georgia peaches

Alaska pipeline

Maine fishing and lobster industry

# LOCATION, LOCATION

**W**hy is New York City at the mouth of the Hudson River and not 300 km inland? Why are there more farms in Iowa than in Alaska? What's the reason for growing lots of peaches in Georgia but not in California's Death Valley? It's all about location. The landforms, climate, soil, and resources in an area determine where cities and farms grow and what people connected with them do.

## LANDFORMS ARE KEY

When many American cities were founded hundreds of years ago, waterways were the best means of transportation. Old cities such as New York City and Boston are located on deep harbors where ships could land with people and goods. Rivers also were major highways centuries ago. They still are.

Topography and soil also play a role in where activities such as farming take root. States such as Iowa and Illinois have many farms because they have flat land and fertile soil. Growing crops is more difficult in mountainous areas or where soil is stony and poor.

## CLIMATE AND SOIL

Climate limits the locations of cities and farms, as well. The fertile soil and warm, moist climate of Georgia make it a perfect place to grow peaches. California's Death Valley can't support such crops because it's a hot, dry desert.

## RESOURCES RULE

The location of an important natural resource can change the rules. A gold deposit or an oil field can cause a town to grow in a place where the topography, soil, and climate are not favorable. For example, thousands of people now live in parts of Alaska only because of the great supply of oil there. Maine has a harsh climate and poor soil. But people settled along its coast because they could catch lobsters and fish in the nearby North Atlantic.

The rules that govern where towns grow and where people live are different now than they used to be. Often information, not goods, moves from place to place on computers that can be anywhere. But as long as people farm, use minerals, and transport goods from place to place, the natural environment and natural resources will always help determine where people are and what they do.

**Research** Why was your community built where it is? Research its history. What types of economic activity were important when it was founded? Did topography, climate, or resources determine its location? Design a Moment in History to share your information.

Science Online

For more information, visit glencoe.com

## Reviewing Main Ideas

### Section 1  Landforms

1. The three main types of landforms are plains, plateaus, and mountains.

2. Plains are large, flat areas. Plateaus are relatively flat, raised areas of land made up of nearly horizontal rocks that have been uplifted. Mountains rise high above the surrounding land.

### Section 2  Viewpoints

1. Latitude and longitude form an imaginary grid system that enables points on Earth to be located exactly.

2. Latitude is the distance in degrees north or south of the equator. Longitude is the distance in degrees east or west of the prime meridian.

3. Earth is divided into 24 time zones. Each time zone represents a 1-h difference. The International Date Line separates different calendar days.

### Section 3  Maps

1. Mercator, Robinson, and conic projections are made by transferring points and lines on a globe's surface onto paper.

2. Topographic maps show the elevation of Earth's surface. Geologic maps show the types of rocks that make up Earth's surface.

3. Remote sensing is a way of collecting information from a distance. Satellites are important remote-sensing devices.

## Visualizing Main Ideas

*Copy and complete the following concept map on landforms.*

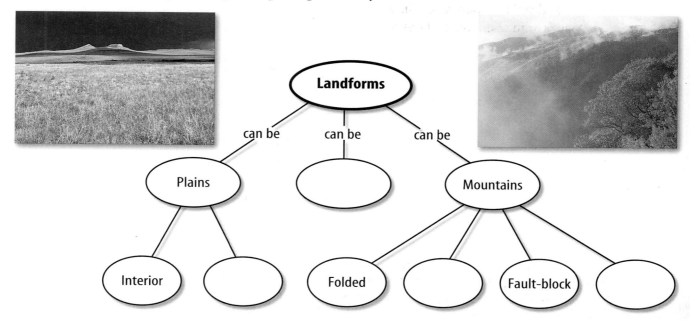

## Using Vocabulary

conic projection p. 165
contour line p. 166
equator p. 160
fault-block
    mountain p. 158
folded mountain p. 157
latitude p. 160
longitude p. 161
map legend p. 168

map scale p. 168
plain p. 154
plateau p. 156
prime meridian p. 161
topographic map p. 166
upwarped
    mountain p. 158
volcanic mountain p. 159

*For each set of terms below, choose the one term that does not belong and explain why it does not belong.*

1. upwarped mountain—equator—volcanic mountain

2. plain—plateau—prime meridian

3. topographic map—contour line—volcanic mountain

4. prime meridian—equator—folded mountain

5. fault-block mountain—upwarped mountain—plateau

## Checking Concepts

*Choose the word or phrase that best answers the question.*

6. What makes up about 50 percent of all land areas in the United States?
   A) plateaus
   B) plains
   C) mountains
   D) volcanoes

7. Which type of map shows changes in elevation at Earth's surface?
   A) conic
   B) topographic
   C) Robinson
   D) Mercator

8. How many degrees apart are the 24 time zones?
   A) 10°
   B) 34°
   C) 15°
   D) 25°

**Use the photo below to answer question 9.**

9. What kind of mountains are the Grand Tetons of Wyoming?
   A) fault-block
   B) volcanic
   C) upwarped
   D) folded

10. Landsat satellites collect data by using
    A) sonar
    B) echolocation
    C) sound waves.
    D) light waves.

11. Which type of map is most distorted at the poles?
    A) conic
    B) topographic
    C) Robinson
    D) Mercator

12. Where is the north pole located?
    A) 0°N
    B) 180°N
    C) 50°N
    D) 90°N

13. What is measured with respect to sea level?
    A) contour interval
    B) elevation
    C) conic projection
    D) sonar

14. What kind of map shows rock types making up Earth's surface?
    A) topographic
    B) Robinson
    C) geologic
    D) Mercator

15. Which major U.S. landform includes the Grand Canyon?
    A) Great Plains
    B) Great Basin
    C) Colorado Plateau
    D) Gulf Coastal Plain

Vocabulary Puzzlemaker glencoe.com

## Thinking Critically

**16. Explain** how a topographic map of the Atlantic Coastal Plain differs from a topographic map of the Rocky Mountains.

**17. Determine** If you left Korea early Wednesday morning and flew to Hawaii, on what day of the week would you arrive?

**Use the illustration below to answer question 18.**

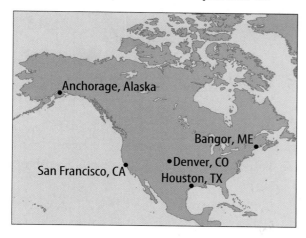

**18. Determine** Using the map above, arrange these cities in order from the city with the earliest time to the one with the latest time on a given day: Anchorage, Alaska; San Francisco, California; Bangor, Maine; Denver, Colorado; Houston, Texas.

**19. Describe** how a map with a scale of 1:50,000 is different from a map with a scale of 1:24,000.

**20. Compare and contrast** Mercator, Robinson, and conic map projections.

**21. Form Hypotheses** You are visiting a mountain in the northwest part of the United States. The mountain has steep sides and is not part of a mountain range. A crater can be seen at the top of the mountain. Hypothesize about what type of mountain you are visiting.

**22. Concept Map** Copy and complete the following concept map about parts of a topographic map.

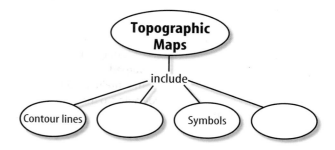

## Performance Activities

**23. Poem** Create a poem about one type of landform. Include characteristics of the landform in your poem. How can the shape of your poem add meaning to your poem? Display your poem with those of your classmates.

*Hot Words Hot Topics:* Bk (24) p. 91; (25) pp. 91, 406

## Applying Math

**24. Calculate** If you were flying directly south from the north pole and reached 70° north latitude, how many more degrees of latitude would you pass over before reaching the south pole? Illustrate and label a diagram to support your answer.

**Use the map below to answer question 25.**

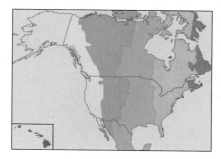

**25. Calculate** If it is 2:00 P.M. in Orlando, Florida, what time is it in Los Angeles, California? In Anchorage, Alaska? In your hometown?

**Part I**

*Record your answers on the answer sheet provided by your teacher or on a sheet of paper.*

**Use the map below to answer question 1.**

**1** Which of the following is shown above?
   (1) cross section    (3) topographic map
   (2) geologic map    (4) road map

**2** Which landform is a relatively flat area that has high elevation?
   (1) mountain    (3) coastal plain
   (2) interior plain    (4) plateau

**3** Which of the following can provide detailed information about your position on Earth's surface?
   (1) prime meridian
   (2) global positioning system
   (3) International Date Line
   (4) LandSat 7

**4** What connects points of equal elevation on a map?
   (1) legend
   (2) series
   (3) scale
   (4) contour line

**5** Which type of mountain forms when rock layers are squeezed and bent?
   (1) fault-block mountains
   (2) upwarped mountains
   (3) folded mountains
   (4) volcanic mountains

**Use the illustration below to answer questions 6–8. The numbers on the drawing represent meters above sea level.**

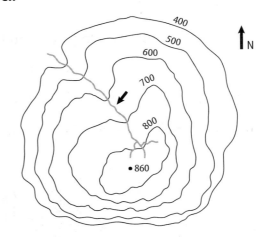

**6** Which side of the feature has the steepest slope?
   (1) north side    (3) west side
   (2) east side    (4) south side

**7** What is the highest elevation on the feature?
   (1) 800 meters    (3) 860 meters
   (2) 960 meters    (4) 700 meters

**8** What does the line that is marked by the arrow represent?
   (1) a contour line    (3) a high ridge
   (2) a stream    (4) a glacier

**9** Which type of map is made by projecting points and lines from a globe onto a cone?
   (1) Mercator projection
   (2) conic projection
   (3) Robinson projection
   (4) geologic map

**10** Which are useful for measuring position north or south of the equator?
   (1) lines of latitude
   (2) lines of longitude
   (3) index contours
   (4) map legends

**Part II**

*Record your answers on the answer sheet provided by your teacher or on a separate sheet of paper.*

**11** What is a time zone? How are time zones determined around the world? Why are they needed?

**12** Which type of map would you use to find the location of a layer of coal at Earth's surface? Why?

**13** Why are lines of latitude sometimes called parallels?

**14** List the locations on Earth that represent 0° latitude, 90°N latitude, and 90°S latitude.

**Use the map below to answer questions 15–16.**

**15** Where do mountains, plateaus, and plains occur in the United States? Describe these regions and how they were formed.

**16** Take the role of a fur trader, pioneer, or explorer. Write three journal entries that give a general description of how the landforms change across the United States.

**17** Why is remote sensing important to society? What types of information are obtained?

**18** Why are computers often used to make maps?

**19** Why might you experience jet lag if you travel across the United States on a plane? Predict which direction it would be more difficult to adjust to jet lag—when traveling from Hawaii to New York or New York to Hawaii. Support your answer with an example of each situation.

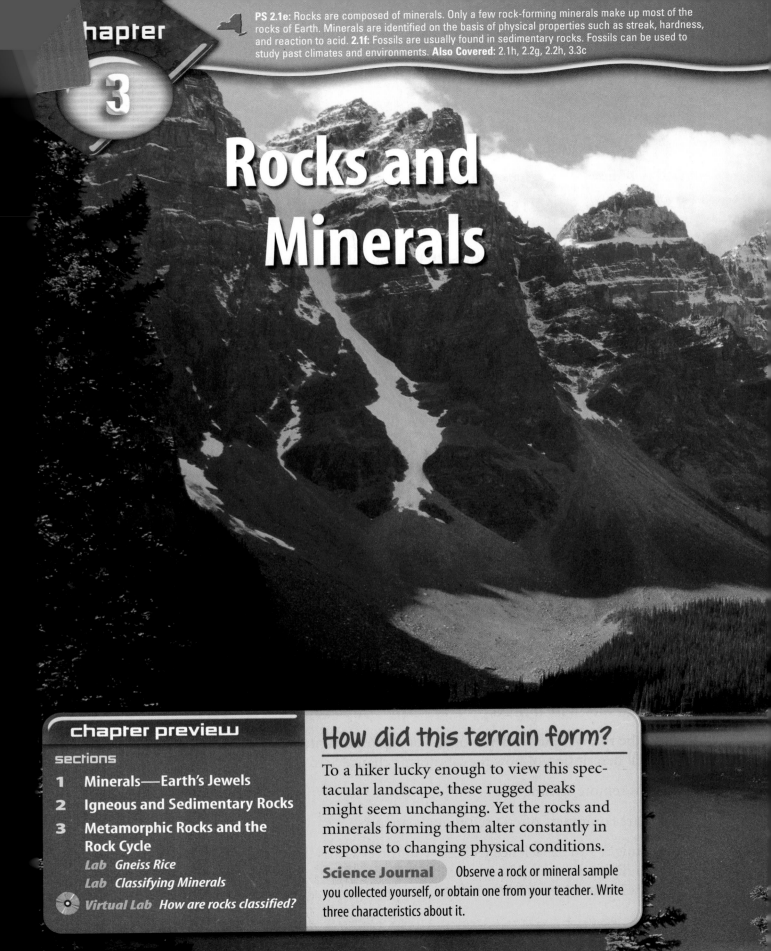

chapter

3

**PS 2.1e:** Rocks are composed of minerals. Only a few rock-forming minerals make up most of the rocks of Earth. Minerals are identified on the basis of physical properties such as streak, hardness, and reaction to acid. **2.1f:** Fossils are usually found in sedimentary rocks. Fossils can be used to study past climates and environments. **Also Covered:** 2.1h, 2.2g, 2.2h, 3.3c

# Rocks and Minerals

## chapter preview

### sections

## How did this terrain form?

To a hiker lucky enough to view this spectacular landscape, these rugged peaks might seem unchanging. Yet the rocks and minerals forming them alter constantly in response to changing physical conditions.

**Science Journal**    Observe a rock or mineral sample you collected yourself, or obtain one from your teacher. Write three characteristics about it.

# Start-Up Activities

## Observe a Rock

Upon reaching the top, you have a chance to look more closely at the rock you've been climbing. First, you notice that it sparkles in the Sun because of the silvery specks that are stuck in the rock. Looking closer, you also see clear, glassy pieces and pink, irregular chunks. What is the rock made of? How did it get here?

1. Obtain a sparkling rock from your teacher. You also will need a magnifying lens.

2. Observe the rock with the magnifying lens. Your job is to observe and record as many of the features of the rock as you can.

3. Return the rock to your teacher.

4. Describe your rock so other students could identify it from a variety of rocks.

5. **Think Critically** How do the parts of the rock fit together to form the whole thing? Describe this in your Science Journal and make a drawing. Be sure to label the colors and shapes in your drawing.

**Science Online** Preview this chapter's content and activities at glencoe.com

**Rocks and Minerals** Make the following Foldable to compare and contrast the characteristics of rocks and minerals.

**STEP 1** Fold one sheet of paper lengthwise.

**STEP 2** Fold into thirds.

**STEP 3** Unfold and draw overlapping ovals. Cut the top sheet along the folds.

**STEP 4** Label the ovals as shown.

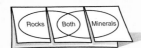

**Construct a Venn Diagram** As you read the chapter, list the characteristics unique to rocks under the left tab, those unique to minerals under the right tab, and those characteristics common to both under the middle tab.

# section 1

# Minerals—Earth's Jewels

## as you read

### *What* You'll Learn
- **Identify** the difference between a mineral and a rock.
- **Describe** the properties that are used to identify minerals.

### *Why* It's Important
Minerals are basic substances of nature that humans use for a variety of purposes.

### ⊘ Review Vocabulary
**physical property:** any characteristic of a material that you can observe without changing the identity of the material

### New Vocabulary
- mineral
- gem
- rock
- ore
- crystal

## What is a mineral?

Suppose you are planning an expedition to find minerals (MIH nuh rulz). Where would you look? Do you think you'll have to crawl into a cave or brave the depths of a mine? Well, put away your flashlight. You can find minerals in your own home—in the salt shaker and in your pencil. Metal pots, glassware, and ceramic dishes are products made from minerals. Minerals and products made from them, shown in **Figure 1,** surround you.

**Minerals Defined** **Minerals** are inorganic, solid materials found in nature. *Inorganic* means they usually are not formed by plants or animals. You could go outside and find minerals that occur as gleaming crystals—or as small grains in ordinary rocks. X-ray patterns of a mineral show an orderly arrangement of atoms that looks something like a garden trellis. Evidence of this orderly arrangement is the beautiful crystal shape often seen in minerals. The particular chemical makeup and arrangement of the atoms in the crystal is unique to each mineral. **Rocks,** such as the one used in the Launch Lab, usually are made of two or more minerals. Each mineral has unique characteristics you can use to identify it. So far, more than 4,000 minerals have been identified.

**Figure 1** You use minerals every day—maybe without even realizing it. Minerals are used to make many common objects.

The mineral quartz is used to make the glass that you use every day.

The "lead" in a pencil is not really lead. It is the mineral graphite.

**How do minerals form?** Minerals form in several ways. One way is from melted rock material inside Earth called magma. As magma cools, atoms combine in orderly patterns to form minerals. Minerals also form from magma that reaches Earth's surface. Magma at Earth's surface is called lava.

Evaporation can form minerals. Just as salt crystals appear when seawater evaporates, other dissolved minerals, such as gypsum, can crystallize. A process called precipitation (prih sih puh TAY shun) can form minerals, too. Water can hold only so much dissolved material. Any extra separates and falls out as a solid. Large areas of the ocean floor are covered with manganese nodules that formed in this way. These metallic spheres average 25 cm in diameter. They crystallized directly from seawater containing metal atoms.

**Figure 2** This cluster of fluorite crystals formed from a solution rich in dissolved minerals.

**Formation Clues** Sometimes you can tell how a mineral formed by how it looks. Large mineral grains that fit together like a puzzle seem to show up in rocks formed from slow-cooling magma. If you see large, perfectly formed crystals, it means the mineral had plenty of space in which to grow. This is a sign they may have formed in open pockets within the rock.

The crystals you see in **Figure 2** grew this way from a solution that was rich in dissolved minerals. To figure out how a mineral was formed, you have to look at the size of the mineral crystal and how the crystals fit together.

## Properties of Minerals

The cheers are deafening. The crowd is jumping and screaming. From your seat high in the bleachers, you see someone who is wearing a yellow shirt and has long, dark hair in braids, just like a friend you saw this morning. You're sure it's your friend only when she turns and you recognize her smile. You've identified your friend by physical properties that set her apart from other people—her clothing, hair color and style, and facial features. Each mineral, too, has a set of physical properties that can be used to identify it. Most common minerals can be identified with items you have around the house and can carry in your pocket, such as a penny or a steel file. With a little practice you can learn to recognize mineral shapes, too. Next you will learn about properties that help you identify minerals.

**Physical Setting**

**2.1e  Discuss** several ways minerals can form.

**INTEGRATE Life Science**

**Bone Composition** Bones, such as those found in humans and horses, contain tiny crystals of the mineral apatite. Research apatite and report your findings to your class.

**Figure 3** The mineral pyrite often forms crystals with six faces. **Determine** *why pyrite also is called "fool's gold."*

**Crystals** All minerals have an orderly pattern of atoms. The atoms making up the mineral are arranged in a repeating pattern. Solid materials that have such a pattern of atoms are called **crystals.** Sometimes crystals have smooth growth surfaces called crystal faces. The mineral pyrite commonly forms crystals with six crystal faces, as shown in **Figure 3.**

✔ **Reading Check** *What distinguishes crystals from other types of solid matter?*

**Cleavage and Fracture** Another clue to a mineral's identity is the way it breaks. Minerals that split into pieces with smooth, regular planes that reflect light are said to have cleavage (KLEE vihj). The mica sample in **Figure 4A** shows cleavage by splitting into thin sheets. Splitting mica along a cleavage surface is similar to peeling off a piece of presliced cheese. Cleavage is caused by weaknesses within the arrangement of atoms that make up the mineral.

Not all minerals have cleavage. Some break into pieces with jagged or rough edges. Instead of neat slices, these pieces are shaped more like hunks of cheese torn from an unsliced block. Materials that break this way, such as quartz, have what is called fracture (FRAK chur). **Figure 4C** shows the fracture of flint.

**Figure 4** Some minerals have one or more directions of cleavage. If minerals do not break along flat surfaces, they have fracture.

**A** Minerals in the mica group have one direction of cleavage and can be peeled off in sheets.

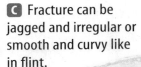

**B** The mineral halite, also called rock salt, has three directions of cleavage at right angles to each other.
**Infer** *Why might grains of rock salt look like little cubes?*

**C** Fracture can be jagged and irregular or smooth and curvy like in flint.

**Figure 5** The mineral calcite can form in a variety of colors. The colors are caused by slight impurities.

**Color** The reddish-gold color of a new penny shows you that it contains copper. The bright yellow color of sulfur is a valuable clue to its identity. Sometimes a mineral's color can help you figure out what it is. But color also can fool you. The common mineral pyrite (PI rite) has a shiny, gold color similar to real gold—close enough to disappoint many prospectors during the California Gold Rush in the 1800s. Because of this, pyrite also is called fool's gold. While different minerals can look similar in color, the same mineral can occur in a variety of colors. The mineral calcite, for example, can occur in many different colors, as shown in **Figure 5.**

**Streak and Luster** Scraping a mineral sample across an unglazed, white tile, called a streak plate, produces a streak of color, as shown in **Figure 6.** Oddly enough, the streak is not necessarily the same color as the mineral itself. This streak of powdered mineral is more useful for identification than the mineral's color. Gold prospectors could have saved themselves a lot of heartache if they had known about the streak test. Pyrite makes a greenish-black or brownish-black streak, but gold makes a yellow streak.

Is the mineral shiny? Dull? Pearly? Words like these describe another property of minerals, called luster. Luster describes how light reflects from a mineral's surface. If it shines like a metal, the mineral has metallic (muh TA lihk) luster. Nonmetallic minerals can be described as having pearly, glassy, dull, or earthy luster. You can use color, streak, and luster to help identify minerals.

**Figure 6** Streak is the color of the powdered mineral. The mineral hematite has a characteristic reddish-brown streak.
**Explain** *how you obtain a mineral's streak.*

| Mineral | Hardness | Hardness of Common Objects |
|---|---|---|
| Talc | 1 (softest) | |
| Gypsum | 2 | fingernail (2.5) |
| Calcite | 3 | copper penny (3.0) |
| Fluorite | 4 | iron nail (4.5) |
| Apatite | 5 | glass (5.5) |
| Feldspar | 6 | steel file (6.5) |
| Quartz | 7 | streak plate (7) |
| Topaz | 8 | |
| Corundum | 9 | |
| Diamond | 10 (hardest) | |

**Table 1 Mohs Scale**

**Hardness** As you investigate different minerals, you'll find that some are harder than others. Some minerals, like talc, are so soft that they can be scratched with a fingernail. Others, like diamond, are so hard that they can be used to cut almost anything else.

In 1822, an Austrian geologist named Friedrich Mohs also noticed this property of minerals. He developed a way to classify minerals by their hardness. The Mohs scale, shown in **Table 1,** classifies minerals from 1 (softest) to 10 (hardest). You can determine hardness by trying to scratch one mineral with another to see which is harder. For example, fluorite (4 on the Mohs scale) will scratch calcite (3 on the scale), but fluorite cannot scratch apatite (5 on the scale). You also can use a homemade mineral identification kit—a copper penny, a nail, and a small glass plate with smooth edges. Simply find out what scratches what. Is the mineral hard enough to scratch a penny? Will it scratch glass?

**Specific Gravity** Some minerals are heavier for their size than others. Specific gravity compares the weight of a mineral with the weight of an equal volume of water. Pyrite—or fool's gold—is about five times heavier than water. Pure gold is more than 19 times heavier than water. You could easily sense this difference by holding each one in your hand. Measuring specific gravity is another way you can identify minerals.

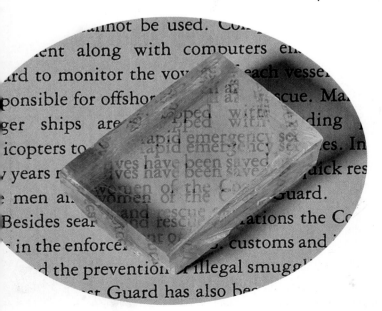

**Figure 7** Calcite has the unique property of double refraction.

**Other Properties** Some minerals have other unusual properties that can help identify them. The mineral magnetite will attract a magnet. The mineral calcite has two unusual properties. It will fizz when it comes into contact with an acid like dilute HCl. Also, if you look through a clear calcite crystal, you will see a double image, as shown in **Figure 7.** Scientists taste some minerals to identify them, but you should not try this yourself. Halite, also called rock salt, has a salty taste.

Together, all of the properties you have read about are used to identify minerals. Learn to use them and you can be a mineral detective.

# Common Minerals

Rocks that make up huge mountain ranges are made of minerals. But only a small number of the more than 4,000 minerals make up most rocks. These minerals often are called the rock-forming minerals. If you can recognize these minerals, you will be able to identify most rocks. Other minerals are much rarer. However, some of these rare minerals also are important because they are used as gems or they are ore minerals, which are sources of valuable metals.

Most of the rock-forming minerals are silicates (SIH luh kaytz), which contain the elements silicon and oxygen. The mineral quartz is pure silica ($SiO_2$). More than half of the minerals in Earth's crust are types of a silicate mineral called feldspar. Other important rock-forming minerals are carbonates—compounds containing carbon and oxygen. The carbonate mineral calcite makes up most of the common rock limestone.

**✔ Reading Check** *Why is the silicate mineral feldspar important?*

Other common minerals can be found in rocks that formed at the bottom of ancient, evaporating seas. Rock comprised of the mineral gypsum is abundant in many places, and rock salt, made of the mineral halite, underlies large parts of the Midwest.

## Mini LAB

**Classifying Minerals**

**Procedure**

1. Touch a **magnet** to samples of **quartz, calcite, hornblende,** and **magnetite.** Record which mineral attracts the magnet.
2. With a **dropper,** apply a small amount of **dilute hydrochloric acid (HCl)** to each sample.
3. Rinse the samples with **water.**

**Analysis**

1. Describe how each mineral reacted to the tests in steps 1 and 2.
2. Describe in a data table the other physical properties of the four minerals.

## Applying Science

### How hard are these minerals?

**S**ome minerals, like diamonds, are hard. Others, like talc, are soft. How can you determine the hardness of a mineral?

#### Identifying the Problem

The table at the right shows the results of a hardness test done using some common items as tools (a fingernail, copper penny, nail, and steel file) to scratch certain minerals (halite, turquoise, emerald, ruby, and graphite). The testing tools are listed at the top from softest (fingernail) to hardest (steel file). The table shows which minerals were scratched by which tools. Examine the table to determine the relative hardness of each mineral.

| Hardness Test | | | | |
|---|---|---|---|---|
| **Mineral** | **Fingernail** | **Penny** | **Nail** | **Steel File** |
| Turquoise | N | N | Y | Y |
| Halite | N | Y | Y | Y |
| Ruby | N | N | N | N |
| Graphite | Y | Y | Y | Y |
| Emerald | N | N | N | N |

#### Solving the Problem

1. Is it possible to rank the five minerals from softest to hardest using the data in the table above? Why or why not?
2. What method could you use to determine whether the ruby or the emerald is harder?

**Figure 8** The beauty of gem-quality minerals often is enhanced by cutting and polishing them.

This garnet crystal is encrusted with other minerals but still shines a deep red.

Cut garnet is a prized gemstone.

**Science Online**

**Topic: Gem Locations**
Visit glencoe.com to find Web links to information about the geography of gems.

**Activity** Select a continent, such as Africa, and list three examples of gems found there. Locate mining operations for each of these gems on a map for your class.

**Gems** Which would you rather win, a diamond ring or a quartz ring? A diamond ring would be more valuable. Why? The diamond in a ring is a kind of mineral called a gem. **Gems** are minerals that are rare and can be cut and polished, giving them a beautiful appearance, as shown in **Figure 8.** This makes them ideal for jewelry. To be gem quality, most minerals must be clear with few or no blemishes or cracks. A gem also must have a beautiful luster or color. Few minerals meet these standards. That's why the ones that do are rare and valuable.

**The Making of a Gem** One reason why gems are so rare is that they are formed under special conditions. Diamond, for instance, is a form of the element carbon. Scientists can make synthetic diamonds in laboratories, but they must use extremely high pressures. These pressures are greater than any found within Earth's crust. Therefore, scientists suggest that diamond forms deep in Earth's mantle. It takes a certain kind of volcanic eruption to bring a diamond close to Earth's surface, where miners can find it. This type of eruption forces magma from the mantle toward the surface of Earth at high speeds, bringing diamond along with it. This type of magma is called kimberlite magma. **Figure 9** shows a rock from a kimberlite deposit in South Africa that was mined for diamond. Kimberlite deposits are found in the necks of some ancient volcanoes.

**Figure 9** Diamonds sometimes are found in kimberlite deposits.

**Figure 10** Mining is expensive. To be profitable, ores must be found in large deposits or rich veins. Copper ore is obtained from this mine in Arizona.
**List** *three advantages of recycling metals.*

**Physical Setting**

2.1e, 3.3c **Define** in your own words, the seven different properties used to identify minerals.

**Ores** A mineral is called an **ore** if it contains enough of a useful substance that it can be sold for a profit. Many of the metals that humans use come from ores. For example, the iron used to make steel comes from the mineral hematite, lead for batteries is produced from galena, and the magnesium used in vitamins comes from dolomite. Ores of these useful metals must be extracted from Earth in a process called mining. A copper mine is shown in **Figure 10.**

Scrap metal often is reused or recycled to help reduce the rate that minerals are extracted from Earth. Because minerals may take millions of years to form, they are considered a nonrenewable resource. Conservation efforts can decrease mining and production costs, preserve resources, and reduce the volume of landscape disrupted when minerals are extracted from Earth.

**Ore Processing** After an ore has been mined, it must be processed to extract the desired mineral or element. **Figure 11** shows a copper smelting plant that melts the ore and then separates and removes most of the unwanted materials. After this smelting process, copper can be refined, which means that it is purified. Then it is processed into many materials that you use every day. Examples of useful copper products include sheet-metal products, electrical wiring in cars and homes, and just about anything electronic. Some examples of copper products are shown in **Figure 12.**

**Figure 11** This smelter in Montana heats and melts copper ore.
**Explain** *why smelting is necessary to process copper ore.*

**Figure 12** Many metal objects you use every day are made with copper.
**List** *other metals that are used to produce everyday objects.*

**Minerals Around You** Now you have a better understanding of minerals and their uses. Can you name five things in your classroom that come from minerals? Can you go outside and find a mineral right now? You will find that minerals are all around you and that you use minerals every day. Next, you will look at rocks, which are Earth materials made up of combinations of minerals.

## section 1 review

### Summary

**What is a mineral?**

- Many everyday products are made from minerals.
- Minerals form in several ways, such as crystallizing from magma or from solutions rich in dissolved materials.

**Properties of Minerals**

- Minerals are identified by observing their physical properties.
- Some minerals exhibit unusual physical properties, such as reaction to acid, formation of a double image, or magnetism.

**Common Minerals**

- Of the more than 4,000 minerals known, only a small number make up most rocks.
- Gems are highly prized mineral specimens often used as decorative pieces in jewelry or other items.

### Self Check

1. **Explain** the difference between a mineral and a rock. Name five common rock-forming minerals.

2. **List** five properties that are used most commonly to identify minerals.

3. **Describe** an event that must occur in order for diamond to reach Earth's surface. Where in Earth is diamond formed?

4. **Describe** the steps of mining, smelting, and refining that are used to extract minerals or elements from ores. When is a mineral considered to be an ore?

5. **Think Critically** Would you want to live close to a working gold mine? Explain.

*Hot Words Hot Topics*: Bk 2 (6) pp. 145-146

### Applying Math

6. **Use Percentages** In 1996, the United States produced approximately 2,340,000 metric tons of refined copper. In 1997, about 2,440,000 metric tons of refined copper were produced. Compared to the 1996 amount, copper production increased by what percentage in 1997?

**More Section Review** glencoe.com

# section 2

# Igneous and Sedimentary Rocks

## Igneous Rock

A rocky cliff, a jagged mountain peak, and a huge boulder probably all look solid and permanent to you. Rocks seem as if they've always been here and always will be. But little by little, things change constantly on Earth. New rocks form, and old rocks wear away. Such processes produce three main kinds of rocks—igneous, sedimentary, and metamorphic.

The deeper you go into the interior of Earth, the higher the temperature is and the greater the pressure is. Deep inside Earth, it is hot enough to melt rock. **Igneous** (IHG nee us) **rocks** form when melted rock material from inside Earth cools. The cooling and hardening that result in igneous rock can occur on Earth, as seen in **Figure 13,** or underneath Earth's surface. When melted rock material cools on Earth's surface, it makes an **extrusive** (ehk STREW sihv) igneous rock. When the melt cools below Earth's surface, **intrusive** (ihn TREW sihv) igneous rock forms.

**Chemical Composition** The chemicals in the melted rock material determine the color of the resulting rock. If it contains a high percentage of silica and little iron, magnesium, or calcium, the rock generally will be light in color. Light-colored igneous rocks are called granitic (gra NIH tihk) rocks. If the silica content is far less, but it contains more iron, magnesium, or calcium, a dark-colored or basaltic (buh SAWL tihk) rock will result. Intrusive igneous rocks often are granitic, and extrusive igneous rocks often are basaltic. These two categories are important in classifying igneous rocks.

**Figure 13** Sakurajima is a volcano in Japan. During the 1995 eruption, molten rock material and solid rock were thrown into the air.

**Obsidian Uses** Humans have developed uses for obsidian from ancient through modern times. Research how people have used obsidian. Include information on where it has been found, processed, and distributed.

**Rocks from Lava** Extrusive igneous rocks form when melted rock material cools on Earth's surface. When the melt reaches Earth's surface, it is called lava. Lava cools quickly before large mineral crystals have time to form. That's why extrusive igneous rocks usually have a smooth, sometimes glassy appearance.

Extrusive igneous rocks can form in two ways. In one way, volcanoes erupt and shoot out lava and ash. Also, large cracks in Earth's crust, called fissures (FIH shurz), can open up. When they do, the lava oozes out onto the ground or into water. Oozing lava from a fissure or a volcano is called a lava flow. In Hawaii, lava flows are so common that you can observe one almost every day. Lava flows are quickly exposed to air or water. The fastest cooling lava forms no grains at all. This is how obsidian, a type of volcanic glass, forms. Lava trapping large amounts of gas can cool to form igneous rocks containing many holes.

**Reading Check** *What is a fissure?*

**Figure 14** Extrusive igneous rocks form at Earth's surface. Intrusive igneous rocks form inside Earth. Wind and water can erode rocks to expose features such as dikes, sills, and volcanic necks.

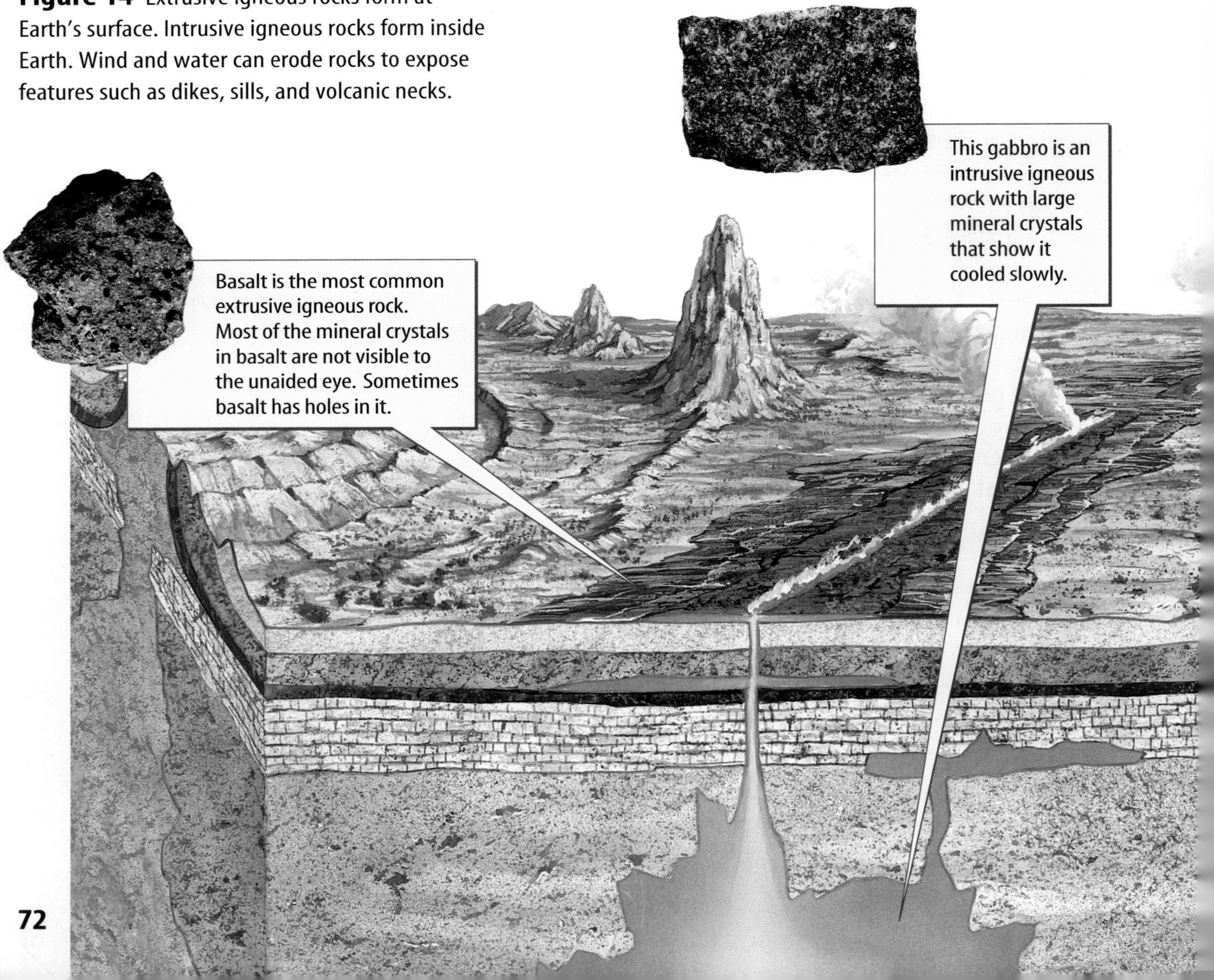

This gabbro is an intrusive igneous rock with large mineral crystals that show it cooled slowly.

Basalt is the most common extrusive igneous rock. Most of the mineral crystals in basalt are not visible to the unaided eye. Sometimes basalt has holes in it.

**Rocks from Magma** Some melted rock material never reaches Earth's surface. Such underground molten material is called magma. Intrusive igneous rocks are produced when magma cools below the surface of Earth, as shown in **Figure 14.**

Intrusive igneous rocks form when a huge glob of magma from inside Earth is forced upward toward the surface but never reaches it. It's similar to when a helium balloon rises and gets stopped by the ceiling. This hot mass of rock material sits under the surface and cools slowly over millions of years until it is solid. The cooling is so slow that the minerals in the magma have time to form large crystals. Intrusive igneous rocks generally have large crystals that are easy to see. Some extrusive igneous rocks do not have large crystals that you can see easily. Others are a mixture of small crystals and larger, visible crystals. **Figure 15** shows some igneous rock features.

**Reading Check** *How do intrusive and extrusive rocks appear different?*

**Thermal Energy** The extreme heat found inside Earth has several sources. Some is left over from Earth's formation, and some comes from radioactive isotopes that constantly emit heat while they decay deep in Earth's interior. Research to find detailed explanations of these heat sources. Use your own words to explain them in your Science Journal.

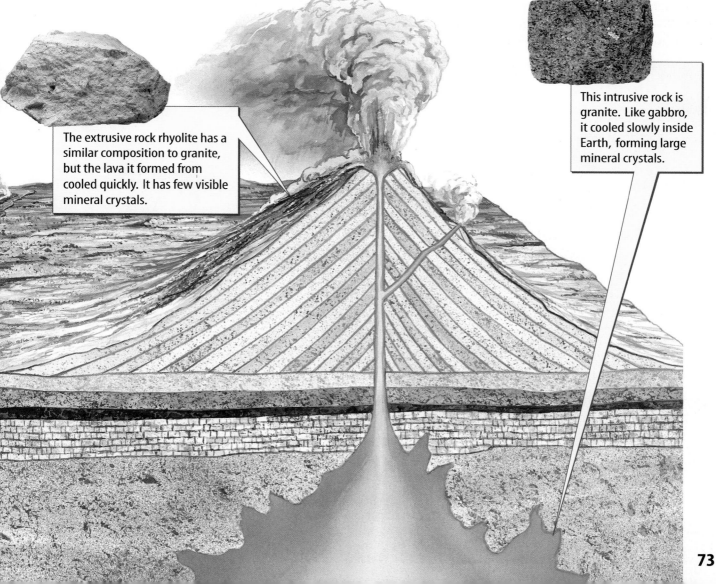

The extrusive rock rhyolite has a similar composition to granite, but the lava it formed from cooled quickly. It has few visible mineral crystals.

This intrusive rock is granite. Like gabbro, it cooled slowly inside Earth, forming large mineral crystals.

**Figure 15**

Intrusive igneous rocks are formed when a mass of magma is forced upward toward Earth's surface and then cools before emerging. The magma cools in a variety of ways. Eventually the rocks may be uplifted and erosion may expose them at Earth's surface. A selection of these formations is shown here.

▶ This dike in Israel's Negev Desert formed when magma squeezed into cracks that cut across rock layers.

▶ A batholith is a very large igneous rock body that forms when rising magma cools below the ground. Towering El Capitan, right, is just one part of a huge batholith. It looms over the entrance to the Yosemite Valley.

▲ Sills such as this one in Death Valley, California, form when magma is forced into spaces that run parallel to rock layers.

▶ Volcanic necks like Shiprock, New Mexico, form when magma hardens inside the vent of a volcano. Because the volcanic rock in the neck is harder than the volcanic rock in the volcano's cone, only the volcanic neck remains after erosion wears the cone away.

# Sedimentary Rocks

Pieces of broken rock, shells, mineral grains, and other materials make up what is called sediment (SE duh munt). The sand you squeeze through your toes at the beach is one type of sediment. As shown in **Figure 16,** sediment can collect in layers to form rocks. These are called **sedimentary** (sed uh MEN tuh ree) **rocks.** Rivers, ocean waves, mudslides, and glaciers can carry sediment. Sediment also can be carried by the wind. When sediment is dropped, or deposited, by wind, ice, gravity, or water, it collects in layers. After sediment is deposited, it begins the long process of becoming rock. Most sedimentary rocks take thousands to millions of years to form. The changes that form sedimentary rocks occur continuously. As with igneous rock, there are several kinds of sedimentary rocks. They fall into three main categories.

**Figure 16** The layers in these rocks are the different types of sedimentary rocks that have been exposed at Sedona, in Arizona. **Explain** what causes the layers seen in sedimentary rocks.

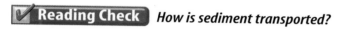 **Reading Check** *How is sediment transported?*

**Detrital Rocks** When you mention sedimentary rocks, most people think about rocks like sandstone, which is a detrital (dih TRI tuhl) rock. Detrital rocks, shown in **Figure 17,** are made of grains of minerals or other rocks that have moved and been deposited in layers by water, ice, gravity, or wind. Other minerals dissolved in water act to cement these particles together. The weight of sediment above them also squeezes or compacts the layers into rock.

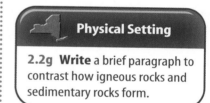

**Physical Setting**

**2.2g Write** a brief paragraph to contrast how igneous rocks and sedimentary rocks form.

**Figure 17** Four types of detrital sedimentary rocks include shale, siltstone, sandstone, and conglomerate.

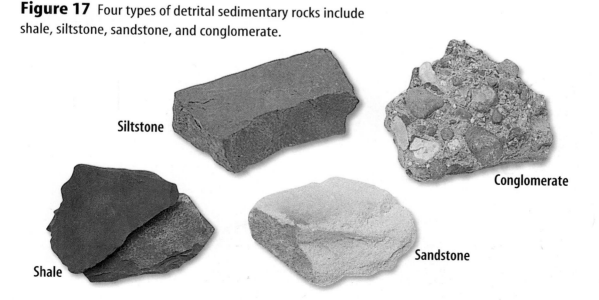

Siltstone

Conglomerate

Shale

Sandstone

## Modeling How Fossils Form Rocks

**Procedure** 🧤 📋 ✂️

1. Fill a small **aluminum pie pan** with pieces of broken **macaroni**. These represent various fossils.
2. Mix 50 mL of **white glue** into 250 mL of **water**. Pour this solution over the macaroni and set it aside to dry.
3. When your fossil rock sample has set, remove it from the pan and compare it with an actual **fossil limestone** sample.

**Analysis**

1. Explain why you used the glue solution and what this represents in nature.
2. Using whole macaroni samples as a guide, match the macaroni "fossils" in your "rock" to the intact macaroni. Draw and label them in your **Science Journal**.

*Try at Home*

**Identifying Detrital Rocks** To identify a detrital sedimentary rock, you use the size of the grains that make up the rock. The smallest, clay-sized grains feel slippery when wet and make up a rock called shale. Silt-sized grains are slightly larger than clay. These make up the rougher-feeling siltstone. Sandstone is made of yet larger, sand-sized grains. Pebbles are larger still. Pebbles mixed and cemented together with other sediment make up rocks called conglomerates (kun GLAHM ruts).

**Chemical Rocks** Some sedimentary rocks form when seawater, loaded with dissolved minerals, evaporates. Chemical sedimentary rock also forms when mineral-rich water from geysers, hot springs, or salty lakes evaporates, as shown in **Figure 18.** As the water evaporates, layers of the minerals are left behind. If you've ever sat in the Sun after swimming in the ocean, you probably noticed salt crystals on your skin. The seawater on your skin evaporated, leaving behind deposits of halite. The halite was dissolved in the water. Chemical rocks form this way from evaporation or other chemical processes.

**Organic Rocks** Would it surprise you to know that the chalk your teacher is using on the chalkboard might also be a sedimentary rock? Not only that, but coal, which is used as a fuel to produce electricity, also is a sedimentary rock.

Chalk and coal are examples of the group of sedimentary rocks called organic rocks. Organic rocks form over millions of years. Living matter dies, piles up, and then is compressed into rock. If the rock is produced from layers of plants piled on top of one another, it is called coal. Organic sedimentary rocks also form in the ocean and usually are classified as limestone.

**Figure 18** The minerals left behind after a geyser erupts form layers of chemical rock.

**Figure 19** There are a variety of organic sedimentary rocks.

The pyramids in Egypt are made from fossiliferous limestone.

A thin slice through the limestone shows that it contains many small fossils.

**Fossils** Chalk and other types of fossiliferous limestone are made from the fossils of millions of tiny organisms, as shown in **Figure 19.** A fossil is the remains or trace of a once-living plant or animal. A dinosaur bone and footprint are both fossils.

## section 2 review

### Summary

**Igneous Rock**

- The chemistry of an igneous rock often is indicated by its color.

- Starting materials that form igneous rocks include lava and magma.

**Sedimentary Rocks**

- Sedimentary rocks form as layers. They originate because wind, water, and ice transport and deposit sediment on Earth's surface.

- Some rocks have grainy textures because they are composed of rock, mineral, or organic fragments cemented together by mineral-rich solutions.

- Other sedimentary rocks appear crystalline as they form directly from mineral-rich solutions.

### Self Check

1. **Compare** and **contrast** the ways in which extrusive and intrusive igneous rocks are formed.

2. **Diagram** how each of the three kinds of sedimentary rock forms. List one example of each kind of rock: detrital, chemical, and organic.

3. **List** in order from smallest to largest the grain sizes used to describe detrital rocks.

4. **Think Critically** Why do igneous rocks that solidify underground cool so slowly?

#### Applying Skills

5. **Communicate** Research a national park where volcanic activity has taken place. Read about the park and the features that you'd like to see. Then describe the volcanic features in your Science Journal. Be sure to explain how each feature formed.

**PS 2.2g:** Rocks are classified according to their method of formation. The three classes of rocks are sedimentary, metamorphic, and igneous. Most rocks show characteristics that give clues to their formation conditions.
**Also Covered:** TPS 2.1h, 2.2h

# section 3

# Metamorphic Rocks and the Rock Cycle

## as you read

### *What* You'll Learn

- **Describe** the conditions needed for metamorphic rocks to form.
- **Explain** how all rocks are linked by the rock cycle.

### *Why* It's Important

Metamorphic rocks and the rock cycle show that Earth is a constantly changing planet.

### 🔎 Review Vocabulary

**pressure:** force applied over a given area

### New Vocabulary

- metamorphic rock
- foliated
- nonfoliated
- rock cycle

## New Rock from Old Rock

Many physical changes on and within Earth are at work, constantly changing rocks. From low-temperature processes such as weathering and erosion, to high-temperature conditions that form molten rock material, new rocks are always forming. There are conditions in between those that form igneous and sedimentary rock that also produce new rocks. Pressures and temperatures increase as rocks are compressed or buried deeply, which can change the chemistry and grain sizes of rocks without even melting them. These conditions often happen where Earth's tectonic plates collide to form mountains, like those shown in **Figure 20.**

It can take millions of years for rocks to change. That's the amount of time that often is necessary for extreme pressure to build while rocks are buried deeply or continents collide. Sometimes existing rocks are cooked when magma is forced upward into Earth's crust, changing their mineral crystals. All these events can make new rocks out of old rocks.

✅ **Reading Check** *What events can change rocks?*

**Figure 20** The rocks of the Labrador Peninsula in Canada were squeezed into spectacular folds. This photo was taken during the space shuttle *Challenger* mission *STS-41G* in 1984.

**Figure 21** High pressure and temperature can cause existing rocks to change into new metamorphic rocks. **A** Granite can change to gneiss. **B** The sedimentary rock sandstone can become quartzite, and **C** limestone can change to marble.

## Metamorphic Rocks
Do you recycle your plastic milk jugs? After the jugs are collected, sorted, and cleaned, they are heated and squeezed into pellets. The pellets later can be made into useful new products. It takes millions of years, but rocks get recycled, too. This process usually occurs thousands of meters below Earth's surface where temperatures and pressures are high. New rocks that form when existing rocks are heated or squeezed but are not melted are called **metamorphic** (me tuh MOR fihk) **rocks.** The word *metamorphic* means "change of form." This describes well how some rocks take on a whole new look when they are under great temperatures and pressures.

 **Reading Check** *What does the word metamorphic mean?*

**Figure 21** shows three kinds of rocks and what they change into when they are subjected to the temperatures, pressures, and hot fluids involved in metamorphism. Not only do the resulting rocks look different, they have recrystallized and might be chemically changed, too. The minerals often align in a distinctive way.

**Physical Setting**

**2.2g Sequence** the steps a rock might undergo to become a metamorphic rock. Analyze how this would be different if the rock melted.

**Figure 22** There are many different types of metamorphic rocks.

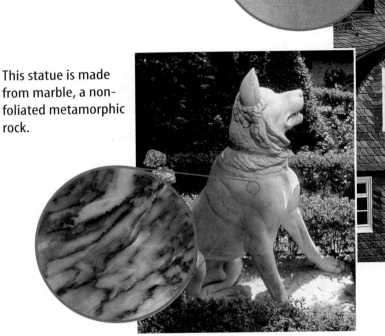

This statue is made from marble, a nonfoliated metamorphic rock.

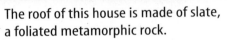

The roof of this house is made of slate, a foliated metamorphic rock.

**Science Online**

**Topic: Rock Types**
Visit glencoe.com for Web links to information about types of metamorphic rocks.

**Activity** Make a two-column table with *Foliated* and *Nonfoliated* as table headings at the top. Find three examples of each of these metamorphic rock classifications. List minerals commonly found in each example.

**Types of Changed Rocks** New metamorphic rocks can form from any existing type of rock—igneous, sedimentary, or metamorphic. A physical characteristic helpful for classifying all rocks is the texture of the rocks. This term refers to the general appearance of the rock. Texture differences in metamorphic rocks divide them into two main groups—foliated (FOH lee ay tud) and nonfoliated, as shown in **Figure 22.**

**Foliated** rocks have visible layers or elongated grains of minerals. The term *foliated* comes from the Latin *foliatus*, which means "leafy." These minerals have been heated and squeezed into parallel layers, or leaves. Many foliated rocks have bands of different-colored minerals. Slate, gneiss (NISE), phyllite (FIH lite), and schist (SHIHST) are all examples of foliated rocks.

**Nonfoliated** rocks do not have distinct layers or bands. These rocks, such as quartzite, marble, and soapstone, often are more even in color than foliated rocks. If the mineral grains are visible at all, they do not seem to line up in any particular direction. Quartzite forms when the quartz sand grains in sandstone recrystallize after they are squeezed and heated. You can form ice crystals in a similar way if you squeeze a snowball. The presssure from your hands creates grains of ice inside the ball.

# The Rock Cycle

Rocks are changing constantly from one type to another. If you wanted to describe these processes to someone, how would you do it? Scientists have created a model called the **rock cycle** to describe how different kinds of rock are related to one another and how rocks change from one type to another. Each rock is on a continuing journey through the rock cycle, which is shown in diagram form in **Figure 23.** A trip through the rock cycle can take millions of years.

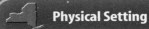

**Physical Setting**

**2.2g, 2.2h** Refer to the rock cycle to design a creative 10-step flow chart to show how magma might be transformed into different types of rocks and back into magma.

**Figure 23** This diagram of the rock cycle shows how rocks are recycled constantly from one kind of rock to another.

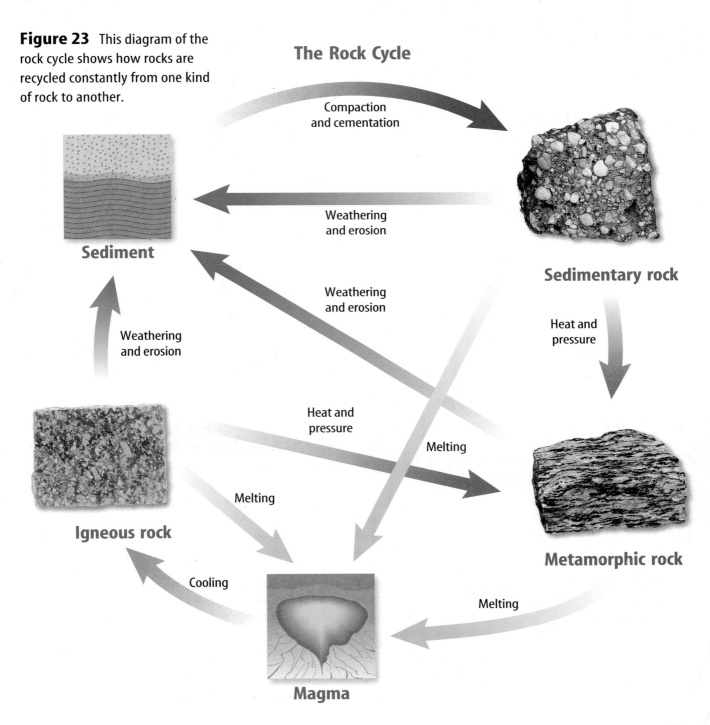

The Rock Cycle

**Figure 24** This lava in Hawaii is flowing into the ocean and cooling rapidly.

**The Journey of a Rock** Pick any point on the diagram of the rock cycle in **Figure 23,** and you will see how a rock in that part of the cycle could become any other kind of rock. Start with a blob of lava that oozes to the surface and cools, as shown in **Figure 24.** It forms an igneous rock. Wind, rain, and ice wear away at the rock, breaking off small pieces. These pieces are called sediment. Streams and rivers carry the sediment to the ocean, where it piles up over time. The weight of sediment above compresses the pieces below. Mineral-rich water seeps through the sediment and glues, or cements, it together. It becomes a sedimentary rock. If this sedimentary rock is buried deeply, pressure and heat inside Earth can change it into a metamorphic rock. Metamorphic rock deep inside Earth can melt and begin the cycle again. Rocks on Earth are changed over millions of years. These processes are taking place right now.

 **Reading Check** *Describe how a metamorphic rock might change into an igneous rock.*

## section 3 review

### Summary

**New Rock from Old Rock**

- Changing conditions can cause new minerals to form, or the same minerals to change form as they align and recrystallize.
- Large-scale formation of metamorphic rock often occurs where tectonic plates collide.
- Metamorphic rocks sometimes are classified according to the textures they exhibit.
- Metamorphic rock textures can be foliated or nonfoliated.

**The Rock Cycle**

- Processes that are part of the rock cycle change rocks slowly through time.
- Igneous, sedimentary, and metamorphic rocks constantly are changing and exchanging matter through processes such as melting, weathering, and changing temperature and pressure.
- There is no beginning and no end to the rock cycle.

### Self Check

1. **Identify** two factors that can produce metamorphic rocks.
2. **List** examples of foliated and nonfoliated rocks. Explain the difference between the two types of metamorphic rocks.
3. **Explain** Igneous rocks and metamorphic rocks can form at high temperatures and pressures. What is the difference between these two rock types?
4. **Explain** what the rock cycle describes.
5. **Think Critically** Trace the journey of a piece of granite through the rock cycle. Explain how this rock could be changed from an igneous rock to a sedimentary rock and then to a metamorphic rock.

### Applying Skills

6. **Use a Spreadsheet** Using a spreadsheet program, create a data table to list the properties of rocks and minerals that you have studied in this chapter. After you've made your table, cut and paste the rows to group like rocks and minerals together.

**More Section Review** glencoe.com

# Gneiss Rice

You know that metamorphic rocks often are layered. But did you realize that individual mineral grains can change in orientation? This means that the grains can line up in certain directions. You'll experiment with rice grains in clay to see how foliation is produced.

## ⓘ *Real-World Question*

What conditions will cause an igneous rock to change into a metamorphic rock?

### Goals

- ■ **Investigate** ways rocks are changed.
- ■ **Model** a metamorphic rock texture.

### Materials

rolling pin
lump of modeling clay
uncooked rice (wild rice, if available) (200 g)
granite sample
gneiss sample

### Safety Precautions

**WARNING:** *Do not taste, eat, or drink any materials used in the lab.*

## ⓘ *Procedure*

1. **Sketch** the granite specimen in your Science Journal. Be sure that your sketch clearly shows the arrangement of the mineral grains.

2. Pour the rice onto the table. Roll the ball of clay in the rice. Some of the rice will stick to the outside of the ball. Knead the ball until the rice is spread out fairly evenly. Roll and knead the ball again, and repeat until your clay sample has lots of "minerals" distributed throughout it.

3. Using the rolling pin, roll the clay until it is about 0.5 cm thick. Don't roll it too hard. The grains of rice should be pointing in different directions. Draw a picture of the clay in your Science Journal.

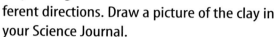

4. Take the edge of the clay closest to you and fold it toward the edge farthest from you. Roll the clay in the direction you folded it. Fold and roll the clay in the same direction several more times. Flatten the lump to 0.5 cm in thickness again. Draw what you observe in your "rock" and in the gneiss sample in your Science Journal.

## ⓘ *Conclude and Apply*

1. **Describe** What features did the granite and the first lump of clay have in common?

2. **Explain** what force caused the positions of rice grains in the lump of clay to change. How is this process similar to and different from what happens in nature?

### *C*ommunicating
#### Your Data

Refer to your Science Journal diagrams and the rock samples provided for you in this lab and make a poster relating this lab to processes in the rock cycle. Be sure to include diagrams of what you did, as well as information on how similar events occur in nature. **For more help, refer to the** Science Skill Handbook.

# Classifying Minerals

## ◉ Real-World Question

Hiking along a trail, you encounter what looks like an interesting mineral. You notice that it is uniform in color and shows distinct crystal faces. You think it must be valuable and want to identify it, so you open a guidebook to rocks and minerals. What observations must you make in order to identify it? What tests can you perform in the field?

## ◉ Procedure

1. Copy the data table into your Science Journal. Based on your observations and hardness tests, you will fill in columns 2 through 6. In the sixth column—"Scratches which samples?"—you will list the number of each mineral sample that this sample is able to scratch. This information will allow you to rank each sample from softest to hardest. Comparing these ranks to Mohs scale should help identify the mineral.

2. Obtain a classroom set of minerals.

### Goals
- **Test** and observe important mineral characteristics.

### Materials
set of minerals
magnifying lens
putty knife
streak plate
Mohs scale
minerals field guide

### Safety Precautions

**WARNING:** *Be careful when using a knife. Never taste any materials used in a lab.*

3. **Observe** each sample and conduct appropriate tests to complete as much of your data table as possible. Consult the *Minerals* Reference Handbook at the back of this book to help fill in the last column.

| Mineral Characteristics | | | | | | | |
|---|---|---|---|---|---|---|---|
| Sample Number | Crystal Shape | Cleavage/ Fracture | Color | Streak and Luster | Scratches which samples? | Hardness Rank | Mineral Name |
| 1 | | | | | | | |
| 2 | | | | | | | |
| 3 | | Do not write in this book. | | | | | |
| 4 | | | | | | | |
| 5 | | | | | | | |
| ... | | | | | | | |
| No. of samples | | | | | | | |

## ◉ Analyze Your Data

1. **Identify** each mineral based on the information in your data table.

2. **Evaluate** Did you need all of the information in the table to identify each mineral? Explain why or why not.

3. **Explain** which characteristics were easy to determine. Which were somewhat more difficult?

## ◉ Conclude and Apply

1. **Evaluate** Were some characteristics more useful as indicators than others?

2. **Apply** Would you be able to identify minerals in the field after doing this activity? Which characteristics would be easy to determine on the spot? Which would be difficult?

3. **Describe** how your actions in this lab are similar to those of a scientist. What additional work might a scientist have done to identify these unknown minerals?

**Communicating Your Data**

**Create** a visually appealing poster showing the minerals in this lab and the characteristics that were useful for identifying each one. Be sure to include informative labels on your poster.

# Going for the Gold

### A time line history of the accidental discovery of gold in California

**Sutter's Mill**

**1840**
California is a quiet place. Only a few hundred people live in the small town of San Francisco.

**1848**
On January 24, Marshall notices something glinting in the water. He hits it with a rock. Marshall knows that "fool's gold" shatters when hit. But this shiny metal bends. After more tests, Sutter and Marshall decide it is gold! They try to keep the discovery a secret, but word leaks out.

**1850**
California becomes the thirty-first state.

**1864**
California's gold rush ends. The rich surface deposits are largely exhausted.

**1880**
His pension ended, Marshall is forced to earn a living through various odd jobs, receiving charity, and by selling his autograph. He attempts a lecture tour, but is unsuccessful.

**1885**
James Marshall dies with barely enough money to cover his funeral.

1840    1850    1860    1870    1880    1890

**1847**
John Sutter hires James Marshall to build a sawmill on his ranch. Marshall and local Native Americans work quickly to harness the water power of the American River.

**1849**
The Gold Rush hits! A flood of people from around the world descends on northern California. Many people become wealthy—but not Marshall or Sutter. Because Sutter doesn't have a legal claim to the land, the U.S. government claims it.

**1854**
A giant nugget of gold, the largest known to have been discovered in California, is found in Calaveras County.

**1872**
As thanks for his contribution to California's growth, the state legislature awards Marshall $200 a month for two years. This pension is renewed until 1878.

**1890**
California builds a bronze statue to honor Marshall.

MARSHALL

**Research** Trace the history of gold from ancient civilizations to the present. How was gold used in the past? How is it used in the present? What new uses for gold have been discovered? Report to the class.

## Reviewing Main Ideas

### Section 1 Minerals—Earth's Jewels

1. Minerals are inorganic solid materials found in nature. They have a definite chemical makeup, and an orderly arrangement of atoms. Rocks are combinations of two or more minerals.

2. Physical properties of minerals are observed to help identify them.

3. Gems are minerals that are rare and beautiful.

4. Ores of useful materials must be mined and processed to extract the desired substance.

### Section 2 Igneous and Sedimentary Rocks

1. Igneous rocks form when melted rock material from inside Earth cools and hardens.

Extrusive rocks form above Earth's surface. Intrusive rocks solidify beneath the surface.

2. Sedimentary rocks formed from mineral or rock fragments are called detrital rocks.

3. Rocks formed as mineral-rich water evaporates are examples of chemical rocks. Rocks composed of fossils or plant remains are organic rocks.

### Section 3 Metamorphic Rocks and the Rock Cycle

1. Metamorphic rocks form as a result of changing temperature, pressure, and fluid conditions inside Earth.

2. The rock cycle describes how all rocks are subject to constant change.

## Visualizing Main Ideas

*Copy and complete the concept map using the following terms and phrases:* extrusive, organic, foliated, intrusive, chemical, nonfoliated, detrital, metamorphic, *and* sedimentary.

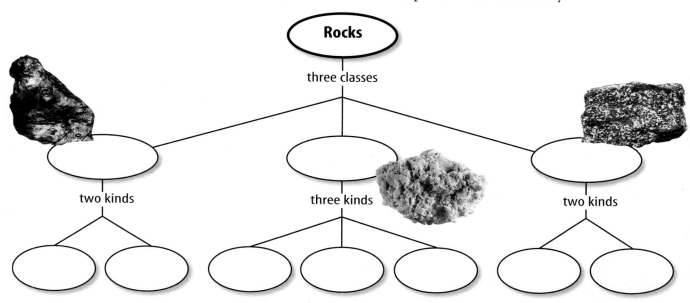

Rocks
three classes

two kinds

three kinds

two kinds

## Using Vocabulary

| | |
|---|---|
| crystal p.64 | mineral p.62 |
| extrusive p.71 | nonfoliated p.80 |
| foliated p.80 | ore p.69 |
| gem p.68 | rock p.62 |
| igneous rock p.71 | rock cycle p.81 |
| intrusive p.71 | sedimentary rock p.75 |
| metamorphic rock p.79 | |

*Explain the difference between each pair of vocabulary words.*

1. mineral—rock
2. crystal—gem
3. cleavage—fracture
4. hardness—streak
5. rock—rock cycle
6. intrusive—extrusive
7. igneous rock—metamorphic rock
8. foliated—nonfoliated
9. rock—ore
10. metamorphic rock—sedimentary rock

## Checking Concepts

*Choose the word or phrase that best answers the question.*

11. When do metamorphic rocks form?
    **A)** when layers of sediment are deposited
    **B)** when lava solidifies in seawater
    **C)** when particles of rock break off at Earth's surface
    **D)** when heat and pressure change rocks

12. Which of the following must be true for a substance to be considered a mineral?
    **A)** It must be organic.
    **B)** It must be glassy.
    **C)** It must be a gem.
    **D)** It must be naturally occurring.

**Use the illustration below to answer question 13.**

13. What kind of rocks are produced by volcanic eruptions?
    **A)** detrital     **C)** organic
    **B)** foliated     **D)** extrusive

14. Which is true about how all detrital rocks form?
    **A)** form from grains of preexisting rocks
    **B)** form from lava
    **C)** form by evaporation
    **D)** form from plant remains

15. Which of the following describes what rocks usually are composed of?
    **A)** pieces
    **B)** minerals
    **C)** fossil fuels
    **D)** foliations

16. How can sedimentary rocks be classified?
    **A)** foliated or nonfoliated
    **B)** gems or ores
    **C)** extrusive or intrusive
    **D)** detrital, chemical, or organic

17. Which is true of all minerals?
    **A)** They are inorganic solids.
    **B)** They have a hardness of 4 or greater.
    **C)** They have a glassy luster.
    **D)** They can scratch a penny.

## Thinking Critically

18. **Classify** Is a sugar crystal a mineral? Explain.

19. **List** some reasons why metal deposits in Antarctica are not considered to be ores.

20. **Describe** How is it possible to find pieces of gneiss, granite, and basalt in a single conglomerate?

21. **Predict** Would you expect to find a well-preserved dinosaur bone in a metamorphic rock like schist? Explain.

22. **Explain** how the mineral quartz could be in an igneous rock and in a sedimentary rock.

23. **Classify** Your teacher gives you two clear minerals. What quick test could you do in order to determine which is halite and which is calcite?

24. **Concept Map** Copy and complete this concept map about minerals.

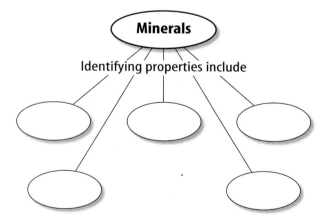

25. **Test a Hypothesis** Suppose your teacher gives you a glass plate, a nail, a copper penny, and a bar magnet. Using a word processing program on a computer, describe how you would use these items to determine the hardness and special property of the mineral magnetite. Refer to Mohs scale in **Table 1** for help.

## Performance Activities

26. **Make Models** Determine what materials and processes you would need to use to set up a working model of the rock cycle. Describe the ways in which your model is accurate and the ways in which it falls short. Present your model to the class.

*Hot Words Hot Topics:* Bk 2 (27) p. 194; (28) p. 194; (29) p. 397

## Applying Math

**Use the table below to answer questions 27–29.**

### Modified Wentworth Scale, after Lane et. al., 1947

| Grain Sizes (mm) | U.S. Standard Sieve Series | Grain Types | |
|---|---|---|---|
| — 2 — | No. 10 — | very coarse | |
| 1 | No. 18 | coarse | |
| 0.500 | No. 35 | medium | SAND |
| 0.250 | No. 60 | fine | |
| 0.125 | No. 120 | very fine | |
| — 0.062 — | No. 230 — | coarse | |
| 0.031 | — | medium | |
| 0.016 | — | fine | SILT |
| 0.008 | — | very fine | |
| — 0.004 — | — | coarse | |
| 0.002 | — | medium | |
| 0.001 | — | | CLAY |

27. **Grain Type** According to the table, if a rock contains grains that are 0.5 mm in dimension, what type of grains are they?

28. **Filtering** Which U.S. standard sieve would you use to filter out all sediment in a sample less than one-fourth of one millimeter?

29. **Grain Size** A siltstone contains grains that range in size from 0.031 to 0.008 mm. Convert this size range from millimeters to micrometers.

**Part I**

*Record your answers on the answer sheet provided by your teacher or on a sheet of paper.*

**Use the photo below to answer question 1.**

when boats cannot be used. Complex communicatio equipment along with computers enables the Coa Guard to monitor the vo... ...each vessel. Cutters a responsible for offshor... ...cue. Many of the larger ships are... ...ding pads f helicopters to... ...rapid emergency s... ...es. In the pa few years... ...ves have been save... ...ick response the men an... women of the... ...uard.
    Besides sear... and res... ...ations the Coast Gua aids in the enforce... ...customs and immigratio laws and the prevention... illegal smuggling. Since 19... the U.S. Coast Guard has also been involved in maki...

**1** Which special property is illustrated by the piece of calcite shown above?
(1) magnetism
(2) double refraction
(3) reaction to acid
(4) salty taste

**2** What forms when lava cools so quickly that crystals cannot form?
(1) volcanic glass  (3) bauxite
(2) intrusive rock  (4) a gem

**3** Which is the color of powdered mineral?
(1) hardness  (3) cleavage
(2) luster  (4) streak

**4** Varieties of which mineral are most abundant in Earth's crust?
(1) quartz  (3) feldspar
(2) calcite  (4) gypsum

**5** What is a solid material that has an orderly, repeating pattern of atoms?
(1) crystal
(2) gem
(3) ore
(4) rock

**6** Which feature is a tabular body of igneous rock that is parallel to surrounding rock layers?
(1) sill  (3) batholith
(2) volcanic neck  (4) dike

**7** Which type of rock is made mostly of clay?
(1) conglomerate  (3) siltstone
(2) shale  (4) sandstone

**Use the diagram below to answer questions 8–9.**

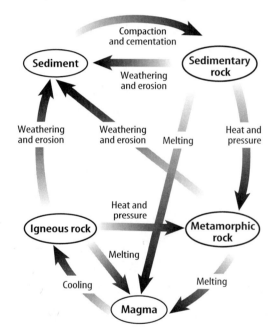

**8** Which changes sediment into sedimentary rock?
(1) weathering and erosion
(2) heat and pressure
(3) compaction and cementation
(4) melting

**9** Which type of rock forms when magma cools?
(1) sedimentary
(2) chemical
(3) metamorphic
(4) igneous

Part II

*Record your answers on the answer sheet provided by your teacher or on a sheet of paper.*

**10** How is a rock different from a mineral?

**11** How do organic sedimentary rocks form? List one example of an organic sedimentary rock.

**12** How can minerals be identified by their physical properties?

**Use the table below to answer questions 13–15.**

| World Gold Production (metric tons) | | |
|---|---|---|
| **Country** | **2001 Production** | **2002 Production** |
| United States | 335 | 300 |
| Australia | 285 | 280 |
| Canada | 160 | 160 |
| China | 185 | 175 |
| Indonesia | 130 | 170 |
| Peru | 138 | 140 |
| Russia | 152 | 170 |
| South Africa | 402 | 395 |
| Other countries | 783 | 740 |
| World total | 2,570 | 2,530 |

**13** Identify which single country produced the most gold in 2002. How many more metric tons did this country produce than the United States?

**14** How many fewer metric tons did the U.S. produce in 2002 than in 2001?

**15** What percentage of 2002 world gold production came from the United States?

**16** Why are minerals important to society?

**17** Compare and contrast mineral cleavage and mineral fracture.

**18** Why must ores be processed after they are mined?

**19** Why do sedimentary rocks occur in layers?

**20** Describe how a layer of rock containing fossils could be present in a mountain wall that is several thousand feet above sea level.

## chapter 4

PS 2.1g: The dynamic processes that wear away Earth's surface include weathering and erosion. 2.1h: The process of weathering breaks down rocks to form sediment. Soil consists of sediment, organic material, water, and air. **Also Covered:** PS 2.1i

# Weathering and Erosion

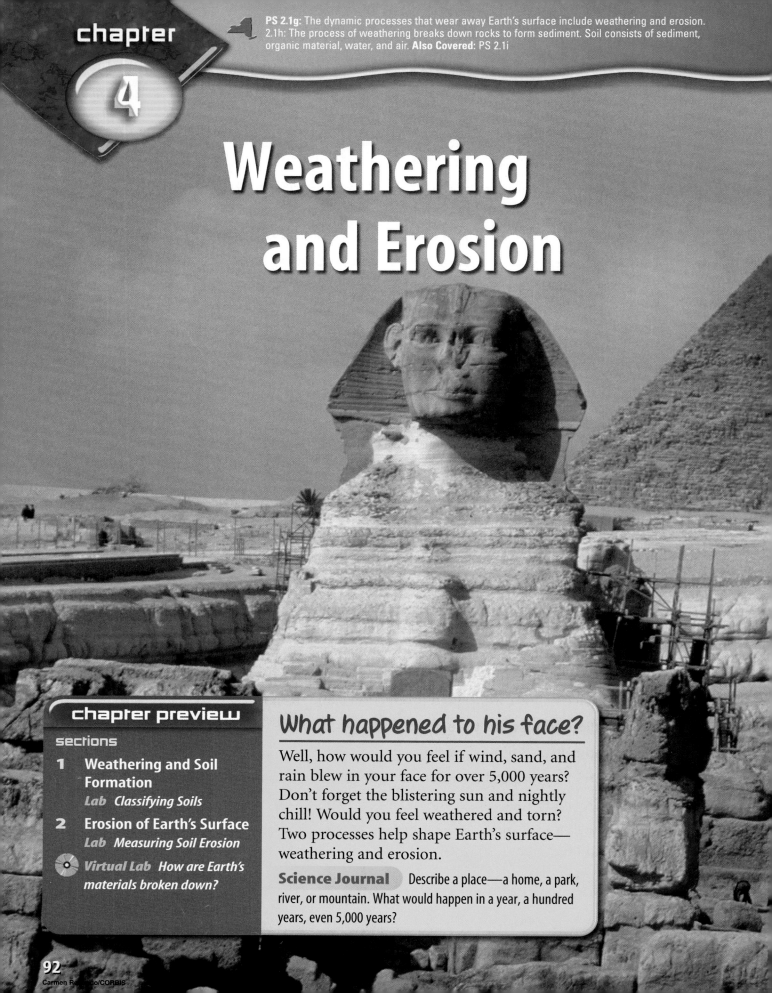

## What happened to his face?

Well, how would you feel if wind, sand, and rain blew in your face for over 5,000 years? Don't forget the blistering sun and nightly chill! Would you feel weathered and torn? Two processes help shape Earth's surface—weathering and erosion.

**Science Journal**   Describe a place—a home, a park, river, or mountain. What would happen in a year, a hundred years, even 5,000 years?

# Start-Up Activities

## Water's Force

The Grand Canyon is 446 km long, up to 29 km wide, and up to 1,829 m deep. The water of the Colorado River carved the canyon out of rock by wearing away particles and carrying them away for millions of years. Over time, erosion has shaped and reshaped Earth's surface many times. In this lab, you will explore how running water formed the Grand Canyon.

1. Fill a bread pan with packed sand and form a smooth, even surface.

2. Place the bread pan in a plastic wash tub. Position one end of the washtub in a sink under the faucet.

3. Place a brick or wood block under the end of the bread pan beneath the faucet.

4. Turn on the water to form a steady trickle of water falling into the pan and observe for 10 min. The washtub should catch the eroded sand.

5. **Think Critically** In your Science Journal, draw a top view picture of the erosion pattern formed in the sand by the running water. Write a paragraph describing what the sand would look like if you had left the water running overnight.

**Weathering and Erosion**
Make the following Foldable to compare and contrast weathering and erosion.

**STEP 1** Fold one sheet of paper lengthwise.

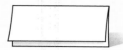

**STEP 2** Fold into thirds.

**STEP 3** Unfold and draw overlapping ovals. Cut the top sheet along the folds.

**STEP 3** Label the ovals as shown.

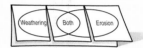

**Construct a Venn Diagram** As you read the chapter, list the characteristics unique to weathering under the left tab, those unique to erosion under the right tab, and those characteristics common to both under the middle tab.

Preview this chapter's content and activities at glencoe.com

# Weathering and Soil Formation

## as you read

### *What* You'll Learn

- **Identify** processes that break rock apart.
- **Describe** processes that chemically change rock.
- **Explain** how soil evolves.

### *Why* It's Important

Soil forms when rocks break apart and change chemically. Soil is home to many organisms, and most plants need soil in order to grow.

### ⊙ Review Vocabulary

**acid rain:** acidic moisture, with a pH below 5.6

### New Vocabulary

- weathering
- mechanical weathering
- chemical weathering
- soil
- topography

## Weathering

Have you noticed potholes in roadways and broken concrete in sidewalks and curbs? When a car rolls over a pothole in the road in late winter or when you step over a broken sidewalk, you know things aren't as solid or permanent as they look. Holes in roads and broken sidewalks show that solid materials can be changed by nature. **Weathering** is a mechanical or chemical surface process that breaks rocks into smaller pieces. Freezing and thawing, oxygen in the air, and even plants and animals can affect the stability of rock. These are some of the things that cause rocks on Earth's surface to weather, and in some cases, to become soils.

## Mechanical Weathering

When a sidewalk breaks apart, a large slab of concrete is broken into many small pieces. The concrete looks the same. It's just broken apart. This is similar to mechanical weathering of rocks. **Mechanical weathering** breaks rocks into smaller pieces without changing them chemically. The small pieces are identical in composition to the original rock, as shown in **Figure 1.** Two of the many causes of mechanical weathering are ice wedging and living organisms.

**Figure 1** The forces of mechanical weathering break apart rocks. **Describe** *how you know that the smaller pieces of granite were produced by mechanical weathering.*

**Figure 2** Over time, freezing water can break apart rock.

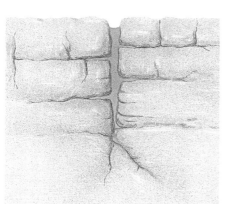
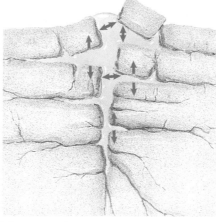
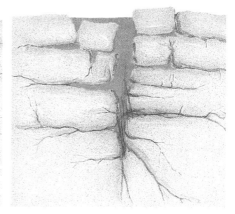

Water seeps into cracks. The deeper the cracks are, the deeper water can seep in.

The water freezes and expands, forcing the cracks to open further.

The ice melts. If the temperature falls below freezing again, the process will repeat itself.

**Ice Wedging** In some areas of the world, air temperature drops low enough to freeze water. Then, when the temperature rises, the ice thaws. This freezing and thawing cycle breaks up rocks. How can this happen? When it rains or snow melts, water seeps into cracks in rocks. If the temperature drops below freezing, ice crystals form. As the crystals grow, they take up more space than the water did because when water freezes, its molecules move apart. This expansion exerts pressure on the rocks. With enough force, the rocks will crack further and eventually break apart, as shown in **Figure 2.** Ice wedging also causes potholes to form in roadways.

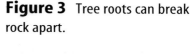 *Explain how ice wedging can break rock apart.*

**Plants and Animals** Plants and animals also cause mechanical weathering. As shown in **Figure 3,** plants can grow in what seem to be the most inconvenient places. Their roots grow deep into cracks in rock where water collects. As they grow, roots become thicker and longer, slowly exerting pressure and wedging rock apart.

Gophers and prairie dogs also weather rock—as do other animals that burrow in the ground. As they burrow through sediment or soft sedimentary rock, animals break rock apart. They also push some rock and sediment to the surface where another kind of weathering, called chemical weathering, takes place more rapidly.

**Figure 3** Tree roots can break rock apart.

**Figure 4** Chemical weathering changes the chemical composition of minerals and rocks.
**Describe** *how kaolinite is different from feldspar.*

**Elements in Feldspar**

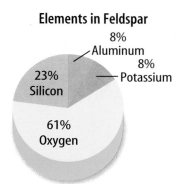

8% Aluminum
8% Potassium
23% Silicon
61% Oxygen

**Elements in Kaolinite**

12% Aluminum
12% Silicon
23% Hydrogen
53% Oxygen

Feldspar crystals react with carbonic acid.

The mineral kaolinite is formed.

**Physical Setting**

**2.1g, 2.1h** Use a Venn diagram to define, compare, and contrast chemical weathering and mechanical weathering.

# Chemical Weathering

**Chemical weathering** occurs when the chemical composition of rock changes. This kind of weathering is rapid in tropical regions where it's moist and warm most of the time. Because desert areas have little rainfall and polar regions have low temperatures, chemical weathering occurs slowly in these areas. **Table 1** summarizes the rates of chemical weathering for different climates. Two important causes of chemical weathering are natural acids and oxygen.

 **Reading Check** *Why is chemical weathering rapid in the tropics?*

 **Natural Acids** Some rocks react chemically with natural acids in the environment. When water mixes with carbon dioxide in air or soil, for example, carbonic acid forms. Carbonic acid can change the chemical composition of minerals in rocks, as shown in **Figure 4.**

Although carbonic acid is weak, it reacts chemically with many rocks. Vinegar reacts with the calcium carbonate in chalk, dissolving it. In a similar way, when carbonic acid comes in contact with rocks like limestone, dolomite, and marble, they dissolve. Other rocks also weather when exposed to carbonic acid.

| Table 1 Rates of Weathering | |
|---|---|
| **Climate** | **Chemical Weathering** |
| Hot and dry | Slow |
| Hot and wet | Fast |
| Cold and dry | Slow |
| Cold and wet | Slow |

**Plant Acids** Plant roots also produce acid that reacts with rocks. Many plants produce a substance called tannin. In solution, tannin forms tannic acid. This acid dissolves some minerals in rocks. When minerals dissolve, the remaining rock is weakened, and it can break into smaller pieces. The next time you see moss or other plants growing on rock, as shown in **Figure 5,** peel back the plant. You'll likely see discoloration of the rock where plant acids are reacting chemically with some of the minerals in the rock.

**Figure 5** Moss growing on rocks can cause chemical weathering.

**Effect of Oxygen** When you see rusty cars, reddish soil, or reddish stains on rock, you are witnessing oxidation, the effects of chemical changes caused by oxygen. When iron-containing materials such as steel are oxidized, a chemical reaction causes the material to rust. Rocks chemically weather in a similar way. When some iron-containing minerals are exposed to oxygen, they can weather to minerals that are like rust. This leaves the rock weakened, and it can break apart. As shown in **Figure 6,** some rocks also can be colored red or orange when iron-bearing minerals in them react with oxygen.

**Figure 6** Oxidation occurs in rocks and cars.

Even a tiny amount of iron in rock can combine with oxygen and form a reddish iron oxide.

The iron contained in metal objects such as this truck also can combine with oxygen and form a reddish iron oxide called rust.

## Mini LAB

### Dissolving Rock with Acids

**Procedure**

**WARNING:** *Do not remove goggles until lab cleanup and handwashing are completed.*

1. Use an **eyedropper** to put several drops of **vinegar** on pieces of **chalk** and **limestone.** Observe the results with a **magnifying lens.**
2. Put several drops of **5% hydrochloric acid** on the chalk and limestone. Observe the results.

**Analysis**

1. Describe the effect of the hydrochloric acid and vinegar on chalk and limestone.
2. Research what type of acid vinegar contains.

| Table 2 Factors that Affect Soil Formation | | | | |
|---|---|---|---|---|
| **Parent Rock** | **Slope of Land** | **Climate** | **Time** | **Organisms** |

## Soil

Is soil merely dirt under your feet, or is it something more important? **Soil** is a mixture of weathered rock, organic matter, water, and air that supports the growth of plant life. Organic matter includes decomposed leaves, twigs, roots, and other material. Many factors affect soil formation.

**Parent Rock** As listed in **Table 2,** one factor affecting soil formation is the kind of parent rock that is being weathered. For example, where limestone is chemically weathered, clayey soil is common because clay is left behind when the limestone dissolves. In areas where sandstone is weathered, sandy soil forms.

**The Slope of the Land** The **topography,** or surface features, of an area also influence the types of soils that develop. You've probably noticed that on steep hillsides, soil has little chance of developing. This is because rock fragments move downhill constantly. However, in lowlands where the land is flat, wind and water deposit fine sediments that help form thick soils.

**Climate** Climate affects soil evolution, too. If rock weathers quickly, deep soils can develop rapidly. This is more likely to happen in tropical regions where the climate is warm and moist. Climate also affects the amount of organic material in soil. Soils in desert climates contain little organic material. However, in warm, humid climates, vegetation is lush and much organic material is present. When plants and animals die, decomposition by fungi and bacteria begins. The result is the formation of a dark-colored material called humus, as shown in the soil profile in **Figure 7.** Most of the organic matter in soil is humus. Humus helps soil hold water and provides nutrients that plants need to grow.

## Mini LAB

### Analyzing Soils
**Procedure**
1. Obtain a sample of **soil** from near your home.
2. Spread the soil out over a piece of **newspaper.**
3. Carefully sort through the soil. Separate out organic matter from weathered rock.
4. Wash hands thoroughly after working with soils.

**Analysis**
1. Besides the organic materials and the remains of weathered rock, what else is present in the soil?
2. Is some of the soil too fine-grained to tell if it is organic or weathered rock?

**Try at Home**

**Time** It takes time for rocks to weather. It can take thousands of years for some soils to form. As soils develop, they become less like the rock from which they formed. In young soils, the parent rock determines the soil characteristics. As weathering continues, however, the soil resembles the parent rock less and less. Thicker, well-developed soils often are found in areas where weathering has gone on undisturbed for a long period of time. For this to happen, soil materials must not be eroded away and new sediment must not be deposited over the land's surface too quickly.

**Organisms** Organisms influence soil development. Lichens are small organisms that consist of an alga and a fungus that live together for mutual benefit. You may have seen lichens in the form of multicolored patches growing on tree branches or cliff faces. Interestingly, lichens can grow directly on rock. As they grow, they take nutrients from the rock that they are starting to break down, forming a thin soil. After a soil has formed, many types of plants such as grasses and trees can grow.

The roots of these plants further break down the parent rock. Dead plant material such as leaves accumulates and adds organic matter to the soil. Some plants contribute more organic matter to soil than others. For example, soil under grassy areas often is richer in organic matter than soil developing under forests. This is why some of the best farmland in the midwestern United States is where grasslands used to be.

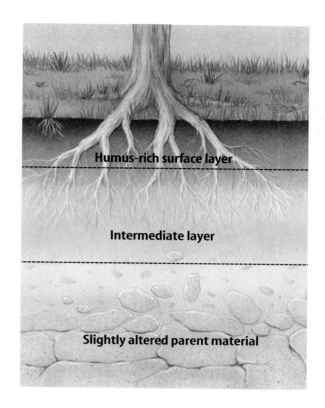

Humus-rich surface layer

Intermediate layer

Slightly altered parent material

**Figure 7** Soils contain layers that are created by weathering, the flow of water and chemicals, and the activities of organisms. **Explain** *what part microorganisms play in soil development.*

---

## section 1 review

### Summary

**Mechanical Weathering**
- The freezing and thawing cycle breaks up rocks.
- Plants' roots and burrowing animals can break rocks apart.

**Chemical Weathering**
- Some rocks react chemically with natural acids.

**Soil**
- A factor affecting soil formation is the kind of parent rock that is being weathered.

### Self Check

1. **Describe** how rocks are mechanically weathered.
2. **Name** two agents of chemical weathering.
3. **Explain** how carbonic acid weather rocks.
4. **Describe** how soil forms. What factors are important?
5. **Think Critically** How could climate affect rates of mechanical weathering? What about chemical weathering? How are the two kinds of weathering related?

**Applying Skills**
6. **Compare and contrast** mechanical weathering caused by ice and growing roots.

---

# Classifying Soils

Not all soils are the same. Geologists and soil scientists classify soils based on the amounts and kinds of particles they contain.

## ▶ Real-World Question

How is soil texture determined?

### Goals
■ **Classify** a soil using an identification key.
■ **Observe** soil with a stereomicroscope.

### Materials
soil sample
stereomicroscope
*magnifying lens
*Alternate materials

### Safety Precautions

## ▶ Procedure

1. Place a small sample of moistened soil between your fingers. Then follow the directions in the classification key below.
   a. Slide your fingers back and forth past each other. If your sample feels gritty, go to **b.** If it doesn't feel gritty, go to **c.**
   b. If you can mold the soil into a firm ball, it's sandy loam soil. If you cannot mold it into a firm ball, it's sandy soil.
   c. If your sample is sticky, go to **d.** If your sample isn't sticky, go to **e.**
   d. If your sample can be molded into a long, thin ribbon, it's clay soil. If your soil can't be molded into a long, thin ribbon, it's clay loam soil.
   e. If your sample is smooth, it's silty loam soil. If it isn't smooth, it's loam soil.

2. After classifying your soil sample, examine it under a microscope. Draw the particles and any other materials that you see.

3. Wash your hands thoroughly after you are finished working with soils.

## ▶ Conclude and Apply

1. **Determine** the texture of your soil sample.
2. **Describe** two characteristics of loam soil.
3. **Describe** two features of sandy loam soil.
4. **Record Observations** Based on your observations with the stereomicroscope, what types of particles and other materials did you see? Did you observe any evidence of the activities of organisms?

### Communicating Your Data

Compare your conclusions with those of other students in your class. **For more help, refer to the** Science Skill Handbook.

# section
## 2

# Erosion of Earth's Surface

## Agents of Erosion

Imagine looking over the rim of the Grand Canyon at the winding Colorado River below or watching the sunset over Utah's famous arches. Features such as these are spectacular examples of Earth's natural beauty, but how can canyons and arches form in solid rock? These features and many other natural landforms are a result of erosion of Earth's surface. **Erosion** is the wearing away and removal of rock or sediment. Erosion occurs because gravity, ice, wind, and water sculpt Earth's surface.

## Gravity

Gravity is a force that pulls every object toward every other object. Gravity pulls everything on Earth toward its center. As a result, water flows downhill and rocks tumble down slopes. When gravity alone causes rock or sediment to move down a slope, the erosion is called **mass movement.** Mass movements can occur anywhere there are hills or mountains. One place where they often occur is near volcanoes, as shown in **Figure 8.** Creep, slump, rock slides, and mudflows are four types of mass movements, as seen in **Figure 9.**

### as you read

**What You'll Learn**
- **Identify** agents of erosion.
- **Describe** the effects of erosion.

**Why It's Important**
Erosion shapes Earth's surface.

**Review Vocabulary**
**deposition:** dropping of sediments occurs when an agent of erosion can no longer carry its load

**New Vocabulary**
- erosion
- mass movement
- creep
- slump
- deflation
- abrasion
- runoff

**Figure 8** The town of Weed, California, was built on top of a landslide that moved down the volcano known as Mount Shasta.

**Figure 9**

When the relentless tug of gravity causes a large chunk of soil or rock to move downhill—either gradually or with sudden speed—the result is what geologists call a mass movement. Weathering and water often contribute to mass movements. Several kinds are shown here.

**A CREEP** When soil on a slope moves very slowly downhill, a mass movement called creep occurs. Some of the trees at right have been gradually bent because of creep's pressure on their trunks.

**B SLUMP** This cliff in North Dakota shows the effects of the mass movement known as slump. Slumping often occurs after earthquakes or heavy and prolonged rains.

**C ROCK SLIDES** When rocks break free from the side of a cliff or a mountain, they crash down in what is called a rock slide. Rock slides, like the one at the left in Yosemite National Park, can occur with little warning.

**D MUDFLOWS** A Japanese town shows the devastation that a fourth type of mass movement—a mudflow—can bring. When heavy moisture saturates sediments, mudflows can develop, sending a pasty mix of water and sediment downhill over the ground's surface.

**Creep** The process in which sediments move slowly downhill, as shown in **Figure 9A,** is called **creep.** Creep is common where freezing and thawing occur. As ice expands in soil, it pushes sediments up. Then as soil thaws, the sediments move farther downslope. **Figure 10** shows how small particles of sediment can creep downslope. Over time, creep can move large amounts of sediment, possibly causing damage to some structures. Do you live in an area where you can see the results of creep?

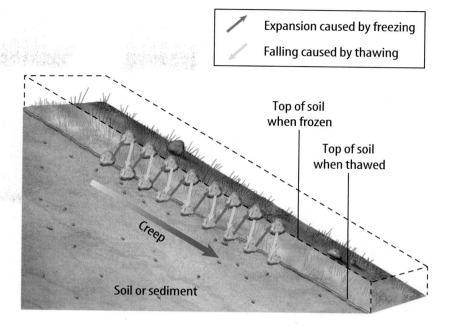

↗ Expansion caused by freezing
↗ Falling caused by thawing

Top of soil when frozen

Top of soil when thawed

Creep

Soil or sediment

**Slump** A **slump** occurs when a mass of rock or sediment moves downhill, leaving a curved scar, as shown in **Figure 9B.** Slumps are most common in thick layers of loose sediment, but they also form in sedimentary rock. Slumps frequently occur on slopes that have been undercut by erosion, such as those above the bases of cliffs that have been eroded by waves. Slumping of this kind is common along the coast of Southern California, where it threatens to destroy houses and other buildings.

**Rock Slides** Can you imagine millions of cubic meters of rock roaring down a mountain at speeds greater than 250 km/h? This can happen when a rock slide occurs. During a rock slide layers of rock break loose from slopes and slide to the bottom. The rock layers often bounce and break apart during movement. This produces a huge, jumbled pile of rocks at the bottom of the slope, as you can see in **Figure 9C.** Rock slides can be destructive, sometimes destroying entire villages or causing hazards on roads in mountainous areas.

**Mudflows** Where heavy rains or melting snow and ice saturate sediments, mudflows, as shown in **Figure 9D,** can develop. A mudflow is a mass of wet sediment that flows downhill over the ground surface. Some mudflows can be thick and flow slowly downhill at rates of a few meters per day. Other mudflows can be much more fluid and move downslope at speeds approaching 160 km/h. This type of mudflow is common on some volcanoes.

**Reading Check** *What is the slowest of the four kinds of mass movement?*

**Figure 10** When soil freezes, particles are lifted. When it thaws, the particles are pulled downhill by gravity. Eventually, large amounts of sediment are moved by this process.

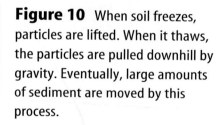
INTEGRATE
**Physics**

**Mass Movement** Slumps and rock slides often occur when sediment becomes saturated by rain. Water between sediment grains helps lift up overlying rock and sediment. This makes it easier for the sediment to overcome the forces holding it in place. Can you think of a way some slopes might be protected from slumps and rock slides? Explain.

**Figure 11** Glaciers form in cold regions.

Continental glaciers are located near the poles, in Antarctica and Greenland.

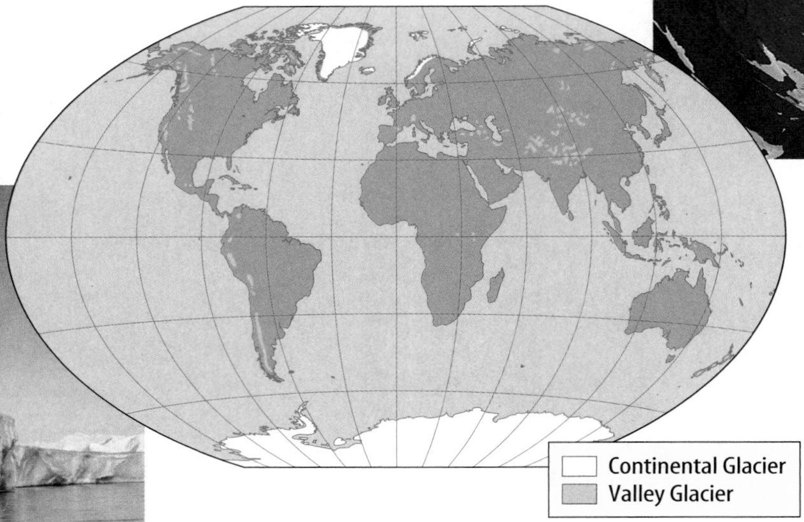

Valley glaciers are found at high elevations on many continents.

| Continental Glacier |
| Valley Glacier |

**Topic: Glacial Erosion and Deposition**

Visit glencoe.com for Web links to information about glacial erosion and deposition.

**Activity** Research glacial erosion and describe how it has affected the topography in an area.

## Ice

In some parts of the world, ice is an agent of erosion. In cold regions, more snow might fall than melt. Over many years, the snow can accumulate to form large, deep masses of ice called glaciers. When the ice in a glacier becomes thick enough, its own weight causes it to flow downhill under the influence of gravity. As glaciers move over Earth's surface, they erode materials from some areas and deposit sediment in other areas. **Figure 11** shows the two kinds of glaciers—continental glaciers and valley glaciers.

Today, continental glaciers in polar regions cover about ten percent of Earth. These glaciers are so large and thick that they can bury mountain ranges. Valley glaciers are much smaller and are located in high mountains where the average temperature isn't warm enough to melt the ice sheets. The average flow rate of a valley glacier is 0.01 to 2.0 meters per day, but during a surge, they can flow up to 100 meters per day.

**Glacial Erosion** Glaciers can erode rock in two different ways. If the underlying rock has cracks in it, the ice can pull out pieces of rock. This causes the rock to erode slowly. Loose pieces of rock freeze into the bottom of the glacier and are dragged along as the glacier moves. As these different-sized fragments of rock are dragged over Earth's surface, they scratch the rock below like giant sheets of sandpaper. This scratching is the second way that glaciers can erode rock. Scratching produces large grooves or smaller striations in the rock underneath. The scratching also can wear rock into a fine powder called rock flour.

**Figure 12** Many high-altitude areas owe their distinctive appearance to glacial erosion.

Mountain glaciers can carve bowl-shaped depressions called cirques.

Glaciers can widen valleys, giving them a U-shaped profile.

**Effects of Glacial Erosion** Glacial erosion of rock can be a powerful force shaping Earth's surface. In mountains, valley glaciers can remove rock from the mountaintops to form large bowls, called cirques (SURKS), and steep peaks. When a glacier moves into a stream valley, it erodes rock along the valley sides, producing a wider, U-shaped valley. These features are shown in **Figure 12.** Continental glaciers also shape Earth's surface. These glaciers can scour large lakes and completely remove rock layers from the land's surface.

**Glacial Deposition** Glaciers also can deposit sediments. When stagnant glacier ice melts or when ice melts at the bottom of a flowing glacier or along its edges, the sediment the ice was carrying gets left behind on Earth's surface. This sediment, deposited directly from glacier ice, is called till. Till is a mixture of different-sized particles, ranging from clay to large boulders.

As you can imagine, a lot of melting occurs around glaciers, especially during summer. So much water can be produced that streams often flow away from the glacier. These streams carry and deposit sediment. Sand and gravel deposits laid down by these streams, shown in **Figure 13,** are called outwash. Unlike till, outwash usually consists of particles that are all about the same size.

**Figure 13** This valley in New Zealand has been filled with outwash.
**Explain** *how you could distinguish outwash from till.*

**Figure 14** In a desert, where small particles have been carried away by wind, larger sediments called desert pavement remain behind.

# Wind

If you've had sand blow into your eyes, you've experienced wind as an agent of erosion. When wind blows across loose sediments like silt and sand, it lifts and carries it. As shown in **Figure 14,** wind often leaves behind particles too heavy to move. This erosion of the land by wind is called **deflation.** Deflation can lower the land's surface by several meters.

Wind that is carrying sediment can wear down, or abrade, other rocks just as a sandblasting machine would do. **Abrasion** is a form of erosion that can make pits in rocks and produce smooth, polished surfaces. Abrasion is common in some deserts and in some cold regions with strong winds.

✓ **Reading Check** *How does abrasion occur?*

When wind blows around some irregular feature on Earth's surface, such as a rock or clump of vegetation, it slows down. This causes sand carried by the wind to be deposited. If this sand deposit continues to grow, a sand dune like that shown in **Figure 15** might form. Sand dunes move when wind carries sand up one side of the dune and it avalanches down the other, as shown in **Figure 15.**

Sometimes, wind carries only fine sediment called silt. When this sediment is deposited, an accumulation of silt called loess (LOOS) can blanket Earth's surface. Loess is as fine as talcum powder. Loess often is deposited downwind of large deserts and deflated glacial outwash deposits.

**Figure 15** Wind transportation of sand creates sand dunes.

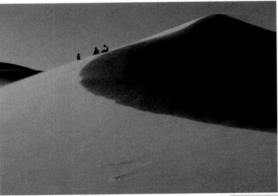

Sand dunes do not remain in one location—they migrate.

As wind blows over a sand dune, sand blows up the windward side and tumbles down the other side. In this way, a sand dune migrates across the land.

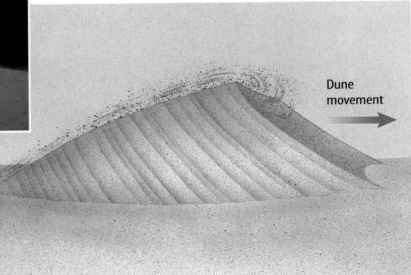

Dune movement

# Water

You probably have seen muddy water streaming down a street after a heavy rain. You might even have taken off your shoes and waded through the water. Water that flows over Earth's surface is called **runoff.** Runoff is an important agent of erosion, especially if the water is moving fast. The more speed water has, the more material it can carry with it. Water can flow over Earth's surface in several different ways, as you will soon discover.

**Sheet Flow** As raindrops land on Earth's surface, they break up clumps of soil and loosen small grains of sediment. If these raindrops are falling on a sloped land surface, a thin sheet of water might begin to move downhill. You have observed something similar if you've ever washed a car and seen sheets of water flowing over the hood, as shown in **Figure 16.** When water flows downhill as a thin sheet, it is called sheet flow. This thin sheet of water can carry loose sediment grains with it, causing erosion of the land. This erosion is called sheet erosion.

**Figure 16** Water flows over the hood of a car as a thin sheet. **Describe** *how this is similar to sheet flow on Earth's surface.*

## Applying Science

### Can evidence of sheet erosion be seen in a farm field?

If you've ever traveled through parts of your state where there are farms, you might have seen bare, recently cultivated fields. Perhaps the soil was prepared for planting a crop of corn, oats, or soybeans. Do you think sheet erosion can visibly affect the soil in farm fields?

**Identifying the Problem**

The top layer of most soils is much darker than layers beneath because it contains more organic matter. This layer is the first to be removed from a slope by sheet flow. How does the photo show evidence of sheet erosion?

**Solving the Problem**

1. Observe the photo and write a description of it in your Science Journal.

2. Infer why some areas of the field are darker colored than others are. Where do you think the highest point(s) are in this field?
3. Make a generalization about the darker areas of the field.

**Figure 17** Gullies often form on vegetation-free slopes.

**Topic: Power of Water**
Visit glencoe.com for Web links to information about the erosional force of running water.

**Activity** Research your watershed and see if the topography was shaped by running water.

**Figure 18** Streams that flow down steep slopes such as this one in Yosemite National Park often have white-water rapids and waterfalls.

**Rills and Gullies** Where a sheet of water flows around obstacles and becomes deeper, rills can form. Rills are small channels cut into the sediment at Earth's surface. These channels carry more sediment than can be moved by sheet flow. In some cases, a network of rills can form on a slope after just one heavy rain. Large amounts of sediment can be picked up and carried away by rills.

As runoff continues to flow through the rills, more sediment erodes and the channel widens and deepens. When the channels get to be about 0.5 m across, they are called gullies, as shown in **Figure 17.**

**Streams** Gullies often connect to stream channels. Streams can be so small that you could jump to the other side or large enough for huge river barges to transport products along their course. Most streams have water flowing through them continually, but some have water only during part of the year.

In mountainous and hilly regions, as in **Figure 18,** streams flow down steep slopes. These streams have a lot of energy and often cut into the rock beneath their valleys. This type of stream typically has white-water rapids and may have waterfalls. As streams move out of the mountains and onto flatter land, they begin to flow more smoothly. The streams might snake back and forth across their valley, eroding and depositing sediments along their sides. All streams eventually must flow into the ocean or a large lake. The level of water in the ocean or lake determines how deeply a river can erode.

**Shaping Earth's Surface** In the Launch Lab, you saw a small model of erosion by a stream. Streams are the most important agent of erosion on Earth. They shape more of Earth's surface than ice, wind, or gravity. Over long periods of time, water moving in a stream can have enough power to cut large canyons into solid rock. Many streams together can sculpt the land over a wide region, forming valleys and leaving some rock as hills. Streams also shape the land by depositing sediment. Rivers can deposit sandbars along their course, and can build up sheets of sand across their valleys. When rivers enter oceans or lakes, the water slows and sediment is deposited. This can form large accumulations of sediment called deltas, as in **Figure 19.** The city of New Orleans is built on the delta formed by the Mississippi River.

**Figure 19** A triangular area of sediment near the mouth of a river is called a delta. Ancient deltas that are now dry land are often excellent places to grow crops.

## Effects of Erosion

All agents of erosion change Earth's surface. Rock and sediment are removed from some areas only to be deposited somewhere else. Where material is removed, canyons, valleys, and mountain cirques can form. Where sediment accumulates, deltas, sandbars, sand dunes, and other features make up the land.

## section 2 review

### Summary

**Gravity**

- Erosion of rock or sediment, moved down a slope by gravity, is called mass movement.
- Creep, slump, rock slides, and mudflows are four types of mass movement.

**Ice**

- Glaciers move over Earth's surface, eroding materials from some areas and depositing sediments in other areas.

**Wind**

- Deflation and abrasion are two common forms of wind erosion.

**Water**

- Runoff is water flowing over Earth's surface.
- Water erosion can create sheet erosion, rills, gullies, streams, valleys, and canyons.

### Self Check

1. **Describe** four agents of erosion. Which of these is the fastest? The slowest? Explain your answers.
2. **Explain** the difference between deflation and abrasion.
3. **Describe** how a cirque forms.
4. **Explain** When do streams deposit sediments? When do streams erode sediments?
5. **Think Critically** Why might a river that was eroding and depositing sediment along its sides start to cut into Earth to form a canyon?

*Hot Words Hot Topics*: Bk 2 (6) pp. 277, 292-294, 397

### Applying Math

6. **Solve One-Step Equations** If wind is eroding an area at a rate of 2 mm per year and depositing it in a smaller area at a rate of 7 mm per year, how much lower will the first area be in meters after 2 thousand years? How much higher will the second area be?

## Design Your Own

# Measuring Soil Erosion

## Goals

- **Design** an experiment to measure soil loss from grass-covered soil and from soil without grass cover.
- **Calculate** the percent of soil loss with and without grass cover.

## Possible Materials

blocks of wood
*books*
paint trays (2)
soil
grass sod
water
pails (2)
1,000-mL beaker
triple-beam balance
calculator
watch
*Alternate materials*

## Safety Precautions

Wash your hands thoroughly when you are through working with soils.

## ◉ Real-World Question

During urban highway construction, surface mining, forest harvesting, or agricultural cultivation, surface vegetation is removed from soil. These practices expose soil to water and wind. Does vegetation significantly reduce soil erosion? How much does vegetation reduce soil erosion?

## ◉ Form a Hypothesis

Based on what you've read and observed, hypothesize about how a grassy field will have less erosion than a field that is bare soil.

## Test Your Hypothesis

**Make a Plan**

1. As a group, agree upon the hypothesis and decide how you will test it. Identify which results challenge or confirm the hypothesis.

2. **List** the steps you will need to take to test your hypothesis. Describe exactly what you will do in each step.

3. **Prepare** a data table in your Science Journal to record your observations.

4. Read over the entire experiment to make sure all steps are in logical order, and that you have all necessary materials.

5. **Identify** all constants and variables and the control of the experiment. A control is a standard for comparing the results of an experiment. One possible control for this experiment would be the results of the treatment of an uncovered soil sample.

**Follow Your Plan**

1. Make sure your teacher approves your plan before you start.

2. Carry out the experiment step by step as planned.

3. While doing the experiment, record your observations and complete the data table in your Science Journal.

| Vegetation and Erosion | | | |
|---|---|---|---|
| | **(A) Mass of Soil at Start** | **(B) Mass of Eroded Soil** | **% of Soil Loss (B/A) × 100** |
| Covered soil sample | *Do not write in this book.* | | |
| Uncovered soil sample | | | |

## Analyze Your Data

1. **Compare** the percent of soil loss from each soil sample.

2. **Compare** your results with those of other groups.

3. What was your control in this experiment? Why is it a control?

4. Which were the variables you kept constant? Which did you vary?

## Conclude and Apply

1. Did the results support your hypothesis? Explain.

2. **Infer** what effect other types of plants would have in reducing soil erosion. Do you think that grass is better or worse than most other plants at reducing erosion? Explain your answer.

Acid rain is destroying some of the world's most famous monuments

# CRUMBLING MONUMENTS

The Taj Mahal in India, the Acropolis in Greece, and the Colosseum in Italy have stood for centuries. They've survived wars, souvenir-hunters, and natural weathering from wind and rain. But now, something far worse threatens their existence—acid rain. Over the last few decades, this form of pollution has eaten away at some of history's greatest monuments.

Most of these structures are made of sandstone, limestone, and marble. Acid rain causes the calcium in these stones to form calcium sulfate, or gypsum.

**Acid rain has not been kind to this Mayan figure.**

Gypsum's powdery little blotches are sometimes called "marble cancer." When it rains, the gypsum washes away, along with some of the surface of the monument.

In Agra, India, the smooth, white marble mausoleum called the Taj Mahal has stood since the seventeenth century. But acid rain is making the surface of the building yellow and flaky. The pollution is caused by hundreds of factories surrounding Agra that emit damaging chemicals.

What moisture, molds, and the roots of vegetation couldn't do in 1,500 years, acid rain is doing in a few decades. It is destroying the Mayan ruins of Mexico. Acid rain is causing statues to crumble and paintings on walls to flake off.

Acid rain is a huge problem affecting national monuments and treasures in just about every urban location in the world. These include the Capitol building in Washington, D.C., churches in Germany, and stained-glass windows in Sweden. In London, acid rain has forced workers to repair and replace so much of Westminster Abbey that the structure is becoming a mere copy of the original.

Throughout the world, acid rain has weathered many structures more in the last 20 years than in the 2,000 years before. This is one reason some steps have been taken in Europe and the United States to reduce emissions from the burning of fossil fuels. If these laws don't work, many irreplaceable art treasures may be gone forever.

**Identify** What are some famous monuments and buildings in the United States? Brainstorm a list with your class. Then choose a monument and, using your school's media center or the Science Online address, learn more about it. Is acid rain affecting it in any way?

Science Online

**For more information, visit glencoe.com**

## Reviewing Main Ideas

### Section 1 Weathering and Soil Formation

1. Weathering includes processes that break down rock.

2. During mechanical weathering, physical processes break rock into smaller pieces.

3. During chemical weathering, the chemical composition of rocks is changed.

4. Soil evolves over time from weathered rock. Parent rock, topography, climate, and organisms affect soil formation.

### Section 2 Erosion of Earth's Surface

1. Erosion is the wearing away and removal of rock or sediment.

2. Agents of erosion include gravity, ice, wind, and water. Downslope movement of a portion of the land's surface is called mass movement.

3. All agents of erosion move rock and sediment. When energy of motion decreases, sediment is deposited.

4. Erosion and deposition determine the shape of the land.

## Visualizing Main Ideas

*Copy and fill in the following table, which compares erosion and deposition by different agents.*

| Erosion and Deposition | | |
|---|---|---|
| **Erosional Agent** | **Evidence of Erosion** | **Evidence of Deposition** |
| Gravity | | material piled at bottom of slopes |
| Ice | cirques, striations, U-shaped valleys | |
| Wind | | sand dunes, loess |
| Surface water | rills, gullies, stream valleys | |

## Using Vocabulary

| | |
|---|---|
| abrasion  p.106 | mechanical weathering |
| chemical weathering | p.94 |
| p.96 | runoff  p.107 |
| creep  p.103 | slump  p.103 |
| deflation  p.106 | soil  p.98 |
| erosion  p.101 | topography  p.98 |
| mass movement  p.101 | weathering  p.94 |

*Use each of the following pairs of terms in a sentence.*

1. chemical weathering—mechanical weathering

2. erosion—weathering

3. deflation—runoff

4. mass movement—weathering

5. soil—abrasion

6. soil—erosion

7. mass movement—mechanical weathering

8. weathering—chemical weathering

9. creep—slump

10. topography—runoff

## Checking Concepts

*Choose the word or phrase that best answers the question.*

11. Which of the following agents of erosion forms U-shaped valleys?
    A) gravity      C) ice
    B) surface water  D) wind

12. In which of these places is chemical weathering most rapid?
    A) deserts
    B) mountains
    C) polar regions
    D) tropical regions

13. Which of the following forms when carbon dioxide combines with water?
    A) calcium carbonate
    B) carbonic acid
    C) tannic acid
    D) dripstone

14. Which process causes rocks to weather to a reddish color?
    A) oxidation      C) carbon dioxide
    B) deflation      D) frost action

15. Which type of mass movement occurs when sediments slowly move downhill because of freezing and thawing?
    A) creep        C) slump
    B) rock slide     D) mudflow

16. Which of the following helps form cirques and U-shaped valleys?
    A) rill erosion    C) deflation
    B) ice wedging    D) till

17. What is windblown, fine sediment called?
    A) till         C) loess
    B) outwash       D) delta

18. Which of the following refers to water that flows over Earth's surface?
    A) runoff        C) weathering
    B) slump        D) till

19. Which of the following is an example of chemical weathering?
    A) Plant roots grow in cracks in rock and break the rock apart.
    B) Freezing and thawing of water widens cracks in rocks.
    C) Wind blows sand into rock, scratching the rock.
    D) Oxygen causes iron-bearing minerals in rock to break down.

20. Which one of the following erosional agents creates desert pavement?
    A) wind         C) water
    B) gravity       D) ice

Vocabulary Puzzlemaker glencoe.com

## Thinking Critically

**21. Explain** why mass movement is more common after a heavy rainfall.

**22. Describe** how climate affects the development of soils.

**23. Explain** how some mass movement could be prevented.

**24. Describe** why chemical weathering would not be rapid in Antarctica.

**25. Describe** why caves form only in certain types of rock.

**26. Recognize Cause and Effect** Explain how water creates stream valleys.

**27. Form hypotheses** about how deeply water could erode and about how deeply glaciers could erode.

**28. Recognize Cause and Effect** Explain how valley glaciers create U-shaped valleys.

**29. Classify** the following by the agent that deposits each: sand dune, delta, till, and loess.

**30. Concept Map** Copy and complete the concept map showing the different types of mass movements.

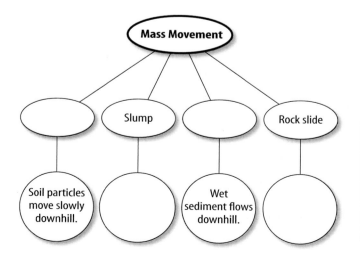

## Performance Activities

**31. Poster** Use photographs from old magazines to make a poster that illustrates different kinds of weathering and erosion. Display your poster in your classroom.

**32. Model** Use polystyrene, cardboard, and clay to make a model of a glacier. Include a stream of meltwater leading away from the glacier. Use markers to label the areas of erosion and deposition. Show and label areas where till and outwash sediments could be found. Display your model in your classroom.

*Hot Words Hot Topics:* Bk 2 (33) pp. 194, 277; (34) pp. 277, 292–294

## Applying Math

**Use the table below to answer questions 33–34.**

| Loss and Formation of Topsoil | | |
|---|---|---|
| Years Soil Erodes | Topsoil Lost (cm) | Years to Re-create Soil Lost |
| 10 | 1 | 500 |
| 15 | 1.5 | |
| 20 | 2 | **Do not write in this book.** |
| 25 | 2.5 | |
| 30 | 3 | |
| 40 | 4.5 | |

**33. Formation of Topsoil** In a given region, it takes 500 years to form 1 cm of topsoil. For the past 20 years, the area has lost 1 cm of topsoil every 10 years because of erosion. If erosion stops today, how long will it take to re-create the lost topsoil? How long will it take to re-create the topsoil lost in 15, 25, and 30 years?

**34. Weather's Affect** In the 30th year, climate changes and precipitation increases, causing a new erosion rate of 1.5 cm every 10 years. How many years will it now take to re-create the topsoil lost at the end of 40 years?

*Record your answers on the answer sheet provided by your teacher or on a sheet of paper.*

**1** Which is an example of mechanical weathering?
(1) creep
(2) ice wedging
(3) oxidation
(4) slump

**2** Which forms as a glacier moves into a stream valley?
(1) cirque
(2) outwash
(3) U-shaped valley
(4) V-shaped valley

**3** Which factor in soil formation deals with the slope of the land?
(1) climate
(2) parent rock
(3) time
(4) topography

**4** Which is a mixture of weathered rock, organic matter, water, and air?
(1) humus
(2) organisms
(3) parent rock
(4) soil

**5** Which type of erosion occurs when a thin sheet of water flows downhill?
(1) creep
(2) gulley erosion
(3) runoff
(4) sheet erosion

**6** What causes potholes to form in roadways?
(1) creep
(2) ice wedging
(3) oxidation
(4) slump

**Use the photo below to answer questions 7–8.**

**7** Which form of mass movement is shown in this picture?
(1) creep
(2) mudflow
(3) rockslide
(4) slump

**8** Which agent of erosion causes this?
(1) gravity
(2) ice
(3) water
(4) wind

**9** What form of mass movement occurs when a pasty mix of water and sediment moves downhill?
(1) creep
(2) mudflow
(3) rockslide
(4) slump

**10** What type of erosion is similar to using sandpaper to smooth the edges of wood?
(1) abrasion
(2) creep
(3) deflation
(4) runoff

**Part II**

*Record your answers on the answers sheet provided by your teacher or on a sheet of paper.*

**11** How do lichens growing on rocks contribute to soil development?

**Use the illustration below to answer question 12.**

**12** Using the diagram, explain how a sand dune moves.

**13** What type of mass movement causes problems along the Southern California coast? Support your reasoning with examples.

**14** Compare and contrast chemical and mechanical weathering.

**15** How do freeze and thaw cycles contribute to both weathering and erosion?

**16** What types of glaciers are there and how do they erode the land? Support your reasoning with examples.

**Use to the photo below to answer question 17.**

**17** What type of erosion is pictured here? How can this type of erosion help to carry harmful chemicals that are deposited in the soil to rivers, lakes and oceans?

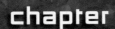

**LE 3.2c:** Many thousands of layers of sedimentary rock provide evidence for the long history of Earth and for the long history of changing lifeforms whose remains are found in the rocks. Recently deposited rock layers are more likely to contain fossils resembling existing species. **Also Covered:** LE 3.2b, PS 2.1f, 2.2c, 3.3a

# Clues to Earth's Past

## Reading the Past

The pages of Earth's history, much like the pages of human history, can be read if you look in the right place. Unlike the pages of a book, the pages of Earth's past are written in stone. In this chapter you will learn how to read the pages of Earth's history to understand what the planet was like in the distant past.

**Science Journal**   List three fossils that you would expect to find a million years from now in the place you live today.

# Start-Up Activities

## Clues to Life's Past

Fossil formation begins when dead plants or animals are buried in sediment. In time, if conditions are right, the sediment hardens into sedimentary rock. Parts of the organism are preserved along with the impressions of parts that don't survive. Any evidence of once-living things contained in the rock record is a fossil.

1. Fill a small jar (about 500 mL) one-third full of plaster of paris. Add water until the jar is half full.

2. Drop in a few small shells.

3. Cover the jar and shake it to model a swift, muddy stream.

4. Now model the stream flowing into a lake by uncovering the jar and pouring the contents into a paper or plastic bowl. Let the mixture sit for an hour.

5. Crack open the hardened plaster to locate the model fossils.

6. **Think Critically** Remove the shells from the plaster and study the impressions they made. In your Science Journal, list what the impressions would tell you if found in a rock.

**Age of Rocks** Make the following Foldable to help you understand how scientists determine the age of a rock.

**STEP 1** Fold a sheet of paper in half lengthwise.

**STEP 2** Fold paper down 2.5 cm from the top. (Hint: From the tip of your index finger to your middle knuckle is about 2.5 cm.)

**STEP 3** Open and draw lines along the 2.5-cm fold. Label as shown.

Determining Age | Absolute or Relative

**Summarize in a Table** As you read the chapter, in the left column, list four different ways in which one could determine the age of a rock. In the right column, note whether each method gives an absolute or a relative age.

Preview this chapter's content and activities at glencoe.com

LE 3.2b: Extinction of a species occurs when the environment changes and the adaptive characteristics of a species are insufficient to permit its survival. Fossils are evidence that a great variety of species existed in the past. **PS 2.1f:** Fossils are usually found in sedimentary rocks. **Also Covered:** LE 3.2c

# Fossils

## Traces of the Distant Past

A giant crocodile lurks in the shallow water of a river. A herd of *Triceratops* emerges from the edge of the forest and cautiously moves toward the river. The dinosaurs are thirsty, but danger waits for them in the water. A large bull *Triceratops* moves into the river. The others follow.

Does this scene sound familiar to you? It's likely that you've read about dinosaurs and other past inhabitants of Earth. But how do you know that they really existed or what they were like? What evidence do humans have of past life on Earth? The answer is fossils. Paleontologists, scientists who study fossils, can learn about extinct animals from their fossil remains, as shown in **Figure 1.**

**Figure 1** Scientists can learn how dinosaurs looked and moved using fossil remains. A skeleton can then be reassembled and displayed in a museum.

# Formation of Fossils

**Fossils** are the remains, imprints, or traces of prehistoric organisms. Fossils have helped scientists determine approximately when life first appeared, when plants and animals first lived on land, and when organisms became extinct. Fossils are evidence of not only when and where organisms once lived, but also how they lived.

For the most part, the remains of dead plants and animals disappear quickly. Scavengers eat and scatter the remains of dead organisms. Fungi and bacteria invade, causing the remains to rot and disappear. If you've ever left a banana on the counter too long, you've seen this process begin. In time, compounds within the banana cause it to break down chemically and soften. Microorganisms, such as bacteria, cause it to decay. What keeps some plants and animals from disappearing before they become fossils? Which organisms are more likely to become fossils?

**Figure 2** These fossil shark teeth are hard parts. Soft parts of animals do not become fossilized as easily.

**Conditions Needed for Fossil Formation** Whether or not a dead organism becomes a fossil depends upon how well it is protected from scavengers and agents of physical destruction, such as waves and currents. One way a dead organism can be protected is for sediment to bury the body quickly. If a fish dies and sinks to the bottom of a lake, sediment carried into the lake by a stream can cover the fish rapidly. As a result, no waves or scavengers can get to it and tear it apart. The body parts then might be fossilized and included in a sedimentary rock like shale. However, quick burial alone isn't always enough to make a fossil.

Organisms have a better chance of becoming fossils if they have hard parts such as bones, shells, or teeth. One reason is that scavengers are less likely to eat these hard parts. Hard parts also decay more slowly than soft parts do. Most fossils are the hard parts of organisms, such as the fossil teeth in **Figure 2.**

# Types of Preservation

Perhaps you've seen skeletal remains of *Tyrannosaurus rex* towering above you in a museum. You also have some idea of what this dinosaur looked like because you've seen illustrations. Artists who draw *Tyrannosaurus rex* and other dinosaurs base their illustrations on fossil bones. What preserves fossil bones?

## Mini LAB

### Predicting Fossil Preservation

**Procedure**
1. Take a brief walk outside and observe your neighborhood.
2. Look around and notice what kinds of plants and animals live nearby.

**Analysis**
1. Predict what remains from your time might be preserved far into the future.
2. Explain what conditions would need to exist for these remains to be fossilized.

**Figure 3** Opal and various minerals have replaced original materials and filled the hollow spaces in this permineralized dinosaur bone. **Explain** *why this fossil retained the shape of the original bone.*

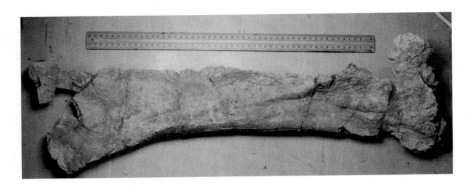

**Mineral Replacement** Most hard parts of organisms such as bones, teeth, and shells have tiny spaces within them. In life, these spaces can be filled with cells, blood vessels, nerves, or air. When the organism dies and the soft materials inside the hard parts decay, the tiny spaces become empty. If the hard part is buried, groundwater can seep in and deposit minerals in the spaces. **Permineralized remains** are fossils in which the spaces inside are filled with minerals from groundwater. In permineralized remains, some original material from the fossil organism's body might be preserved—encased within the minerals from groundwater. It is from these original materials that DNA, the chemical that contains an organism's genetic code, can sometimes be recovered.

Sometimes minerals replace the hard parts of fossil organisms. For example, a solution of water and dissolved silica (the compound $SiO_2$) might flow into and through the shell of a dead organism. If the water dissolves the shell and leaves silica in its place, the original shell is replaced.

Often people learn about past forms of life from bones, wood, and other remains that became permineralized or replaced with minerals from groundwater, as shown in **Figure 3,** but many other types of fossils can be found.

**Figure 4** Graptolites lived hundreds of millions of years ago and drifted on currents in the oceans. These organisms often are preserved as carbon films.

**Carbon Films** The tissues of organisms are made of compounds that contain carbon. Sometimes fossils contain only carbon. Fossils usually form when sediments bury a dead organism. As sediment piles up, the organism's remains are subjected to pressure and heat. These conditions force gases and liquids from the body. A thin film of carbon residue is left, forming a silhouette of the original organism called a **carbon film. Figure 4** shows the carbonized remains of graptolites, which were small marine animals. Graptolites have been found in rocks as old as 500 million years.

**Coal** In swampy regions, large volumes of plant matter accumulate. Over millions of years, these deposits become completely carbonized, forming coal. Coal is an important fuel source, but since the structure of the original plant is usually lost, it cannot reveal as much about the past as other kinds of fossils.

**Reading Check** *In what sort of environment does coal form?*

**Molds and Casts** In nature, impressions form when seashells or other hard parts of organisms fall into a soft sediment such as mud. The object and sediment are then buried by more sediment. Compaction, together with cementation, which is the deposition of minerals from water into the pore spaces between sediment particles, turns the sediment into rock. Other open pores in the rock then let water and air reach the shell or hard part. The hard part might decay or dissolve, leaving behind a cavity in the rock called a **mold.** Later, mineral-rich water or other sediment might enter the cavity, form new rock, and produce a copy or **cast** of the original object, as shown in **Figure 5.**

**Coal Mining** Many of the first coal mines in the United States were located in eastern states like Pennsylvania and West Virginia. In your Science Journal, discuss how the environments of the past relate to people's lives today.

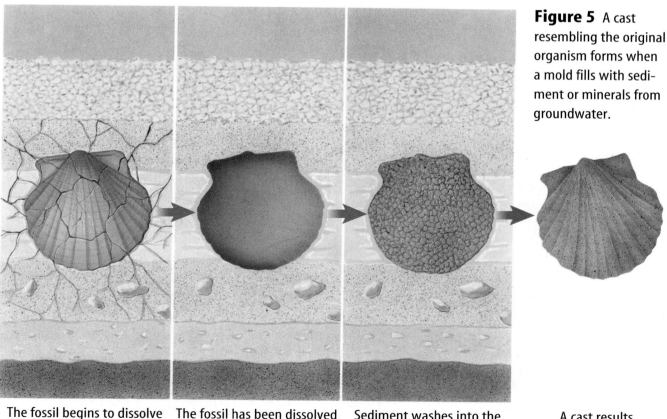

**Figure 5** A cast resembling the original organism forms when a mold fills with sediment or minerals from groundwater.

The fossil begins to dissolve as water moves through spaces in the rock layers.

The fossil has been dissolved away. The harder rock once surrounding it forms a mold.

Sediment washes into the mold and is deposited, or mineral crystals form.

A cast results.

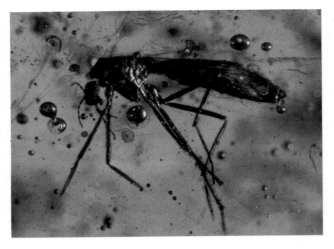

**Figure 6** The original soft parts of this mosquito have been preserved in amber for millions of years.

**Original Remains** Sometimes conditions allow original soft parts of organisms to be preserved for thousands or millions of years. For example, insects can be trapped in amber, a hardened form of sticky tree resin. The amber surrounds and protects the original material of the insect's exoskeleton from destruction, as shown in **Figure 6.** Some organisms, such as the mammoth, have been found preserved in frozen ground in Siberia. Original remains also have been found in natural tar deposits, such as the La Brea tar pits in California.

**Trace Fossils** Do you have a handprint in plaster that you made when you were in kindergarten? If so, it's a record that tells something about you. From it, others can guess your size and maybe your weight at that age. Animals walking on Earth long ago left similar tracks, such as those in **Figure 7.** Trace fossils are fossilized tracks and other evidence of the activity of organisms. In some cases, tracks can tell you more about how an organism lived than any other type of fossil. For example, from a set of tracks at Davenport Ranch, Texas, you might be able to learn something about the social life of sauropods, which were large, plant-eating dinosaurs. The largest tracks of the herd are on the outer edges and the smallest are on the inside. These tracks led some scientists to hypothesize that adult sauropods surrounded their young as they traveled—perhaps to protect them from predators. A nearby set of tracks might mean that another type of dinosaur, an allosaur, was stalking the herd.

**Figure 7** Tracks made in soft mud, and now preserved in solid rock, can provide information about animal size, speed, and behavior.

The dinosaur track below is from the Glen Rose Formation in north-central Texas.

The tracks to the right are located on a Navajo reservation in Arizona.

**Trails and Burrows** Other trace fossils include trails and burrows made by worms and other animals. These, too, tell something about how these animals lived. For example, by examining fossil burrows you can sometimes tell how firm the sediment the animals lived in was. As you can see, fossils can tell a great deal about the organisms that have inhabited Earth.

**Reading Check** *How are trace fossils different from fossils that are the remains of an organism's body?*

## Index Fossils

One thing you can learn by studying fossils is that species of organisms have changed over time. Some species of organisms inhabited Earth for long periods of time without changing. Other species changed a lot in comparatively short amounts of time. It is these organisms that scientists use as index fossils.

**Index fossils** are the remains of species that existed on Earth for relatively short periods of time, were abundant, and were widespread geographically. Because the organisms that became index fossils lived only during specific intervals of geologic time, geologists can estimate the ages of rock layers based on the particular index fossils they contain. However, not all rocks contain index fossils. Another way to approximate the age of a rock layer is to compare the spans of time, or ranges, over which more than one fossil appears. The estimated age is the time interval where fossil ranges overlap, as shown in **Figure 8.**

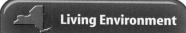
**Living Environment**

**3.2c** *Recently deposited rock layers are more likely to contain fossils resembling existing species.* **Support** this statement with a sketch of several layers of sedimentary rock containing fossils. Explain how index fossils are used to date the ages of rock layers.

**Figure 8** The fossils in a sequence of sedimentary rock can be used to estimate the ages of each layer. The chart shows when each organism inhabited Earth.

**Explain** *why it is possible to say that the middle layer of rock was deposited between 440 million and 410 million years ago.*

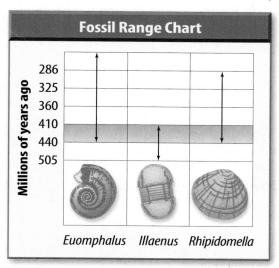

Fossil Range Chart

Millions of years ago

286 325 360 410 440 505

Euomphalus   Illaenus   Rhipidomella

**Ancient Ecology**
Ecology is the study of how organisms interact with each other and with their environment. Some paleontologists study the ecology of ancient organisms. Discuss the kinds of information you could use to determine how ancient organisms interacted with their environment.

# Fossils and Ancient Environments

Scientists can use fossils to determine what the environment of an area was like long ago. Using fossils, you might be able to find out whether an area was land or whether it was covered by an ocean at a particular time. If the region was covered by ocean, it might even be possible to learn the depth of the water. What clues about the depth of water do you think fossils could provide?

Fossils also are used to determine the past climate of a region. For example, rocks in parts of the eastern United States contain fossils of tropical plants. The environment of this part of the United States today isn't tropical. However, because of the fossils, scientists know that it was tropical when these plants were living. **Figure 9** shows that North America was located near the equator when these fossils formed.

**Figure 9** The equator passed through North America 310 million years ago. At this time, warm, shallow seas and coal swamps covered much of the continent, and ferns like the *Neuropteris,* below, were common.

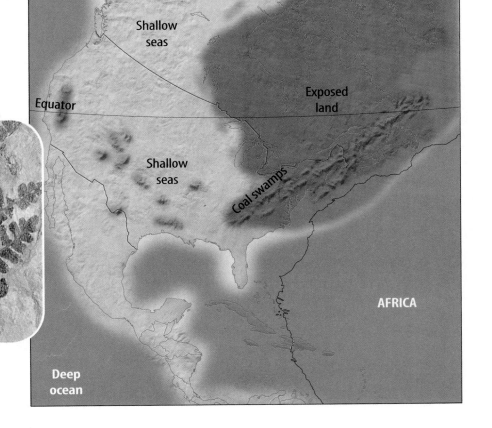

**Shallow Seas** How would you explain the presence of fossilized crinoids—animals that lived in shallow seas—in rocks found in what is today a desert? **Figure 10** shows a fossil crinoid and a living crinoid. When the fossil crinoids were alive, a shallow sea covered much of western and central North America. The crinoid hard parts were included in rocks that formed from the sediments at the bottom of this sea. Fossils provide information about past life on Earth and also about the history of the rock layers that contain them. Fossils can provide information about the ages of rocks and the climate and type of environment that existed when the rocks formed.

**Figure 10** The crinoid on the left lived in warm, shallow seas that once covered part of North America. Crinoids like the one on the right typically live in warm, shallow waters in the Pacific Ocean.

## section 1 review

### Summary

**Formation of Fossils**

- Fossils are the remains, imprints, or traces of past organisms.
- Fossilization is most likely if the organism had hard parts and was buried quickly.

**Fossil Preservation**

- Permineralized remains have open spaces filled with minerals from groundwater.
- Thin carbon films remain in the shapes of dead organisms.
- Hard parts dissolve to leave molds.
- Trace fossils are evidence of past activity.

**Index Fossils**

- Index fossils are from species that were abundant briefly, but over wide areas.
- Scientists can estimate the ages of rocks containing index fossils.

**Fossils and Ancient Environments**

- Fossils tell us about the environment in which the organisms lived.

### Self Check

1. **Describe** the typical conditions necessary for fossil formation.
2. **Explain** how a fossil mold is different from a fossil cast.
3. **Discuss** how the characteristics of an index fossil are useful to geologists.
4. **Describe** how carbon films form.
5. **Think Critically** What can you say about the ages of two widely separated layers of rock that contain the same type of fossil?

### Applying Skills

6. **Communicate** what you learn about fossils. Visit a museum that has fossils on display. Make an illustration of each fossil in your Science Journal. Write a brief description, noting key facts about each fossil and how each fossil might have formed.
7. **Compare and contrast** original remains with other kinds of fossils. What kinds of information would only be available from original remains? Are there any limitations to the use of original remains?

LE 3.2c: Many thousands of layers of sedimentary rock provide evidence for the long history of Earth and for the long history of changing lifeforms whose remains are found in the rocks. Recently deposited rock layers are more likely to contain fossils resembling existing species. **Also Covered:** PS 2.2c.

# Relative Ages of Rocks

**as you read**

### *What* You'll Learn

- **Describe** methods used to assign relative ages to rock layers.
- **Interpret** gaps in the rock record.
- **Give** an example of how rock layers can be correlated with other rock layers.

### *Why* It's Important

Being able to determine the age of rock layers is important in trying to understand a history of Earth.

### Review Vocabulary

**sedimentary rock:** rock formed when sediments are cemented and compacted or when minerals are precipitated from solution

### New Vocabulary

- principle of superposition
- relative age
- unconformity

## Superposition

Imagine that you are walking to your favorite store and you happen to notice an interesting car go by. You're not sure what kind it is, but you remember that you read an article about it. You decide to look it up. At home you have a stack of magazines from the past year, as seen in **Figure 11.**

You know that the article you're thinking of came out in the January edition, so it must be near the bottom of the pile. As you dig downward, you find magazines from March, then February. January must be next. How did you know that the January issue of the magazine would be on the bottom? To find the older edition under newer ones, you applied the principle of superposition.

**Oldest Rocks on the Bottom** According to the **principle of superposition,** in undisturbed layers of rock, the oldest rocks are on the bottom and the rocks become progressively younger toward the top. Why is this the case?

**Figure 11** The pile of magazines illustrates the principle of superposition. According to this principle, the oldest rock layer (or magazine) is on the bottom.

**Rock Layers** Sediment accumulates in horizontal beds, forming layers of sedimentary rock. The first layer to form is on the bottom. The next layer forms on top of the previous one. Because of this, the oldest rocks are at the bottom. However, forces generated by mountain formation sometimes can turn layers over. When layers have been turned upside down, it's necessary to use other clues in the rock layers to determine their original positions and relative ages.

## Relative Ages

Now you want to look for another magazine. You're not sure how old it is, but you know it arrived after the January issue. You can find it in the stack by using the principle of relative age.

The **relative age** of something is its age in comparison to the ages of other things. Geologists determine the relative ages of rocks and other structures by examining their places in a sequence. For example, if layers of sedimentary rock are offset by a fault, which is a break in Earth's surface, you know that the layers had to be there before a fault could cut through them. The relative age of the rocks is older than the relative age of the fault. Relative age determination doesn't tell you anything about the age of rock layers in actual years. You don't know if a layer is 100 million or 10,000 years old. You only know that it's younger than the layers below it and older than the fault cutting through it.

**Other Clues Help** Determination of relative age is easy if the rocks haven't been faulted or turned upside down. For example, look at **Figure 12.** Which layer is the oldest? In cases where rock layers have been disturbed you might have to look for fossils and other clues to date the rocks. If you find a fossil in the top layer that's older than a fossil in a lower layer, you can hypothesize that layers have been turned upside down by folding during mountain building.

**Science Online**

**Topic: Relative Dating**
Visit glencoe.com for Web links to information about relative dating of rocks and other materials.

**Activity** Imagine yourself at an archaeological dig. You have found a rare artifact and want to know its age. Make a list of clues you might look for to provide a relative date and explain how each would allow you to approximate the artifact's age.

**Living Environment**

**3.2c Discuss** the principle of superposition and how the relative age of a rock cannot tell scientists exactly how old the rock is.

**Figure 12** In a stack of undisturbed sedimentary rocks, the oldest rocks are at the bottom. This stack of rocks can be folded by forces within Earth.
**Explain** *how you can tell if an older rock is above a younger one.*

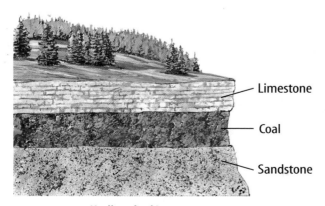

**Undisturbed Layers**

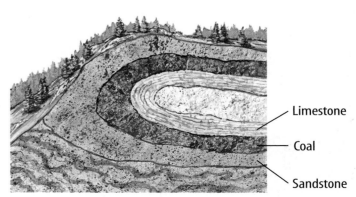

**Folded Layers**

**Figure 13** An angular unconformity results when horizontal layers cover tilted, eroded layers.

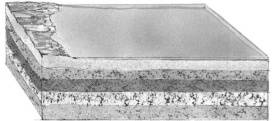

**A** Sedimentary rocks are deposited originally as horizontal layers.

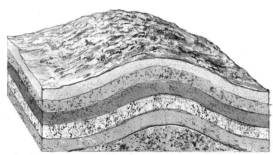

**B** The horizontal rock layers are tilted as forces within Earth deform them.

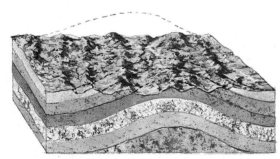

**C** The tilted layers erode.

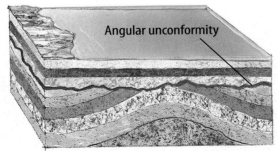

Angular unconformity

**D** An angular unconformity results when new layers form on the tilted layers as deposition resumes.

# Unconformities

A sequence of rock is a record of past events. But most rock sequences are incomplete—layers are missing. These gaps in rock sequences are called **unconformities** (un kun FOR muh teez). Unconformities develop when agents of erosion such as running water or glaciers remove rock layers by washing or scraping them away.

**Reading Check** *How do unconformities form?*

**Angular Unconformities** Horizontal layers of sedimentary rock often are tilted and uplifted. Erosion and weathering then wear down these tilted rock layers. Eventually, younger sediment layers are deposited horizontally on top of the tilted and eroded layers. Geologists call such an unconformity an angular unconformity. **Figure 13** shows how angular unconformities develop.

**Disconformity** Suppose you're looking at a stack of sedimentary rock layers. They look complete, but layers are missing. If you look closely, you might find an old surface of erosion. This records a time when the rocks were exposed and eroded. Later, younger rocks formed above the erosion surface when deposition of sediment began again. Even though all the layers are parallel, the rock record still has a gap. This type of unconformity is called a disconformity. A disconformity also forms when a period of time passes without any new deposition occurring to form new layers of rock.

**Nonconformity** Another type of unconformity, called a nonconformity, occurs when metamorphic or igneous rocks are uplifted and eroded. Sedimentary rocks are then deposited on top of this erosion surface. The surface between the two rock types is a nonconformity. Sometimes rock fragments from below are incorporated into sediments deposited above the nonconformity. All types of unconformities are shown in **Figure 14.**

## Figure 14

An unconformity is a gap in the rock record caused by erosion or a pause in deposition. There are three major kinds of unconformities—nonconformity, angular unconformity, and disconformity.

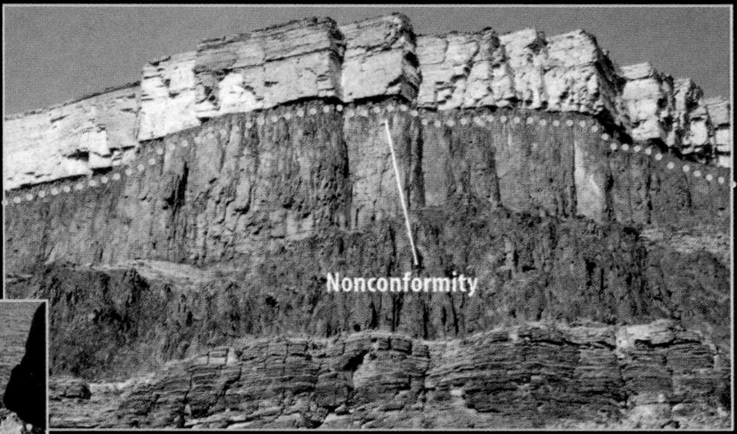

Nonconformity

▲ In a nonconformity, horizontal layers of sedimentary rock overlie older igneous or metamorphic rocks. A nonconformity in Big Bend National Park, Texas, is shown above.

Angular unconformity

▲ An angular unconformity develops when new horizontal layers of sedimentary rock form on top of older sedimentary rock layers that have been folded by compression. An example of an angular unconformity at Siccar Point in southeastern Scotland is shown above.

▼ A disconformity develops when horizontal rock layers are exposed and eroded, and new horizontal layers of rock are deposited on the eroded surface. The disconformity shown below is in the Grand Canyon.

Disconformity

## Matching Up Rock Layers

Suppose you're studying a layer of sandstone in Bryce Canyon in Utah. Later, when you visit Canyonlands National Park, Utah, you notice that a layer of sandstone there looks just like the sandstone in Bryce Canyon, 250 km away. Above the sandstone in the Canyonlands is a layer of limestone and then another sandstone layer. You return to Bryce Canyon and find the same sequence—sandstone, limestone, and sandstone. What do you infer? It's likely that you're looking at the same layers of rocks in two different locations. **Figure 15** shows that these rocks are parts of huge deposits that covered this whole area of the western United States. Geologists often can match up, or correlate, layers of rocks over great distances.

**Evidence Used for Correlation** It's not always easy to say that a rock layer exposed in one area is the same as a rock layer exposed in another area. Sometimes it's possible to walk along the layer for kilometers and prove that it's continuous. In other cases, such as at the Canyonlands area and Bryce Canyon as seen in **Figure 16,** the rock layers are exposed only where rivers have cut through overlying layers of rock and sediment. How can you show that the limestone sandwiched between the two layers of sandstone in Canyonlands is likely the same limestone as at Bryce Canyon? One way is to use fossil evidence. If the same types of fossils were found in the limestone layer in both places, it's a good indication that the limestone at each location is the same age, and, therefore, one continuous deposit.

**Reading Check** *How do fossils help show that rocks at different locations belong to the same rock layer?*

**Figure 15** These rock layers, exposed at Hopi Point in Grand Canyon National Park, Arizona, can be correlated, or matched up, with rocks from across large areas of the western United States.

Canyonlands National Park

UTAH

Bryce Canyon National Park

Grand Canyon National Park

ARIZONA

Canyonlands National Park

Bryce Canyon National Park

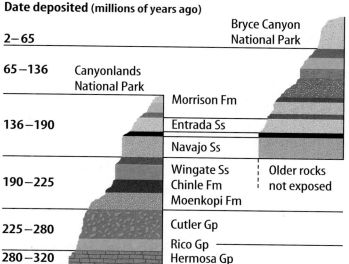

**Date deposited** (millions of years ago)

| Date | Canyonlands formations | Bryce Canyon formations |
|---|---|---|
| 2–65 | | Wasatch Fm |
| 65–136 | | Kaiparowits Fm |
| | | Straight Cliffs Ss |
| 136–190 | Morrison Fm | Dakota Ss |
| | Entrada Ss | Winsor Fm |
| | | Entrada Ss |
| | Navajo Ss | Carmel Fm |
| | | Navajo Ss |
| 190–225 | Wingate Ss | Older rocks not exposed |
| | Chinle Fm | |
| | Moenkopi Fm | |
| 225–280 | Cutler Gp | |
| | Rico Gp | |
| 280–320 | Hermosa Gp | |

**Figure 16** Geologists have named the many rock layers, or formations, in Canyonlands and in Bryce Canyon, Utah. They also have correlated some formations between the two canyons.
**List** the labeled layers present at both canyons.

Can layers of rock be correlated in other ways? Sometimes determining relative ages isn't enough and other dating methods must be used. In Section 3, you'll see how the numerical ages of rocks can be determined and how geologists have used this information to estimate the age of Earth.

## section 2 review

### Summary

**Superposition**
- Superposition states that in undisturbed rock, the oldest layers are on the bottom.

**Relative Ages**
- Rock layers can be ranked by relative age.

**Unconformities**
- Angular unconformities are new layers deposited over tilted and eroded rock layers.
- Disconformities are gaps in the rock record.
- Nonconformities divide uplifted igneous or metamorphic rock from new sedimentary rock.

**Matching Up Rock Layers**
- Rocks from different areas may be correlated if they are part of the same layer.

### Self Check

1. **Discuss** how to find the oldest paper in a stack of papers.
2. **Explain** the concept of relative age.
3. **Illustrate** a disconformity.
4. **Describe** one way to correlate similar rock layers.
5. **Think Critically** Explain the relationship between the concept of relative age and the principle of superposition.

#### Applying Skills

6. **Interpret data** to determine the oldest rock bed. A sandstone contains a 400-million-year-old fossil. A shale has fossils that are over 500 million years old. A limestone, below the sandstone, contains fossils between 400 million and 500 million years old. Which rock bed is oldest? Explain.

# Relative Ages

Which of your two friends is older? To answer this question, you'd need to know their relative ages. You wouldn't need to know the exact age of either of your friends—just who was born first. The same is sometimes true for rock layers.

 **Real-World Question**

Can you determine the relative ages of rock layers?

**Goals**
■ **Interpret** illustrations of rock layers and other geological structures and determine the relative order of events.

**Materials**
paper        pencil

 **Procedure**

1. **Analyze Figures A** and **B.**
2. Make a sketch of **Figure A.** On it, identify the relative age of each rock layer, igneous intrusion, fault, and unconformity. For example, the shale layer is the oldest, so mark it with a 1. Mark the next-oldest feature with a 2, and so on.
3. Repeat step 2 for **Figure B.**

 **Conclude and Apply**

**Figure A**

1. **Identify** the type of unconformity shown. Is it possible that there were originally more layers of rock than are shown?
2. **Describe** how the rocks above the fault moved in relation to rocks below the fault.
3. **Hypothesize** how the hill on the left side of the figure formed.

Figure B

4. Is it possible to conclude if the igneous intrusion on the left is older or younger than the unconformity nearest the surface?
5. **Describe** the relative ages of the two igneous intrusions. How did you know?
6. **Hypothesize** which two layers of rock might have been much thicker in the past.

**Compare** your results with other students' results. **For more help, refer to the** Science Skill Handbook.

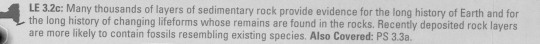

**LE 3.2c:** Many thousands of layers of sedimentary rock provide evidence for the long history of Earth and for the long history of changing lifeforms whose remains are found in the rocks. Recently deposited rock layers are more likely to contain fossils resembling existing species. **Also Covered:** PS 3.3a.

## section 3

# Absolute Ages of Rocks

## Absolute Ages

As you sort through your stack of magazines looking for that article about the car you saw, you decide that you need to restack them into a neat pile. By now, they're in a jumble and no longer in order of their relative age, as shown in **Figure 17.** How can you stack them so the oldest are on the bottom and the newest are on top? Fortunately, magazine dates are printed on the cover. Thus, stacking magazines in order is a simple process. Unfortunately, rocks don't have their ages stamped on them. Or do they? **Absolute age** is the age, in years, of a rock or other object. Geologists determine absolute ages by using properties of the atoms that make up materials.

## Radioactive Decay

**INTEGRATE Physics** Atoms consist of a dense central region called the nucleus, which is surrounded by a cloud of negatively charged particles called electrons. The nucleus is made up of protons, which have a positive charge, and neutrons, which have no electric charge. The number of protons determines the identity of the element, and the number of neutrons determines the form of the element, or isotope. For example, every atom with a single proton is a hydrogen atom. Hydrogen atoms can have no neutrons, a single neutron, or two neutrons. This means that there are three isotopes of hydrogen.

**✓ Reading Check** *What particles make up an atom's nucleus?*

Some isotopes are unstable and break down into other isotopes and particles. Sometimes a lot of energy is given off during this process. The process of breaking down is called **radioactive decay.** In the case of hydrogen, atoms with one proton and two neutrons are unstable and tend to break down. Many other elements have stable and unstable isotopes.

### as you read

**What You'll Learn**
- **Identify** how absolute age differs from relative age.
- **Describe** how the half-lives of isotopes are used to determine a rock's age.

**Why It's Important**
Events in Earth's history can be better understood if their absolute ages are known.

**⊙ Review Vocabulary**
**isotopes:** atoms of the same element that have different numbers of neutrons

**New Vocabulary**
- absolute age
- radioactive decay
- half-life
- radiometric dating
- uniformitarianism

**Figure 17** The magazines that have been shuffled through no longer illustrate the principle of superposition.

## Modeling Carbon-14 Dating

### Procedure

1. Count out 80 **red jelly beans.**
2. Remove half the red jelly beans and replace them with **green jelly beans.**
3. Continue replacing half the red jelly beans with green jelly beans until only 5 red jelly beans remain. Count the number of times you replace half the red jelly beans.

### Analysis

1. How did this activity model the decay of carbon-14 atoms?
2. How many half lives of carbon-14 did you model during this activity?
3. If the atoms in a bone experienced the same number of half lives as your jelly beans, how old would the bone be?

**Figure 18** In beta decay, a neutron changes into a proton by giving off an electron. This electron has a lot of energy and is called a beta particle.

In the process of alpha decay, an unstable parent isotope nucleus gives off an alpha particle and changes into a new daughter product. Alpha particles contain two neutrons and two protons.

**Alpha and Beta Decay** In some isotopes, a neutron breaks down into a proton and an electron. This type of radioactive decay is called beta decay because the electron leaves the atom as a beta particle. The nucleus loses a neutron but gains a proton. When the number of protons in an atom is changed, a new element forms. Other isotopes give off two protons and two neutrons in the form of an alpha particle. Alpha and beta decay are shown in **Figure 18.**

**Half-Life** In radioactive decay reactions, the parent isotope undergoes radioactive decay. The daughter product is produced by radioactive decay. Each radioactive parent isotope decays to its daughter product at a certain rate. Based on this decay rate, it takes a certain period of time for one half of the parent isotope to decay to its daughter product. The **half-life** of an isotope is the time it takes for half of the atoms in the isotope to decay. For example, the half-life of carbon-14 is 5,730 years. So it will take 5,730 years for half of the carbon-14 atoms in an object to change into nitrogen-14 atoms. You might guess that in another 5,730 years, all of the remaining carbon-14 atoms will decay to nitrogen-14. However, this is not the case. Only half of the atoms of carbon-14 remaining after the first 5,730 years will decay during the second 5,730 years. So, after two half-lives, one fourth of the original carbon-14 atoms still remain. Half of them will decay during another 5,730 years. After three half-lives, one eighth of the original carbon-14 atoms still remain. After many half-lives, such a small amount of the parent isotope remains that it might not be measurable.

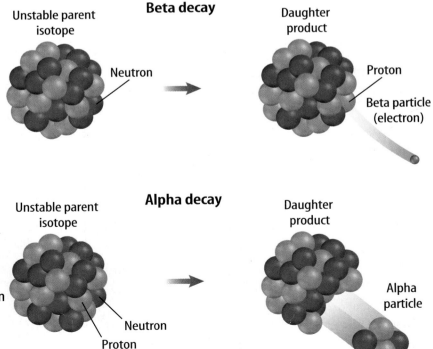

# Radiometric Ages

Decay of radioactive isotopes is like a clock keeping track of time that has passed since rocks have formed. As time passes, the amount of parent isotope in a rock decreases as the amount of daughter product increases, as in **Figure 19.** By measuring the ratio of parent isotope to daughter product in a mineral and by knowing the half-life of the parent, in many cases you can calculate the absolute age of a rock. This process is called **radiometric dating.**

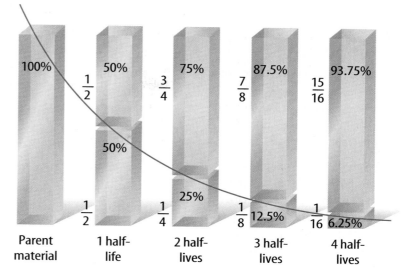

**Figure 19** During each half-life, one half of the parent material decays to the daughter product. **Explain** *how one uses both parent and daughter material to estimate age.*

A scientist must decide which parent isotope to use when measuring the age of a rock. If the object to be dated seems old, then the geologist will use an isotope with a long half-life. The half-life for the decay of potassium-40 to argon-40 is 1.25 billion years. As a result, this isotope can be used to date rocks that are many millions of years old. To avoid error, conditions must be met for the ratios to give a correct indication of age. For example, the rock being studied must still retain all of the argon-40 that was produced by the decay of potassium-40. Also, it cannot contain any contamination of daughter product from other sources. Potassium-argon dating is good for rocks containing potassium, but what about other things?

**Radiocarbon Dating** Carbon-14 is useful for dating bones, wood, and charcoal up to 75,000 years old. Living things take in carbon from the environment to build their bodies. Most of that carbon is carbon-12, but some is carbon-14, and the ratio of these two isotopes in the environment is always the same. After the organism dies, the carbon-14 slowly decays. By determining the amounts of the isotopes in a sample, scientists can evaluate how much the isotope ratio in the sample differs from that in the environment. For example, during much of human history, people built campfires. The wood from these fires often is preserved as charcoal. Scientists can determine the amount of carbon-14 remaining in a sample of charcoal by measuring the amount of radiation emitted by the carbon-14 isotope in labs like the one in **Figure 20.** Once they know the amount of carbon-14 in a charcoal sample, scientists can determine the age of the wood used to make the fire.

**Living Environment**

**3.2c Summarize** how scientists can determine the absolute age of rock through radiometric age.

**Figure 20** Radiometric ages are determined in labs like this one.

**Age Determinations** Aside from carbon-14 dating, rocks that can be radiometrically dated are mostly igneous and metamorphic rocks. Most sedimentary rocks cannot be dated by this method. This is because many sedimentary rocks are made up of particles eroded from older rocks. Dating these pieces only gives the age of the preexisting rock from which it came.

**The Oldest Known Rocks** Radiometric dating has been used to date the oldest rocks on Earth. These rocks are about 3.96 billion years old. By determining the age of meteorites, and using other evidence, scientists have estimated the age of Earth to be about 4.5 billion years. Earth rocks greater than 3.96 billion years old probably were eroded or changed by heat and pressure.

**✔ Reading Check** *Why can't most sedimentary rocks be dated radiometrically?*

## Applying Science

### When did the Iceman die?

Carbon-14 dating has been used to date charcoal, wood, bones, mummies from Egypt and Peru, the Dead Sea Scrolls, and the Italian Iceman. The Iceman was found in 1991 in the Italian Alps, near the Austrian border. Based on carbon-14 analysis, scientists determined that the Iceman is 5,300 years old. Determine approximately in what year the Iceman died.

| Half-Life of Carbon-14 | |
|---|---|
| Percent Carbon-14 | Years Passed |
| 100 | 0 |
| 50 | 5,730 |
| 25 | 11,460 |
| 12.5 | 17,190 |
| 6.25 | 22,920 |
| 3.125 | |

**Reconstruction of Iceman**

### Identifying the Problem

The half-life chart shows the decay of carbon-14 over time. Half-life is the time it takes for half of a sample to decay. Fill in the years passed when only 3.125 percent of carbon-14 remain. Is there a point at which no carbon-14 would be present? Explain.

### Solving the Problem

1. Estimate, using the data table, how much carbon-14 still was present in the Iceman's body that allowed scientists to determine his age.
2. If you had an artifact that originally contained 10.0 g of carbon-14, how many grams would remain after 17,190 years?

# Uniformitarianism

Can you imagine trying to determine the age of Earth without some of the information you know today? Before the discovery of radiometric dating, many people estimated that Earth is only a few thousand years old. But in the 1700s, Scottish scientist James Hutton estimated that Earth is much older. He used the principle of **uniformitarianism.** This principle states that Earth processes occurring today are similar to those that occurred in the past. Hutton's principle is often paraphrased as "the present is the key to the past."

Hutton observed that the processes that changed the landscape around him were slow, and he inferred that they were just as slow throughout Earth's history. Hutton hypothesized that it took much longer than a few thousand years to form the layers of rock around him and to erode mountains that once stood kilometers high. **Figure 21** shows Hutton's native Scotland, a region shaped by millions of years of geologic processes.

Today, scientists recognize that Earth has been shaped by two types of change: slow, everyday processes that take place over millions of years, and violent, unusual events such as the collision of a comet or asteroid about 65 million years ago that might have caused the extinction of the dinosaurs.

**Figure 21** The rugged highlands of Scotland were shaped by erosion and uplift.

## section 3 review

### Summary

**Absolute Ages**

- The absolute age is the actual age of an object.

**Radioactive Decay**

- Some isotopes are unstable and decay into other isotopes and particles.
- Decay is measured in half-lives, the time it takes for half of a given isotope to decay.

**Radiometric Ages**

- By measuring the ratio of parent isotope to daughter product, one can determine the absolute age of a rock.
- Living organisms less than 75,000 years old can be dated using carbon-14.

**Uniformitarianism**

- Processes observable today are the same as the processes that took place in the past.

### Self Check

1. **Evaluate** the age of rocks. You find three undisturbed rock layers. The middle layer is 120 million years old. What can you say about the ages of the layers above and below it?

2. **Determine** the age of a fossil if it had only one eighth of its original carbon-14 content remaining.

3. **Explain** the concept of uniformitarianism.

4. **Describe** how radioactive isotopes decay.

5. **Think Critically** Why can't scientists use carbon-14 to determine the age of an igneous rock?

   *Hot Words Hot Topics:* Bk 2 (6) p. 194

#### Applying Math

6. **Make and use a table** that shows the amount of parent material of a radioactive element that is left after four half-lives if the original parent material had a mass of 100 g.

## Model and Invent

# Trace Fossils

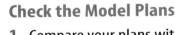

**Goals**
- **Construct** a model of trace fossils.
- **Describe** the information that you can learn from looking at your model.

**Possible Materials**
construction paper
wire
plastic (a fairly rigid type)
scissors
plaster of paris
toothpicks
sturdy cardboard
clay
pipe cleaners
glue

**Safety Precautions**

## ◉ *Real-World Question*

Trace fossils can tell you a lot about the activities of organisms that left them. They can tell you how an organism fed or what kind of home it had. How can you model trace fossils that can provide information about the behavior of organisms? What materials can you use to model trace fossils? What types of behavior could you show with your trace fossil model?

## ◉ *Make a Model*

1. **Decide** how you are going to make your model. What materials will you need?

2. **Decide** what types of activities you will demonstrate with your model. Were the organisms feeding? Resting? Traveling? Were they predators? Prey? How will your model indicate the activities you chose?

3. What is the setting of your model? Are you modeling the organism's home? Feeding areas? Is your model on land or water? How can the setting affect the way you build your model?

4. Will you only show trace fossils from a single species or multiple species? If you include more than one species, how will you provide evidence of any interaction between the species?

### Check the Model Plans

1. Compare your plans with those of others in your class. Did other groups mention details that you had forgotten to think about? Are there any changes you would like to make to your plan before you continue?

2. Make sure your teacher approves your plan before you continue.

### ▶ Test Your Model

1. Following your plan, construct your model of trace fossils.

2. Have you included evidence of all the behaviors you intended to model?

### ▶ Analyze Your Data

1. **Evaluate** Now that your model is complete, do you think that it adequately shows the behaviors you planned to demonstrate? Is there anything that you think you might want to do differently if you were going to make the model again?

2. **Describe** how using different kinds of materials might have affected your model. Can you think of other materials that would have allowed you to show more detail than you did?

### ▶ Conclude and Apply

1. **Compare and contrast** your model of trace fossils with trace fossils left by real organisms. Is one more easily interpreted than the other? Explain.

2. **List** behaviors that might not leave any trace fossils. Explain.

### Communicating Your Data

Ask other students in your class or another class to look at your model and describe what information they can learn from the trace fossils. Did their interpretations agree with what you intended to show?

## The World's Oldest Fish Story

*A catch-of-the-day set science on its ears*

Camouflage marks

First dorsal fin

Second dorsal fin

Pectoral fin

Anal fin

Pelvic fin

Some scientists call the coelacanth "Old Four Legs." It got its nickname because the fish has paired fins that look something like legs.

On a December day in 1938, just before Christmas, Marjorie Courtenay-Latimer went to say hello to her friends on board a fishing boat that had just returned to port in South Africa. Courtenay-Latimer, who worked at a museum, often went aboard her friends' ship to check out the catch. On this visit, she received a surprise Christmas present—an odd-looking fish. As soon as the woman spotted its strange blue fins among the piles of sharks and rays, she knew it was special.

Courtenay-Latimer took the fish back to her museum to study it. "It was the most beautiful fish I had ever seen, five feet long, and a pale mauve blue with iridescent silver markings," she later wrote. Courtenay-Latimer sketched it and sent the drawing to a friend of hers, J. L. B. Smith.

Smith was a chemistry teacher who was passionate about fish. After a time, he realized it was a coelacanth (SEE luh kanth). Fish experts knew that coelacanths had first appeared on Earth 400 million years ago. But the experts thought the fish were extinct. People had found fossils of coelacanths, but

no one had seen one alive. It was assumed that the last coelacanth species had died out 65 million years ago. They were wrong. The ship's crew had caught one by accident.

Smith figured there might be more living coelacanths. So he decided to offer a reward for anyone who could find a living specimen. After 14 years of silence, a report came in that a coelacanth had been caught off the east coast of Africa.

Today, scientists know that there are at least several hundred coelacanths living in the Indian Ocean, just east of central Africa. Many of these fish live near the Comoros Islands. The coelacanths live in underwater caves during the day but move out at night to feed. The rare fish are now a protected species. With any luck, they will survive for another hundred million years.

**Write** a short essay describing the discovery of the coelacanths and describe the reaction of scientists to this discovery.

Science online

For more information, visit glencoe.com

## Reviewing Main Ideas

### Section 1 Fossils

1. Fossils are more likely to form if hard parts of the dead organisms are buried quickly.

2. Some fossils form when original materials that made up the organisms are replaced with minerals. Other fossils form when remains are subjected to heat and pressure, leaving only a carbon film behind. Some fossils are the tracks or traces left by ancient organisms.

### Section 2 Relative Ages of Rocks

1. The principle of superposition states that, in undisturbed layers, older rocks lie underneath younger rocks.

2. Unconformities, or gaps in the rock record, are due to erosion or periods of time during which no deposition occurred.

3. Rock layers can be correlated using rock types and fossils.

### Section 3 Absolute Ages of Rocks

1. Absolute dating provides an age in years for the rocks.

2. The half-life of a radioactive isotope is the time it takes for half of the atoms of the isotope to decay into another isotope.

## Visualizing Main Ideas

*Copy and complete the following concept map on fossils.*

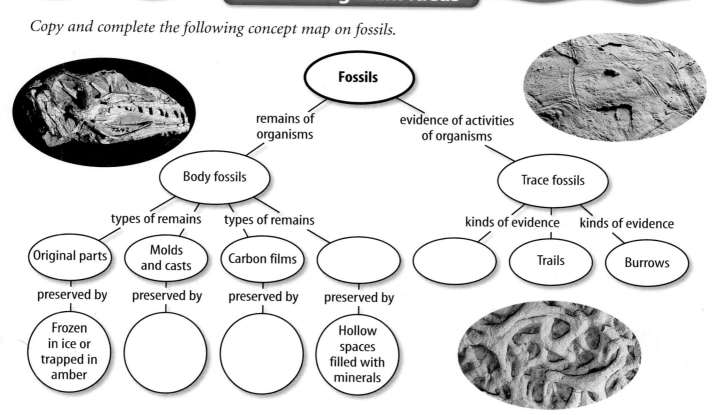

## Using Vocabulary

absolute age  p. 135
carbon film  p. 122
cast  p. 123
fossil  p. 121
half-life  p. 136
index fossil  p. 125
mold  p. 123
permineralized remains
  p. 122

principle of superposition
  p. 128
radioactive decay  p. 135
radiometric dating  p. 137
relative age  p. 129
unconformity  p. 130
uniformitarianism  p. 139

*Write an original sentence using the vocabulary word to which each phrase refers.*

1. thin film of carbon preserved as a fossil

2. older rocks lie under younger rocks

3. processes occur today as they did in the past

4. gap in the rock record

5. time needed for half the atoms to decay

6. fossil organism that lived for a short time

7. gives the age of rocks in years

8. minerals fill spaces inside fossil

9. a copy of a fossil produced by filling a mold with sediment or crystals

## Checking Concepts

*Choose the word or phrase that best answers the question.*

10. What is any evidence of ancient life called?
    **A)** half-life        **C)** unconformity
    **B)** fossil          **D)** disconformity

11. Which of the following conditions makes fossil formation more likely?
    **A)** buried slowly
    **B)** attacked by scavengers
    **C)** made of hard parts
    **D)** composed of soft parts

12. What are cavities left in rocks when a shell or bone dissolves called?
    **A)** casts          **C)** original remains
    **B)** molds          **D)** carbon films

13. To say "the present is the key to the past" is a way to describe which of the following principles?
    **A)** superposition    **C)** radioactivity
    **B)** succession      **D)** uniformitarianism

14. A fault can be useful in determining which of the following for a group of rocks?
    **A)** absolute age    **C)** radiometric age
    **B)** index age       **D)** relative age

15. Which of the following is an unconformity between parallel rock layers?
    **A)** angular unconformity
    **B)** fault
    **C)** disconformity
    **D)** nonconformity

**Use the illustration below to answer question 16.**

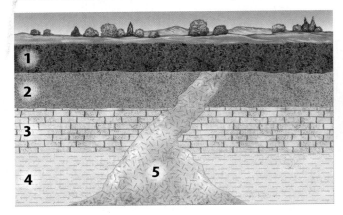

16. Which of the following puts the layers in order from oldest to youngest?
    **A)** 5-4-3-2-1      **C)** 2-3-4-5-1
    **B)** 1-2-3-4-5      **D)** 4-3-2-5-1

17. Which process forms new elements?
    **A)** superposition
    **B)** uniformitarianism
    **C)** permineralization
    **D)** radioactive decay

Vocabulary Puzzlemaker glencoe.com

## Thinking Critically

**18. Explain** why the fossil record of life on Earth is incomplete. Give some reasons why.

**19. Infer** Suppose a lava flow was found between two sedimentary rock layers. How could you use the lava flow to learn about the ages of the sedimentary rock layers? *(Hint: Most lava contains radioactive isotopes.)*

**20. Infer** Suppose you're correlating rock layers in the western United States. You find a layer of volcanic ash deposits. How can this layer help you in your correlation over a large area?

**21. Recognize Cause and Effect** Explain how some woolly mammoths could have been preserved intact in frozen ground. What conditions must have persisted since the deaths of these animals?

**22. Classify** each of the following fossils in the correct category in the table below: *dinosaur footprint, worm burrow, dinosaur skull, insect in amber, fossil woodpecker hole,* and *fish tooth.*

| Types of Fossils | |
|---|---|
| Trace Fossils | Body Fossils |
| Do not write in this book. | |

**23. Compare and contrast** the three different kinds of unconformities. Draw sketches of each that illustrate the features that identify them.

**24. Describe** how relative and absolute ages differ. How might both be used to establish ages in a series of rock layers?

**25. Discuss** uniformitarianism in the following scenario. You find a shell on the beach, and a friend remembers seeing a similar fossil while hiking in the mountains. What does this suggest about the past environment of the mountain?

## Performance Activities

**26. Illustrate** Create a model that allows you to explain how to establish the relative ages of rock layers.

**27. Use a Classification System** Start your own fossil collection. Label each find as to type, approximate age, and the place where it was found. Most state geological surveys can provide you with reference materials on local fossils.

*Hot Words Hot Topics*: Bk 2 (28): p. 120; (29) p. 199

## Applying Math

**28. Calculate** how many half-lives have passed in a rock containing one-eighth the original radioactive material and seven-eighths of the daughter product.

**Use the graphs below to answer question 29.**

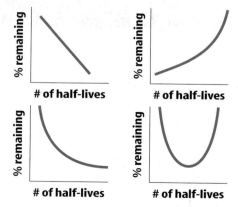

**29. Interpret Data** Which of the above curves best illustrates radioactive decay?

## Part I

*Record your answers on the answer sheet provided by your teacher or on a sheet of paper.*

**Use the photo below to answer question 1.**

1 Which type of fossil preservation is shown above?
(1) trace fossil
(2) original remains
(3) carbon film
(4) permineralized remains

2 Which principle states that the oldest rock layer is found at the bottom in an undisturbed stack of rock layers?
(1) half-life
(2) absolute dating
(3) superposition
(4) uniformitarianism

3 Which type of scientist studies fossils?
(1) meteorologist
(2) chemist
(3) astronomer
(4) paleontologist

4 Which are the remains of species that existed on Earth for relatively short periods of time, were abundant, and were widespread geographically?
(1) trace fossils
(2) index fossils
(3) carbon films
(4) body fossils

5 Which term means matching up rock layers in different places?
(1) superposition
(2) correlation
(3) uniformitarianism
(4) absolute dating

6 Which of the following is least likely to be found as a fossil?
(1) clam shell
(2) shark tooth
(3) snail shell
(4) jellyfish imprint

7 Which type of fossil preservation is a thin carbon silhouette of the original organism?
(1) cast
(2) carbon film
(3) mold
(4) permineralized remains

8 Which isotope is useful for dating wood and charcoal that is less than about 75,000 years old?
(1) carbon-14
(2) potassium-40
(3) uranium-238
(4) argon-40

**Use the diagram below to answer questions 9–11.**

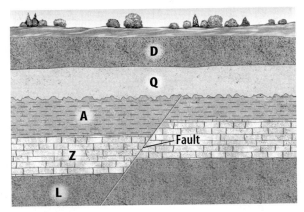

9 Which sequence of letters describes the rock layers in the diagram from oldest to youngest?
(1) D, Q, A, Z, L
(2) L, Z, A, Q, D
(3) Z, L, A, D, Q
(4) Q, D, L, Z, A

10 What does the wavy line between layers A and Q represent?
(1) a disconformity
(2) a fault
(3) a nonconformity
(4) an angular unconformity

11 Which of the following correctly describes the relative age of the fault?
(1) younger than A, but older than Q
(2) younger than Z, but older than L
(3) younger than Q, but older than A
(4) younger than D, but older than Q

**Part II**

*Record your answers on the answer sheet provided by your teacher or on a sheet of paper.*

**12** How is a fossil cast different from a fossil mold?

**13** Describe the principle of uniformitarianism.

**14** Explain how the original remains of an insect can be preserved as a fossil in amber.

**15** Use the terms *isotope, nucleus,* and *half-life* to describe the process of radioactive decay.

**Use the table below to answer questions 16 and 17.**

| Number of Half-lives | Parent Isotope Remaining (%) |
|:---:|:---:|
| 1 | 100 |
| 2 | X |
| 3 | 25 |
| 4 | 12.5 |
| 5 | Y |

**16** What value should replace the letter X in the table above? What value should replace the letter Y in the table above?

**17** Explain the relationship between the number of half-lives that have elapsed and the amount of parent isotope remaining.

**18** Why are index fossils useful for estimating the age of rock layers?

**Examine the graph below and answer questions 19 and 20.**

**Relationship Between Sediment Burial Rate and Potential for Remains to Become Fossils**

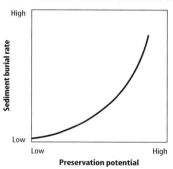

**19** How does the potential for remains to be preserved change as the rate of burial by sediment increases? Why do you think this relationship exists?

**20** What other factors affect the potential for the remains of organisms to become fossils?

**21** How could a fossil of an organism that lived in ocean water millions of years ago be found in the middle of North America?

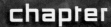

**PS 2.1c:** The rock at Earth's surface forms a nearly continuous shell around Earth called the lithosphere.
**2.2a:** The interior of Earth is hot. Heat flow and movement of material within Earth cause sections of Earth's crust to move. This may result in earthquakes, volcanic eruption, and the creation of mountains and ocean basins. **Also Covered:** PS 2.2b, 2.2c, 2.2d, 2.2e, 2.2f

# Plate Tectonics

## Will this continent split?

Ol Doinyo Lengai is an active volcano in the East African Rift Valley, a place where Earth's crust is being pulled apart. If the pulling continues over millions of years, Africa will separate into two landmasses. In this chapter, you'll learn about rift valleys and other clues that the continents move over time.

**Science Journal** Pretend you're a journalist with an audience that assumes the continents have never moved. Write about the kinds of evidence you'll need to convince people otherwise.

# Start-Up Activities

## Reassemble an Image

Can you imagine a giant landmass that broke into many separate continents and Earth scientists working to reconstruct Earth's past? Do this lab to learn about clues that can be used to reassemble a supercontinent.

1. Collect interesting photographs from an old magazine.

2. You and a partner each select one photo, but don't show them to each other. Then each of you cut your photos into pieces no smaller than about 5 cm or 6 cm.

3. Trade your cut-up photo for your partner's.

4. Observe the pieces, and reassemble the photograph your partner has cut up.

5. **Think Critically** Write a paragraph describing the characteristics of the cut-up photograph that helped you put the image back together. Think of other examples in which characteristics of objects are used to match them up with other objects.

 **Preview this chapter's content and activities at** glencoe.com

**Plate Tectonics** Make the following Foldable to help identify what you already know, what you want to know, and what you learned about plate tectonics.

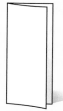 **STEP 1** Fold a vertical sheet of paper from side to side. Make the front edge about 1.25 cm shorter than the back edge.

**STEP 2** Turn lengthwise and fold into thirds.

**STEP 3** Unfold and cut only the layer along both folds to make three tabs.

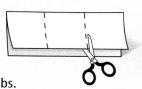

**STEP 4** Label each tab.

Know?  Like to know?  Learned?

**Identify Questions** Before you read the chapter, write what you already know about plate tectonics under the left tab of your Foldable, and write questions about what you'd like to know under the center tab. After you read the chapter, list what you learned under the right tab.

# Continental Drift

**as you read**

### *What* You'll Learn

- **Describe** the hypothesis of continental drift.
- **Identify** evidence supporting continental drift.

### *Why* It's Important

The hypothesis of continental drift led to plate tectonics—a theory that explains many processes in Earth.

### 🔎 Review Vocabulary

**continent:** one of the six or seven great divisions of land on the globe

### New Vocabulary

- continental drift
- Pangaea

## Evidence for Continental Drift

If you look at a map of Earth's surface, you can see that the edges of some continents look as though they could fit together like a puzzle. Other people also have noticed this fact. For example, Dutch mapmaker Abraham Ortelius noted the fit between the coastlines of South America and Africa more than 400 years ago.

**Pangaea** German meteorologist Alfred Wegener (VEG nur) thought that the fit of the continents wasn't just a coincidence. He suggested that all the continents were joined together at some time in the past. In a 1912 lecture, he proposed the hypothesis of continental drift. According to the hypothesis of **continental drift,** continents have moved slowly to their current locations. Wegener suggested that all continents once were connected as one large landmass, shown in **Figure 1,** that broke apart about 200 million years ago. He called this large landmass **Pangaea** (pan JEE uh), which means "all land."

**✓ Reading Check** *Who proposed continental drift?*

**Figure 1** This illustration represents how the continents once were joined to form Pangaea. This fitting together of continents according to shape is not the only evidence supporting the past existence of Pangaea.

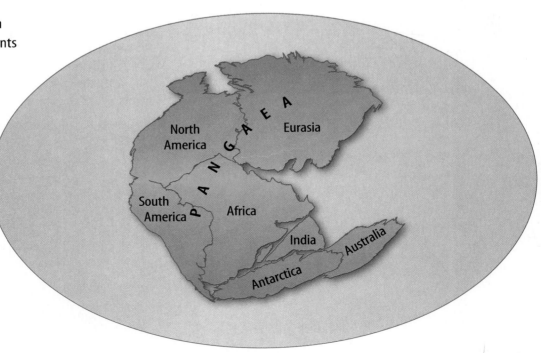

**A Controversial Idea** Wegener's ideas about continental drift were controversial. It wasn't until long after Wegener's death in 1930 that his basic hypothesis was accepted. The evidence Wegener presented hadn't been enough to convince many people during his lifetime. He was unable to explain exactly how the continents drifted apart. He proposed that the continents plowed through the ocean floor, driven by the spin of Earth. Physicists and geologists of the time strongly disagreed with Wegener's explanation. They pointed out that continental drift would not be necessary to explain many of Wegener's observations. Other important observations that came later eventually supported Wegener's earlier evidence.

**Fossil Clues** Besides the puzzlelike fit of the continents, fossils provided support for continental drift. Fossils of the reptile *Mesosaurus* have been found in South America and Africa, as shown in **Figure 2.** This swimming reptile lived in freshwater and on land. How could fossils of *Mesosaurus* be found on land areas separated by a large ocean of salt water? It probably couldn't swim between the continents. Wegener hypothesized that this reptile lived on both continents when they were joined.

> **Reading Check** *How do* Mesosaurus *fossils support the past existence of Pangaea?*

**Science Online**

**Topic: Continental Drift**
Visit glencoe.com for Web links to information about the continental drift hypothesis.

**Activity** Research and write a brief report about the initial reactions, from the public and scientific communities, toward Wegener's continental drift hypothesis.

**Figure 2** Fossil remains of plants and animals that lived in Pangaea have been found on more than one continent.
**Evaluate** *How do the locations of* Glossopteris, Mesosaurus, Kannemeyerid, Labyrinthodont, *and other fossils support Wegener's hypothesis of continental drift?*

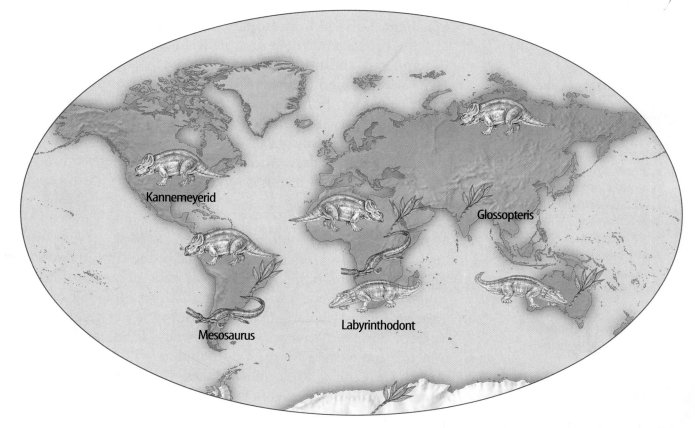

Kannemeyerid

Glossopteris

Mesosaurus

Labyrinthodont

**Figure 3** This fossil plant, *Glossopteris,* grew in a temperate climate.

## Interpreting Fossil Data

**Procedure**
1. Build a three-layer landmass using **clay** or **modeling dough.**
2. Mold the clay into mountain ranges.
3. Place similar "**fossils**" into the clay at various locations around the landmass.
4. Form five continents from the one landmass. Also, form two smaller landmasses out of different clay with different mountain ranges and fossils.
5. Place the five continents and two smaller landmasses around the room.
6. Have someone who did not make or place the landmasses make a model that shows how they once were positioned.
7. Return the clay to its container so it can be used again.

**Analysis**
What clues were useful in reconstructing the original landmass?

**Try at Home**

**A Widespread Plant** Another fossil that supports the hypothesis of continental drift is *Glossopteris* (glahs AHP tur us). **Figure 3** shows this fossil plant, which has been found in Africa, Australia, India, South America, and Antarctica. The presence of *Glossopteris* in so many areas also supported Wegener's idea that all of these regions once were connected and had similar climates.

**Climate Clues** Wegener used continental drift to explain evidence of changing climates. For example, fossils of warm-weather plants were found on the island of Spitsbergen in the Arctic Ocean. To explain this, Wegener hypothesized that Spitsbergen drifted from tropical regions to the arctic. Wegener also used continental drift to explain evidence of glaciers found in temperate and tropical areas. Glacial deposits and rock surfaces scoured and polished by glaciers are found in South America, Africa, India, and Australia. This shows that parts of these continents were covered with glaciers in the past. How could you explain why glacial deposits are found in areas where no glaciers exist today? Wegener thought that these continents were connected and partly covered with ice near Earth's south pole long ago.

**Rock Clues** If the continents were connected at one time, then rocks that make up the continents should be the same in locations where they were joined. Similar rock structures are found on different continents. Parts of the Appalachian Mountains of the eastern United States are similar to those found in Greenland and western Europe. If you were to study rocks from eastern South America and western Africa, you would find other rock structures that also are similar. Rock clues like these support the idea that the continents were connected in the past.

250 million years ago

135 million years ago

Present day

# How could continents drift?

Although Wegener provided evidence to support his hypothesis of continental drift, he couldn't explain how, when, or why these changes, shown in **Figure 4,** took place. The idea suggested that lower-density, continental material somehow had to plow through higher-density, ocean-floor material. The force behind this plowing was thought to be the spin of Earth on its axis—a notion that was quickly rejected by physicists. Because other scientists could not provide explanations either, Wegener's idea of continental drift was initially rejected. The idea was so radically different at that time that most people closed their minds to it.

Rock, fossil, and climate clues were the main types of evidence for continental drift. After Wegener's death, more clues were found, largely because of advances in technology, and new ideas that related to continental drift were developed. You'll learn about a new idea, seafloor spreading, in the next section.

**Figure 4** These computer models show the probable course the continents have taken. On the far left is their position 250 million years ago. In the middle is their position 135 million years ago. At right is their current position.

 **Physical Setting**

**2.2d Analyze** how rock, fossil, and climate clues are the main types of evidence for continental drift. Explain how the puzzle shapes of the continents helped support Wegener's hypothesis that the continents were once one large land mass.

## section 1 review

### Summary

**Evidence for Continental Drift**

- Alfred Wegener proposed in his hypothesis of continental drift that all continents were once connected as one large landmass called Pangaea.
- Evidence of continental drift came from fossils, signs of climate change, and rock structures from different continents.

**How could continents drift?**

- During his lifetime, Wegener was unable to explain how, when, or why the continents drifted.
- After his death, advances in technology permitted new ideas to be developed to help explain his hypothesis.

### Self Check

1. **Explain** how Wegener used climate clues to support his hypothesis of continental drift.

2. **Describe** how rock clues were used to support the hypothesis of continental drift.

3. **Summarize** the ways that fossils helped support the hypothesis of continental drift.

4. **Think Critically** Why would you expect to see similar rocks and rock structures on two landmasses that were connected at one time.

### Applying Skills

5. **Compare and contrast** the locations of fossils of the temperate plant *Glossopteris,* as shown in **Figure 2,** with the climate that exists at each location today.

# Seafloor Spreading

**as you read**

## *What* You'll Learn

- **Explain** seafloor spreading.
- **Recognize** how age and magnetic clues support seafloor spreading.

## *Why* It's Important

Seafloor spreading helps explain how continents moved apart.

🔍 **Review Vocabulary**
**seafloor:** portion of Earth's crust that lies beneath ocean waters

**New Vocabulary**
- seafloor spreading

## Mapping the Ocean Floor

If you were to lower a rope from a boat until it reached the seafloor, you could record the depth of the ocean at that particular point. In how many different locations would you have to do this to create an accurate map of the seafloor? This is exactly how it was done until World War I, when the use of sound waves was introduced by German scientists to detect submarines. During the 1940s and 1950s, scientists began using sound waves on moving ships to map large areas of the ocean floor in detail. Sound waves echo off the ocean bottom—the longer the sound waves take to return to the ship, the deeper the water is.

Using sound waves, researchers discovered an underwater system of ridges, or mountains, and valleys like those found on the continents. In some of these underwater ridges are rather long rift valleys where volcanic eruptions and earthquakes occur from time to time. Some of these volcanoes actually are visible above the ocean surface. In the Atlantic, the Pacific, and in other oceans around the world, a system of ridges, called the mid-ocean ridges, is present. These underwater mountain ranges, shown in **Figure 5,** stretch along the center of much of Earth's ocean floor. This discovery raised the curiosity of many scientists. What formed these mid-ocean ridges?

✔ **Reading Check** *How were mid-ocean ridges discovered?*

**Figure 5** As the seafloor spreads apart at a mid-ocean ridge, new seafloor is created. The older seafloor moves away from the ridge in opposite directions.

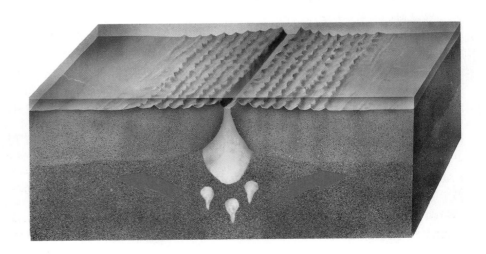

**The Seafloor Moves** In the early 1960s, Princeton University scientist Harry Hess suggested an explanation. His now-famous theory is known as **seafloor spreading.** Hess proposed that hot, less dense material below Earth's crust rises toward the surface at the mid-ocean ridges. Then, it flows sideways, carrying the seafloor away from the ridge in both directions, as seen in **Figure 5.**

As the seafloor spreads apart, magma is forced upward and flows from the cracks. It becomes solid as it cools and forms new seafloor. As new seafloor moves away from the mid-ocean ridge, it cools, contracts, and becomes denser. This denser, colder seafloor sinks, helping to form the ridge. The theory of seafloor spreading was later supported by the following observations.

 **Reading Check** *How does new seafloor form at mid-ocean ridges?*

## Evidence for Spreading

In 1968, scientists aboard the research ship *Glomar Challenger* began gathering information about the rocks on the seafloor. *Glomar Challenger* was equipped with a drilling rig that allowed scientists to drill into the seafloor to obtain rock samples. Scientists found that the youngest rocks are located at the mid-ocean ridges. The ages of the rocks become increasingly older in samples obtained farther from the ridges, adding to the evidence for seafloor spreading.

Using submersibles along mid-ocean ridges, new seafloor features and life-forms also were discovered there, as shown in **Figure 6.** As molten material is forced upward along the ridges, it brings heat and chemicals that support exotic life-forms in deep, ocean water. Among these are giant clams, mussels, and tube worms.

 **Magnetic Clues** Earth's magnetic field has a north and a south pole. Magnetic lines, or directions, of force leave Earth near the south pole and enter Earth near the north pole. During a magnetic reversal, the lines of magnetic force run the opposite way. Scientists have determined that Earth's magnetic field has reversed itself many times in the past. These reversals occur over intervals of thousands or even millions of years. The reversals are recorded in rocks forming along mid-ocean ridges.

**Figure 6** Many new discoveries have been made on the seafloor. These giant tube worms inhabit areas near hot water vents along mid-ocean ridges.

**Physical Setting**

**2.2a Summarize** how the theory of seafloor spreading supports the concept that sections of Earth's crust move.

**Curie Point** Find out what the Curie point is and describe in your Science Journal what happens to iron-bearing minerals when they are heated to the Curie point. Explain how this is important to studies of seafloor spreading.

■ Normal magnetic polarity
■ Reverse magnetic polarity

**Figure 7** Changes in Earth's magnetic field are preserved in rock that forms on both sides of mid-ocean ridges.
**Explain** *why this is considered to be evidence of seafloor spreading.*

**Magnetic Time Scale** Iron-bearing minerals, such as magnetite, that are found in the rocks of the seafloor can record Earth's magnetic field direction when they form. Whenever Earth's magnetic field reverses, newly forming iron minerals will record the magnetic reversal.

Using a sensing device called a magnetometer (mag nuh TAH muh tur) to detect magnetic fields, scientists found that rocks on the ocean floor show many periods of magnetic reversal. The magnetic alignment in the rocks reverses back and forth over time in strips parallel to the mid-ocean ridges, as shown in **Figure 7.** A strong magnetic reading is recorded when the polarity of a rock is the same as the polarity of Earth's magnetic field today. Because of this, normal polarities in rocks show up as large peaks. This discovery provided strong support that seafloor spreading was indeed occurring. The magnetic reversals showed that new rock was being formed at the mid-ocean ridges. This helped explain how the crust could move—something that the continental drift hypothesis could not do.

## section 2 review

### Summary

**Mapping the Ocean Floor**

- Mid-ocean ridges, along the center of the ocean floor, have been found by using sound waves, the same method once used to detect submarines during World War I.
- Harry Hess suggested, in his seafloor spreading hypothesis, that the seafloor moves.

**Evidence for Spreading**

- Scientists aboard *Glomar Challenger* provided evidence of spreading by discovering that the youngest rocks are located at ridges and become increasingly older farther from the ridges.
- Magnetic alignment of rocks, in alternating strips that run parallel to ridges, indicates reversals in Earth's magnetic field and provides further evidence of seafloor spreading.

### Self Check

1. **Summarize** What properties of iron-bearing minerals on the seafloor support the theory of seafloor spreading?
2. **Explain** how the ages of the rocks on the ocean floor support the theory of seafloor spreading.
3. **Summarize** How did Harry Hess's hypothesis explain seafloor movement?
4. **Explain** why some partly molten material rises toward Earth's surface.
5. **Think Critically** The ideas of Hess, Wegener, and others emphasize that Earth is a dynamic planet. How is seafloor spreading different from continental drift?

*Hot Words Hot Topics*: Bk 2 (6) pp. 277, 292–294

### Applying Math

6. **Solve One-Step Equations** North America is moving about 1.25 cm per year away from a ridge in the middle of the Atlantic Ocean. Using this rate, how much farther apart will North America and the ridge be in 200 million years?

**More Section Review** glencoe.com

# Seafloor Spreading Rates

How did scientists use their knowledge of seafloor spreading and magnetic field reversals to reconstruct Pangaea? Try this lab to see how you can determine where a continent may have been located in the past.

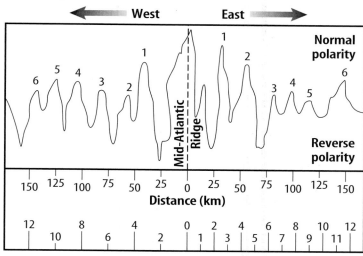

## Real-World Question

Can you use clues, such as magnetic field reversals on Earth, to help reconstruct Pangaea?

### Goals

■ **Interpret** data about magnetic field reversals. Use these magnetic clues to reconstruct Pangaea.

### Materials

metric ruler
pencil

## Procedure

1. Study the magnetic field graph above. You will be working only with normal polarity readings, which are the peaks above the baseline in the top half of the graph.

2. Place the long edge of a ruler vertically on the graph. Slide the ruler so that it lines up with the center of peak 1 west of the Mid-Atlantic Ridge.

3. **Determine** and record the distance and age that line up with the center of peak 1 west. Repeat this process for peak 1 east of the ridge.

4. **Calculate** the average distance and age for this pair of peaks.

5. Repeat steps 2 through 4 for the remaining pairs of normal-polarity peaks.

6. **Calculate** the rate of movement in cm per year for the six pairs of peaks. Use the formula rate = distance/time. Convert kilometers to centimeters. For example, to calculate a rate using normal-polarity peak 5, west of the ridge:

$$\text{rate} = \frac{125 \text{ km}}{10 \text{ million years}} = \frac{12.5 \text{ km}}{\text{million years}} = \frac{1,250,000 \text{ cm}}{1,000,000 \text{ years}} = 1.25 \text{ cm/year}$$

## Conclude and Apply

1. **Compare** the age of igneous rock found near the mid-ocean ridge with that of igneous rock found farther away from the ridge.

2. If the distance from a point on the coast of Africa to the Mid-Atlantic Ridge is approximately 2,400 km, calculate how long ago that point in Africa was at or near the Mid-Atlantic Ridge.

3. How could you use this method to reconstruct Pangaea?

**section**

**3**

PS 2.2e: The Theory of Plate Tectonics explains how the "solid" lithosphere consists of a series of plates that "float" on the partially molten section of the mantle. Convection cells within the mantle may be the driving force for the movement of the plates. **Also Covered:** PS 2.1c, 2.2b, 2.2c, 2.2f

# Theory of Plate Tectonics

## as you read

### *What* You'll Learn

- **Compare and contrast** different types of plate boundaries.
- **Explain** how heat inside Earth causes plate tectonics.
- **Recognize** features caused by plate tectonics.

### *Why* It's Important

Plate tectonics explains how many of Earth's features form.

### ⚙ Review Vocabulary

**converge:** to come together
**diverge:** to move apart
**transform:** to convert or change

### New Vocabulary

- plate tectonics
- plate
- lithosphere
- asthenosphere
- convection current

## Plate Tectonics

The idea of seafloor spreading showed that more than just continents were moving, as Wegener had thought. It was now clear to scientists that sections of the seafloor and continents move in relation to one another.

**Plate Movements**  In the 1960s, scientists developed a new theory that combined continental drift and seafloor spreading. According to the theory of **plate tectonics,** Earth's crust and part of the upper mantle are broken into sections. These sections, called **plates,** move on a plasticlike layer of the mantle. The plates can be thought of as rafts that float and move on this layer.

**Composition of Earth's Plates**  Plates are made of the crust and a part of the upper mantle, as shown in **Figure 8.** These two parts combined are the **lithosphere** (LIH thuh sfihr). This rigid layer is about 100 km thick and generally is less dense than material underneath. The plasticlike layer below the lithosphere is called the **asthenosphere** (as THE nuh sfihr). The rigid plates of the lithosphere float and move around on the asthenosphere.

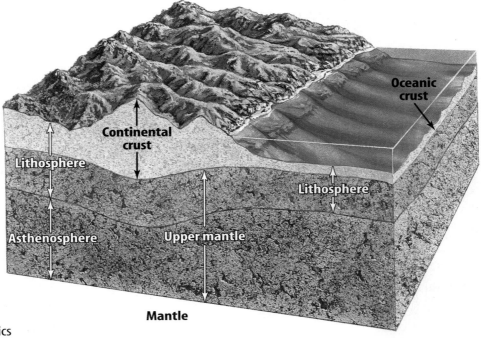

**Figure 8** Plates of the lithosphere are composed of oceanic crust, continental crust, and rigid upper mantle.

Oceanic crust

Continental crust

Lithosphere

Lithosphere

Asthenosphere

Upper mantle

Mantle

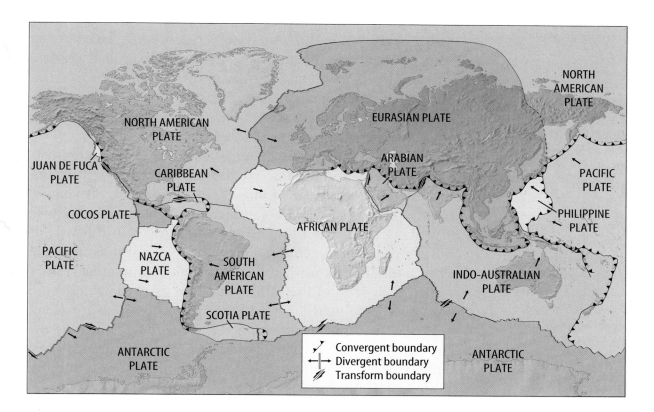

# Plate Boundaries

When plates move, they can interact in several ways. They can move toward each other and converge, or collide. They also can pull apart or slide alongside one another. When the plates interact, the result of their movement is seen at the plate boundaries, as in **Figure 9.**

**✔ Reading Check** *What are the general ways that plates interact?*

Movement along any plate boundary means that changes must happen at other boundaries. What is happening to the Atlantic Ocean floor between the North American and African Plates? Compare this with what is happening along the western margin of South America.

**Plates Moving Apart** The boundary between two plates that are moving apart is called a divergent boundary. You learned about divergent boundaries when you read about seafloor spreading. In the Atlantic Ocean, the North American Plate is moving away from the Eurasian and the African Plates, as shown in **Figure 9.** That divergent boundary is called the Mid-Atlantic Ridge. The Great Rift Valley in eastern Africa might become a divergent plate boundary. There, a valley has formed where a continental plate is being pulled apart. **Figure 10** shows a side view of what a rift valley might look like and illustrates how the hot material rises up where plates separate.

**Figure 9** This diagram shows the major plates of the lithosphere, their direction of movement, and the type of boundary between them. **Analyze and Conclude** *Based on what is shown in this figure, what is happening where the Nazca Plate meets the Pacific Plate?*

**Physical Setting**

**2.2f** *Plates may collide, move apart, or slide past one another.* **Predict** what physical evidence you might observe as Earth's plates interact.

**Topic: Earthquakes and Volcanoes**

Visit glencoe.com for Web links to recent news or magazine articles about earthquakes and volcanic activity related to plate tectonics.

**Activity** Prepare a group demonstration about recent volcanic and earthquake events. Divide tasks among group members. Find and copy maps, diagrams, photographs, and charts to highlight your presentation. Emphasize the locations of events and the relationship to plate tectonics.

**Plates Moving Together** If new crust is being added at one location, why doesn't Earth's surface keep expanding? As new crust is added in one place, it disappears below the surface at another. The disappearance of crust can occur when seafloor cools, becomes denser, and sinks. This occurs where two plates move together at a convergent boundary.

When an oceanic plate converges with a less dense continental plate, the denser oceanic plate sinks under the continental plate. The area where an oceanic plate subducts, or goes down, into the mantle is called a subduction zone. Some volcanoes form above subduction zones. **Figure 10** shows how this type of convergent boundary creates a deep-sea trench where one plate bends and sinks beneath the other. High temperatures cause rock to melt around the subducting slab as it goes under the other plate. The newly formed magma is forced upward along these plate boundaries, forming volcanoes. The Andes mountain range of South America contains many volcanoes. They were formed at the convergent boundary of the Nazca and the South American Plates.

## Applying Science

### How well do the continents fit together?

Recall the Launch Lab you performed at the beginning of this chapter. While you were trying to fit pieces of a cut-up photograph together, what clues did you use?

**Identifying the Problem**

Take a copy of a map of the world and cut out each continent. Lay them on a tabletop and try to fit them together, using techniques you used in the Launch Lab. You will find that the pieces of your Earth puzzle—the continents—do not fit together well. Yet, several of the areas on some continents fit together extremely well.

Take out another world map—one that shows the continental shelves as well as the continents. Copy it and cut out the continents, this time including the continental shelves.

**Solving the Problem**

1. Does including the continental shelves solve the problem of fitting the continents together?

2. Why should continental shelves be included with maps of the continents?

## Figure 10

By diverging at some boundaries and converging at others, Earth's plates are continually—but gradually—reshaping the landscape around you. The Mid-Atlantic Ridge, for example, was formed when the North and South American Plates pulled apart from the Eurasian and African Plates (see globe). Some features that occur along plate boundaries—rift valleys, volcanoes, and mountain ranges—are shown on the right and below.

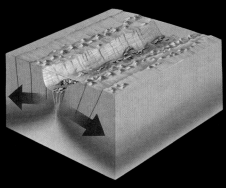

**A RIFT VALLEY** When continental plates pull apart, they can form rift valleys. The African continent is separating now along the East African Rift Valley.

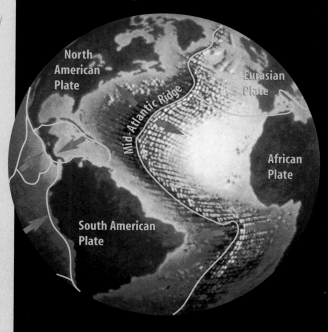

North American Plate

Eurasian Plate

Mid-Atlantic Ridge

African Plate

South American Plate

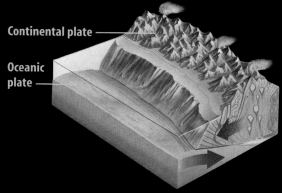

Continental plate

Oceanic plate

**SUBDUCTION** Where oceanic and continental plates collide, the oceanic plate plunges beneath the less dense continental plate. As the plate descends, molten rock (yellow) forms and rises toward the surface, creating volcanoes.

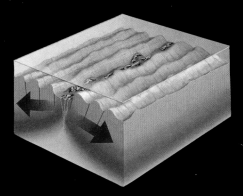

**SEAFLOOR SPREADING** A mid-ocean ridge, like the Mid-Atlantic Ridge, forms where oceanic plates continue to separate. As rising magma (yellow) cools, it forms new oceanic crust.

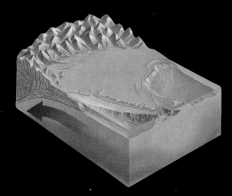

**CONTINENTAL COLLISION** Where two continental plates collide, they push up the crust to form mountain ranges such as the Himalaya.

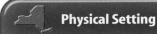
**Physical Setting**

**2.2f Analyze** the movement of Earth's plates at a divergent boundary, convergent boundary, and a transform boundary.

**Where Plates Collide** A subduction zone also can form where two oceanic plates converge. In this case, the colder, older, denser oceanic plate bends and sinks down into the mantle. The Mariana Islands in the western Pacific are a chain of volcanic islands formed where two oceanic plates collide.

Usually, no subduction occurs when two continental plates collide, as shown in **Figure 10.** Because both of these plates are less dense than the material in the asthenosphere, the two plates collide and crumple up, forming mountain ranges. Earthquakes are common at these convergent boundaries. However, volcanoes do not form because there is no, or little, subduction. The Himalaya in Asia are forming where the Indo-Australian Plate collides with the Eurasian Plate.

**Where Plates Slide Past Each Other** The third type of plate boundary is called a transform boundary. Transform boundaries occur where two plates slide past one another. They move in opposite directions or in the same direction at different rates. When one plate slips past another suddenly, earthquakes occur. The Pacific Plate is sliding past the North American Plate, forming the famous San Andreas Fault in California, as seen in **Figure 11.** The San Andreas Fault is part of a transform plate boundary. It has been the site of many earthquakes.

**Figure 11** The San Andreas Fault in California occurs along the transform plate boundary where the Pacific Plate is sliding past the North American Plate.

Overall, the two plates are moving in roughly the same direction. **Explain** *Why, then, do the red arrows show movement in opposite directions?*

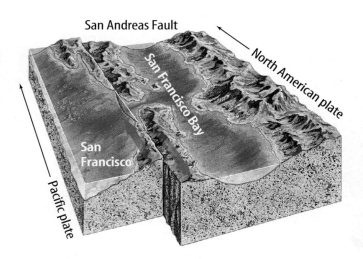

This photograph shows an aerial view of the San Andreas Fault.

# Causes of Plate Tectonics

Many new discoveries have been made about Earth's crust since Wegener's day, but one question still remains. What causes the plates to move? Scientists now think they have a good idea. They think that plates move by the same basic process that occurs when you heat soup.

**Convection Inside Earth** Soup that is cooking in a pan on the stove contains currents caused by an unequal distribution of heat in the pan. Hot, less dense soup is forced upward by the surrounding, cooler, denser soup. As the hot soup reaches the surface, it cools and sinks back down into the pan. This entire cycle of heating, rising, cooling, and sinking is called a **convection current.** A version of this same process, occurring in the mantle, is thought to be the force behind plate tectonics. Scientists suggest that differences in density cause hot, plasticlike rock to be forced upward toward the surface.

**Moving Mantle Material** Wegener wasn't able to come up with an explanation for why plates move. Today, researchers who study the movement of heat in Earth's interior have proposed several possible explanations. All of the hypotheses use convection in one way or another. It is, therefore, the transfer of heat inside Earth that provides the energy to move plates and causes many of Earth's surface features. One hypothesis is shown in **Figure 12.** It relates plate motion directly to the movement of convection currents. According to this hypothesis, convection currents cause the movements of plates.

## Mini LAB

### Modeling Convection Currents

**Procedure**

1. Pour **water** into **a clear, colorless casserole dish** until it is 5 cm from the top.
2. Center the dish on a **hot plate** and heat it. **WARNING:** *Wear thermal mitts to protect your hands.*
3. Add a few drops of **food coloring** to the water above the center of the hot plate.
4. Looking from the side of the dish, observe what happens in the water.
5. Illustrate your observations in your **Science Journal.**

**Analysis**

1. Determine whether any currents form in the water.
2. Infer what causes the currents to form.

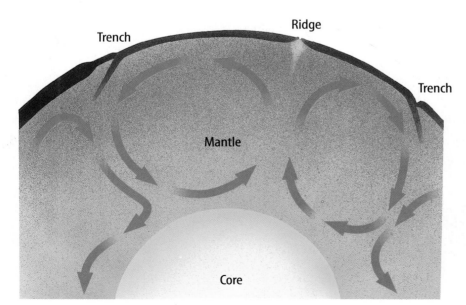

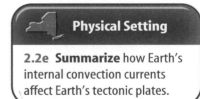

**Physical Setting**

**2.2e Summarize** how Earth's internal convection currents affect Earth's tectonic plates.

**Figure 12** In one hypothesis, convection currents occur throughout the mantle. Such convection currents (see arrows) are the driving force of plate tectonics.

## Features Caused by Plate Tectonics

Earth is a dynamic planet with a hot interior. This heat leads to convection, which powers the movement of plates. As the plates move, they interact. The interaction of plates produces forces that build mountains, create ocean basins, and cause volcanoes. When rocks in Earth's crust break and move, energy is released in the form of seismic waves. Humans feel this release as earthquakes. You can see some of the effects of plate tectonics in mountainous regions, where volcanoes erupt, or where landscapes have changed from past earthquake or volcanic activity.

**Reading Check** *What happens when seismic energy is released as rocks in Earth's crust break and move?*

**Normal Faults and Rift Valleys** Tension forces, which are forces that pull apart, can stretch Earth's crust. This causes large blocks of crust to break and tilt or slide down the broken surfaces of crust. When rocks break and move along surfaces, a fault forms. Faults interrupt rock layers by moving them out of place. Entire mountain ranges can form in the process, called fault-block mountains, as shown in **Figure 13.** Generally, the faults that form from pull-apart forces are normal faults—faults in which the rock layers above the fault move down when compared with rock layers below the fault.

Rift valleys and mid-ocean ridges can form where Earth's crust separates. Examples of rift valleys are the Great Rift Valley in Africa, and the valleys that occur in the middle of mid-ocean ridges. Examples of mid-ocean ridges include the Mid-Atlantic Ridge and the East Pacific Rise.

**Figure 13** Fault-block mountains can form when Earth's crust is stretched by tectonic forces. The arrows indicate the directions of moving blocks.

**Name** *the type of force that occurs when Earth's crust is pulled in opposite directions.*

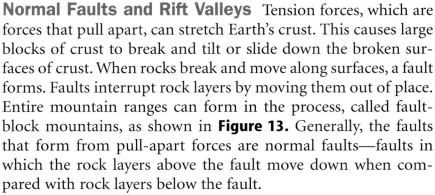

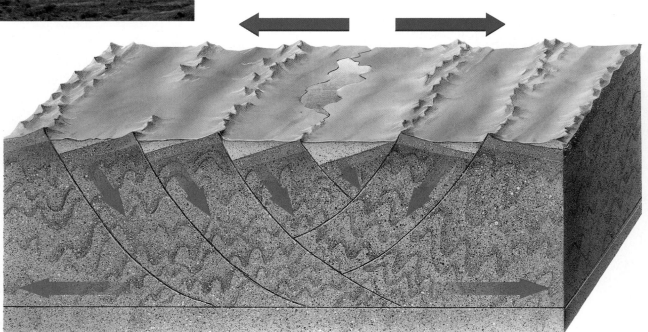

**Mountains and Volcanoes** Compression forces squeeze objects together. Where plates come together, compression forces produce several effects. As continental plates collide, the forces that are generated cause massive folding and faulting of rock layers into mountain ranges such as the Himalaya, shown in **Figure 14,** or the Appalachian Mountains. The type of faulting produced is generally reverse faulting. Along a reverse fault, the rock layers above the fault surface move up relative to the rock layers below the fault.

**✓ Reading Check** *What features occur where plates converge?*

As you learned earlier, when two oceanic plates converge, the denser plate is forced beneath the other plate. Curved chains of volcanic islands called island arcs form above the sinking plate. If an oceanic plate converges with a continental plate, the denser oceanic plate slides under the continental plate. Folding and faulting at the continental plate margin can thicken the continental crust to produce mountain ranges. Volcanoes also typically are formed at this type of convergent boundary.

**Volcanologist** This person's job is to study volcanoes in order to predict eruptions. Early warning of volcanic eruptions gives nearby residents time to evacuate. Volcanologists also educate the public about the hazards of volcanic eruptions and tell people who live near volcanoes what they can do to be safe in the event of an eruption. Volcanologists travel all over the world to study new volcanic sites.

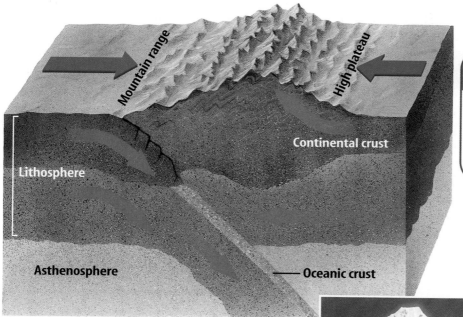

Mountain range

High plateau

Continental crust

Lithosphere

Asthenosphere

Oceanic crust

**Physical Setting**

**2.2c** *Scientists study geologic evidence that suggests past crustal movement.* **Identify** three types of evidence that suggest past crustal movement.

**Figure 14** The Himalaya still are forming today as the Indo-Australian Plate collides with the Eurasian Plate.

**Figure 15** Most of the movement along a strike-slip fault is parallel to Earth's surface. When movement occurs, human-built structures along a strike-slip fault are offset, as shown here in this road.

**Direction of Forces** In which directions do forces act at convergent, divergent, and transform boundaries? Demonstrate these forces using wooden blocks or your hands.

**Strike-Slip Faults** At transform boundaries, two plates slide past one another without converging or diverging. The plates stick and then slide, mostly in a horizontal direction, along large strike-slip faults. In a strike-slip fault, rocks on opposite sides of the fault move in opposite directions, or in the same direction at different rates. This type of fault movement is shown in **Figure 15.** One such example is the San Andreas Fault. When plates move suddenly, vibrations are generated inside Earth that are felt as an earthquake.

Earthquakes, volcanoes, and mountain ranges are evidence of plate motion. Plate tectonics explains how activity inside Earth can affect Earth's crust differently in different locations. You've seen how plates have moved since Pangaea separated. Is it possible to measure how far plates move each year?

## Testing for Plate Tectonics

Until recently, the only tests scientists could use to check for plate movement were indirect. They could study the magnetic characteristics of rocks on the seafloor. They could study volcanoes and earthquakes. These methods supported the theory that the plates have moved and still are moving. However, they did not provide proof—only support—of the idea.

New methods had to be discovered to be able to measure the small amounts of movement of Earth's plates. One method, shown in **Figure 16,** uses lasers and a satellite. Now, scientists can measure exact movements of Earth's plates of as little as 1 cm per year.

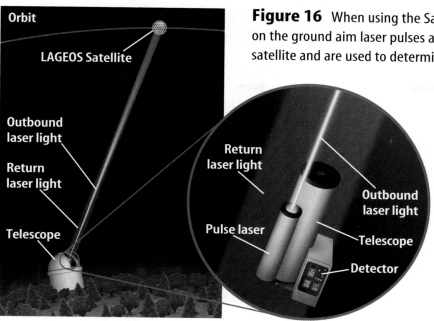

**Figure 16** When using the Satellite Laser Ranging System, scientists on the ground aim laser pulses at a satellite. The pulses reflect off the satellite and are used to determine a precise location on the ground.

Orbit

LAGEOS Satellite

Outbound laser light

Return laser light

Telescope

Return laser light

Pulse laser

Outbound laser light

Telescope

Detector

**Current Data** Satellite Laser Ranging System data show that Hawaii is moving toward Japan at a rate of about 8.3 cm per year. Maryland is moving away from England at a rate of 1.7 cm per year. Using such methods, scientists have observed that the plates move at rates ranging from about 1 cm to 12 cm per year.

## section 3 review

### Summary

**Plate Tectonics**

- The theory of plate tectonics states that sections of the seafloor and continents move as plates on a plasticlike layer of the mantle.

**Plate Boundaries**

- The boundary between two plates moving apart is called a divergent boundary.
- Plates move together at a convergent boundary.
- Transform boundaries occur where two plates slide past one another.

**Causes of Plate Tectonics**

- Convection currents are thought to cause the movement of Earth's plates.

**Features Caused by Plate Tectonics**

- Tension forces cause normal faults, rift valleys, and mid-ocean ridges at divergent boundaries.
- At convergent boundaries, compression forces cause folding, reverse faults, and mountains.
- At transform boundaries, two plates slide past one another along strike-slip faults.

### Self Check

1. **Describe** what occurs at plate boundaries that are associated with seafloor spreading.

2. **Describe** three types of plate boundaries where volcanic eruptions can occur.

3. **Explain** how convection currents are related to plate tectonics.

4. **Think Critically** Using **Figure 9** and a world map, determine what natural disasters might occur in Iceland. Also determine what disasters might occur in Tibet. Explain why some Icelandic disasters are not expected to occur in Tibet.

#### Applying Skills

5. **Predict** Plate tectonic activity causes many events that can be dangerous to humans. One of these events is a seismic sea wave, or tsunami. Learn how scientists predict the arrival time of a tsunami in a coastal area.

6. **Use a Word Processor** Write three separate descriptions of the three basic types of plate boundaries— divergent boundaries, convergent boundaries, and transform boundaries. Then draw a sketch of an example of each boundary next to your description.

# Use the Internet

# Predicting Tectonic Activity

## Goals

- **Research** the locations of earthquakes and volcanic eruptions around the world.
- **Plot** earthquake epicenters and the locations of volcanic eruptions.
- **Predict** locations that are tectonically active based on a plot of the locations of earthquake epicenters and active volcanoes.

## Data Source

**Science** online

Visit internet labs at **glencoe.com** for more information about earthquake and volcano sites, and data from other students.

## Real-World Question

The movement of plates on Earth causes forces that build up energy in rocks. The release of this energy can produce vibrations in Earth that you know as earthquakes. Earthquakes occur every day. Many of them are too small to be felt by humans, but each event tells scientists something more about the planet. Active volcanoes can do the same and often form at plate boundaries.

Can you predict tectonically active areas by plotting locations of earthquake epicenters and volcanic eruptions?

Think about where earthquakes and volcanoes have occurred in the past. Make a hypothesis about whether the locations of earthquake epicenters and active volcanoes can be used to predict tectonically active areas.

## Make a Plan

1. Make a data table in your Science Journal like the one shown.

2. Collect data for earthquake epicenters and volcanic eruptions for at least the past two weeks. Your data should include the longitude and latitude for each location. For help, refer to the data sources given on the opposite page.

| Locations of Epicenters and Eruptions | | |
|---|---|---|
| Earthquake Epicenter/ Volcanic Eruption | Longitude | Latitude |
| | | |
| Do not write in this book. | | |
| | | |

## Follow Your Plan

1. Make sure your teacher approves your plan before you start.

2. **Plot** the locations of earthquake epicenters and volcanic eruptions on a map of the world. Use an overlay of tissue paper or plastic.

3. After you have collected the necessary data, predict where the tectonically active areas on Earth are.

4. **Compare and contrast** the areas that you predicted to be tectonically active with the plate boundary map shown in **Figure 9.**

## Analyze Your Data

1. What areas on Earth do you predict to be the locations of tectonic activity?

2. How close did your prediction come to the actual location of tectonically active areas?

## Conclude and Apply

1. How could you make your predictions closer to the locations of actual tectonic activity?

2. Would data from a longer period of time help? Explain.

3. What types of plate boundaries were close to your locations of earthquake epicenters? Volcanic eruptions?

4. **Explain** which types of plate boundaries produce volcanic eruptions. Be specific.

### Communicating Your Data

Find this lab using the link below. Post your data in the table provided. **Compare** your data to those of other students. Combine your data with those of other students and **plot** these combined data on a map to recognize the relationship between plate boundaries, volcanic eruptions, and earthquake epicenters.

Science Online
glencoe.com

# Listening In
## by Gordon Judge

I'm just a bit of seafloor on this mighty solid sphere.
With no mind to be broadened, I'm quite content
    down here.
The mantle churns below me, and the sea's in turmoil, too;
But nothing much disturbs me, I'm rock solid through
    and through.

I do pick up occasional low-frequency vibrations –
(I think, although I can't be sure, they're sperm whales'
    conversations).
I know I shouldn't listen in, but what else can I do?
It seems they are all studying for degrees from the OU.

They've mentioned me in passing, as their minds begin
    improving:

I think I've heard them say
    "The theory says the sea-
    floor's moving…".
They call it "Plate Tectonics", this
    new theory in their noddle.
If they would only ask me, I
    could tell them it's all
    twaddle….

But, how can I be moving, when I know full well myself
That I'm quite firmly anchored to a continental shelf?
"Well, the continent is moving, too; you're *pushing* it,
    you see,"
I hear those OU whales intone, hydro-acoustically….

Well, thank you very much, OU. You've upset my
    composure.
Next time you send your student whales to look at
    my exposure
I'll tell them it's a load of tosh: it's *they* who move,
    not me,
Those arty-smarty blobs of blubber, clogging up the sea!

## Understanding Literature

**Point of View** Point of view refers to the perspective from which an author writes. This poem begins, "I'm just a bit of seafloor…." Right away, you know that the poem, or story, is being told from the point of view of the speaker, or the "first person." What effect does the first-person narration have on the story?

## Respond to the Reading

1. Who is narrating the poem?
2. Why might the narrator think he or she hasn't moved?
3. **Linking Science and Writing** Using the first-person point of view, write an account from the point of view of a living or nonliving thing.

Volcanoes can occur where two plates move toward each other. When an oceanic plate and a continental plate collide, a volcano will form. Subduction zones occur when one plate sinks under another plate. Rocks melt in the zones where these plates converge, causing magma to move upward and form volcanic mountains.

## Reviewing Main Ideas

### Section 1 Continental Drift

1. Alfred Wegener suggested that the continents were joined together at some point in the past in a large landmass he called Pangaea. Wegener proposed that continents have moved slowly, over millions of years, to their current locations.

2. The puzzlelike fit of the continents, fossils, climatic evidence, and similar rock structures support Wegener's idea of continental drift. However, Wegener could not explain what process could cause the movement of the landmasses.

### Section 2 Seafloor Spreading

1. Detailed mapping of the ocean floor in the 1950s showed underwater mountains and rift valleys.

2. In the 1960s, Harry Hess suggested seafloor spreading as an explanation for the formation of mid-ocean ridges.

3. The theory of seafloor spreading is supported by magnetic evidence in rocks and by the ages of rocks on the ocean floor.

### Section 3 Theory of Plate Tectonics

1. In the 1960s, scientists combined the ideas of continental drift and seafloor spreading to develop the theory of plate tectonics. The theory states that the surface of Earth is broken into sections called plates that move around on the asthenosphere.

2. Currents in Earth's mantle called convection currents transfer heat in Earth's interior. It is thought that this transfer of heat energy moves plates.

3. Earth is a dynamic planet. As the plates move, they interact, resulting in many of the features of Earth's surface.

## Visualizing Main Ideas

*Copy and complete the concept map below about continental drift, seafloor spreading, and plate tectonics.*

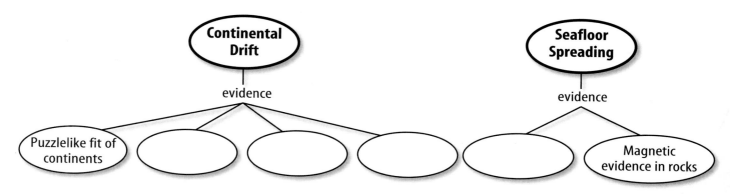

## Using Vocabulary

| | |
|---|---|
| asthenosphere p. 158 | Pangaea p. 150 |
| continental drift p. 150 | plate p. 158 |
| convection current p. 163 | plate tectonics p. 158 |
| lithosphere p. 158 | seafloor spreading p. 155 |

*Each phrase below describes a vocabulary term from the list. Write the term that matches the phrase describing it.*

1. plasticlike layer below the lithosphere

2. idea that continents move slowly across Earth's surface

3. large, ancient landmass that consisted of all the continents on Earth

4. composed of oceanic or continental crust and upper mantle

5. explains locations of mountains, trenches, and volcanoes

6. theory proposed by Harry Hess that includes processes along mid-ocean ridges

## Checking Concepts

*Choose the word or phrase that best answers the question.*

7. Which layer of Earth contains the asthenosphere?
    **A)** crust  **C)** outer core
    **B)** mantle  **D)** inner core

8. What type of plate boundary is the San Andreas Fault part of?
    **A)** divergent  **C)** convergent
    **B)** subduction  **D)** transform

9. What hypothesis states that continents slowly moved to their present positions on Earth?
    **A)** subduction  **C)** continental drift
    **B)** erosion  **D)** seafloor spreading

**Use the illustration below to answer question 10.**

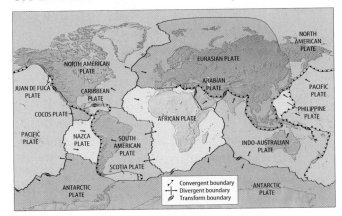

10. Which plate is subducting beneath the South American Plate?
    **A)** Nazca  **C)** North American
    **B)** African  **D)** Indo-Australian

11. Which of the following features are evidence that many continents were at one time near Earth's south pole?
    **A)** glacial deposits  **C)** volcanoes
    **B)** earthquakes  **D)** mid-ocean ridges

12. What evidence in rocks supports the theory of seafloor spreading?
    **A)** plate movement
    **B)** magnetic reversals
    **C)** subduction
    **D)** convergence

13. Which type of plate boundary is the Mid-Atlantic Ridge a part of?
    **A)** convergent  **C)** transform
    **B)** divergent  **D)** subduction

14. What theory states that plates move around on the asthenosphere?
    **A)** continental drift
    **B)** seafloor spreading
    **C)** subduction
    **D)** plate tectonics

## Thinking Critically

**15. Infer** Why do many earthquakes but few volcanic eruptions occur in the Himalaya?

**16. Explain** Glacial deposits often form at high latitudes near the poles. Explain why glacial deposits have been found in Africa.

**17. Describe** how magnetism is used to support the theory of seafloor spreading.

**18. Explain** why volcanoes do not form along the San Andreas Fault.

**19. Explain** why the fossil of an ocean fish found on two different continents would not be good evidence of continental drift.

**20. Form Hypotheses** Mount St. Helens in the Cascade Range is a volcano. Use **Figure 9** and a U.S. map to hypothesize how it might have formed.

**21. Concept Map** Make an events-chain concept map that describes seafloor spreading along a divergent plate boundary. Choose from the following phrases: *magma cools to form new seafloor, convection currents circulate hot material along divergent boundary,* and *older seafloor is forced apart.*

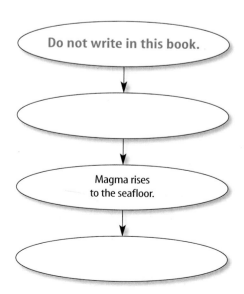

Do not write in this book.

Magma rises
to the seafloor.

## Performance Activities

**22. Observe and Infer** In the MiniLab called "Modeling Convection Currents," you observed convection currents produced in water as it was heated. Repeat the experiment, placing sequins, pieces of wood, or pieces of rubber bands into the water. How do their movements support your observations and inferences from the MiniLab?

*Hot Words Hot Topics*: Bk 2 (23) pp. 277, 292-294; (24) p. 277; (25) pp. 277, 292-294

## Applying Math

**23. A Growing Rift** Movement along the African Rift Valley is about 2.1 cm per year. If plates continue to move apart at this rate, how much larger will the rift be (in meters) in 1,000 years? In 15,500 years?

**Use the illustration below to answer questions 24 and 25.**

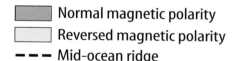

Normal magnetic polarity
Reversed magnetic polarity
Mid-ocean ridge

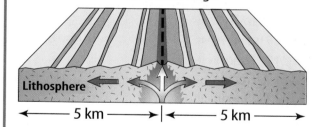

Lithosphere

←— 5 km —→|←— 5 km —→

**24. New Seafloor** 10 km of new seafloor has been created in 50,000 years, with 5 km on each side of a mid-ocean ridge. What is the rate of movement, in km per year, of each plate? In cm per year?

**25. Use a Ratio** If 10 km of seafloor were created in 50,000 years, how many kilometers of seafloor were created in 10,000 years? How many years will it take to create a total of 30 km of seafloor?

**Part I**

*Record your answers on the answer sheet
provided by your teacher or on a sheet of paper.*

**Use the illustration below to answer question 1.**

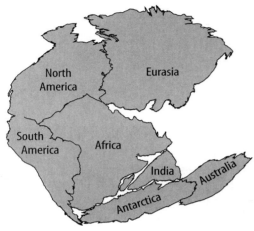

**1** What is the name of the ancient supercontinent shown above?
(1) Pangaea
(2) Gondwanaland
(3) Laurasia
(4) North America

**2** Who developed the continental drift hypothesis?
(1) Harry Hess
(2) J. Tuzo Wilson
(3) Alfred Wegener
(4) W. Jason Morgan

**3** Which term refers to sections of Earth's crust and part of the upper mantle?
(1) asthenosphere
(2) plate
(3) lithosphere
(4) core

**4** About how fast do plates move?
(1) a few millimeters each year
(2) a few centimeters each year
(3) a few meters each year
(4) a few kilometers each year

**5** Where do Earth's plates slide past each other?
(1) convergent boundaries
(2) divergent boundaries
(3) transform boundaries
(4) subduction zones

**Study the diagram below before answering questions 6 and 7.**

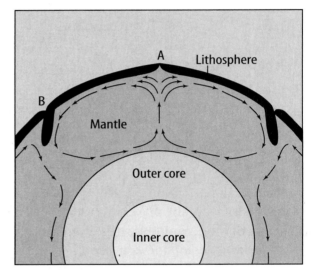

**6** Suppose that the arrows in the diagram represent patterns of convection in Earth's mantle. Which type of plate boundary is most likely to occur along the region labeled "A"?
(1) transform
(2) reverse
(3) convergent
(4) divergent

**7** Which statement is true of the region marked "B" on the diagram?
(1) Plates move past each other sideways.
(2) Plates move apart and volcanoes form.
(3) Plates move toward each other and volcanoes form.
(4) Plates are not moving.

**Part II**

*Record your answers on the answer sheet provided by your teacher or on a sheet of paper.*

**8** Compare and contrast an ocean trench to a mid-ocean range.

**Use the graph below to answer questions 9–11.**

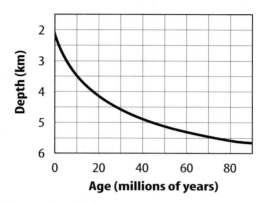

**Relationship Between Depth and Age of Seafloor**

**9** Use the graph to estimate the average depth below the ocean of ocean crust that has just formed.

**10** Estimate the average depth of ocean crust that is 60 million years old.

**11** Describe how the depth of ocean crust is related to the age of ocean crust.

**Use the illustration below to answer question 12.**

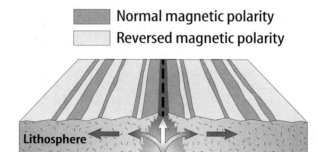

Normal magnetic polarity
Reversed magnetic polarity

Lithosphere

**12** Examine the diagram above. Explain what the magnetic stripes found in the ocean crust can tell a geologist.

**13** Explain the theory of plate tectonics.

**14** What evidence do we have that supports the hypothesis of continental drift?

**15** What happened to the continents that made up Pangaea after it started to break up?

**16** What are the three types of motion that occur at plate boundaries? Describe each motion.

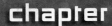 

PS 2.2a: Heat flow and movement of material within Earth cause sections of Earth's crust to move. This may result in earthquakes, volcanic eruption, and the creation of mountains and ocean basins. **2.2b:** Analysis of earthquake wave data (vibrational disturbances) leads to the conclusion that there are layers within Earth. **Also Covered:** PS 2.2c, 2.2e, 2.2f.

# Earthquakes and Volcanoes

## Earth's upset stomach?

Rivers of boiling lava poured down the mountain, engulfing small buildings and threatening a lodge after a series of earthquakes awakened this volcano. What causes Earth to behave this way? Are earthquakes and volcanoes related?

**Science Journal** Are earthquakes and volcanoes completely unrelated, or could there be a possible connection? Propose several ideas that might explain what causes these events.

# Start-Up Activities

## Construct with Strength

One of the greatest dangers associated with an earthquake occurs when people are inside buildings during the event. In the following lab, you will see how construction materials can be used to help strengthen a building.

1. Using wooden blocks, construct a building with four walls. Place a piece of cardboard over the four walls as a ceiling.
2. Gently shake the table under your building. Describe what happens.
3. Reconstruct the building. Wrap large rubber bands around each section, or wall, of blocks. Then wrap large rubber bands around the entire building.
4. Gently shake the table again.
5. **Think Critically** In your Science Journal, note any differences you observed as the two buildings were shaken. Hypothesize how the construction methods you used in this activity might be applied to the construction of real buildings.

Preview this chapter's content and activities at glencoe.com

**Earthquakes and Volcanoes** Make the following Foldable to help you compare and contrast the characteristics of earthquakes and volcanoes.

**STEP 1** Draw a mark at the midpoint of a vertical sheet of paper.

**STEP 2** **Turn** the paper horizontally and **fold** the outside edges in to touch at the midpoint mark.

**STEP 3** Draw a volcano on one flap and label the flap *Volcanoes*. Draw an earthquake on the other flap and label it *Earthquakes*. The inside portion should be labeled *Both* and include characteristics that both events share.

**Analyze and Critique** Before you read the chapter, write what you know about earthquakes and volcanoes on the back of each flap. As you read the chapter, add more information about earthquakes and volcanoes.

# section 1

# Earthquakes

## as you read

### *What* You'll Learn

- **Explain** how earthquakes are caused by a buildup of strain in Earth's crust.
- **Compare and contrast** primary, secondary, and surface waves.
- **Recognize** earthquake hazards and how to prepare for them.

### *Why* It's Important

Studying earthquakes will help you learn where they might occur and how you can prepare for their hazards.

### 🔍 Review Vocabulary

**energy:** the ability to cause change

### New Vocabulary

- earthquake
- fault
- seismic wave
- focus
- epicenter
- seismograph
- magnitude
- tsunami
- seismic safe

## What causes earthquakes?

If you've gone for a walk in the woods lately, maybe you picked up a stick along the way. If so, did you try to bend or break it? If you've ever bent a stick slowly, you might have noticed that it changes shape but usually springs back to normal form when you stop bending it. If you continue to bend the stick, you can do it for only so long before it changes permanently. When this elastic limit is passed, the stick may break, as shown in **Figure 1.** When the stick snaps, you can feel vibrations in the stick.

**Elastic Rebound** As hard as they seem, rocks act in much the same way when forces push or pull on them. If enough force is applied, rocks become strained, which means they change shape. They may even break, and the ends of the broken pieces may snap back. This snapping back is called elastic rebound.

Rocks usually change shape, or deform, slowly over long periods of time. As they are strained, potential energy builds up in them. This energy is released suddenly by the action of rocks breaking and moving. Such breaking, and the movement that follows, causes vibrations that move through rock or other earth materials. If they are large enough, these vibrations are felt as **earthquakes.**

✔️ **Reading Check** *What is an earthquake?*

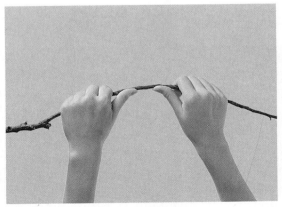

When a stick is bent, potential energy is stored in the stick.

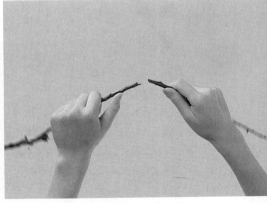

The energy is released as vibrations when the stick breaks.

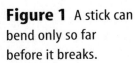

**Figure 1** A stick can bend only so far before it breaks.

**Figure 2** When rocks change shape by breaking, faults form. The type of fault formed depends on the type of stress exerted on the rock.

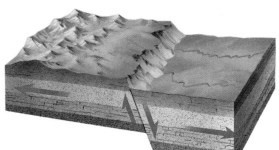

**A** When rocks are pulled apart, a normal fault may form.

**B** When rocks are compressed, a reverse fault may form.

**C** When rocks are sheared, a strike-slip fault may form.

## Types of Faults

When a section of rock breaks, rocks on either side of the break along which rocks move might move as a result of elastic rebound. The surface of such a break along which rocks move is called a **fault**. Several types of faults exist. The type that forms depends on how forces were applied to the rocks.

When rocks are pulled apart under tension forces, normal faults form, as shown in **Figure 2A.** Along a normal fault, rock above the fault moves down compared to rock below the fault. Compression forces squeeze rocks together, like an accordion. Compression might cause rock above a fault to move up compared to rock below the fault. This movement forms reverse faults, as shown in **Figure 2B.** As illustrated in **Figure 2C,** rock experiencing shear forces can break to form a strike-slip fault. Shear forces cause rock on either side of a strike-slip fault to move past one another in opposite directions along Earth's surface. You could infer the motion of a strike-slip fault while walking along and observing an offset feature, such as a displaced fence line, on Earth's surface.

Where do the forces come from that cause rocks to deform by bending or breaking? Why do faults form and why do earthquakes occur in certain areas? As you'll learn later in this chapter, forces inside Earth are caused by the constant motion of plates, or sections, of Earth's crust and upper mantle.

### Mini LAB

**Observing Deformation**

**WARNING:** *Do not taste or eat any lab materials. Wash hands when finished.*

**Procedure**
1. Remove the wrapper from three bars of **taffy.**
2. Hold a bar of taffy lengthwise between your hands and gently push on it from opposite directions.
3. Hold another bar of taffy and pull it in opposite directions.

**Analysis**
1. Which of the procedures that you performed on the taffy involved applying tension? Which involved applying compression?
2. Infer how to apply a shear stress to the third bar of taffy.

**Figure 3** During an earthquake, several types of seismic waves form. Primary and secondary waves travel in all directions from the focus and can travel through Earth's interior. Surface waves travel at shallow depths and along Earth's surface.
**Infer** *Which seismic waves are the most destructive?*

# Making Waves

Do you recall the last time you shouted for a friend to save you a seat on the bus? When you called out, energy was transmitted through the air to your friend, who interpreted the familiar sound of your voice as belonging to you. These sound waves were released by your vocal cords and were affected by your tongue and mouth. They traveled outward through the air. Earthquakes also release waves. Earthquake waves are transmitted through materials in Earth and along Earth's surface. Earthquake waves are called **seismic waves.** In the two-page activity, you'll make waves similar to seismic waves by moving a coiled spring toy.

**Earthquake Focus and Epicenter** Movement along a fault releases strain energy. Strain energy is potential energy that builds up in rock when it is bent. When this potential energy is released, it moves outward from the fault in the form of seismic waves. The point inside Earth where this movement first occurs and energy is released is called the **focus** of an earthquake, as shown in **Figure 3.** The point on Earth's surface located directly above the earthquake focus is called the **epicenter** of the earthquake.

**Reading Check** *Where is the focus of an earthquake located?*

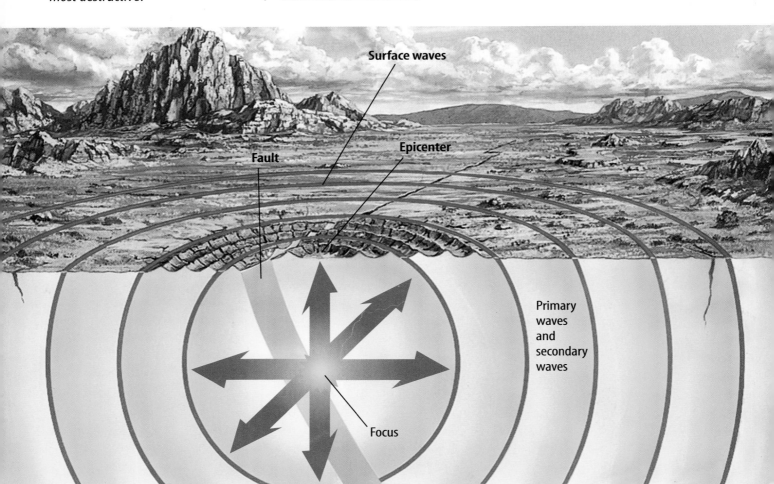

Surface waves

Fault

Epicenter

Primary waves and secondary waves

Focus

**Seismic Waves** After they are produced at the focus, seismic waves travel away from the focus in all directions, as illustrated in **Figure 3.** Some seismic waves travel throughout Earth's interior, and others travel along Earth's surface. The surface waves cause the most damage during an earthquake event.

Primary waves, also known as P-waves, travel the fastest through rock material by causing particles in the rock to move back and forth, or vibrate, in the same direction as the waves are moving. Secondary waves, known as S-waves, move through rock material by causing particles in the rock to vibrate at right angles to the direction in which the waves are moving. P- and S-waves travel through Earth's interior. Studying them has revealed much information about Earth's interior.

Surface waves are the slowest and largest of the seismic waves, and they cause most of the destruction during an earthquake. The movements of surface waves are complex. Some surface waves move along Earth's surface in a manner that moves rock and soil in a backward rolling motion. They have been observed moving across the land like waves of water. Some surface waves vibrate in a side-to-side, or swaying, motion parallel to Earth's surface. This motion can be particularly devastating to human-built structures.

## Learning from Earthquakes

On your way to lunch tomorrow, suppose you were to walk twice as fast as your friend does. What would happen to the distance between the two of you as you walked to the lunchroom? The distance between you and your friend would become greater the farther you walked, and you would arrive first. Using this same line of reasoning, scientists use the different speeds of seismic waves and their differing arrival times to calculate the distance to an earthquake epicenter.

**Earthquake Measurements** Seismologists are scientists who study earthquakes and seismic waves. The instrument they use to obtain a record of seismic waves from all over the world is called a **seismograph,** shown in the top photo of **Figure 4.**

One type of seismograph has a drum holding a roll of paper on a fixed frame. A pendulum with an attached pen is suspended from the frame. When seismic waves are received at the station, the drum vibrates but the pendulum remains at rest. The pen on the pendulum traces a record of the vibrations on the paper. The height of the lines traced on the paper is a measure of the energy released by the earthquake, also known as its **magnitude.**

**Figure 4** Scientists study seismic waves using seismographs located around the world.

This seismograph records incoming seismic waves using a fixed mass.

Some seismographs collect and store data on a computer.

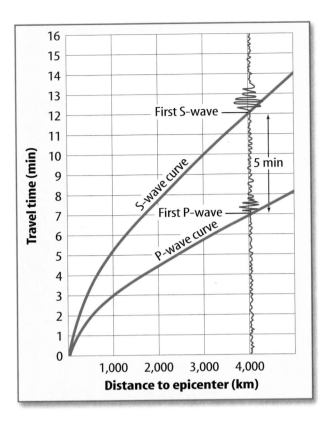

**Figure 5** P-waves and S-waves travel at different speeds. These speeds are used to determine how close a seismograph station is to an earthquake.

**Figure 6** After distances from at least three seismograph stations are determined, they are plotted as circles with radii equal to these distances on a map. The epicenter is the point at which the circles intersect.

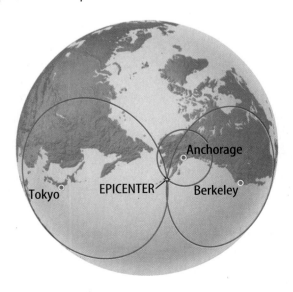

**Epicenter Location** When seismic-wave arrival times are recorded at a seismograph station, the distance from that station to the epicenter can be determined. The farther apart the arrival times for the different waves are, the farther away the earthquake epicenter is. This difference is shown by the graph in **Figure 5.** Using this information, scientists draw a circle with a radius equal to the distance from the earthquake for each of at least three seismograph stations, as illustrated in **Figure 6.** The point where the three circles meet is the location of the earthquake epicenter. Data from many stations normally are used to determine an epicenter location.

## How strong are earthquakes?

As shown in **Table 1,** major earthquakes cause much loss of life. For example, on September 20, 1999, a major earthquake struck Taiwan, leaving more than 2,400 people dead, more than 8,700 injured, and at least 100,000 homeless. Sometimes earthquakes are felt and can cause destruction in areas hundreds of kilometers away from their epicenters. The Mexico City earthquake in 1985 is an example of this. The movement of the soft sediment underneath Mexico City caused extensive damage to this city, even though the epicenter was nearly 400 km away.

**The Richter Scale** Richter (RIHK tur) magnitude is based on measurements of amplitudes, or heights, of seismic waves as recorded on seismographs. Richter magnitude describes how much energy an earthquake releases. For each increase of 1.0 on the Richter scale, the amplitude of the highest recorded seismic wave increases by 10. However, about 32 times more energy is released for every increase of 1.0 on the scale. For example, an earthquake with a magnitude of 7.5 releases about 32 times more energy than one with a magnitude of 6.5, and the wave height for a 7.5-magnitude quake is ten times higher than for a quake with a magnitude of 6.5.

**Earthquake Damage** Another way to measure earthquakes is available. The modified Mercalli intensity scale measures the intensity of an earthquake. Intensity is a measure of the amount of structural and geologic damage done by an earthquake in a specific location. The range of intensities spans Roman numerals I through XII. The amount of damage done depends on several factors—the strength of the earthquake, the nature of the surface material, the design of structures, and the distance from the epicenter. An intensity-I earthquake would be felt only by a few people under ideal conditions. An intensity-VI earthquake would be felt by everyone. An intensity-XII earthquake would cause major destruction to human-built structures and Earth's surface. The 1994 earthquake in Northridge, California was a Richter magnitude 6.7, and its intensity was listed at IX. An intensity-IX earthquake causes considerable damage to buildings and could cause cracks in the ground.

**Table 1 Strong Earthquakes**

| Year | Location | Magnitude | Deaths |
|------|----------|-----------|--------|
| 1989 | Loma Prieta, CA | 7.1 | 62 |
| 1990 | Iran | 7.7 | 50,000 |
| 1993 | Guam | 8.1 | none |
| 1993 | Maharashtra, India | 6.4 | 30,000 |
| 1994 | Northridge, CA | 6.7 | 61 |
| 1995 | Kobe, Japan | 6.8 | 5,378 |
| 1999 | Taiwan | 7.7 | 2,400 |
| 2000 | Indonesia | 7.9 | 103 |
| 2001 | India | 7.7 | 20,000 |
| 2003 | Iran | 6.6 | 30,000 |

**Tsunamis** Most damage from an earthquake is caused by surface waves. Buildings can crack or fall down. Elevated bridges and highways can collapse. However, people living near the seashore must protect themselves against another hazard from earthquakes. When an earthquake occurs on the ocean floor, the sudden movement pushes against the water and powerful water waves are produced. These waves can travel outward from the earthquake thousands of kilometers in all directions.

When these seismic sea waves, or **tsunamis,** are far from shore, their energy is spread out over large distances and great water depths. The wave heights of tsunamis are less than a meter in deep water, and large ships can ride over them and not even know it. In the open ocean, the speed of tsunamis can reach 950 km/h. However, when tsunamis approach land, the waves slow down and their wave heights increase as they encounter the bottom of the seafloor. This creates huge tsunami waves that can be as much as 30 m in height. Just before a tsunami crashes to shore, the water near a shoreline may move rapidly out toward the sea. If this should happen, there is immediate danger that a tsunami is about to strike. **Figure 7** illustrates the behavior of a tsunami as it approaches the shore.

**Science** online

**Topic: Earthquake Magnitude**
Visit glencoe.com for Web links to information about determining earthquake magnitudes.

**Activity** Create a table that compares the damage in dollars, the magnitude, and the general location of six recent earthquakes.

**Physical Setting**

**2.2f Discuss** how a tsunami is evidence of movement at plate boundaries.

## Figure 7

The diagram below shows stages in the development of a tsunami. A tsunami is an ocean wave that is usually generated by an earthquake and is capable of inflicting great destruction.

▶ **TSUNAMI ALERT** The red dots on this map show the tide monitoring stations that make up part of the Tsunami Warning System for the Pacific Ocean. The map shows approximately how long it would take for tsunamis that originate at different places in the Pacific to reach Hawaii. Each ring represents two hours of travel time.

**TSUNAMI WARNING SYSTEM**

**Displacement**

**A** The vibrations set off by a sudden movement along a fault in Earth's crust are transferred to the water's surface and spread across the ocean in a series of long waves.

**B** The waves travel across the ocean at speeds ranging from about 500 to 950 km/h

**C** When a tsunami wave reaches shallow water, friction slows it down and causes it to roll up into a wall of water—sometimes 30 m high—before it breaks against the shore.

**Tsunami Warning System buoy**

# Earthquake Safety

You've just read about the destruction that earthquakes cause. Fortunately, there are ways to reduce the damage and the loss of life associated with earthquakes.

Learning the earthquake history of an area is one of the first things to do to protect yourself. If the area you are in has had earthquakes before, chances are it will again and you can prepare for that.

**Is your home seismic safe?** What could you do to make your home earthquake safe? As shown in **Figure 8,** it's a good idea to move all heavy objects to lower shelves so they can't fall on you. Make sure your gas hot-water heater and appliances are well secured. A new method of protecting against fire is to place sensors on your gas line that would shut off the gas when the vibrations of an earthquake are felt.

In the event of an earthquake, keep away from all windows and avoid anything that might fall on you. Watch for fallen power lines and possible fire hazards. Collapsed buildings and piles of rubble can contain many sharp edges, so keep clear of these areas.

**Seismic-Safe Structures** If a building is considered **seismic safe,** it will be able to stand up against the vibrations caused by most earthquakes. Residents in earthquake-prone areas are constantly improving the way structures are built. Since 1971, stricter building codes have been enforced in California. Older buildings have been reinforced. Many high-rise office buildings now stand on huge steel-and-rubber supports that could enable them to ride out the vibrations of an earthquake. Underground water and gas pipes are replaced with pipes that will bend during an earthquake. This can help prevent broken gas lines and therefore reduce damage from fires.

Seismic-safe highways have cement pillars with spiral reinforcing rods placed within them. One structure that was severely damaged in the 1989 Loma Prieta, California earthquake was Interstate Highway 880. The collapsed highway was due to be renovated to make it seismic safe. It was built in the 1950s and did not have spiral reinforcing rods in its concrete columns. When the upper highway went in one direction, the lower one went in the opposite direction. The columns collapsed and the upper highway came down onto the lower one.

**Figure 8** You can minimize your risk of getting hurt by preparing for an earthquake in advance.

Placing heavy or breakable objects on lower shelves means they won't fall too far during an earthquake.

Vibration sensors on gas lines shut off the supply of gas automatically during an earthquake. **Draw Conclusions** *What hazard can be prevented if the gas is turned off?*

**Figure 9** One way to monitor changes along a fault is to detect any movement that occurs.

**Predicting Earthquakes** Imagine how many lives could be saved if only the time and location of a major earthquake could be predicted. Because most injuries from earthquakes occur when structures fall on top of people, it would help if people could be warned to move outside of buildings.

Researchers try to predict earthquakes by noting changes that precede them. That way, if such changes are observed again, an earthquake warning may be issued.

For example, movement along faults is monitored using laser-equipped, distance-measuring devices, such as the one shown in **Figure 9.** Changes in groundwater level or in electrical properties of rocks under stress have been measured by some scientists. Some people even study rock layers that have been affected by ancient earthquakes. Whether any of these studies will lead to the accurate and reliable prediction of earthquakes, no one knows. A major problem is that no single change in Earth occurs for all earthquakes. Each earthquake is unique.

Long-range forecasts predict whether an earthquake of a certain magnitude is likely to occur in a given area within 30 to 100 years. Forecasts of this nature are used to update building codes to make a given area more seismic safe.

## section 1 review

### Summary

**What causes earthquakes?**
- The sudden release of energy in rock and the resulting movement causes an earthquake.
- Faults are breaks in rocks along which movement occurs.

**Making Waves**
- The focus is where an earthquake occurs. The epicenter is directly above it.
- Earthquakes generate seismic waves.

**How strong are earthquakes?**
- The Richter Scale measures magnitude.
- The modified Mercalli scale measures intensity.

**Earthquake Safety**
- Structures can be made seismic safe.

### Self Check

1. **Explain** what happens to rocks after their elastic limit is passed.
2. **Identify** Which seismic waves cause most of the damage during an earthquake?
3. **Apply** What has been done to make structures more seismic safe?
4. **Summarize** How can seismic waves be used to determine an earthquake's epicenter?
5. **Think Critically** Explain how a magnitude-8.0 earthquake could be classified as a low-intensity earthquake.

#### Applying Skills

6. **Make and Use Tables** Use **Table 1** to research the earthquakes that struck Indonesia in 2000, Loma Prieta, California in 1989, and Iran in 1990. Why was there such a great difference in the number of deaths?

# section 2

# Volcanoes

## How do volcanoes form?

Much like air bubbles that are forced upward toward the bottom of an overturned bottle of denser syrup, molten rock material, or magma, is forced upward toward Earth's surface by denser surrounding rock. Rising magma eventually can lead to an eruption, where magma, solids, and gas are spewed out to form cone-shaped mountains called **volcanoes.** As magma flows onto Earth's surface through a vent, or opening, it is called **lava.** Volcanoes have circular holes near their summits called craters. Lava and other volcanic materials can be expelled through a volcano's crater.

Some explosive eruptions throw lava and rock thousands of meters into the air. Bits of rock or solidified lava dropped from the air are called tephra. Tephra varies in size from volcanic ash to cinders to larger rocks called bombs or blocks.

**Where Plates Collide** Some volcanoes form because of collision of large plates of Earth's crust and upper mantle. This process has produced a string of volcanic islands, much like those illustrated in **Figure 10,** which includes Montserrat. These islands are forming as plates made up of oceanic crust and mantle collide. The older and denser oceanic plate subducts, or sinks beneath, the less dense plate, as shown in **Figure 10.** When one plate sinks under another plate, rock in and above the sinking plate melts, forming chambers of magma. This magma is the source for volcanic eruptions that have formed the Caribbean Islands.

**as you read**

*What* **You'll Learn**

- **Explain** how volcanoes can affect people.
- **Describe** how types of materials are produced by volcanoes.
- **Compare** how three different volcano forms develop.

*Why* **It's Important**

Volcanic eruptions can cause serious consequences for humans and other organisms.

**Review Vocabulary**
**plate:** a large section of Earth's crust and rigid upper mantle that moves around on the asthenosphere

**New Vocabulary**
- volcano
- lava
- shield volcano
- cinder cone volcano
- composite volcano

**Physical Setting**

**2.2a, 2.2f Sequence** the events that lead to the eruption of a volcano at a convergent plate boundary.

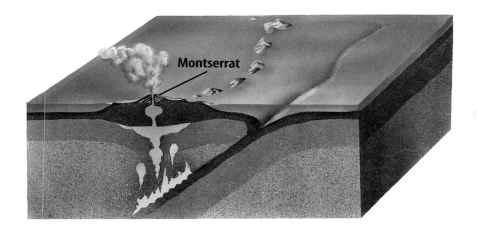

Montserrat

**Figure 10** A string of Caribbean Islands known as the Lesser Antilles formed because of subduction. The island of Montserrat is among these.

**Figure 11** Several volcanic hazards are associated with explosive activity.

Volcanic ash blanketing an area can cause collapse of structures or—when mixed with precipitation—mudflows.

Objects in the path of a pyroclastic flow are subject to complete destruction.

## Mini LAB

### Modeling an Eruption

**Procedure**

1. Place **red-colored gelatin** into a **self-sealing plastic bag** until the bag is half full.
2. Seal the bag and press the gelatin to the bottom of the bag.
3. Put a hole in the bottom of the bag with a **pin.**

**Analysis**

1. What parts of a volcano do the gelatin, the plastic bag, and the hole represent?
2. What force in nature did you mimic as you moved the gelatin to the bottom of the bag?
3. What factors in nature cause this force to increase and lead to an eruption?

**Try at Home**

**Eruptions on a Caribbean Island** Soufrière (soo free UR) Hills volcano on the island of Montserrat was considered dormant until recently. However, in 1995, Soufrière Hills volcano surprised its inhabitants with explosive activity. In July 1995, plumes of ash soared to heights of more than 10,000 m. This ash covered the capital city of Plymouth and many other villages, as shown at left in **Figure 11.**

Every aspect of a once-calm tropical life changed when the volcano erupted. Glowing avalanches and hot, boiling mudflows destroyed villages and shut down the main harbor of the island and its airport. During activity on July 3, 1998, volcanic ash reached heights of more than 14,000 m. This ash settled over the entire island and was followed by mudflows brought on by heavy rains.

Pyroclastic flows are another hazard for inhabitants of Montserrat. They can occur anytime on any side of the volcano. Pyroclastic flows are massive avalanches of hot, glowing rock flowing on a cushion of intensely hot gases, as shown at right in **Figure 11.** Speeds at which these flows travel can reach 200 km/h.

More than one half of Montserrat has been converted to a barren wasteland by the volcano. Virtually all of the farmland is now unusable, and most of the island's business and leisure centers are gone. Many of the inhabitants of the island have been evacuated to England, surrounding islands, or northern Montserrat, which is considered safe from volcanic activity.

**Volcanic Risks** According to the volcanic-risk map shown in **Figure 12,** inactive volcanic centers exist at Silver Hill, Centre Hill, and South Soufrière Hills. The active volcano, Soufrière Hills volcano, is located just north of South Soufrière Hills. The risk map shows different zones of the island where inhabitants still are able to stay and locations from which they have been evacuated. Twenty people who had ignored evacuation orders were killed by pyroclastic flows from the June 25, 1997, event. These are the first and only deaths that have occurred since July 1995.

## Forms of Volcanoes

As you have learned, volcanoes can cause great destruction. However, volcanoes also add new rock to Earth's crust with each eruption. The way volcanoes add this new material to Earth's surface varies greatly. Different types of eruptions produce different types of volcanoes.

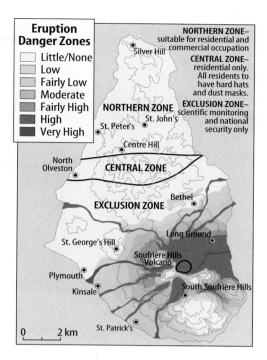

 **What determines how a volcano erupts?** Some volcanic eruptions are violent, while during others lava flows out quietly around a vent. The composition of the magma plays a big part in determining the manner in which energy is released during a volcanic eruption. Lava that contains more silica, which is a compound consisting of silicon and oxygen, tends to be thicker and is more resistant to flow. Lava containing more iron and magnesium and less silica tends to flow easily. The amount of water vapor and other gases trapped in the lava also influences how lava erupts.

When you shake a bottle of carbonated soft drink before opening it, the pressure from the gas in the drink builds up and is released suddenly when the container is opened. Similarly, steam builds pressure in magma. This pressure is released as magma rises toward Earth's surface and eventually erupts. Sticky, silica-rich lava tends to trap water vapor and other gases.

Water is carried down from the surface of Earth into the mantle when one plate subducts beneath another, as in the case of the Lesser Antilles volcanoes. In hotter regions of Earth's interior, part of a descending plate and nearby rock will melt to form magma. The magma produced is more silica rich than the rock that melts to form the magma. Superheated steam produces tremendous pressure in such thick, silica-rich magmas. After enough pressure builds up, an eruption occurs. The type of lava and the gases contained in that lava determine the type of eruption that occurs.

**Figure 12** A volcanic risk map for Montserrat was prepared to warn inhabitants and visitors about unsafe areas on the island.

**Topic: Montserrat Volcano**
Visit glencoe.com for Web links to an update of data on Soufrière Hills volcano on Montserrat.

**Activity** Compare the recent activity of the Soufrière Hills volcano to another recently active volcano. Gather your findings into a table and include dates as well as amount of area destroyed in your report.

**Figure 13** Volcanic landforms vary greatly in size and shape.

**NE–SW across Mauna Loa, Hawaii**

**A** The fluid nature of basaltic lava has produced extensive flows at Mauna Loa, Hawaii—the largest active volcano on Earth.

**Cinder cone volcano**

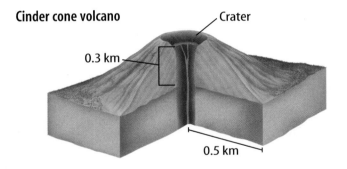

Crater

0.3 km

0.5 km

**N–S View across Sunset Crater, Arizona**

**B** Sunset Crater is small and steep along its flanks—typical of a cinder cone. Compare the scale given for Sunset Crater with that shown in Figure 13A.

**Shield volcano**

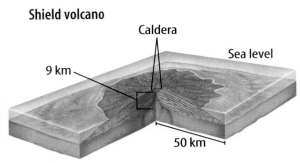

Caldera

Sea level

9 km

50 km

## Shield Volcanoes

Basaltic lava, which is high in iron and magnesium and low in silica, flows in broad, flat layers. The buildup of basaltic layers forms a broad volcano with gently sloping sides called a **shield volcano.** Shield volcanoes, shown in **Figure 13A,** are the largest type of volcano. They form where magma is being forced up from extreme depths within Earth, or in areas where Earth's plates are moving apart. The separation of plates enables magma to be forced upward to Earth's surface.

**Reading Check** *What materials are shield volcanoes composed of?*

## Cinder Cone Volcanoes

Rising magma accumulates gases on its way to the surface. When the gas builds up enough pressure, it erupts. Moderate to violent eruptions throw volcanic ash, cinders, and lava high into the air. The lava cools quickly in midair and the particles of solidified lava, ash, and cinders fall back to Earth. This tephra forms a relatively small cone of volcanic material called a **cinder cone volcano.** Cinder cones are usually less than 300 m in height and often form in groups near other larger volcanoes. Because the eruption is powered by the high gas content, it usually doesn't last long. After the gas is released, the force behind the eruption is gone. Sunset Crater, an example of a cinder cone near Flagstaff, Arizona, is shown in **Figure 13B.**

**Composite Volcanoes** Steep-sided mountains composed of alternating layers of lava and tephra are **composite volcanoes**. They sometimes erupt violently, releasing large quantities of ash and gas. This forms a tephra layer of solid materials. Then a quieter eruption forms a lava layer.

Composite volcanoes form where one plate sinks beneath another. Soufrière Hills volcano is an example of a composite volcano. Another volcanic eruption from a composite volcano was the May 1980 eruption of Mount St. Helens in the state of Washington. It erupted explosively, spewing ash that fell on regions hundreds of kilometers away from the volcano. A composite volcano is shown in **Figure 13C**.

**C** Composite cones are intermediate in size and shape compared to shield volcanoes and cinder cone volcanoes.

Mount Rainier, Washington

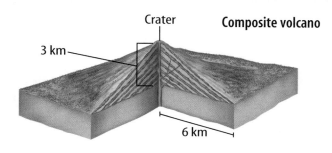

Crater    **Composite volcano**

3 km

6 km

**Fissure Eruptions** Magma that is highly fluid can ooze from cracks or fissures in Earth's surface. This is the type of magma that usually is associated with fissure eruptions. The lava that erupts has a low viscosity, which means it can flow freely across the land to form flood basalts. Flood basalts that have been exposed to erosion for millions of years can become large, relatively flat landforms known as lava plateaus, as shown in **Figure 13D**. The Columbia River Plateau in the northwestern United States was formed about 15 million years ago when several fissures erupted and the flows built up layer upon layer.

**D** No modern example compares with the extensive flood basalts making up the Columbia River Plateau.

## Table 2 Seven Selected Eruptions in History

| Volcano (Year) | Type | Eruptive Force | Silica Content | Gas Content | Eruption Products |
|---|---|---|---|---|---|
| Krakatau, Indonesia (1883) | composite | high | high | high | gas, cinders, ash |
| Katmai, Alaska (1912) | composite | high | high | high | lava, ash, gas |
| Paricutín, Mexico (1943) | cinder cone | moderate | high | low | gas, cinders, ash |
| Helgafell, Iceland (1973) | cinder cone | moderate | low | high | gas, ash |
| Mount St. Helens, Washington (1980) | composite | high | high | high | gas, ash |
| Kilauea Iki, Hawaii (1989) | shield | low | low | low | gas, lava |
| Soufrière Hills, Montserrat (1995–) | composite | high | high | high | gas, ash, rocks |

You have read about some variables that control the type of volcanic eruption that will occur. Examine **Table 2** for a summary of these important factors. In the next section, you'll learn that the type of magma produced is associated with properties of Earth's plates and how these plates interact.

## section 2 review

### Summary

**How do volcanoes form?**

- Some volcanoes form as two or more large plates collide.
- The Caribbean Islands formed from volcanic eruptions as one plate sinks under another plate.

**Forms of volcanoes**

- Lava high in silica produces explosive eruptions, lava low in silica but high in iron and magnesium produces more fluid eruptions.
- The amount of water vapor and gases impacts how volcanoes erupt.
- The types of volcanoes include shield, cinder cone and composite volcanoes, and fissure eruptions.

### Self Check

1. **Identify** Which types of lava eruptions cover the largest area on Earth's surface?
2. **Describe** the processes that have led to the formation of the Soufrière Hills volcano.
3. **Explain** why a cinder cone has steep sides?
4. **List** What types of materials are volcanoes like Mount St. Helens made of?
5. **Think Critically** Why is silica-rich magma explosive?

*Hot Words Hot Topics*: Bk 2 (6) pp. 92, 397

#### Applying Math

6. **Solve One-Step Equations** Mauna Loa in Hawaii rises 9 km above the seafloor. Sunset Crater in Arizona rises to an elevation of 300 m. How many times higher is Mauna Loa than Sunset Crater?

**More Section Review** glencoe.com

# Disruptive Eruptions

A volcano's structure can influence how it erupts. Some volcanoes have only one central vent, while others have numerous fissures that allow lava to escape. Materials in magma influence its viscosity, or how it flows. If magma is a thin fluid—not viscous—gases can escape easily. But if magma is thick—viscous—gases cannot escape as easily. This builds up pressure within a volcano.

## Real-World Question

What determines the explosiveness of a volcanic eruption?

### Goals

■ **Infer** how a volcano's opening contributes to how explosive an eruption might be.

■ **Hypothesize** how the viscosity of magma can influence an eruption.

### Materials

plastic film canisters
baking soda (NaHCO₃)
vinegar (CH₃COOH)

50-mL graduated
cylinder
teaspoon

### Safety Precautions

This lab should be done outdoors. Goggles must be worn at all times. The caps of the film canisters fly off due to the chemical reaction that occurs inside them. Never put anything in your mouth while doing the experiment.

## Procedure

1. Watch your teacher demonstrate this lab before attempting to do it yourself.

2. Add 15 mL of vinegar to a film canister.

3. Place 1 teaspoon of baking soda in the film

canister's lid, using it as a type of plate.

4. Place the lid on top of the film canister, but do not cap it. The baking soda will fall into the vinegar. Move a safe distance away. Record your observations in your Science Journal.

5. Clean out your film canister and repeat the lab, but this time cap the canister quickly and tightly. Record your observations.

## Conclude and Apply

1. **Identify** Which of the two labs models a more explosive eruption?

2. **Explain** Was the pressure greater inside the canister during the first or second lab? Why?

3. **Explain** What do the bubbles have to do with the explosion? How do they influence the pressure in the container?

4. **Infer** If the vinegar were a more viscous substance, how would the eruption be affected?

### Communicating Your Data

**Research** three volcanic eruptions that have occurred in the past five years. Compare each eruption to one of the eruption styles you modeled in this lab. Communicate to your class what you learn.

**section**

**3**

PS 2.2a: The interior of Earth is hot. Heat flow and movement of material within Earth cause sections of Earth's crust to move. This may result in earthquakes, volcanic eruption, and the creation of mountains and ocean basins. **Also Covered:** PS 2.2e, 2.2f.

# Earthquakes, Volcanoes, and Plate Tectonics

**as you read**

### *What* You'll Learn

- **Explain** how the locations of volcanoes and earthquake epicenters are related to tectonic plate boundaries.
- **Explain** how heat within Earth causes Earth's plates to move.

### *Why* It's Important

Most volcanoes and earthquakes are caused by the motion and interaction of Earth's plates.

### Review Vocabulary

**asthenosphere:** plasticlike layer of mantle under the lithosphere

### New Vocabulary

- rift
- hot spot

## Earth's Moving Plates

At the beginning of class, your teacher asks for volunteers to help set up the cafeteria for a special assembly. You and your classmates begin to move the tables carefully, like the students shown in **Figure 14.** As you move the tables, two or three of them crash into each other. Think about what could happen if the students moving those tables kept pushing on them. For a while one or two of the tables might keep another from moving. However, if enough force were used, the tables would slide past one another. One table might even slide up on top of another. It is because of this possibility that your teacher has asked that you move the tables carefully.

The movement of the tables and the possible collisions among them is like the movement of Earth's crust and uppermost mantle, called the lithosphere. Earth's lithosphere is broken into separate sections, or plates. When these plates move around, they collide, move apart, or slide past each other. The movement of these plates can cause vibrations known as earthquakes and can create conditions that cause volcanoes to form.

**Figure 14** Like the tables pictured here, Earth's plates are in contact with one another and can slide beneath each other. The way Earth's plates interact at boundaries is an important factor in the locations of earthquakes and volcanoes.

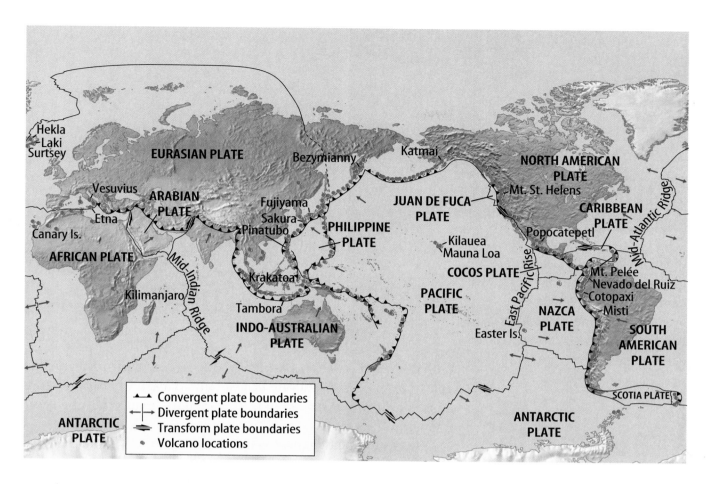

## Where Volcanoes Form

A plot of the location of plate boundaries and volcanoes on Earth shows that most volcanoes form along plate boundaries. Examine the map in **Figure 15.** Can you see how this indicates that plate tectonics and volcanic activity are related? Perhaps the energy involved in plate tectonics is causing magma to form deep under Earth's surface. You'll recall that the Soufrière Hills volcano formed where plates converge. Plate movement often explains why volcanoes form in certain areas.

**Divergent Plate Boundaries** Tectonic plates move apart at divergent plate boundaries. As the plates separate, long cracks called **rifts** form between them. Rifts contain fractures that serve as passageways for magma originating in the mantle. Rift zones account for most of the places where lava flows onto Earth's surface. Fissure eruptions often occur along rift zones. These eruptions form lava that cools and solidifies into basalt, the most abundant type of rock in Earth's crust.

 *Where does magma along divergent boundaries originate?*

**Figure 15** Earth's lithosphere is divided into about 13 major plates. Where plates collide, separate, and slip past one another at plate boundaries, interesting geological activity results.

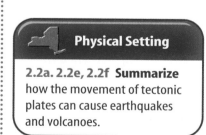

### Physical Setting

**2.2a. 2.2e, 2.2f Summarize** how the movement of tectonic plates can cause earthquakes and volcanoes.

**Figure 16** The Hawaiian Islands have formed, and continue to form, as the Pacific Plate moves over a hot spot. The arrow shows that the Pacific Plate is moving north-northwest.

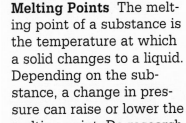

**INTEGRATE Chemistry**

**Melting Points** The melting point of a substance is the temperature at which a solid changes to a liquid. Depending on the substance, a change in pressure can raise or lower the melting point. Do research to find out how pressure affects the formation of magma in a mantle plume in a process called decompression melting.

**Convergent Plate Boundaries** A common location for volcanoes to form is along convergent plate boundaries. More dense oceanic plates sink beneath less dense plates that they collide with. This sets up conditions that form volcanoes.

When one plate sinks beneath another, basalt and sediment on an oceanic plate move down into the mantle. Water from the sediment and altered basalt lowers the melting point of the surrounding rock. Heat in the mantle causes part of the sinking plate and overlying mantle to melt. This melted material then is forced upward. Volcanoes have formed in this way all around the Pacific Ocean, where the Pacific Plate, among others, collides with several other plates. This belt of volcanoes surrounding the Pacific Ocean is called the Pacific Ring of Fire.

**Hot Spots** The Hawaiian Islands are volcanic islands that have not formed along a plate boundary. In fact, they are located well within the Pacific Plate. What process causes them to form? Large bodies of magma, called **hot spots,** are forced upward through Earth's mantle and crust, as shown in **Figure 16.** Scientists suggest that this is what is occurring at a hot spot that exists under the present location of Hawaii.

**✓ Reading Check** *What is a hot spot?*

Volcanoes on Earth usually form along rift zones, subduction zones (where one plate sinks beneath another), or over hot spots. At each of these locations, magma from deep within Earth is forced upward toward the surface. Lava breaks through and flows out, where it piles up into layers or forms a volcanic cone.

# Moving Plates Cause Earthquakes

Place two notebooks on your desk with the page edges facing each other. Then push them together slowly. The individual sheets of paper gradually will bend upward from the stress. If you continue to push on the notebooks, one will slip past the other suddenly. This sudden movement is like an earthquake.

Now imagine what would happen if tectonic plates were moving like the notebooks. What would happen if the plates collided and stopped moving? Forces generated by the locked-up plates would cause strain to build up. Both plates would begin to deform until the elastic limit was passed. The breaking and elastic rebound of the deformed material would produce vibrations felt as earthquakes.

Earthquakes often occur where tectonic plates come together at a convergent boundary, where tectonic plates move apart at a divergent boundary, and where tectonic plates grind past each other, called a transform boundary.

### Earthquake Locations

If you look at a map of earthquakes, you'll see that most occur in well-known belts. About 80 percent of them occur in the Pacific Ring of Fire—the same belt in which many of Earth's volcanoes occur. If you compare **Figure 17** with **Figure 15,** you will notice a definite relationship between earthquake epicenters and tectonic plate boundaries. Movement of the plates produces forces that generate the energy to cause earthquakes.

**Friction** Friction is a force that opposes the motion of two objects in contact. Do research to find out different types of friction in a literary and figurative sense.

**Figure 17** Locations of earthquakes that have occurred between 1990 and 2000 are plotted below.

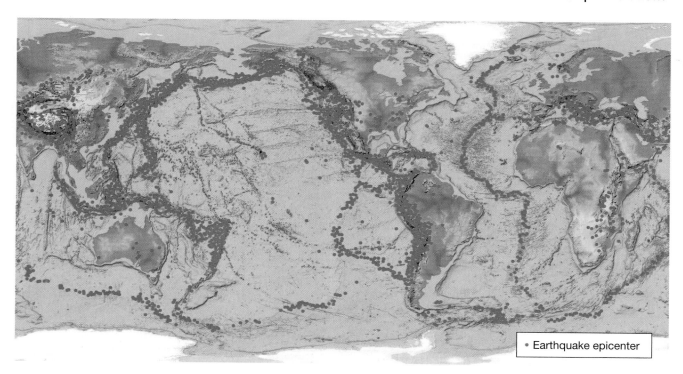

• Earthquake epicenter

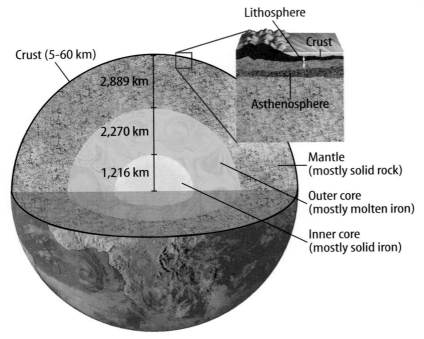

Crust (5-60 km)

Lithosphere

Crust

2,889 km

Asthenosphere

2,270 km

1,216 km

Mantle (mostly solid rock)

Outer core (mostly molten iron)

Inner core (mostly solid iron)

**Figure 18** Seismic waves generated by earthquakes allow researchers to figure out the structure and composition of Earth's layers.

*Hot Words Hot Topics*: Bk 2 (1) pp. 135, 276–278; (2) pp. 135, 276–278

## Earth's Plates and Interior

Researchers have learned much about Earth's interior and plate tectonics by studying seismic waves. The way in which seismic waves pass through a material depends on the properties of that material. Seismic wave speeds, and how they travel through different levels in the interior, have allowed scientists to map out the major layers of Earth, as shown in **Figure 18.**

For example, the asthenosphere was discovered when seismologists noted that seismic waves slowed when they reached the base of the lithosphere of the Earth. This partially molten layer forms a warmer, softer layer over which the colder, brittle, rocky plates move.

## Applying Math — Calculate

**P-WAVE TRAVEL TIME** There is a relationship between the density of a region in Earth and the velocity of P-waves. How can you calculate the time it would take P-waves to travel 100 km in the crust of Earth?

### Density and Wave Velocity

| Region | Density | P-Wave Velocity |
|---|---|---|
| Crust | 2.8 g/cm$^3$ | 6 km/s |
| Upper mantle | 3.3 g/cm$^3$ | 8 km/s |

### Solution

**1** *This is what you know:*
- velocity: $v = 6$ km/s
- distance: $d = 100$ km

**2** *This is what you need to find:*
How long would it take a P wave to travel?

**3** *This is the procedure you need to use:*
- $t = d/v$
- $t = (100$ km$)/(6$ km/s$) = 16.7$ s

**4** *Check your answer:*
Solve $v = d/t = (100$ km$)/(16.7\ s) = 6$ km/s

### Practice Problems

1. Calculate the time it takes P-waves to travel 300 km in the upper mantle.

2. How long will it take a P-wave to travel 500 km in the crust?

 **For more practice, visit** glencoe.com

**What is driving Earth's plates?** There are several hypotheses about where all the energy comes from to power the movement of Earth's plates.

In one case, mantle material deep inside Earth is heated by Earth's core. This hot, less dense rock material is forced toward the surface. The hotter, rising mantle material eventually cools. The cooler material then sinks into the mantle toward Earth's core, completing the convection current. Convection currents inside Earth, shown in **Figure 19,** provide the mechanism for plate motion, which then produces the conditions that cause volcanoes and earthquakes. Sometimes magma is forced up directly within a plate. Volcanic activity in Yellowstone National Park is caused by a hot spot beneath the North American Plate. Such hot spots might be related to larger-scale convection in Earth's mantle.

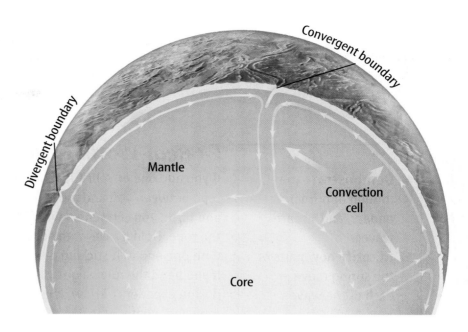

**Figure 19** Convection of material in Earth's interior drives the motion of tectonic plates.

---

## section 3 review

### Summary

**Earth's Moving Plates**

- Earth's lithosphere is broken into plates that move around the planet.

**Where Volcanoes Form**

- Plates move apart at divergent plate boundaries, creating fissure eruptions.
- Plates collide at convergent plate boundaries.
- Many volcanoes form at convergent plate boundaries.
- Volcanoes may also form along rift zones, subduction zones, or over hot spots.

**Moving Plates Cause Earthquakes**

- Earthquakes often form at plate boundaries.
- Seismic waves have been used to determine the characteristics of Earth's interior.
- Convection currently may drive tectonic plate movement.

### Self Check

1. **Identify** Along which type of plate boundary has the Soufrière Hills volcano formed?

2. **Predict** At which type of plate boundary does rift-volcanism occur?

3. **Explain** how volcanoes in Hawaii form.

4. **Recognize Cause and Effect** Why do most deep earthquakes occur at convergent boundaries?

5. **Think Critically** Subduction occurs where plates converge. This causes water-rich sediment and altered rock to be forced down to great depths. Explain how water can help form a volcano.

#### Applying Skills

6. **Form Hypotheses** Write a hypothesis concerning the type of lava that will form a hot spot volcano. Consider that magma in a hot spot comes from deep inside Earth's mantle.

---

# Seismic Waves

## ⦿ Real-World Question

If you and one of your friends hold a long piece of rope between you and move one end of the rope back and forth, you can send a wave through the length of the rope. Hold a ruler at the edge of a table securely with one end of it sticking out from the table's edge. If you bend the ruler slightly and then release it, what do you experience? How does what you see in the rope and what you feel in the ruler relate to seismic waves? How do seismic waves differ?

## ⦿ Procedure

1. Copy the following data table in your Science Journal.
2. Tie a small piece of yarn or string to every tenth coil of the spring.
3. Place the spring on a smooth, flat surface. Stretch it so it is about 2 m long (1 m for shorter springs).
4. Hold your end of the spring firmly. Make a wave by having your partner snap the spring from side to side quickly.
5. **Record** your observations in your Science Journal and draw the wave you and your partner made in the data table.
6. Have your lab partner hold his or her end of the spring firmly. Make a wave by quickly pushing your end of the spring toward your partner and bringing it back to its original position.

### Goals

- **Demonstrate** the motion of primary, secondary, and surface waves.
- **Identify** how parts of the spring move in each of the waves.

### Materials

coiled spring toy
yarn or string
metric ruler

### Safety Precautions

| Comparing Seismic Waves | | | |
|---|---|---|---|
| Observation of Wave | Observation of Yarn or String | Drawing | Wave Type |
| | Do not write in this book. | | |
| | | | |
| | | | |

7. **Record** your observations of the wave and of the yarn or string and draw the wave in the data table.

8. Have your lab partner hold his or her end of the spring firmly. Move the spring off of the table. Gently move your end of the spring side to side while at the same time moving it in a rolling motion, first up and away and then down and toward your partner.

9. **Record** your observations and draw the wave in the data table.

## ▶ Conclude and Apply

1. Based on your observations, determine which of the waves that you and your partner have generated demonstrates a primary, or pressure, wave. Record in your data table and explain why you chose the wave you did.

2. Do the same for the secondary, or shear wave, and for the surface wave. Explain why you chose the wave you did.

3. **Explain** Based on your observations of wave motion, which of the waves that you and your partner generated probably would cause the most damage during an earthquake?

4. **Observe** What was the purpose of the yarn or string?

5. **Compare and contrast** the motion of the yarn or string when primary and secondary waves travel through the spring. Which of these waves is a compression wave? Explain your answer.

6. **Compare and Contrast** Which wave most closely resembled wave motion in a body of water? How was it different? Explain.

### Communicating Your Data

**Compare** your conclusions with those of other students in your class. **For more help, refer to the** Science Skill Handbook.

# quake

## The 1906 San Francisco earthquake taught people valuable lessons

It struck without warning. "We found our-selves staggering and reeling. It was as if the earth was slipping gently from under our feet. Then came the sickening swaying of the earth that threw us flat upon our faces. We struggled in the street. We could not get on our feet. Then it seemed as though my head were split with the roar that crashed into my ears. Big buildings were crumbling as one might crush a biscuit in one's hand."

That's how survivor P. Barrett described the San Francisco earthquake of 1906. Duration of the quake on the morning of April 18—one minute. Yet, in that short time, Earth opened a gaping hole stretching more than 430 km. The tragic result was one of the worst natural disasters in U.S. history.

Fires caused by falling chimneys and fed by broken gas mains raged for three days. Despite the estimated 3,000 deaths and enormous devas-tation to San Francisco, the earthquake did have a positive effect. It led to major building changes that would help protect people and property from future quakes.

Computers analyze information from seismo-graphs that have helped to map the San Andreas Fault—the area along which many California earthquakes take place. This information is help-ing scientists better understand how and when earthquakes might strike.

The 1906 quake also has led to building codes that require stronger construction materials for homes, offices, and bridges. Laws have been passed saying where hospitals, homes, and nuclear power plants can be built—away from soft ground and away from the San Andreas Fault.

Even today, scientists can't predict an earth-quake. But thanks to what they learned from the 1906 quake—and others—people are safer today than ever before.

**Write** Prepare a diary entry pretending to be a person who experienced the 1906 San Francisco earthquake. Possible events to include in your entry: What were you doing at 5:15 A.M.? What began to happen around you? What did you see and hear?

Science Online

For more information, visit glencoe.com

## Reviewing Main Ideas

### Section 1 Earthquakes

1. Earthquakes occur whenever rocks inside Earth pass their elastic limit, break, and experience elastic rebound.

2. Seismic waves are vibrations inside Earth. P- and S-waves travel in all directions away from the earthquake focus. Surface waves travel along the surface.

3. Earthquakes are measured by their magnitudes—the amount of energy they release—and by their intensity—the amount of damage they produce.

### Section 2 Volcanoes

1. The Soufrière Hills volcano is a composite volcano formed by converging plates.

2. The way a volcano erupts is determined by the composition of the lava and the amount of water vapor and other gases in the lava.

3. Three different forms of volcanoes are shield volcanoes, cinder cone volcanoes, and composite volcanoes.

### Section 3 Earthquakes, Volcanoes, and Plate Tectonics

1. The locations of volcanoes and earthquake epicenters are related to the locations of plate boundaries.

2. Volcanoes occur along rift zones, subduction zones, and at hot spots.

3. Most earthquakes occur at convergent, divergent, and transform plate boundaries.

## Visualizing Main Ideas

*Copy and complete the following table comparing characteristics of shield, composite, and cinder cone volcanoes.*

**Volcanoes**

| Characteristic | Shield Volcano | Cinder Cone Volcano | Composite Volcano |
|---|---|---|---|
| Relative size | large | | |
| Nature of eruption | | | moderate to high eruptive force |
| Materials extruded | lava, gas | cinders, gas | |
| Composition of lava | | | high silica |
| Ability of lava to flow | | low | variable |

## Using Vocabulary

| | |
|---|---|
| cinder cone volcano p. 190 | magnitude p. 181 |
| composite volcano p. 191 | rift p. 195 |
| earthquake p. 178 | seismic safe p. 185 |
| epicenter p. 180 | seismic wave p. 180 |
| fault p. 179 | seismograph p. 181 |
| focus p. 180 | shield volcano p. 190 |
| hot spot p. 196 | tsunami p. 183 |
| lava p. 187 | volcano p. 187 |

*Explain the differences between the vocabulary words in each of the following sets.*

1. fault—earthquake

2. shield volcano—composite volcano

3. focus—epicenter

4. seismic wave—seismograph

5. tsunami—seismic wave

6. epicenter—earthquake

7. cinder cone volcano—shield volcano

## Checking Concepts

*Choose the word or phrase that best answers the question.*

8. Which type of plate boundary caused the formation of the Soufrière Hills volcano?
   **A)** divergent      **C)** rift
   **B)** transform      **D)** convergent

9. What is a cone-shaped mountain that is built from layers of lava?
   **A)** volcano       **C)** vent
   **B)** lava flow     **D)** crater

10. What is the cause of the volcanoes on Hawaii?
    **A)** rift zone
    **B)** hot spot
    **C)** divergent plate boundary
    **D)** convergent plate boundary

11. Which type of lava flows easily?
    **A)** silica-rich    **C)** basaltic
    **B)** composite     **D)** smooth

12. Which type of volcano is built from alternating layers of lava and tephra?
    **A)** shield         **C)** lava dome
    **B)** cinder cone    **D)** composite

13. Which type of volcano is relatively small with steep sides?
    **A)** shield         **C)** lava dome
    **B)** cinder cone    **D)** composite

14. Which seismic wave moves through Earth at the fastest speed?
    **A)** primary wave
    **B)** secondary wave
    **C)** surface wave
    **D)** tsunami

15. Which of the following is a wave of water caused by an earthquake under the ocean?
    **A)** primary wave
    **B)** secondary wave
    **C)** surface wave
    **D)** tsunami

**Use the illustration below to answer question 16.**

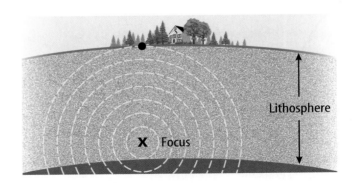

16. What is the point on Earth's surface directly above an earthquake's focus?
    **A)** earthquake center
    **B)** epicenter
    **C)** fault
    **D)** focus

**Vocabulary Puzzlemaker** glencoe.com

## Thinking Critically

**17. Infer** Why does the Soufrière Hills volcano erupt so explosively?

**18. Compare and contrast** composite and cinder cone volcanoes.

**19. Explain** how the composition of magma can affect the way a volcano erupts.

**20. Evaluate** What factors determine an earthquake's intensity on the modified Mercalli scale?

**21. Compare and contrast** magnitude and intensity.

**22. Make Models** Select one of the three forms of volcanoes and make a model, using appropriate materials.

**23. Draw Conclusions** You are flying over an area that has just experienced an earthquake. You see that most of the buildings are damaged or destroyed and much of the surrounding countryside is disrupted. What level of intensity would you conclude for this earthquake?

**24. Concept Map** Copy and complete this concept map on examples of features produced along plate boundaries. Use the following terms: *Mid-Atlantic Ridge, Soufrière Hills volcano, divergent, San Andreas Fault, convergent,* and *transform.*

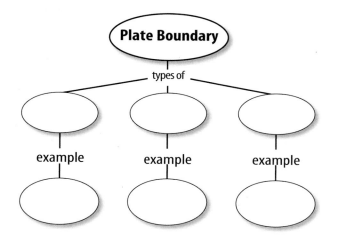

## Performance Activities

**25. Oral Presentation** Research the earthquake or volcano history of your state or community. Find out how long ago your area experienced earthquake- or volcano-related problems. Present your findings in a speech to your class.

*Hot Words Hot Topics:* Bk 2 (26) p. 199; (27) p. 199

## Applying Math

**Use the graph below to answer questions 26 and 27.**

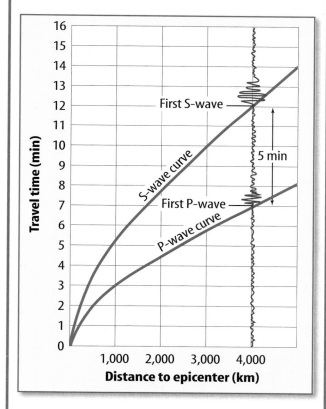

**26. Earthquake Epicenter** If a P-wave arrives at a seismograph station at 9:07 AM and the S-wave arrives at the same seismograph station at 9:09 AM, about how far is that station from the epicenter of the earthquake?

**27. Arrival Time** A seismograph station is 2,500 km from the epicenter of an earthquake. What is the difference in time between the P-wave arrival time and the S-wave arrival time?

## Part I

*Record your answers on the answer sheet provided by your teacher or on a sheet of paper.*

**Use the table below to answer questions 1 and 2.**

| Plate Boundaries | | |
|---|---|---|
| Plate | Number of convergent boundaries | Number of divergent boundaries |
| African | 1 | 4 |
| Antarctic | 1 | 2 |
| Indo-Australian | 4 | 2 |
| Eurasian | 4 | 1 |
| North American | 2 | 1 |
| Pacific | 6 | 2 |
| South American | 2 | 1 |

**1** Which plate has the most spreading boundaries?
(1) African
(2) Indo-Australian
(3) Pacific
(4) Antarctic

**2** If composite volcanoes often form along convergent boundaries, which plate should be surrounded by the most composite volcanoes?
(1) Pacific           (3) Eurasian
(2) Antarctic       (4) Indo-Australian

**3** Which of the following best describes a fault?
(1) the point on Earth's surface located directly above the earthquake focus
(2) the point inside Earth where movement first occurs during an earthquake
(3) the surface of a break in a rock along which there is movement
(4) the snapping back of a rock that has been strained by force

**4** Waves created by earthquakes that travel through Earth's interior and along Earth's surface are called
(1) sound waves.
(2) energy waves.
(3) light waves.
(4) seismic waves.

**5** Volcanoes are associated with all of the following areas EXCEPT
(1) rift zones.
(2) epicenters.
(3) subduction zones.
(4) hot spots.

**Use the figure below to answer question 6 and 7.**

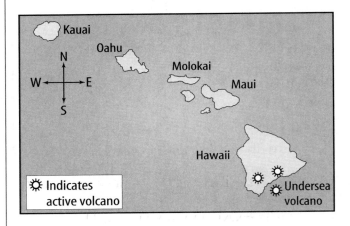

**6** In which direction is the Pacific Plate moving?
(1) north-northwest
(2) north-northeast
(3) south-southwest
(4) south-southeast

**7** Which of the following islands is the oldest?
(1) Kauai
(2) Molokai
(3) Maui
(4) Hawaii

**Part II**

*Record your answers on the answer sheet provided by your teacher or on a sheet of paper.*

**8** What is an earthquake?

**Use the figure below to answer questions 9 and 10.**

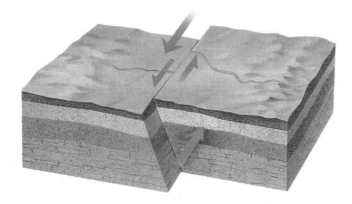

**9** Identify the type of fault shown here. Explain how this type of fault is formed.

**10** What is a tsunami? What happens when a tsunami enters shallow water?

**11** The lava of a particular volcano is high in silica and water vapor and other gases. What kind of eruptive force will likely result from this volcano?

**12** Suppose a tsunami begins near the Aleutian Islands in Alaska. The wave reaches the Hawaiian Islands, a distance of 3800 km, 5 hours later. At what speed is the wave traveling?

**13** What is a seismograph? How does it work?

**Use the figure below to answer question 14.**

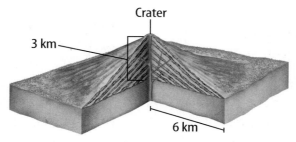

Crater

3 km

6 km

**14** Which type of volcano is shown in the figure? Explain how you know this. Where does this type of volcano form?

**15** Explain the relationship between faults and earthquakes.

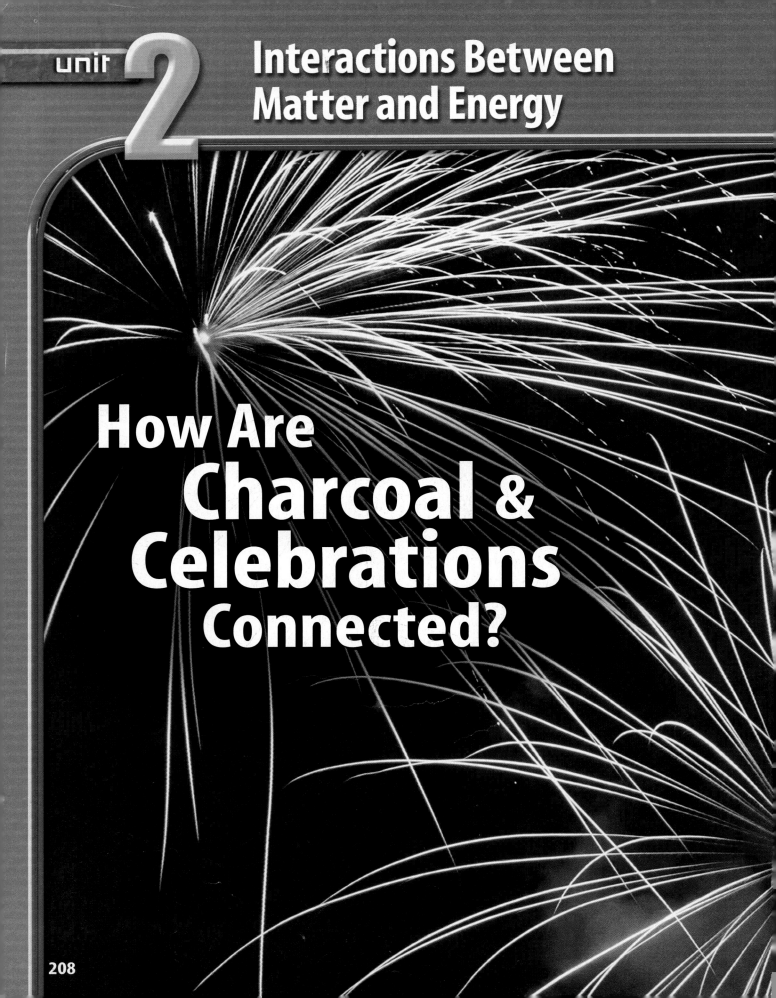

# How Are **Charcoal & Celebrations** Connected?

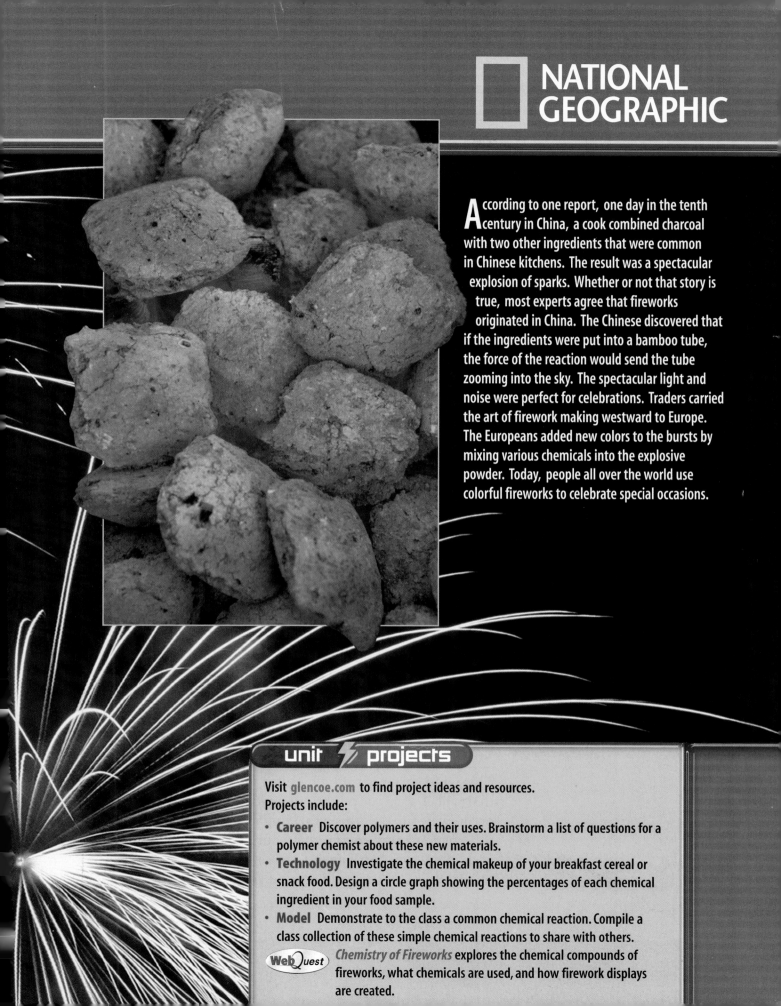

# NATIONAL GEOGRAPHIC

According to one report, one day in the tenth century in China, a cook combined charcoal with two other ingredients that were common in Chinese kitchens. The result was a spectacular explosion of sparks. Whether or not that story is true, most experts agree that fireworks originated in China. The Chinese discovered that if the ingredients were put into a bamboo tube, the force of the reaction would send the tube zooming into the sky. The spectacular light and noise were perfect for celebrations. Traders carried the art of firework making westward to Europe. The Europeans added new colors to the bursts by mixing various chemicals into the explosive powder. Today, people all over the world use colorful fireworks to celebrate special occasions.

## unit ⚡ projects

Visit **glencoe.com** to find project ideas and resources.
Projects include:

- **Career** Discover polymers and their uses. Brainstorm a list of questions for a polymer chemist about these new materials.
- **Technology** Investigate the chemical makeup of your breakfast cereal or snack food. Design a circle graph showing the percentages of each chemical ingredient in your food sample.
- **Model** Demonstrate to the class a common chemical reaction. Compile a class collection of these simple chemical reactions to share with others.

**WebQuest** *Chemistry of Fireworks* explores the chemical compounds of fireworks, what chemicals are used, and how firework displays are created.

**PS 4.4a:** Different forms of electromagnetic energy have different wavelengths. **4.4b:** Light passes through some materials, sometimes refracting in the process. Materials absorb and reflect light, and may transmit light. To see an object, light from that object, emitted by or reflected from it, must enter the eye. **Also Covered:** 4.4c

# Waves, Sound, and Light

## Ups and Downs

This wind surfer is riding high for now, but that will change soon. The energy carried by ocean waves makes this a thrilling ride, but other waves carry energy, too. Sound waves and light waves carry energy that enable you to hear and see the world around you.

**Science Journal**   Write a short paragraph describing water waves you have seen.

# Start-Up Activities

## Wave Properties

If you drop a pebble into a pool of water, you notice how the water rises and falls as waves spread out in all directions. How could you describe the waves? In this lab you'll make a model of one type of wave. By describing the model, you'll learn about some properties of all waves.

1. Make a model of a wave by forming a piece of thick string about 50-cm long into a series of *S* shapes with an up and down pattern.

2. Compare the wave you made with those of other students. Notice how many peaks you have in your wave.

3. Reform your wave so that you have a different number of peaks.

4. **Think Critically** Write a description of your wave model. How did the distance between the peaks change as the number of peaks increased?

Preview this chapter's content and activities at glencoe.com

---

**Waves** Make the following Foldable to compare and contrast the characteristics of transverse and compressional waves.

**STEP 1** **Fold** one sheet of lengthwise paper in half.

**STEP 2** **Fold** into thirds.

**STEP 3** **Unfold and draw** overlapping ovals. **Cut** the top sheet along the folds.

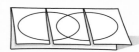

**STEP 4** **Label** the ovals as shown.

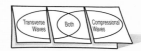

**Construct a Venn Diagram** As you read the chapter, list the characteristics unique to transverse waves under the left tab, those unique to compressional waves under the right tab, and those characteristics common to both under the middle tab.

# section

## 1

# Waves

**as you read**

*What* You'll Learn

■ **Explain** how waves transport energy.
■ **Distinguish** among transverse, compressional, and electromagnetic waves.
■ **Describe** the properties of waves.
■ **Describe** reflection, refraction, and diffraction of waves.

*Why* It's Important

Devices such as televisions, radios, and cell phones receive and transmit information by waves.

🔍 **Review Vocabulary**
**density:** the mass per cubic meter of a substance

**New Vocabulary**
● wave
● transverse wave
● compressional wave
● wavelength
● frequency
● law of reflection
● refraction
● diffraction

## What are waves?

When you float in the pool on a warm summer day, the up-and-down movement of the water tells you waves are moving past. Sometimes the waves are so strong they almost push you over. Other times, the waves just gently rock you. You know about water waves because you can see and feel their movement, but there are other types of waves, also. Different types of waves carry signals to televisions and radios. Sound and light waves move all around you and enable you to hear and see. Waves are even responsible for the damage caused by earthquakes.

**Waves Carry Energy, not Matter** A **wave** is a disturbance that moves through matter or space. Waves carry energy from one place to another. You can see that the waves in **Figure 1** carry energy by the way they crash against the rocks. In water waves, the energy is transferred by water molecules. When a wave moves, it may seem that the wave carries matter from place to place as the wave moves.

But that's not what really happens. When waves travel through solids, liquids, and gases, matter is not carried along with the waves. The movement of the fishing bob in **Figure 1** transfers energy to nearby water molecules. The energy is then passed from molecule to molecule as the wave spreads out. The wave disturbance moves outward, but the locations of the water molecules hardly change at all.

The energy carried by ocean waves can break rocks.

The movement of the fishing bob produces water waves that carry energy through the water.

**Figure 1** Waves carry energy from place to place without carrying matter.

# Types of Waves

Waves usually are produced by something moving back and forth, or vibrating. It is the energy of the vibrating object that waves carry outward. This energy can spread out from the vibrating object in different types of waves. Some waves, known as mechanical waves, can travel only through matter. Other waves called electromagnetic waves can travel either through matter or through empty space.

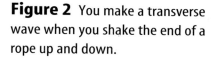

Crest

Direction wave moves

Trough

Direction rope moves

**Figure 2** You make a transverse wave when you shake the end of a rope up and down.

**Transverse Waves** One type of mechanical wave is a transverse wave, shown in **Figure 2**. A **transverse wave** causes particles in matter to move back and forth at right angles to the direction in which the wave travels. If you tie a rope to a door handle and shake the end of the rope up and down, transverse waves travel through the rope.

High points in the wave are called crests. Low points are called troughs. The series of crests and troughs forms a transverse wave. The crests and troughs travel along the rope, but the particles in the rope move only up and down.

**Compressional Waves** Another type of mechanical wave is a compressional wave. **Figure 3** shows a compressional wave traveling along a spring coil. A **compressional wave** causes particles in matter to move back and forth along the same direction in which the wave travels.

In **Figure 3** the places where the coils are squeezed together are called compressions. The places where the coils are spread apart are called rarefactions. The series of compressions and rarefactions forms a compressional wave. The compressions and rarefactions travel along the spring, but the coils move only back and forth.

 *How does matter move in a compressional wave?*

**Physical Setting**

**4.4c** *Energy of the vibrating object is carried outward by the waves.* **Discuss** how this statement applies to both earthquakes and ripples on a pond.

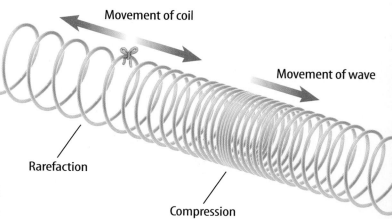

Movement of coil

Movement of wave

Rarefaction

Compression

**Figure 3** A wave on a spring coil is an example of a compressional wave.

**Seismic waves** move through the ground during an earthquake. Some of these waves are compressional, and others are transverse. The seismic waves that cause most damage to buildings are a kind of rolling waves. These rolling waves are a combination of compressional and transverse waves.

**Electromagnetic Waves** Light, radio waves, and X rays are examples of electromagnetic waves. Just like waves on a rope, electromagnetic waves are transverse waves. However, electromagnetic waves contain electric and magnetic parts that vibrate up and down perpendicular to the direction the wave travels.

## Properties of Waves

The properties that waves have depend on the vibrations that produce the waves. For example, if you move a pencil slowly up and down in a bowl of water, the waves produced by the pencil's motion will be small and spread apart. If you move the pencil rapidly, the waves will be larger and close together.

**Wavelength** The distance between one point on a wave and the nearest point moving with the same speed and direction is the **wavelength. Figure 4** shows how the wavelengths of transverse and compressional waves are measured. The wavelength of a transverse wave is the distance between two adjacent crests or two adjacent troughs. The wavelength of a compressional wave is the distance between two adjacent compressions or rarefactions.

**Frequency** The **frequency** of a wave is the number of wavelengths that pass by a point each second. If you were watching a transverse wave on a rope, the frequency of the wave would be the number of crests or troughs that pass you each second. In the same way, the frequency of a compressional wave is the number of compressions or rarefactions that would pass by each second.

**Figure 4** The wavelength of a transverse wave is the distance from crest to crest or from trough to trough. The wavelength of a compressional wave is the distance from compression to compression or rarefaction to rarefaction.

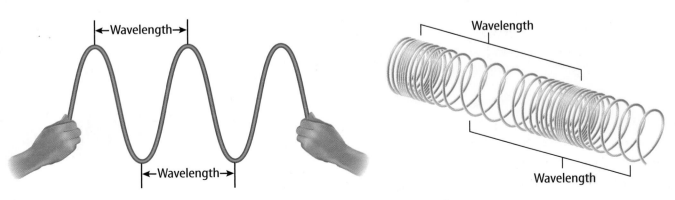

## Amplitude of a Transverse Wave
Waves have another property called amplitude. Suppose you shake the end of a rope by moving your hand up and down a large distance. Then you make a transverse wave with high crests and deep troughs. The wave you've made has a large amplitude. The amplitude of a transverse wave is half the distance between a crest and trough as shown in **Figure 5.** As the distance between crests and troughs increases, the amplitude of a transverse wave increases.

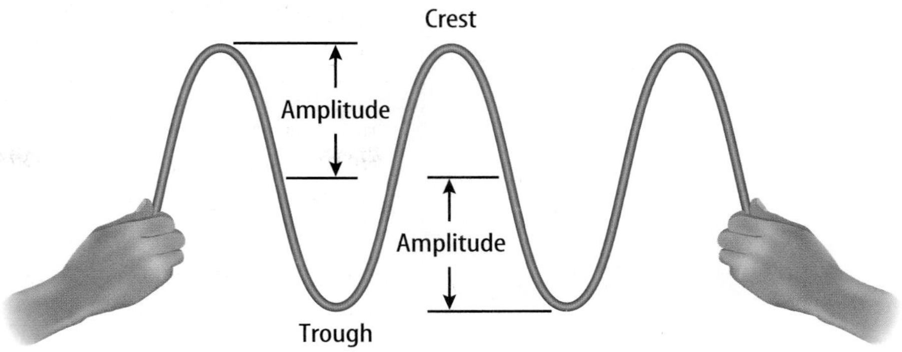

## Amplitude of a Compressional Wave
The amplitude of a compressional wave depends on the density of material in compressions and rarefactions as shown in **Figure 6.** Compressional waves with greater amplitude have compressions that are more squeezed together and rarefactions that are more spread apart. For example, in a spring, squeezing some coils together more tightly causes the nearby coils to be more spread apart.

**Reading Check** *What is the amplitude of a compressional wave?*

## Amplitude and Energy
The vibrations that produce a wave transfer energy to the wave. The more energy a wave carries, the larger its amplitude. By moving your hand up and down a larger distance in making a wave on a rope, you transfer more energy to the wave. Seismic waves are produced by vibrations in Earth's crust that cause earthquakes. The more energy these waves have, the larger their amplitudes and the more damage they cause as they travel along Earth's surface.

Crest

Amplitude

Amplitude

Trough

**Figure 5** The amplitude of a transverse wave depends on the height of the crests or the depth of the troughs.

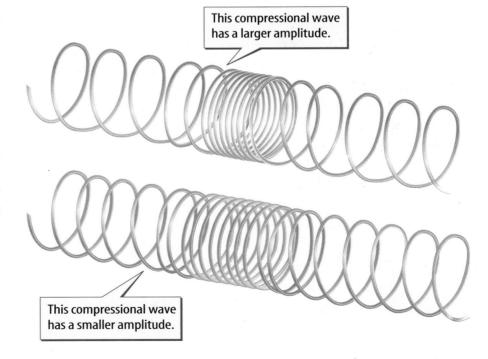

This compressional wave has a larger amplitude.

This compressional wave has a smaller amplitude.

**Figure 6** The amplitude of a compressional wave depends on the density of the material in the compressions and rarefactions.

**Wave Speed** The speed of a wave depends on the medium in which the wave travels. The faster waves travel, the more crests or compressions pass by you each second. You can calculate the speed of a wave if you know its wavelength and frequency using the equation below.

**Physical Setting**

**4.4c Analyze** how vibrational waves move at different speeds in different materials. Support your reasoning with examples.

### Wave Speed Equation

**wave speed** (in m/s) = **wavelength** (in m) × **frequency** (in Hz)

$$v = \lambda f$$

In this equation, $v$ is the symbol for wave speed and $f$ is the symbol for frequency. The SI unit for frequency is the hertz, abbreviated Hz. One hertz equals one vibration per second, or one wavelength passing a point in one second. One hertz is equal to the unit $1/s$. The wavelength is represented by the Greek letter lambda, $\lambda$, and is measured in meters.

*Hot Words Hot Topics*: Bk 2 (1) pp. 132–136, 276–278; (2) pp. 132–136, 276–278

## Applying Math     Solve a Simple Equation

**SPEED OF SOUND** A sound wave produced by a lightning bolt has a frequency of 34 Hz and a wavelength of 10.0 m. What is the speed of the sound wave?

### Solution

**1** *This is what you know:*
- wavelength: $\lambda = 10$ m
- frequency: $f = 34$ Hz

**2** *This is what you need to find:*   wave speed: $v = ?$ m/s

**3** *This is the procedure you need to use:*   Substitute the known values for wavelength and frequency into the wave speed equation and calculate the wave speed:

$$v = \lambda f = (10.0 \text{ m})(34 \text{ Hz})$$
$$= 340 \text{ m} \times \text{Hz} = 340 \text{ m} \times (1/s) = 340 \text{ m/s}$$

**4** *Check your answer:*   Divide your answer by the wavelength 10.0 m. The result should be the given frequency 34 Hz.

### Practice Problems

1. Waves on a string have a wavelength of 0.55 m. If the frequency of the waves is 6.0 Hz, what is the wave speed?

2. If the frequency of a sound wave in water is 15,000 Hz, and the sound wave travels through water at a speed of 1,500 m/s, what is the wavelength?

**Science**Online   For more practice, visit glencoe.com

# Waves Can Change Direction

Waves don't always travel in a straight line. When you look into a mirror, you use the mirror to make light waves change direction. Waves can change direction when they travel from one material to another. The waves can reflect (bounce off a surface), refract (change direction), or diffract (bend around an obstacle).

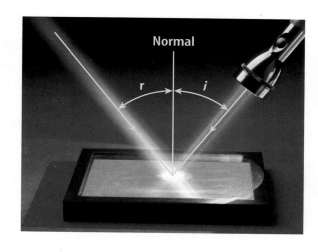

**Figure 7** All waves obey the law of reflection. The angle of reflection, *r*, always equals the angle of incidence, *i*.

**The Law of Reflection** When waves reflect off a surface, they always obey the law of reflection, as shown in **Figure 7.** A line that makes an angle of 90 degrees with a surface is called the normal to the surface. According to **law of reflection,** the angle that the incoming wave makes with the normal equals the angle that the outgoing wave makes with the normal.

**Refraction** The speed of the wave depends on properties of the material through which it travels. A light wave, for example, travels faster through air than it does through water. **Figure 8** shows that a change in a wave's speed changes the direction in which the wave travels. When the light wave moves from air to water, it slows down. This change in speed causes the light wave to bend. **Refraction** is the change in direction of a wave when it changes speed as it travels from one material to another.

**Figure 8** Refraction occurs when a wave changes speed. Light waves change direction when they slow down as they pass from air to water.

## Mini LAB

### Refraction of Light

**Procedure**
1. Fill a **drinking glass** about half full with water.
2. Place a **pencil** in the glass. Describe the appearance of the pencil.
3. Slowly add water to the glass. Describe how the appearance of the pencil changes.

**Analysis**
1. How does the appearance of the pencil depend on the level of water in the glass?
2. Where do the light waves coming from the pencil change speed?
3. **Infer** how the appearance of the pencil and the change in speed of the light waves are related.

*Try at Home*

**Diffraction** Waves can change direction by **diffraction,** which is the bending of waves around an object. In **Figure 9,** the water waves are not completely blocked by the obstacle, but instead bend around the obstacle.

The amount of diffraction or bending of the wave depends on the size of the obstacle the wave encounters. If the size of the obstacle is much larger than the wavelength, very little diffraction occurs. Then there is a shadow behind the object where there are no waves.

As the wavelength increases compared with the size of the obstacle, the amount of diffraction increases. The amount of diffraction is greatest if the wavelength is much larger than the obstacle.

**Figure 9** The amount of diffraction or bending around an obstacle depends on the size of the obstacle and the wavelength of the wave.

**Diffraction of Sound and Light** The wavelengths of sound waves are similar to the size of objects around you, but the wavelength of light waves are much shorter. As a result, you can hear people talking in a room with an open door even though you can't see them.

## section 1 review

### Summary

**Wave Energy**
- Waves transport energy without transporting matter.

**Types of Waves**
- Transverse waves cause particles in a material to move back and forth at right angles to the direction the waves travel.
- Compressional waves cause particles in a material to move back and forth along the same direction the waves travel.
- Electromagnetic waves are transverse waves that can travel through empty space.

**Wave Properties**
- A wave can be described by its wavelength, frequency, and amplitude.
- The energy carried by a wave increases as the amplitude of the wave increases.
- The speed of a wave, $v$, equals its wavelength, $\lambda$, multiplied by its frequency, $f$:
$$v = \lambda f$$
- Reflection, refraction, or diffraction can cause waves to change direction.

### Self Check

1. **Analyze** How can waves transport energy without transporting matter from place to another?

2. **Explain** how the spacing between coils of a spring changes if the amplitude of compressional waves traveling along the spring increases.

3. **Predict** how the wavelength of waves traveling with the same speed would change if the frequency of the waves increases.

4. **Apply** Two similar-sized stones, one heavy and one light, are dropped from the same height into a pond. Explain why the impact of the heavy stone would produce waves with higher amplitude than the impact of the light stone would.

5. **Think Critically** Water waves produced by a speed boat strike a floating inner tube. Describe the motion of the inner tube as the waves pass by.

*Hot Words Hot Topics*: Bk 2 (6) pp. 132–136, 276–278; (7) pp. 132–136, 276–278

#### Applying Math

6. **Calculate Wave Speed** Find the speed of a wave with a wavelength of 0.2 m and a frequency of 1.5 Hz.

7. **Calculate Wavelength** Find the wavelength of a wave with a speed of 3.0 m/s and a frequency of 0.5 Hz.

# Sound Waves

## Making Sound Waves

How does the motion of a drummer's drumsticks produce sound waves? The impact of the sticks on the head of a drum causes the drum head to vibrate. These vibrations transfer energy to nearby air particles, producing sound waves in air. You can hear the sound because energy from the drums travels as sound waves to your ears. Every sound you hear is caused by something vibrating. For example, when you talk, tissues in your throat vibrate in different ways to form sounds.

**Sound Waves are Compressional Waves** Sound waves produced by a vibrating object are compressional waves. **Figure 10** shows how the vibrating drum produces compressional waves. When the drummer hits the drum, the head of the drum vibrates. Nearby air particles vibrate with the same frequency as the frequency of vibrations. The drum head moving outward compresses nearby air particles. The drum head moving inward causes rarefactions in nearby air particles. The inward and outward movement of the drum head produces the same pattern of compressions and rarefactions in the air particles.

Sound waves can only travel through matter. The energy carried by a sound wave is transferred by the collisions between the particles in the material the wave is traveling in. A spaceship traveling outside Earth's atmosphere, for example, does not make any sound outside the ship.

*What* **You'll Learn**

- **Describe** how sound waves are produced.
- **Explain** how sound waves travel through matter.
- **Describe** the relationship between loudness and sound intensity.
- **Explain** how humans hear sound.

*Why* **It's Important**

A knowledge of sound helps you understand how to protect your hearing.

**Review Vocabulary**
**perception:** a recognition, sense, or understanding of something

**New Vocabulary**
- intensity
- pitch
- reverberation

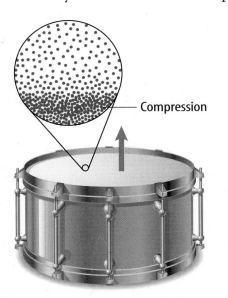

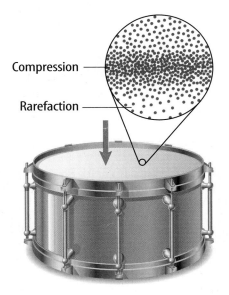

Compression

Compression

Rarefaction

**Figure 10** A vibrating drumhead produces a sound wave. The drum head produces a compression each time it moves upward and a rarefaction each time it moves downward.

| Table 1  Speed of Sound in Different Materials | |
| --- | --- |
| Material | Speed (m/s) |
| Air (20°C) | 343 |
| Glass | 5,640 |
| Steel | 5,940 |
| Water (25°C) | 1,493 |
| Seawater (25°C) | 1,533 |
| Rubber | 1,600 |
| Diamond | 12,000 |
| Iron | 5,130 |

**Figure 11** The loudness of a sound depends on the amount of energy the sound waves carry.

# The Speed of Sound

Like all waves, the speed of sound depends on the matter through which it travels. Sound waves travel faster through solids and liquids. **Table 1** shows the speed of sound in different materials.

The speed of sound through a material increases as the temperature of the material increases. The effect of temperature is greatest in gases. For example, the speed of sound in air increases from about 330 m/s to about 350 m/s as the air temperature increases from 0° to 30°C.

 **Reading Check**  *How does temperature affect the speed of sound through a material?*

# The Loudness of Sound

What makes a sound loud or soft? The girl in **Figure 11** can make a loud sound by clapping the cymbals together sharply. She can make a soft sound by clapping the cymbals together gently. The difference is the amount of energy the girl gives to the cymbals. Loud sounds have more energy than soft sounds.

**Intensity**  The amount of energy that a wave carries past a certain area each second is the **intensity** of the sound. **Figure 12** shows how the intensity of sound from the cymbals decreases with distance. A person standing close when the girl claps the cymbals would hear an intense sound. The sound would be less intense for someone standing farther away. The intensity of sound waves is related to the amplitude. Sound with a greater amplitude also has a greater intensity.

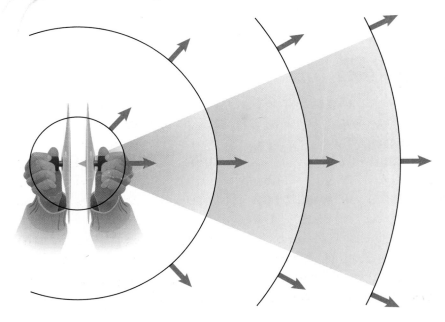

**Figure 12** The intensity of a sound wave decreases as the wave spreads out from the source of the sound. The energy the wave carries is spread over a larger area.

## Loudness in Decibels

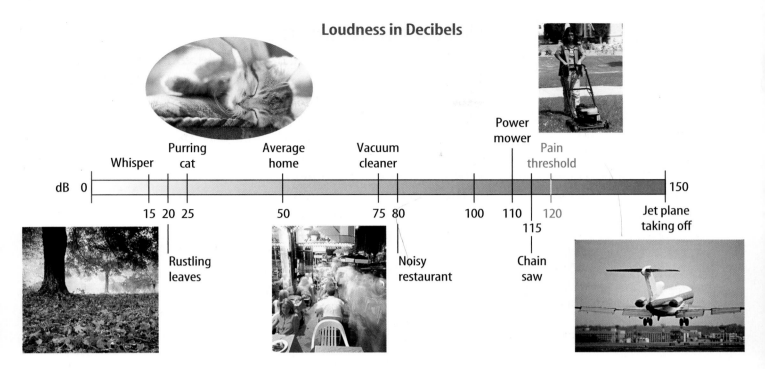

**The Decibel Scale and Loudness** The intensity of sound waves is measured in units of decibels (dB), as shown in **Figure 13.** The softest sound a person can hear has an intensity of 0 dB. Normal conversation has an intensity of about 50 dB. Sound with intensities of about 120 dB or higher are painful to people.

Loudness is the human perception of the intensity of sound waves. Each increase of 10 dB in intensity multiplies the energy of the sound waves ten times. Most people perceive this as a doubling of the loudness of the sound. An intensity increase of 20 dB corresponds to a hundred times the energy and an increase in loudness of about four times.

 *How much has the energy of a sound wave changed if its intensity has increased by 30 dB?*

## Frequency and Pitch

The frequency of sound waves is determined by the frequency of the vibrations that produce the sound. Recall that wave frequency is measured in units of hertz (Hz), which is the number of vibrations each second. On the musical scale, the note C has a frequency of 262 Hz. The note E has a frequency of 330 Hz. People are usually able to hear sounds with frequencies between about 20 Hz and 20,000 Hz.

**Pitch** is the human perception of the frequency of sound. The sounds from a tuba have a low pitch and the sounds from a flute have a high pitch. Sounds with low frequencies have low pitch and sounds with high frequencies have high pitch.

**Figure 13** The intensity of sound is measured on the decibel scale.
**Infer** *how many times louder a power mower is compared to a noisy restaurant.*

**Hearing Damage**
Prolonged exposure to sounds above 85 dB can damage your hearing. Research to find out the danger of noise levels you might experience at activities such as loud music concerts or basketball games.

# Hearing and the Ear

The ear is a complex organ that can detect a wide range of sounds. You may think that the ear is just the structure that you see on the side of your head. However, the ear can be divided into three parts—the outer ear, the middle ear, and the inner ear. **Figure 14** shows the different parts of the human ear.

**The Outer Ear** The outer ear is a sound collector. It consists of the part that you can see and the ear canal. The visible part is shaped somewhat like a funnel. This shape helps the visible part collect sound waves and direct them into the ear canal.

**The Middle Ear** The middle air is a sound amplifier. It consists of the ear drum and three tiny bones called the hammer, the anvil, and the stirrup. Sound waves that pass through the ear canal cause the eardrum to vibrate. Theses vibrations are transmitted to the three small bones, which amplify the vibrations.

**The Inner Ear** The inner ear contains the cochlea. The cochlea is filled with fluid and is lined with tiny hair-like cells. Vibrations of the stirrup bone are transmitted to the hair cells. The movement of the hair cells produce signals that travel to your brain, where they are interpreted as sound.

**Physical Setting**

4.4c **Explain** why sound cannot travel in a vacuum.

**Figure 14** The human ear can be divided into three parts. The outer ear is the sound collector, the middle ear is the sound amplifier, and the inner ear is the sound interpreter.

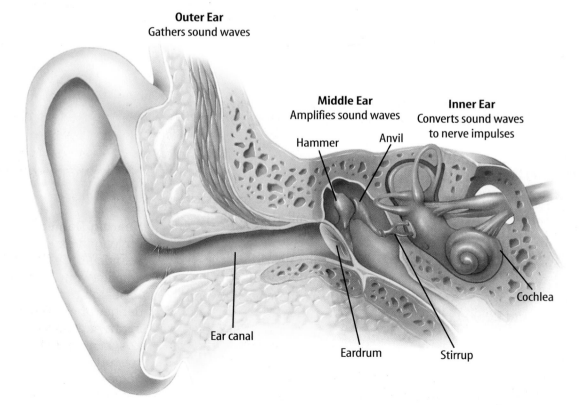

**Outer Ear**
Gathers sound waves

**Middle Ear**
Amplifies sound waves

**Inner Ear**
Converts sound waves to nerve impulses

Hammer

Anvil

Ear canal

Eardrum

Stirrup

Cochlea

# The Reflection of Sound

Have you ever stood in an empty room and heard echoes when you talked very loudly? Echoes are sounds that reflect off surfaces. Repeated echoes are called **reverberation.** Concert halls and auditoriums are designed with soft materials on the ceilings and walls to avoid too much reverberation. Theaters like the one in **Figure 15** often have curtains on the walls because sounds won't reflect off soft surfaces. The curtains absorb the energy of the sound waves.

The reflection of sound can be used to locate or identify objects. Echolocation is the process of locating objects by bouncing sounds off them. Bats, dolphins, and other animals emit short, high-frequency sound waves toward a certain area. By interpreting the reflected waves, the animals can locate and determine properties of other animals. Doctors use reflection of sound waves in medicine. Computers can analyze ultrasonic waves that reflect off body parts to produce an internal picture of the body. These pictures help doctors monitor pregnancies, heart problems, and other medical conditions.

**Figure 15** A modern concert hall contains materials that absorb sound waves to control reverberation and other sound reflections.

## section 2 review

### Summary

**Making Sound Waves**

- Sound waves are compressional waves produced by something vibrating.
- The speed of sound waves depends on the material in which the waves travel and its temperature.

**Loudness and Pitch**

- The intensity of a wave is the amount of energy the wave transports each second across a unit surface.
- The intensity of sound waves is measured in units of decibels.
- Loudness is the human perception of sound intensity.
- Pitch is the human perception of the frequency of a sound.

**Hearing Sound**

- You hear a sound when a sound wave reaches your ear and causes structures in your ear to vibrate.

### Self Check

1. **Explain** why you hear a sound when you clap your hands together.
2. **Predict** whether sound will would travel faster in air in the summer or in the winter.
3. **Compare and contrast** the sound waves produced by someone whispering and someone shouting.
4. **Describe** how vibrations produced in your ear by a sound wave enable you to hear the sound.
5. **Think Critically** Vibrations cause sounds, yet if you move your hand back and forth through the air, you don't hear a sound. Explain.

*Hot Words Hot Topics*: Bk 2(6) pp. 106, 292; 7: pp. 87–88

### Applying Math

6. **Calculate a Ratio** How many times louder is a sound wave with an intensity of 50 dB than a sound wave with an intensity of 20 dB?
7. **Calculate Increase in Intensity** If the energy carried by a sound wave is multiplied by a thousand times, by what factor does the intensity of the sound wave increase?

# Sound Waves in Matter

In this lab you can hear differences in sound when the sound waves travel through various materials.

## Real-World Question

How does the movement of sound waves through different materials affect the sounds we hear?

### Goals

■ **Notice** the variations in sound when sound waves travel through different materials.

■ **Infer** what property of the materials cause the sound waves to produce a different sound.

### Materials

150-mL beakers (4)    corn syrup
water                 pencil
vegetable oil

### Safety Precautions

## Procedure

1. Fill a beaker to the 140-mL line with water. Fill another beaker with 140 mL of vegetable oil. Fill a third beaker with 140 mL of corn syrup. Leave the fourth beaker empty.

2. Hold the pencil securely and tap the side of the beaker about halfway down from its rim. Use the metal band near the end of the pencil to make a clear sound.

3. Pay careful attention to the pitch of the sound. Notice whether the sound continues for a moment after the tap or if it stops suddenly. Write a description of the sound you hear in your data table.

4. Repeat steps 3 and 4 for the remaining beakers. You may wish to tap each beaker several times to be sure you hear the sound well.

5. **Compare** the sounds made by the beaker filled with air and the beaker filled with the different liquids.

## Conclude and Apply

1. **List** the materials in the beakers in order of increasing density.

2. **Infer** how the pitch of the sound changes as the density of the material in the beaker increases.

3. How does the density of the material in the beaker affect how long the sound continued to be heard after the beaker was tapped?

### Communicating Your Data

Compare your results with other students in your class.

PS 4.4a: Different forms of electromagnetic energy have different wavelengths. Some examples of electromagnetic energy are microwaves, infrared light, visible light, ultraviolet light, X-rays, and gamma rays.
**Also Covered:** PS 4.4b

# Light

## Waves in Empty Space

On a clear night you might see the Moon shining brightly, as in **Figure 16.** Like other waves, light waves can travel through matter, but light waves are different from water waves and sound waves. Light from the Moon has traveled through space that contains almost no matter. You can see light from the moon, distant stars, and galaxies because light is an electromagnetic wave. **Electromagnetic waves** are waves that can travel through matter or through empty space.

**The Speed of Light** Have you ever seen a movie where a spaceship travels faster than the speed of light? In reality, nothing travels faster than the speed of light. In empty space, light travels at a speed of about 300,000 km/s. Light travels so fast that light emitted from the Sun travels 150 million km to Earth in only about eight and a half minutes.

However, when light travels in matter, it interacts with the atoms and molecules in the material and slows down. As a result, light travels fastest in empty space, and travels slowest in solids. In glass, for example, light travels about 197,000 km/s.

**Wavelength and Frequency of Light** Can you guess how long a wavelength of light is? Wavelengths of light are usually expressed in units of nanometers (nm). One nanometer is equal to one billionth of a meter. For example, green light has a wavelength of about 500 nm, or 500 billionths of a meter. A light wave with this wavelength has a frequency of 600 trillion Hz.

**as you read**

*What* **You'll Learn**
- **Identify** the properties of light waves.
- **Describe** the electromagnetic spectrum.
- **Describe** the types of electromagnetic waves that travel from the Sun to Earth.
- **Explain** human vision and color perception.

*Why* **It's Important**

Light is necessary for vision. Other electromagnetic waves are used in devices such as cell phones and microwave ovens.

**Review Vocabulary**
**spectrum:** a range of values or properties

**New Vocabulary**
- electromagnetic waves
- electromagnetic spectrum
- infrared waves
- ultraviolet waves

**Figure 16** The Moon reflects light from the Sun. These light waves travel through space to reach your eyes.
**Infer** *whether a sound wave could travel from the Moon to Earth.*

**Figure 17** A light wave is a transverse wave that contains vibrating electric and magnetic fields. The fields vibrate at right angles to the direction the wave travels.

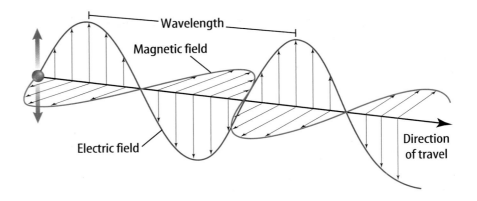

Wavelength

Magnetic field

Electric field

Direction of travel

**Science** nline

**Topic: Lasers**
Visit glencoe.com for Web links to information about why the intensity of light emitted by lasers makes them useful.

**Activity** Write a short paragraph describing three uses for lasers.

# Properties of Light Waves

Light waves, and all electromagnetic waves, are transverse waves. Recall that a wave on a rope is a transverse wave that causes the rope to move at right angles to the direction the wave is traveling. An electromagnetic wave traveling through matter also can cause matter to move at right angles to the direction the wave is moving.

An electromagnetic wave contains an electric part and a magnetic part, as shown in **Figure 17.** Both parts are called fields and vibrate at right angles to the wave motion. The number of times the electric and magnetic parts vibrate each second is the frequency of the wave. The wavelength is the distance between the crests or troughs of the vibrating electric or magnetic parts.

**Intensity of Light Waves** The intensity of waves is a measure of the amount of energy that the waves carry. For light waves, the intensity determines the brightness of the light. A dim light has lower intensity because the waves carry less energy. However, as you move away from a light source, the energy spreads out and the intensity decreases.

✔ **Reading Check** *What determines the intensity of light waves?*

# The Electromagnetic Spectrum

Light waves aren't the only kind of electromagnetic waves. In fact, there is an entire spectrum of electromagnetic waves, as shown in **Figure 18.** The **electromagnetic spectrum** is the complete range of electromagnetic wave frequencies and wavelengths. At one end of the spectrum the waves have low frequency, long wavelength, and low energy. At the other end of the spectrum the waves have high frequency, short wavelength, and high energy. All of the waves—from radio waves to visible light to gamma rays—are the same kind of waves. They differ from each other only by their frequencies, wavelengths, and energy.

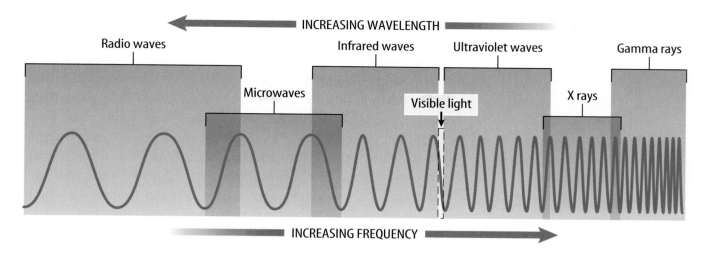

INCREASING WAVELENGTH

Radio waves | Microwaves | Infrared waves | Ultraviolet waves | Gamma rays

Visible light | X rays

INCREASING FREQUENCY

## Radio Waves and Microwaves

The waves that carry radio and television signals to your home are radio waves. The wavelengths of radio waves are greater than about 0.3 meters. Some are even thousands of meters long. The shortest radio waves are called microwaves. These waves have a wavelength between about 0.3 meters and 0.001 meters. You use these waves when you cook food in a microwave oven. Microwaves are also used to transmit information to and from cell phones.

## Infrared Waves

When you use a remote control, infrared waves travel from the remote to a receiver on your television. **Infrared waves** have wavelengths between 0.001 meters and 700 billionths of a meter. All warm bodies emit infrared waves. Because of this, law enforcement officials and military personnel sometimes use special night goggles that are sensitive to infrared waves. These goggles can be used to help locate people in the dark.

## Visible Light and Color

The range of electromagnetic waves between 700 and 400 billionths of a meter is special, because that is the range of wavelengths people can see. Electromagnetic waves in this range are called visible light. **Figure 19** shows how different wavelengths correspond to different colors of light. White light, like the light from the Sun or a flashlight, is really a combination of different colors. You can see this by using a prism to separate white light into different colors. When the light passes through the prism, the different wavelengths of light are bent different amounts. Violet light is bent the most because it has the shortest wavelength. Red light is bent the least.

**Reading Check** *What range of wavelengths of electromagnetic waves can people see?*

**Figure 18** Electromagnetic waves have a range of frequencies and wavelengths called the electromagnetic spectrum.
**Infer** *how the frequency of electromagnetic waves change as their wavelength decreases.*

**Figure 19** Visible light waves are electromagnetic waves with a narrow range of wavelengths from about 700 to 400 billionths of a meter. The color of visible light waves depends on their wavelength.
**Determine** *the color of the visible light waves with the highest frequency.*

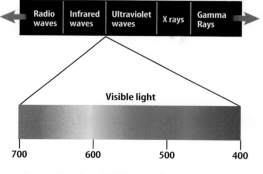

Radio waves | Infrared waves | Ultraviolet waves | X rays | Gamma Rays

Visible light

700   600   500   400

Wavelength (billionths of a meter)

**Ultraviolet Waves** Electromagnetic waves with wavelengths between about 400 billionths and 10 billionths of a meter are **ultraviolet waves.** These wavelengths are shorter than those of visible light. Ultraviolet waves carry more energy than visible light waves. Sunlight that reaches Earth's surface contains a small fraction of ultraviolet waves. These waves can cause sunburn if skin is exposed to sunlight for too long. Excessive exposure to ultraviolet waves can permanently damage skin, and in some cases cause skin cancer. However, some exposure to ultraviolet waves is needed for your body to make vitamin D, which helps form healthy bones and teeth.

**X Rays and Gamma Rays** The electromagnetic waves with the highest energy, highest frequency, and shortest wavelengths are X rays and gamma rays. If you've ever broken a bone, the doctor probably took an X ray to examine the injured area. X rays are energetic enough to pass through the body. X rays pass through soft tissues, but are blocked by denser body parts, such as bones. This enables images to be made of internal body parts. Gamma rays are even more energetic than X rays. One use of gamma rays is in the food industry to kill bacteria that might increase the rate of spoilage of food.

**Electromagnetic Waves from the Sun** Most of the energy emitted by the Sun is in the form of ultraviolet, visible, and infrared waves, as shown in **Figure 20.** These waves carry energy away from the Sun and spread out in all directions. Only a tiny fraction of this energy reaches Earth. Most of the ultraviolet waves from the Sun are blocked by Earth's atmosphere. As a result, almost all energy from the Sun that reaches Earth's surface is carried by infrared and visible electromagnetic waves.

**Figure 20** About 49 percent of the electromagnetic waves emitted by the Sun are infrared waves, about 43 percent are visible light, and about 7 percent are ultraviolet waves.

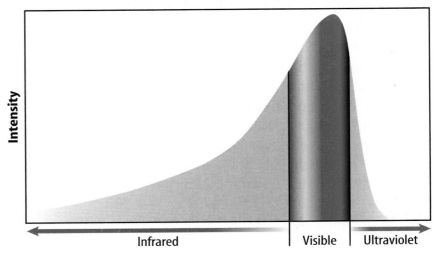

**Electromagnetic Waves from the Sun**

Intensity

Infrared | Visible | Ultraviolet

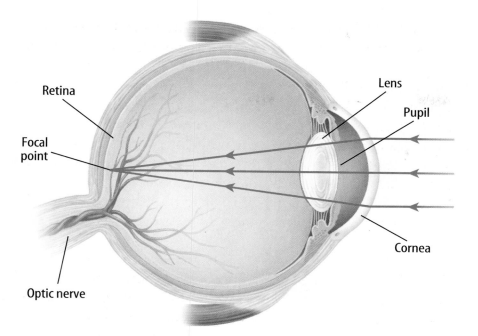

Retina

Focal point

Optic nerve

Lens

Pupil

Cornea

**Figure 21** The cornea and the lens focus light waves that enter your eye so that a sharp image is formed on the retina. Special cells in the retina cause signals to be sent to the brain when they are struck by light.

# The Eye and Seeing Light

You see an object when light emitted or reflected from the object enters your eye, as shown in **Figure 21.** Light waves first pass through a transparent layer called the cornea (KOR nee uh), and then the transparent lens. The lens is flexible and changes shape to enable you to focus on objects that are nearby and far away, as shown in **Figure 22.** However, sometimes the eye is unable to form sharp images of both nearby and distant objects, as shown in **Figure 23** on the next page.

**Why do objects have color?** When light waves strike an object, some of the light waves are reflected. The wavelengths of the light waves that are reflected determine the object's color. For example, a red rose reflects light waves that have wavelengths in the red part of the visible spectrum. The color of objects that emit light is determined by the wavelengths of light that they emit. A neon sign appears to be red because it emits red light waves.

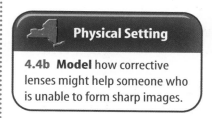

**Physical Setting**

**4.4b Model** how corrective lenses might help someone who is unable to form sharp images.

**Figure 22** The shape of the lens changes when you focus on nearby and distant objects.

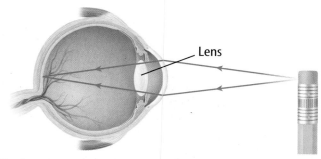

The lens becomes flatter when you focus on a distant object.

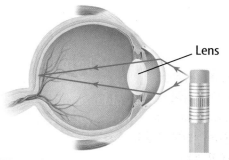

The lens becomes more curved when you focus on an object nearby.

## Figure 23

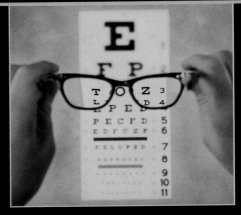

In a human eye, light waves pass through the transparent cornea and the lens of the eye. The cornea and the lens cause light waves from an object to be focused on the retina, forming a sharp image. However, vision problems result when a sharp image is not formed on the retina. The two most common vision problems are farsightedness and nearsightedness.

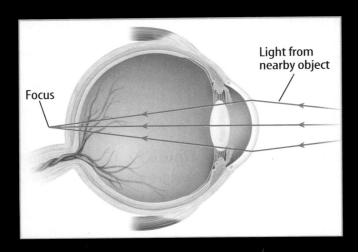

Focus

Light from distant object

◄ **Nearsightedness** A person that is nearsighted can see nearby objects clearly, but distant objects seem blurry. Nearsightedness results if the eyeball is too long, so that light waves from far away objects are brought to a focus before they reach the retina. This vision problem usually is corrected by wearing glasses or contact lenses. Laser surgery also is used to correct nearsightedness by reshaping the cornea.

Focus

Light from nearby object

◄ **Farsightedness** A farsighted person can see distant objects clearly, but cannot focus clearly on nearby objects. Farsightedness results if the eyeball is too short, so light waves from nearby objects have not been brought to a focus when they strike the retina.

► **Farsightedness** also can be corrected by wearing glasses. People commonly become farsighted as they get older because of changes in the lens of the eye. Laser surgery sometimes is used to correct farsightedness.

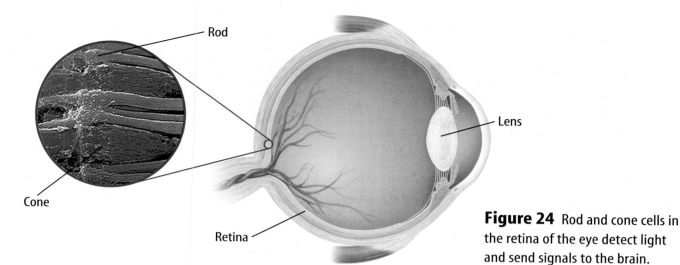

Rod

Lens

Cone

Retina

**Figure 24** Rod and cone cells in the retina of the eye detect light and send signals to the brain.

**Rod and Cone Cells** The retina contains over a hundred million light-sensitive cells called rods and cones, shown in **Figure 24.** Rod cells are sensitive to dim light, and cone cells enable you to see colors. There are three types of cone cells. One type is sensitive to red and yellow light, another type is sensitive to green and yellow light, and the third type is sensitive to blue and violet light. The combination of the signals sent to the brain by all three types of cone cells forms the color image that you see.

 **Physical Setting**

**4.4b Hypothesize** how the rods and cones might be different in someone who is red-green color blind as compared to someone with normal vision.

## section 3 review

### Summary

**Light and Electromagnetic Waves**

- Light waves are electromagnetic waves. These waves travel through empty space at a speed of 300,000 km/s.

- Electromagnetic waves are transverse waves made of vibrating electric and magnetic fields.

- Radio waves, infrared waves, visible light, ultraviolet waves, X rays, and gamma rays form the electromagnetic spectrum.

- Most of the electromagnetic waves emitted by the Sun are infrared waves, visible light, and ultraviolet waves.

**Color and Vision**

- The color of an object is the color of the light the object emits or reflects.

- You see an object when light waves emitted or reflected by the object enter your eye and strike the retina.

- Rod cells and cone cells in the retina of the eye are light-sensitive cells that send signals to the brain when light strikes them.

### Self Check

1. **Identify** the electromagnetic waves with the longest wavelengths and the electromagnetic waves with the shortest wavelengths.

2. **Describe** the difference between radio waves, visible light, and gamma rays.

3. **Compare and contrast** the rod cells and the cone cells in the retina of the human eye.

4. **Explain** why most of the electromagnetic waves emitted by the Sun that strike Earth's surface are infrared and visible light waves.

5. **Think Critically** Explain why the brightness of the light emitted by a flashlight decreases as the flashlight moves farther away from you.

### Applying Skills

6. **Make a Concept Map** Design a concept map to show the sequence of events that occurs when you see a blue object.

7. **Recognize Cause and Effect** Why does light travel faster through empty space than it does through matter?

# Bending Light

## Goals

- **Compare and contrast** the reflection, refraction, and transmission of light.
- **Observe** how the refraction of white light can produce different colors of light.

## Materials

small piece of cardboard
scissors
tape
flashlight
flat mirror
clear plastic CD case
250-mL beaker
prism

## Safety Precautions

## ◉ Real-World Question

What happens to light waves when they strike the boundary between two materials? Some of the light waves might be reflected from the boundary and some of the waves might travel into the second material. These light waves can change direction and be refracted in the second material. Transmission occurs when the light waves finally pass through the second material. What happens to light waves when they strike a boundary between air and other materials?

## ◉ Procedure

1. Make a data table similar to the one shown below.

### Bending of Light by Different Surfaces

| Surface | How Beam is Affected | Colors Formed |
|---------|---------------------|---------------|
| Mirror | | |
| CD case | Do not write in this book. | |
| Water | | |
| Prism | | |

2. Cut a slit about 3 cm long and 2 mm wide in a circular piece of cardboard. Tape the cardboard to the face of the flashlight.

3. In a darkened room, shine the flashlight at an angle toward the mirror. Determine whether the flashlight beam is reflected, refracted, or transmitted. Look at the color of the light beam after it strikes the mirror. Has the white light been changed into different colors of light? Record your observations on the chart.

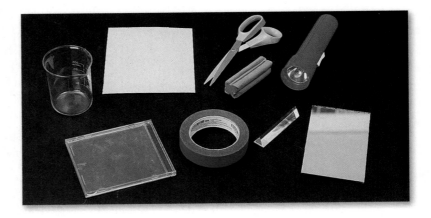

4. Remove the clear plastic front from an empty CD case. Shine the flashlight at an angle toward the plastic. Does transmission occur? Record your observations about how the direction of the beam changes and colors of the light.

5. Fill the beaker with water. Shine the flashlight toward the side of the beaker so that the light shines through the water. Move the light beam from side to side. Record your observations.

6. Shine the flashlight toward a side of the prism. Move the light beam around until you see the outgoing beam spread into different colors. Record your observations.

## ▶ Analyze Your Data

1. For which objects did reflection occur? For which objects did refraction occur? For which objects did transmission occur?

2. For which objects did refraction cause the flashlight beam to be separated into different colors?

## ▶ Conclude and Apply

1. **Compare and contrast** the behavior of light waves when they strike the mirror and the CD case.

2. **Explain** why the beam that passes through the CD case does or does not change direction.

3. **Describe** how the light beam changes after it passes through the prism.

### Communicating Your Data

Create a sketch showing how light refracts in a prism and divides into different colors.

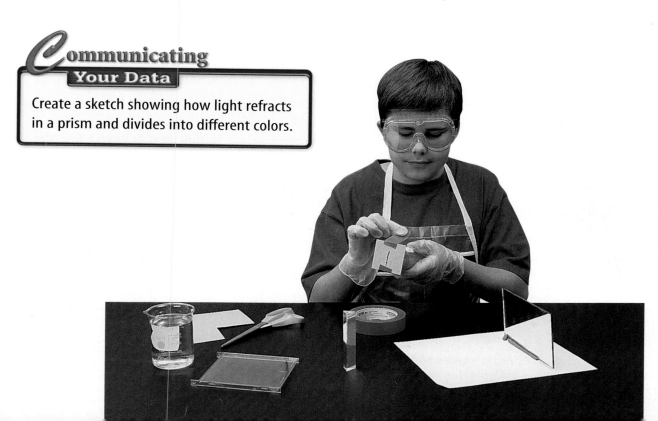

# Jansky's Merry-Go-Round

**B**efore the first radio signals were sent across the Atlantic Ocean in 1902, ships could only communicate if they could see one another. Being able to communicate using radio waves was a real breakthrough. But it wasn't without its problems—namely lots of static. Around 1930, Bell Labs was trying to improve radio communication by using radio waves with shorter wavelengths—between 10 and 20 m. They put Karl Jansky to work finding out what might be causing the static.

**Karl Jansky built the first radiotelescope.**

## An Unexpected Discovery

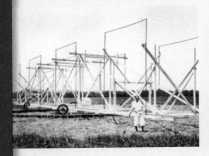

**This antenna built by Janksy detected radio waves from the Milky Way galaxy.**

Jansky built an antenna to receive radio waves with a wavelength of about 14.5 m. He mounted it on a turntable so that he could rotate it in any direction. His coworkers called it "Jansky's merry-go-round."

After recording signals for several months, Jansky found that there were three types of static. Two were caused by nearby and distant thunderstorms.

But the third was totally unexpected. It seemed to come from the center of our Milky Way galaxy! Jansky wanted to follow up on this unexpected discovery, but Bell Labs had the information it wanted. They were in the telephone business, not astronomy!

## A New Branch of Astronomy

Fortunately, other scientists were fascinated with Jansky's find. Grote Reber built a "radiotelescope" in his Illinois backyard. He confirmed Jansky's discovery and did the first systematic survey of radio waves from space. The field of radioastronomy was born.

Previously, astronomers could observe distant galaxies only by gathering the light arriving from their stars. But they couldn't see past the clouds of gas and small particles surrounding the galaxies. Radio waves emitted by a galaxy can penetrate much of the gas and dust in space. This allows radio astronomers to make images of galaxies and other objects they can't see. As a result, Radio astronomy has revealed previously invisible objects such as quasars and pulsars.

**The blue-white colors in this image are all you could see without radio waves.**

**Experiment** Research how astronomers convert the radio waves received by radio telescopes into images of galaxies and stars.

## Reviewing Main Ideas

### Section 1 Waves

1. Waves carry energy from place to place without transporting matter.

2. Transverse waves move particles in matter at right angles to the direction in which the waves travel.

3. Compressional waves move particles back and forth along the same direction in which the waves travel.

4. The speed of a wave equals its wavelength multiplied by its frequency.

### Section 2 Sound Waves

1. Sound waves are compressional waves produced by something vibrating.

2. The intensity of sound waves is measured in units of decibels.

3. You hear sound when sound waves reach your ear and cause parts of the ear to vibrate.

### Section 3 Light

1. Electromagnetic waves are transverse waves that can travel in matter or empty space.

2. Light waves are electromagnetic waves.

3. The range of frequencies and wavelengths of electromagnetic waves forms the electromagnetic spectrum.

4. You see an object when light waves emitted or reflected by the object enter your eye and strike light-sensitive cells inside the eye.

## Visualizing Main Ideas

*Copy and complete the following concept map on waves.*

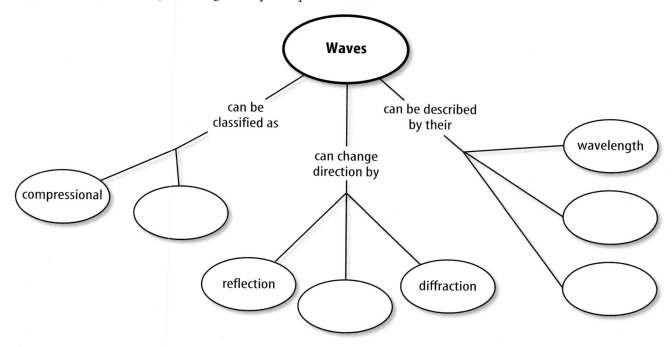

## Using Vocabulary

compressional wave p. 213
diffraction p. 218
electromagnetic
   spectrum p. 226
electromagnetic
   waves p. 225
frequency p. 214
infrared waves p. 227
intensity p. 220

law of reflection p. 217
pitch p. 221
refraction p. 217
reverberation p. 223
transverse wave p. 213
ultraviolet waves p. 228
wave p. 212
wavelength p. 214

*Complete each statement using a word(s) from the vocabulary list above.*

1. The bending of a wave when it moves from one material into another is _____.

2. The bending of waves around an object is due to _____.

3. The _____ is the complete range of electromagnetic wave frequencies and wavelengths.

4. The amount of energy that a wave carries past a certain area each second is the _____.

5. In a(n) _____, the particles in the material move at right angles to the direction the wave moves.

6. The _____ of a wave is the number of wavelengths that pass a point each second.

7. In a _____, particles in the material move back and forth along the direction of wave motion.

## Checking Concepts

*Choose the word or phrase that best answers the question.*

8. If the distance between the crest and trough of a wave is 0.6 m, what is the wave's amplitude?
   **A)** 0.3 m     **C)** 0.6 m
   **B)** 1.2 m     **D)** 2.4

9. Which of the following are units for measuring frequency?
   **A)** decibels     **C)** meters
   **B)** hertz     **D)** meters/second

10. Through which of these materials does sound travel fastest?
    **A)** empty space     **C)** steel
    **B)** water     **D)** air

11. An increase in a sound's pitch corresponds to an increase in what other property?
    **A)** intensity     **C)** wavelength
    **B)** frequency     **D)** loudness

12. Soft materials are sometimes used in concert halls to prevent what effect?
    **A)** refraction     **C)** compression
    **B)** diffraction     **D)** reverberation

13. Which of the following are not transverse waves?
    **A)** radio waves     **C)** sound waves
    **B)** infrared waves     **D)** visible light

14. Which of the following wave properties determines the energy carried by a wave?
    **A)** amplitude     **C)** wavelength
    **B)** frequency     **D)** wave speed

15. Which of the following best describes why refraction of a wave occurs when the wave travels from one material into another?
    **A)** The wavelength increases.
    **B)** The speed of the wave changes.
    **C)** The amplitude increases.
    **D)** The frequency decreases.

16. What produces waves?
    **A)** sound     **C)** transfer of energy
    **B)** heat     **D)** vibrations

17. Which of the following has wavelengths longer than the wavelengths of visible light?
    **A)** X rays     **C)** radio waves
    **B)** gamma rays     **D)** ultraviolet waves

## Thinking Critically

**18. Infer** Radio waves broadcast by a radio station strike your radio and your ear. Infer whether the human ear can hear radio waves. What evidence supports your conclusion?

**19. Solve an Equation** Robotic spacecraft on Mars have sent radio signals back to Earth. The distance from Mars to Earth, at its greatest, is about 401,300,000 km. About how many minutes would it take a signal to reach Earth from that distance?

**20. Recognize Cause and Effect** When a musician plucks a string on a guitar it produces sound with a certain pitch. If the musician then presses down on the string and plucks it, the sound produced has a shorter wavelength. How does the pitch of the sound change?

**21. Interpret Scientific Illustrations** One way that radio waves can carry signals to radios is by varying the amplitude of the wave. This is known as amplitude modulation (AM). Another way is by varying the frequency. This is called frequency modulation (FM). Which of the waves below shows AM, and which shows FM? Explain.

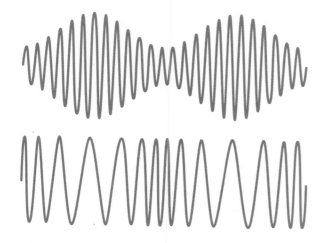

**22. Infer** When light passes through a prism, infer how the amount of bending of a light wave depends on the frequency of the light wave. How does the amount of bending depend on the wavelength of the light wave?

**23. Describe** how the lenses in your eyes change shape when you first look at your wristwatch to read the time, and then look at a mountain in the distance.

## Performance Activities

**24. Poster** Investigate a musical instrument to find out how it produces sound. Make a poster showing the instrument and describing how it works.

**25. Model** Make an instrument out of common materials. Present the instrument to the class, and explain how it can produce different pitches.

*Hot Words Hot Topics*: Bk 2 (26) pp. 106, 292; (27) pp. 132–136, 276–278; (28) pp. 132–136, 276–278; (29) pp. 132–136, 276–278

## Applying Math

**26. Noise Levels** A noisy restaurant has an intensity of about 80 dB, and a lawn mower has an intensity of about 110 dB. How many times louder does the lawn mower noise seem?

**27. Wavelength of Sound** Sound waves with a frequency of 150 Hz travel at a speed of 340 m/s. What is the wavelength of the sound waves?

**28. Ultrasound** Physicians sometimes use high-frequency sound waves to diagnose and monitor medical conditions. A typical frequency for the sound waves is about 5,000,000.0 Hz. Sound travels through soft body tissue at about 1500.0 m/s. What is the wavelength of the sound waves?

**29. Frequency of Radio Waves** Find the frequency of radio waves that have a wavelength of 15 m if they are traveling at a speed of 300,000,000 m/s.

**Part I**

*Record your answers on the answer sheet provided by your teacher or on a sheet of paper.*

**1** Which of the following terms refers to the bending of waves around objects?
(1) diffraction
(2) reflection
(3) refraction
(4) transmission

**Use the table below to answer questions 2 and 3.**

| Speed of Sound in Different Materials | |
|---|---|
| **Material** | **Speed (m/s)** |
| Air (20°C) | 343 |
| Glass | 5,640 |
| Steel | 5,940 |
| Water (25°C) | 1,493 |
| Seawater (25°C) | 1,533 |

**2** The table above shows the speed of sound through different materials. About how far can sound travel in air in 2.38 s if the air temperature is 20°C?
(1) 144 m          (3) 684 m
(2) 343 m          (4) 816 m

**3** Sound travels 2,146 m through a material in 1.4 seconds. What is the material?
(1) air (20°C)          (3) water (25°C)
(2) glass          (4) seawater (25°C)

**4** Which of the following are not able to travel through empty space?
(1) gamma rays
(2) ultraviolet waves
(3) sound waves
(4) light waves

**5** Which of the following is a true statement?
(1) Waves do not transport the matter through which they travel.
(2) Waves can transport matter through solids, liquids, and gases, but not through empty space.
(3) Waves can transport matter through liquids and solids, but not through gases or empty space.
(4) Sound and water waves can transport matter, but light waves can't.

**Use the following table to answer questions 6 and 7.**

| Decibel Scale | |
|---|---|
| **Sound Source** | **Loudness (dB)** |
| jet plane taking off | 150 |
| running lawn mower | 100 |
| average home | 50 |
| whisper | 15 |

**6** The table above shows typical sound intensity values on a decibel scale. Which of the following would you expect to be the approximate sound intensity of a noisy restaurant?
(1) 20 dB          (3) 80 dB
(2) 40 dB          (4) 120 dB

**7** What sound intensity level would you expect to be painful to most humans?
(1) 30 dB          (3) 90 dB
(2) 60 dB          (4) 120 dB

**8** What is the maximum range of sound frequencies that humans can hear?
(1) 0 to 150 Hz          (3) 20 to 5000 H4
(2) 0 to 200 Hz          (4) 20 to 20,000 Hz

### Part II

*Record your answers on the answer sheet provided by your teacher or on a sheet of paper.*

**9** Why do concert halls often have drapes or other soft material on the walls?

**10** Why do you sometimes hear thunder at about the same time you see the flash of lightning, but other times you hear the thunder after the flash?

**11** You hear thunder 3.0 seconds after you see a lightning flash. Later you hear thunder 2.5 seconds after you see a flash. If the sound travels at 340 m/s, how much closer was the second lightning strike than the first one?

**12** The speed of all electromagnetic waves through space is 300,000,000 m/s. What is the frequency of a radio wave that has a wavelength of 10 m?

**13** Compare and contrast light waves and sound waves.

**14** Name the different types of electromagnetic waves from longest to shortest wavelength. Give an example of each type.

**15** Describe compressional and transverse waves. Explain the difference between them.

**16** Explain why sound travels faster through some types of matter than through others. How does temperature affect the speed of sound through a material?

**Use the photograph below to answer questions 17 and 18.**

**17** The girl in the photograph above produces sound by clapping cymbals together. Describe how the cymbals produce sound.

**18** What determines the intensity of the sound that the girl produces with the cymbals? How does this affect whether the sound is loud or soft?

**19** If you stand near a large tree, you can hear someone talking on the other side of the tree. Explain why you can hear the person, but can't see them.

**PS 3.1a:** Substances have characteristic properties. **3.1c:** The motion of particles helps to explain the phases (states) of matter as well as changes from one phase to another. The phase in which matter exists depends on the attractive forces among its particles. **Also Covered:** PS 3.1d, 3.1e, 3.1f, 3.1g, 3.2a, 3.2c, 3.2e

# Matter and Its Changes

## An Underwater Flame?

Wendy Craig Duncan carried the Olympic flame underwater on the way to the 2000 Summer Olympics in Sydney, Australia. How many different states of matter can you find in this picture? In this chapter, you will learn about the four states of matter, and the physical and chemical properties of matter.

**Science Journal**   How many states of matter do you see in this photo? List as many as you can.

# Start-Up Activities

## Can you classify pennies by their properties?

Your teacher has given you a collection of pennies. It is your task to separate these pennies into groups. In this chapter, you will learn how to identify things based on their physical and chemical properties. With an understanding of these principles of matter, you will discover how things are classified or put into groups.

1. Observe the collection of pennies.
2. Choose a characteristic that will allow you to separate the pennies into groups.
3. Classify and sort each penny based on the chosen feature. Tally your data in a frequency table.
4. Explain how you classified the pennies. Compare your system of classification with those of others in the classroom.
5. **Think Critically** Write a paragraph in your Science Journal explaining how your group classified its pennies. What other requirements could have been used to classify the pennies?

 **Preview this chapter's content and activities at** glencoe.com

**Study Organizer**

**Properties of Matter** Make the following Foldable to help you organize your thoughts into clear categories about properties of matter.

**STEP 1** **Draw** a mark at the midpoint of a sheet of paper along the side edge. Then **fold** the top and bottom edges in to touch the midpoint.

**STEP 2** **Fold** in half from side to side.

**STEP 3** **Turn** the paper vertically. **Open and cut** along the inside fold lines to form four tabs.

**STEP 4** **Label** each tab as shown.

**Classify** Before you read the chapter, define each term on the front of the tabs. As you read the chapter, correct your definitions and write about each under the appropriate tab. Use the information in your Foldable to compare and contrast physical and chemical properties of matter. Write about each on the back of the tabs.

# section 1

# Physical Properties and Changes

as you read

## *What* You'll Learn

- **Identify** physical properties of matter.
- **Explain** why materials with different masses have different densities.
- **Observe** water displacement to determine volume.
- **Describe** the states of matter.
- **Determine** how temperature changes affect substances.
- **Classify** matter using physical properties.

## *Why* It's Important

Observing physical properties will help you interpret the world around you.

### 🔎 Review Vocabulary
**mass:** amount of matter in an object

### New Vocabulary

- physical property
- matter
- physical change

- density
- states of matter
- melting point
- boiling point

**Figure 1** For safety reasons, in the laboratory you usually use only two of your senses—sight and hearing. Many chemicals can be dangerous to touch, taste, and smell.

## Using Your Senses

As you look in your empty wallet and realize that your allowance isn't coming anytime soon, you decide to get an after-school job. You've been hired at the new grocery store that will open next month. They are getting everything ready for the grand opening, and you will be helping make decisions about where things will go and how they will be arranged.

When you come into a new situation or have to make any kind of decision, what do you usually do first? Most people would make some observations. Observing involves seeing, hearing, tasting, touching, and smelling.

Whether in a new job or in the laboratory, you use your senses to observe materials. Any characteristic of a material that can be observed or measured without changing the identity of the material is a **physical property.** However, it is important to never taste, touch, or smell any of the materials being used in the lab without guidance, as noted in **Figure 1.** For safety reasons you will rely mostly on other observations.

Watch

Listen

Do NOT touch

Do NOT smell

Do NOT taste

**Figure 2** The identity of the material does not necessarily depend on its color. Each of these bottles is made of high-density polyethylene (HDPE).
**Describe** *a physical change that can be applied to the bottles.*

# Physical Properties

On the first day of your new job, the boss gives you an inventory list and a drawing of the store layout. She explains that every employee is going to give his or her input as to how the merchandise should be arranged. Where will you begin?

You decide that the first thing you'll do is make some observations about the items on the list. One of the key senses used in observing physical properties is sight, so you go shopping to look at what you will be arranging.

**Color and Shape** Everything that you can see, touch, smell, or taste is matter. **Matter** is anything that has mass and takes up space. What things do you observe about the matter on your inventory list? The list already is organized by similarity of products, so you go to an aisle and look.

Color is the first thing you notice. The laundry detergent bottles you are looking at come in every color. Maybe you will organize them in the colors of the rainbow. You make a note and look more closely. Each bottle or box has a different shape. Some are square, some rectangular, and some are a free-form shape. You could arrange the packages by their shape.

When the plastic used to make the packaging is molded, it changes shape. However, the material is still plastic. This type of change is called a physical change. It is important to realize that in a **physical change,** the physical properties of a substance change, but the identity of the substance does not change. Notice **Figure 2.** The detergent bottles are made of high-density polyethylene regardless of the differences in the physical properties of color or shape.

 **Reading Check** *What is matter?*

**Physical Setting**

**3.1a, 3.1g Define** *physical property,* then list six characteristic properties that can be observed.

**Topic: Physical Properties**
Visit glencoe.com for Web links to information about classifying matter by its physical properties.

**Activity** Choose three objects in the room around you. Try to describe them using as many different physical properties as you can. Pass your description to another classmate and see if they are able to identify the object.

**Length and Mass** Some properties of matter can be identified by using your senses, and other properties can be measured. How much is there? How much space does it take up?

One useful and measurable physical property is length. Length is measured using a ruler, meterstick, or tape measure, as shown in **Figure 3.** Objects can be classified by their length. For example, you could choose to organize the French bread in the bakery section of your store by the length of the loaf. But, even though the dough has been shaped in different lengths, it is still French bread.

Back in the laundry aisle, you notice a child struggling to lift one of the boxes of detergent. That raises a question. How much detergent is in each box? Mass is a physical property that describes the amount of material in an object. Some of the boxes are heavy, but, the formula of the detergent hasn't changed from the small box to the large box. Organizing the boxes by mass is another option.

**Volume and Density** Mass isn't the only physical property that describes how much of something you have. Another measurement is volume. Volume measures the amount of space an object takes up. Liquids usually are measured by volume. The juice bottles on your list could be organized by volume.

Another measurable physical property related to mass and volume is **density**—the amount of mass a material has in a given volume. You notice this property when you try to lift two things of equal volume that have different masses. Density is found by dividing the mass of an object by its volume.

$$\text{density} = \text{mass/volume, or } D = m/V$$

**Figure 3** The length of any object can be measured with the appropriate tool.
**Describe** *how you would measure the length of your school building.*

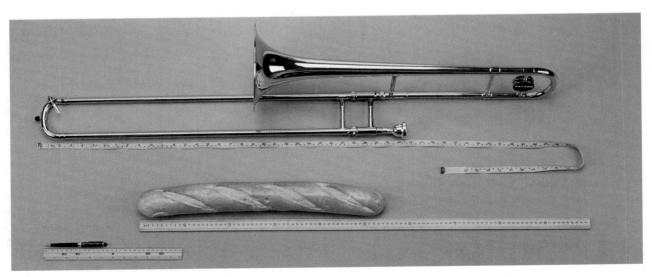

**Figure 4** These balls take up about the same space, but the bowling ball on the left has more mass than the kickball on the right. Therefore, the bowling ball is more dense.

**Same Volume, Different Mass** **Figure 4** shows two balls that are the same size but not the same mass. The bowling ball is more dense than the kickball. The customers of your grocery store will notice the density of their bags of groceries if the baggers load all of the canned goods in one bag and put all of the cereal and napkins in the other.

The density of a material stays the same as long as pressure and temperature stay the same. Water at room temperature has a density of 1.00 g/cm$^3$. However, when you do change the temperature or pressure, the density of a material can change. Water kept in the freezer at 0°C is in the form of ice. The density of that ice is 0.9168 g/cm$^3$. Has the identity of water changed? No, but something has changed.

 *What two properties are related in the measurement of density?*

## States of Matter

How does water change when it goes from 20°C to 0°C? It changes from a liquid to a solid. The four **states of matter** are solid, liquid, gas, and plasma (PLAZ muh). The state of matter of a substance depends on its temperature and pressure. Three of these states of matter are things you talk about or experience every day, but the term *plasma* might be unfamiliar. The plasma state occurs at very high temperatures and is found in fluorescent (floo RE sunt) lightbulbs, the atmosphere, and in lightning strikes.

As you look at the products to shelve in your grocery store, you might make choices of classification based on the state of matter. The state of matter of a material is another physical property. The liquid juices all will be in one place, and the solid, frozen juice concentrates will be in another.

**Determining Volume**

**Procedure**
1. Find **three objects of the same size.** For example: a marble, a rubber ball, and a wood sphere.
2. Fill a **100-mL graduated cylinder** with 50 mL of **water.**
3. Submerge one object into the graduated cylinder and record the new water level. Empty the graduated cylinder.
4. Repeat steps 2 and 3 for the remaining two objects.

**Analysis**
1. Which of the three items displaced the most water? Which displaced the least?
2. What does this tell you about the volume of the objects?
3. What other quantities would you measure to determine the density of each object?

**Physical Setting**

**3.1d, 3.1e, 3.1f** *The motion of particles helps to explain the phases (states) of matter as well as changes from one state to another.* **Sketch** *and label the motion of particles in each of the four states of matter.*

**Moving Particles** Matter is made up of moving particles. The state of matter is determined by how much energy the particles have. The particles of a solid vibrate in a fixed position. They remain close together and give the solid a definite shape and volume. The particles of a liquid are moving much faster and have enough energy to slide past one another. This allows a liquid to take the shape of its container. The particles of a gas are moving so quickly that they have enough energy to move freely away from other particles. The particles of a gas take up as much space as possible and will spread out to fill any container. **Figure 5** illustrates the differences in the states of water.

Particles of matter move faster as higher temperatures are applied. To demonstrate this, fill one beaker with cold water and another with very hot water. Add ten drops of food coloring. Observe in which beaker the color becomes uniform first.

**Changes of State** You witness a change of state when you place ice cubes in a cup and they melt. You still have water but in another form. The opposite physical change happens when you put liquid water in ice-cube trays and pop them in your freezer. The water doesn't change identity—only the state it is in.

For your job, you will need to make some decisions based on the ability of materials to change state. You don't want all the frozen items thawing out and becoming slushy liquid. You also don't want some of the liquids to get so cold that they freeze.

**Figure 5** Water can be in three different states: solid, liquid, and gas. The molecules in ice are tightly packed and vibrate in place, but in liquid water they can slip past each other because they have more energy to move. In water vapor, they move freely all around the container with even more energy.

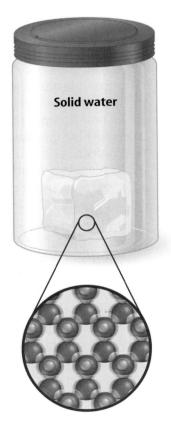

Solid water

Liquid water

Gaseous water

**Melting and Boiling Points** At what temperature will water in the form of ice change into a liquid? The temperature at which a solid becomes a liquid is its **melting point.** The melting point of a pure substance does not change with the amount of the substance. This means that a small sliver of ice and a block of ice the size of a house both will melt at 0°C. Lead always melts at 327.5°C. When a substance melts, it changes from a solid to a liquid. This is a physical change, and the melting point is a physical property.

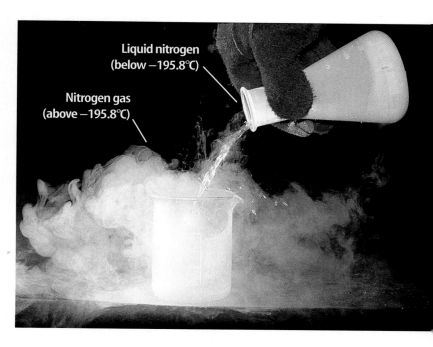

Liquid nitrogen
(below −195.8°C)

Nitrogen gas
(above −195.8°C)

At what temperature will liquid water change to a gas? The **boiling point** is the temperature at which a substance in the liquid state becomes a gas. Each pure substance has a unique boiling point at atmospheric pressure. The boiling point of water is 100°C at atmospheric pressure. The boiling point of nitrogen is −195.8°C, so it changes to a gas when it warms after being spilled into the open air, as shown in **Figure 6.** The boiling point, like the melting point, does not depend on the amount of the substance.

**Figure 6** When liquid nitrogen is poured from a flask, you see an instant change to gas because nitrogen's boiling point is −195.8°C, which is much lower than room temperature.

 **Reading Check** *What physical change takes place at the boiling point?*

However, the boiling point and melting point can help to identify a substance. If you observe a clear liquid that boils at 56.1°C at atmospheric pressure, it is not water. Water boils at 100°C. If you know the boiling points and melting points of substances, you can classify substances based on those properties.

## Metallic Properties

Other physical properties allow you to classify substances as metals. You already have seen how you can classify things as solids, liquids, or gases or according to color, shape, length, mass, volume, or density. What properties do metals have?

**How do metals look?** Often the first thing you notice about something that is a metal is its shiny appearance. This is due to the way light is reflected from the surface of the metal. This shine is called luster. New handlebars on a bike have a metallic luster. Words to describe the appearance of nonmetallic objects are *pearly, milky,* or *dull.*

**INTEGRATE Language Arts**

**Rock Descriptions** When geologists describe rocks, they use specific terms that have meaning to all other scientists who read their descriptions. To describe the appearance of a rock or mineral, they use the following terms: *metallic, adamantine, vitreous, resinous, pearly, silky,* and *greasy.* Research these terms and write a definition and example of each in your Science Journal.

**Figure 7** This artist has taken advantage of the ductility of metal by choosing wire as the medium for this sculpture.

**Uses of Metals** Metals can be used in unique ways because of some of the physical properties they have. For example, many metals can be hammered, pressed, or rolled into thin sheets. This property of metals is called malleability (mal lee uh BIH luh tee). The malleability of copper makes it an ideal choice for artwork such as the Statue of Liberty. Many metals can be drawn into wires as shown in **Figure 7.** This property is called ductility (duk TIH luh tee). The wires in buildings and most electrical equipment and household appliances are made from copper. Silver and platinum are also ductile.

You probably observe another physical property of some metals every day when you go to the refrigerator to get milk or juice for breakfast. Your refrigerator door is made of metal. Some metals respond to magnets. Most people make use of that property and put reminder notes, artwork, and photos on their refrigerators. Some metals have groups of atoms that can be affected by the force of a magnet, and they are attracted to the magnet because of that force. The magnet in **Figure 8** is being used to select metallic objects.

**Figure 8** This junkyard magnet pulls scrap metal that can be salvaged from the rest of the debris. It is sorting by a physical property.

At the grocery store, your employer might think about these properties of metals as she looks at grocery carts and thinks about shelving. Malleable carts can be dented. How could the shelf's attraction of magnets be used to post advertisements or weekly specials? Perhaps the prices could be fixed to the shelves with magnetic numbers. After you observe the physical properties of an object, you can make use of those properties.

# Using Physical Properties

In the previous pages, many physical properties were discussed. These physical properties—such as appearance, state, shape, length, mass, volume, ability to attract a magnet, density, melting point, boiling point, malleability, and ductility—can be used to help you identify, separate, and classify substances.

For example, salt can be described as a white solid. Each salt crystal, if you look at it under a microscope, could be described as having a three-dimensional cubic structure. You can measure the mass, volume, and density of a sample of salt or find out if it would attract a magnet. These are examples of how physical properties can be used to identify a substance.

**Sorting and Separating** When you do laundry, you sort according to physical properties. Perhaps you sort by color. When you select a heat setting on an iron, you classify the clothes by the type of fabric. When miners during the Gold Rush panned for gold, they separated the dirt and rocks by the density of the particles. **Figure 9** shows a coin sorter that separates the coins based on their size. Iron filings can be separated from sand by using a magnet.

 **INTEGRATE Life Science** Scientists who work with animals use physical properties or characteristics to determine the identity of a specimen. They do this by using a tool called a dichotomous (di KAH tuh mus) key. The term *dichotomous* refers to two parts or divisions. Part of a dichotomous key for identifying hard-shelled crabs is shown on the next page in **Figure 10.** To begin the identification of your unknown animal, you are given two choices. Your animal will match only one of the choices. In the key in **Figure 10,** you are to determine whether or not your crab lives in a borrowed shell. Based on your answer, you are either directed to another set of choices or given the name of the crab you are identifying.

**Figure 9** Coins can be sorted by their physical properties. Sorting by size is used here.
**Identify** *three other properties that can be used to sort coins.*

---

**Physical Setting**

**3.1d, 3.1e, 3.1f Design** a chart to compare the physical properties of gas, liquid, and solid using volume and shape in a container.

|  | Definite Volume | Definite Shape |
|---|---|---|
| Gas |  | no |
| Liquid | yes |  |
| Solid |  |  |

---

# NATIONAL GEOGRAPHIC VISUALIZING DICHOTOMOUS KEYS

**Figure 10**

Whether in the laboratory or in the field, scientists often encounter substances or organisms that they cannot immediately identify. One approach to tracking down the identity of such "unknowns" is to use a dichotomous key, such as the one shown. The key is designed so a user can compare physical properties or characteristics of the unknown substance or organism—in this case, a crab—with characteristics of known organisms in a stepwise manner. With each step, a choice must be made. Each choice leads to subsequent steps that guide the user through the key until a positive identification is made.

### Dichotomous Key

| | | |
|---|---|---|
| 1. | A. Lives in a "borrowed" shell (usually some type of snail shell) | Hermit Crab |
| | B. Does not live in a "borrowed" shell | go to #2 |
| 2. | A. Shell completely overlaps the walking legs | Box Crab |
| | B. Walking legs are exposed | Kelp Crab |

Can you identify the three crabs shown here by following this dichotomous key?

**Everyday Examples** Identification by physical properties is a subject in science that is easy to observe in the real world. Suppose you volunteer to help your friend choose a family pet. While visiting the local animal shelter, you spot a cute dog. The dog looks like the one in **Figure 11.** You look at the sign on the cage. It says that the dog is male, one to two years old, and its breed is unknown. You and your friend wonder what breed of dog he is. What kind of information do you and your friend need to figure out the dog's breed? First, you need a thorough description of the physical properties of the dog. What does the dog look like? Second, you need to know the descriptions of various breeds of dogs. Then you can match up the description of the dog with the correct breed. The dog you found is a white, medium-sized dog with large black spots on his back. He also has black ears and a black mask around his eyes. The manager of the shelter tells you that the dog is close to full-grown. What breed is the dog?

**Narrowing the Options** To find out, you may need to research the various breeds of dogs and their descriptions. Often, determining the identity of something that is unknown is easiest by using the process of elimination. You figure out all of the breeds the dog can't be. Then your list of possible breeds is smaller. Upon looking at the descriptions of various breeds, you eliminate small dog and large dog breeds. You also eliminate breeds that do not contain white dogs. With the remaining breeds, you might look at photos to see which ones most resemble your dog. Scientists use similar methods to determine the identities of living and nonliving things.

**Figure 11** Physical descriptions are used to determine the identities of unknown things.
**Observe** *What physical properties can be used to describe this dog?*

## section 1 review

### Summary

**Physical Properties**
- Physical properties include color, shape, length, mass, volume, and density.

**States of Matter**
- There are four states of matter.
- Matter can change from one state of matter to another.
- State of matter is determined by how much energy the particles have.

**Using Physical Properties**
- Substances can be classified according to their physical properties.

### Self Check

1. **Identify** the physical properties of this textbook.
2. **List** the four states of matter. Describe each and give an example.
3. **Explain** how water might have two different densities.
4. **Think Critically** Which evaporates more quickly— rubbing alcohol that has been refrigerated or unrefrigerated?

*Hot Words Hot Topics*: Bk 2 (5) pp. 276–278

### Applying Math

5. **Solve One-Step Equations** Nickel has a density of 9.8 g/cm$^3$. Lead has a density of 11.3 g/cm$^3$. If both samples have a volume of 4 cm$^3$, what are the masses of each?

# section 2

# Chemical Properties and Changes

## as you read

### *What* You'll Learn

- **Recognize** chemical properties.
- **Identify** chemical changes.
- **Classify** matter according to chemical properties
- **Describe** the law of conservation of mass.

### *Why* It's Important

Knowing the chemical properties will allow you to distinguish differences in matter.

### 🕮 Review Vocabulary

**heat:** a form of energy that flows from a warmer object to a cooler object

### New Vocabulary

- chemical property
- chemical change
- law of conservation of mass

## Ability to Change

It is time to celebrate. You and your coworkers have cooperated in classifying all of the products and setting up the shelves in the new grocery store. The store manager agrees to a celebration party and campfire at the nearby park. Several large pieces of firewood and some small pieces of kindling are needed to start the campfire. After the campfire, all that remains of the wood is a small pile of ash. Where did the wood go? What property of the wood is responsible for this change?

All of the properties that you observed and used for classification in the first section were physical properties that you could observe easily. In addition, even when those properties changed, the identity of the object remained the same. Something different seems to have happened in the bonfire example.

Some properties do indicate a change of identity for the substances involved. A **chemical property** is any characteristic that gives a substance the ability to undergo a change that results in a new substance. **Figure 12** shows some properties of substances that can be observed only as they undergo a chemical change.

 **Reading Check** *What does a chemical property give a substance the ability to do?*

**Figure 12** These are four examples of chemical properties.

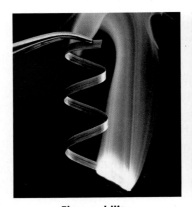

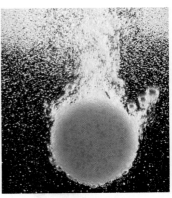

**Flammability**          **Reacts with oxygen**          **Reacts with light**          **Reacts with water**

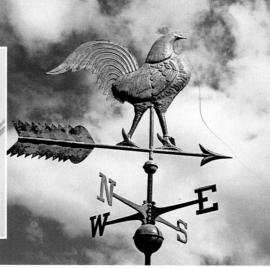

An untreated iron gate will rust.

Silver dishes develop tarnish.

# Common Chemical Properties

You don't have to be in a laboratory to see the changes that take place because of chemical properties. These are called chemical changes. A **chemical change** is a change in the identity of a substance due to the chemical properties of that substance. A new substance or substances are formed as a result of such a change.

The campfire you enjoyed to celebrate the opening of the grocery store resulted in chemical changes. The oxygen in the air reacted with the wood to form a new substance called ash. Wood can burn. This chemical property is called flammability. Some products have warnings on their labels about keeping them away from heat and flame because of the flammability of the materials. Sometimes after a campfire you see stones that didn't burn around the edge of the ashes. These stones have the chemical property of being incombustible.

**Common Reactions** An unpainted iron gate, such as the one shown in **Figure 13,** will rust in time. The rust is a result of oxygen in the air reacting with the iron and causing corrosion. The corrosion produces a new substance called iron oxide, also known as rust. Other chemical reactions occur when metals interact with other elements. The middle photo shows tarnish, the grayish-brown film that develops on silver when it reacts with sulfur in the air. The ability to react with oxygen or sulfur is a chemical property. The photo on the right shows another example of this chemical property.

Have you ever sliced an apple or banana and left it sitting on the table? The brownish coloring that you notice is a chemical change that occurs between the fruit and the oxygen in the air. Those who work in the produce department at the grocery store must be careful with any fruit they slice to use as samples. Although nothing is wrong with brown apples, they don't look appetizing.

**Figure 13** Many kinds of interactions with oxygen can occur. Copper sculptures develop a green patina, which is a mixture of copper compounds.

**Enzyme Research**
Researchers have discovered an enzyme in fruit that is involved in the browning process. They are doing experiments to try to grow grapevines in which the level of this enzyme, polyphenol oxidase (PPO), is reduced. This could result in grapes that do not brown as quickly. Write a paragraph in your Science Journal about why this would be helpful to fruit growers, store owners, and customers.

**Heat and Light** Vitamins often are dispensed in dark-brown bottles. Do you know why? Many vitamins will change when exposed to light. This is a chemical property. They are protected in those colored bottles from undergoing a chemical change with light.

Some substances are sensitive to heat and will undergo a chemical change only when heated or cooled. One example is limestone. Limestone is generally thought of as unreactive. Some limestone formations have been around for centuries without changing. However, if limestone is heated, it goes through a chemical change and produces carbon dioxide and lime, a chemical used in many industrial processes. The chemical property in this case is the ability to change when heated.

Another chemical property is the ability to change with electrical contact. Electricity can cause a change in some substances and decompose some compounds. Water is one of those compounds that can be broken down with electricity.

## Something New

The important difference in a chemical change is that a new substance is formed. Because of chemical changes, you can enjoy many things in life that you would not have experienced without them. What about that perfect, browned marshmallow you roasted at the campfire? A chemical change occurred as a result of the fire to make the taste and the appearance different.

Sugar is normally a white, crystalline substance, but after you heat it over a flame, it turns to a dark-brown caramel. A new substance has been formed. Sugar also can undergo a chemical change when sulfuric acid is added to it. The new substance has obviously different properties from the original, as shown in **Figure 14.**

If eggs, sugar, flour, and other ingredients didn't change chemically through baking, you couldn't enjoy birthday cake. Cake begins as liquid and ends as solid. The baked cake clearly has different properties.

**Physical Setting**

**3.2c** *During a chemical change, substances react in characteristic ways to form new substances with different physical and chemical properties.*
**Support** this statement with three specific examples of a chemical change.

**Figure 14** When sugar and sulfuric acid combine, a chemical change occurs and a new substance forms. During this reaction, the mixture foams and a toxic gas is released, leaving only water and air-filled carbon behind.

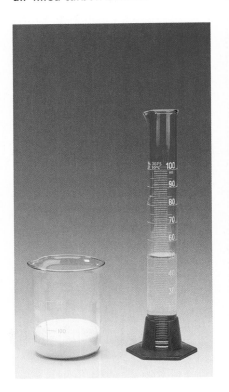

**Signs of Change** How do you know that you have a new substance? Is it just because it looks different? You could put a salad in a blender and it would look different, but a chemical change would not have occurred. You still would have lettuce, carrots, and any other vegetables that were there to begin with.

You can look for signs when evaluating whether you have a new substance as a result of a chemical change. Look at the piece of birthday cake in **Figure 15.** When a cake bakes, gas bubbles form and grow within the ingredients. Bubbles are a sign that a chemical change has taken place. When you look closely at a piece of cake, you can see the airholes left from the bubbles.

Other signs of change include the production of heat, light, smoke, change in color, and sound. Which of these signs of change would you have seen or heard during the campfire?

**Figure 15** The evidence of a chemical change in the cake is the holes left by the air bubbles that were produced during baking. **Identify** *other examples of a chemical change.*

**Is it reversible?** One other way to determine whether a physical change or a chemical change has occurred is to decide whether or not you can reverse the change by simple physical means. Physical changes usually can be reversed easily. For example, melted butter can become solid again if it is placed in the refrigerator. A figure made of modeling clay, like the one in **Figure 16,** can be smashed to fit back into a container. However, chemical changes can't be reversed using physical means. For example, the ashes in a fireplace cannot be put back together to make the logs that you had to start with. Can you find the egg in a cake? Where is the white flour?

**✓ Reading Check** *What kind of change can be reversed easily?*

**Figure 16** A change such as molding clay can be undone easily.

| Table 1 Comparing Properties | |
| --- | --- |
| **Physical Properties** | color, shape, length, mass, volume, density, state, ability to attract a magnet, melting point, boiling point, malleability, ductility |
| **Chemical Properties** | flammability; reacts with: oxygen, water, vinegar, etc.; reacts in the presence of electricity, light, heat, etc. |

## Classifying According to Chemical Properties

Classifying according to physical properties is often easier than classifying according to chemical properties. **Table 1** summarizes the two kinds of properties. The physical properties of a substance are easily observed, but the chemical properties can't be observed without changing the substance. However, once you know the chemical properties, you can classify and identify matter based on those properties. For example, if you try to burn what looks like a piece of wood but find that it won't burn, you can rule out the possibility that it is wood.

In a grocery store, the products sometimes are separated according to their flammability or sensitivity to light or heat. You don't often see the produce section in front of big windows where heat and light come in. The fruit and vegetables would undergo a chemical change and ripen too quickly. You also won't find the lighter fluid and rubbing alcohol near the bakery or other places where heat and flame could be present.

Architects and product designers have to take into account the chemical properties of materials when they design buildings and merchandise. For example, children's sleepwear and bedding can't be made of a flammable fabric. Also, some of the architects designing the most modern buildings are choosing materials like titanium because it does not react with oxygen like many other metals do.

## The Law of Conservation of Mass

It was so convenient to turn the firewood into the small pile of ash left after the campfire. You began with many kilograms of flammable substances but ended up with just a few kilograms of ash. Could this be a solution to the problems with landfills and garbage dumps? Why not burn all the trash? If you could make such a reduction without creating undesirable materials, this would be a great solution.

**Mass Is Not Destroyed** Before you celebrate your discovery, think this through. Did mass really disappear during the fire? It appears that way when you compare the mass of the pile of ashes to the mass of the firewood you started with. The **law of conservation of mass** states that the mass of what you end with is always the same as the mass of what you start with.

This law was first investigated about 200 years ago, and many investigations since then have proven it to be true. One experiment done by French scientist Antoine Lavoisier was a small version of a campfire. He determined that a fire does not make mass disappear or truly get rid of anything. The question, however, remains. Where did the mass go? The ashes aren't heavy enough to account for the mass of all of the pieces of firewood.

**Where did the mass go?** If you look at the campfire example more closely, you see that the law of conservation of mass is true. When flammable materials burn, they combine with oxygen. Ash, smoke, and gases are produced. The smoke and gases escape into the air. If you could measure the mass of the oxygen and all of the original firewood that was burned and compare it to the remaining mass of the ash, smoke, and gas, they would be equal.

**Physical Setting**

**3.2e Summarize** a creative chemical reaction that is an example of the law of conservation of mass.

## Applying Science

### Do light sticks conserve mass?

Light sticks often are used on Halloween to light the way for trick-or-treaters. They make children visible to drivers. They also are used as toys, for camping, marking trails, emergency traffic problems, by the military, and they work well underwater. A light stick contains two chemicals in separate tubes. When you break the inner tube, the two chemicals react producing a greenish light. The chemicals are not toxic, and they will not catch fire.

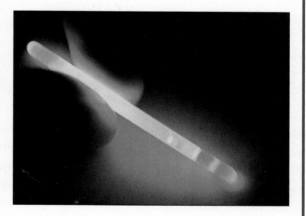

### Identifying the Problem

In all reactions that occur in the world, mass is never lost or gained. This is the law of conservation of mass. An example of this phenomenon is the light stick. How can you prove this?

### Solving the Problem

Describe how you could show that a light stick does not gain or lose mass when you allow the reaction to take place. Is this reaction a chemical or physical change? What is your evidence?

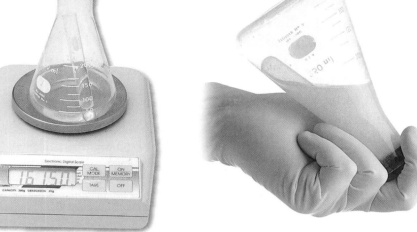
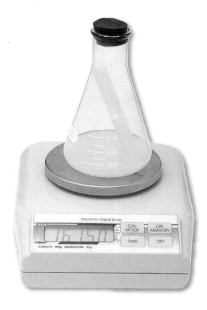

**Figure 17** This reaction demonstrates the law of conservation of mass. Although a chemical change has occurred and new substances were made, the mass remained constant.

**Before and After** Mass is not destroyed or created during any chemical change. The law of conservation of mass is demonstrated in **Figure 17.** In the first photo, you see one substance in the flask and a different substance contained in a test tube inside the flask. The total mass is 16.150 g. In the second photo, the flask is turned upside down. This allows the two substances to mix and react. Because the flask is sealed, nothing is allowed to escape. In the third photo, the flask is placed on the balance again and the total mass is determined to be 16.150 g. If no mass is lost or gained, what happens in a reaction? Instead of disappearing or appearing, the particles in the substances rearrange into different combinations with different properties.

## section 2 review

### Summary

**Common Chemical Properties**

- A new substance, or substances, form(s) as a result of a chemical change.
- Exposure to oxygen, heat, and light can cause chemical reactions.

**Something New**

- Physical changes can be reversed. Chemical changes cannot be reversed.
- Substances can be classified according to their chemical properties.

**The Law of Conservation of Mass**

- Mass is not gained or lost during a chemical reaction.

### Self Check

1. **Define** What is a chemical property? Give four examples.
2. **Identify** some of the signs that a chemical change has occurred.
3. **Think Critically** You see a bright flash and then flames during a class demonstration. Is this an example of a physical change or a chemical change? Explain.

*Hot Words Hot Topics*: Bk 2 (4) pp. 130–131

### Applying Math

4. **Solving One-Step Equations** A student heats 4.00 g of a blue compound, which reacts completely to produce 2.56 g of a white compound and an unknown amount of colorless gas. What is the mass of this gas?

**More Section Review** glencoe.com

# Liquid Layers

Why must you shake up a bottle of Italian salad dressing before using it? Have you observed how the liquids in some dressings separate into two distinct layers? In this lab, you will experiment with creating layers of liquids.

## ◉ Real-World Question

What would several liquids and solids of different densities look like when put into the same container?

### Goals

- **Create** layers of liquids using liquids of different densities.
- **Observe** where solids of different densities will rest in the liquid layers.
- **Infer** the densities of the different materials.

### Materials

| | |
|---|---|
| 250-mL beaker | corn oil |
| graduated cylinder | rubbing alcohol |
| corn syrup | penny |
| glycerin | wood sphere |
| water | rubber ball |

### Safety Precautions

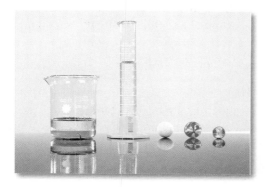

## ◉ Procedure

1. Pour 40 mL of corn syrup into your beaker.
2. Slowly pour 40 mL of glycerin into the beaker. Allow the glycerin to trickle down the sides of the container and observe.
3. Slowly pour 40 mL of water into the beaker and observe.
4. Repeat step 3 with 40 mL of corn oil and then 40 mL of rubbing alcohol.
5. Carefully drop the penny, wood sphere, and rubber ball into the beaker and observe where these items come to a stop.

## ◉ Conclude and Apply

1. **Draw and Label** In your Science Journal, draw a picture of the liquids and solids in your beaker. Label your diagram.
2. **Describe** what happened to the five liquids when you poured them into the beaker. Why did the liquids behave this way?
3. If water has a density of 1 g/cm$^3$, infer the relative densities of the rest of the materials.
4. **List** the liquids and solids in order from the highest density to the lowest density.

### 𝒞ommunicating Your Data

Draw a labeled poster of the substances you placed in your beaker. Research the densities of each substance and include these densities on your poster. **For more help, refer to the** Science Skill Handbook.

## LAB

### Design Your Own

# Fr🦇it Salad Favorites

**Goals**

■ **Design** an experiment that identifies physical changes and chemical changes in fruit.

■ **Observe** whether chemical changes can be controlled.

**Possible Materials**

bananas

apples

pears

plastic or glass mixing
  bowls (2)

lemon/water solution
  (500 mL)

paring knife

**Safety Precautions**

**WARNING:** *Be careful when working with sharp objects. Always keep hands away from sharp blades. Never eat anything in the laboratory.*

## 🔵 Real-World Question

When you are looking forward to enjoying a tasty, sweet fruit salad at a picnic, the last thing you want to see is brown fruit in the bowl. What can you do about this problem? Your teacher has given you a few different kinds of fruit. It is your task to perform a test in which you will observe a physical change and a chemical change. Can a chemical change be controlled?

## 🔵 Form a Hypothesis

Based on your reading and observations, state a hypothesis about whether you can control a chemical change.

## 🔵 Test Your Hypothesis

**Make a Plan**

1. As a group, agree upon the hypothesis and decide how you will test it. Identify what results will confirm the hypothesis.

2. **List** each of the steps you will need in order to test your hypothesis. Be specific. Describe exactly what you will do in each step. List all of your materials.

3. Prepare a data table in your Science Journal or on a computer for your observations.

4. Read the entire investigation to make sure all steps are in logical order.

5. **Identify** all constants, variables, and controls of the investigation.

### Follow Your Plan

1. Ask your teacher to approve your plan and choice of constants, variables and controls before you start.
2. Perform the investigation as planned.
3. While doing the investigation, record your observations and complete the data table you prepared in your Science Journal.

## ⊙ Analyze Your Data

1. **Compare and contrast** the changes you observe in the control and the test fruit.
2. **Compare** your results with those of other groups.
3. What was your control in this investigation?
4. What are your variables?
5. Did you encounter any problems carrying out the investigation?
6. Do you have any suggestions for changes in a future investigation?

## ⊙ Conclude and Apply

1. Did the results support your hypothesis? Explain.
2. **Describe** what effect refrigerating the two salads would have on the fruit.
3. What will you do with the fruit from this experiment? Could it be eaten?

### Communicating Your Data

**Write** a page for an illustrated cookbook explaining the benefits you found in this experiment. Include drawings and a step-by-step procedure. **For more help, refer to the** Science Skill Handbook.

# The Road to Understanding Matter

## What a Ride!

Front wheel drive, a powerful motor, and a smooth ride are characteristics to look for in an automobile. This car, developed by Nippondenso, packs it all under a gold plated hood. At 4.78 mm long, this car is about the size of a grain of rice! Created to show the power and potential of technology applied to unimaginably small objects, this car demonstrates a fraction of the knowledge scientists have gained in exploring matter on a very small scale.

## Matter Mileposts

Philosophers and scientists have speculated about the building blocks of matter for centuries. Around 425 B.C., the Greek Democritis used the term "atomos" to describe the indivisible particles making up matter of all types.

While early thinkers typically lacked the ability to test their theories, later technological advances applied to the study of matter moved science from the realm of the philosophical to the quantitative. In the 1700's, scientists experimented with gases, a type of matter difficult to confine and hard to study. Their findings eliminated the last of the old Greek notions and laid the foundation for modern chemistry.

It was the work of French scientist Antoine Lavoisier (1743–1794) which earned him the title "Father of Modern Chemistry." By focusing on measurable, quantifiable data, he forever changed the way science was conducted. Lavoisier's experiments with gases led to the development of the law of conservation of mass, a cornerstone of modern chemistry which helps explain what happens to matter during chemical change.

## A Changing Road Map

In the 1930's, scientists used the first particle accelerators to reveal the composition of the atom. These machines accelerate subatomic particles, like electrons, to speeds close to the speed of light. Collisions at this speed cause these particles to shatter, and provide the opportunity to detect and analyze the smaller particles which comprise them.

Once thought to be the smallest building blocks, the proton, neutron, and electron are now joined by other subatomic particles groups, including quarks. Scientists currently believe the quark is the most fundamental particle. Studying particles created in particle accelerators is difficult because most exist for less than a billionth of a second.

As the technology behind these powerful machines advances, current hypotheses will undergo revision. The nature of scientific study is to build upon and extend, while sometimes uprooting, commonly held theories. Experimentation to discover the building blocks of matter is no exception.

**Investigate** Research the two types of particle accelerators. Compare how they work and their sizes. Describe what scientists learn about atomic structure using these machines. Use the link to the right or your school's media center to get started.

Science online

**For more information, visit glencoe.com**

## Reviewing Main Ideas

### Section 1 Physical Properties and Changes

1. Any characteristic of a material that can be observed or measured is a physical property.

2. The four states of matter are solid, liquid, gas, and plasma. The state of matter is determined by the energy the particles have.

3. Color, shape, length, mass, volume, density, melting point, boiling point, are common physical properties.

4. In a physical change the properties of a substance change but the identity of the substance always stays the same.

5. You can classify materials according to their physical properties.

### Section 2 Chemical Properties and Changes

1. Chemical properties give a substance the ability to undergo a chemical change.

2. Common chemical properties include: ability to burn, reacts with oxygen, reacts with heat or light, and breaks down with electricity.

3. In a chemical change substances combine to form a new material.

4. The mass of the products of a chemical change is always the same as the mass of what you started with.

5. A chemical change results in a substance with a new identity, but matter is not created or destroyed.

## Visualizing Main Ideas

*Copy and complete the following table comparing properties of different objects.*

| Properties of Matter | | |
|---|---|---|
| **Type of Matter** | **Physical Properties** | **Chemical Properties** |
| Log | | |
| Pillow | | |
| Bowl of cookie dough | Do not write in this book. | |
| Book | | |
| Glass of orange juice | | |

## Using Vocabulary

boiling point p. 247
chemical change p. 253
chemical property p. 252
density p. 244
law of conservation
  of mass p. 257

matter p. 243
melting point p. 247
physical change p. 243
physical property p. 242
states of matter p. 245

*Fill in the blanks with the correct vocabulary word or words.*

1. The _____ is the temperature at which matter in a solid state changes to a liquid.

2. _____ is a measure of the mass of an object in a given volume.

3. A(n) _____ is easily observed or measured without changing the object.

4. _____ result in a new substance and cannot be reversed by physical means.

5. Solid, liquid, and gas are all examples of _____.

## Checking Concepts

*Choose the word or phrase that best answers the question.*

6. Which of the following is an example of a physical change?
   A) tarnishing
   B) rusting
   C) burning
   D) melting

7. Which of the following is a sign that a chemical change has occurred?
   A) smoke
   B) broken pieces
   C) change in shape
   D) change in state

8. When iron reacts with oxygen, what substance is produced?
   A) tarnish
   B) rust
   C) patina
   D) ashes

9. What statement describes the physical property of density?
   A) the distance between two points
   B) how light is reflected from an object's surface
   C) the amount of mass for a given volume
   D) the amount of space an object takes up

10. Which of the choices below describes a boiling point?
    A) a chemical property
    B) a chemical change
    C) a physical property
    D) a color change

11. What property is described by the ability of metals to be hammered into sheets?
    A) mass
    B) density
    C) volume
    D) malleability

12. Which of these is a chemical property?
    A) size
    B) density
    C) flammability
    D) volume

13. Which describes what volume is?
    A) the area of a square
    B) the amount of space an object takes up
    C) the distance between two points
    D) the temperature at which boiling begins

14. What kind of change results in a new substance being produced?
    A) chemical
    B) mass
    C) physical
    D) change of state

15. What is conserved during any change?
    A) color
    B) volume
    C) identity
    D) mass

## Thinking Critically

**16. Explain** Use the law of conservation of mass to explain what happens to atoms when they combine to form a new substance.

**17. Describe** the four states of matter. How are they different?

**18. Observe** A globe is placed on your desk and you are asked to identify its physical properties. How would you describe the globe?

**19. Evaluate** What information do you need to know about a material to find its density?

**20. Classify** the following as a chemical or physical change: an egg breaks, a newspaper burns in the fireplace, a dish of ice cream is left out and melts, and a loaf of bread is baked.

**21. Draw Conclusions** List the physical and chemical properties and changes that describe the process of scrambling eggs.

**22. Infer** Concrete is formed through a chemical reaction of sand, gravel, crushed stones, and water. Do the starting materials have the same properties as the end materials? Give two examples to support your response.

**23. Describe** In terms of particle movement explain how increasing temperature changes water in the solid state.

**24. Concept Map** Use a spider map to organize and define physical properties of matter. Include the concepts of color, shape, length, density, mass, states of matter, volume, density, melting point, and boiling point.

## Performance Activities

**25. Comic Strip** Create a comic strip demonstrating a chemical change in a substance. Include captions and drawings that demonstrate your understanding of the law of conservation of mass.

*Hot Words Hot Topics*: Bk 2 (26) pp. 276–278; (27) p. 194; (28) pp. 276–278

## Applying Math

**26. Measure in SI** Find the density of the piece of lead that has a mass of 49.01 g and a volume of 4.5 cm$^3$.

**Use the table below to answer question 27.**

| Density | | | |
|---|---|---|---|
| Sample | Mass | Volume | Density |
| A | 3.0 g | 6.5 cm$^3$ | |
| B | 1.2 g | 1.1 cm$^3$ | |
| C | 4.5 g | | 0.88 g/cm$^3$ |
| D | 125 g | | 0.36 g/cm$^3$ |
| E | | 85 cm$^3$ | 2.3 g/cm$^3$ |
| F | | 10 cm$^3$ | 0.75 g/cm$^3$ |

**27. Density** Copy and complete the table by supplying the missing information.

**28. Density** Using the formula for density evaluate if two samples with the same volume, but different densities will have the same mass. Give two sample calculations to support your answer.

*Record your answers on the answer sheet provided by your teacher or on a sheet of paper.*

**1** Which of these is NOT a physical property?
(1) volume
(2) mass
(3) density
(4) flammability

**Use the illustration below to answer questions 2 and 3.**

**2** Which statement about the bowling ball and the kickball shown above is TRUE?
(1) These balls have nearly equal densities.
(2) These balls have nearly equal masses.
(3) These balls have nearly equal volumes.
(4) One of these balls exists as a different state of matter than the other.

**3** A hole is punched in the kickball. Most of the air escapes and the ball collapses and shrinks. What happens to the ball?
(1) The mass of the ball increases.
(2) The volume of the ball decreases.
(3) The volume of the ball increases.
(4) The mass of the ball does not change.

**4** Which term is a physical property that describes the amount of matter in an object?
(1) mass
(2) density
(3) volume
(4) state of matter

**5** Which step in the process of making a cake results in a chemical change?
(1) breaking an egg and removing the contents from the shell
(2) melting butter
(3) mixing sugar and flour
(4) baking a cake in the oven

**Use the illustration below to answer questions 6 and 7.**

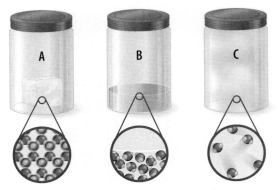

**6** The particles in the jar labeled A represent a
(1) solid         (3) gas.
(2) liquid        (4) plasma.

**7** If the material in the jars are all a form of $H_2O$, then jar C must be
(1) liquid water      (3) ice.
(2) water vapor       (4) pure oxygen.

**8** When mercury (II) oxide, HgO, is heated, liquid mercury (Hg) and oxygen ($O_2$) are produced.

| $2HgO \rightarrow 2Hg + O_2$ | |
|---|---|
| Beginning mass of HgO | 216 grams |
| Mass of Hg after heating | 200 grams |
| Mass of $O_2$ after heating | ? grams |

According to the law of conservation of mass, what mass of $O_2$ is generated?
(1) 0 g          (3) 200 g
(2) 216 g        (4) 16 g

*Record your answers on the answer sheet provided by your teacher or on a sheet of paper.*

9 Choose an object in the room and describe its physical properties as completely as possible.

10 Compare the density of two sponges: Dry Sponge A has a mass of 60 g. Moist Sponge B has a mass of 90 g. The volume of each sponge is 180 cm$^3$.

11 Describe the key properties of metals. Identify something you own which is made of metal. How has a metallic property made it possible to create or use this item?

**Use the photos below to answer questions 12 and 13.**

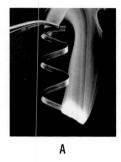
A

B

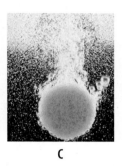
C

12 What type of change is occurring in each picture? Describe the signs of the change.

13 How do chemical and physical changes differ? What signs indicate a chemical change? What signs indicate a physical change?

14 You are asked to determine the identity of an unknown element. How will you use the properties of the element to discover its identity?

15 Based on the way particles move in solid, liquid, and gas phases of matter, describe what happens when solid water (ice) gradually changes to water as a gas (water vapor).

**Use the graph below to answer questions 16 and 17.**

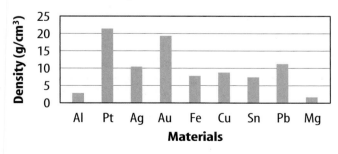

**Density of Materials at 20° Celsius**

16 Rank the materials shown from most to least dense.

17 Imagine the graph had the title: *Density of Materials at 5° Celsius.* How and why would the graph look different?

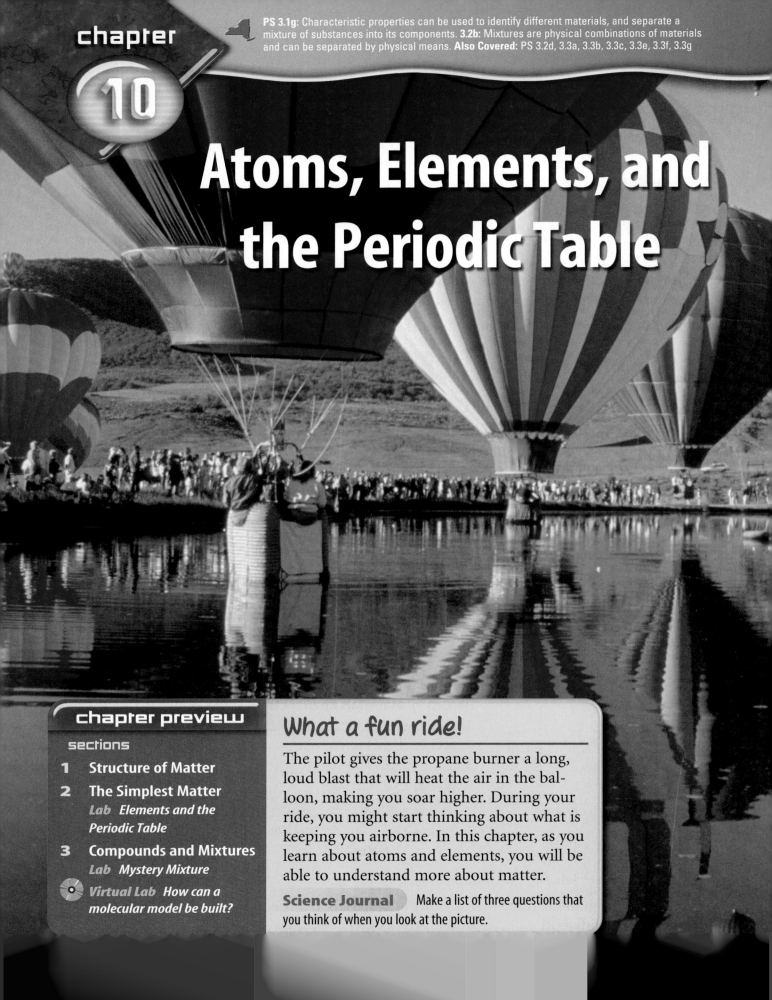

**chapter**

**10**

PS 3.1g: Characteristic properties can be used to identify different materials, and separate a mixture of substances into its components. **3.2b:** Mixtures are physical combinations of materials and can be separated by physical means. **Also Covered:** PS 3.2d, 3.3a, 3.3b, 3.3c, 3.3e, 3.3f, 3.3g

# Atoms, Elements, and the Periodic Table

## What a fun ride!

The pilot gives the propane burner a long, loud blast that will heat the air in the balloon, making you soar higher. During your ride, you might start thinking about what is keeping you airborne. In this chapter, as you learn about atoms and elements, you will be able to understand more about matter.

**Science Journal**   Make a list of three questions that you think of when you look at the picture.

# Start-Up Activities

## Observe Matter

You've just finished playing basketball. You're hot and thirsty. You reach for your bottle of water and take a drink. Releasing your grip, you notice that the bottle is nearly empty. Is the bottle really almost empty? According to the dictionary, *empty* means "containing nothing." When you have finished all the water in the bottle, will it be empty or full? 👓 🧤

1. Wad up a dry paper towel or tissue and tape it to the inside of a plastic cup as shown.

2. Fill a bowl or sink with water. Turn the cup upside down and slowly push the cup straight down into the water as far as you can.

3. Slowly raise the cup straight up and out of the water. Remove the paper towel or tissue paper and examine it.

4. **Think Critically** In your Science Journal, describe the lab and its results. Explain what you think happened. Was anything in the cup besides the paper? If so, what was it?

**Atoms, Elements, and the Periodic Table** Make the following Foldable to help you identify the main ideas about atoms, elements, compounds, and mixtures.

**STEP 1** **Draw** a mark at the midpoint of a sheet of paper along the side edge. Then **fold** the top and bottom edges in to touch the midpoint.

**STEP 2** **Fold** in half from side to side.

**STEP 3** **Open** and cut along the inside fold lines to form four tabs.

**STEP 4** **Label** each tab as shown.

**Read and Write** As you read the chapter, list several everyday examples of atoms, elements, compounds, and mixtures on the back of the appropriate tab.

**Preview this chapter's content and activities at** glencoe.com

269

# section

## 1

# Structure of Matter

### *What* You'll Learn

- **Describe** characteristics of matter.
- **Identify** what makes up matter.
- **Identify** the parts of an atom.
- **Compare** the models that are used for atoms.

### *Why* It's Important

Matter makes up almost everything we see—and much of what we can't see.

### ⓘ Review Vocabulary

**density:** the mass of an object divided by its volume

### New Vocabulary

- matter
- atom
- law of conservation of matter
- electron
- nucleus
- proton
- neutron

## What is matter?

Is a glass with some water in it half empty or half full? Actually, neither is correct. The glass is completely full—half full of water and half full of air. What is air? Air is a mixture of several gases, including nitrogen and oxygen, which are kinds of matter. **Matter** is anything that has mass and takes up space. So, even though you can't see it or hold it in your hand, air is matter. What about all the things you can see, taste, smell, and touch? Most are made of matter, too. Look at the things pictured in **Figure 1** and determine which of them are matter.

## What isn't matter?

You can see the words on this page because of the light from the Sun or from a fixture in the room. Does light have mass or take up space? What about the warmth from the Sun or the heat from the heater in your classroom? Light and heat do not take up space, and they have no mass. Therefore, they are not forms of matter. Emotions, thoughts, and ideas are not matter either. Does this information change your mind about the items in **Figure 1**?

✓ **Reading Check** *Why is air matter, but light is not?*

**Figure 1** A rainbow is formed when light filters through the raindrops, a plant grows from a seed in the ground, and a statue is sculpted from bronze.
**Identify** *which are matter.*

## Figure 2  Early Beliefs About the Composition of Matter

| Many Indian Philosophers (1,000 B.C.) | Kashyapa, an Indian Philosopher (1,000 B.C.) | Many Greek Philosophers (500–300 B.C.) | Democritus (380 B.C.) | Aristotle (330 B.C.) | Chinese Philosophers (300 B.C.) |
|---|---|---|---|---|---|
| • Ether—an invisible substance that filled the heavens<br>• Earth<br>• Water<br>• Air<br>• Fire | • Five elements broken down into smaller units called parmanu<br>• Parmanu of earth elements are heavier than air elements | • Earth<br>• Water<br>• Air<br>• Fire | • Tiny individual particles he called *atomos*<br>• Empty space through which atoms move<br>• Each substance composed of one type of *atomos* | • Empty space could not exist<br>• Earth<br>• Water<br>• Air<br>• Fire | • Metal<br>• Earth<br>• Water<br>• Air<br>• Fire |

## What makes up matter?

Suppose you cut a chunk of wood into smaller and smaller pieces. Do the pieces seem to be made of the same matter as the large chunk you started with? If you could cut a small enough piece, would it still have the same properties as the first chunk? Would you reach a point where the last cut resulted in a piece that no longer resembled the first chunk? Is there a limit to how small a piece can be? For centuries, people have asked questions like these and wondered what matter is made of.

**An Early Idea** Democritus, who lived from about 460 B.C. to 370 B.C., was a Greek philosopher who thought the universe was made of empty space and tiny bits of stuff. He believed that the bits of stuff were so small they could no longer be divided into smaller pieces. He called these tiny pieces atoms. The term *atom* comes from a Greek word that means "cannot be divided." Today an **atom** is defined as a small particle that makes up most types of matter. **Figure 2** shows the difference between Democritus's ideas and those of other early scientists and philosophers. Democritus thought that different types of atoms existed for every type of matter and that the atom's identity explained the characteristics of each type of matter. Democritus's ideas about atoms were a first step toward understanding matter. However, his ideas were not accepted for over 2,000 years. It wasn't until the early 1800s that scientists built upon the concept of atoms to form the current atomic theory of matter.

**INTEGRATE History**

**Atomism** Historians note that Leucippus developed the idea of the atom around 440 B.C. He and his student, Democritus, refined the idea of the atom years later. Their concept of the atom was based on five major points: (1) all matter is made of atoms, (2) there are empty spaces between atoms, (3) atoms are complete solids, (4) atoms do not have internal structure, and (5) atoms are different in size, shape, and weight.

**Figure 3** When wood burns, matter is not lost. The total mass of the wood and the oxygen it combines with during a fire equals the total mass of the ash, water vapor, carbon dioxide, and other gases produced.
**Infer** *When you burn wood in a fireplace, what is the source of oxygen?*

wood + oxygen = ash + gases + water vapor

### Investigating the Unseen

**Procedure**
1. Your teacher will give you a **sealed shoe box** that contains **one or more items.**
2. Try to find out how many and what kinds of items are inside the box. You cannot look inside the box. The only observations you can make are by handling the box.

**Analysis**
1. How many items do you infer are in the box? Sketch the apparent shapes of the items and identify them if you can.
2. Compare your procedure with how scientists perform experiments and make models to find out more about the atom.

**Lavoisier's Contribution** Lavoisier (la VWAH see ay), a French chemist who lived about 2,000 years after Democritus, also was curious about matter—especially when it changed form. Before Lavoisier, people thought matter could appear and disappear because of the changes they saw as matter burned or rusted. You might have thought that matter can disappear if you've ever watched wood burn in a fireplace or at a bonfire. Lavoisier showed that wood and the oxygen it combines with during burning have the same mass as the ash, water, carbon dioxide, and other gases that are produced, as shown in **Figure 3**. In a similar way, an iron bar, oxygen, and water have the same mass as the rust that forms when they interact. From Lavoisier's work came the **law of conservation of matter,** which states that matter is not created or destroyed—it only changes form.

## Models of the Atom

Models are often used for things that are too small or too large to be observed or that are too difficult to be understood easily. One way to make a model is to make a smaller version of something large. If you wanted to design a new sailboat, would you build a full-sized boat and hope it would float? It would be more efficient, less expensive, and safer to build and test a smaller version first. Then, if it didn't float, you could change your design and build another model. You could keep trying until the model worked.

In the case of atoms, scientists use large models to explain something that is too small to be looked at. These models of the atom were used to explain data or facts that were gathered experimentally. As a result, these models are also theories.

**Dalton's Atomic Model** In the early 1800s, an English schoolteacher and chemist named John Dalton studied the experiments of Lavoisier and others. Dalton thought he could design an atomic model that explained the results of those experiments. Dalton's atomic model was a set of ideas—not a physical object. Dalton believed that matter was made of atoms that were too small to be seen by the human eye. He also thought that each type of matter was made of only one kind of atom. For example, gold atoms make up a gold nugget and give a gold ring its shiny appearance. Likewise, iron atoms make up an iron bar and give it unique properties, and so on. Because predictions using Dalton's model were supported by data, the model became known as the atomic theory of matter.

**Sizes of Atoms** Atoms are so small it would take about 1 million of them lined up in a row to equal the thickness of a human hair. For another example of how small atoms are, look at **Figure 4.** Imagine you are holding an orange in your hand. If you wanted to be able to see the individual atoms on the orange's surface, the size of the orange would have to be increased to the size of Earth. Then, imagine the Earth-sized orange covered with billions and billions of marbles. Each marble would represent one of the atoms on the skin of the orange. No matter what kind of model you use to picture it, the result is the same—an atom is an extremely small particle of matter.

**Figure 4** If this orange were as large as Earth, each of its atoms would be marble-sized.

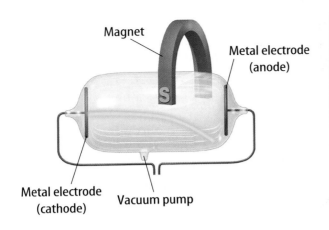

Magnet

Metal electrode (anode)

Metal electrode (cathode)

Vacuum pump

**Figure 5** In Thomson's experiment, the magnet caused the cathode rays inside the tube to bend. **Describe** *what you think would happen to the cathode rays if the magnet were removed.*

**Topic: Subatomic Particles**
Visit glencoe.com for Web links to information about particles that make up atoms.

**Activity** Can any of the particles be divided further? Display your data in a table.

**Discovering the Electron** One of the many pioneers in the development of today's atomic model was J.J. Thomson, an English scientist. He conducted experiments using a cathode ray tube, which is a glass tube sealed at both ends out of which most of the air has been pumped. Thomson's tube had a metal plate at each end. The plates were connected to a high-voltage electrical source that gave one of the plates—the anode—a positive charge and the other plate—the cathode—a negative charge. During his experiments, Thomson observed rays that traveled from the cathode to the anode. These cathode rays were bent by a magnet, as seen in **Figure 5,** showing that they were made up of particles that had mass and charge. Thomson knew that like charges repel each other and opposite charges attract each other. When he saw that the rays traveled toward a positively charged plate, he concluded that the cathode rays were made up of negatively charged particles. These invisible, negatively charged particles are called **electrons.**

**Reading Check** *Why were the cathode rays in Thomson's cathode ray tube bent by a magnet?*

Try to imagine Thomson's excitement at this discovery. He had shown that atoms are not too tiny to divide after all. Rather, they are made up of even smaller subatomic particles. Other scientists soon built upon Thomson's results and found that the electron had a small mass. In fact, an electron is 1/1,837 the mass of the lightest atom, the hydrogen atom. In 1906, Thomson received the Nobel Prize in Physics for his work on the discovery of the electron.

Matter that has an equal amount of positive and negative charge is said to be neutral—it has no net charge. Because most matter is neutral, Thomson pictured the atom as a ball of positive charge with electrons embedded in it. It was later determined that neutral atoms contained an equal number of positive and negative charges.

**Thomson's Model** Thomson's model, shown in **Figure 6,** can be compared to chocolate chips spread throughout a ball of cookie dough. However, the model did not provide all the answers to the questions that puzzled scientists about atoms.

**Rutherford—The Nucleus** Scientists still had questions about how the atom was arranged and about the presence of positively charged particles. In about 1910, a team of scientists led by Ernest Rutherford worked on these questions. In their experiment, they bombarded an extremely thin piece of gold foil with alpha particles. Alpha particles are tiny, high-energy, positively charged particles that he predicted would pass through the foil. Most of the particles passed straight through the foil as if it were not there at all. However, other particles changed direction, and some even bounced back. Rutherford thought the result was so remarkable that he later said, "It was almost as incredible as if you had fired a 15-inch shell at a piece of tissue paper, and it came back and hit you."

**Positive Center** Rutherford concluded that because so many of the alpha particles passed straight through the gold foil, the atoms must be made of mostly empty space. However, because some of the positively charged alpha particles bounced off something, the gold atoms must contain some positively charged object concentrated in the midst of this empty space. Rutherford called the positively charged, central part of the atom the **nucleus** (NEW klee us). He named the positively charged particles in the nucleus **protons**. He also suggested that electrons were scattered in the mostly empty space around the nucleus, as shown in **Figure 7.**

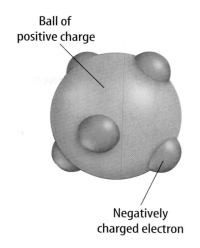

Ball of positive charge

Negatively charged electron

**Figure 6** Thomson's model shows the atom as electrons embedded in a ball of positive charge.
**Explain** *how Thomson knew atoms contained positive and negative charges.*

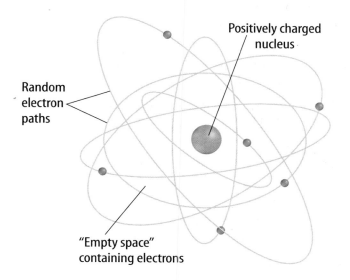

Positively charged nucleus

Random electron paths

"Empty space" containing electrons

**Figure 7** Rutherford concluded that the atom must be mostly empty space in which electrons travel in random paths around the nucleus. He also thought the nucleus of the atom must be small and positively charged.
**Identify** *where most of the mass of an atom is concentrated.*

**Discovering the Neutron** Rutherford had been puzzled by one observation from his experiments with nuclei. After the collisions, the nuclei seemed to be heavier. Where did this extra mass come from? James Chadwick, a student of Rutherford's, answered this question. The alpha particles themselves were not heavier. The atoms that had been bombarded had given off new particles. Chadwick experimented with these new particles and found that, unlike electrons, the paths of these particles were not affected by an electric field. To explain his observations, he said that these particles came from the nucleus and had no charge. Chadwick called these uncharged particles **neutrons** (NEW trahnz). His proton-neutron model of the atomic nucleus is still accepted today.

## Improving the Atomic Model

Early in the twentieth century, a scientist named Niels Bohr found evidence that electrons in atoms are arranged according to energy levels. The lowest energy level is closest to the nucleus and can hold only two electrons. Higher energy levels are farther from the nucleus and can contain more electrons. To explain these energy levels, some scientists thought that the electrons might orbit an atom's nucleus in paths that are specific distances from the nucleus, as shown in **Figure 8.** This is similar to how the planets orbit the Sun.

**The Modern Atomic Model** As a result of continuing research, scientists now realize that because electrons have characteristics that are similar to waves and particles, their energy levels are not defined, planet-like orbits around the nucleus. Rather, it seems most likely that electrons move in what is called the atom's electron cloud, as shown in **Figure 9.**

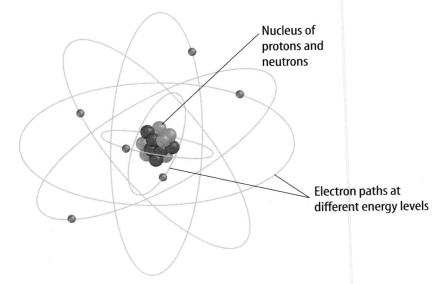

Nucleus of protons and neutrons

Electron paths at different energy levels

**Figure 8** This simplified Bohr model shows a nucleus of protons and neutrons and electron paths based on energy levels.

**The Electron Cloud** The electron cloud is a spherical cloud of varying density surrounding the nucleus. The varying density shows where an electron is more or less likely to be. Atoms with electrons in higher energy levels have electron clouds of different shapes that also show where those electrons are likely to be. Generally, the electron cloud has a radius 10,000 times that of the nucleus.

**Further Research** By the 1930s, it was recognized that matter was made up of atoms, which were, in turn, made up of protons, neutrons, and electrons. But scientists, called physicists, continued to study the basic parts of this atom. Today, they have succeeded in breaking down protons and neutrons into even smaller particles called quarks. These particles can combine to make other kinds of tiny particles, too. The six types of quarks are *up, down, strange, charmed, top,* and *bottom.* Quarks have fractional electric charges of $+2/3$ or $-1/3$, unlike the $+1$ charge of a proton or the $-1$ charge of an electron. Research will continue as new discoveries are made about the structure of matter.

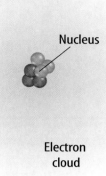

Nucleus

Electron cloud

**Figure 9** This model of the atom shows the electrons moving around the nucleus in a region called an electron cloud. The dark cloud of color represents the area where the electron is more likely to be found.
**Infer** *What does the intensity of color near the nucleus suggest?*

## section 1 review

### Summary

**What is matter?**
- Matter is anything that has mass and takes up space.
- Matter is composed of atoms.

**Models of the Atom**
- Democritus introduced the idea of an atom. Lavoisier showed matter is neither created nor destroyed, just changed.
- Dalton's ideas led to the atomic theory of matter.
- Thomson discovered the electron.
- Rutherford discovered protons exist in the nucleus.
- Chadwick discovered the neutron.

**Improving the Atomic Model**
- Niels Bohr suggested electrons move in energy levels.
- More recent physicists introduced the idea of the electron cloud and were able to break down protons and neutrons into smaller particles called quarks.

### Self Check

1. **List** five examples of matter and five examples that are not matter. Explain your answers.
2. **Describe** and name the parts of the atom.
3. **Explain** why the word *atom* was an appropriate term for Democritus's idea.
4. **Think Critically** When neutrons were discovered, were these neutrons created in the experiment? How does Lavoisier's work help answer this question?
5. **Explain** the law of conservation of matter using your own examples.
6. **Think Critically** How is the electron cloud model different from Bohr's atomic model?

#### Applying Skills

7. **Classify** each scientist and his contribution according to the type of discovery each person made. Explain why you grouped certain scientists together.
8. **Evaluate Others' Data and Conclusions** Analyze, review, and critique the strengths and weaknesses of Thomson's "cookie dough" theory using the results of Rutherford's gold foil experiment.

PS 3.3f: There are more than 100 elements. Elements combine in a multitude of ways to produce compounds that account for all living and nonliving substances. Few elements are found in their pure form. 3.3g: The periodic table is one useful model for classifying elements. **Also Covered:** PS 3.2d, 3.3e

# section 2

# The Simplest Matter

## The Elements

Have you watched television today? TV sets are common, yet each one is a complex system. The outer case is made mostly of plastic, and the screen is made of glass. Many of the parts that conduct electricity are metals or combinations of metals. Other parts in the interior of the set contain materials that barely conduct electricity. All of the different materials have one thing in common: they are made up of even simpler materials. In fact, if you had the proper equipment, you could separate the plastics, glass, and metals into these simpler materials.

**One Kind of Atom** Eventually, though, you would separate the materials into groups of atoms. At that point, you would have a collection of elements. An **element** is matter made of only one kind of atom. At least 115 elements are known and about 90 of them occur naturally on Earth. These elements make up gases in the air, minerals in rocks, and liquids such as water. Examples of naturally occurring elements include the oxygen and nitrogen in the air you breathe and the metals gold, silver, aluminum, and iron. The other elements are known as synthetic elements. These elements have been made in nuclear reactions by scientists with machines called particle accelerators, like the one shown in **Figure 10.** Some synthetic elements have important uses in medical testing and are found in smoke detectors and heart pacemaker batteries.

**Figure 10** The Tevatron has a circumference of 6.3 km—a distance that allows particles to accelerate to high speeds. These high-speed collisions can create synthetic elements.

**Figure 11** When you look for information in the library, a system of organization called the Dewey Decimal Classification System helps you find a book quickly and efficiently.

| Dewey Decimal Classification System | |
|---|---|
| 000 | Computers, information and general reference |
| 100 | Philosophy and psychology |
| 200 | Religion |
| 300 | Social sciences |
| 400 | Languages |
| 500 | Science |
| 600 | Technology |
| 700 | Arts and recreation |
| 800 | Literature |
| 900 | History and geography |

## The Periodic Table

Suppose you go to a library, like the one shown in **Figure 11,** to look up information for a school assignment. How would you find the information? You could look randomly on shelves as you walk up and down rows of books, but the chances of finding your book would be slim. To avoid such haphazard searching, some libraries use the Dewey Decimal Classification System to categorize and organize their volumes and to help you find books quickly and efficiently.

**Charting the Elements** Chemists have created a chart called the periodic table of the elements to help them organize and display the elements. **Figure 12** shows how scientists changed their model of the periodic table over time.

On the inside back cover of this book, you will find a modern version of the periodic table. Each element is represented by a chemical symbol that contains one to three letters. The symbols are a form of chemical shorthand that chemists use to save time and space—on the periodic table as well as in written formulas. The symbols are an important part of an international system that is understood by scientists everywhere.

The elements are organized on the periodic table by their properties. There are rows and columns that represent relationships between the elements. The rows in the table are called periods. The elements in a row have the same number of energy levels. The columns are called groups. The elements in each group have similar properties related to their structure. They also tend to form similar bonds.

**Science** nline

**Topic: New Elements**
Visit glencoe.com for Web links to information about new elements.

**Activity** Research physical properties of two synthetic elements.

# VISUALIZING THE PERIODIC TABLE

## Figure 12

The familiar periodic table that adorns many science classrooms is based on a number of earlier efforts to identify and classify the elements. In the 1790s, one of the first lists of elements and their compounds was compiled by French chemist Antoine-Laurent Lavoisier, who is shown in the background picture with his wife and assistant, Marie Anne. Three other tables are shown here.

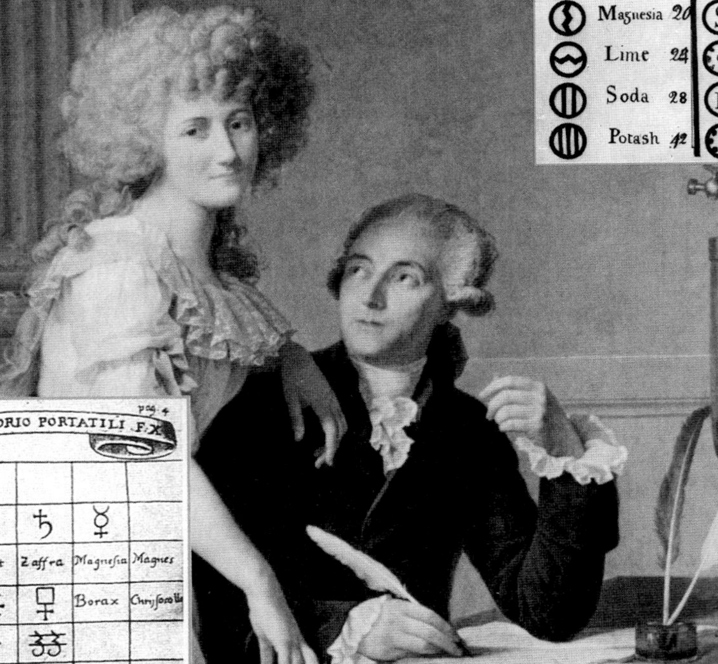

John Dalton (Britain, 1803) used symbols to represent elements. His table also assigned masses to each element.

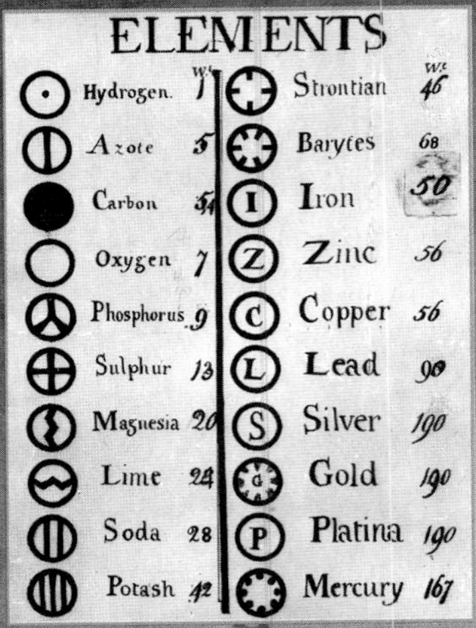

ELEMENTS

| | Wt | | Wt |
|---|---|---|---|
| Hydrogen. | 1 | Strontian | 46 |
| Azote | 5 | Barytes | 68 |
| Carbon | 54 | Iron | 50 |
| Oxygen | 7 | Zinc | 56 |
| Phosphorus | 9 | Copper | 56 |
| Sulphur | 13 | Lead | 90 |
| Magnesia | 20 | Silver | 190 |
| Lime | 24 | Gold | 190 |
| Soda | 28 | Platina | 190 |
| Potash | 42 | Mercury | 167 |

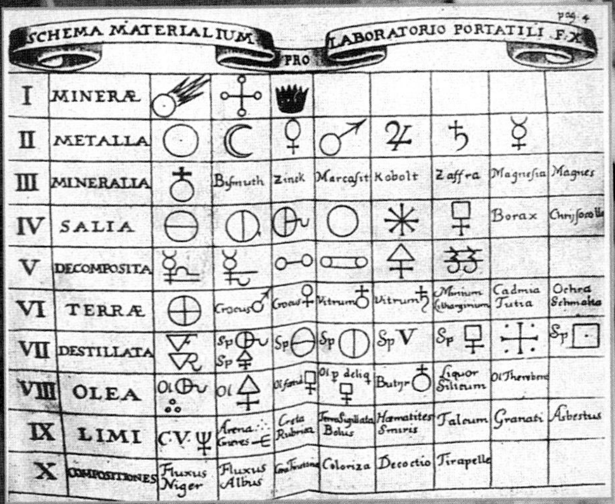


An early alchemist put together this table of elements and compounds. Some of the symbols have their origin in astrology.

Dmitri Mendeleev (Russia, 1869) arranged the 63 elements known to exist at that time into groups based on their chemical properties and atomic weights. He left gaps for elements he predicted were yet to be discovered.

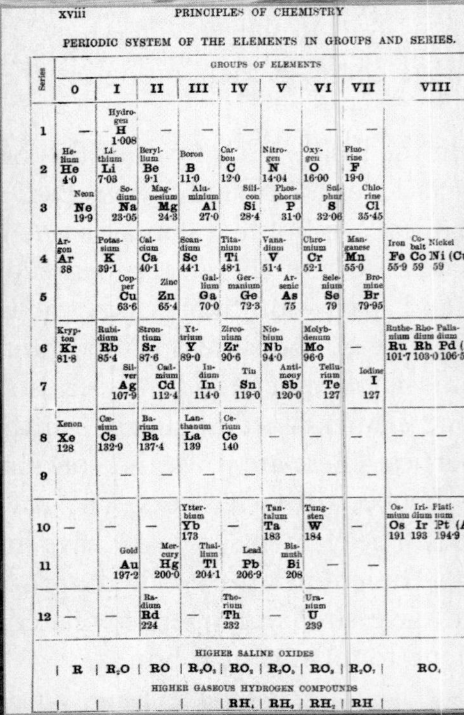

xviii PRINCIPLES OF CHEMISTRY

PERIODIC SYSTEM OF THE ELEMENTS IN GROUPS AND SERIES.

| Series | GROUPS OF ELEMENTS 0 | I | II | III | IV | V | VI | VII | VIII |
|---|---|---|---|---|---|---|---|---|---|
| 1 | — | Hydrogen H 1·008 | — | — | — | — | — | — | |
| 2 | Helium He 4·0 | Lithium Li 7·03 | Beryllium Be 9·1 | Boron B 11·0 | Carbon C 12·0 | Nitrogen N 14·04 | Oxygen O 16·00 | Fluorine F 19·0 | |
| 3 | Neon Ne 19·9 | Sodium Na 23·05 | Magnesium Mg 24·3 | Aluminium Al 27·0 | Silicon Si 28·4 | Phosphorus P 31·0 | Sulphur S 32·06 | Chlorine Cl 35·45 | |
| 4 | Argon Ar 38 | Potassium K 39·1 | Calcium Ca 40·1 | Scandium Sc 44·1 | Titanium Ti 48·1 | Vanadium V 51·4 | Chromium Cr 52·1 | Manganese Mn 55·0 | Iron Fe 55·9, Cobalt Co 59, Nickel Ni (Cu) 59 |
| 5 | | Copper Cu 63·6 | Zinc Zn 65·4 | Gallium Ga 70·0 | Germanium Ge 72·3 | Arsenic As 75 | Selenium Se 79 | Bromine Br 79·95 | |
| 6 | Krypton Kr 81·8 | Rubidium Rb 85·4 | Strontium Sr 87·6 | Yttrium Y 89·0 | Zirconium Zr 90·6 | Niobium Nb 94·0 | Molybdenum Mo 96·0 | — | Ruthenium Ru 101·7, Rhodium Rh 103·0, Palladium Pd (Ag) 106·5 |
| 7 | | Silver Ag 107·9 | Cadmium Cd 112·4 | Indium In 114·0 | Tin Sn 119·0 | Antimony Sb 120·0 | Tellurium Te 127 | Iodine I 127 | |
| 8 | Xenon Xe 128 | Cæsium Cs 132·9 | Barium Ba 137·4 | Lanthanum La 139 | Cerium Ce 140 | — | — | — | — — — |
| 9 | | — | — | — | — | — | — | — | |
| 10 | — | — | — | Ytterbium Yb 173 | — | Tantalum Ta 183 | Tungsten W 184 | — | Osmium Os 191, Iridium Ir 193, Platinum Pt (Au) 194·9 |
| 11 | | Gold Au 197·2 | Mercury Hg 200·0 | Thallium Tl 204·1 | Lead Pb 206·9 | Bismuth Bi 208 | — | — | |
| 12 | — | — | Radium Rd 224 | — | Thorium Th 232 | — | Uranium U 239 | | |
| HIGHER SALINE OXIDES | R | $R_2O$ | RO | $R_2O_3$ | $RO_2$ | $R_2O_5$ | $RO_3$ | $R_2O_7$ | $RO_4$ |
| HIGHER GASEOUS HYDROGEN COMPOUNDS | | | | | $RH_4$ | $RH_3$ | $RH_2$ | RH | |

# Identifying Characteristics

Each element is different and has unique properties. These differences can be described in part by looking at the relationships between the atomic particles in each element. The periodic table contains numbers that describe these relationships.

**Number of Protons and Neutrons** Look up the element chlorine on the periodic table found on the inside back cover of your book. Cl is the symbol for chlorine, as shown in **Figure 13,** but what are the two numbers? The top number is the element's **atomic number.** It tells you the number of protons in the nucleus of each atom of that element. Every atom of chlorine, for example, has 17 protons in its nucleus.

 **Reading Check** *What are the atomic numbers for Cs, Ne, Pb, and U?*

**Isotopes** Although the number of protons changes from element to element, every atom of the same element has the same number of protons. However, the number of neutrons can vary even for one element. For example, some chlorine atoms have 18 neutrons in their nucleus while others have 20. These two types of chlorine atoms are chlorine-35 and chlorine-37. They are called **isotopes** (I suh tohps), which are atoms of the same element that have different numbers of neutrons.

You can tell someone exactly which isotope you are referring to by using its mass number. An atom's **mass number** is the number of protons plus the number of neutrons it contains. The numbers 35 and 37, which were used to refer to chlorine, are mass numbers. Hydrogen has three isotopes with mass numbers of 1, 2, and 3. They are shown in **Figure 14.** Each hydrogen atom always has one proton, but in each isotope the number of neutrons is different.

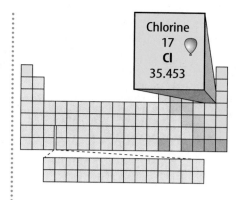

**Figure 13** The periodic table block for chlorine shows its symbol, atomic number, and atomic mass.
**Determine** *if chlorine atoms are more or less massive than carbon atoms.*

 **Physical Setting**

**3.3e, 3.3f, 3.3g Analyze** the periodic table. Describe how scientists find this organized chart helpful when working with elements.

**Figure 14** Three isotopes of hydrogen are known to exist. They have zero, one, and two neutrons in addition to their one proton. Protium, with only the one proton, is the most abundant isotope.

1 Proton
0 Neutrons

1 Proton
1 Neutron

1 Proton
2 Neutrons

Protium

Deuterium

Tritium

**Circle Graph Showing Abundance of Chlorine Isotopes**

Average atomic mass = 35.45 u

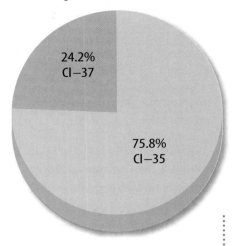

24.2%
Cl−37

75.8%
Cl−35

**Figure 15** If you have 1,000 atoms of chlorine, about 758 will be chlorine-35 and have a mass of 34.97 u each. About 242 will be chlorine-37 and have a mass of 36.97 u each. The total mass of the 1,000 atoms is 35,454 u, so the average mass of one chlorine atom is about 35.45 u.

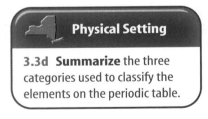
**Figure 16** The artisan is chasing, or chiseling, the malleable metal into the desired form.

**Atomic Mass** The **atomic mass** is the weighted average mass of the isotopes of an element. The atomic mass is the number found below the element symbol in **Figure 13.** The unit that scientists use for atomic mass is called the atomic mass unit, which is given the symbol u. It is defined as 1/12 the mass of a carbon-12 atom.

The calculation of atomic mass takes into account the different isotopes of the element. Chlorine's atomic mass of 35.45 u could be confusing because there aren't any chlorine atoms that have that exact mass. About 76 percent of chlorine atoms are chlorine-35 and about 24 percent are chlorine-37, as shown in **Figure 15.** The weighted average mass of all chlorine atoms is 35.45 u.

## Classification of Elements

Elements fall into three general categories—metals, metalloids (ME tuh loydz), and nonmetals. The elements in each category have similar properties.

**Metals** generally have a shiny or metallic luster and are good conductors of heat and electricity. All metals, except mercury, are solids at room temperature. Metals are malleable (MAL yuh bul), which means they can be bent and pounded into various shapes. The beautiful form of the shell-shaped basin in **Figure 16** is a result of this characteristic. Metals are also ductile, which means they can be drawn into wires without breaking. If you look at the periodic table, you can see that most of the elements are metals.

**Other Elements** Nonmetals are elements that are usually dull in appearance. Most are poor conductors of heat and electricity. Many are gases at room temperature, and bromine is a liquid. The solid nonmetals are generally brittle, meaning they cannot change shape easily without breaking. The nonmetals are essential to the chemicals of life. More than 97 percent of your body is made up of various nonmetals, as shown in **Figure 17.** You can see that, except for hydrogen, the nonmetals are found on the right side of the periodic table.

**Metalloids** are elements that have characteristics of metals and nonmetals. On the periodic table, metalloids are found between the metals and nonmetals. All metalloids are solids at room temperature. Some metalloids are shiny and many are conductors, but they are not as good at conducting heat and electricity as metals are. Some metalloids, such as silicon, are used to make the electronic circuits in computers, televisions, and other electronic devices.

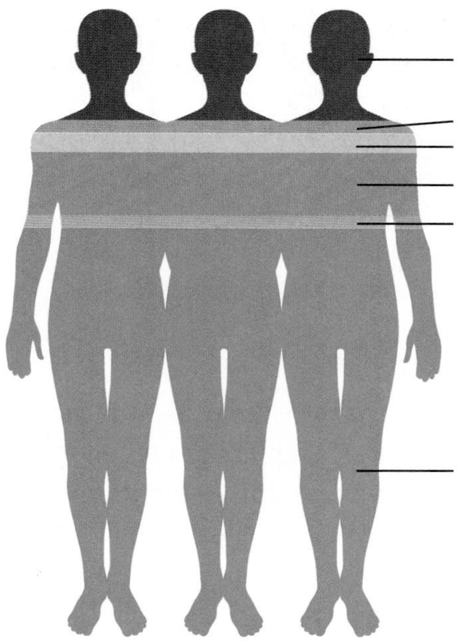

Carbon 18.5%
Calcium 1.5%
Nitrogen 3.2%
Hydrogen 9.5%
Other elements 2.3%
Oxygen 65%

**Figure 17** You are made up of mostly nonmetals.

☑ **Reading Check** *What is a metalloid?*

## section 2 review

### Summary

**The Elements**

- An element is matter made of only one type of atom.
- Some elements occur naturally on Earth. Synthetic elements are made in nuclear reactions in particle accelerators.
- Elements are divided into three categories based on certain properties.

**The Periodic Table**

- The periodic table arranges and displays all known elements in an orderly way.
- Each element has a chemical symbol.

**Identifying Characteristics**

- Each element has a unique number of protons, called the atomic mass number.
- Isotopes of an element are important when determining the atomic mass of an element.

### Self Check

1. **Explain** some of the uses of metals based on their properties.
2. **Describe** the difference between atomic number and atomic mass.
3. **Define** the term *isotope.* Explain how two isotopes of an element are different.
4. **Identify** the isotopes of hydrogen.
5. **Think Critically** Describe how to find the atomic number for the element oxygen. Explain what this information tells you about oxygen.

*Hot Words Hot Topics*: Bk 2 (6) p. 91

#### Applying Math

6. **Simple Equation** An atom of niobium has a mass number of 93. How many neutrons are in the nucleus of this atom? An atom of phosphorus has 15 protons and 15 neutrons in the nucleus. What is the mass number of this isotope?

# Elements and the Periodic Table

The periodic table organizes the elements, but what do they look like? What are they used for? In this lab, you'll examine some elements and share your findings with your classmates.

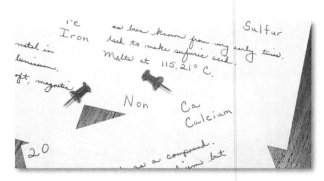

## ◉ Real-World Question

What are some of the characteristics and purposes of the chemical elements?

### Goals
- ■ **Classify** the chemical elements.
- ■ **Organize** the elements into the groups and periods of the periodic table.

### Materials
| | |
|---|---|
| colored markers | large bulletin board |
| large index cards | 8½-in × 14-in paper |
| Merck Index | thumbtacks |
| encyclopedia | *pushpins |
| *other reference | |
| materials | *Alternate materials |

### Safety Precaution

**WARNING:** *Use care when handling sharp objects.*

## ◉ Procedure

1. Select the assigned number of elements from the list provided by your teacher.

2. **Design** an index card for each of your selected elements. On each card, mark the element's atomic number in the upper left-hand corner and write its symbol and name in the upper right-hand corner.

3. **Research** each of the elements and write several sentences on the card about its appearance, its other properties, and its uses.

4. **Classify** each of your elements as a metal, a metalloid, or a nonmetal based upon its properties.

5. **Write** the appropriate classification on each of your cards using the colored marker chosen by your teacher.

6. Work with your classmates to make a large periodic table. Use thumbtacks to attach your cards to a bulletin board in their proper positions on the periodic table.

7. **Draw** your own periodic table. Place the elements' symbols and atomic numbers in the proper locations on your table.

## ◉ Conclude and Apply

1. **Interpret** the class data and classify the elements into the categories metal, metalloid, and nonmetal. Highlight each category in a different color on your periodic table.

2. **Predict** the properties of a yet-undiscovered element located directly under francium on the periodic table.

# section 3

# Compounds and Mixtures

## Substances

Scientists classify matter in several ways that depend on what it is made of and how it behaves. For example, matter that has the same composition and properties throughout is called a **substance.** Elements, such as a bar of gold or a sheet of aluminum, are substances. When different elements combine, other substances are formed.

**Compounds** What do you call the colorless liquid that flows from the kitchen faucet? You probably call it water, but maybe you've seen it written $H_2O$. The elements hydrogen and oxygen exist as separate, colorless gases. However, these two elements can combine, as shown in **Figure 18,** to form the compound water, which is different from the elements that make it up. A **compound** is a substance whose smallest unit is made up of atoms of more than one element bonded together.

Compounds often have properties that are different from the elements that make them up. Water is distinctly different from the elements that make it up. It is also different from another compound made from the same elements. Have you ever used hydrogen peroxide ($H_2O_2$) to disinfect a cut? This compound is a different combination of hydrogen and oxygen and has different properties from those of water.

Water is a nonirritating liquid that is used for bathing, drinking, cooking, and much more. In contrast, hydrogen peroxide carries warnings on its labels such as *Keep Hydrogen Peroxide Out of the Eyes.* Although it is useful in solutions for cleaning contact lenses, it is not safe for your eyes as it comes from the bottle.

## as you read

*What* **You'll Learn**
■ **Identify** the characteristics of a compound.
■ **Compare and contrast** different types of mixtures.

*Why* **It's Important**
The food you eat, the materials you use, and all matter can be classified by compounds or mixtures.

🔎 **Review Vocabulary**
**formula:** shows which elements and how many atoms of each make up a compound

**New Vocabulary**
● substance      ● mixture
● compound

**Figure 18** A space shuttle is powered by the reaction between liquid hydrogen and liquid oxygen. The reaction produces a large amount of energy and the compound water.
**Explain** *why a car that burns hydrogen rather than gasoline would be friendly to the environment.*

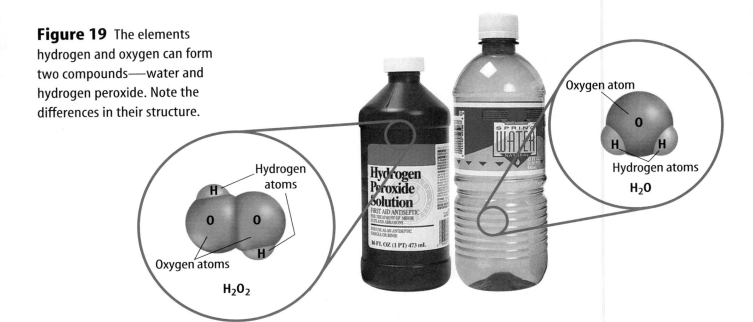

**Figure 19** The elements hydrogen and oxygen can form two compounds—water and hydrogen peroxide. Note the differences in their structure.

Hydrogen atoms

Oxygen atoms

$H_2O_2$

Oxygen atom

Hydrogen atoms

$H_2O$

## Mini LAB

### Comparing Compounds

**Procedure**

1. Collect the following substances—**granular sugar, rubbing alcohol,** and **salad oil.**
2. Observe the color, appearance, and state of each substance. Note the thickness or texture of each substance.
3. Stir a spoonful of each substance into separate **glasses** of **hot tap water** and observe.

**Analysis**

1. Compare the different properties of the substances.
2. The formulas of the three substances are made of only carbon, hydrogen, and oxygen. Infer how they can have different properties.

Try at Home

**Compounds Have Formulas** What's the difference between water and hydrogen peroxide? $H_2O$ is the chemical formula for water, and $H_2O_2$ is the formula for hydrogen peroxide. The formula tells you which elements make up a compound as well as how many atoms of each element are present. Look at **Figure 19.** The subscript number written below and to the right of each element's symbol tells you how many atoms of that element exist in one unit of that compound. For example, hydrogen peroxide has two atoms of hydrogen and two atoms of oxygen. Water is made up of two atoms of hydrogen and one atom of oxygen.

Carbon dioxide, $CO_2$, is another common compound. Carbon dioxide is made up of one atom of carbon and two atoms of oxygen. Carbon and oxygen also can form the compound carbon monoxide, CO, which is a gas that is poisonous to all warm-blooded animals. As you can see, no subscript is used when only one atom of an element is present. A given compound always is made of the same elements in the same proportion. For example, water always has two hydrogen atoms for every oxygen atom, no matter what the source of the water is. No matter what quantity of the compound you have, the formula of the compound always remains the same. If you have 12 atoms of hydrogen and six atoms of oxygen, the compound is still written $H_2O$, but you have six molecules of $H_2O$ ($6 H_2O$), not $H_{12}O_6$. The formula of a compound communicates its identity and makeup to any scientist in the world.

✓ **Reading Check** *Propane has three carbon and eight hydrogen atoms. What is its chemical formula?*

# Mixtures

When two or more substances (elements or compounds) come together but don't combine to make a new substance, a **mixture** results. Unlike compounds, the proportions of the substances in a mixture can be changed without changing the identity of the mixture. For example, if you put some sand into a bucket of water, you have a mixture of sand and water. If you add more sand or more water, it's still a mixture of sand and water. Its identity has not changed. Air is another mixture. Air is a mixture of nitrogen, oxygen, and other gases, which can vary at different times and places. Whatever the proportion of gases, it is still air. Even your blood is a mixture that can be separated, as shown in **Figure 20,** by a machine called a centrifuge.

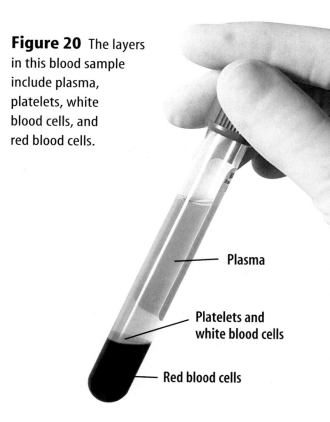

**Figure 20** The layers in this blood sample include plasma, platelets, white blood cells, and red blood cells.

Plasma

Platelets and white blood cells

Red blood cells

**✔ Reading Check** *How do the proportions of a mixture relate to its identity?*

---

## Applying Science

### What's the best way to desalt ocean water?

You can't drink ocean water because it contains salt and other suspended materials. Or can you? In many areas of the world where drinking water is in short supply, methods for getting the salt out of salt water are being used to meet the demand for fresh water. Use your problem-solving skills to find the best method to use in a particular area.

| Methods for Desalting Ocean Water | | | |
|---|---|---|---|
| Process | Amount of Water a Unit Can Desalt in a Day (m³) | Special Needs | Number of People Needed to Operate |
| Distillation | 1,000 to 200,000 | lots of energy to boil the water | many |
| Electrodialysis | 10 to 4,000 | stable source of electricity | 1 to 2 persons |

**Identifying the Problem**

The table above compares desalting methods. In distillation, the ocean water is heated. Pure water boils off and is collected, and the salt is left behind. Electrodialysis uses an electric current to pull salt particles out of water.

**Solving the Problem**

1. What method(s) might you use to desalt the water for a large population where energy is plentiful?
2. What method(s) would you choose to use in a single home?

**Figure 21** Mixtures are part of your everyday life.

**Physical Setting**

**3.2b Compare and contrast** *mixture* to *compound*. Support your reasoning with an example of each.

**Science** nline

**Topic: Mixtures**
Visit glencoe.com for Web links to information about separating mixtures.

**Activity** Describe the difference between mixtures and compounds.

**INTEGRATE**
**Life Science**
Your blood is a mixture made up of elements and compounds. It contains white blood cells, red blood cells, water, and a number of dissolved substances. The different parts of blood can be separated and used by doctors in different ways. The proportions of the substances in your blood change daily, but the mixture does not change its identity.

**Separating Mixtures** Sometimes you can use a liquid to separate a mixture of solids. For example, if you add water to a mixture of sugar and sand, only the sugar dissolves in the water. The sand then can be separated from the sugar and water by pouring the mixture through a filter. Heating the remaining solution will separate the water from the sugar.

At other times, separating a mixture of solids of different sizes might be as easy as pouring them through successively smaller sieves or filters. A mixture of marbles, pebbles, and sand could be separated in this way.

**Homogeneous or Heterogeneous** Mixtures, such as the ones shown in **Figure 21,** can be classified as homogeneous or heterogeneous. *Homogeneous* means "the same throughout." You can't see the different parts in this type of mixture. In fact, you might not always know that homogeneous mixtures are mixtures because you can't tell by looking. Which mixtures in **Figure 21** are homogeneous? No matter how closely you look, you can't see the individual parts that make up air or the parts of the mixture called brass in the lamp shown. Homogeneous mixtures can be solids, liquids, or gases.

A heterogeneous mixture has larger parts that are different from each other. You can see the different parts of a heterogeneous mixture, such as sand and water. How many heterogeneous mixtures are in **Figure 21?** A pepperoni and mushroom pizza is a tasty kind of heterogeneous mixture. Other examples of this kind of mixture include tacos, vegetable soup, a toy box full of toys, or a toolbox full of nuts and bolts.

**INTEGRATE
Earth Science**

**Rocks and Minerals**
Scientists called geologists study rocks and minerals. A mineral is composed of a pure substance. Rocks are mixtures and can be described as being homogeneous or heterogeneous. Research to learn more about rocks and minerals and note some examples of homogeneous and heterogeneous rocks in your Science Journal.

## section 3 review

### Summary

**Substances**

- A substance can be either an element or a compound.
- A compound contains more than one kind of element bonded together.
- A chemical formula shows which elements and how many atoms of each make up a compound.

**Mixtures**

- A mixture contains substances that are not chemically bonded together.
- There are many ways to separate mixtures, based on their physical properties.
- Homogeneous mixtures are those that are the same throughout. These types of mixtures can be solids, liquids, or gases.
- Heterogeneous mixtures have larger parts that are different from each other.

### Self Check

1. **List** three examples of compounds and three examples of mixtures. Explain your choices.

2. **Determine** A container contains a mixture of sand, salt, and pebbles. How can each substance be separated from the others?

3. **Think Critically** Explain whether your breakfast was a compound, a homogeneous mixture, or a heterogeneous mixture.

#### Applying Skills

4. **Compare and contrast** compounds and mixtures based on what you have learned from this section.

5. **Use a Database** Use a computerized card catalog or database to find information about one element from the periodic table. Include information about the properties and uses of the mixtures and/or compounds in which the element is frequently found.

# Mystery Mixture

## Goals

- **Test** for the presence of certain compounds.
- **Decide** which of these compounds are present in an unknown mixture.

## Materials

test tubes (4)
cornstarch
powdered sugar
baking soda
mystery mixture
small scoops (3)
dropper bottles (2)
iodine solution
white vinegar
hot plate
250-mL beaker
water (125 mL)
test-tube holder
small pie pan

## Safety Precautions

**WARNING:** *Use caution when handling hot objects. Substances could stain or burn clothing. Be sure to point the test tube away from your face and your classmates while heating.*

## Real-World Question

You will encounter many compounds that look alike. For example, a laboratory stockroom is filled with white powders. It is important to know what each is. In a kitchen, cornstarch, baking powder, and powdered sugar are compounds that look alike. To avoid mistaking one for another, you can learn how to identify them. Different compounds can be identified by using chemical tests. For example, some compounds react with certain liquids to produce gases. Other combinations produce distinctive colors. Some compounds have high melting points. Others have low melting points. How can the compounds in an unknown mixture be identified by experimentation?

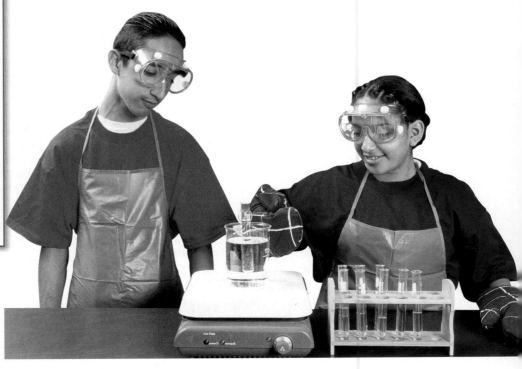

## Procedure

1. Copy the data table into your Science Journal. Record your results carefully for each of the following steps.

2. Place a small scoopful of cornstarch on the pie pan. Do the same for the sugar and baking soda making separate piles. Add a drop of vinegar to each. Wash and dry the pan after you record your observations.

3. Again, place a small scoopful of cornstarch, sugar, and baking soda on the pie pan. Add a drop of iodine solution to each one. Wash and dry the pan after you record your observations.

4. Again place a small scoopful of each compound in a separate test tube. Hold the test tube with the test-tube holder and with an oven mitt. Gently heat the test tube in a beaker of boiling water on a hot plate.

5. Follow steps 2 through 4 to test your mystery mixture for each compound.

### Identifying Presence of Compounds

| Substance to Be Tested | Fizzes with Vinegar | Turns Blue with Iodine | Melts When Heated |
|---|---|---|---|
| Cornstarch | | | |
| Sugar | | Do not write in this book. | |
| Baking soda | | | |
| Mystery mix | | | |

## Analyze Your Data

**Identify** from your data table which compound(s) you have.

## Conclude and Apply

1. **Describe** how you decided which substances were in your unknown mixture.

2. **Explain** how you would be able to tell if all three compounds were not in your mystery substance.

3. **Draw a Conclusion** What would you conclude if you tested baking powder from your kitchen and found that it fizzed with vinegar, turned blue with iodine, and did not melt when heated?

### Communicating Your Data

Make a different data table to display your results in a new way. **For more help, refer to the** Science Skill Handbook.

# Ancient Views of Matter

air

## Two cultures observed the world around them differently

water

The world's earliest scientists were people who were curious about the world around them and who tried to develop explanations for the things they observed. This type of observation and inquiry flourished in ancient cultures such as those found in India and China. Read on to see how the ancient Indians and Chinese defined matter.

### Indian Ideas

To Indians living about 3,000 years ago, the world was made up of five elements: fire, air, earth, water, and ether, which they thought of as an unseen substance that filled the heavens. Building upon this concept, the early Indian philosopher Kashyapa (kah SHI ah pah) proposed that the five elements could be broken down into smaller units called parmanu (par MAH new). Parmanu were similar to atoms in that they were too small to be seen but still retained the properties of the original element. Kashyapa also believed that each type of parmanu had unique physical and chemical properties.

metal

Parmanu of earth elements, for instance, were heavier than parmanu of air elements. The different properties of the parmanu determined the characteristics of a substance. Kashyapa's ideas about matter are similar to those of the Greek philosopher Democritus, who lived centuries after Kashyapa.

### Chinese Ideas

The ancient Chinese also broke matter down into five elements: fire, wood, metal, earth, and water. Unlike the early Indians, however, the Chinese believed that the elements constantly changed form. For example, wood can be burned and thus changes to fire. Fire eventually dies down and becomes ashes, or earth. Earth gives forth metals from the ground. Dew or water collects on these metals, and the water then nurtures plants that grow into trees, or wood.

fire

This cycle of constant change was explained in the fourth century B.C. by the philosopher Tsou Yen. Yen, who is known as the founder of Chinese scientific thought, wrote that all changes that took place in nature were linked to changes in the five elements.

earth

---

**Research** Write a brief paragraph that compares and contrasts the ancient Indian and Chinese views of matter. How are they different? Similar? Which is closer to the modern view of matter? Explain.

Science Online

For more information, visit glencoe.com

### Reviewing Main Ideas

**Section 1** **Structure of Matter**

1. Matter is anything that occupies space and has mass.

2. Matter is made up of atoms.

3. Atoms are made of smaller parts called protons, neutrons, and electrons.

4. Many models of atoms have been created as scientists try to discover and define the atom's internal structure. Today's model has a central nucleus with the protons and neutrons, and an electron cloud surrounding it.

**Section 2** **The Simplest Matter**

1. Elements are the building blocks of matter.

2. An element's atomic number tells how many protons its atoms contain, and its atomic mass tells the average mass of its atoms.

3. Isotopes are two or more atoms of the same element that have different numbers of neutrons.

**Section 3** **Compounds and Mixtures**

1. Compounds are substances that are produced when elements combine. Compounds contain specific proportions of the elements that make them up.

2. Mixtures are combinations of compounds and elements that have not formed new substances. Their proportions can change.

### Visualizing Main Ideas

*Copy and complete the following concept map.*

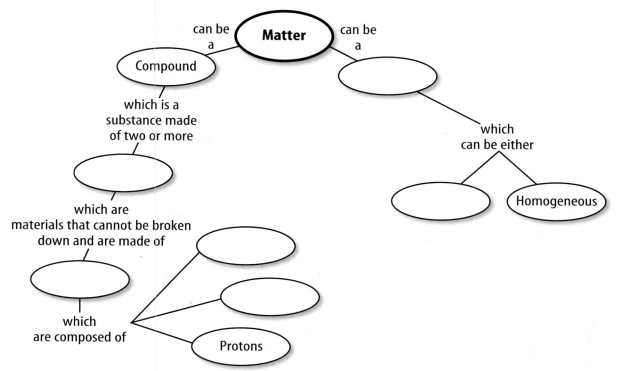

## Using Vocabulary

| | |
|---|---|
| atom p.271 | matter p.270 |
| atomic mass p.282 | metal p.282 |
| atomic number p.281 | metalloid p.283 |
| compound p.289 | mixture p.287 |
| electron p.274 | neutron p.276 |
| element p.278 | nonmetal p.283 |
| isotope p.281 | nucleus p.275 |
| law of conservation | proton p.275 |
| of matter p.272 | substance p.285 |
| mass number p.281 | |

*Fill in the blanks with the correct vocabulary word or words.*

1. The _____ is the particle in the nucleus of the atom that carries a positive charge and is counted to identify the atomic number.

2. The new substance formed when elements combine chemically is a(n) _____.

3. Anything that has mass and takes up space is _____.

4. The particles in the atom that account for most of the mass of the atom are protons and _____.

5. Elements that are shiny, malleable, ductile, good conductors of heat and electricity, and make up most of the periodic table are _____.

## Checking Concepts

*Choose the word or phrase that best answers the question.*

6. What is a solution an example of?
   A) element
   B) heterogeneous mixture
   C) compound
   D) homogeneous mixture

7. The nucleus of one atom contains 12 protons and 12 neutrons, while the nucleus of another atom contains 12 protons and 16 neutrons. What are the atoms?
   A) chromium atoms
   B) two different elements
   C) two isotopes of an element
   D) negatively charged

8. What is a compound?
   A) a mixture of chemicals and elements
   B) a combination of two or more elements
   C) anything that has mass and occupies space
   D) the building block of matter

9. What does the atom consist of?
   A) electrons, protons, and alpha particles
   B) neutrons and protons
   C) electrons, protons, and neutrons
   D) elements, protons, and electrons

10. In an atom, where is an electron located?
    A) in the nucleus with the proton
    B) on the periodic table of the elements
    C) with the neutron
    D) in a cloudlike formation surrounding the nucleus

11. How is matter defined?
    A) the negative charge in an atom
    B) anything that has mass and occupies space
    C) the mass of the nucleus
    D) sound, light, and energy

12. What are two atoms that have the same number of protons called?
    A) metals
    B) nonmetals
    C) isotopes
    D) metalloids

13. Which is a heterogeneous mixture?
    A) air         C) a salad
    B) brass       D) apple juice

**Use the illustration below to answer questions 14 and 15.**

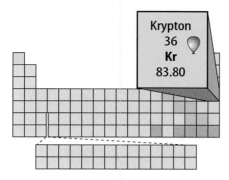

Krypton
36
**Kr**
83.80

**14.** Using the figure above, krypton has
  **A)** an atomic number of 84.
  **B)** an atomic number of 36.
  **C)** an atomic mass of 36.
  **D)** an atomic mass of 72.

**15.** From the figure, the element krypton is
  **A)** a solid.       **C)** a mixture.
  **B)** a liquid.      **D)** a gas.

## Thinking Critically

**16. Analyze Information** A chemical formula is written to indicate the makeup of a compound. What is the ratio of sulfur atoms to oxygen atoms in $SO_2$?

**17. Determine** which element contains seven protons.

**18. Describe** Using the periodic table, what are the atomic numbers for carbon, sodium, and nickel?

**19. Explain** how cobalt-60 and cobalt-59 can be the same element but have different mass numbers.

**20. Analyze Information** What did Rutherford's gold foil experiment tell scientists about atomic structure?

**21. Predict** Suppose Rutherford had bombarded aluminum foil with alpha particles instead of the gold foil he used in his

experiment. What observations do you predict Rutherford would have made? Explain your prediction.

**22. Draw Conclusions** You are shown a liquid that looks the same throughout. You're told that it contains more than one type of element and that the proportion of each varies throughout the liquid. Is this an element, a compound, or a mixture?

**Use the illustrations below to answer question 23.**

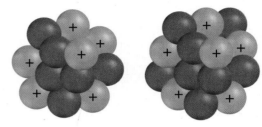

**23. Interpret Scientific Illustrations** Look at the two carbon atoms above. Explain whether or not the atoms are isotopes.

**24. Explain** how the atomic mass of an element is determined.

## Performance Activities

**25. Newspaper Article** As a newspaper reporter in the year 1896, you have heard about the discovery of the electron. Research and write an article about the scientist and the discovery.

*Hot Words Hot Topics*: Bk 2 (26) pp. 91, 194; (27) p. 292

## Applying Math

**26. Atomic Mass** Krypton has six naturally occurring isotopes with atomic masses of 78, 80, 82, 83, 84, and 86. Make a table of the number of protons, electrons, and neutrons in each isotope.

**27. Atomic Ratio** A researcher is analyzing two different compounds, sulfuric acid ($H_2SO_4$) and hydrogen peroxide ($H_2O_2$). What is the ratio of hydrogen to oxygen in sulfuric acid? What is the ratio of hydrogen to oxygen in hydrogen peroxide?

**Part I**

*Record your answers on the answer sheet provided by your teacher or on a sheet of paper.*

1 Which of the scientists below introduced the idea that matter is made up of tiny, individual bits called atoms?
(1) Arrhenius
(2) Avogadro
(3) Chadwick
(4) Democritus

**Use the illustration below to answer questions 2 and 3.**

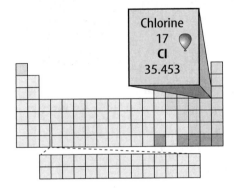

Chlorine
17
Cl
35.453

2 The periodic table block shown above lists properties of the element chlorine. What does the number 35.453 mean?
(1) the number of neutrons and in every chlorine atom
(2) the number of neutrons and protons in every chlorine atom
(3) the average number of neutrons in a chlorine atom
(4) the average number of neutrons and protons in a chlorine atom

3 According to the periodic table block, how many electrons does an uncharged atom of chlorine have?
(1) 17
(2) 18
(3) 35
(4) 36

4 Which of the following scientists envisioned the atom as a ball of positive charge with electrons embedded in it, much like chocolate chips spread through cookie dough?
(1) Crookes
(2) Dalton
(3) Thomson
(4) Rutherford

**Use the illustration below to answer questions 5 and 6.**

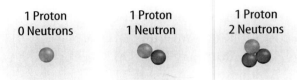

1 Proton
0 Neutrons

1 Proton
1 Neutron

1 Proton
2 Neutrons

5 Which of the following correctly identifies the three atoms shown in the illustration above?
(1) hydrogen, lithium, sodium
(2) hydrogen, helium, lithium
(3) hydrogen, helium, helium
(4) hydrogen, hydrogen, hydrogen

6 What is the mass number for each of the atoms shown in the illustration?
(1) 0, 1, 2
(2) 1, 1, 1
(3) 1, 2, 2
(4) 1, 2, 3

7 Which of the following are found close to the right side of the periodic table?
(1) metals
(2) lanthanides
(3) nonmetals
(4) metalloids

8 Which of the following is a characteristic that is typical of a solid, nonmetal element?
(1) shiny
(2) brittle
(3) good heat conductor
(4) good electrical conductor

**Part II**

*Record your answers on the answer sheet provided by your teacher or on a sheet of paper.*

**9** Analyze why electrons are more likely to be in an energy level close to the nucleus. Support your reasoning.

**10** Describe Dalton's ideas about the composition of matter, including the relationship between atoms and elements.

**Use the illustration below to answer questions 11 and 12.**

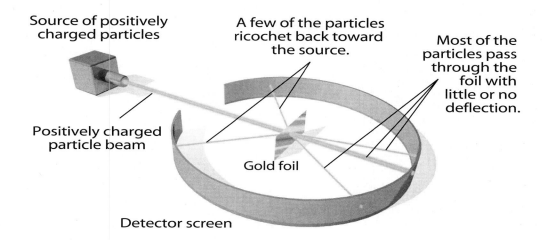

Source of positively charged particles

A few of the particles ricochet back toward the source.

Most of the particles pass through the foil with little or no deflection.

Positively charged particle beam

Gold foil

Detector screen

**11** The illustration above shows Rutherford's gold foil experiment. Describe the setup shown. What result did Rutherford expect from his experiment?

**12** What is the significance of the particles that reflected back from the gold foil? How did Rutherford explain his results?

**13** Describe three possible methods for separating mixtures. Give an example for each method.

**14** What are the rows and columns on the periodic table called? How are elements in the rows similar, and how are elements in the columns similar?

**15** Describe how Thomson was able to show that cathode rays were streams of particles, not light.

**16** Describe how the mass numbers, or atomic masses, listed on the periodic table for the elements are calculated.

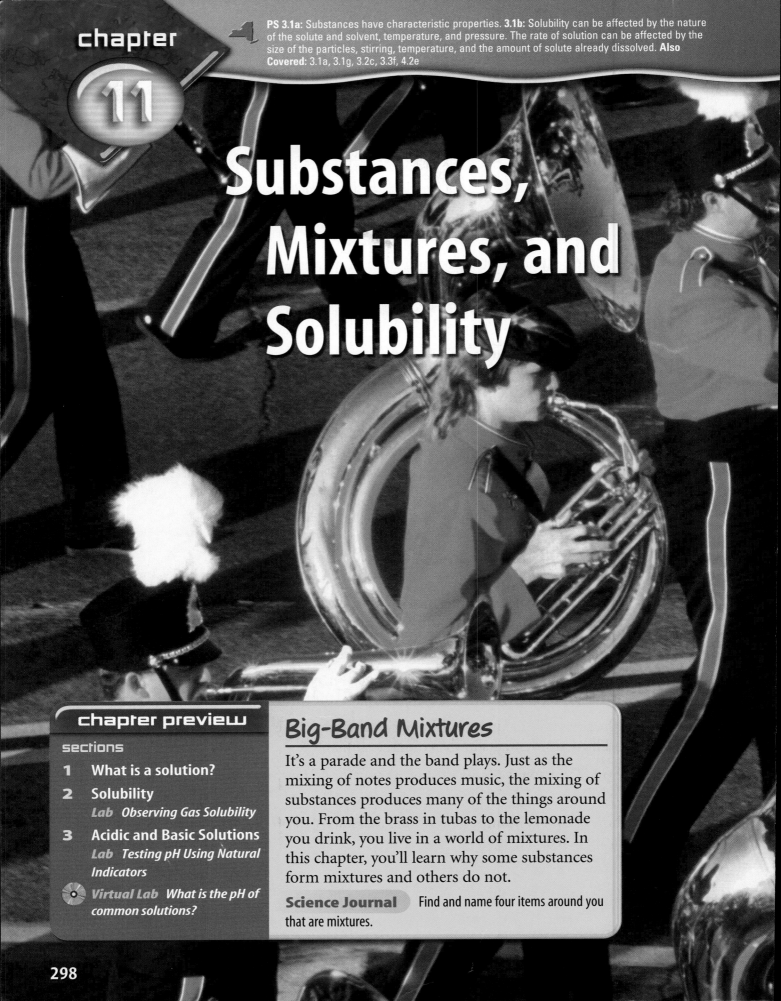

PS 3.1a: Substances have characteristic properties. **3.1b:** Solubility can be affected by the nature of the solute and solvent, temperature, and pressure. The rate of solution can be affected by the size of the particles, stirring, temperature, and the amount of solute already dissolved. **Also Covered:** 3.1a, 3.1g, 3.2c, 3.3f, 4.2e

# Substances, Mixtures, and Solubility

## chapter preview

## Big-Band Mixtures

It's a parade and the band plays. Just as the mixing of notes produces music, the mixing of substances produces many of the things around you. From the brass in tubas to the lemonade you drink, you live in a world of mixtures. In this chapter, you'll learn why some substances form mixtures and others do not.

**Science Journal** Find and name four items around you that are mixtures.

# Start-Up Activities

## Particle Size and Dissolving Rates

Why do drink mixes come in powder form? What would happen if you dropped a big chunk of drink mix into the water? Would it dissolve quickly? Powdered drink mix dissolves faster in water than chunks do because it is divided into smaller particles, exposing more of the mix to the water. See for yourself how particle size affects the rate at which a substance dissolves.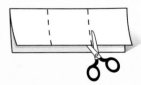

1. Pour 400 mL of water into each of two 600-mL beakers.

2. Carefully grind a bouillon cube into powder using a mortar and pestle.

3. Place the bouillon powder into one beaker and drop a whole bouillon cube into the second beaker.

4. Stir the water in each beaker for 10 s and observe.

5. **Think Critically** Write a paragraph in your Science Journal comparing the color of the two liquids and the amount of undissolved bouillon at the bottom of each beaker. How does the particle size affect the rate at which a substance dissolves?

**Solutions** Make the following Foldable to help classify solutions based on their common features.

**STEP 1** Fold a vertical sheet of paper from side to side. Make the front edge about 1.25 cm shorter than the back edge.

**STEP 2** Turn lengthwise and fold into thirds.

**STEP 3** Unfold and cut only the top layer along both folds to make three tabs.

**STEP 4** Label each tab as shown.

| Solid Solutions | Liquid Solutions | Gaseous Solutions |

**Find Main Ideas** As you read the chapter, classify solutions based on their states and list them under the appropriate tabs. On your Foldable, circle the solutions that are acids and underline the solutions that are bases.

**Science Online** Preview this chapter's content and activities at glencoe.com

# section

## 1

# What is a solution?

## as you read

### *What* You'll Learn

- **Distinguish** between substances and mixtures.
- **Describe** two different types of mixtures.
- **Explain** how solutions form.
- **Describe** different types of solutions.

### *Why* It's Important

The air you breathe, the water you drink, and even parts of your body are all solutions.

### Review Vocabulary

**proton:** positively charged particle located in the nucleus of an atom

### New Vocabulary

- substance
- heterogeneous mixture
- homogeneous mixture
- solution    • solvent
- solute    • precipitate

## Substances

Water, salt water, and pulpy orange juice have some obvious differences. These differences can be explained by chemistry. Think about pure water. No matter what you do to it physically—freeze it, boil it, stir it, or strain it—it still is water. On the other hand, if you boil salt water, the water turns to gas and leaves the salt behind. If you strain pulpy orange juice, it loses its pulp. How does chemistry explain these differences? The answer has to do with the chemical compositions of the materials.

**Atoms and Elements**   Recall that atoms are the basic building blocks of matter. Each atom has unique chemical and physical properties which are determined by the number of protons it has. For example, all atoms that have eight protons are oxygen atoms. A **substance** is matter that has the same fixed composition and properties. It can't be broken down into simpler parts by ordinary physical processes, such as boiling, grinding, or filtering. Only a chemical process can change a substance into one or more new substances. **Table 1** lists some examples of physical and chemical processes. An element is an example of a pure substance; it cannot be broken down into simpler substances. The number of protons in an element, like oxygen, are fixed—it cannot change unless the element changes.

| Table 1  Examples of Physical and Chemical Processes | |
|---|---|
| **Physical Processes** | **Chemical Processes** |
| Boiling | Burning |
| Changing pressure | Reacting with other chemicals |
| Cooling | Reacting with light |
| Sorting | |

**Compounds**   Water is another example of a substance. It is always water even when you boil it or freeze it. Water, however, is not an element. It is an example of a compound which is made of two or more elements that are chemically combined. Compounds also have fixed compositions. The ratio of the atoms in a compound is always the same. For example, when two hydrogen atoms combine with one oxygen atom, water is formed. All water—whether it's in the form of ice, liquid, or steam—has the same ratio of hydrogen atoms to oxygen atoms.

Separation by magnetism          Separation by straining

Figure 1 Mixtures can be separated by physical processes.
**Explain** *why the iron-sand mixture and the pulpy lemonade are not pure substances.*

## Mixtures

Imagine drinking a glass of salt water. You would know right away that you weren't drinking pure water. Like salt water, many things are not pure substances. Salt water is a mixture of salt and water. Mixtures are combinations of substances that are not bonded together and can be separated by physical processes. For example, you can boil salt water to separate the salt from the water. If you had a mixture of iron filings and sand, you could separate the iron filings from the sand with a magnet. **Figure 1** shows some mixtures being separated.

Unlike compounds, mixtures do not always contain the same proportions of the substances that they are composed of. Lemonade is a mixture that can be strong tasting or weak tasting, depending on the amounts of water and lemon juice that are added. It also can be sweet or sour, depending on how much sugar is added. But whether it is strong, weak, sweet, or sour, it is still lemonade.

**Heterogeneous Mixtures** It is easy to tell that some things are mixtures just by looking at them. A watermelon is a mixture of fruit and seeds. The seeds are not evenly spaced through the whole melon—one bite you take might not have any seeds in it and another bite might have several seeds. A type of mixture where the substances are not mixed evenly is called a **heterogeneous** (he tuh ruh JEE nee us) **mixture.** The different areas of a heterogeneous mixture have different compositions. The substances in a heterogeneous mixture are usually easy to tell apart, like the seeds from the fruit of a watermelon. Other examples of heterogeneous mixtures include a bowl of cold cereal with milk and the mixture of pens, pencils, and books in your backpack.

**Science** nline

**Topic: Desalination**
Visit glencoe.com for Web links to information about how salt is removed from salt water to provide drinking water.

**Activity** Compare and contrast the two most common methods used for desalination.

Sugar

Water

**Homogeneous Mixtures** Your shampoo contains many ingredients, but you can't see them when you look at the shampoo. It is the same color and texture throughout. Shampoo is an example of a homogeneous (hoh muh JEE nee us) mixture. A **homogeneous mixture** contains two or more substances that are evenly mixed on a molecular level but still are not bonded together. Another name for a homogeneous mixture is a **solution.** The sugar and water in the frozen pops shown in **Figure 2,** are a solution—the sugar is evenly distributed in the water, and you can't see the sugar.

**Figure 2** Molecules of sugar and water are evenly mixed in frozen pops.

**Reading Check** *What is another name for a homogeneous mixture?*

# How Solutions Form

How do you make sugar water for a hummingbird feeder? You might add sugar to water and heat the mixture until the sugar disappears. The sugar molecules would spread out until they were evenly spaced throughout the water, forming a solution. This is called dissolving. The substance that dissolves—or seems to disappear—is called the **solute.** The substance that dissolves the solute is called the **solvent.** In the hummingbird feeder solution, the solute is the sugar and the solvent is water. The substance that is present in the greatest quantity is the solvent.

**Figure 3** Minerals and soap react to form soap scum, which comes out of the water solution and coats the tiles of a shower.

**Forming Solids from Solutions** Under certain conditions, a solute can come back out of its solution and form a solid. This process is called crystallization. Sometimes this occurs when the solution is cooled or when some of the solvent evaporates. Crystallization is the result of a physical change. When some solutions are mixed, a chemical reaction occurs, forming a solid. This solid is called a **precipitate** (prih SIH puh tayt). A precipitate is the result of a chemical change. Precipitates probably have formed in your sink or shower because of chemical reactions. Minerals that are dissolved in tap water react chemically with soap. The product of this reaction leaves the water as a precipitate called soap scum, shown in **Figure 3.**

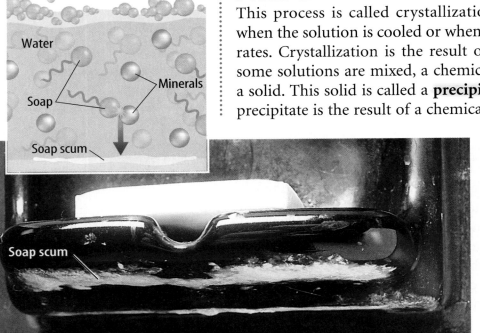

Water

Minerals

Soap

Soap scum

Soap scum

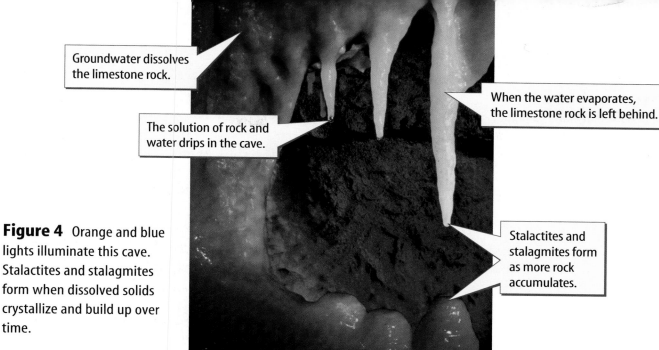

Groundwater dissolves the limestone rock.

When the water evaporates, the limestone rock is left behind.

The solution of rock and water drips in the cave.

Stalactites and stalagmites form as more rock accumulates.

**Figure 4** Orange and blue lights illuminate this cave. Stalactites and stalagmites form when dissolved solids crystallize and build up over time.

**INTEGRATE Environment**

Stalactites and stalagmites in caves are formed from solutions, as shown in **Figure 4.** First, minerals dissolve in water as it flows through rocks at the top of the cave. This solution of water and dissolved minerals drips from the ceiling of the cave. When drops of the solution evaporate from the roof of the cave, the minerals are left behind. They create the hanging rock formations called stalactites. When drops of the solution fall onto the floor of the cave and evaporate, they form stalagmites. Very often, a stalactite develops downward while a stalagmite develops upward until the two meet. One continuous column of minerals is formed. This process will be discussed later.

## Types of Solutions

So far, you've learned about types of solutions in which a solid solute dissolves in a liquid solvent. But solutions can be made up of different combinations of solids, liquids, and gases, as shown in **Table 2.**

| Table 2  Examples of Common Solutions | | | |
|---|---|---|---|
| | **Solvent/ State** | **Solute/ State** | **State of Solution** |
| **Earth's atmosphere** | nitrogen/gas | oxygen/gas<br>carbon dioxide/gas<br>argon/gas | gas |
| **Ocean water** | water/liquid | salt/solid<br>oxygen/gas<br>carbon dioxide/gas | liquid |
| **Carbonated beverage** | water/liquid | carbon dioxide/gas | liquid |
| **Brass** | copper/solid | zinc/solid | solid |

**Figure 5** Acetic acid (a liquid), carbon dioxide (a gas), and drink-mix crystals (a solid) can be dissolved in water (a liquid). *Determine whether one liquid solution could contain all three different kinds of solute.*

## Liquid Solutions

You're probably most familiar with liquid solutions like the ones shown in **Figure 5,** in which the solvent is a liquid. The solute can be another liquid, a solid, or even a gas. You've already learned about liquid-solid solutions such as sugar water and salt water. When discussing solutions, the state of the solvent usually determines the state of the solution.

**Liquid-Gas Solutions** Carbonated beverages are liquid-gas solutions—carbon dioxide is the gaseous solute, and water is the liquid solvent. The carbon dioxide gas gives the beverage its fizz and some of its tartness. The beverage also might contain other solutes, such as the compounds that give it its flavor and color.

✔ **Reading Check** *What are the solutes in a carbonated beverage?*

**Liquid-Liquid Solutions** In a liquid-liquid solution, both the solvent and the solute are liquids. Vinegar, which you might use to make salad dressing, is a liquid-liquid solution made of 95 percent water (the solvent) and 5 percent acetic acid (the solute).

## Gaseous Solutions

In gaseous solutions, a smaller amount of one gas is dissolved in a larger amount of another gas. This is called a gas-gas solution because both the solvent and solute are gases. The air you breathe is a gaseous solution. Nitrogen makes up about 78 percent of dry air and is the solvent. The other gases are the solutes.

**Figure 6** Metal alloys can contain either metal or nonmetal solutes dissolved in a metal solvent.

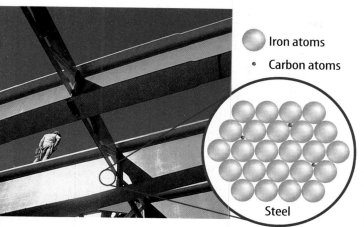

Iron atoms
Carbon atoms

Copper atoms
Zinc atoms

Brass

Steel

Steel is a solid solution of the metal iron and the non-metal carbon.

Brass is a solid solution made of copper and zinc.

**Solid Solutions** In solid solutions, the solvent is a solid. The solute can be a solid, liquid, or gas. The most common solid solutions are solid-solid solutions—ones in which the solvent and the solute are solids. A solid-solid solution made from two or more metals is called an alloy. It's also possible to include elements that are not metals in alloys. For example, steel is an alloy that has carbon dissolved in iron. The carbon makes steel much stronger and yet more flexible than iron. Two alloys are shown in **Figure 6.**

## section 1 review

### Summary

**Substances**

- Elements are substances that cannot be broken down into simpler substances.
- A compound is made up of two or more elements bonded together.

**Mixtures and Solutions**

- Mixtures are either heterogeneous or homogeneous.
- Solutions have two parts—solute and solvent.
- Crystallization and precipitation are two ways that solids are formed from solutions.

**Types of Solutions**

- The solutes and solvents can be solids, liquids, or gases.

### Self Check

1. **Compare and contrast** substances and mixtures. Give two examples of each.
2. **Describe** how heterogeneous and homogeneous mixtures differ.
3. **Explain** how a solution forms.
4. **Identify** the common name for a solid-solid solution of metals.
5. **Think Critically** The tops of carbonated-beverage cans usually are made with a different aluminum alloy than the pull tabs are made with. Explain.

#### Applying Skills

6. **Compare and contrast** the following solutions: a helium-neon laser, bronze (a copper-tin alloy), cloudy ice cubes, and ginger ale.

# section

## 2 Solubility

### *What* You'll Learn

- **Explain** why water is a good general solvent.
- **Describe** how the structure of a compound affects which solvents it dissolves in.
- **Identify** factors that affect how much of a substance will dissolve in a solvent.
- **Describe** how temperature affects reaction rate.
- **Explain** how solute particles affect physical properties of water.

### *Why* It's Important

How you wash your hands, clothes, and dishes depends on which substances can dissolve in other substances.

### ⊙ Review Vocabulary
**polar bond:** a bond resulting from the unequal sharing of electrons

### New Vocabulary
- aqueous
- solubility
- saturated
- concentration

## Water—The Universal Solvent

In many solutions, including fruit juice and vinegar, water is the solvent. A solution in which water is the solvent is called an **aqueous** (A kwee us) solution. Because water can dissolve so many different solutes, chemists often call it the universal solvent. To understand why water is such a great solvent, you must first know a few things about atoms and bonding.

**Molecular Compounds** When certain atoms form compounds, they share electrons. Sharing electrons is called covalent bonding. Compounds that contain covalent bonds are called molecular compounds, or molecules.

If a molecule has an even distribution of electrons, like the one in **Figure 7,** it is called nonpolar. The atoms in some molecules do not have an even distribution of electrons. For example, in a water molecule, two hydrogen atoms share electrons with a single oxygen atom. However, as **Figure 7** shows, the electrons spend more time around the oxygen atom than they spend around the hydrogen atoms. As a result, the oxygen portion of the water molecule has a partial negative charge and the hydrogen portions have a partial positive charge. The overall charge of the water molecule is neutral. Such a molecule is said to be polar, and the bonds between its atoms are called polar covalent bonds.

**Figure 7** Some atoms share electrons to form covalent bonds.

Two atoms of hydrogen share their electrons equally. Such a molecule is nonpolar.

(Partial negative charge)

The electrons spend more time around the oxygen atom than the hydrogen atoms. Such a molecule is polar.

(Partial positive charge)

**Ionic Bonds** Some atoms do not share electrons when they join with other atoms to form compounds. Instead, these atoms lose or gain electrons. When they do, the number of protons and electrons within an atom are no longer equal, and the atom becomes positively or negatively charged. Atoms with a charge are called ions. Bonds between ions that are formed by the transfer of electrons are called ionic bonds, and the compound that is formed is called an ionic compound. Table salt is an ionic compound that is made of sodium ions and chloride ions. Each sodium atom loses one electron to a chlorine atom and becomes a positively charged sodium ion. Each chlorine atom gains one electron from a sodium atom, becoming a negatively charged chloride ion.

**Reading Check** *How does an ionic compound differ from a molecular compound?*

**How Water Dissolves Ionic Compounds** Now think about the properties of water and the properties of ionic compounds as you visualize how an ionic compound dissolves in water. Because water molecules are polar, they attract positive and negative ions. The more positive part of a water molecule—where the hydrogen atoms are—is attracted to negatively charged ions. The more negative part of a water molecule—where the oxygen atom is—attracts positive ions. When an ionic compound is mixed with water, the different ions of the compound are pulled apart by the water molecules. **Figure 8** shows how sodium chloride dissolves in water.

**Solutions** Seawater is a solution that contains nearly every element found on Earth. Most elements are present in tiny quantities. Sodium and chloride ions are the most common ions in seawater. Several gases, including oxygen, nitrogen, and carbon dioxide, also are dissolved in seawater.

**Figure 8** Water dissolves table salt because its partial charges are attracted to the charged ions in the salt.

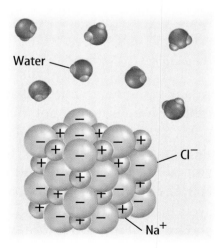

The partially negative oxygen in the water molecule is attracted to a positive sodium ion.

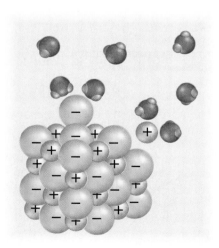

The partially positive hydrogen atoms in another water molecule are attracted to a negative chloride ion.

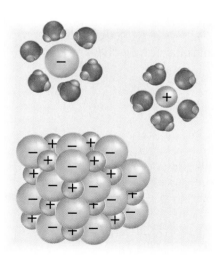

The sodium and chloride ions are pulled apart from each other, and more water molecules are attracted to them.

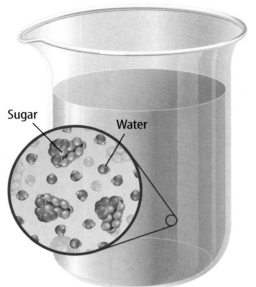

**Figure 9** Sugar molecules that are dissolved in water spread out until they are spaced evenly in the water.

**Figure 10** Water and oil do not mix because water molecules are polar and oil molecules are nonpolar.

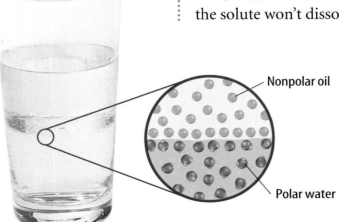

Nonpolar oil

Polar water

## How Water Dissolves Molecular Compounds

Can water also dissolve molecular compounds that are not made of ions? Water does dissolve molecular compounds, such as sugar, although it doesn't break each sugar molecule apart. Water simply moves between different molecules of sugar, separating them. Like water, a sugar molecule is polar. Polar water molecules are attracted to the positive and negative portions of the polar sugar molecules. When the sugar molecules are separated by the water and spread throughout it, as **Figure 9** shows, they have dissolved.

## What will dissolve?

When you stir a spoonful of sugar into iced tea, all of the sugar dissolves but none of the metal in the spoon does. Why does sugar dissolve in water, but metal does not? A substance that dissolves in another is said to be soluble in that substance. You would say that the sugar is soluble in water but the metal of the spoon is insoluble in water, because it does not dissolve readily.

**Like Dissolves Like** When trying to predict which solvents can dissolve which solutes, chemists use the rule of "like dissolves like." This means that polar solvents dissolve polar solutes and nonpolar solvents dissolve nonpolar solutes. In the case of sugar and water, both are made up of polar molecules, so sugar is soluble in water. In the case of salt and water, the sodium and chloride ion pair is like the water molecule because it has a positive charge at one end and a negative charge at the other end.

**Reading Check** *What does "like dissolves like" mean?*

On the other hand, if a solvent and a solute are not similar, the solute won't dissolve. For example, oil and water do not mix. Oil molecules are nonpolar, so polar water molecules are not attracted to them. If you pour vegetable oil into a glass of water, the oil and the water separate into layers instead of forming a solution, as shown in **Figure 10.** You've probably noticed the same thing about the oil-and-water mixtures that make up some salad dressings. The oil stays on the top. Oils generally dissolve better in solvents that have nonpolar molecules.

# How much will dissolve?

Even though sugar is soluble in water, if you tried to dissolve 1 kg of sugar into one small glass of water, not all of the sugar would dissolve. **Solubility** (sahl yuh BIH luh tee) is a measurement that describes how much solute dissolves in a given amount of solvent. The solubility of a material has been described as the amount of the material that can dissolve in 100 g of solvent at a given temperature. Some solutes are highly soluble, meaning that a large amount of solute can be dissolved in 100 g of solvent. For example, 63 g of potassium chromate can be dissolved in 100 g of water at 25°C. On the other hand, some solutes are not very soluble. For example, only 0.00025 g of barium sulfate will dissolve in 100 g of water at 25°C. When a substance has an extremely low solubility, like barium sulfate does in water, it usually is considered insoluble.

**Reading Check** *What is an example of a substance that is considered to be insoluble in water?*

**Solubility in Liquid-Solid Solutions** Did you notice that the temperature was included in the explanation about the amount of solute that dissolves in a quantity of solvent? The solubility of many solutes changes if you change the temperature of the solvent. For example, if you heat water, not only does the sugar dissolve at a faster rate, but more sugar can dissolve in it. However, some solutes, like sodium chloride and calcium carbonate, do not become more soluble when the temperature of water increases. The graph in **Figure 11** shows how the temperature of the solvent affects the solubility of some solutes.

**Solubility in Liquid-Gas Solutions** Unlike liquid-solid solutions, an increase in temperature decreases the solubility of a gas in a liquid-gas solution. You might notice this if you have ever opened a warm carbonated beverage and it bubbled up out of control while a chilled one barely fizzed. Carbon dioxide is less soluble in a warm solution. What keeps the carbon dioxide from bubbling out when it is sitting at room temperature on a supermarket shelf? When a bottle is filled, extra carbon dioxide gas is squeezed into the space above the liquid, increasing the pressure in the bottle. This increased pressure increases the solubility of gas and forces most of it into the solution. When you open the cap, the pressure is released and the solubility of the carbon dioxide decreases.

**Reading Check** *Why does a bottle of carbonated beverage go "flat" after it has been opened for a few days?*

**Figure 11** The solubility of some solutes changes as the temperature of the solvent increases.
**Use a Graph** *According to the graph, is it likely that warm ocean water contains any more sodium chloride than cold ocean water does?*

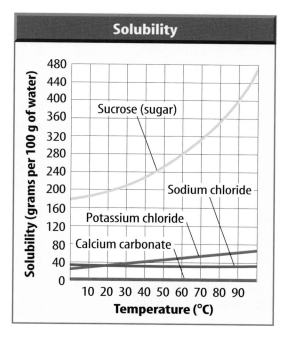

**Solubility**

Solubility (grams per 100 g of water)

Sucrose (sugar)

Sodium chloride

Potassium chloride

Calcium carbonate

480 440 400 360 320 280 240 200 160 120 80 40 0

10 20 30 40 50 60 70 80 90

Temperature (°C)

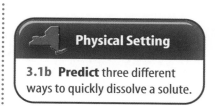

**Physical Setting**

**3.1b Predict** three different ways to quickly dissolve a solute.

## Mini LAB

### Observing Chemical Processes

**Procedure**

1. Pour **two small glasses of milk.**
2. Place one glass of milk in the **refrigerator.** Leave the second glass on the counter.
3. Allow the milk to sit overnight. **WARNING:** *Do not drink the milk that sat out overnight.*
4. On the following day, smell both glasses of milk. Record your observations.

### Analysis

1. Compare and contrast the smell of the refrigerated milk to the non-refrigerated milk.
2. Explain why refrigeration is needed.

**Try at Home**

**Figure 12** The Dead Sea has an extremely high concentration of dissolved minerals. When the water evaporates, the minerals are left behind and form pillars.

**Saturated Solutions** If you add calcium carbonate to 100 g of water at 25°C, only 0.0014 g of it will dissolve. Additional calcium carbonate will not dissolve. Such a solution—one that contains all of the solute that it can hold under the given conditions—is called a **saturated** solution. **Figure 12** shows a saturated solution. If a solution is a liquid-solid solution, the extra solute that is added will settle to the bottom of the container. It's possible to make solutions that have less solute than they would need to become saturated. Such solutions are unsaturated. An example of an unsaturated solution is one containing 50 g of sugar in 100 g of water at 25°C. That's much less than the 204 g of sugar the solution would need to be saturated.

A hot solvent usually can hold more solute than a cool solvent can. When a saturated solution cools, some of the solute usually falls out of the solution. But if a saturated solution is cooled slowly, sometimes the excess solute remains dissolved for a period of time. Such a solution is said to be supersaturated, because it contains more than the normal amount of solute.

## Rate of Dissolving

Solubility does not tell you how fast a solute will dissolve—it tells you only how much of a solute will dissolve at a given temperature. Some solutes dissolve quickly, but others take a long time to dissolve. A solute dissolves faster when the solution is stirred or shaken or when the temperature of the solution is increased. These methods increase the rate at which the surfaces of the solute come into contact with the solvent. Increasing the area of contact between the solute and the solvent can also increase the rate of dissolving. This can be done by breaking up the solute into smaller pieces, which increases the surface area of the solute that is exposed to the solvent.

**INTEGRATE Chemistry**

Molecules are always moving and colliding. The collisions must take place for chemical processes to occur. The chemical processes take place at a given rate of reaction. Temperature has a large effect on that rate. The higher the temperature, the more collisions occur and the higher the rate of reaction. The opposite is also true. The lower the temperature, the less collisions occur and the lower the rate of reaction. Refrigerators are an example of slowing the reaction rate—and therefore the chemical process—down to prevent food spoilage.

# Concentration

What makes strong lemonade strong and weak lemonade weak? The difference between the two drinks is the amount of water in each one compared to the amount of lemon. The lemon is present in different concentrations in the solution. The **concentration** of a solution tells you how much solute is present compared to the amount of solvent. You can give a simple description of a solution's concentration by calling it either concentrated or dilute. These terms are used when comparing the concentrations of two solutions with the same type of solute and solvent. A concentrated solution has more solute per given amount of solvent than a dilute solution.

**Measuring Concentration** Can you imagine a doctor ordering a dilute intravenous, or IV, solution for a patient? Because dilute is not an exact measurement, the IV could be made with a variety of amounts of medicine. The doctor would need to specify the exact concentration of the IV solution to make sure that the patient is treated correctly.

**Pharmacist** Doctors rely on pharmacists to formulate IV solutions. Pharmacists begin with a concentrated form of the drug, which is supplied by pharmaceutical companies. This is the solute of the IV solution. The pharmacist adds the correct amount of solvent to a small amount of the solute to achieve the concentration requested by the doctor. There may be more than one solute per IV solution in varying concentrations.

## Applying Science

### How can you compare concentrations?

A solute is a substance that can be dissolved in another substance called a solvent. Solutions vary in concentration, or strength, depending on the amount of solute and solvent being used. Fruit drinks are examples of such a solution. Stronger fruit drinks appear darker in color and are the result of more drink mix being dissolved in a given amount of water. What would happen if more water were added to the solution?

| Glucose Solutions (g/100 mL) | | |
|---|---|---|
| Solute Glucose (g) | Solvent Water (mL) | Solution Concentration of Glucose (%) |
| 2 | 100 | 2 |
| 4 | 100 | 4 |
| 10 | 100 | 10 |
| 20 | 100 | 20 |

**Identifying the Problem**

The table on the right lists different concentration levels of glucose solutions, a type of carbohydrate your body uses as a source of energy. The glucose is measured in grams, and the water is measured in milliliters.

**Solving the Problem**

A physician writes a prescription for a patient to receive 1,000 mL of a 20 percent solution of glucose. How many grams of glucose must the pharmacist add to 1,000 mL of water to prepare this 20 percent concentration level?

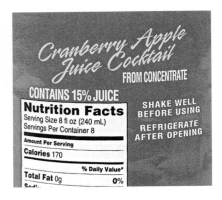

**Figure 13** Concentrations can be stated in percentages.
**Identify** *the percentage of this fruit drink that is water, assuming there are no other dissolved substances.*

One way of giving the exact concentration is to state the percentage of the volume of the solution that is made up of solute. Labels on fruit drinks show their concentration like the one in **Figure 13.** When a fruit drink contains 15 percent fruit juice, the remaining 85 percent of the drink is water and other substances such as sweeteners and flavorings. This drink is more concentrated than another brand that contains 10 percent fruit juice, but it's more dilute than pure juice, which is 100 percent juice. Another way to describe the concentration of a solution is to give the percentage of the total mass that is made up of solute.

**Effects of Solute Particles** All solute particles affect the physical properties of the solvent, such as its boiling point and freezing point. The effect that a solute has on the freezing or boiling point of a solvent depends on the number of solute particles.

When a solvent such as water begins to freeze, its molecules arrange themselves in a particular pattern. Adding a solute such as sodium chloride to this solvent changes the way the molecules arrange themselves. To overcome this interference of the solute, a lower temperature is needed to freeze the solvent.

When a solvent such as water begins to boil, the solvent molecules are gaining enough energy to move from the liquid state to the gaseous state. When a solute such as sodium chloride is added to the solvent, the solute particles interfere with the evaporation of the solvent particles. More energy is needed for the solvent particles to escape from the liquid, and the boiling point of the solution will be higher.

## section 2 review

### Summary

**The Universal Solvent**

- Water is known as the universal solvent.
- A molecule that has an even distribution of electrons is a nonpolar molecule.
- A molecule that has an uneven distribution of electrons is a polar molecule.
- A compound that loses or gains electrons is an ionic compound.

**Dissolving a Substance**

- Chemists use the rule "like dissolves like."

**Concentration**

- Concentration is the quantity of solute present compared to the amount of solvent.

### Self Check

1. **Identify** the property of water that makes it the universal solvent.
2. **Describe** the two methods to increase the rate at which a substance dissolves.
3. **Infer** why it is important to add sodium chloride to water when making homemade ice cream.
4. **Think Critically** Why can the fluids used to dry-clean clothing remove grease even when water cannot?

**Applying Skills**

5. **Recognize Cause and Effect** Why is it more important in terms of reaction rate to take groceries straight home from the store when it is 25°C than when it is 2°C?

# LAB

# Observing Gas Solubility

On a hot day, a carbonated beverage will cool you off. If you leave the beverage uncovered at room temperature, it quickly loses its fizz. However, if you cap the beverage and place it in the refrigerator, it will still have its fizz hours later. In this lab you will explore why this happens.

## Real-World Question

What effect does temperature have on the fizz, or carbon dioxide, in your carbonated beverage?

### Goals

■ **Observe** the effect that temperature has on solubility of a gas in a liquid.

■ **Compare** the amount of carbon dioxide released at room temperature and in hot tap water.

### Materials

carbonated beverages in plastic bottles, thoroughly chilled (2)

balloons (2)          *ruler
tape                  container
fabric tape measure   hot tap water
*string               *Alternative materials

### Safety Precautions

**WARNING:** *DO NOT point the bottles at anyone at any time during the lab.*

## Procedure

1. Carefully remove the caps from the thoroughly chilled plastic bottles one at a time. Create as little agitation as possible.

2. Quickly cover the opening of each bottle with an uninflated balloon.

3. Use tape to secure and tightly seal the balloons to the top of the bottles.

4. Gently agitate one bottle from side to side for two minutes. Measure the circumference of the balloon.

**WARNING:** *Contents under pressure can cause serious accidents. Be sure to wear safety goggles, and DO NOT point the bottles at anyone.*

5. Gently agitate the second bottle in the same manner as in step 4. Then, place the bottle in a container of hot tap water for ten minutes. Measure the circumference of the balloon.

## Conclude and Apply

1. **Contrast** the relative amounts of carbon dioxide gas released from the cold and the warm carbonated beverages.

2. **Infer** Why does the warmed carbonated beverage release a different amount of carbon dioxide than the chilled one?

### Communicating Your Data

Compare the circumferences of your balloons with those of members of your class. **For more help, refer to the** Science Skill Handbook.

# section 3

# Acidic and Basic Solutions

## as you read

### *What* You'll Learn

- **Compare** acids and bases and their properties.
- **Describe** practical uses of acids and bases.
- **Explain** how pH is used to describe the strength of an acid or base.
- **Describe** how acids and bases react when they are brought together.

### *Why* It's Important

Many common products, such as batteries and bleach, work because of acids or bases.

### ⊙ Review Vocabulary

**physical property:** any characteristic of a material that can be seen or measured without changing the material

### New Vocabulary

- acid
- hydronium ion
- base
- pH
- indicator
- neutralization

## Acids

What makes orange juice, vinegar, dill pickles, and grapefruit tangy? Acids cause the sour taste of these and other foods. **Acids** are substances that release positively charged hydrogen ions, $H^+$, in water. When an acid mixes with water, the acid dissolves, releasing a hydrogen ion. The hydrogen ion then combines with a water molecule to form a hydronium ion, as shown in **Figure 14. Hydronium ions** are positively charged and have the formula $H_3O^+$.

**Properties of Acidic Solutions** Sour taste is one of the properties of acidic solutions. The taste allows you to detect the presence of acids in your food. However, even though you can identify acidic solutions by their sour taste, you should never taste anything in the laboratory, and you should never use taste to test for the presence of acids in an unknown substance. Many acids can cause serious burns to body tissues.

Another property of acidic solutions is that they can conduct electricity. The hydronium ions in an acidic solution can carry the electric charges in a current. This is why some batteries contain an acid. Acidic solutions also are corrosive, which means they can break down certain substances. Many acids can corrode fabric, skin, and paper. The solutions of some acids also react strongly with certain metals. The acid-metal reaction forms metallic compounds and hydrogen gas, leaving holes in the metal in the process.

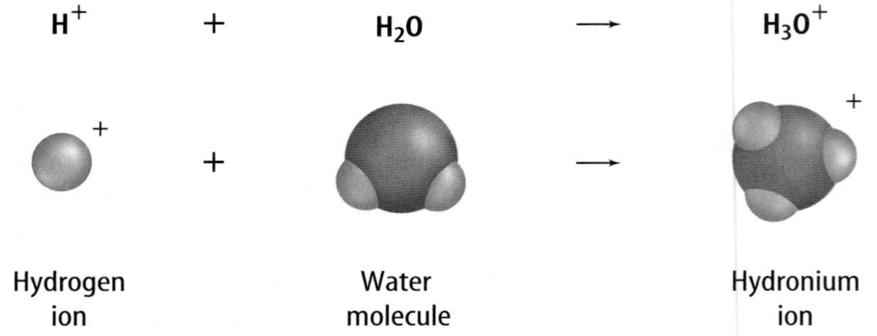

$$H^+ \quad + \quad H_2O \quad \longrightarrow \quad H_3O^+$$

**Figure 14** One hydrogen ion can combine with one water molecule to form one positively charged hydronium ion.
**Identify** *what kinds of substances are sources of hydrogen ions.*

Hydrogen ion    Water molecule    Hydronium ion

**Figure 15** Each of these products contains an acid or is made with the help of an acid.
**Describe** how your life would be different if acids were not available to make these products.

**Uses of Acids** You're probably familiar with many acids. Vinegar, which is used in salad dressing, contains acetic acid. Lemons, limes, and oranges have a sour taste because they contain citric acid. Your body needs ascorbic acid, which is vitamin C. Ants that sting inject formic acid into their victims.

**Figure 15** shows other products that are made with acids. Sulfuric acid is used in the production of fertilizers, steel, paints, and plastics. Acids often are used in batteries because their solutions conduct electricity. For this reason, it sometimes is referred to as battery acid. Hydrochloric acid, which is known commercially as muriatic acid, is used in a process called pickling. Pickling is a process that removes impurities from the surfaces of metals. Hydrochloric acid also can be used to clean mortar from brick walls. Nitric acid is used in the production of fertilizers, dyes, and plastics.

**Acid in the Environment** Carbonic acid plays a key role in the formation of caves and of stalactites and stalagmites. Carbonic acid is formed when carbon dioxide in soil is dissolved in water. When this acidic solution comes in contact with calcium carbonate—or limestone rock—it can dissolve it, eventually carving out a cave in the rock. A similar process occurs when acid rain falls on statues and eats away at the stone, as shown in **Figure 16.** When this acidic solution drips from the ceiling of the cave, water evaporates and carbon dioxide becomes less soluble, forcing it out of solution. The solution becomes less acidic and the limestone becomes less soluble, causing it to come out of solution. These solids form stalactites and stalagmites.

## Mini LAB

### Observing a Nail in a Carbonated Drink

**Procedure**
1. Observe the initial appearance of an **iron nail.**
2. Pour enough **carbonated soft drink** into a **cup or beaker** to cover the nail.
3. Drop the nail into the soft drink and observe what happens.
4. Leave the nail in the soft drink overnight and observe it again the next day.

**Analysis**
1. Describe what happened when you first dropped the nail into the soft drink and the appearance of the nail the following day.
2. Based upon the fact that the soft drink was carbonated, explain why you think the drink reacted with the nail as you observed.

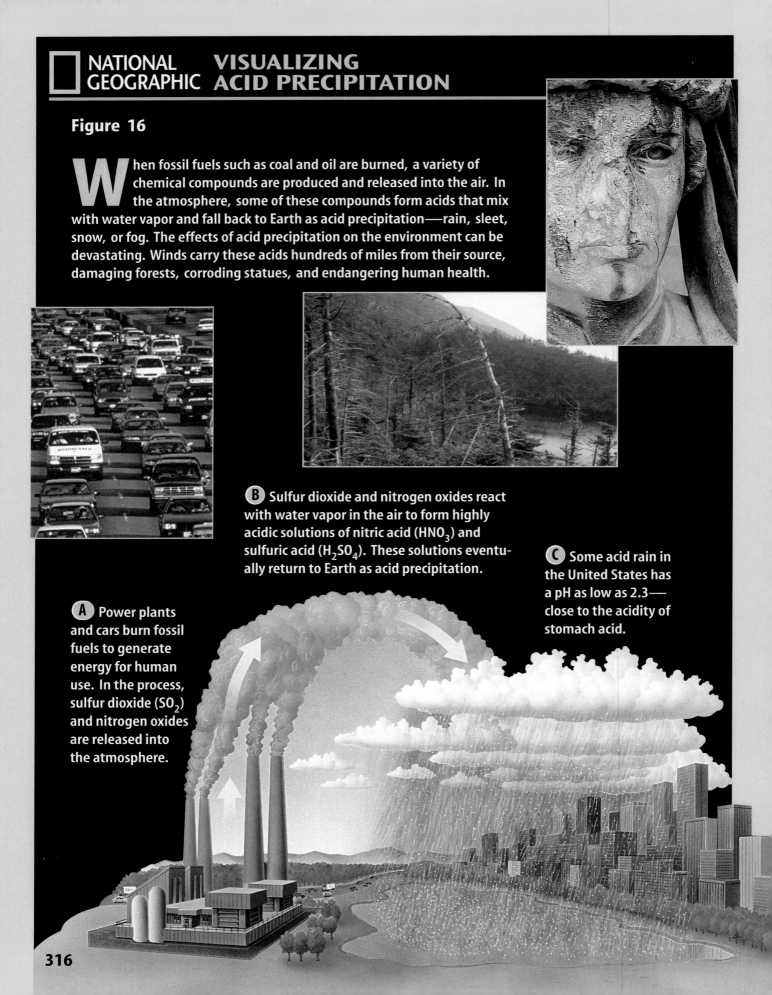

## Figure 16

**W**hen fossil fuels such as coal and oil are burned, a variety of chemical compounds are produced and released into the air. In the atmosphere, some of these compounds form acids that mix with water vapor and fall back to Earth as acid precipitation—rain, sleet, snow, or fog. The effects of acid precipitation on the environment can be devastating. Winds carry these acids hundreds of miles from their source, damaging forests, corroding statues, and endangering human health.

**B** Sulfur dioxide and nitrogen oxides react with water vapor in the air to form highly acidic solutions of nitric acid ($HNO_3$) and sulfuric acid ($H_2SO_4$). These solutions eventually return to Earth as acid precipitation.

**C** Some acid rain in the United States has a pH as low as 2.3— close to the acidity of stomach acid.

**A** Power plants and cars burn fossil fuels to generate energy for human use. In the process, sulfur dioxide ($SO_2$) and nitrogen oxides are released into the atmosphere.

# Bases

People often use ammonia solutions to clean windows and floors. These solutions have different properties from those of acidic solutions. Ammonia is called a base. **Bases** are substances that can accept hydrogen ions. When bases dissolve in water, some hydrogen atoms from the water molecules are attracted to the base. A hydrogen atom in the water molecule leaves behind the other hydrogen atom and oxygen atom. This pair of atoms is a negatively charged ion called a hydroxide ion. A hydroxide ion has the formula $OH^-$. Most bases contain a hydroxide ion, which is released when the base dissolves in water. For example, sodium hydroxide is a base with the formula NaOH. When NaOH dissolves in water, a sodium ion and the hydroxide ion separate.

**Science Online**

**Topic: Calcium Hydroxide**
Visit glencoe.com for Web links to information about the uses for calcium hydroxide.

**Activity** Describe the chemical reaction that converts limestone (calcium carbonate) to calcium hydroxide.

**Properties of Basic Solutions** Most soaps are bases, so if you think about how soap feels, you can figure out some of the properties of basic solutions. Basic solutions feel slippery. Acids in water solution taste sour, but bases taste bitter—as you know if you have ever accidentally gotten soap in your mouth.

Like acids, bases are corrosive. Bases can cause burns and damage tissue. You should never touch or taste a substance to find out whether it is a base. Basic solutions contain ions and can conduct electricity. Basic solutions are not as reactive with metals as acidic solutions are.

**Uses of Bases** Many uses for bases are shown in **Figure 17.** Bases give soaps, ammonia, and many other cleaning products some of their useful properties. The hydroxide ions produced by bases can interact strongly with certain substances, such as dirt and grease.

Chalk and oven cleaner are examples of familiar products that contain bases. Your blood is a basic solution. Calcium hydroxide, often called lime, is used to mark the lines on athletic fields. It also can be used to treat lawns and gardens that have acidic soil. Sodium hydroxide, known as lye, is a strong base that can cause burns and other health problems. Lye is used to make soap, clean ovens, and unclog drains.

**Figure 17** Many products, including soaps, cleaners, and plaster contain bases or are made with the help of bases.

**pH Levels** Most life-forms can't exist at extremely low pH levels. However, some bacteria thrive in acidic environments. Acidophils are bacteria that exist at low pH levels. These bacteria have been found in the Hot Springs of Yellowstone National Park in areas with pH levels ranging from 1 to 3.

# What is pH?

You've probably heard of pH-balanced shampoo or deodorant, and you might have seen someone test the pH of the water in a swimming pool. **pH** is a measure of how acidic or basic a solution is. The pH scale ranges from 0 to 14. Acidic solutions have pH values below 7. A solution with a pH of 0 is very acidic. Hydrochloric acid can have a pH of 0. A solution with a pH of 7 is neutral, meaning it is neither acidic nor basic. Pure water is neutral. Basic solutions have pH values above 7. A solution with a pH of 14 is very basic. Sodium hydroxide can have a pH of 14. **Figure 18** shows where various common substances fall on the pH scale.

The pH of a solution is related directly to its concentrations of hydronium ions ($H_3O^+$) and hydroxide ions ($OH^-$). Acidic solutions have more hydronium ions than hydroxide ions. Neutral solutions have equal numbers of the two ions. Basic solutions have more hydroxide ions than hydronium ions.

 **Reading Check** *In a neutral solution, how do the numbers of hydronium ions and hydroxide ions compare?*

**pH Scale** The pH scale is not a simple linear scale like mass or volume. For example, if one book has a mass of 2 kg and a second book has a mass of 1 kg, the mass of the first book is twice that of the second. However, a change of 1 pH unit represents a tenfold change in the acidity of the solution. For example, if one solution has a pH of 1 and a second solution has a pH of 2, the first solution is not twice as acidic as the second—it is ten times more acidic. To determine the difference in pH strength, use the following calculation: $10^n$, where $n =$ the difference between pHs. For example: pH3 − pH1 = 2, $10^2 = 100$ times more acidic.

**Figure 18** The pH scale classifies a solution as acidic, basic, or neutral.

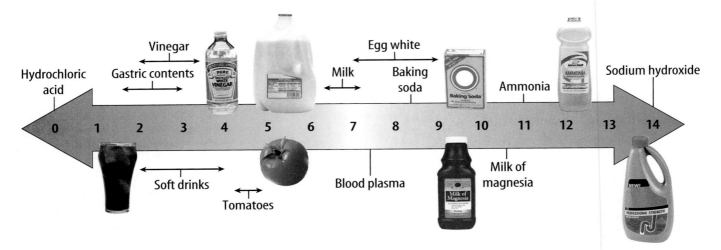

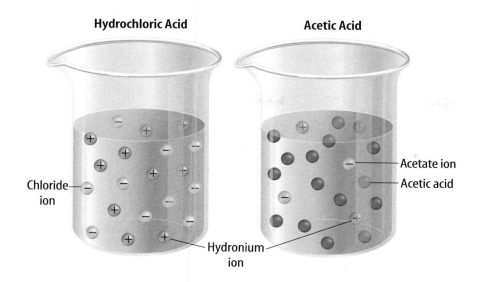

**Hydrochloric Acid**

**Acetic Acid**

Chloride ion

Acetate ion
Acetic acid

Hydronium ion

**Figure 19** Hydrochloric acid separates into ions more readily than acetic acid does when it dissolves in water. Therefore, hydrochloric acid exists in water as separated ions. Acetic acid exists in water almost entirely as molecules.

**Strengths of Acids and Bases** You've learned that acids give foods a sour taste but also can cause burns and damage tissue. The difference between food acids and the acids that can burn you is that they have different strengths. The acids in food are fairly weak acids, while the dangerous acids are strong acids. The strength of an acid is related to how easily the acid separates into ions, or how easily a hydrogen ion is released, when the acid dissolves in water. Look at **Figure 19.** In the same concentration, a strong acid—like hydrochloric acid—forms more hydronium ions in solution than a weak acid does—like acetic acid. More hydronium ions means the strong-acid solution has a lower pH than the weak-acid solution. Similarly, the strength of a base is related to how easily the base separates into ions, or how easily a hydroxide ion is released, when the base dissolves in water. The relative strengths of some common acids and bases are shown in **Table 3.**

**Physical Setting**

**3.1a, 3.2c Design** a chart to compare acids to bases. Include how each reacts chemically to water, general physical and chemical characteristics, and neutralization.

✔ **Reading Check** *What determines the strength of an acid or a base?*

An acid containing more hydrogen atoms, such as carbonic acid, $H_2CO_3$, is not necessarily stronger than an acid containing fewer hydrogen atoms, such as nitric acid, $HNO_3$. An acid's strength is related to how easily a hydrogen ion separates—not to how many hydrogen atoms it has. For this reason, nitric acid is stronger than carbonic acid.

| Table 3  Strengths of Some Acids and Bases | | |
|---|---|---|
| | **Acid** | **Base** |
| **Strong** | hydrochloric (HCl)<br>sulfuric ($H_2SO_4$)<br>nitric ($HNO_3$) | sodium hydroxide (NaOH)<br>potassium hydroxide (KOH) |
| **Weak** | acetic ($CH_3COOH$)<br>carbonic ($H_2CO_3$)<br>ascorbic ($H_2C_6H_6O_6$) | ammonia ($NH_3$)<br>aluminum hydroxide ($Al(OH)_3$)<br>iron (III) hydroxide ($Fe(OH)_3$) |

## Indicators

What is a safe way to find out how acidic or basic a solution is? **Indicators** are compounds that react with acidic and basic solutions and produce certain colors, depending on the solution's pH.

Because they are different colors at different pHs, indicators can help you determine the pH of a solution. Some indicators, such as litmus, are soaked into paper strips. When litmus paper is placed in an acidic solution, it turns red. When placed in a basic solution, litmus paper turns blue. Some indicators can change through a wide range of colors, with each different color appearing at a different pH value.

## Neutralization

Perhaps you've heard someone complain about heartburn or an upset stomach after eating spicy food. To feel better, the person might have taken an antacid. Think about the word *antacid* for a minute. How do antacids work?

Heartburn or stomach discomfort is caused by excess hydrochloric acid in the stomach. Hydrochloric acid helps break down the food you eat, but too much of it can irritate your stomach or digestive tract. An antacid product, often made from the base magnesium hydroxide, $Mg(OH)_2$, neutralizes the excess acid. **Neutralization** (new truh luh ZAY shun) is the reaction of an acid with a base. It is called this because the properties of both the acid and base are diminished, or neutralized. In most cases, the reaction produces a water and a salt. **Figure 20** illustrates the relative amounts of hydronium and hydroxide ions between pH 0 and pH 14.

✔ **Reading Check** *What are the products of neutralization?*

**Topic: Indicators**

Visit glencoe.com for Web links to information about the types of pH indicators.

**Activity** Describe how plants can act as indicators in acidic and basic solutions.

**Figure 20** The pH of a solution is more acidic when greater amounts of hydronium ions are present.
**Define** *what makes a pH 7 solution neutral.*

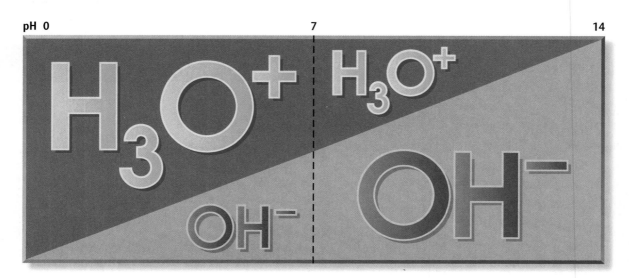

pH 0         7         14

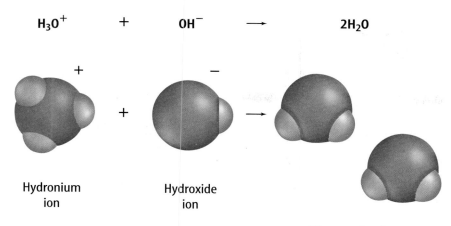

$$H_3O^+ \quad + \quad OH^- \quad \longrightarrow \quad 2H_2O$$

$+$     $+$     $-$

Hydronium ion     Hydroxide ion

Water molecules

**Figure 21** When acidic and basic solutions react, hydronium and hydroxide ions react to form water.
**Determine** *why the pH of the solution changes.*

**How does neutralization occur?** Recall that every water molecule contains two hydrogen atoms and one oxygen atom. As **Figure 21** shows, when one hydronium ion reacts with one hydroxide ion, the product is two water molecules. This reaction occurs during acid-base neutralization. Equal numbers of hydronium ions from the acidic solution and hydroxide ions from the basic solution react to produce water. Pure water has a pH of 7, which means that it's neutral.

✔ **Reading Check** *What happens to acids and bases during neutralization?*

## section 3 review

### Summary

**Acids and Bases**

- Acids are substances that release positively charged hydrogen ions in water.
- Substances that accept hydrogen ions in water are bases.
- Acidic and basic solutions can conduct electricity.

**pH**

- pH measures how acidic or basic a solution is.
- The scale ranges from 0 to 14.

**Neutralization**

- Neutralization is the interaction between an acid and a base to form water and a salt.

### Self Check

1. **Identify** what ions are produced by acids in water and bases in water. Give two properties each of acids and bases.

2. **Name** three acids and three bases and list an industrial or household use of each.

3. **Explain** how the concentration of hydronium ions and hydroxide ions are related to pH.

4. **Think Critically** In what ways might a company that uses a strong acid handle an acid spill on the factory floor?

*Hot Words Hot Topics*: Bk 2 (5) pp. 91, 169

### Applying Math

5. **Solve One-Step Equations** How much more acidic is a solution with a pH of 2 than one with a pH of 6? How much more basic is a solution with a pH of 13 than one with a pH of 10?

# Testing pH Using Natural Indicators

## Goals

- **Determine** the relative acidity or basicity of several common solutions.
- **Compare** the strengths of several common acids and bases.

## Materials

small test tubes (9)
test-tube rack
concentrated red cabbage juice in a dropper bottle
labeled bottles containing:
   household ammonia,
   baking soda solution,
   soap solution,
   0.1*M* hydrochloric acid
   solution, white vinegar,
   colorless carbonated
   soft drink, borax soap
   solution, distilled water
grease pencil
droppers (9)

## Safety Precautions

**WARNING:** *Many acids and bases are poisonous, can damage your eyes, and can burn your skin. Wear goggles and gloves AT ALL TIMES. Tell your teacher immediately if a substance spills. Wash your hands after you finish but before removing your goggles.*

## Real-World Question

You have learned that certain substances, called indicators, change color when the pH of a solution changes. The juice from red cabbage is a natural indicator. How do the pH values of various solutions compare to each other? How can you use red cabbage juice to determine the relative pH of several solutions?

## Procedure

1. **Design** a data table to record the names of the solutions to be tested, the colors caused by the added cabbage juice indicator, and the relative strengths of the solutions.

2. Mark each test tube with the identity of the acid or base solution it will contain.

3. Half-fill each test tube with the solution to be tested.
   **WARNING:** *If you spill any liquids on your skin, rinse the area immediately with water. Alert your teacher if any liquid spills in the work area or on your skin.*

4. Add ten drops of the cabbage juice indicator to each of the solutions to be tested. Gently agitate or wiggle each test tube to mix the cabbage juice with the solution.

5. **Observe** and record the color of each solution in your data table.

| Determining pH Values | |
|---|---|
| **Cabbage Juice Color** | **Relative Strength of Acid or Base** |
| | strong acid |
| | medium acid |
| | weak acid |
| | neutral |
| | weak base |
| | medium base |
| | strong base |

## Analyze Your Data

1. **Compare** your observations with the table above. Record in your data table the relative acid or base strength of each solution you tested.

2. **List** the solutions by pH value starting with the most acidic and finishing with the most basic.

## Conclude and Apply

1. **Classify** which solutions were acidic and which were basic.

2. **Identify** which solution was the weakest acid. The strongest base? The closest to neutral?

3. **Predict** what ion might be involved in the cleaning process based upon your data for the ammonia, soap, and borax soap solutions.

## Form a Hypothesis

Form a hypothesis that explains why the borax soap solution was less basic than an ammonia solution of approximately the same concentration.

### Communicating
#### Your Data

Use your data to create labels for the solutions you tested. Include the relative strength of each solution and any other safety information you think is important on each label. **For more help, refer to the** Science Skill Handbook.

# SCIENCE Stats

## Salty Solutions

### Did you know...

**...Seawater is certainly a salty solution.** Ninety-nine percent of all salt ions in the sea are sodium, chlorine, sulfate, magnesium, calcium, and potassium. The major gases in the sea are nitrogen, oxygen, carbon dioxide, argon, neon, and helium.

**...Tears and saliva have a lot in common.** Both are salty solutions that protect you from harmful bacteria, keep tissues moist, and help spread nutrients. Bland-tasting saliva, however, is 99 percent water. The remaining one percent is a combination of many ions, including sodium and several proteins.

**...The largest salt lake** in the United States is the Great Salt Lake. It covers more than 4,000 km² in Utah and is up to 13.4 m deep. The Great Salt Lake and the Salt Lake Desert were once part of the enormous, prehistoric Lake Bonneville, which was 305 m deep at some points.

**Applying Math** At its largest, Lake Bonneville covered about 32,000 km². What percentage of that area does the Great Salt Lake now cover?

*Hot Words Hot Topics*: Bk 2 (Stats) pp. 142–143, 356

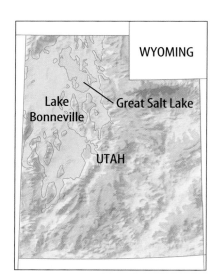

WYOMING

Lake Bonneville — Great Salt Lake

UTAH

**...Salt can reduce pain.** Gargled salt water is a disinfectant; it fights the bacteria that cause some sore throats.

### Graph It

Visit glencoe.com to research and learn about other elements in seawater. Create a graph that shows the amounts of the ten most common elements in 1 L of seawater.

## Reviewing Main Ideas

### Section 1 What is a solution?

1. Elements and compounds are pure substances, because their compositions are fixed. Mixtures are not pure substances.

2. Heterogeneous mixtures are not mixed evenly. Homogeneous mixtures, also called solutions, are mixed evenly on a molecular level.

3. Solutes and solvents can be gases, liquids, or solids, combined in many different ways.

### Section 2 Solubility

1. Because water molecules are polar, they can dissolve many different solutes. Like dissolves like.

2. Temperature and pressure can affect solubility.

3. Solutions can be unsaturated, saturated, or supersaturated, depending on how much solute is dissolved compared to the solubility of the solute in the solvent.

4. The concentration of a solution is the amount of solute in a particular volume of solvent.

### Section 3 Acidic and Basic Solutions

1. Acids release H+ ions and produce hydronium ions when they are dissolved in water. Bases accept H+ ions and produce hydroxide ions when dissolved in water.

2. pH expresses the concentrations of hydronium ions and hydroxide ions in aqueous solutions.

3. In a neutralization reaction, an acid reacts with a base to form water and a salt.

## Visualizing Main Ideas

*Copy and complete the concept map on the classification of matter.*

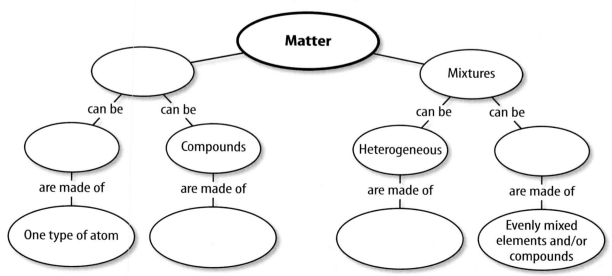

# chapter 11 Review

## Using Vocabulary

acid p.314
aqueous p.306
base p.317
concentration p.311
heterogeneous mixture p.301
homogeneous mixture p.302
hydronium ion p.314
indicator p.320

neutralization p.320
pH p.318
precipitate p.302
saturated p.310
solubility p.309
solute p.302
solution p.302
solvent p.302
substance p.300

*Fill in the blanks with the correct vocabulary word.*

1. A base has a(n) _____ value above 7.

2. A measure of how much solute is in a solution is its _____.

3. The amount of a solute that can dissolve in 100 g of solvent is its _____.

4. The _____ is the substance that is dissolved to form a solution.

5. The reaction between an acidic and basic solution is called _____.

6. A(n) _____ has a fixed composition.

## Checking Concepts

*Choose the word or phrase that best answers the question.*

7. Which of the following is a solution?
   A) pure water
   B) an oatmeal-raisin cookie
   C) copper
   D) vinegar

8. What type of compounds will not dissolve in water?
   A) polar          C) nonpolar
   B) ionic          D) charged

9. What type of molecule is water?
   A) polar          C) nonpolar
   B) ionic          D) precipitate

10. When chlorine compounds are dissolved in pool water, what is the water?
    A) the alloy
    B) the solvent
    C) the solution
    D) the solute

11. A solid might become less soluble in a liquid when you decrease what?
    A) particle size     C) temperature
    B) pressure          D) container size

12. Which acid is used in the industrial process known as pickling?
    A) hydrochloric      C) sulfuric
    B) carbonic          D) nitric

13. A solution is prepared by adding 100 g of solid sodium hydroxide, NaOH, to 1,000 mL of water. What is the solid NaOH called?
    A) solution          C) solvent
    B) solute            D) mixture

14. Given equal concentrations, which of the following will produce the most hydronium ions in an aqueous solution?
    A) a strong base     C) a strong acid
    B) a weak base       D) a weak acid

15. Bile, an acidic body fluid used in digestion, has a high concentration of hydronium ions. Predict its pH.
    A) 11                C) less than 7
    B) 7                 D) greater than 7

16. When you swallow an antacid, what happens to your stomach acid?
    A) It is more acidic.
    B) It is concentrated.
    C) It is diluted.
    D) It is neutralized.

## Thinking Critically

**17. Infer** why deposits form in the steam vents of irons in some parts of the country.

**18. Explain** if it is possible to have a dilute solution of a strong acid.

**19. Draw Conclusions** Antifreeze is added to water in a car's radiator to prevent freezing in cold months. It also prevents overheating or boiling. Explain how antifreeze does both.

**Use the illustration below to answer question 20.**

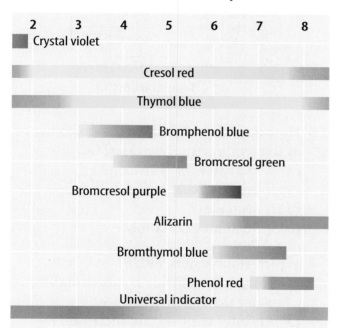

**20. Interpret** Chemists use a variety of indicators. Using the correct indicator is important. The color change must occur at the proper pH or the results could be misleading. Looking at the indicator chart, what indicators could be used to produce a color change at both pH 2 and pH 8?

**21. Explain** Water molecules can break apart to form $H^+$ ions and $OH^-$ ions. Water is known as an amphoteric substance, which is something that can act as an acid or a base. Explain how this can be so.

**22. Describe** how a liquid-solid solution forms. How is this different from a liquid-gas solution? How are these two types of solutions different from a liquid-liquid solution? Give an example of each with your description.

**23. Compare and contrast** examples of heterogeneous and homogeneous mixtures from your daily life.

**24. Form a Hypotheses** A warm carbonated beverage seems to fizz more than a cold one when it is opened. Explain this based on the solubility of carbon dioxide in water.

## Performance Activities

**25. Poem** Write a poem that explains the difference between a substance and a mixture.

*Hot Words Hot Topics:* Bk 2 (26) p. 199; (27) p. 199

## Applying Math

**Use the graph below to answer question 26.**

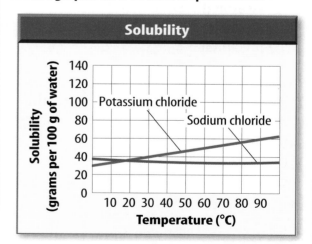

**26. Solubility** Using the solubility graph above, estimate the solubilities of potassium chloride and sodium chloride in grams per 100 g of water at 80°C.

**27. Juice Concentration** You made a one-liter (1,000 mL) container of juice. How much concentrate, in mL, did you add to make a concentration of 18 percent?

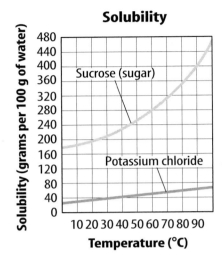

### Part I

*Record your answers on the answer sheet provided by your teacher or on a sheet of paper.*

**Use the illustration below to answer questions 1 and 2.**

### Composition of Earth's Atmosphere

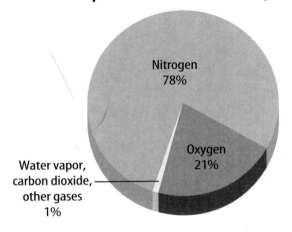

**Use the illustration below to answer questions 4 and 5.**

**1** Which term best describes Earth's atmosphere?
(1) saturated
(2) solution
(3) precipitate
(4) indicator

**2** Which of these is the solvent in Earth's atmosphere?
(1) nitrogen
(2) oxygen
(3) water vapor
(4) carbon dioxide

**3** What characteristic do aqueous solutions share?
(1) They contain more than three solutes.
(2) No solids or gases are present as solutes in them.
(3) All are extremely concentrated.
(4) Water is the solvent in them.

**4** How does the solubility of sucrose change as the temperature increases?
(1) It increases.
(2) It does not change.
(3) It decreases.
(4) It fluctuates randomly.

**5** Which statement is TRUE?
(1) Potassium chloride is more soluble in water than sucrose.
(2) As water temperature increases, the solubility of potassium chloride decreases.
(3) Sucrose is more soluble in water than potassium chloride.
(4) Water temperature has no effect on the solubility of these two chemicals.

**6** Which of these is a property of acidic solutions?
(1) They taste sour.
(2) They feel slippery.
(3) They are in many cleaning products.
(4) They taste bitter.

**Part II**

*Record your answers on the answer sheet provided by your teacher or on a sheet of paper.*

**7** Give the pH of the solutions vinegar, blood plasma, and ammonia. Compare the acidities of soft drinks, tomatoes, and milk.

**Use the illustration below to answer questions 8 and 9.**

**8** How can you tell that the matter in this bowl is a mixture?

**9** What kind of mixture is this? Define this type of mixture, and give three additional examples.

**10** Explain why a solute broken into small pieces will dissolve more quickly than the same type and amount of solute in large chunks.

**Use the illustration below to answer questions 11 and 12.**

(Partial negative charge)

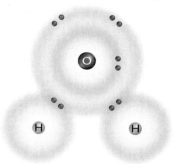

(Partial positive charge)

**11** The diagram shows a water molecule. Use the distribution of electrons to describe this molecule's polarity.

**12** Explain how the polarity of water molecules makes water effective in dissolving ionic compounds.

**13** Marble statues and building facades in many of the world's cities weather more quickly today than when first constructed. Explain how the pH of water plays a role in this process.

**chapter**

**12**

PS 3.2c: During a chemical change, substances react in characteristic ways to form new substances with different physical and chemical properties. **3.2e:** The Law of Conservation of Mass states that during an ordinary chemical reaction matter cannot be created or destroyed. **Also Covered:** PS 3.3d, 4.3a

# Chemical Reactions

## What chemical reactions happen at chemical plants?

Chemical plants like this one provide the starting materials for thousands of chemical reactions. The compact discs you listen to, personal items, such as shampoo and body lotion, and medicines all have their beginnings in a chemical plant.

**Science Journal** What additional types of products do you think are manufactured in a chemical plant?

# Start-Up Activities

## Identify a Chemical Reaction

You can see substances changing every day. Fuels burn, giving energy to cars and trucks. Green plants convert carbon dioxide and water into oxygen and sugar. Cooking an egg or baking bread causes changes too. These changes are called chemical reactions. In this lab you will observe a common chemical change.

**WARNING:** *Do not touch the test tube. It will be hot. Use extreme caution around an open flame. Point test tubes away from you and others.*

1. Place 3 g of sugar into a large test tube.
2. Carefully light a laboratory burner.
3. Using a test-tube holder, hold the bottom of the test tube just above the flame for 45 s or until something happens with the sugar.
4. Observe any change that occurs.
5. **Think Critically** Describe in your Science Journal the changes that took place in the test tube. What do you think happened to the sugar? Was the substance that remained in the test tube after heating the same as the substance you started with?

**Chemical Reaction** Make the following Foldable to help you understand chemical reactions.

**STEP 1** Fold a vertical sheet of notebook paper in half lengthwise.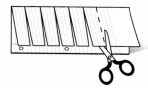

**STEP 2** Cut along every third line of only the top layer to form tabs.

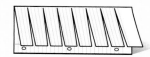

**STEP 3** Label each tab.

**Research Information** Before you read the chapter, write several questions you have about chemical reactions on the front of the tabs. As you read, add more questions. Under the tabs of your Foldable, write answers to the questions you recorded on the tabs.

Science Online | **Preview this chapter's content and activities at** glencoe.com

**PS 3.2c:** During a chemical change, substances react in characteristic ways to form new substances with different physical and chemical properties. Examples of chemical changes include burning of wood, cooking of an egg, rusting of iron, and souring of milk. **Also Covered:** PS 3.2d, 3.2e, 3.3d, 4.3a.

# Chemical Formulas and Equations

## *What* You'll Learn

- **Determine** whether or not a chemical reaction is occurring.
- **Determine** how to read and understand a balanced chemical equation.
- **Examine** some reactions that release energy and others that absorb energy.
- **Explain** the law of conservation of mass.

## *Why* It's Important

Chemical reactions warm your home, cook your meals, digest your food, and power cars and trucks.

### Review Vocabulary

**atom:** the smallest piece of matter that still retains the property of the element

### New Vocabulary

- chemical reaction
- reactant
- product
- chemical equation
- endothermic reaction
- exothermic reaction

## Physical or Chemical Change?

You can smell a rotten egg and see the smoke from a campfire. Signs like these tell you that a chemical reaction is taking place. Other evidence might be less obvious, but clues are always present to announce that a reaction is under way.

Matter can undergo two kinds of changes—physical and chemical. Physical changes in a substance affect only physical properties, such as its size and shape, or whether it is a solid, liquid, or gas. For example, when water freezes, its physical state changes from liquid to solid, but it's still water.

In contrast, chemical changes produce new substances that have properties different from those of the original substances. The rust on a bike's handlebars, for example, has properties different from those of the metal around it. Another example is the combination of two liquids that produce a precipitate, which is a solid, and a liquid. The reaction of silver nitrate and sodium chloride forms solid silver chloride and liquid sodium nitrate. A process that produces chemical change is a **chemical reaction.**

To compare physical and chemical changes, look at the newspaper shown in **Figure 1.** If you fold it, you change its size and shape, but it is still newspaper. Folding is a physical change. If you use it to start a fire, it will burn. Burning is a chemical change because new substances result. How can you recognize a chemical change? **Figure 2** shows what to look for.

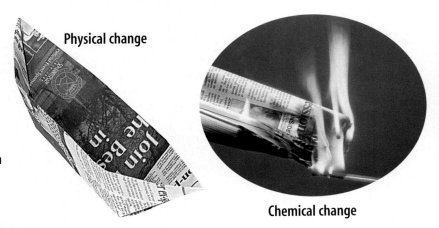

**Physical change**

**Chemical change**

**Figure 1** Newspaper can undergo both physical and chemical changes.

# NATIONAL GEOGRAPHIC VISUALIZING CHEMICAL REACTIONS

## Figure 2

Chemical reactions take place when chemicals combine to form new substances. Your senses—sight, taste, hearing, smell, and touch—can help you detect chemical reactions in your environment.

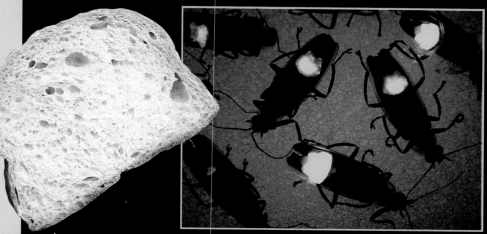

▼ **TASTE** A boy grimaces after sipping milk that has gone sour due to a chemical reaction.

▲ **SIGHT** When you spot a firefly's bright glow, you are seeing a chemical reaction in progress—two chemicals are combining in the firefly's abdomen and releasing light in the process. The holes in a slice of bread are visible clues that sugar molecules were broken down by yeast cells in a chemical reaction that produces carbon dioxide gas. The gas caused the bread dough to rise.

▲ **SMELL AND TOUCH** Billowing clouds of acrid smoke and waves of intense heat indicate that chemical reactions are taking place in this burning forest.

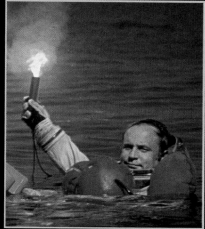

▲ **HEARING** A Russian cosmonaut hoists a flare into the air after landing in the ocean during a training exercise. The hissing sound of the burning flare is the result of a chemical reaction.

# Chemical Equations

To describe a chemical reaction, you must know which substances react and which substances are formed in the reaction. The substances that react are called the reactants (ree AK tunts). **Reactants** are the substances that exist before the reaction begins. The substances that form as a result of the reaction are called the **products.**

When you mix baking soda and vinegar, a vigorous chemical reaction occurs. The mixture bubbles and foams up inside the container, as you can see in **Figure 3.**

Baking soda and vinegar are the common names for the reactants in this reaction, but they also have chemical names. Baking soda is the compound sodium hydrogen carbonate (often called sodium bicarbonate), and vinegar is a solution of acetic (uh SEE tihk) acid in water. What are the products? You saw bubbles form when the reaction occurred, but is that enough of a description?

**Describing What Happens** Bubbles tell you that a gas has been produced, but they don't tell you what kind of gas. Are bubbles of gas the only product, or do some atoms from the vinegar and baking soda form something else? What goes on in the chemical reaction can be more than what you see with your eyes. Chemists try to find out which reactants are used and which products are formed in a chemical reaction. Then, they can write it in a shorthand form called a chemical equation. A **chemical equation** tells chemists at a glance the reactants, products, physical state, and the proportions of each substance present. This is very important as you will see later.

**✓ Reading Check** *What does a chemical equation tell chemists?*

**Figure 3** The bubbles tell you that a chemical reaction has taken place.
**Predict** *how you might find out whether a new substance has formed.*

| Table 1  Reactions Around the Home | | |
| --- | --- | --- |
| **Reactants** | | **Products** |
| Baking soda + Vinegar | → | Gas + White solid |
| Charcoal + Oxygen | → | Ash + Gas +Heat |
| Iron + Oxygen + Water | → | Rust |
| Silver + Hydrogen sulfide | → | Black tarnish + Gas |
| Gas (kitchen range) + Oxygen | → | Gas + Heat |
| Sliced apple + Oxygen | → | Apple turns brown |

**Using Words**  One way you can describe a chemical reaction is with an equation that uses words to name the reactants and products. The reactants are listed on the left side of an arrow, separated from each other by plus signs. The products are placed on the right side of the arrow, also separated by plus signs. The arrow between the reactants and products represents the changes that occur during the chemical reaction. When reading the equation, the arrow is read as *produces*.

You can begin to think of processes as chemical reactions even if you do not know the names of all the substances involved. **Table 1** can help you begin to think like a chemist. It shows the word equations for chemical reactions you might see around your home. See how many other reactions you can find. Look for the signs you have learned that indicate a reaction might be taking place. Then, try to write them in the form shown in the table.

**Using Chemical Names**  Many chemicals used around the home have common names. For example, acetic acid dissolved in water is called vinegar. Some chemicals, such as baking soda, have two common names—it also is known as sodium bicarbonate. However, chemical names are usually used in word equations instead of common names. In the baking soda and vinegar reaction, you already know the chemical names of the reactants—sodium hydrogen carbonate and acetic acid. The names of the products are sodium acetate, water, and carbon dioxide. The word equation for the reaction is as follows.

Acetic acid + Sodium hydrogen carbonate →
Sodium acetate + Water + Carbon dioxide

**Autumn Leaves** A color change can indicate a chemical reaction. When leaves change colors in autumn, the reaction may not be what you expect. The bright yellow and orange are always in the leaves, but masked by green chlorophyll. When the growth season ends, more chlorophyll is broken down than produced. The orange and yellow colors become visible.

## Observing the Law of Conservation of Mass

**Procedure** 🌊 🧤 🔧 🥽

1. Place a piece of **steel wool** into a **medium test tube.** Seal the end of the test tube with a **balloon.**
2. Find the mass.
3. Using a test-tube holder, heat the bottom of the tube for two minutes in a **hot water bath** provided by your teacher. Allow the tube to cool completely.
4. Find the mass again.

**Analysis**

1. What did you observe that showed a chemical reaction took place?
2. Compare the mass before and after the reaction.
3. Why was it important for the test tube to be sealed?

**Using Formulas** The word equation for the reaction of baking soda and vinegar is long. That's why chemists use chemical formulas to represent the chemical names of substances in the equation. You can convert a word equation into a chemical equation by substituting chemical formulas for the chemical names. For example, the chemical equation for the reaction between baking soda and vinegar can be written as follows:

$$CH_3COOH + NaHCO_3 \rightarrow CH_3COONa + H_2O + CO_2$$

| Acetic acid (vinegar) | Sodium hydrogen carbonate (baking soda) | Sodium acetate | Water | Carbon dioxide |

**Subscripts** When you look at chemical formulas, notice the small numbers written to the right of the atoms. These numbers, called subscripts, tell you the number of atoms of each element in that compound. For example, the subscript 2 in $CO_2$ means that each molecule of carbon dioxide has two oxygen atoms. If an atom has no subscript, it means that only one atom of that element is in the compound, so carbon dioxide has only one carbon atom.

## Conservation of Mass

What happens to the atoms in the reactants when they are converted into products? According to the law of conservation of mass, the mass of the products must be the same as the mass of the reactants in that chemical reaction. This principle was first stated by the French chemist Antoine Lavoisier (1743–1794), who is considered the first modern chemist. Lavoisier used logic and scientific methods to study chemical reactions. He proved by his experiments that nothing is lost or created in chemical reactions.

He showed that chemical reactions are much like mathematical equations. In math equations, the right and left sides of the equation are numerically equal. Chemical equations are similar, but it is the number and kind of atoms that are equal on the two sides. Every atom that appears on the reactant side of the equation also appears on the product side, as shown in **Figure 4.** Atoms are never lost or created in a chemical reaction; however, they do change partners.

**Figure 4** The law of conservation of mass states that the number and kind of atoms must be equal for products and reactants.

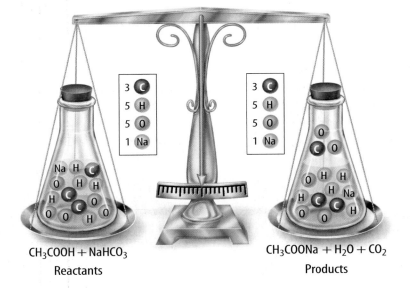

CH₃COOH + NaHCO₃
Reactants

CH₃COONa + H₂O + CO₂
Products

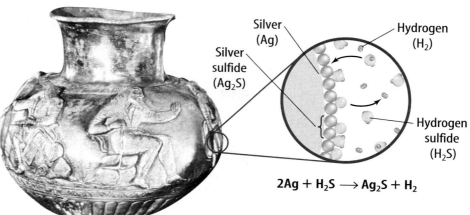

**Figure 5** Keeping silver bright takes frequent polishing, especially in homes heated by gas. Sulfur compounds found in small concentrations in natural gas react with silver, forming black silver sulfide, $Ag_2S$.

Silver (Ag)

Silver sulfide ($Ag_2S$)

Hydrogen ($H_2$)

Hydrogen sulfide ($H_2S$)

$$2Ag + H_2S \longrightarrow Ag_2S + H_2$$

# Balancing Chemical Equations

When you write the chemical equation for a reaction, you must observe the law of conservation of mass. Look back at **Figure 4.** It shows that when you count the number of carbon, hydrogen, oxygen, and sodium atoms on each side of the arrow in the equation, you find equal numbers of each kind of atom. This means the equation is balanced and the law of conservation of mass is observed.

Not all chemical equations are balanced so easily. For example, silver tarnishes, as in **Figure 5,** when it reacts with sulfur compounds in the air, such as hydrogen sulfide. The following unbalanced equation shows what happens when silver tarnishes.

| Ag | + | $H_2S$ | → | $Ag_2S$ | + | $H_2$ |
| Silver | | Hydrogen sulfide | | Silver sulfide | | Hydrogen |

**Count the Atoms** Count the number of atoms of each type in the reactants and in the products. The same numbers of hydrogen and sulfur atoms are on each side, but one silver atom is on the reactant side and two silver atoms are on the product side. This cannot be true. A chemical reaction cannot create a silver atom, so this equation does not represent the reaction correctly. Place a 2 in front of the reactant Ag and check to see if the equation is balanced. Recount the number of atoms of each type.

$$2Ag + H_2S \rightarrow Ag_2S + H_2$$

The equation is now balanced. There are an equal number of silver atoms in the reactants and the products. When balancing chemical equations, numbers are placed before the formulas as you did for Ag. These are called coefficients. However, never change the subscripts written to the right of the atoms in a formula. Changing these numbers changes the identity of the compound.

**Science**  **nline**

**Topic: Chemical Equations**
Visit glencoe.com for Web links to information about chemical equations and balancing them.

**Activity** Find a chemical reaction that takes place around your home or school. Write a chemical equation describing it.

# Energy in Chemical Reactions

Often, energy is released or absorbed during a chemical reaction. The energy for the welding torch in **Figure 6** is released when hydrogen and oxygen combine to form water.

$$2H_2 + O_2 \rightarrow 2H_2O + energy$$

**Energy Released** Where does this energy come from? To answer this question, think about the chemical bonds that break and form when atoms gain, lose, or share electrons. When such a reaction takes place, bonds break in the reactants and new bonds form in the products. In reactions that release energy, the products are more stable, and their bonds have less energy than those of the reactants. The extra energy is released in various forms—light, sound, and heat.

*Hot Words Hot Topics*: Bk 2 (1) p. 92; (2) p. 92

## Applying Math    Balancing Equations

**CONSERVING MASS** Methane and oxygen react to form carbon dioxide, water, and heat. You can see how mass is conserved by balancing the equation: $CH_4 + O_2 \rightarrow CO_2 + H_2O$.

### Solution

**1** *This is what you know:*

The number of atoms of C, H, and O in reactants and products.

**2** *This is what you need to do:*

Make sure that the reactants and products have equal numbers of atoms of each element. Start with the reactant having the greatest number of atoms.

| Reactants | Products | Action |
|---|---|---|
| $CH_4 + O_2$ have 4 H atoms | $CO_2 + H_2O$ have 2 H atoms | Need 2 more H atoms in Products Multiply $H_2O$ by 2 to give 4 H atoms |
| $CH_4 + O_2$ have 2 O atoms | $CO_2 + H_2O$ have 4 O atoms | Need 2 more O atoms in Reactants Multiply $O_2$ by 2 to give 4 O atoms |

The balanced equation is $CH_4 + 2O_2 \rightarrow CO_2 + 2H_2O$.

**3** *Check your answer:*

Count the carbons, hydrogens, and oxygens on each side.

### Practice Problems

**1.** Balance the equation $Fe_2O_3 + CO \rightarrow Fe_3O_4 + CO_2$.

**2.** Balance the equation $Al + I_2 \rightarrow AlI_3$.

Science online | For more practice, visit glencoe.com

**Figure 6** This welding torch burns hydrogen and oxygen to produce temperatures above 3,000°C. It can even be used underwater.
**Identify** *the products of this chemical reaction.*

**Energy Absorbed** What happens when the reverse situation occurs? In reactions that absorb energy, the reactants are more stable, and their bonds have less energy than those of the products.

$$2H_2O \; + \; energy \; \rightarrow \; 2H_2 \; + \; O_2$$
Water       Hydrogen  Oxygen

In this reaction the extra energy needed to form the products can be supplied in the form of electricity, as shown in **Figure 7.**

As you have seen, reactions can release or absorb energy of several kinds, including electricity, light, sound, and heat. When heat energy is gained or lost in reactions, special terms are used. **Endothermic** (en doh THUR mihk) **reactions** absorb heat energy. **Exothermic** (ek soh THUR mihk) **reactions** release heat energy. You may notice that the root word *therm* refers to heat, as it does in thermos bottles and thermometers.

**Heat Released** You might already be familiar with several types of reactions that release heat. Burning is an exothermic chemical reaction in which a substance combines with oxygen to produce heat along with light, carbon dioxide, and water.

 *What type of chemical reaction is burning?*

**Rapid Release** Sometimes energy is released rapidly. For example, charcoal lighter fluid combines with oxygen in the air and produces enough heat to ignite a charcoal fire within a few minutes.

**Figure 7** Electrical energy is needed to break water into its components. This is the reverse of the reaction that takes place in the welding torch shown in **Figure 6.**

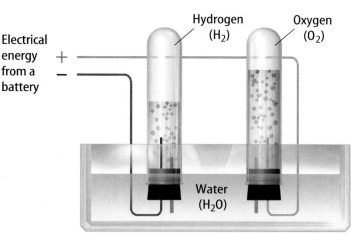

**Fast reaction**

**Figure 8** Two exothermic reactions are shown. The charcoal fire to cook the food was started when lighter fluid combined rapidly with oxygen in air. The iron in the wheelbarrow combined slowly with oxygen in the air to form rust.

**Slow reaction**

**Slow Release** Other materials also combine with oxygen but release heat so slowly that you cannot see or feel it happen. This is the case when iron combines with oxygen in the air to form rust. The slow heat release from a reaction also is used in heat packs that can keep your hands warm for several hours. Fast and slow energy release are compared in **Figure 8.**

**Heat Absorbed** Some chemical reactions and physical processes need to have heat energy added before they can proceed. An example of an endothermic physical process that absorbs heat energy is the cold pack shown in **Figure 9.**

The heavy plastic cold pack holds ammonium nitrate and water. The two substances are separated by a plastic divider. When you squeeze the bag, you break the divider so that the ammonium nitrate dissolves in the water. The dissolving process absorbs heat energy, which must come from the surrounding environment—the surrounding air or your skin after you place the pack on the injury.

**Figure 9** The heat energy needed to dissolve the ammonium nitrate in this cold pack comes from the surrounding environment.

**Energy in the Equation** The word *energy* often is written in equations as either a reactant or a product. Energy written as a reactant helps you think of energy as a necessary ingredient for the reaction to take place. For example, electrical energy is needed to break up water into hydrogen and oxygen. It is important to know that energy must be added to make this reaction occur.

Similarly, in the equation for an exothermic reaction, the word *energy* often is written along with the products. This tells you that energy is released. You include energy when writing the reaction that takes place between oxygen and methane in natural gas when you cook on a gas range, as shown in **Figure 10.** This heat energy cooks your food.

**Figure 10** Energy from a chemical reaction is used to cook.
**Determine** *if energy is used as a reactant or a product in this reaction.*

$$CH_4 + 2O_2 \rightarrow CO_2 + 2H_2O + energy$$

Methane  Oxygen    Carbon    Water
                   dioxide

Although it is not necessary, writing the word *energy* can draw attention to an important aspect of the equation.

## section 1 review

### Summary

**Physical or Chemical Change?**

- Matter can undergo physical and chemical changes.
- A chemical reaction produces chemical changes.

**Chemical Equations**

- A chemical equation describes a chemical reaction.
- Chemical formulas represent chemical names for substances.
- A balanced chemical equation has the same number of atoms of each kind on both sides of the equation.

**Energy in Chemical Reactions**

- Endothermic reactions absorb heat energy.
- Exothermic reactions release heat energy.

### Self Check

1. **Determine** if each of these equations is balanced. Why or why not?
   a. $Ca + Cl_2 \rightarrow CaCl_2$
   b. $Zn + Ag_2S \rightarrow ZnS + Ag$

2. **Describe** what evidence might tell you that a chemical reaction has occurred.

3. **Think Critically** After a fire, the ashes have less mass and take up less space than the trees and vegetation before the fire. How can this be explained in terms of the Law of Conservation of Mass?

 *Hot Words Hot Topics:* Bk 2 (4) p. 178, 292

#### Applying Math

4. **Calculate** The equation for the decomposition of silver oxide is $2Ag_2O \rightarrow 4Ag + O_2$. Set up a ratio to calculate the number of oxygen molecules released when 1 g of silver oxide is broken down. There are $2.6 \times 10^{21}$ molecules in 1 g of silver oxide.

# section 2

# Rates of Chemical Reactions

## as you read

## *What* You'll Learn

- **Determine** how to describe and measure the speed of a chemical reaction.
- **Identify** how chemical reactions can be speeded up or slowed down.

## *Why* It's Important

Speeding up useful reactions and slowing down destructive ones can be helpful.

## 🔁 Review Vocabulary

**state of matter:** physical property that is dependent on temperature and pressure and occurs in four forms—solid, liquid, gas, or plasma

## New Vocabulary

- activation energy
- rate of reaction
- concentration
- inhibitor
- catalyst
- enzyme

## How Fast?

Fireworks explode in rapid succession on a summer night. Old copper pennies darken slowly while they lie forgotten in a drawer. Cooking an egg for two minutes instead of five minutes makes a difference in the firmness of the yolk. The amount of time you leave coloring solution on your hair must be timed accurately to give the color you want. Chemical reactions are common in your life. However, notice from these examples that time has something to do with many of them. As you can see in **Figure 11,** not all chemical reactions take place at the same rate.

Some reactions, such as fireworks or lighting a campfire, need help to get going. You may also notice that others seem to start on their own. In this section, you will also learn about factors that make reactions speed up or slow down once they get going.

**Figure 11** Reaction speeds vary greatly. Fireworks are over in a few seconds. However, the copper coating on pennies darkens slowly as it reacts with substances it touches.

# Activation Energy—Starting a Reaction

Before a reaction can start, molecules of the reactants have to bump into each other, or collide. This makes sense because to form new chemical bonds, atoms have to be close together. But, not just any collision will do. The collision must be strong enough. This means the reactants must smash into each other with a certain amount of energy. Anything less, and the reaction will not occur. Why is this true?

To form new bonds in the product, old bonds must break in the reactants, and breaking bonds takes energy. To start any chemical reaction, a minimum amount of energy is needed. This energy is called the **activation energy** of the reaction.

**☑ Reading Check** *What term describes the minimum amount of energy needed to start a reaction?*

What about reactions that release energy? Is there an activation energy for these reactions too? Yes, even though they release energy later, these reactions also need enough energy to start.

One example of a reaction that needs energy to start is the burning of gasoline. You have probably seen movies in which a car plunges over a cliff, lands on the rocks below, and suddenly bursts into flames. But if some gasoline is spilled accidentally while filling a gas tank, it probably will evaporate harmlessly in a short time.

Why doesn't this spilled gasoline explode as it does in the movies? The reason is that gasoline needs energy to start burning. That is why there are signs at filling stations warning you not to smoke. Other signs advise you to turn off the ignition, not to use mobile phones, and not to reenter the car until fueling is complete.

This is similar to the lighting of the Olympic Cauldron, as shown in **Figure 12.** Cauldrons designed for each Olympics contain highly flammable materials that cannot be extinguished by high winds or rain. However, they do not ignite until the opening ceremonies when a runner lights the cauldron using a flame that was kindled in Olympia, Greece, the site of the original Olympic Games.

**Science Online**

**Topic: Olympic Torch**

Visit glencoe.com for Web links to information about the Olympic Torch.

**Activity** With each new Olympics, the host city devises a new Olympic Torch. Research the process that goes into developing the torch and the fuel it uses.

**Physical Setting**

**3.1b, 3.2c** *The rate of a solution can be affected by the size of the particles, stirring, temperature, and the amount of solute already dissolved.* **Predict** *how these same factors might affect the rate of a chemical reaction.*

**Figure 12** Most fuels need energy to ignite. The Olympic Torch, held by Cathy Freeman in the 2000 Olympics, provided the activation energy required to light the fuel in the cauldron.

**Figure 13** The diminishing amount of wax in this candle as it burns indicates the rate of the reaction.

# Reaction Rate

Many physical processes are measured in terms of a rate. A rate tells you how much something changes over a given period of time. For example, the rate or speed at which you run or ride your bike is the distance you move divided by the time it took you to move that distance. You may jog at a rate of 8 km/h.

Chemical reactions have rates, too. The **rate of reaction** tells how fast a reaction occurs after it has started. To find the rate of a reaction, you can measure either how quickly one of the reactants is consumed or how quickly one of the products is created, as in **Figure 13**. Both measurements tell how the amount of a substance changes per unit of time.

**Reading Check** *What can you measure to determine the rate of a reaction?*

Reaction rate is important in industry because the faster the product can be made, the less it usually costs. However, sometimes fast rates of reaction are undesirable such as the rates of reactions that cause food spoilage. In this case, the slower the reaction rate, the longer the food will stay edible. What conditions control the reaction rate, and how can the rate be changed?

**Temperature Changes Rate** You can keep the food you buy at the store from spoiling so quickly by putting it in the refrigerator or freezer, as in **Figure 14.** Food spoiling is a chemical reaction. Lowering the temperature of the food slows the rate of this reaction.

**Figure 14** Refrigerated foods must be kept below a certain temperature to slow spoilage. These grapes prove that spoilage, a chemical reaction, has occurred.

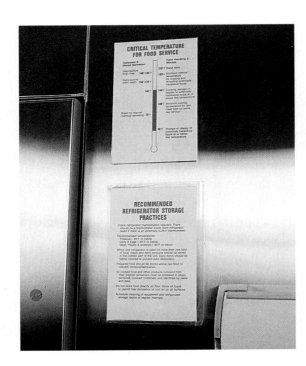

Meat and fish decompose faster at higher temperatures, producing toxins that can make you sick. Keeping these foods chilled slows the decomposition process. Bacteria grow faster at higher temperatures, too, so they reach dangerous levels sooner. Eggs may contain such bacteria, but the heat required to cook eggs also kills bacteria, so hard-cooked eggs are safer to eat than soft-cooked or raw eggs.

**Temperature Affects Rate** Most chemical reactions speed up when temperature increases. This is because atoms and molecules are always in motion, and they move faster at higher temperatures, as shown in **Figure 15.** Faster molecules collide with each other more often and with greater energy than slower molecules do, so collisions are more likely to provide enough energy to break the old bonds. This is the activation energy.

The high temperature inside an oven speeds up the chemical reactions that turn a liquid cake batter into a more solid, spongy cake. This works the other way, too. Lowering the temperature slows down most reactions. If you set the oven temperature too low, your cake will not bake properly.

**Concentration Affects Rate** The closer reactant atoms and molecules are to each other, the greater the chance of collisions between them and the faster the reaction rate. It's like the situation shown in **Figure 16.** When you try to walk through a crowded train station, you're more likely to bump into other people than if the station were not so crowded. The amount of substance present in a certain volume is called the **concentration** of that substance. If you increase the concentration, you increase the number of particles of a substance per unit of volume.

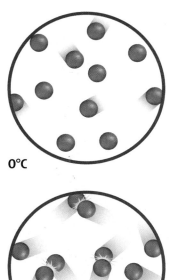

0°C

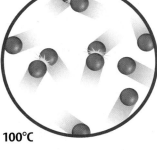

100°C

**Figure 15** Molecules collide more frequently at higher temperatures than at lower temperatures. This means they are more likely to react.

Collisions are more frequent in a concentrated solution.

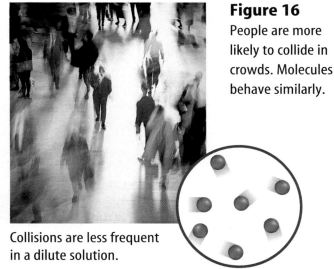

**Figure 16**
People are more likely to collide in crowds. Molecules behave similarly.

Collisions are less frequent in a dilute solution.

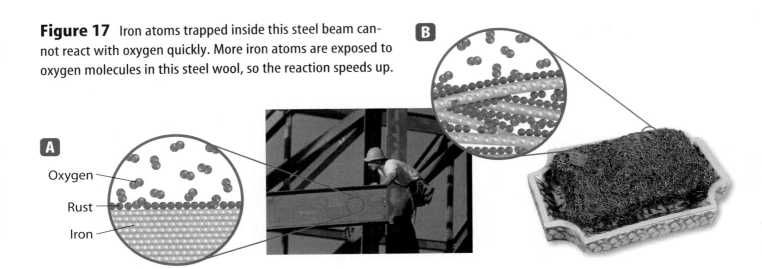

**Figure 17** Iron atoms trapped inside this steel beam cannot react with oxygen quickly. More iron atoms are exposed to oxygen molecules in this steel wool, so the reaction speeds up.

A

Oxygen

Rust

Iron

B

## Mini LAB

### Identifying Inhibitors

**Procedure**
1. Look at the ingredients listed on **packages of cereals** and **crackers** in your kitchen.
2. Note the preservatives listed. These are chemical inhibitors.
3. Compare the date on the box with the approximate date the box was purchased to estimate shelf life.

**Analysis**
1. What is the average shelf life of these products?
2. Why is increased shelf life of such products important?

Try at Home

**Surface Area Affects Rate** The exposed surface area of reactant particles also affects how fast the reaction can occur. You can quickly start a campfire with small twigs, but starting a fire with only large logs would probably not work.

Only the atoms or molecules in the outer layer of the reactant material can touch the other reactants and react. **Figure 17A** shows that when particles are large, most of the iron atoms are stuck inside and can't react. In **Figure 17B,** more of the reactant atoms are exposed to the oxygen and can react.

## Slowing Down Reactions

Sometimes reactions occur too quickly. For example, food and medications can undergo chemical reactions that cause them to spoil or lose their effectiveness too rapidly. Luckily, these reactions can be slowed down.

A substance that slows down a chemical reaction is called an **inhibitor.** An inhibitor makes the formation of a certain amount of product take longer. Some inhibitors completely stop reactions. Many cereals and cereal boxes contain the compound butylated hydroxytoluene, or BHT. The BHT slows the spoiling of the cereal and increases its shelf life.

**Figure 18** BHT, an inhibitor, is found in many cereals and cereal boxes.

# Speeding Up Reactions

Is it possible to speed up a chemical reaction? Yes, you can add a catalyst (KAT uh lihst). A **catalyst** is a substance that speeds up a chemical reaction. Catalysts do not appear in chemical equations, because they are not changed permanently or used up. A reaction using a catalyst will not produce more product than a reaction without a catalyst, but it will produce the same amount of product faster.

✔ **Reading Check** *What does a catalyst do in a chemical reaction?*

How does a catalyst work? Many catalysts speed up reaction rates by providing a surface for the reaction to take place. Sometimes the reacting molecules are held in a particular position that favors reaction. Other catalysts reduce the activation energy needed to start the reaction. When the activation energy is reduced, the reaction rate increases.

## Catalytic Converters

Catalysts are used in the exhaust systems of cars and trucks to aid fuel combustion. The exhaust passes through the catalyst, often in the form of beads coated with metals such as platinum or rhodium. Catalysts speed the reactions that change incompletely burned substances that are harmful, such as carbon monoxide, into less harmful substances, such as carbon dioxide. Similarly, hydrocarbons are changed into carbon dioxide and water. The result of these reactions is cleaner air. These reactions are shown in **Figure 19.**

**INTEGRATE History**

**Breathe Easy** The Clean Air Act of 1970 required the reduction of 90 percent of automobile tailpipe emissions. The reduction of emissions included the amount of hydrocarbons and carbon monoxide released. Automakers did not have the technology to meet this new standard. After much hard work, the result of this legislation was the introduction of the catalytic converter in 1975.

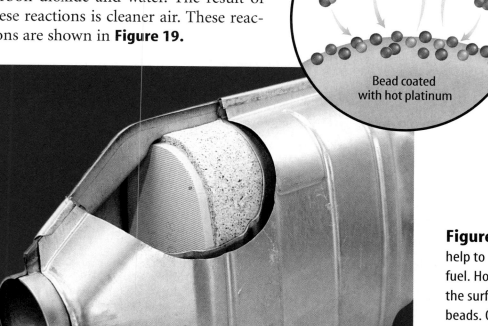

**Figure 19** Catalytic converters help to complete combustion of fuel. Hot exhaust gases pass over the surfaces of metal-coated beads. On the surface of the beads, carbon monoxide and hydrocarbons are converted to $CO_2$ and $H_2O$.

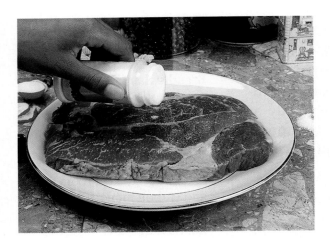

**Figure 20** The enzymes in meat tenderizer break down protein in meat, making it more tender.

**Enzymes Are Specialists** Some of the most effective catalysts are at work in thousands of reactions that take place in your body. These catalysts, called **enzymes,** are large protein molecules that speed up reactions needed for your cells to work properly. They help your body convert food to fuel, build bone and muscle tissue, convert extra energy to fat, and even produce other enzymes.

These are complex reactions. Without enzymes, they would occur at rates that are too slow to be useful or they would not occur at all. Enzymes make it possible for your body to function. Like other catalysts, enzymes function by positioning the reacting molecules so that their structures fit together properly. Enzymes are a kind of chemical specialist—enzymes exist to carry out each type of reaction in your body.

**Other Uses** Enzymes work outside your body, too. One class of enzymes, called proteases (PROH tee ay ses), specializes in protein reactions. They work within cells to break down large, complex molecules called proteins. The meat tenderizer shown in **Figure 20** contains proteases that break down protein in meat, making it more tender. Contact lens cleaning solutions also contain proteases that break down proteins from your eyes that can collect on your lenses and cloud your view.

## section 2 review

### Summary

**Chemical Reactions**

- To form new bonds in the product, old bonds must break in the reactants. This takes energy.
- Activation energy is the minimum quantity of energy needed to start a reaction.

**Reaction Rate**

- The rate of reaction tells you how fast a reaction occurs.
- Temperature, concentration, and surface area affect the rate of reaction.

**Inhibitors and Catalysts**

- Inhibitors slow down reactions. Catalysts speed up reactions.
- Enzymes are catalysts that speed up or slow down reactions for your cells.

### Self Check

1. **Describe** how you can measure reaction rates.
2. **Explain** in the general reaction A + B + energy → C, how the following will affect the reaction rate.
   a. increasing the temperature
   b. decreasing the reactant concentration
3. **Describe** how catalysts work to speed up chemical reactions.
4. **Think Critically** Explain why a jar of spaghetti sauce can be stored for weeks on the shelf in the market but must be placed in the refrigerator after it is opened.

*Hot Words Hot Topics*: Bk 2 (5) pp. 276–278, 292–296

### Applying Math

5. **Solve One-Step Equations** A chemical reaction is proceeding at a rate of 2 g of product every 45 s. How long will it take to obtain 50 g of product?

# Physical or Chemical Change?

## Real-World Question

Matter can undergo two kinds of changes—physical and chemical. A physical change affects the physical properties. When a chemical change takes place, a new product is produced. How can a scientist tell if a chemical change took place?

### Goals

■ **Determine** if a physical or chemical change took place.

### Materials

500-mL Erlenmeyer flask
1,000-mL graduated cylinder
one-hole stopper with 15-cm length of glass tube inserted
1,000-mL beaker
45-cm length of rubber (or plastic) tubing
stopwatch or clock with second hand
weighing dish          balance
baking soda           vinegar

### Safety Precautions

**WARNING:** *Vinegar (acetic acid) may cause skin and eye irritation.*

## Procedure

1. Measure 300 mL of water. Pour water into 500-mL Erlenmeyer flask.

2. Weigh 5 g of baking soda. Carefully pour the baking soda into the flask. Swirl the flask until the solution is clear.

3. Insert the rubber stopper with the glass tubing into the flask.

4. Measure 600 mL of water and pour into the 1,000-mL beaker.

5. Attach one end of the rubber tubing to the top of the glass tubing. Place the other end of the rubber tubing in the beaker. Be sure the rubber tubing remains under the water.

6. Remove the stopper from the flask. Carefully add 80 mL of vinegar to the flask. Replace the stopper.

7. Count the number of bubbles coming into the beaker for 20 s. Repeat this two more times.

8. Record your data in your Science Journal.

## Conclude and Apply

1. **Describe** what you observed in the flask after the acid was added to the baking soda solution.

2. **Classify** Was this a physical or chemical change? How do you know?

3. **Analyze Results** Was this process endothermic or exothermic?

4. **Calculate** the average reaction rate based on the number of bubbles per second.

### Communicating Your Data

Compare your results with those of other students in your class.

## Design Your Own

# Exothermic or Endothermic?

**Goals**

■ **Design** an experiment to test whether a reaction is exothermic or endothermic.

■ **Measure** the temperature change caused by a chemical reaction.

**Possible Materials**

test tubes (8)
test-tube rack
3% hydrogen peroxide solution
raw liver
raw potato
thermometer
stopwatch
clock with second hand
25-mL graduated cylinder

**Safety Precautions**

**WARNING:** *Hydrogen peroxide can irritate skin and eyes and damage clothing.* Be careful when handling glass thermometers. Test tubes containing hydrogen peroxide should be placed and kept in racks. Dispose of materials as directed by your teacher. Wash your hands when you complete this lab.

### ▶ Real-World Question

Energy is always a part of a chemical reaction. Some reactions need energy to start. Other reactions release energy into the environment. What evidence can you find to show that a reaction between hydrogen peroxide and liver or potato is exothermic or endothermic? Think about the difference between these two types of reactions.

### ▶ Form a Hypothesis

Make a hypothesis that describes how you can use the reactions between hydrogen peroxide and liver or potato to determine whether a reaction is exothermic or endothermic.

### ▶ Test Your Hypothesis

**Make a Plan**

1. As a group, look at the list of materials. Decide which procedure you will use to test your hypothesis, and which measurements you will make.

2. **Decide** how you will detect the heat released to the environment during the reaction. Determine how many measurements you will need to make during a reaction.

3. You will get more accurate data if you repeat each experiment several times. Each repeated experiment is called a trial. Use the average of all the trials as your data for supporting your hypothesis.

4. **Decide** what the variables are and what your control will be.

5. **Copy** the data table in your Science Journal before you begin to carry out your experiment.

**Follow Your Plan**

1. Make sure your teacher approves your plan before you start.

2. Carry out your plan.

3. **Record** your measurements immediately in your data table.

4. **Calculate** the averages of your trial results and record them in your Science Journal.

### Analyze Your Data

1. Can you infer that a chemical reaction took place? What evidence did you observe to support this?

2. **Identify** what the variables were in this experiment.

3. **Identify** the control.

**Temperature After Adding Liver/Potato**

| Trial | Temperature After Adding Liver (°C) | | Temperature After Adding Potato (°C) | |
|---|---|---|---|---|
| | Starting | After_____min | Starting | After_____min |
| 1 | | | | |
| 2 | | Do not write in this book. | | |
| 3 | | | | |
| 4 | | | | |

### Conclude and Apply

1. Do your observations allow you to distinguish between an exothermic reaction and an endothermic reaction? Use your data to explain your answer.

2. Where do you think that the energy involved in this experiment came from? Explain your answer.

### Communicating Your Data

**Compare** the results obtained by your group with those obtained by other groups. Are there differences? **Explain** how these might have occurred.

# Synthetic Diamonds

**Natural Diamond**

## Almost the Real Thing

**Synthetic Diamond**

Diamonds are the most dazzling, most dramatic, most valuable natural objects on Earth. Strangely, these beautiful objects are made of carbon, the same material graphite—the stuff found in pencils—is made of. So why is a diamond hard and clear and graphite soft and black? A diamond's hardness is a result of how strongly its atoms are linked. What makes a diamond transparent is the way its crystals are arranged. The carbon in a diamond is almost completely pure, with trace amounts of boron and nitrogen in it. These elements account for the many shades of color found in diamonds.

A diamond is the hardest naturally occurring substance on Earth. It's so hard, only a diamond can scratch another diamond. Diamonds are impervious to heat and household chemicals. Their crystal structure allows them to be split (or crushed) along particular lines.

Diamonds are made when carbon is squeezed at high pressures and temperatures in Earth's upper mantle, about 150 km beneath the surface. At that depth, the temperature is about 1,400°C, and the pressure is about 55,000 atmospheres greater than the pressure at sea level.

As early as the 1850s, scientists tried to convert graphite into diamonds. It wasn't until 1954 that researchers produced the first synthetic diamonds by compressing carbon under extremely high pressure and heat. Scientists converted graphite powder into tiny diamond crystals using pressure of more than 68,000 atm, and a temperature of about 1,700°C for about 16 hours.

Synthetic diamonds are human-made, but they're not fake. They have all the properties of natural diamonds, from hardness to excellent heat conductivity. Experts claim to be able to detect synthetics because they contain tiny amounts of metal (used in their manufacturing process) and have a different luminescence than natural diamonds. In fact, most synthetics are made for industrial use. One major reason is that making small synthetic diamonds is cheaper than finding small natural ones. The other reason is that synthetics can be made to a required size and shape. Still, if new techniques bring down the cost of producing large, gem-quality synthetic diamonds, they may one day compete with natural diamonds as jewelry.

**Research** Investigate the history of diamonds—natural and synthetic. Explain the differences between them and their uses. Share your findings with the class.

**Science Online**

**For more information, visit glencoe.com**

## Reviewing Main Ideas

### Section 1 — Formulas and Chemical Equations

1. Chemical reactions often cause observable changes, such as a change in color or odor, a release or absorption of heat or light, or a release of gas.

2. A chemical equation is a shorthand method of writing what happens in a chemical reaction. Chemical equations use symbols to represent the reactants and products of a reaction, and sometimes show whether energy is produced or absorbed.

3. The law of conservation of mass requires that the same number of atoms of each element be in the products as in the reactants of a chemical equation. This is true in every balanced chemical equation.

### Section 2 — Rates of Chemical Reactions

1. The rate of reaction is a measure of how quickly a reaction occurs.

2. All reactions have an activation energy—a certain minimum amount of energy required to start the reaction.

3. The rate of a chemical reaction can be influenced by the temperature, the concentration of the reactants, and the exposed surface area of the reactant particles.

4. Catalysts can speed up a reaction without being used up. Inhibitors slow down the rate of reaction.

5. Enzymes are protein molecules that act as catalysts in your body's cells.

## Visualizing Main Ideas

*Copy and complete the following concept map on chemical reactions.*

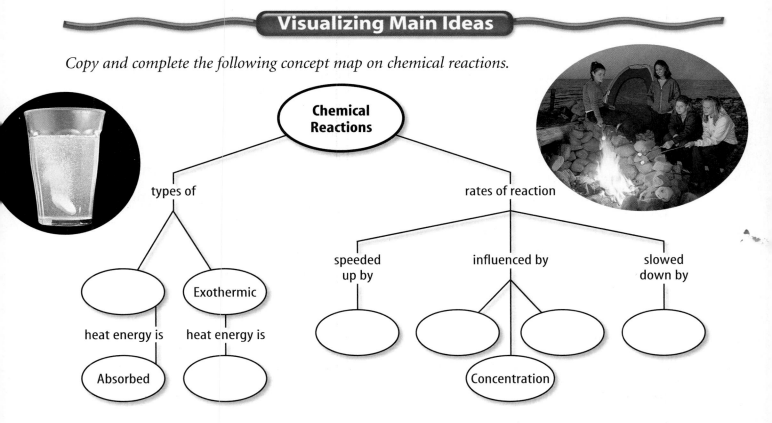

## Using Vocabulary

| | |
|---|---|
| activation energy p. 343 | enzyme p. 348 |
| catalyst p. 347 | exothermic reaction p. 339 |
| chemical equation p. 334 | inhibitor p. 346 |
| chemical reaction p. 332 | product p. 334 |
| concentration p. 345 | rate of reaction p. 344 |
| endothermic reaction p. 339 | reactant p. 334 |

*Explain the differences between the vocabulary terms in each of the following sets.*

1. exothermic reaction—endothermic reaction

2. activation energy—rate of reaction

3. reactant—product

4. catalyst—inhibitor

5. concentration—rate of reaction

6. chemical equation—reactant

7. inhibitor—product

8. catalyst—chemical equation

9. rate of reaction—enzyme

## Checking Concepts

*Choose the word or phrase that best answers the question.*

10. Which statement about the law of conservation of mass is NOT true?
    A) The mass of reactants must equal the mass of products.
    B) All the atoms on the reactant side of an equation are also on the product side.
    C) The reaction creates new types of atoms.
    D) Atoms are not lost, but are rearranged.

11. To slow down a chemical reaction, what should you add?
    A) catalyst          C) inhibitor
    B) reactant          D) enzyme

12. Which of these is a chemical change?
    A) Paper is shredded.
    B) Liquid wax turns solid.
    C) A raw egg is broken.
    D) Soap scum forms.

13. Which of these reactions releases heat energy?
    A) unbalanced        C) exothermic
    B) balanced          D) endothermic

14. A balanced chemical equation must have the same number of which of these on both sides of the equation?
    A) atoms             C) molecules
    B) reactants         D) compounds

15. What does NOT affect reaction rate?
    A) balancing         C) surface area
    B) temperature       D) concentration

16. Which is NOT a balanced equation?
    A) $CuCl_2 + H_2S \rightarrow CuS + 2HCl$
    B) $AgNO_3 + NaI \rightarrow AgI + NaNO_3$
    C) $2C_2H_6 + 7O_2 \rightarrow 4CO_2 + 6H_2O$
    D) $MgO + Fe \rightarrow Fe_2O_3 + Mg$

17. Which is NOT evidence that a chemical reaction has occurred?
    A) Milk tastes sour.
    B) Steam condenses on a cold window.
    C) A strong odor comes from a broken egg.
    D) A slice of raw potato darkens.

18. Which of the following would decrease the rate of a chemical reaction?
    A) increase the temperature
    B) reduce the concentration of a reactant
    C) increase the concentration of a reactant
    D) add a catalyst

19. Which of these describes a catalyst?
    A) It is a reactant.
    B) It speeds up a reaction.
    C) It appears in the chemical equation.
    D) It can be used in place of an inhibitor.

## Thinking Critically

**20. Cause and Effect** Pickled cucumbers remain edible much longer than fresh cucumbers do. Explain.

**21. Analyze** A beaker of water in sunlight becomes warm. Has a chemical reaction occurred? Explain.

**22. Distinguish** if $2Ag + S$ is the same as $Ag_2S$. Explain.

**23. Infer** Apple slices can be kept from browning by brushing them with lemon juice. Infer what role lemon juice plays in this case.

**24. Draw a Conclusion** Chili can be made using ground meat or chunks of meat. Which would you choose, if you were in a hurry? Explain.

**Use the graph below to answer question 25.**

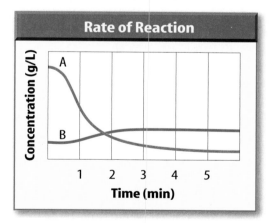

Rate of Reaction

**25. Interpret Scientific Illustrations** The two curves on the graph represent the concentrations of compounds A (blue) and B (red) during a chemical reaction.
  **a.** Which compound is a reactant?
  **b.** Which compound is a product?
  **c.** During which time period is the concentration of the reactant changing most rapidly?

**26. Form a Hypothesis** You are cleaning out a cabinet beneath the kitchen sink and find an unused steel wool scrub pad that has rusted completely. Will the remains of this pad weigh more or less than when it was new? Explain.

## Performance Activities

**27. Poster** Make a list of the preservatives in the food you eat in one day. Present your findings to your class in a poster.

*Hot Words Hot Topics:* Bk 2 (28) p. 199; (29) p. 92; (30) pp. 142–143; (31) pp. 178, 292–294

## Applying Math

**Use the graph below to answer question 28.**

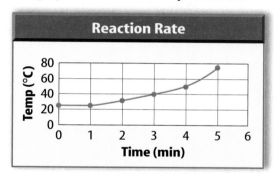

Reaction Rate

**28. Reaction Rates** In the reaction graph above, how long does it take the reaction to reach 50°C?

**29. Chemical Equation** In the following chemical equation, $3Na + AlCl_3 \longrightarrow 3NaCl + Al$, how many aluminum molecules will be produced if you have 30 molecules of sodium?

**30. Catalysis** A zinc catalyst is used to reduce the reaction time by 30%. If the normal time for the reaction to finish is 3 h, how long will it take with the catalyst?

**31. Molecules** Silver has $6.023 \times 10^{23}$ molecules per 107.9 g. How many molecules are there if you have
  **a.** 53.95 g?
  **b.** 323.7 g?
  **c.** 10.79 g?

**Part I**

*Record your answers on the answer sheet*
*provided by your teacher or on a sheet of paper.*

**Use the photo below to answer questions 1 and 2.**

**1** The photograph shows the reaction of copper (Cu) with silver nitrate ($AgNO_3$) to produce copper nitrate ($Cu(NO_3)_2$) and silver (Ag). The chemical equation that describes this reaction is the following:

$$2AgNO_3 + Cu \rightarrow Cu(NO_3)_2 + 2Ag$$

What term describes what is happening in the reaction?
(1) catalyst
(2) chemical change
(3) inhibitor
(4) physical change

**2** Which of the following terms describes the copper on the left side of the equation?
(1) reactant
(2) catalyst
(3) enzyme
(4) product

**3** Which of the following terms best describes a chemical reaction that absorbs heat energy?
(1) catalytic
(2) exothermic
(3) endothermic
(4) acidic

**4** What should be balanced in a chemical equation?
(1) electrons
(2) atoms
(3) molecules
(4) molecules and atoms

**Use the photo below to answer questions 5 and 6.**

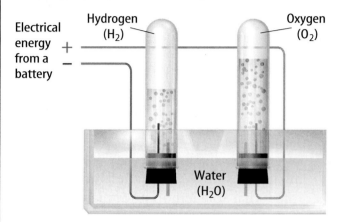

**5** The photograph above shows a demonstration of electrolysis, in which water is broken down into hydrogen and oxygen. Which of the following is the best way to write the chemical equation for this process?
(1) $H_2O + energy \rightarrow H_2 + O_2$
(2) $H_2O + energy \rightarrow 2H_2 + O_2$
(3) $2H_2O + energy \rightarrow 2H_2 + O_2$
(4) $2H_2O + energy \rightarrow 2H_2 + 2O_2$

**6** For each atom of hydrogen that is present before the reaction begins, how many atoms of hydrogen are present after the reaction?
(1) 1
(2) 2
(3) 4
(4) 8

**7** What is the purpose of an inhibitor in a chemical reaction?
(1) decrease the shelf life of food
(2) increase the surface area
(3) decrease the speed of a chemical reaction
(4) increase the speed of a chemical reaction

# NATIONAL GEOGRAPHIC

**B**ack in the 1800s, a mysterious disease called beriberi affected people in certain parts of Asia. One day, a doctor in Indonesia noticed some chickens staggering around, a symptom often seen in people with beriberi. It turned out that the chickens had been eating white rice—the same kind of rice that was being eaten by human beriberi sufferers. White rice has had the outer layers, including the bran, removed. When the sick chickens were fed rice that still had its bran, they quickly recovered. It turned out that the same treatment worked for people with beriberi! Research eventually showed that rice bran contains a vitamin, $B_1$, which is essential for good health. Today, white rice usually is "vitamin-enriched" to replace $B_1$ and other nutrients lost in processing.

## unit ⚡ projects

Visit **glencoe.com** to find project ideas and resources.
Projects include:

- **History** Contribute to a class "remedy journal" with interesting, out-dated medical treatments, and how techniques have improved.
- **Technology** Investigate rare and interesting medical conditions, including their history, characteristics, and treatments. Present a colorful poster with photos and information for class display.
- **Model** Research and create a menu that includes vitamin-rich foods. Prepare a sample and a recipe card for a class food fair.

 *New Research in Cells* provides an opportunity to explore current research on cells and how different cells work in the human body. Questions and answers lead to a summary paragraph of the new

**chapter**

**13**

**LE 1.1b:** The way in which cells function is similar in all living things. Cells grow and divide, producing more cells. Cells take in nutrients, which they use to provide energy for the work that cells do and to make the materials that a cell or an organism needs. **Also Covered:** 1.1a, 1.1c, 1.1d, 1.1e, 1.1f, 1.1g, 1.2a

# Cells—The Units of Life

## Life's Building Blocks

If you look closely, you can see that these frogs and crocodiles are made up of small, plastic building blocks. Similarly, living organisms also are made up of small building blocks. The building block of all living things is the cell.

**Science Journal**   Describe how plastic building blocks fit together to build a larger structure.

# Start-Up Activities

## Observe Onion Cells

An active, organized world is inside you and in all other living things. Yet it is a world that you usually can't see with just your eyes. Make the magnifier in the lab below to help you see how living things are organized.

1. Cut a 2-cm hole in the middle of an index card. Tape a piece of plastic wrap over the hole.

2. Turn down about 1 cm of the two shorter sides of the card, then stand it up.

3. Place a piece of onion skin on a microscope slide, then put it directly under the hole in the card.

4. Put a drop of water on the plastic wrap. Look through the water drop and observe the piece of onion. Draw what you see.

5. **Think Critically** In your Science Journal, describe how the onion skin looked when viewed with your magnifier.

**Compare Cells** Make the following Foldable to help you see how plant and animal cells are similar and different.

**STEP 1** **Fold** a vertical sheet of paper in half from top to bottom.

**STEP 2** **Fold** in half from side to side with the fold at the top.

**STEP 3** **Unfold** the paper once. **Cut** only the fold of the top flap to make two tabs. **Turn** the paper vertically and **draw** on the front tabs as shown.

Plant Cell

Animal Cell

**Read and Write** Before you read the chapter, write what you know about each of these cells. As you read the chapter, add to or correct what you have written under the tabs. Compare and contrast the two types of cells.

 Preview this chapter's content and activities at glencoe.com

LE 1.1a: Living things are composed of cells. Cells provide structure and carry on major functions to sustain life. Cells are usually microscopic in size. **1.1c** Most cells have cell membranes, genetic material, and cytoplasm. Some cells have a cell wall and/or chloroplasts. Many cells have a nucleus. **Also Covered:** LE 1.1b

# The World of Cells

**as you read**

*What* **You'll Learn**

■ **Discuss** the cell theory.
■ **Identify** some of the parts of animal and plant cells.
■ **Explain** the functions of different cell parts.

*Why* **It's Important**

Cells carry out the activities of life.

⊙ **Review Vocabulary**

**theory:** an explanation of things or events based on scientific knowledge that is the result of many observations and experiments

**New Vocabulary**
● bacteria
● cell membrane
● cell wall
● cytoplasm
● organelle
● nucleus
● vacuole
● mitochondria
● photosynthesis
● chloroplast

## Importance of Cells

A cell is the smallest unit of life in all living things. Cells are important because they are organized structures that help living things carry on the activities of life, such as the breakdown of food, movement, growth, and reproduction. Different cells have different jobs in living things. Some plant cells help move water and other substances throughout the plant. White blood cells, found in humans and many other animals, help fight diseases. Plant cells, white blood cells, and all other cells are alike in many ways.

**Cell Theory** Because most cells are small, they were not observed until microscopes were invented. In 1665, scientist Robert Hooke, using a microscope that he made, observed tiny, boxlike things in a thin slice of cork, as shown in **Figure 1.** He called them cells because they reminded him of the small, boxlike rooms called cells, where monks lived.

Throughout the seventeenth and eighteenth centuries, scientists observed many living things under microscopes. Their observations led to the development of the cell theory. The three main ideas of the cell theory are:

1. All living things are made of one or more cells.

2. The cell is the basic unit of life in which the activities of life occur.

3. All cells come from cells that already exist.

**Figure 1** Robert Hooke designed this microscope and drew the cork cells he observed.

**The Microscopic Cell** All the living things pictured in **Figure 2** are made up of cells. The smallest organisms on Earth are **bacteria.** They are one-celled organisms, which means they are made up of only one cell.

**✓ Reading Check** *How many cells does each bacterium have?*

Larger organisms are made of many cells. These cells work together to complete all of the organism's life activities. The living things that you see every day—trees, dogs, insects, people—are many-celled organisms. Your body contains more than 10 trillion (10,000,000,000,000) cells.

**Microscopes** Scientists have viewed and studied cells for about 300 years. In that time, they have learned a lot about cells. Better microscopes have helped scientists learn about the differences among cells. Some modern microscopes allow scientists to study the small features that are inside cells.

**INTEGRATE Physics** The microscope used in most classrooms is called a compound light microscope. In this type of microscope, light passes through the object you are looking at and then through two or more lenses. The lenses enlarge the image of the object. How much an image is enlarged depends on the powers of the eyepiece and the objective lens. The power—a number followed by an ✕—is found on each lens. For example, a power of 10✕ means that the lens can magnify something to ten times its actual size. The magnification of a microscope is found by multiplying the powers of the eyepiece and the objective lens.

**Figure 2** All living things are made up of cells.

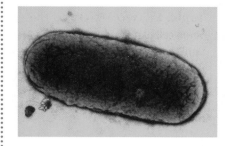

*E. coli*—a bacterium—is a one-celled organism.

Plant cells are different from animal cells.

Human cells are similar to other animal cells like those in cats and turtles.

# What are cells made of?

As small as cells are, they are made of even smaller parts, each doing a different job. A cell can be compared to a bakery. The activities of a bakery are inside a building. Electricity is used to run the ovens and other equipment, power the lights, and heat the building. The bakery's products require ingredients such as dough, sugar, and fillings, that must be stored, assembled, and baked. The bakery's products are packaged and shipped to different locations. A manager is in charge of the entire operation. The manager makes a plan for every employee of the bakery and a plan for every step of making and selling the baked goods.

A living cell operates in a similar way. Like the walls of the bakery, a cell has a boundary. Inside this boundary, the cell's life activities take place. These activities must be managed. Smaller parts inside the cell can act as storage areas. The cell also has parts that use ingredients such as oxygen, water, minerals, and other nutrients. Some cell parts can release energy or make substances that are necessary for maintaining life. Some substances leave the cell and are used elsewhere in the organism.

**Figure 3** These are some of the parts of an animal cell that perform the activities necessary for life.

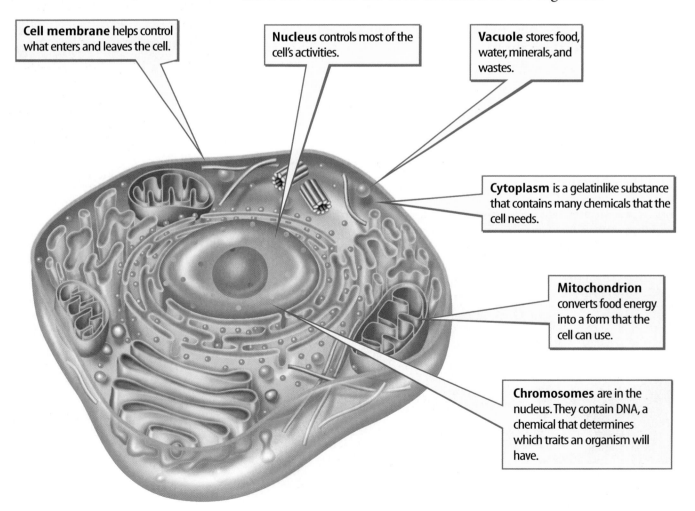

**Cell membrane** helps control what enters and leaves the cell.

**Nucleus** controls most of the cell's activities.

**Vacuole** stores food, water, minerals, and wastes.

**Cytoplasm** is a gelatinlike substance that contains many chemicals that the cell needs.

**Mitochondrion** converts food energy into a form that the cell can use.

**Chromosomes** are in the nucleus. They contain DNA, a chemical that determines which traits an organism will have.

**Outside the Cell** The **cell membrane,** shown in **Figure 3,** is a flexible structure that holds the cell together, similar to the walls of the bakery. The cell membrane forms a boundary between the cell and its environment. It also helps control what goes into and comes out of the cell. Some cells, like those in plants, algae, fungi, and many types of bacteria, also have a structure outside the cell membrane called a **cell wall,** shown in **Figure 4.** The cell wall helps support and protect these cells.

**Inside the Cell** The inside of a cell is filled with a gelatinlike substance called **cytoplasm** (SI tuh pla zum). Approximately two-thirds of the cytoplasm is water, but it also contains many chemicals that are needed by the cell. Like the work area inside the bakery, the cytoplasm is where the cell's activities take place.

**Organelles** Except for bacterial cells, cells contain **organelles** (or guh NELZ) like those in **Figure 3** and **Figure 4.** These specialized cell parts can move around in the cytoplasm and perform activities that are necessary for life. You could think of these organelles as the employees of the cell because each type of organelle does a different job. In bacteria, most cell activities occur in the cytoplasm.

**INTEGRATE Chemistry**

**Phospholipids** The cell membrane is a double layer of complex molecules called phospholipids (fahs foh LIH pudz). Research to find the elements that are in these molecules. Find those elements on the periodic table at the back of this book.

**Living Environment**

**1.1a, 1.1b, 1.1c Design** a comparison chart of the organelles of an animal cell and a plant cell. Briefly describe the job of each organelle.

**Figure 4** Most plant cells contain the same types of organelles as in animal cells. Plant cells also have a cell wall and chloroplasts.

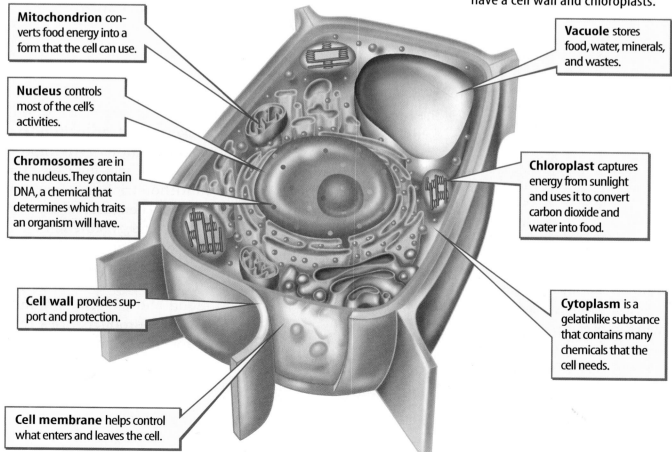

**Mitochondrion** converts food energy into a form that the cell can use.

**Nucleus** controls most of the cell's activities.

**Chromosomes** are in the nucleus. They contain DNA, a chemical that determines which traits an organism will have.

**Cell wall** provides support and protection.

**Cell membrane** helps control what enters and leaves the cell.

**Vacuole** stores food, water, minerals, and wastes.

**Chloroplast** captures energy from sunlight and uses it to convert carbon dioxide and water into food.

**Cytoplasm** is a gelatinlike substance that contains many chemicals that the cell needs.

## Mini LAB

**Modeling a Cell**

**Procedure**

1. Collect **household materials such as clay, cardboard, yarn, buttons, dry macaroni,** or other objects.
2. Using the objects that you collected, make a three-dimensional model of an animal or plant cell.
3. On a separate sheet of **paper,** make a key to the materials in your cell model.

**Analysis**

1. What does each part of your cell model do?
2. Have someone look at your model. Which of the cell parts could they identify without using the key?
3. How could you improve your model?

*Try at Home*

**The Nucleus** A bakery's manager follows a business plan to make sure that the business runs smoothly. A business plan describes how the business should operate. These plans could include how many donuts are made and what kinds of pies are baked.

The hereditary material of the cell is like the bakery's manager. It directs most of the cell's activities. In the cells of organisms except bacteria, the hereditary material is in an organelle called the **nucleus** (NEW klee us). Inside the nucleus are chromosomes (KROH muh zohmz). They contain a plan for the cell, similar to the bakery's business plan. Chromosomes contain an important chemical called DNA. It determines which traits an organism will have, such as the shape of a plant's leaves or the color of your eyes.

**✓ Reading Check** *Which important chemical determines the traits of an organism?*

**Storage** Pantries, closets, refrigerators, and freezers store food and other supplies that a bakery needs. Trash cans hold garbage until it can be picked up. In cells, food, water, and other substances are stored in balloonlike organelles in the cytoplasm called **vacuoles** (VA kyuh wohlz). Some vacuoles store wastes until the cell is ready to get rid of them. Plant cells usually have a large vacuole that stores water and other substances.

## Energy and the Cell

Electrical energy or the energy in natural gas is converted to heat energy by the bakery's ovens. The heat then is used to bake the breads and other bakery products. Cells need energy, too. Cells, except bacteria, have organelles called **mitochondria** (mi tuh KAHN dree uh)(singular, *mitochondrion*). An important process called cellular respiration (SEL yuh lur • res puh RAY shun) takes place inside a mitochondrion as shown in **Figure 5.** Cellular respiration is a series of chemical reactions in which energy stored in food is converted to a form of energy that the cell can use. This energy is released as food and oxygen combine. Waste products of this process are carbon dioxide and water. All cells with mitochondria use the energy from cellular respiration to do all of their work.

**Figure 5** Inside a mitochondrion, food energy is changed into a form of energy that a cell can use.
**Infer** *what happens to the water and carbon dioxide produced by mitochondria in human cells.*

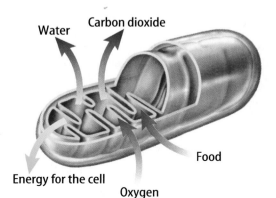

Water

Carbon dioxide

Energy for the cell

Oxygen

Food

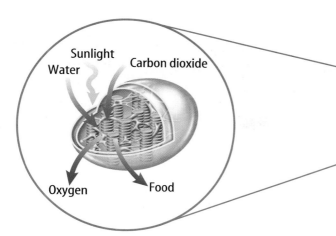

Sunlight
Water
Carbon dioxide
Oxygen
Food

**Nature's Solar Energy Factories** Animals obtain food from their surroundings. A cow grazes in a pasture. A bird pecks at worms, and a dog eats from a bowl. Have you ever seen a plant eat anything? How do plants get energy-rich food?

Plants, algae, and many types of bacteria make food through a process called **photosynthesis** (foh toh SIHN thuh sus). Most photosynthesis in plants occurs in leaf cells. Inside these cells are green organelles called **chloroplasts** (KLOR uh plasts). Most leaves are green because their cells contain so many chloroplasts. During plant photosynthesis, as shown in **Figure 6,** chloroplasts capture light energy and combine carbon dioxide from the air with water to make food. Energy is stored in food. As the plant needs energy, its mitochondria release the food's energy. The captured light energy is passed to other organisms when they eat organisms that carry on photosynthesis.

**Figure 6** Photosynthesis can take place inside the chloroplasts of plant cells.

**Living Environment**

**1.1a, 1.1b** **Restate** the cell theory in your own words.

## section 1 review

### Summary

**Importance of Cells**

- Cells are organized structures that help living things carry on the activities of life.
- The main ideas behind cells are described in the cell theory.
- Microscopes helped scientists study cells.

**What are cells made of?**

- Different cell parts do different jobs.

**Energy and the Cell**

- Cells need energy to function. This energy comes mainly from cellular respiration.
- Plants, algae, and some bacteria make food through photosynthesis.

### Self Check

1. **List** the three main ideas of the cell theory.
2. **Explain** why the nucleus is so important to the living cell.
3. **Describe** how cells get the energy they need to carry on their activities.
4. **Describe** the purpose of a cell membrane.
5. **Think Critically** Suppose your teacher gave you a slide of an unknown cell. How would you tell whether the cell was from an animal or from a plant?

**Applying Skills**

6. **Compare and contrast** the parts of animal cells and plant cells and the jobs that they do.

# Observing Algae

You might have noticed mats of green algae growing on a pond or clinging to the walls of the aquarium in your classroom. Why are algae green? Like plants, algae contain organelles called chloroplasts. Chloroplasts contain a green pigment called chlorophyll. It captures light energy that is needed to make food. In this lab, you'll describe chloroplasts and other organelles in algal cells.

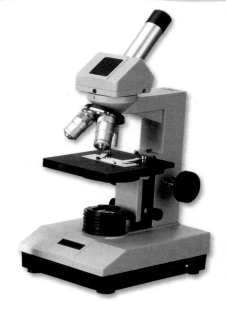

## Real-World Question

What organelles can be seen when viewing algal cells under a microscope?

### Goals
- **Observe** algal cells under a microscope.
- **Identify** cell organelles.

### Materials
microscope      pond water
microscope slides    algae
coverslips       dropper
large jars       colored pencils

### Safety Precautions

**WARNING:** *Thoroughly wash your hands after you have finished this lab.*

## Procedure

1. Fill the tip of a dropper with pond water and thin strands of algae. Use the dropper to place the algae and a drop of water on a microscope slide.
2. Place a coverslip over the water drop and then place the slide on the stage of a microscope.
3. Using the microscope's lowest power objective, focus on the algal strands.
4. Once the algal strands are in focus, switch to a higher power objective and observe several algal cells.
5. **Draw** a colored picture of one of the algal cells, identifying the different organelles in the cell. Label on your drawing the cell wall, chloroplasts, and other organelles you can see.

## Conclude and Apply

1. **List** the organelles you found in each cell.
2. **Explain** the function of chloroplasts.
3. **Infer** why algal cells are essential to all pond organisms.

### Communicating
**Your Data**

Work with three other students to create a collage of algal cell pictures complete with labeled organelles. Create a bulletin board display about algal cells.

**section**

**2**

# The Different Jobs of Cells

## Special Cells for Special Jobs

Choose the right tool for the right job. You might have heard this common expression. The best tool for a job is one that has been designed for that job. For example, you wouldn't use a hammer to saw a board in half, and you wouldn't use a saw to pound in a nail. You can think of your body cells in a similar way.

Cells that make up many-celled organisms, like you, are specialized. Different kinds of specialized cells work as a team to perform the life activities of a many-celled organism.

**Types of Human Cells** Your body is made up of many types of specialized cells. The same is true for other animals. **Figure 7** shows some human cell types. Notice the variety of sizes and shapes. A cell's shape and size can be related to its function.

### as you read

***What* You'll Learn**
- **Discuss** how different cells have different jobs.
- **Explain** the differences among tissues, organs, and organ systems.

***Why* It's Important**
You will understand how different types of cells work together to keep you healthy.

🔎 **Review Vocabulary**
**organism:** anything that possesses all the characteristics of life

**New Vocabulary**
- tissue
- organ system
- organ

**Figure 7** Human cells come in different shapes and sizes.

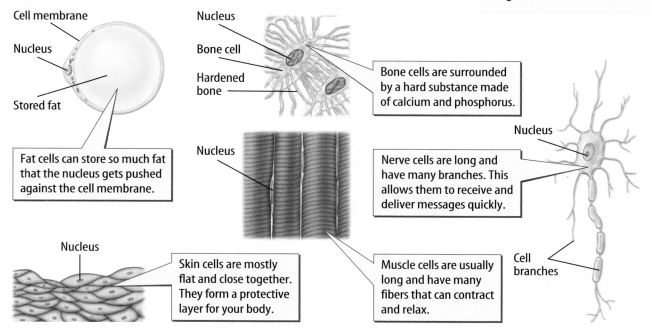

Cell membrane

Nucleus

Stored fat

Fat cells can store so much fat that the nucleus gets pushed against the cell membrane.

Nucleus

Bone cell

Hardened bone

Bone cells are surrounded by a hard substance made of calcium and phosphorus.

Nucleus

Nucleus

Skin cells are mostly flat and close together. They form a protective layer for your body.

Muscle cells are usually long and have many fibers that can contract and relax.

Nucleus

Nerve cells are long and have many branches. This allows them to receive and deliver messages quickly.

Cell branches

**Figure 8** Plants, like animals, have specialized cells.
**Infer** *what process can occur in leaf cells but not in root cells.*

Some leaf cells are brick shaped and contain many chloroplasts.

LM, Magnification: 900×

Many of the cells in stems are long and tube-shaped. They move water and other materials through the plant.

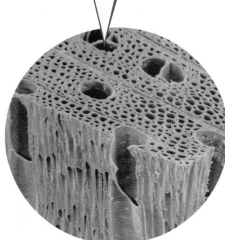

SEM Magnification: 1500×

Most root cells are block shaped and do not contain chloroplasts.

Magnification: 450×

**Types of Plant Cells** Like animals, plants also are made of several different cell types, as shown in **Figure 8.** For instance, plants have different types of cells in their leaves, roots, and stems. Each type of cell has a specific job. Some cells in plant stems are long and tubelike. Together they form a system through which water, food, and other materials move in the plant. Other cells, like those that cover the outside of the stem, are smaller or thicker. They provide strength to the stem.

**✓ Reading Check** *What do long, tubelike cells do in plants?*

# Cell Organization

How well do you think your body would work if all the different cell types were just mixed together in no particular pattern? Could you walk if your leg muscle cells were scattered here and there, each doing its own thing, instead of being grouped together in your legs? How could you think if your brain cells weren't close enough together to communicate with each other? Many-celled organisms are not just mixed-up collections of different types of cells. Cells are organized into systems that, together, perform functions that keep the organism healthy and alive.

*Hot Words Hot Topics*: Bk 2 (1) p. 92; (2) p. 92

**INTEGRATE**
*Career*

**Studying Space**
Astronomers study systems that are found in space. The solar system is just one of many systems that make up the Milky Way Galaxy. Research to learn the education requirements and job description of an astronomer. Write a want ad for an astronomer.

## Applying Math — Solve One-Step Equations

**RED BLOOD CELLS** Each milliliter of blood contains 5 million red blood cells (RBCs). On average, an adolescent has about 3.5 L of blood. On average, how many RBCs are in an adolescent's body?

### Solution

**1** *This is what you know:*
- number of RBCs per 1 mL = 5,000,000
- 1,000 mL = 1 L
- average volume of blood in an adolescent's body = 3.5 L

**2** *This is what you need to find out:*

On average, how many RBCs are in an adolescent's body, $N$?

**3** *This is the procedure you need to use:*
- Use the following equation:
  $N$ = (number of RBCs/1mL) (1,000 mL/1 L) (3.5 L of blood)
- Substitute the known values
  $N$ = (5,000,000 RBCs/1 mL) (1,000 mL/1 L) (3.5 L of blood)
  $N$ = 17,500,000,000 RBCs
- On average, there are 17.5 billion red blood cells in an adolescent's body.

**4** *Check your answer:*

Divide 17,500,000,000 RBCs by 1,000 mL/1 L then divide that answer by 3.5 L, and you should get 5,000,000 RBCs/1 mL.

### Practice Problems

**1.** Each milliliter of blood contains approximately 7,500 white blood cells. How many white blood cells are in the average adolescent's body?

**2.** There are approximately 250,000 platelets in each milliliter of blood. How many platelets are in the average adolescent's body?

 **For more practice, visit** glencoe.com

## Figure 9

Organs are two or more tissue types that work together.
An organ performs a task that no other organ performs.

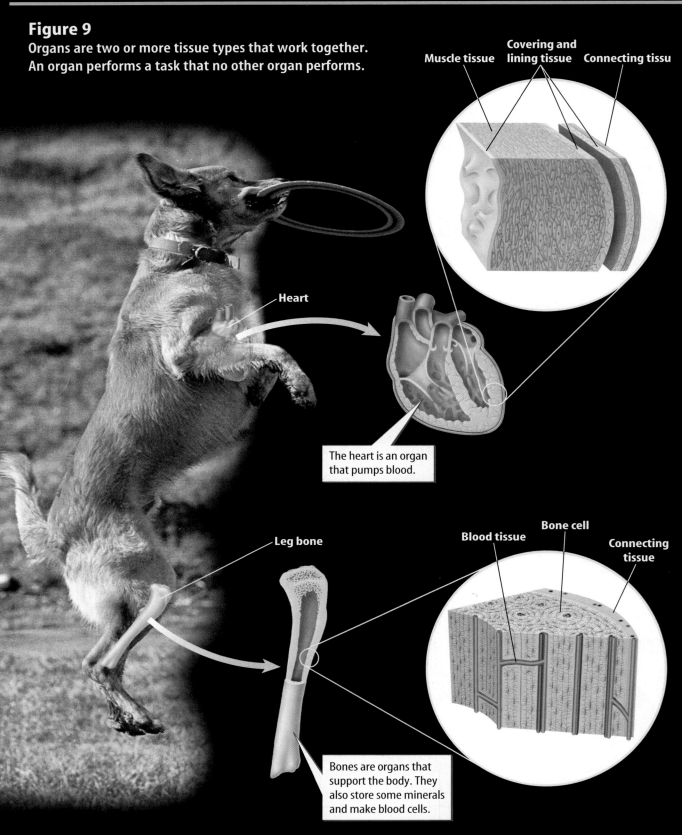

Muscle tissue

Covering and lining tissue

Connecting tissu

Heart

The heart is an organ that pumps blood.

Leg bone

Blood tissue

Bone cell

Connecting tissue

Bones are organs that support the body. They also store some minerals and make blood cells.

**Tissues and Organs** Cells that are alike are organized into tissues (TIH shewz). **Tissues** are groups of similar cells that all do the same sort of work. For example, bone tissue is made up of bone cells, and nerve tissue is made up of nerve cells. Blood, a liquid tissue, includes different types of blood cells.

As important as individual tissues are, they do not work alone. Different types of tissues working together can form a structure called an **organ** (OR gun). For example, the stomach is an organ that includes muscle tissue, nerve tissue, and blood tissue. All of these tissues work together and enable the stomach to perform its digestive functions. Other human organs include the heart and the kidneys.

 **Reading Check** *Which term means "two or more tissue types that work together"?*

**Organ Systems** A group of organs that work together to do a certain job is called an **organ system.** The stomach, mouth, intestines, and liver are involved in digestion. Together, these and several other organs make up the digestive system. Other organ systems found in your body include the respiratory system, the circulatory system, the reproductive system, and the nervous system.

Organ systems also work together, as shown in **Figure 9.** For example, the muscular system has more than 600 muscles that are attached to bones. The contracting cells of muscle tissue cause your bones, which are part of the skeletal system, to move.

**Science** online

**Topic: One-Celled Organisms**
Visit glencoe.com for Web links to information about what types of organisms are made up of only one cell.

**Activity** Create a table that includes images and information about five of these organisms.

 **Physical Setting**

**1.1e, 1.2a Create** a labeled concept web to show the cells which work together to form a tissue. Show the tissues that work together to form an organ. Label a group of organs that work together as an organ system.

---

### section 2 review

#### Summary

**Special Cells for Special Jobs**
- Plant and animal cells come in a variety of sizes and shapes.
- The function of an animal cell can be related to its shape and size.
- The leaves, roots, and stems of plants are made of different types of cells to perform different functions.

**Cell Organization**
- Many-celled organisms are organized into tissues, organs, and organ systems.
- Each organ system performs a specific function that, together with other systems, keeps an organism healthy and alive.

#### Self Check

1. **Describe** three types of cells that are found in the human body.
2. **Compare and contrast** the cells found in a plant's roots, stems, and leaves.
3. **Explain** the difference between a cell and a tissue and between a tissue and an organ.
4. **Think Critically** Why must specialized cells work together as a team?

**Applying Skills**

5. **Concept Map** Make an events-chain concept map of the different levels of cell organization from cell to organ system. Provide an example for each level of organization.

---

# Design Your Own

## Water Movement in Plants

### Goals

■ **Design** an investigation to show where water moves in a plant.

■ **Observe** how long it takes water to move in a plant.

### Possible Materials

fresh stalk of celery with leaves
clear drinking glass
scissors
red food coloring
water

### Safety Precautions

**WARNING:** *Use care when handling sharp objects such as scissors. Avoid getting red food coloring on your clothing.*

### ▶ Real-World Question

When you are thirsty, you can sip water from a glass or drink from a fountain. Plants must get their water in other ways. In most plants, water moves from the soil into cells in the roots. Where does water travel in a plant?

### ▶ Form a Hypothesis

Based on what you already know about how a plant functions, state a hypothesis about where you think water travels in a plant.

### ▶ Test Your Hypothesis

**Make a Plan**

1. As a group, agree upon a hypothesis and decide how you will test it. Identify which results will support the hypothesis.

2. **List** the steps you will need to take to test your hypothesis. Be specific. Describe exactly what you will do in each step. List your materials.

3. Prepare a data table in your Science Journal to record your observations.

4. **Read** the entire investigation to make sure all steps are in logical order.

5. **Identify** all constants, variables, and controls of the investigation.

**Follow Your Plan**

1. Make sure your teacher approves your plan before you start.

2. Carry out the investigation according to the approved plan.

3. While doing the investigation, record your observations and complete the data tables in your Science Journal.

## ◉ Analyze Your Data

1. **Compare** the color of the celery stalk before, during, and after the investigation.
2. **Compare** your results with those of other groups.
3. Make a drawing of the cut stalk. Label your drawing.
4. What was your control in this investigation? What were your variables?

## ◉ Conclude and Apply

1. **Explain** whether the results of this investigation supported your hypothesis.
2. **Infer** why only some of the plant tissue is red.
3. **Explain** what you would do to improve this investigation.
4. **Predict** if other plants have tissues that move water.

### Communicating Your Data

**Write** a report about your investigation. Include illustrations to show how the investigation was performed. Present your report to your class.

# TEST-TUBE TISSUE

## Thanks to advances in science, skin tissue is being "grown" in laboratories

In Chicago, a young woman named Kelly is cooking pasta on her stove. Her clothes catch fire from the gas flame and, in the blink of an eye, 80 percent of her body is severely burned. Will she survive?

Just 20 years ago, the answer to this question probably would have been "no." Fortunately for Kelly, science has come a long way in recent years. Today, there's a very good chance that Kelly might lead a long and healthy life.

Like the brain or the heart, the skin is an organ. In fact, it is the body's largest organ, about 1/12 of your total body weight. Composed of protective layers, skin keeps your internal structure safe from damage, infection, and temperature changes.

Today, just as farmers can grow crops of corn and wheat, scientists can grow human skin. How?

A piece of test skin is removed from its culture.

### Tissue Engineers

Scientists, called tissue engineers, take a piece of skin (no bigger than a quarter) from an undamaged part of the burn victim's body. The skin cells are isolated, mixed with special nutrients, and then they multiply in a culture dish.

After about two to three months, the tissue engineers can harvest sheets of new, smooth skin. These sheets, as large as postcards, are grafted onto the victim's damaged body and promote additional skin growth.

By grafting Kelly's own skin on her body rather than using donor skin—skin from another person or from an animal—doctors avoid at least three potential complications. First, donor skin may not even be available. Second, Kelly's body might perceive the new skin cells from another source to be a danger, and her immune system might reject—or destroy—the transplant. Finally, even if the skin produced from a foreign source is accepted, it may leave extensive scarring.

### Tissue Testing

What else can tissue engineers grow? They produce test skin—skin made in the lab and used to test the effects of cosmetics and chemicals on humans. This skin is eliminating the use of animals for such tests. Also, tissue engineers are working on ways to replace other body parts such as livers, heart valves, and ears, that don't grow back on their own.

**Safety List** Visit the link shown to the right or your media center to learn about fire safety tips, including kitchen safety and escape routes in your home. Make a list and share it with your family.

Science Online

**For more information, visit glencoe.com**

## Reviewing Main Ideas

### Section 1   The World of Cells

1. The cell theory states that all living things are made of one or more cells, the cell is the basic unit of life, and all cells come from other cells.

2. The microscope is an instrument that enlarges the image of an object.

3. All cells are surrounded by a cell membrane and contain hereditary material and cytoplasm. Plant cells have a cell wall outside the cell membrane. Cells, except bacteria, contain organelles.

4. The nucleus directs the cell's activities. Chromosomes contain DNA that determines what kinds of traits an organism will have. Vacuoles store substances.

5. In mitochondria, the process of cellular respiration combines food molecules with oxygen. This series of chemical reactions releases energy for the cell's activities.

6. The energy in light is captured and stored in food molecules during the process of photosynthesis. Plants, algae, and some bacteria make their own food by photosynthesis.

### Section 2   The Different Jobs of Cells

1. Many-celled organisms are made up of different kinds of cells that perform different tasks.

2. Many-celled organisms are organized into tissues, organs, and organ systems that perform specific jobs to keep an organism alive.

## Visualizing Main Ideas

*Copy and complete the following concept map on the parts of a plant cell.*

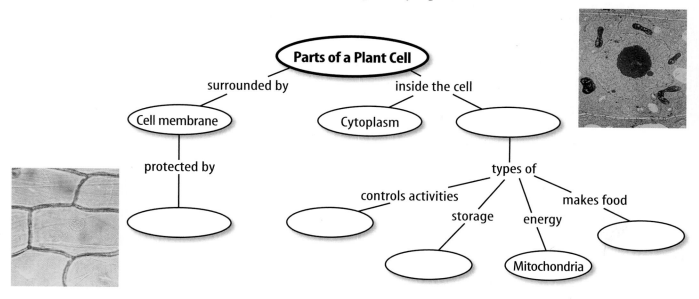

## Using Vocabulary

| | |
|---|---|
| bacteria p. 363 | organ p. 373 |
| cell membrane p. 365 | organ system p. 373 |
| cell wall p. 365 | organelle p. 365 |
| chloroplast p. 367 | photosynthesis p. 367 |
| cytoplasm p. 365 | tissue p. 373 |
| mitochondria p. 366 | vacuole p. 366 |
| nucleus p. 366 | |

*Explain the difference between the terms in the following sets.*

1. mitochondria—chloroplast

2. tissue—organ

3. cell membrane—nucleus

4. organ—organ system

5. nucleus—organelle

6. cytoplasm—nucleus

7. vacuole—mitochondria

8. organ system—tissue

9. organelle—organ

10. cell wall—cell membrane

## Checking Concepts

*Choose the word or phrase that best answers the question.*

11. Which of the following controls what enters and leaves the cell?
    A) mitochondrion
    B) cell membrane
    C) vacuole
    D) nucleus

12. Which of the following are found inside the nucleus of the cell?
    A) vacuoles
    B) chromosomes
    C) chloroplasts
    D) mitochondria

**Use the illustration below to answer questions 13 and 14.**

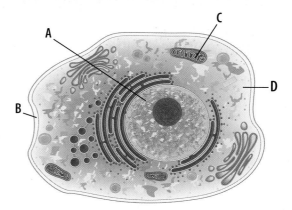

13. Which letter is the gelatinlike substance in a cell that contains water and chemicals?
    A) A          C) C
    B) B          D) D

14. Which structure converts food energy to a form of energy the cell can use?
    A) A          C) C
    B) B          D) D

15. Which of the following terms best describes the stomach?
    A) organelle          C) organ
    B) organ system       D) tissue

16. What does photosynthesis make for a plant?
    A) food          C) water
    B) organs        D) tissues

17. What does DNA do?
    A) makes food
    B) determines traits
    C) converts food to energy
    D) stores substances

18. Which of the following terms is the name of a human organ system?
    A) protective          C) photosynthetic
    B) growth              D) respiratory

19. What cell structure helps support plants?
    A) cell membrane       C) vacuole
    B) cell wall           D) nucleus

## Thinking Critically

**20. Predict** what would happen to a cell if the cell membrane were solid and waterproof.

**21. Describe** what might happen to a cell if all its mitochondria were removed.

**22. Explain** why cells are called the units of life.

**23. Infer** what kinds of animal cells might have a lot of mitochondria present.

**24. Distinguish** between a bacterium and a plant cell.

**25. Compare and contrast** photosynthesis and cellular respiration.

**26. Make and Use Tables** Copy and complete this table about the functions of the following cell parts: *nucleus, cell membrane, mitochondrion, chloroplast,* and *vacuole.*

### Functions of Cell Parts

| Cell Part | Function |
| --- | --- |
|  |  |
| Do not write in this book. | |
|  |  |
|  |  |

**27. Concept Map** Make an events-chain concept map of the following from simple to complex: *small intestine, circular muscle cell, human,* and *digestive system.*

**28. Identify and Manipulate Variables and Controls** Describe an experiment you might do to determine whether water moves into and out of cells.

**29. Recognize Cause and Effect** Why is the brick-like shape of some plant cells important?

## Performance Activities

**30. Skit** Working with three or four classmates, develop a short skit about how a living cell works. Have each group member play the role of a different cell part.

*Hot Words Hot Topics:* Bk 2 (31) p. 92; (32) p. 199; (33)pp. 201–202

## Applying Math

**31. Magnification** A microscope has an eyepiece with a power of 10× and an objective lens with a power of 40×. What is the magnification of the microscope?

**32. Viruses** Use a computer to make a line graph of the following data. At 37°C there are 1.0 million viruses; at 37.5°C, 0.5 milllion; at 37.8°C, 0.25 million; at 38.3°C, 0.1 million; and at 38.9°C, 0.05 million.

**Use the graph below to answer question 33.**

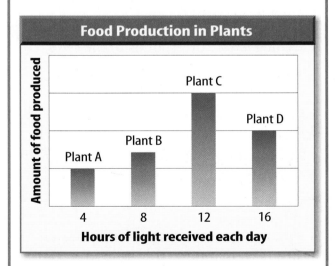

**33. Plant Food Production** Light is necessary for plants to make food. Using the graph above, determine which plant produced the most food. How much light was needed by the plant every day to produce the most food?

**Part I**

*Record your answers on the answer sheet provided by your teacher or on a sheet of paper.*

**1** The idea that all cells come from cells that already exist is part of what theory?
(1) microscopic theory
(2) the basic theory
(3) the Hooke theory
(4) the cell theory

**Use the illustration below to answer questions 2 and 3.**

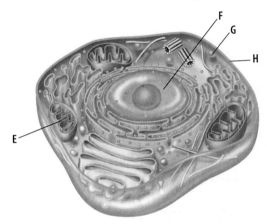

**2** Which letter corresponds to the cell's nucleus?
(1) E　　　　　　(3) G
(2) F　　　　　　(4) H

**3** Which letter corresponds to the part of the cell that helps control what enters and leaves the cell?
(1) E　　　　　　(3) G
(2) F　　　　　　(4) H

**4** Chromosomes contain what important chemical that helps determine the traits of an organism?
(1) DNA　　　　　(3) carbon dioxide
(2) NAD　　　　　(4) oxygen

**5** Which one of the following is an organ?
(1) leg bone　　　　(3) muscle cell
(2) nucleus　　　　(4) bacterium

**6** Which of the following describes plant cells used to move water through the plant?
(1) brick shaped with many chloroplasts
(2) block shaped with no chloroplasts
(3) long with fibers that contract and relax
(4) long and tube-shaped

**7** What are groups of cells that all do the same sort of work called?
(1) organs　　　　(3) tissues
(2) organelles　　　(4) nerves

**Use the illustration below to answer questions 8 and 9.**

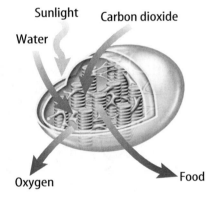

**8** Where would this organelle likely be found?
(1) in your brain　　(3) in a leaf
(2) in your heart　　(4) in your bone

**9** What process is taking place in this organelle?
(1) cellular respiration
(2) photosynthesis
(3) food storage
(4) cell reproduction

**10** Which of the following pairs of organisms would have cells that were the most similar?
(1) a dog and a cat
(2) a turtle and a tree
(3) a carrot and a cat
(4) a fox and a daisy

**Part II**

*Record your answers on the answer sheet provided by your teacher or on a sheet of paper.*

**11** When you breathe out, your breath contains the waste products of carbon dioxide and water. What cellular process produces these wastes?

**12** What two things produced by plants would be important to help keep astronauts alive on a long journey to Mars?

**Use the illustration below to answer questions 13 and 14.**

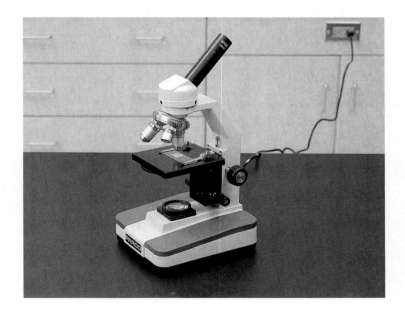

**13** This type of microscope is used in most classrooms. What is the name of this type of microscope?

**14** The magnification of the eyepiece of the microscope above is 10×. A student is looking at a slide of a piece of onion skin. If the magnification of the objective lens used is also 10×, how much is the microscope magnifying the image of the cells in the onion skin?

**15** Name three cellular organelles and describe the role of each.

**16** A caterpillar eats the leaves of a milkweed plant. Explain why the caterpillar, like the milkweed plant, uses captured light energy.

**17** A dog could not jump with just its muscle system. What other system must work with muscles and how do the two systems work together?

**18** Blood carries oxygen to cells. A dog's muscle cells require energy. Explain why a dog's heart might need to pump faster when the dog jumps.

## chapter 14

LE 1.2a: Each system is composed of organs and tissues that perform specific functions and interact with each other. 1.2b: Tissues, organs, and organ systems help to provide all cells with nutrients, oxygen, and waste removal. Also Covered: LE 1.2g, 1.2h, 5.1a, 5.2f

# Support, Movement, and Responses

## chapter preview

### sections

**1** The Skin
*Lab Measuring Skin Surface*

**2** The Muscular System

**3** The Skeletal System

**4** The Nervous System
*Lab Skin Sensitivity*

*Virtual Lab What are the major bones of the human body?*

## How are you like a building?

Buildings are supported and protected by internal and external structures. Your body is supported by your skeleton and protected by your skin. In this chapter, you also will learn how your body senses and responds to the world around you.

**Science Journal** Imagine for a moment that your body does not have a support system. How will you perform your daily activities? Explain your reasoning.

# Start-Up Activities

## Effect of Muscles on Movement

The expression "Many hands make light work" is also true when it comes to muscles in your body. In fact, hundreds of muscles and bones work together to bring about smooth, easy movement. Muscle interactions enable you to pick up a penny or lift a 10-kg weight.

1. Sit on a chair at an empty table and place the palm of one hand under the edge of the table.

2. Push your hand up against the table. Do not push too hard.

3. Use your other hand to feel the muscles located on both sides of your upper arm, as shown in the photo.

4. Next, place your palm on top of the table and push down. Again, feel the muscles in your upper arm.

5. **Think Critically** Describe in your Science Journal how the different muscles in your upper arm were working during each movement.

---

 Support, Movement, and Responses Make the following Foldable to help you understand the functions of skin, muscles, bones, and nerves.

**STEP 1** Fold a sheet of paper in half lengthwise. Make the back edge about 1.25 cm longer than the front edge.

**STEP 2** Fold the paper in half widthwise, twice.

**STEP 3** Unfold and cut only the top layer along the three folds to make four tabs. Label the tabs as shown.

Read and Write As you read this chapter, list the functions that skin, muscles, bones, and nerves have in support, movement, and responses.

 Preview this chapter's content and activities at glencoe.com

# section 1

# The Skin

## as you read

### *What* You'll Learn
- **Distinguish** between the epidermis and dermis of the skin.
- **Identify** the functions of the skin.
- **Explain** how skin protects the body from disease and how it heals itself.

### *Why* It's Important
Skin plays a vital role in protecting your body against injury and disease.

### ⊙ Review Vocabulary
**organ:** a structure, such as the heart, made up of different types of tissues that work together

### New Vocabulary
- epidermis
- dermis
- melanin

## Skin Structures

Your skin is the largest organ of your body. Much of the information you receive about your environment comes through your skin. You can think of your skin as your largest sense organ.

Skin is made up of three layers of tissue—the epidermis, the dermis, and a fatty layer—as shown in **Figure 1.** Each layer is made of different cell types. The **epidermis** is the outer, thinnest layer. The epidermis's outermost cells are dead and water repellent. Thousands of epidermal cells rub off every time you take a shower, shake hands, or scratch your elbow. New cells are produced constantly at the base of the epidermis. These new cells move up and eventually replace those that are rubbed off. The **dermis** is the layer of cells directly below the epidermis. This layer is thicker than the epidermis and contains blood vessels, nerves, muscles, oil and sweat glands, and other structures. Below the dermis is a fatty region that insulates the body. This is where much of the fat is deposited when a person gains weight.

**Figure 1** Hair, sweat glands, and oil glands are part of your body's largest organ.

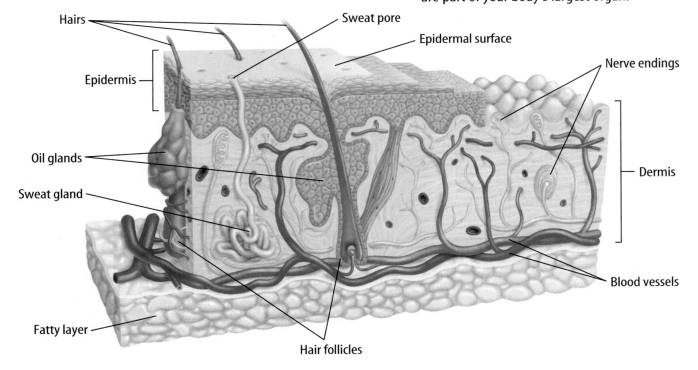

Hairs · Sweat pore · Epidermal surface · Nerve endings · Epidermis · Oil glands · Dermis · Sweat gland · Blood vessels · Fatty layer · Hair follicles

**Melanin** Cells in the epidermis produce the chemical **melanin** (ME luh nun), a pigment that protects your skin and gives it color. The different amounts of melanin produced by cells result in differences in skin color, as shown in **Figure 2.** When your skin is exposed to ultraviolet rays, melanin production increases and your skin becomes darker. Lighter skin tones have less protection. Such skin burns more easily and can be more susceptible to skin cancer.

## Skin Functions

Your skin carries out several major functions, including protection, sensory response, formation of vitamin D, regulation of body temperature, and ridding the body of wastes. The most important function of the skin is protection. The skin forms a protective covering over the body that prevents physical and chemical injury. Some bacteria and other disease-causing organisms cannot pass through skin as long as it is unbroken. Glands in the skin secrete fluids that can damage or destroy some bacteria. The skin also slows water loss from body tissues.

Specialized nerve cells in the skin detect and relay information to the brain. Because of these cells, you are able to sense the softness of a cat, the sharpness of a pin, or the heat of a frying pan.

Another important function of skin is the formation of vitamin D. Small amounts of this vitamin are produced in the presence of ultraviolet light from a fatlike molecule in your epidermis. Vitamin D is essential for good health because it helps your body absorb calcium into your blood from food in your digestive tract.

**INTEGRATE Language Arts**

**High Altitude and Skin** There have been many books written about mountain climbing. Search the library for such a book and find references to the effects of sunlight and weather on the skin at high altitudes. In your Science Journal, list the book title and author and summarize the passage that describes the effects of sunlight and weather on the skin.

**Living Environment**

**1.2a, 1.2h  List** the five major functions of skin.

**Figure 2** Melanin gives skin and eyes their color. The more melanin that is present, the darker the color is. This pigment provides protection from damage caused by harmful light energy.

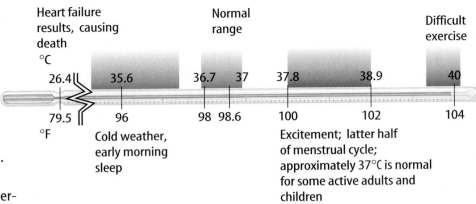

| Heart failure results, causing death | | Normal range | | | | Difficult exercise |
| °C | | | | | | |
| 26.4 | 35.6 | 36.7 | 37 | 37.8 | 38.9 | 40 |
| 79.5 | 96 | 98 | 98.6 | 100 | 102 | 104 |
| °F | Cold weather, early morning sleep | | | Excitement; latter half of menstrual cycle; approximately 37°C is normal for some active adults and children | | |

**Figure 3** Normal human body temperature is about 37°C. Temperature varies throughout the day. The highest body temperature is reached at about 11 A.M. and the lowest at around 4 A.M. At 43°C (109.5°F), fatal bleeding results, causing death.

## Mini LAB

### Recognizing Why You Sweat

**Procedure**
1. Examine the epidermis and the pores of your skin using a **magnifying lens.**
2. Place a **clear-plastic sandwich bag** on your hand. Use **tape** to seal the bag around your wrist. **WARNING:** *Do not wrap the tape too tightly.*
3. Quietly study your textbook for 10 min, then look at your hand. Remove the bag.
4. Describe what happened to your hand while it was inside the bag.

**Analysis**
1. Identify what formed inside the bag. Where did this substance come from?
2. Why does this substance form even when you are not active?

**Heat and Waste Exchange** Humans can withstand a limited range of body temperatures, as shown in **Figure 3.** Your skin plays an important role in regulating your body temperature. Blood vessels in the skin can help release or hold heat. If the blood vessels expand, or dilate, blood flow increases and heat is released. In contrast, less heat is released when the blood vessels constrict. Think of yourself after running—are you flushed red or pale and shivering?

An adult human's dermis has about 3 million sweat glands that help regulate the body's temperature and excrete wastes. When blood vessels dilate, pores open in the skin that lead to the sweat glands. Perspiration, or sweat, moves out onto the skin. Heat transfers from the body to the sweat on the skin. Eventually, this sweat evaporates, removing the heat and cooling the skin. This process eliminates excess heat produced by muscle contractions.

**Reading Check** *What are two functions of sweat glands?*

Wastes are produced when nutrients are broken down in cells. Such wastes, if not removed, can act as poisons. In addition to helping regulate your body's temperature, sweat glands release waste products, such as water and salt. If too much water and salt are released during periods of extreme heat or physical exertion, you might feel light-headed or even faint.

## Skin Injuries and Repair

Your skin often can be bruised, scratched, burned, ripped, or exposed to harsh conditions like cold, dry air. In response, the epidermis produces new cells and the dermis repairs tears. When the skin is injured, disease-causing organisms can enter the body rapidly. An infection often results.

**Bruises** When tiny blood vessels burst under unbroken skin, a bruise results. Red blood cells from these broken blood vessels leak into the surrounding tissue. These blood cells then break down, releasing a chemical called hemoglobin that gradually breaks down into its components, called pigments. The colors of these pigments cause the bruised area to turn shades of blue, red, and purple, as shown in **Figure 4.** Swelling also may occur. As the injury heals, the bruise eventually turns yellow as the pigment in the red blood cells is broken down even more and reenters the bloodstream. After all of the pigment is absorbed into the bloodstream, the bruise disappears and the skin appears normal again.

✔ **Reading Check** *What is the source of the yellow color of a bruise that is healing?*

The body usually can repair bruises and small cuts. What happens when severe burns, some diseases, and surgeries result in injury to large areas of skin? Sometimes there are not enough skin cells left to produce new skin. If not treated, this can lead to rapid water loss from skin and muscle tissues, leading to infection and possibly death. Skin grafts can prevent this. Pieces of skin are cut from one part of a person's body and moved to the injured or burned area where there is no skin. This new graft is kept alive by nearby blood vessels and soon becomes part of the surrounding skin.

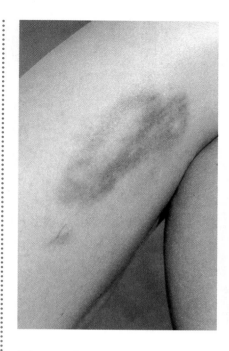

**Figure 4** Bruising occurs when tiny blood vessels beneath the skin burst.
**Infer** *whether this bruise is new or is already healing.*

---

## section 1 review

### Summary

**Skin Structures**
- Skin is the largest organ in your body.
- There are three layers of tissue in skin and each layer is made of different cell types.
- Melanin protects your skin and gives it color.

**Skin Functions**
- The most important function of skin is protection.
- Specialized nerve cells in the skin detect and relay information to the brain.

**Skin Injuries and Repair**
- When skin is injured, disease-causing organisms can enter the body rapidly.
- When skin is damaged, the epidermis produces new cells and the dermis repairs tears.

### Self Check

1. **Compare and contrast** the epidermis and dermis.
2. **Identify** the major functions of the skin.
3. **Describe** the role that your skin plays in regulating body temperature.
4. **Explain** how skin helps prevent disease in the body.
5. **Describe** one way doctors are able to repair severe skin damage from burns, injuries, or surgeries.
6. **Think Critically** Why is a person who has been severely burned in danger of dying from loss of water?

*Hot Words Hot Topics*: Bk 2 (7) p. 135

### Applying Math

7. **Solve One-Step Equations** The skin of eyelids is 0.5 mm thick. On the soles of your feet, skin is up to 0.4 cm thick. How many times thicker is the skin on the soles of your feet compared to your eyelids?

---

# Measuring Skin Surface

Skin covers the entire surface of your body and is your body's largest organ. Skin cells make up a layer of skin about 2 mm thick. How big is this organ?

## ◉ Real-World Question

How much skin covers your body?

### Goals
■ **Estimate** the surface area of skin that covers the body of a middle-school student.

### Materials
10 large sheets of newspaper
scissors
tape
meterstick or ruler

### Safety Precautions

## ◉ Procedure

1. Form groups of three or four, either all female or all male. Select one person from your group to measure the surface area of his or her skin.

2. **Estimate** how much skin covers the average student in your classroom. In your Science Journal, record your estimation.

3. Wrap newspaper snugly around each part of your classmate's body. Overlapping the sheets of paper, use tape to secure the paper. Small body parts, such as fingers and toes, do not need to be wrapped individually. Cover entire hands and feet. Do not cover the face.

4. After your classmate is completely covered with paper, carefully cut the newspaper off his or her body. **WARNING:** *Do not cut any clothing or skin.*

5. Lay all of the overlapping sheets of newspaper on the floor. Using scissors and more tape, cut and piece the paper suit together to form a rectangle.

6. Using a meterstick, measure the length and width of the resulting rectangle. Multiply these two measurements for an estimate of the surface area of your classmate's skin.

## ◉ Conclude and Apply

1. Was your estimation correct? Explain.

2. How accurate are your measurements of your classmate's skin surface area? How could your measurements be improved?

3. **Calculate** the volume of your classmate's skin, using 2 mm as the average thickness and your calculated surface area from this activity.

## 𝒞ommunicating
### Your Data

Using a table, record the estimated skin surface area from all the groups in your class. Find the average surface areas for both males and females. Discuss any differences in these two averages.

**LE 1.2a:** Each system is composed of organs and tissues which perform specific functions and interact with each other. **1.2g:** Locomotion, necessary to escape danger, obtain food and shelter, and reproduce, is accomplished by the interaction of the skeletal and muscular systems, and coordinated by the nervous system.

# The Muscular System

## Movement of the Human Body

Muscles help make all of your daily movements possible. In the process of relaxing, contracting, and providing the force for movements, energy is used and work is done. Imagine how much energy the more than 600 muscles in your body use each day. No matter how still you might try to be, some muscles in your body are always moving. You're breathing, your heart is beating, and your digestive system is working.

**Muscle Control** Your hand, arm, and leg muscles are voluntary. So are the muscles of your face, as shown in **Figure 5.** You can choose to move them or not to move them. Muscles that you are able to control are called **voluntary muscles.** Muscles that you can't control consciously are **involuntary muscles.** They work all day long, all your life. Blood is pumped through blood vessels, and food is moved through your digestive system by the action of involuntary muscles.

✓ **Reading Check** *What is another body activity that is controlled by involuntary muscles?*

**Figure 5** Facial expressions generally are controlled by voluntary muscles. It takes only 13 muscles to smile, but 43 muscles to frown.

**as you read**

*What* **You'll Learn**

- **Identify** the major function of the muscular system.
- **Compare** and contrast the three types of muscles.
- **Explain** how muscle action results in the movement of body parts.

*Why* **It's Important**

The muscular system is responsible for how you move and the production of heat in your body. Muscles also give your body its shape.

🔎 **Review Vocabulary**
**muscle:** an organ that can relax, contract, and provide the force to move bones and body parts

**New Vocabulary**
- voluntary muscle
- involuntary muscle
- tendon

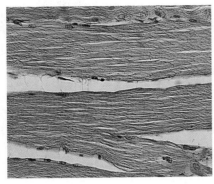

Skeletal muscles move bones. The muscle tissue appears striped, or striated, and is attached to bone.

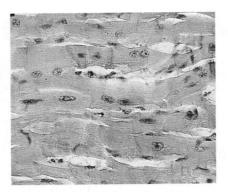

Cardiac muscle is found only in the heart. The muscle tissue has striations.

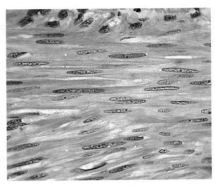

Smooth muscle is found in many of your internal organs, such as the digestive tract. This muscle tissue is nonstriated.

**Figure 6** The three types of muscle tissue are skeletal muscle, cardiac muscle, and smooth muscle.
**Infer** *what type of muscle tissue makes up the walls of veins, which carry blood.*

## Classification of Muscle Tissue

Humans have three types of muscle tissue: skeletal, smooth, and cardiac. Skeletal muscles are voluntary muscles that move bones. They are more common than other muscle types, and are attached to bones by thick bands of tissue called **tendons.** Skeletal muscle cells are striated (STRI ay tud), and when viewed under a microscope, appear striped. You can see the striations in **Figure 6.**

The remaining two types of muscles also are shown in **Figure 6.** Cardiac muscle is found only in the heart. Like skeletal muscle, cardiac muscle is striated. This type of muscle contracts about 70 times per minute every day of your life. Smooth muscles are nonstriated involuntary muscles and are found in your intestines, bladder, blood vessels, and other internal organs.

## Your Body's Simple Machines—Levers

Your skeletal system and muscular system work together when you move, like a machine. A machine, such as a bicycle, is any device that makes work easier. A simple machine does work with only one movement, like a hammer. The hammer is a type of simple machine called a lever, which is a rod or plank that pivots or turns about a point. This point is called a fulcrum. The action of muscles, bones, and joints working together is like a lever. In your body, bones are rods, joints are fulcrums, and contraction and relaxation of muscles provide the force to move body parts. Levers are classified into three types—first class, second class, and third class. Examples of the three types of levers that are found in the human body are shown in **Figure 7.**

## Figure 7

**A**ll three types of levers—first class, second class, and third class—are found in the human body. In the photo below, a tennis player prepares to serve a ball. As shown in the accompanying diagrams, the tennis player's stance demonstrates the operation of all three classes of levers in the human body.

▲ Fulcrum

▼ Effort force

■ Load

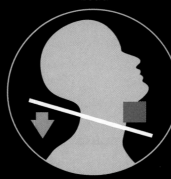

**FIRST-CLASS LEVER**
The fulcrum lies between the effort force and the load. This happens when the tennis player uses his neck muscles to tilt his head back.

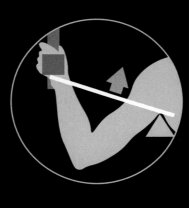

**THIRD-CLASS LEVER**
The effort force is between the fulcrum and the load. This happens when the tennis player flexes the muscles in his arm and shoulder.

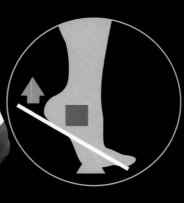

**SECOND-CLASS LEVER**
The load lies between the fulcrum and the effort force. This happens when the tennis player's calf muscles lift the weight of his body up on his toes.

## Working Muscles

How do muscles allow you to move your body? You move because pairs of skeletal muscles work together. When one muscle of a pair of muscles contracts, the other muscle relaxes or returns to its original length, as shown in **Figure 8.** Muscles always pull; they never push. When the muscles on the back of your upper leg contract, they shorten and pull your lower leg back and up. When you straighten your leg, the back muscles lengthen and relax, and the muscles on the front of your upper leg contract. Compare how your leg muscles work with how the muscles of your arms work.

**Changes in Muscles** Over time, muscles can become larger or smaller, depending on whether or not they are used. Also, muscles that are given regular exercise respond quickly to stimuli. Skeletal muscles that do a lot of work, such as those in your writing hand, can become stronger and larger. Some of this change in muscle size is because of an increase in the number of muscle cells. However, most of this change in muscle size is because individual muscle cells become larger. For example, many soccer and basketball players have noticeably larger, defined leg muscles. In contrast, someone who only participates in nonactive pastimes such as watching television or playing computer games, instead of participating in more active pastimes, will have smaller and weaker muscles. Muscles that aren't exercised become smaller in size. Paralyzed muscles also become smaller because they cannot be moved or have limited movement.

**Reading Check** *How do muscles increase their size?*

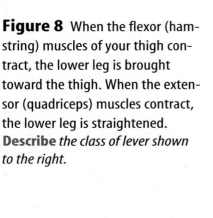

**Living Environment**

**1.2, 1.2b, 1.2c, 1.2d, 1.2e, 1.2f, 1.2g, 1.2h Design** a flow chart to show the systems that interact with each other to allow muscles to exercise, become stronger, and grow.

**Figure 8** When the flexor (hamstring) muscles of your thigh contract, the lower leg is brought toward the thigh. When the extensor (quadriceps) muscles contract, the lower leg is straightened. **Describe** *the class of lever shown to the right.*

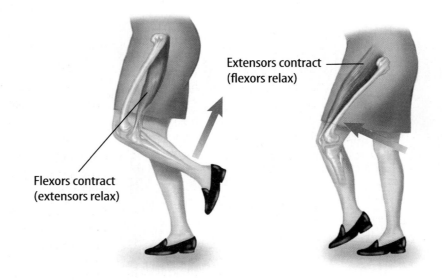

Extensors contract (flexors relax)

Flexors contract (extensors relax)

## How Muscles Move

Your muscles need energy to contract and relax. Your blood carries energy-rich molecules to your muscle cells, where the chemical energy stored in these molecules is released. As the muscle contracts, this released energy changes to mechanical energy (movement) and thermal energy (heat), as shown in **Figure 9.** The heat produced by muscle contractions helps keep your body temperature constant. When the supply of energy-rich molecules in a muscle is used up, the muscle becomes tired and needs to rest. During this resting period, your blood supplies more energy-rich molecules to your muscle cells.

**Figure 9** Chemical energy is needed for muscle activity. During activity, chemical energy supplied by food is changed into mechanical energy (movement) and thermal energy (heat).

 **Reading Check**  *How do muscles obtain energy to contract and relax?*

---

## section 2 review

### Summary

**Movement of the Human Body**

- Muscles contract to move bones and body parts.
- You can control voluntary muscles, but you cannot consciously control involuntary muscles.

**Classification of Muscle Tissue**

- Skeletal muscles are voluntary, smooth muscles control movement of internal organs, and cardiac muscle is striated and involuntary.

**Your Body's Simple Machines—Levers**

- Your muscles, bones, and joints work together like levers to move your body.

**Working Muscles**

- Muscles always pull, and when one muscle of a pair contracts, the other relaxes.
- Chemical energy is needed for muscle activity.

### Self Check

1. **Describe** the function of muscles.
2. **Compare and contrast** the three types of muscle tissue.
3. **Identify** and describe the appearance of the type of muscle tissue found in your heart.
4. **Explain** how your muscles, bones, and joints work together to move your body.
5. **Describe** how a muscle attaches to a bone.
6. **Think Critically**  What happens to your upper arm muscles when you bend your arm at the elbow to eat your favorite sandwich?

#### Applying Skills

7. **Concept Map**  Using a concept map, sequence the activities that take place when you bend your leg at the knee.
8. **Communicate**  Write a paragraph in your Science Journal about the three forms of energy involved in a muscle contraction.

---

# section

## 3

# The Skeletal System

**as you read**

## *What* You'll Learn

- **Identify** five functions of the skeletal system.
- **Compare and contrast** movable and immovable joints.

## *Why* It's Important

You'll begin to understand how each of your body parts moves and what happens that allows you to move them.

## Review Vocabulary

**skeleton:** a framework of living bones that supports your body

### New Vocabulary

- periosteum
- cartilage
- joint
- ligament

## Functions of Your Skeletal System

The skeletal system includes all the bones in your body and has five major functions.

1. The skeleton gives shape and support to your body.

2. Bones protect your internal organs.

3. Major muscles are attached to bones and help them move.

4. Blood cells form in the red marrow of many bones.

5. Major quantities of calcium and phosphorous compounds are stored in the skeleton for later use. Calcium and phosphorus make bones hard.

## Bone Structure

Looking at bone through a magnifying glass will show you that it isn't smooth. Bones have bumps, edges, round ends, rough spots, and many pits and holes. Muscles and ligaments attach to some of the bumps and pits. In your body, blood vessels and nerves enter and leave through the holes in bones. How a bone looks from the inside and the outside is shown in **Figure 10.**

**Figure 10** Bone is made of layers of living tissue.

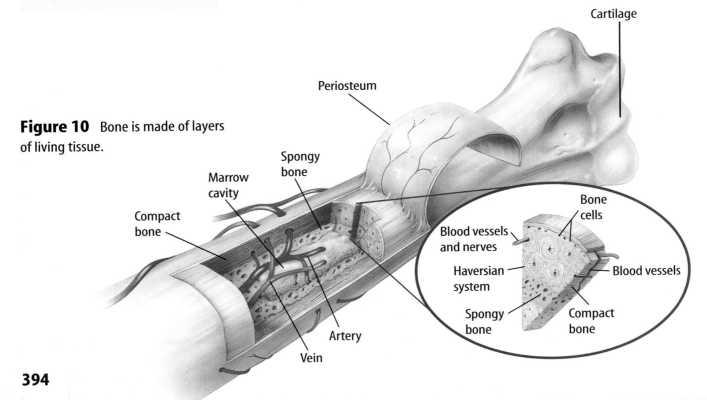

**Bone Tissue** Living bone is an organ made of several different tissues. A living bone's surface is covered with a tough, tight-fitting membrane called the **periosteum** (pur ee AHS tee um). Small blood vessels in the periosteum carry nutrients into the bone and its nerves signal pain. Under the periosteum are compact bone and spongy bone.

Compact bone gives bones strength. It has a framework containing deposits of calcium phosphate that make the bone hard. Spongy bone is located toward the ends of long bones, such as those in your thigh and upper arm. Spongy bone has many small, open spaces that make bones lightweight.

In the centers of long bones are large openings called cavities. These cavities and the spaces in spongy bone are filled with a substance called marrow. Some marrow is yellow and is composed of fat cells. Red marrow produces red blood cells at a rate of 2 million to 3 million cells per second.

**Cartilage** The ends of bones are covered with a smooth, slippery, thick layer of tissue called **cartilage.** Cartilage does not contain blood vessels or minerals. It is flexible and important in joints because it acts as a shock absorber. It also makes movement easier by reducing friction that would be caused by bones rubbing together.

✔ **Reading Check** *What is cartilage?*

# Bone Formation

Your bones have not always been as hard as they are now. Months before your birth, your skeleton was made of cartilage. Gradually, the cartilage broke down and was replaced by bone, as illustrated in **Figure 11.** Bone-forming cells called osteoblasts (AHS tee oh blasts) deposit calcium and phosphorus in bones, making the bone tissue hard. At birth, your skeleton was made up of more than 300 bones. As you developed, some bones fused, or grew together, so that now you have only 206 bones.

Healthy bone tissue is always being formed and re-formed. Osteoblasts build up bone. Another type of bone cell, called an osteoclast, breaks down bone tissue in other areas of the bone. This is a normal process in a healthy person. When osteoclasts break bone down, they release calcium and phosphorus into the bloodstream. These elements are necessary for the working of your body, including the movement of your muscles.

**Topic: Bone Fractures**
Visit glencoe.com for Web links to information about new techniques for treating bone fractures.

**Activity** Using captions, illustrate one technique in your Science Journal.

**Figure 11** Cartilage is replaced slowly by bone as solid tissue grows outward. Over time, the bone reshapes to include blood vessels, nerves, and marrow. **Describe** *the type of bone cell that builds up bone.*

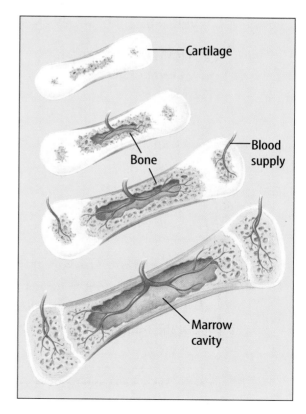

Cartilage

Bone

Blood supply

Marrow cavity

# Joints

What will you do at school today? You may sit at a table, chew and swallow your lunch, or walk to class. All of these motions are possible because your skeleton has joints.

Any place where two or more bones come together is a **joint.** Bones are held in place at joints by a tough band of tissue called a **ligament.** Many joints, such as your knee, are held together by more than one ligament. Muscles move bones by moving joints. The bones in healthy joints are separated by a thin layer of cartilage so that they do not rub against each other as they move.

*Hot Words Hot Topics*: Bk 2 (1) pp. 276–278, 368; 2: pp. 276–278, 368

## Living Environment

**1.2g Draw** a simple sketch of a finger joint. Include bones, ligaments, cartilage, and the periosteum to model the interaction between the skeletal, muscular, circulatory, and nervous systems.

## Applying Math     Estimate

**VOLUME OF BONES** Although bones are not perfectly shaped, many of them are cylindrical. This cylindrical shape allows your bones to withstand great pressure. Estimate the volume of a bone that is 36 cm long and 7 cm in diameter.

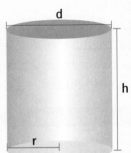

### Solution

**1** *This is what you know:*

The bone has a shape of a cylinder whose height, $h$, measures 36 cm and whose diameter is 7.0 cm.

**2** *This is what you want to find out:*

Volume of the cylinder

**3** *This is the procedure you need to use:*

- Use this equation:
  Volume = $\pi \times$ (radius)$^2 \times$ height, or $V = \pi \times r^2 \times h$
- A radius is one-half the diameter $\left(\frac{1}{2} \times 7 \text{ cm}\right)$, so $r = 3.5$ cm, $h = 36$ cm, and $\pi = 3.14$.
- $V = 3.14 \times (3.5 \text{ cm})^2 \times 36 \text{ cm}$
  $V = 1,384.74 \text{ cm}^3$
- The volume of the bone is approximately 1,384.74 cm$^3$.

**4** *Check your answer:*

Divide your answer by 3.14 and then divide that number by $(3.5)^2$. This number should be the height of the bone.

### Practice Problems

**1.** Estimate the volume of a bone that has a height of 12 cm and a diameter of 2.4 cm.

**2.** If the volume of a bone is 62.8 cm$^3$ and its height is 20 cm, what is its diameter?

 For more practice, visit glencoe.com

**Immovable Joints** Joints are broadly classified as immovable or movable. An immovable joint allows little or no movement. The joints of the bones in your skull and pelvis are classified as immovable joints.

✔ **Reading Check** *How are bones held in place at joints?*

**Movable Joints** All movements, including somersaulting and working the controls of a video game, require movable joints, such as those in **Figure 12.** A movable joint allows the body to make a wide range of motions. There are several types of movable joints—pivot, ball and socket, hinge, and gliding.

In a pivot joint, one bone rotates in a ring of another bone that does not move. Turning your head is an example of a pivot movement. A ball-and-socket joint consists of a bone with a rounded end that fits into a cuplike cavity on another bone. A ball-and-socket joint provides a wider range of motion than a pivot joint does. That's why your legs and arms can swing in almost any direction.

A third type of joint is a hinge joint, which has a back-and-forth movement like hinges on a door. Elbows, knees, and fingers have hinge joints. Hinge joints have a smaller range of motion than the ball-and-socket joint. They are not dislocated, or pulled apart, as easily as a ball-and-socket joint can be.

A fourth type of joint is a gliding joint, in which one part of a bone slides over another bone. Gliding joints also move in a back-and-forth motion and are found in your wrists and ankles and between vertebrae. Gliding joints are used the most in your body. You can't write a word, use a joy stick, or take a step without using one of your gliding joints.

**Figure 12** When a basketball player shoots a ball, several types of joints are in action.
**Name** *other activities that use several types of joints.*

Skull

Immovable joints

Shoulder

Ball-and-socket joint

Vertebrae

Gliding joint

Arm

Pivot joint

Knee

Hinge joint

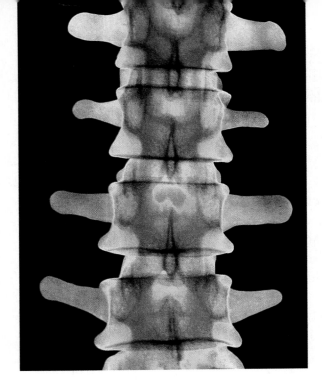

**Figure 13** A colored X ray of the human backbone shows disks of cartilage between the vertebrae.

**Moving Smoothly** When you rub two pieces of chalk together, their surfaces begin to wear away, and they get reshaped. Without the protection of the cartilage at the end of your bones, they also would wear away at the joints. Cartilage helps make joint movement easier. It reduces friction and allows bones to slide more easily over each other. As shown in **Figure 13,** pads of cartilage, called disks, are located between the vertebrae in your back. They act as cushions and prevent injury to your spinal cord. A fluid that comes from nearby blood vessels also lubricates the joint.

**Common Joint Problems** Arthritis is the most common joint problem. The term *arthritis* describes more than 100 different diseases that can damage joints. About one out of every seven people in the United States suffers from arthritis. All forms of arthritis begin with the same symptoms: pain, stiffness, and swelling of the joints.

## section 3 review

### Summary

**Functions of Your Skeletal System**

- The skeletal system includes all the bones in your body and is your body's framework.

**Bone Structure**

- Bones are living organs that need nutrients.
- Compact bone is hard and strong, and spongy bone has many open spaces to make it lightweight.
- Cartilage covers the ends of bones.

**Bone Formation**

- Bone-forming cells deposit calcium and phosphorus to make the bone tissue hard.
- Healthy bone tissue is always being formed and reformed.

**Joints**

- Immovable joints allow little or no movement.
- Movable joints include pivot, ball and socket, hinge, and gliding joints.
- Cartilage helps make joint movement easier.

### Self Check

1. **List** the five major functions of the human skeletal system.
2. **Describe** and give an example of an immovable joint.
3. **Explain** the functions of cartilage in your skeletal system.
4. **Describe** ligaments and their function in the skeletal system.
5. **Think Critically**  A thick band of bone forms around a broken bone as it heals. In time, the thickened band disappears. Explain how this extra bone can disappear over time.

#### Applying Skills

6. **Make and Use Tables**  Use a table to classify the bones of the human body as follows: *long, short, flat,* and *irregular.*
7. **Use graphics software** to make a graph that shows how an adult's bones are distributed: *29 skull bones, 26 vertebrae, 25 ribs, four shoulder bones, 60 arm and hand bones, two hip bones, and 60 leg and feet bones.*

## section 4

# The Nervous System

## How the Nervous System Works

After doing the dishes and finishing your homework, you settle down in your favorite chair and pick up that mystery novel you've been trying to finish. Only three pages to go. . . Who did it? Why did she do it? Crash! You scream. What made that unearthly noise? You turn around to find that your dog's wagging tail has just swept the lamp off the table. Suddenly, you're aware that your heart is racing and your hands are shaking. After a few minutes, your breathing returns to normal and your heartbeat is back to its regular rate. What's going on?

**Responding to Stimuli** The scene described above is an example of how your body responds to changes in its environment. Any internal or external change that brings about a response is called a stimulus (STIHM yuh lus). Each day, you're bombarded by thousands of stimuli, as shown in **Figure 14.** Noise, light, the smell of food, and the temperature of the air are all stimuli from outside your body. Chemical substances such as hormones are examples of stimuli from inside your body. Your body adjusts to changing stimuli with the help of your nervous system.

**as you read**

*What* **You'll Learn**

- **Describe** the basic structure of a neuron and how an impulse moves across a synapse.
- **Compare and contrast** the central and peripheral nervous systems.
- **List** the sensory receptors in each sense organ.
- **Explain** what type of stimulus each sense organ responds to and how.
- **Explain** how drugs affect the body.

*Why* **It's Important**

Your body reacts to your environment because of your nervous system.

**Review Vocabulary**
**homeostasis:** regulation of an organism's internal, life-maintaining conditions despite changes in its environment

**New Vocabulary**
- neuron
- synapse
- central nervous system
- peripheral nervous system

**Figure 14** Stimuli are found everywhere and all the time, even when you're enjoying being with your friends.
**List** *the types of stimuli that are present at this party.*

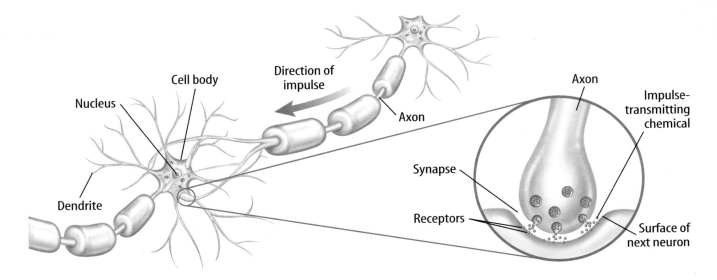

Nucleus
Cell body
Dendrite
Direction of impulse
Axon
Axon
Impulse-transmitting chemical
Synapse
Receptors
Surface of next neuron

**Figure 15** A neuron is made up of a cell body, dendrites, and an axon. An impulse moves in only one direction across a synapse—from an axon to the dendrites or cell body of another neuron.

**Homeostasis** It's amazing how your body handles all these stimuli. Control systems maintain homeostasis. They keep steady, life-maintaining conditions inside your body, despite changes around you. Examples of homeostasis are the regulation of your breathing, heartbeat, and digestion. Your nervous system is one of several control systems used by your body to maintain homeostasis.

## Nerve Cells

The basic functioning units of the nervous system are nerve cells, or **neurons** (NOO rahnz). As shown in **Figure 15,** a neuron is made up of a cell body, branches called dendrites, and axons (AK sahns). Any message carried by a neuron is called an impulse. Your neurons are adapted in such a way that impulses move in only one direction. Dendrites receive impulses from other neurons and send them to the cell body. Axons carry impulses away from the cell body. The end of the axon branches. This allows the impulses to move to many other muscles, neurons, or glands.

Three types of neurons—sensory neurons, motor neurons, and interneurons—transport impulses. Sensory neurons receive information and send impulses to the brain or spinal cord, where interneurons relay these impulses to motor neurons. Motor neurons then conduct impulses from the brain or spinal cord to muscles or glands throughout your body.

**Synapses** Neurons don't touch each other. As an impulse moves from one neuron to another it crosses a small space called a **synapse** (SIH naps). In **Figure 15,** note that when an impulse reaches the end of an axon, the axon releases a chemical. This chemical flows across the synapse and stimulates the impulse in the dendrite of the next neuron.

# The Divisions of the Nervous System

**Figure 16** shows how organs of the nervous system are grouped into two major divisions—the central nervous system (CNS) and the peripheral (puh RIH fuh rul) nervous system (PNS). The **central nervous system** includes the brain and spinal cord. The brain is the control center for all activities in the body. It is made of billions of neurons. The spinal cord is made up of bundles of neurons. An adult's spinal cord is about the width of a thumb and about 43 cm long. Sensory neurons send impulses to the brain or spinal cord.

**Science** nline

**Topic: Nervous System**
Visit glencoe.com for Web links to information about the nervous system.

**Activity** Make a brochure outlining recent medical advances.

**The Peripheral Nervous System** All the nerves outside the CNS that connect the brain and spinal cord to other body parts are part of the **peripheral nervous system.** The PNS includes 12 pairs of nerves from your brain called cranial nerves, and 31 pairs of nerves from your spinal cord called spinal nerves. Spinal nerves are made up of bundles of sensory and motor neurons bound together by connective tissue. They carry impulses from all parts of the body to the brain and from the brain to all parts of your body. A single spinal nerve can have impulses going to and from the brain at the same time. Some nerves contain only sensory neurons, and some contain only motor neurons, but most nerves contain both types of neurons.

## Somatic and Autonomic Systems

The peripheral nervous system has two major divisions. The somatic system controls voluntary actions. It is made up of the cranial and spinal nerves that go from the central nervous system to your skeletal muscles. The autonomic system controls involuntary actions—those not under conscious control—such as your heart rate, breathing, digestion, and glandular functions.

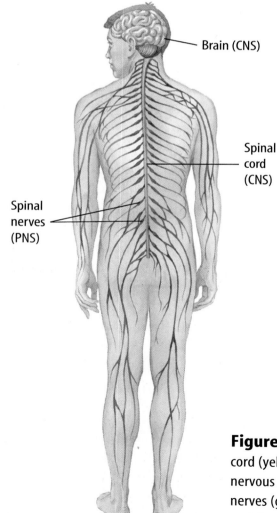

Brain (CNS)

Spinal cord (CNS)

Spinal nerves (PNS)

**Figure 16** The brain and spinal cord (yellow) form the central nervous system (CNS). All other nerves (green) are part of the peripheral nervous system (PNS).

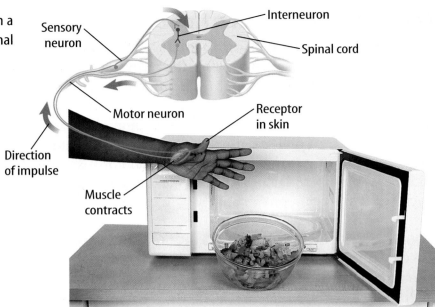

**Figure 17** Your response in a reflex is controlled in your spinal cord, not your brain.

Interneuron

Sensory neuron

Spinal cord

Motor neuron

Receptor in skin

Direction of impulse

Muscle contracts

**Neuron Chemical**
Acetylcholine (uh see tul KOH leen) is a chemical produced by neurons that carries an impulse across a synapse to the next neuron. After the impulse is started, acetylcholine breaks down rapidly. In your Science Journal, make an inference about why the rapid breakdown of acetylcholine is important.

# Safety and the Nervous System

Every mental process and physical action of the body involves structures of the central and peripheral nervous systems. Therefore, any injury to them can be serious. A severe blow to the head can bruise the brain and cause temporary or permanent loss of mental and physical abilities. For example, an injury to the back of the brain could result in the loss of vision.

Although the spinal cord is surrounded by the vertebrae of your spine, spinal cord injuries do occur. They can be just as dangerous as a brain injury. Injury to the spine can bring about damage to nerve pathways and result in paralysis (puh RAH luh suhs), which is the loss of muscle movement. Major causes of head and spinal injuries include automobile, motorcycle, and bicycle accidents, as well as sports injuries. Just like wearing seat belts in automobiles, it is important to wear the appropriate safety gear while playing sports and riding on bicycles and skateboards.

**Reflexes** You experience a reflex if you accidentally touch something sharp, something extremely hot or cold, or when you cough or vomit. A reflex is an involuntary, automatic response to a stimulus. You can't control reflexes because they occur before you know what has happened. A reflex involves a simple nerve pathway called a reflex arc, as illustrated in **Figure 17.**

A reflex allows the body to respond without having to think about what action to take. Reflex responses are controlled in your spinal cord, not in your brain. Your brain acts after the reflex to help you figure out what to do to make the pain stop.

**Reading Check** *Why are reflexes important?*

# The Senses

Sense organs are adapted for intercepting stimuli, such as light rays, sound waves, heat, chemicals, or pressure, and converting them into impulses for the nervous system. Your internal organs have several kinds of sensory receptors that respond to touch, pressure, pain, and temperature and transmit impulses to the brain or spinal cord. In turn, your body responds to this new information. All of your body's senses work together to maintain homeostasis.

Sensory receptors also are located throughout your skin. Your lips are sensitive to heat and can prevent you from drinking something so hot that it would burn you. Pressure-sensitive skin cells warn you of danger and enable you to move to avoid injury.

**Vision** Think about the different kinds of objects you might look at every day. The eye, shown in **Figure 18,** is a sense organ. Your eyes have unique adaptations that usually enable you to see shapes of objects, shadows, and color. It's amazing that at one glance you might see the words on this page, the color illustrations, and your classmate sitting next to you.

How do you see? Light travels in a straight line unless something causes it to refract or change direction. Your eyes have structures that refract light. Two of these structures are the cornea and the lens. As light enters the eye, it passes through the cornea—the transparent section at the front of the eye—and is refracted. Then light passes through a lens and is refracted again. The lens directs the light onto the retina (RET nuh), which is a tissue at the back of the eye that is sensitive to light energy. Two types of cells called rods and cones are found in the retina. Cones respond to bright light and color. Rods respond to dim light. They are used to help you detect shape and movement.

**Figure 18** Light moves through the cornea and the lens—before striking the retina.
**Name** *the structures that enable you to see light.*

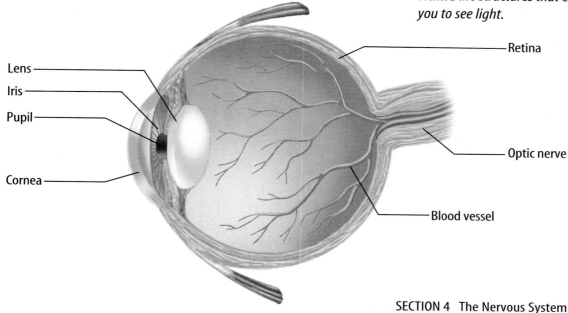

Lens

Iris

Pupil

Cornea

Retina

Optic nerve

Blood vessel

**Images** Light energy stimulates impulses in rods and cones that pass to the optic nerve. This nerve carries the impulses to the vision area of the brain. The image transmitted from the retina to the brain is upside down and reversed. The brain interprets the image correctly, and you see what you are looking at. The brain also interprets the images received by both eyes. It blends them into one image that gives you a sense of distance. This allows you to tell how close or how far away something is.

**Hearing** Whether it's the roar of a rocket launch, the cheers at a football game, or the distant song of a robin in a tree, sound waves are necessary for hearing. Sound is to hearing as light is to vision. When an object vibrates, sound waves are produced. Sound waves can travel through solids, liquids, and gases. When sound waves reach your ear, they usually stimulate nerve cells deep within your ear. Impulses from these cells are sent to the brain. When the sound impulse reaches the hearing area of the brain, it responds and you hear a sound.

**Figure 19** shows that your ear is divided into three sections—the outer ear, middle ear, and inner ear. Your outer ear intercepts sound waves and funnels them down the ear canal to the middle ear. The sound waves cause the eardrum to vibrate much like the membrane on a musical drum vibrates when you tap it. These vibrations then move through three tiny bones called the hammer, anvil, and stirrup. The stirrup bone rests against a second membrane on an opening to the inner ear.

The inner ear includes the cochlea (KOH klee uh) and the semicircular canals. The cochlea is a fluid-filled structure shaped like a snail's shell. When the stirrup vibrates, fluids in the cochlea begin to vibrate. These vibrations bend sensory hair cells in the cochlea, which cause electrical impulses to be sent to the brain by a nerve. Depending on how the nerve endings are stimulated, you hear a different type of sound.

**Living Environment**

**1.2a, 1.2h Discuss** how each of the five senses works to help avoid danger and maintain homeostasis.

**Figure 19** Your ear responds to sound waves and to changes in the position of your head.

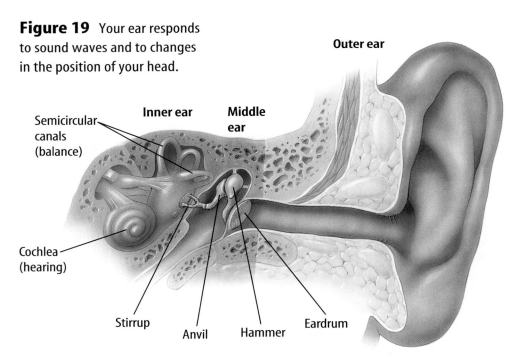

Semicircular canals (balance)

Inner ear

Middle ear

Outer ear

Cochlea (hearing)

Stirrup

Anvil

Hammer

Eardrum

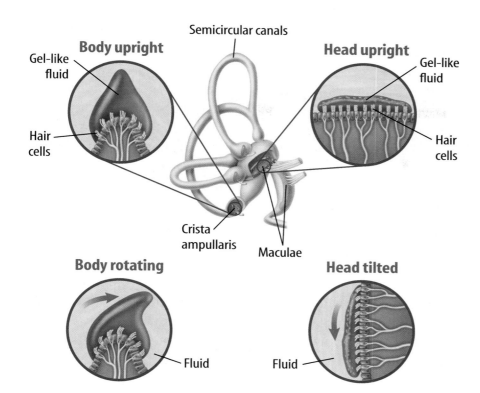

**Body upright**
Gel-like fluid
Hair cells

Semicircular canals

**Head upright**
Gel-like fluid
Hair cells

Crista ampullaris
Maculae

**Body rotating**
Fluid

**Head tilted**
Fluid

**Figure 20** In your inner ear the cristae ampullaris react to rotating movements of your body, and the maculae check the position of your head with respect to the ground. **Explain** *why spinning around makes you dizzy.*

**Balance** Structures in your inner ear also control your body's balance. Structures called the cristae ampullaris (KRIHS tee • am pyew LEER ihs) and the maculae (MA kyah lee), illustrated in **Figure 20,** sense body movement. The cristae ampullaris react to rotating body movements and the maculae responds to the tilt of your head. Both structures contain tiny hair cells. As your body moves, gel-like fluid surrounding the hair cells moves and stimulates the nerve cells at the base of the hair cells. This produces nerve impulses that are sent to the brain, which interprets the body movements. The brain, in turn, sends impulses to skeletal muscles, resulting in other body movements that maintain balance.

**Smell** How can you smell your favorite food? You can smell food because molecules from the food move into the air. If they enter your nasal passages, these molecules stimulate sensitive nerve cells, called olfactory (ohl FAK tree) cells. Olfactory cells are kept moist by mucus. When molecules in the air dissolve in this moisture, the cells become stimulated. If enough molecules are present, an impulse starts in these cells, then travels to the brain where the stimulus is interpreted. If the stimulus is recognized from a previous experience, you can identify the odor. If you don't recognize a particular odor, it is remembered and may be identified the next time you encounter it.

 **Reading Check** *What produces nerve impulses that interpret body movement?*

## Mini LAB

### Observing Balance Control

**Procedure**
1. Place two narrow strips of **paper** on the wall to form two parallel, vertical lines 20–25 cm apart. Have a person stand between them for 3 min, without leaning on the wall.
2. Observe how well balance is maintained.
3. Have the person close his or her eyes, then stand within the lines for 3 min.

**Analysis**
1. When was balance more difficult to maintain? Why?
2. What other factors might cause a person to lose his or her sense of balance?

 Try at Home

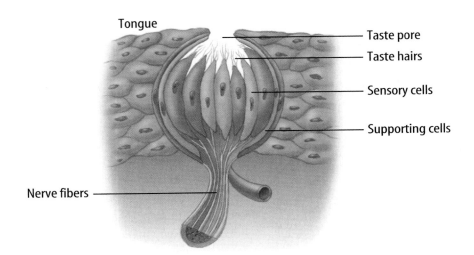

Tongue

Taste pore

Taste hairs

Sensory cells

Supporting cells

Nerve fibers

**Figure 21** Taste buds are made up of a group of sensory cells with tiny taste hairs projecting from them. When food is taken into the mouth, it is dissolved in saliva. This mixture then stimulates receptor sites on the taste hairs, and an impulse is sent to the brain.

**Living Environment**

1.2a, 1.2d, 1.2f, 1.2g, 1.2h
**Summarize** the effects of drugs and alcohol use on human organ systems.

**Taste** Sometimes you taste a new food with the tip of your tongue, it tastes sweet. Then when you chew it, it tastes bitter. Taste buds on your tongue are the major sensory receptors for taste. About 10,000 taste buds all over your tongue enable you to tell one taste from another. Most taste buds respond to several taste sensations. However, certain areas of the tongue are more receptive to one taste than another. The five taste sensations are sweet, salty, sour, bitter, and the taste of MSG (monosodium glutamate).

A taste bud, shown in **Figure 21,** responds to chemical stimuli. In order to taste something, it has to be dissolved in water. Saliva begins this process. When a solution of saliva and food washes over taste buds, impulses are sent to your brain. The brain interprets the impulses, and you identify the tastes.

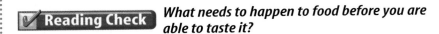
✔ **Reading Check** *What needs to happen to food before you are able to taste it?*

**Smell and Taste** The sense of smell is needed to identify some foods such as chocolate. When saliva in your mouth mixes with chocolate, odors travel up the nasal passage in the back of your throat. Olfactory cells in the nose are stimulated, and the taste and smell of chocolate are sensed. So when you have a stuffy nose and some foods seem tasteless, it may be because the food's molecules are blocked from contacting the olfactory cells in your nasal passages.

## Drugs Affect the Nervous System

Many drugs, such as alcohol and caffeine, directly affect your nervous system. When swallowed, alcohol directly passes into cells of the stomach and small intestine then into the circulatory system. After it is in the circulatory system, it can travel throughout your body. Upon reaching neurons, alcohol moves through their cell membranes and disrupts their normal cell functions. As a result, this drug slows the activities of the central nervous system and is classified as a depressant. Muscle control, judgment, reasoning, memory, and concentration also are impaired. Heavy alcohol use destroys brain and liver cells.

**Stimulants** Any substance that speeds up the activity of the central nervous system is called a stimulant. Caffeine is a stimulant found in coffee, tea, cocoa, and many soft drinks, as shown in **Figure 22.** Too much caffeine can increase heart rate and aggravates restlessness, tremors, and insomnia in some people. It also can stimulate the kidneys to produce more urine.

Do you remember reading at the beginning of this section about being frightened after a lamp was broken? Think again about that scare. The organs of your nervous system control and coordinate responses to maintain homeostasis within your body. This task might be more difficult when your body must cope with the effects of drugs.

**Figure 22** Caffeine, a substance found in colas, coffee, chocolate, and some teas, can cause excitability and sleeplessness.

## section 4 review

### Summary

**How the Nervous System Works**

- The nervous system responds to stimuli to maintain homeostasis.

**Nerve Cells**

- Neurons are the basic functioning units of the nervous system.
- To move from one neuron to another, an impulse crosses a synapse.

**The Divisions of the Nervous System**

- The autonomic system controls involuntary actions like heart rate and breathing.
- The somatic system controls voluntary actions.

**Safety and the Nervous System**

- Reflex responses are automatic and are controlled by the spinal cord.

**The Senses**

- Sense organs respond to stimuli and work together to maintain homeostasis.

**Drugs Affect the Nervous System**

- Drugs can slow or stimulate your nervous system.

### Self Check

1. **Draw and label** the parts of a neuron and describe the function of each part.
2. **Name** the sensory receptors for the eyes, ears, and nose.
3. **Compare and contrast** the central and peripheral nervous systems.
4. **Explain** why you have trouble falling asleep after drinking several cups of hot cocoa.
5. **Identify** the role of saliva in tasting.
6. **Explain** why is it important to have sensory receptors for pain and pressure in your internal organs.
7. **Think Critically** Explain why many medications caution the consumer not to operate heavy machinery.

#### Applying Skills

8. **Communicate** Write a paragraph in your Science Journal that describes what each of the following objects would feel like: ice cube, snake, silk blouse, sandpaper, jelly, and smooth rock.
9. **Make and Use Tables** Organize the information on senses in a table that names the sense organs and which stimuli they respond to.

## Design Your Own

# Skin Sensitivity

## Goals

■ **Observe** the sensitivity to touch on specific areas of the body.

■ **Design** an experiment that tests the effects of a variable, such as how close the contact points are, to determine which body areas can distinguish which stimuli are closest to one another.

## Possible Materials

3-in × 5-in index card
toothpicks
tape
*glue
metric ruler
*Alternate materials

## Safety Precautions

**WARNING:** *Do not apply heavy pressure when touching the toothpicks to the skin of your classmates.*

## ◉ *Real-World Question*

Your body responds to touch, pressure, temperature, and other stimuli. Not all parts of your body are equally sensitive to stimuli. Some areas are more sensitive than others are. For example, your lips are sensitive to heat. This protects you from burning your mouth and tongue. Now think about touch. How sensitive to touch is the skin on various parts of your body ? Which areas can distinguish the smallest amount of distance between stimuli?

## ◉ *Form a Hypothesis*

Based on your experiences, state a hypothesis about which of the following five areas of the body—fingertip, forearm, back of the neck, palm, and back of the hand—you believe to be most sensitive. Rank the areas from 5 (the most sensitive) to 1 (the least sensitive).

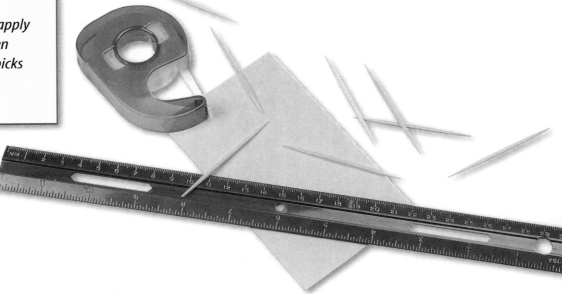

## ⊙ Test Your Hypothesis

**Make a Plan**

1. As a group, agree upon and write the hypothesis statement.

2. As a group, list the steps you need to test your hypothesis. Describe exactly what you will do at each step. Consider the following as you list the steps. How will you know that sight is not a factor? How will you use the card shown on the right to determine sensitivity to touch? How will you determine that one or both points are sensed?

3. Design a data table in your Science Journal to record your observations.

4. Reread your entire experiment to make sure that all steps are in the correct order.

5. Identify constants, variables, and controls of the experiment.

**Follow Your Plan**

1. Make sure your teacher approves your plan before you start.

2. Carry out the experiment as planned.

3. While the experiment is going on, write down any observations that you make and complete the data table in your Science Journal.

## ⊙ Analyze Your Data

1. **Identify** which part of the body tested can distinguish between the closest stimuli.

2. **Compare** your results with those of other groups.

3. Rank body parts tested from most to least sensitive. Did your results from this investigation support your hypothesis? Explain.

## ⊙ Conclude and Apply

1. **Infer** Based on the results of your investigation, what can you infer about the distribution of touch receptors on the skin?

2. **Predict** what other parts of your body would be less sensitive? Explain your predictions.

### Communicating Your Data

**Write** a report to share with your class about body parts of animals that are sensitive to touch.

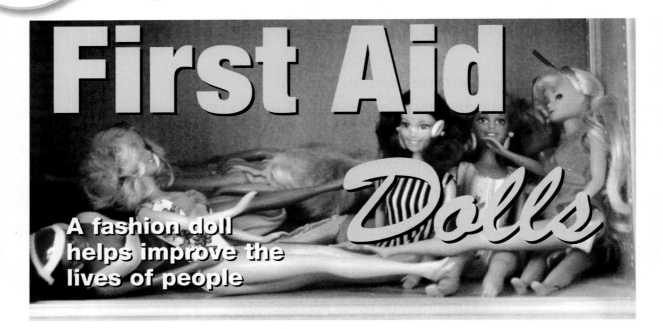

# First Aid Dolls

**A fashion doll helps improve the lives of people**

A fashion doll is doing her part for medical science! It turns out that the plastic joints that make it possible for one type of doll's legs to bend make good joints in prosthetic (artificial) fingers for humans.

Jane Bahor works at Duke University Medical Center in Durham, North Carolina. She makes lifelike body parts for people who have lost legs, arms, or fingers. A few years ago, she met a patient named Jennifer Jordan, an engineering student who'd lost a finger. The artificial finger that Bahor made looked real, but it couldn't bend. She and Jordan began to discuss the problem.

The engineer went home and borrowed one of her sister's dolls. Returning with it to Bahor's office, she and Bahor operated on the fashion doll's legs and removed the knee joints.

"It turns out that the doll's knee joints flexed the same way that human finger joints do," says Bahor. "We could see that using these joints would allow patients more use and flexibility with their 'new' fingers." Because these new prosthetic fingers can bend, the wearers can hold a pen, pick up a cup, or grab a steering wheel.

Bahor called the company that makes the fashion doll and shared the surprising discovery. The toymaker was so impressed that Bahor now has a ten-year supply of plastic knee joints—free of charge! But supplies come from other sources, too. "A Girl Scout troop in New Jersey just sent me a big box of donated dolls for the cause," reports Bahor. "It's really great to have kids' support in this effort."

**Invent** Choose a "problem" you can solve. Need a better place to store your notebooks in your locker, for instance? Use what Bahor calls "commonly found materials" to solve the problem. Then, make a model or a drawing of the problem-solving device.

## Reviewing Main Ideas

### Section 1  The Skin

1. The epidermis produces melanin. Cells at the base of the epidermis produce new skin cells. The dermis contains nerves, sweat and oil glands, and blood vessels.

2. The skin protects the body, reduces water loss, produces vitamin D, and helps to maintain body temperature.

3. Severe skin damage can lead to infection and death if left untreated.

### Section 2  The Muscular System

1. Skeletal muscle is voluntary and moves bones. Smooth muscle is involuntary and controls movement of internal organs. Cardiac muscle is involuntary and located only in the heart.

2. Muscles only can contract. When one skeletal muscle contracts, the other relaxes.

### Section 3  The Skeletal System

1. Bones are living structures that protect, support, make blood, store minerals, and provide for muscle attachment.

2. Joints are either immovable or moveable.

### Section 4  The Nervous System

1. The nervous system responds to stimuli to maintain homeostasis.

2. A neuron is the basic unit of structure and function of the nervous system.

3. A reflex is an automatic response.

4. The central nervous system is the brain and spinal cord. The peripheral nervous system includes cranial and spinal nerves.

5. Your senses enable you to react to your environment.

6. Many drugs affect your nervous system.

## Visualizing Main Ideas

*Copy and complete the following concept map on body movement.*

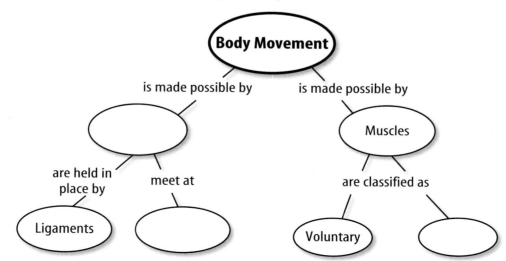

## Using Vocabulary

cartilage p. 395
central nervous system
    p. 401
dermis p. 384
epidermis p. 385
involuntary muscle p. 389
joint p. 396
ligament p. 396

melanin p. 385
neuron p. 400
periosteum p. 395
peripheral nervous
    system p. 401
synapse p. 400
tendon p. 390
voluntary muscle p. 389

*Match the definitions with the correct vocabulary word.*

1. outer layer of skin

2. thick band of tissue that attaches muscle to a bone

3. a muscle that you control

4. basic functioning unit of the nervous system

5. small space across which an impulse moves

6. tough outer covering of bone

7. a tough band of tissue that holds two bones together

## Checking Concepts

*Choose the word or phrase that best answers the question.*

8. Where are blood cells made?
   A) compact bone    C) cartilage
   B) periosteum    D) marrow

9. What are the ends of bones covered with?
   A) cartilage    C) ligaments
   B) tendons    D) muscle

10. Where are human immovable joints found?
    A) at the elbow    C) in the wrist
    B) at the neck    D) in the skull

11. Which vitamin is made in the skin?
    A) A    C) D
    B) B    D) K

12. Which of the following structures helps retain fluids in the body?
    A) bone    C) skin
    B) muscle    D) joint

13. How do impulses cross synapses between neurons?
    A) by osmosis
    B) through interneurons
    C) through a cell body
    D) by a chemical

14. What are the neurons called that detect stimuli in the skin and eyes?
    A) interneurons    C) motor neurons
    B) synapses    D) sensory neurons

15. What does the somatic system of the PNS control?
    A) gland    C) skeletal muscles
    B) heart    D) salivary glands

16. What part of the eye is light finally focused on?
    A) lens    C) pupil
    B) retina    D) cornea

17. Which of the following is in the inner ear?
    A) anvil    C) eardrum
    B) hammer    D) cochlea

**Use the illustration below to answer question 18.**

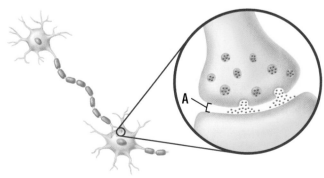

18. What is the name given to A?
    A) axon    C) synapse
    B) dendrite    D) nucleus

Vocabulary Puzzlemaker glencoe.com

## Thinking Critically

**19. Infer** why an infant's skull joints are flexible, but those of a teenager have fused together and are immovable.

**20. Predict** what would happen if a person's sweat glands didn't produce sweat.

**21. Compare and contrast** the functions of ligaments and tendons.

**22. Form a Hypothesis** Your body has about 3 million sweat glands. Make a hypothesis about where these sweat glands are on your body. Are they distributed evenly throughout your body?

**23. Draw Conclusions** If an impulse traveled down one neuron but failed to move on to the next neuron, what might you conclude about the first neuron?

**24. Concept Map** Copy and complete this events-chain concept map to show the correct sequence of the structures through which light passes in the eye.

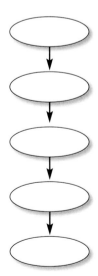

**25. List** what factors a doctor might consider before choosing a method of skin repair for a severe burn victim.

**26. Explain** why skin might not be able to produce enough vitamin D.

## Performance Activities

**27. Illustrate** While walking on a sandy beach, a pain suddenly shoots through your foot. You look down and see that you stepped on the sharp edge of a broken shell. Draw and label the reflex arc that results from this stimulus.

*Hot Words Hot Topics*: Bk 2 (28) pp. 201–202; (29) p. 277

## Applying Math

**Use the graph below to answer question 28.**

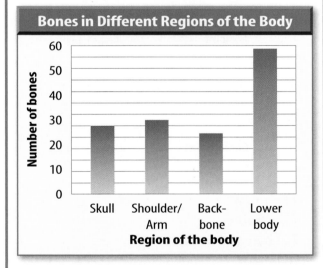

**Bones in Different Regions of the Body**

**28. Bone Tally** The total number of bones in the human body is 206. Approximately what percentage of bones is located in the backbone?

**A)** 2%          **C)** 50%

**B)** 12%         **D)** 75%

**29. Fireworks** You see the flash of fireworks and then four seconds later, you hear the boom. Light travels so fast that you see far away things instantaneously. Sound, on the other hand, travels at 340 m/s. How far away are you from the fireworks?

### Part I

*Record your answers on the answer sheet provided by your teacher or on a sheet of paper.*

**1** Which of the following is NOT released by sweat glands?
(1) water        (3) waste products
(2) salt         (4) oil

**Use the illustration below to answer questions 2 and 3.**

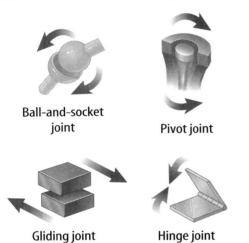

Ball-and-socket joint

Pivot joint

Gliding joint

Hinge joint

**2** Which type of joint do your elbows have?
(1) hinge
(2) gliding
(3) ball and socket
(4) pivot

**3** Which type of joint allows your legs and arms to swing in almost any direction?
(1) hinge
(2) gliding
(3) ball and socket
(4) pivot

**4** An internal or external change that brings about a response is called a
(1) reflex        (3) receptor
(2) stimulus      (4) heartbeat

**Use the table below to answer questions 5 and 6.**

| Drinks | Approximate Blood Alcohol Percentage for Men | | | | | | | |
|--------|------|------|------|------|------|------|------|------|
|        | Body Weight in Kilograms | | | | | | | |
|        | 45.4 | 54.4 | 63.5 | 72.6 | 81.6 | 90.7 | 99.8 | 108.9 |
| 1      | 0.04 | 0.03 | 0.03 | 0.02 | 0.02 | 0.02 | 0.02 | 0.02 |
| 2      | 0.08 | 0.06 | 0.05 | 0.05 | 0.04 | 0.04 | 0.03 | 0.03 |
| 3      | 0.11 | 0.09 | 0.08 | 0.07 | 0.06 | 0.06 | 0.05 | 0.05 |
| 4      | 0.15 | 0.12 | 0.11 | 0.09 | 0.08 | 0.08 | 0.07 | 0.06 |
| 5      | 0.19 | 0.16 | 0.13 | 0.12 | 0.11 | 0.09 | 0.09 | 0.08 |

Subtract 0.01% for each 40 min of drinking. One drink is 40 mL of 80-proof liquor, 355 mL of beer, or 148 mL of table wine.

**5** In Michigan underage drivers can be arrested for drinking and driving if their blood alcohol percentage is more than 0.02 percent. According to the table above, how many drinks would it take for a 72-kg man to exceed this limit?
(1) three         (3) one
(2) two           (4) zero

**6** In some states, the legal blood alcohol percentage limit for driving while under the influence of alcohol is 0.08 percent. According to the table above, how many drinks would it take for a 54-kg man to exceed this limit?
(1) four          (3) two
(2) three         (4) one

**7** A 90-kg man has been tested for blood alcohol content. His blood alcohol percentage is 0.08. Based upon the information in the table, about how much has he had to drink?
(1) three drinks
(2) 120 mL of 80-proof liquor
(3) 396 mL of table wine
(4) 1,420 mL of beer

Part II

*Record your answers on the answer sheet provided by your teacher or on a sheet of paper.*

**8** Explain the difference between voluntary and involuntary muscles.

**Use the table below to answer questions 9–11.**

| Number of Bicycle Deaths per Year | | |
|---|---|---|
| Year | Male | Female |
| 1996 | 654 | 107 |
| 1997 | 712 | 99 |
| 1998 | 658 | 99 |
| 1999 | 656 | 94 |
| 2000 | 605 | 76 |

Data from Insurance Institute for Highway Safety

**9** Head injuries are the most serious injuries that are found in people who died in bicycle accidents. Ninety percent of the deaths were in people who were not wearing bicycle helmets. Using the data in the table, approximately how many of the people (male and female) who died in bicycle accidents in 1998 were wearing bicycle helmets?

**10** In 2000, what percentage of the people who died were women?

**11** Which of the years from 1996 to 2000 had the greatest total number of bicycle deaths?

**12** Explain how bone cells help maintain homeostasis.

**13** Describe the changes that occur in muscles that do a lot of work. Compare these muscles to the muscles of a person who only does inactive pastimes.

**Use the illustration below to answer question 14.**

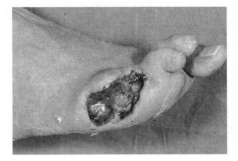

**14** People with diabetes often lose sensation in their feet. Explain why a sore like the one in the photograph might develop if skin sensory receptors were not working properly.

**15** Sam bumped into another player during soccer practice and bruised his leg. Describe the sequence of events from the time of injury until the injury disappears.

**LE 1.2a:** Each system is composed of organs and tissues which perform specific functions and interact with each other. **1.2f:** The circulatory system moves substances to and from cells, where they are needed or produced, responding to changing demands. **Also Covered:** 1.2j

# Circulation

## What does a highway have to do with circulation?

Think of this interchange as a simplified way to visualize how your blood travels through your body. Your complex circulatory system also plays an important role in protecting you from disease.

**Science Journal** Infer how the circulatory system provides your body with the nutrients it needs to stay healthy?

# Start-Up Activities

## Comparing Circulatory and Road Systems

If you look at an aerial view of a road system, as shown in the photograph, you see roads leading in many directions. These roads provide a way to carry people and goods from one place to another. Your circulatory system is like a road system. Just as roads are used to transport goods to homes and factories, your blood vessels transport substances throughout your body.

1. Look at a map of your city, county, or state.

2. Identify roads that are interstates, as well as state and county routes, using the map key.

3. Plan a route to a destination that your teacher describes. Then plan a different return trip.

4. Draw a diagram in your Science Journal showing your routes to and from the destination.

5. **Think Critically** If the destination represents your heart, what do the routes represent? Draw a comparison between a blocked road on your map and a clogged artery in your body.

**Circulation** Your body is supplied with nutrients by blood circulating through your blood vessels. Make the following Foldable to help you organize information about circulation.

**STEP 1** **Fold** a sheet of paper in half lengthwise. Make the back edge about 5 cm longer than the front edge.

**STEP 2** **Turn** the paper so the fold is on the bottom. Then, **fold** it into thirds.

**STEP 3** **Unfold and cut** only the top layer along both folds to make three tabs. **Label** the top of the page *Circulation*, and label the three tabs *Pulmonary*, *Coronary*, and *Systemic*.

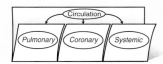

**Read and Write** As you read the chapter, write about each section under its tab.

Preview this chapter's content and activities at glencoe.com

# section 1

# The Circulatory System

### *What* You'll Learn

- **Compare and contrast** arteries, veins, and capillaries.
- **Explain** how blood moves through the heart.
- **Identify** the functions of the pulmonary and systemic circulation systems.

### *Why* It's Important

Your body's cells depend on the blood vessels to bring nutrients and remove wastes.

### Review Vocabulary

**heart:** organ that circulates blood through your body continuously

### New Vocabulary

- atrium
- ventricle
- coronary circulation
- pulmonary circulation
- systemic circulation
- artery
- vein
- capillary

## How Materials Move Through the Body

It's time to get ready for school, but your younger sister is taking a long time in the shower. "Don't use up all the water," you shout. Water is carried throughout your house in pipes that are part of the plumbing system. The plumbing system supplies water for all your needs and carries away wastes. Just as you expect water to flow when you turn on the faucet, your body needs a continuous supply of oxygen and nutrients and a way to remove wastes. In a similar way materials are moved throughout your body by your cardiovascular (kar dee oh VAS kyuh lur) system. It includes your heart, kilometers of blood vessels, and blood.

Blood vessels carry blood to every part of your body, as shown in **Figure 1.** Blood moves oxygen and nutrients to cells and carries carbon dioxide and other wastes away from the cells. Sometimes blood carries substances made in one part of the body to another part of the body where these substances are needed. Movement of materials into and out of your cells occurs by diffusion (dih FYEW zhun) and active transport. Diffusion occurs when a material moves from an area where there is more of it to an area where there is less of it. Active transport is the opposite of diffusion. Active transport requires an input of energy from the cell, but diffusion does not.

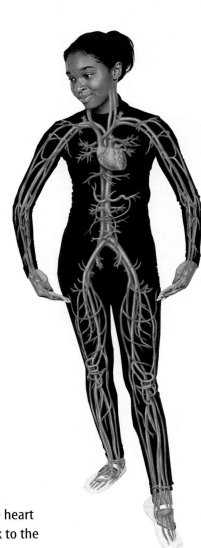

**Figure 1** The blood is pumped by the heart to all the cells of the body and then back to the heart through a network of blood vessels.

# The Heart

Your heart is an organ made of cardiac muscle tissue. It is located behind your breastbone, called the sternum, and between your lungs. Your heart has four compartments called chambers. The two upper chambers are called the right and left **atriums** (AY tree umz). The two lower chambers are called the right and left **ventricles** (VEN trih kulz). During one heartbeat, both atriums contract at the same time. Then, both ventricles contract at the same time. A one-way valve separates each atrium from the ventricle below it. The blood flows only in one direction from an atrium to a ventricle, then from a ventricle into a blood vessel. A wall prevents blood from flowing between the two atriums or the two ventricles. This wall keeps blood rich in oxygen separate from blood low in oxygen. If oxygen-rich blood and oxygen-poor blood were to mix, your body's cells would not get all the oxygen they need.

Scientists have divided the circulatory system into three sections—coronary circulation, pulmonary (PUL muh ner ee) circulation, and systemic circulation. The beating of your heart controls blood flow through each section.

**Coronary Circulation**  Your heart has its own blood vessels that supply it with nutrients and oxygen and remove wastes. **Coronary** (KOR uh ner ee) **circulation,** as shown in **Figure 2,** is the flow of blood to and from the tissues of the heart. When the coronary circulation is blocked, oxygen and nutrients cannot reach all the cells of the heart. This can result in a heart attack.

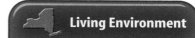
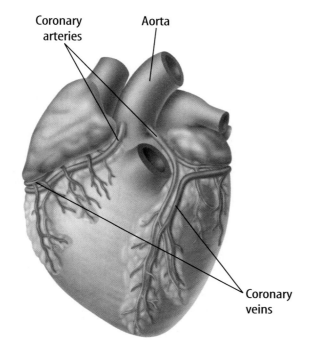

Coronary arteries

Aorta

Coronary veins

**Living Environment**

**1.2f  Describe** the functions of the three categories of the circulatory system.

**Figure 2**  Like the rest of the body, the heart receives the oxygen and nutrients that it needs from the blood. The blood also carries away wastes from the heart's cells. On the diagram, you can see the coronary arteries, which nourish the heart.

Blood, high in carbon dioxide and low in oxygen, returns from the body to the heart. It enters the right atrium through the superior and inferior vena cavae.

Oxygen-rich blood travels from the lungs through the pulmonary veins and into the left atrium. The pulmonary veins are the only veins that carry oxygen-rich blood.

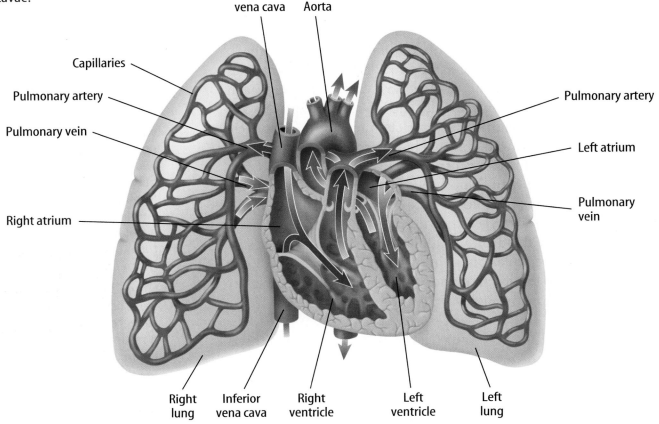

The right atrium contracts, forcing the blood into the right ventricle. When the right ventricle contracts, the blood leaves the heart and goes through the pulmonary arteries to the lungs. The pulmonary arteries are the only arteries that carry blood that is high in carbon dioxide.

The left atrium contracts and forces the blood into the left ventricle. The left ventricle contracts, forcing the blood out of the heart and into the aorta.

**Figure 3** Pulmonary circulation moves blood between the heart and lungs.

**Pulmonary Circulation** The flow of blood through the heart to the lungs and back to the heart is **pulmonary circulation.** Use **Figure 3** to trace the path blood takes through this part of the circulatory system. The blood returning from the body through the right side of the heart and to the lungs contains cellular wastes. The wastes include molecules of carbon dioxide and other substances. In the lungs, gaseous wastes diffuse out of the blood, and oxygen diffuses into the blood. Then the blood returns to the left side of the heart. In the final step of pulmonary circulation, the oxygen-rich blood is pumped from the left ventricle into the aorta (ay OR tuh), the largest artery in your body. Next, the oxygen-rich blood flows to all parts of your body.

**Systemic Circulation** Oxygen-rich blood moves to all of your organs and body tissues, except the heart and lungs, by **systemic circulation,** and oxygen-poor blood returns to the heart. Systemic circulation is the largest of the three sections of your circulatory system. **Figure 4** shows the major arteries (AR tuh reez) and veins (VAYNZ) of the systemic circulation system. Oxygen-rich blood flows from your heart in the arteries of this system. Then nutrients and oxygen are delivered by blood to your body cells and exchanged for carbon dioxide and wastes. Finally, the blood returns to your heart in the veins of the systemic circulation system.

**✓ Reading Check** *What are the functions of the systemic circulation system in your body?*

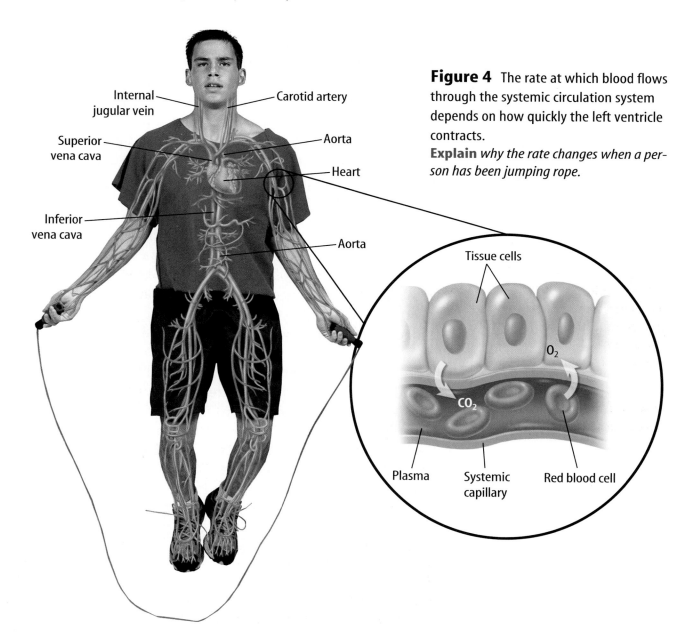

**Figure 4** The rate at which blood flows through the systemic circulation system depends on how quickly the left ventricle contracts.
**Explain** *why the rate changes when a person has been jumping rope.*

Internal jugular vein
Carotid artery
Superior vena cava
Aorta
Heart
Inferior vena cava
Aorta

Tissue cells
$O_2$
$CO_2$
Plasma
Systemic capillary
Red blood cell

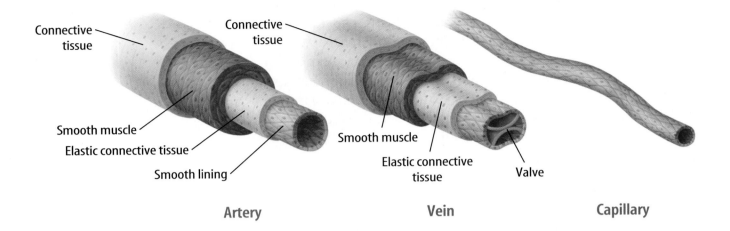

Connective tissue

Connective tissue

Smooth muscle

Elastic connective tissue

Smooth lining

Smooth muscle

Elastic connective tissue

Valve

**Artery**

**Vein**

**Capillary**

**Figure 5** The structures of arteries, veins, and capillaries are different. Valves in veins prevent blood from flowing backward. Capillaries are much smaller. Capillary walls are only one cell thick.

**Living Environment**

**1.2a, 1.2b, 1.2f Predict** how the circulatory system responds to physical exercise and relaxation to help maintain the body's balance and homeostasis.

# Blood Vessels

In the middle 1600s, scientists proved that blood moves in one direction in a blood vessel, like traffic on a one-way street. They discovered that blood moves by the pumping of the heart and flows from arteries to veins. But, they couldn't explain how blood gets from arteries to veins. Using a new invention of that time, the microscope, scientists discovered capillaries (KAP uh ler eez), the connection between arteries and veins.

**Arteries** As blood is pumped out of the heart, it travels through arteries, capillaries, and then veins. **Arteries** are blood vessels that carry blood away from the heart. Arteries, shown in **Figure 5,** have thick, elastic walls made of connective tissue and smooth muscle tissue. Each ventricle of the heart is connected to an artery. The right ventricle is connected to the pulmonary artery, and the left ventricle is attached to the aorta. Every time your heart contracts, blood is moved from your heart into arteries.

**Veins** The blood vessels that carry blood back to the heart are called **veins,** as shown in **Figure 5.** Veins have one-way valves that keep blood moving toward the heart. If blood flows backward, the pressure of the blood against the valves causes them to close. The flow of blood in veins also is helped by your skeletal muscles. When skeletal muscles contract, the veins in these muscles are squeezed and help blood move toward the heart. Two major veins return blood from your body to your heart. The superior vena cava returns blood from your head and neck. Blood from your abdomen and lower body returns through the inferior vena cava.

 **Reading Check** *What are the similarities and differences between arteries and veins?*

**Capillaries** Arteries and veins are connected by microscopic blood vessels called **capillaries**, as shown in **Figure 5.** The walls of capillaries are only one cell thick. You can see capillaries when you have a bloodshot eye. They are the tiny red lines you see in the white area of your eye. Nutrients and oxygen diffuse into body cells through the thin capillary walls. Waste materials and carbon dioxide diffuse from body cells into the capillaries.

## Blood Pressure

 If you fill a balloon with water and then push on it, the pressure moves through the water in all directions, as shown in **Figure 6.** Your circulatory system is like the water balloon. When your heart pumps blood through the circulatory system, the pressure of the push moves through the blood. The force of the blood on the walls of the blood vessels is called blood pressure. This pressure is highest in arteries and lowest in veins. When you take your pulse, you can feel the waves of pressure. This rise and fall of pressure occurs with each heartbeat. Normal resting pulse rates are 60 to 100 heartbeats per minute for adults, and 80 to 100 beats per minute for children.

**Measuring Blood Pressure** Blood pressure is measured in large arteries and is expressed by two numbers, such as 120 over 80. The first number is a measure of the pressure caused when the ventricles contract and blood is pushed out of the heart. This is called the systolic (sihs TAH lihk) pressure. Then, blood pressure drops as the ventricles relax. The second number is a measure of the diastolic (di uh STAH lihk) pressure that occurs as the ventricles fill with blood just before they contract again.

**Controlling Blood Pressure** Your body tries to keep blood pressure normal. Special nerve cells in the walls of some arteries sense changes in blood pressure. When pressure is higher or lower than normal, messages are sent to your brain by these nerve cells. Then messages are sent by your brain to raise or lower blood pressure—by speeding up or slowing the heart rate for example. This helps keep blood pressure constant within your arteries. When blood pressure is constant, enough blood reaches all organs and tissues in your body and delivers needed nutrients to every cell.

**Blood Pressure** Some molecules of nutrients are forced through capillary walls by the force of blood pressure. What is the cause of the pressure? Discuss your answer with a classmate. Then write your answer in your Science Journal.

**Figure 6** When pressure is exerted on a fluid in a closed container, the pressure is transmitted through the liquid in all directions. Your circulatory system is like a closed container.

Water-filled balloon

## Figure 7

**H**ealthy blood vessels have smooth, unobstructed interiors like the one at the right. Atherosclerosis is a disease in which fatty substances build up in the walls of arteries, such as the coronary arteries that supply the heart muscle with oxygen-rich blood. As illustrated below, these fatty deposits can gradually restrict—and ultimately block—the life-giving river of blood that flows through an artery.

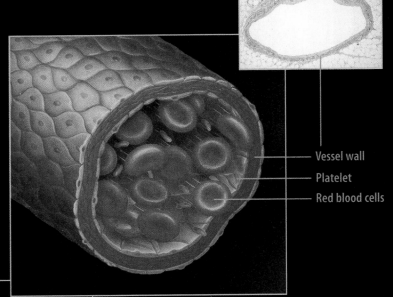

Vessel wall
Platelet
Red blood cells

▲ **HEALTHY ARTERY** The illustration and photo above show a normal functioning artery.

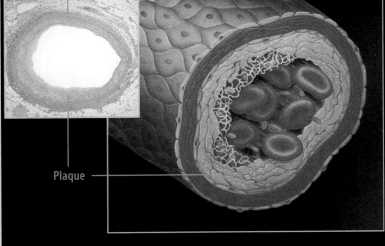

Vessel wall

Plaque

◀ **PARTIALLY CLOGGED ARTERY** The illustration and inset photo at left show fatty deposits, called plaques, that have formed along the artery's inner wall. As the diagram illustrates, plaques narrow the pathway through the artery, restricting and slowing blood flow. As blood supply to the heart muscle cells dwindles, they become starved for oxygen and nutrients.

▶ **NEARLY BLOCKED ARTERY** In the illustration and photo at right, fatty deposits have continued to build. The pathway through the coronary artery has gradually narrowed until blood flow is very slow and nearly blocked. Under these conditions, the heart muscle cells supplied by the artery are greatly weakened. If blood flow stops entirely, a heart attack will result.

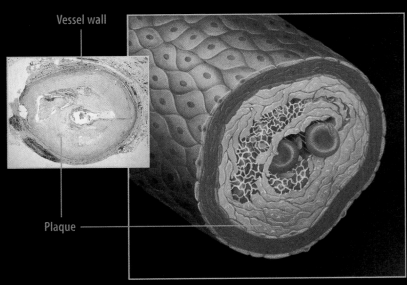

Vessel wall

Plaque

# Cardiovascular Disease

Any disease that affects the cardiovascular system—the heart, blood vessels, and blood—can seriously affect the health of your entire body. People often think of cancer and automobile accidents as the leading causes of death in the United States. However, heart disease is the leading cause of death, when you factor in all age groups.

**Atherosclerosis** One leading cause of heart disease is called atherosclerosis (ah thuh roh skluh ROH sus). In this condition, shown in **Figure 7,** fatty deposits build up on arterial walls. Eating foods high in cholesterol and saturated fats can cause these deposits to form. Atherosclerosis can occur in any artery in the body, but deposits in coronary arteries are especially serious. If a coronary artery is blocked, a heart attack can occur. Open heart surgery may then be needed to correct the problem.

**Hypertension** Another condition of the cardiovascular system is called hypertension (HI pur TEN chun), or high blood pressure. **Figure 8** shows the instruments used to measure blood pressure. When blood pressure is higher than normal most of the time, extra strain is placed on the heart. The heart must work harder to keep blood flowing. One cause of hypertension is atherosclerosis. A clogged artery can increase pressure within the vessel. The walls become stiff and hard, like a metal pipe. The artery walls no longer contract and dilate easily because they have lost their elasticity.

**Heart Failure** Heart failure results when the heart cannot pump blood efficiently. It might be caused when heart muscle tissue is weakened by disease or when heart valves do not work properly. When the heart does not pump blood properly, fluids collect in the arms, legs, and lungs. People with heart failure usually are short of breath and tired.

**☑ Reading Check** *What is heart failure?*

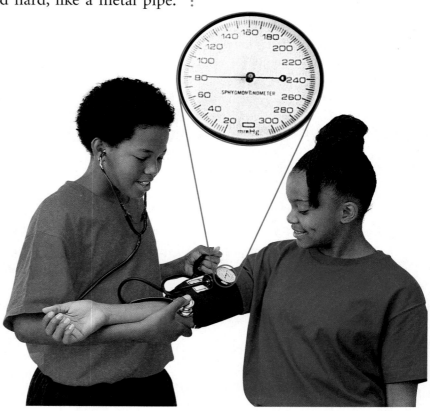

**Figure 8** Blood pressure is measured in large arteries using a blood pressure cuff and stethoscope.

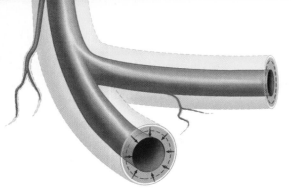

**Figure 9** Nicotine, present in tobacco, contracts blood vessels and causes the body to release hormones that raise blood pressure. **Name** *another substance that raises blood pressure.*

**Preventing Cardiovascular Disease** Having a healthy lifestyle is important for the health of your cardiovascular system. The choices you make to maintain good health may reduce your risk of future serious illness. Regular checkups, a healthful diet, and exercise are part of a heart-healthy lifestyle.

Many diseases, including cardiovascular disease, can be prevented by following a good diet. Choose foods that are low in salt, sugar, cholesterol, and saturated fats. Being overweight is associated with heart disease and high blood pressure. Large amounts of body fat force the heart to pump faster.

Learning to relax and having a regular program of exercise can help prevent tension and relieve stress. Exercise also strengthens the heart and lungs, helps in controlling cholesterol, tones muscles, and helps lower blood pressure.

Another way to prevent cardiovascular disease is to not smoke. Smoking causes blood vessels to contract, as shown in **Figure 9,** and makes the heart beat faster and harder. Smoking also increases carbon monoxide levels in the blood. Not smoking helps prevent heart disease and a number of respiratory system problems, too.

## section 1 review

### Summary

**Cardiovascular System**

- Coronary circulation is the flow of blood to and from the tissues of the heart.
- Pulmonary circulation is the flow of blood through the heart, to the lungs, and back to the heart.
- Oxygen-rich blood is moved to all tissues and organs of the body, except the heart and lungs, by systemic circulation.

**Blood Vessels**

- Arteries carry blood away from the heart.
- Veins carry blood back to the heart.
- Arteries and veins are connected by capillaries.

**Blood Pressure**

- The force of the blood on the walls of the blood vessels is called blood pressure.

**Cardiovascular Disease**

- Atherosclerosis occurs when fatty deposits build up on arterial walls.
- High blood pressure is called hypertension.

### Self Check

1. **Compare and contrast** the structure of the three types of blood vessels.
2. **Explain** the pathway of blood through the heart.
3. **Contrast** pulmonary and systemic circulation. Identify which vessels carry oxygen-rich blood.
4. **Explain** how exercise can help prevent heart disease.
5. **Think Critically** What waste product builds up in blood and cells when the heart is unable to pump blood efficiently?

#### Applying Skills

6. **Concept Map** Make an events-chain concept map to show pulmonary circulation beginning at the right atrium and ending at the aorta.
7. **Use a Database** Research diseases of the circulatory system. Make a database showing what part of the circulatory system is affected by each disease. Categories should include the organs and vessels of the circulatory system.

# The Heart as a Pump

The heart is a pumping organ. Blood is forced through the arteries as heart muscles contract and then relax. This creates a series of waves in blood as it flows through the arteries. These waves are called the pulse. Try this lab to learn how physical activity affects your pulse.

## ▶ Real-World Question

What does the pulse rate tell you about the work of the heart?

### Goals
- ■ **Observe** pulse rate.
- ■ **Compare** pulse rate at rest to rate after jogging.

### Materials
watch or clock with a second hand
*stopwatch
*Alternate materials

### Pulse Rate

| Pulse Rate | Partner's | Yours |
|---|---|---|
| At rest | Do not write in this book. | |
| After jogging | | |

## ▶ Procedure

1. Make a table like the one shown. Use it to record your data.
2. Sit down to take your pulse. Your partner will serve as the recorder.
3. Find your pulse by placing your middle and index fingers over the radial artery in your wrist as shown in the photo.
   **WARNING:** *Do not press too hard.*
4. **Count** each beat of the radial pulse silently for 15 s. Multiply the number of beats by four to find your pulse rate per minute. Have your partner record the number in the data table.
5. Now jog in place for 1 min and take your pulse again. Count the beats for 15 s.
6. **Calculate** this new pulse rate and have your partner record it in the data table.
7. Reverse roles with your partner and repeat steps 2 through 6.
8. **Collect** and record the new data.

## ▶ Conclude and Apply

1. **Describe** why the pulse rate changes.
2. **Infer** what causes the pulse rate to change.
3. **Explain** why the heart is a pumping organ.

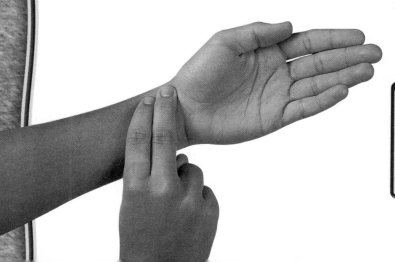

## 𝒞ommunicating
### Your Data

Record the class average for pulse rate at rest and after jogging. Compare the class averages to your data. **For more help, refer to the** Science Skill Handbook.

# Blood

*What* **You'll Learn**

- **Identify** the parts and functions of blood.
- **Explain** why blood types are checked before a transfusion.
- **Give examples** of diseases of blood.

*Why* **It's Important**

Blood plays a part in every major activity of your body.

**Review Vocabulary**

**blood vessels:** Structures that include arteries, veins, and capillaries, which transport blood

**New Vocabulary**

- plasma
- hemoglobin
- platelet

## Functions of Blood

You take a last, deep, calming breath before plunging into a dark, vessel-like tube. The water transports you down the slide much like the way blood carries substances to all parts of your body. Blood has four important functions.

1. Blood carries oxygen from your lungs to all your body cells. Carbon dioxide diffuses from your body cells into your blood. Your blood carries carbon dioxide to your lungs to be exhaled.

2. Blood carries waste products from your cells to your kidneys to be removed.

3. Blood transports nutrients and other substances to your body cells.

4. Cells and molecules in blood fight infections and help heal wounds.

Anything that disrupts or changes these functions affects all the tissues of your body. Can you understand why blood is sometimes called the tissue of life?

## Parts of Blood

As shown in **Figure 10,** blood is a tissue made of plasma (PLAZ muh), platelets (PLAYT luts), and red and white blood cells. Blood makes up about eight percent of your body's total mass. If you weigh 45 kg, you have about 3.6 kg of blood moving through your body. The amount of blood in an adult would fill five 1-L bottles.

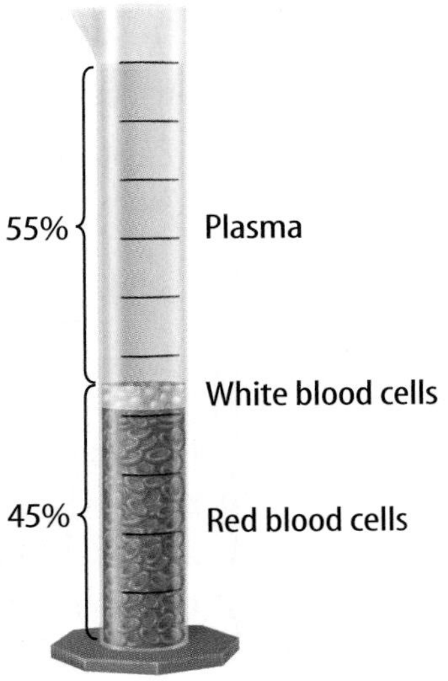

**Plasma** The liquid part of blood is mostly water and is called **plasma.** It makes up more than half the volume of blood. Nutrients, minerals, and oxygen are dissolved in plasma and carried to cells. Wastes from cells are also carried in plasma.

55% — Plasma

White blood cells

45% — Red blood cells

**Figure 10** The blood in this graduated cylinder has separated into its parts. Each part plays a key role in body functions.

**Blood Cells** A cubic millimeter of blood has about five million red blood cells. These disk-shaped blood cells, shown in **Figure 11,** are different from other cells in your body because they have no nuclei. They contain **hemoglobin** (HEE muh gloh bun), which is a molecule that carries oxygen and carbon dioxide, and made of an iron compound that gives blood its red color. Hemoglobin carries oxygen from your lungs to your body cells. Then it carries some of the carbon dioxide from your body cells back to your lungs. The rest of the carbon dioxide is carried in the cytoplasm of red blood cells and in plasma. Red blood cells have a life span of about 120 days. They are made at a rate of 2 million to 3 million per second in the center of long bones like the femur in your thigh. Red blood cells wear out and are destroyed at about the same rate.

In contrast to red blood cells, a cubic millimeter of blood has about 5,000 to 10,000 white blood cells. White blood cells fight bacteria, viruses, and other invaders of your body. Your body reacts to invaders by increasing the number of white blood cells. These cells leave the blood through capillary walls and go into the tissues that have been invaded. Here, they destroy bacteria and viruses and absorb dead cells. The life span of white blood cells varies from a few days to many months.

Circulating with the red and white blood cells are platelets. **Platelets** are irregularly shaped cell fragments that help clot blood. A cubic millimeter of blood can contain as many as 400,000 platelets. Platelets have a life span of five to nine days.

**Topic: White Blood Cells**
Visit glencoe.com for Web links to information about types of human white blood cells and their functions.

**Activity** Write a brief summary describing how white blood cells destroy bacteria and viruses in your Science Journal.

**Living Environment**

**1.2f** *Blood is a tissue.*
**Summarize** in your own words the functions of blood.

**Figure 11** Red blood cells supply your body with oxygen, and white blood cells and platelets have protective roles.

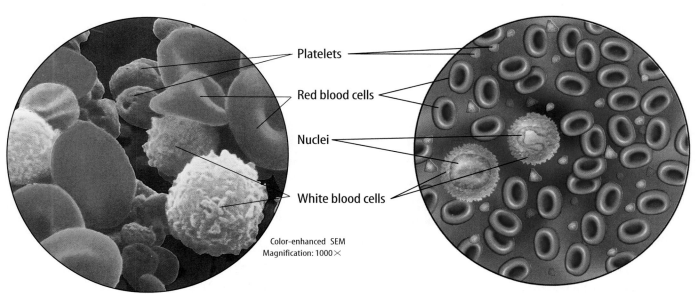

Platelets

Red blood cells

Nuclei

White blood cells

Color-enhanced SEM
Magnification: 1000×

Platelets help stop bleeding. Platelets not only plug holes in small vessels, they also release chemicals that help form filaments of fibrin.

Several types, sizes, and shapes of white blood cells exist. These cells destroy bacteria, viruses, and foreign substances.

**Figure 12** When the skin is damaged, a sticky blood clot seals the leaking blood vessel. Eventually, a scab forms to protect the wound from further damage and allow it to heal.

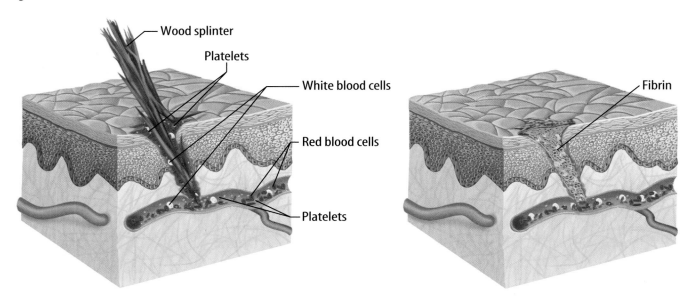

- Wood splinter
- Platelets
- White blood cells
- Red blood cells
- Platelets
- Fibrin

## Modeling Scab Formation

**Procedure**

1. Place a 5-cm × 5-cm square of **gauze** on a piece of **aluminum foil.**
2. Place several drops of a **liquid bandage solution** onto the gauze and let it dry. Keep the liquid bandage away from eyes and mouth.
3. Use a **dropper** to place one drop of **water** onto the area of the liquid bandage. Place another drop of water in another area of the gauze.

**Analysis**

1. Compare the drops of water in both areas.
2. Describe how the treated area of the gauze is like a scab.

# Blood Clotting

You're running with your dog in a park, when all of a sudden you trip and fall down. Your knee starts to bleed, but the bleeding stops quickly. Already the wounded area has begun to heal. Bleeding stops because platelets and clotting factors in your blood make a blood clot that plugs the wounded blood vessels. A blood clot also acts somewhat like a bandage. When you cut yourself, platelets stick to the wound and release chemicals. Then substances called clotting factors carry out a series of chemical reactions. These reactions cause threadlike fibers called fibrin (FI brun) to form a sticky net, as shown in **Figure 12.** This net traps escaping blood cells and plasma and forms a clot. The clot helps stop more blood from escaping. After the clot is in place and becomes hard, skin cells begin the repair process under the scab. Eventually, the scab is lifted off. Bacteria that might get into the wound during the healing process are destroyed by white blood cells.

**✔ Reading Check** *What blood components help form blood clots?*

Most people will not bleed to death from a minor wound, such as a cut or scrape. However, some people have a genetic condition called hemophilia (hee muh FIH lee uh). Their plasma lacks one of the clotting factors that begins the clotting process. A minor injury can be a life threatening problem for a person with hemophilia.

## Table 1  Blood Types

| Blood Type | Antigen | Antibody |
|---|---|---|
| A | A | Anti-B |
| B | B | Anti-A |
| AB | A, B | None |
| O | None | Anti-A, Anti-B |

# Blood Types

Blood clots stop blood loss quickly in a minor wound, but a person with a serious wound might lose a lot of blood and need a blood transfusion. During a blood transfusion, a person receives donated blood or parts of blood. The medical provider must be sure that the right type of blood is given. If the wrong type is given, the red blood cells will clump together. Then, clots form in the blood vessels and the person could die.

**The ABO Identification System** People can inherit one of four types of blood: A, B, AB, or O, as shown in **Table 1.** Types A, B, and AB have chemical identification tags called antigens (AN tih junz) on their red blood cells. Type O red blood cells have no antigens.

Each blood type also has specific antibodies in its plasma. Antibodies are proteins that destroy or neutralize substances that do not belong in or are not part of your body. Because of these antibodies, certain blood types cannot be mixed. This limits blood transfusion possibilities as shown in **Table 2.** If type A blood is mixed with type B blood, the type A antibodies determine that type B blood does not belong there. The type A antibodies cause the type B red blood cells to clump. In the same way, type B antibodies cause type A blood to clump. Type AB blood has no antibodies, so people with this blood type can receive blood from A, B, AB, and O types. Type O blood has both A and B antibodies.

**Reading Check** *Why are people with type O blood called universal donors?*

### Table 2 Blood Transfusion Options

| Type | Can Receive | Can Donate To |
|---|---|---|
| A | O, A | A, AB |
| B | O, B | B, AB |
| AB | all | AB |
| O | O | all |

**Blood Transfusions** The first blood transfusions took place in the 1600s and were from animal to animal, and then from animal to human. In 1818, James Blundell, a British obstetrician, performed the first successful transfusion of human blood to a patient for the treatment of hemorrhage.

**The Rh Factor** Another chemical identification tag in blood is the Rh factor. The Rh factor also is inherited. If the Rh factor is on red blood cells, the person has Rh-positive (Rh+) blood. If it is not present, the person's blood is called Rh-negative (Rh−). If an Rh− person receives a blood transfusion from an Rh+ person, he or she will produce antibodies against the Rh factor. These antibodies can cause Rh+ cells to clump. Clots then form in the blood vessels and the person could die.

When an Rh− mother is pregnant with an Rh+ baby, the mother might make antibodies to the child's Rh factor. Close to the time of birth, Rh antibodies from the mother can pass from her blood into the baby's blood. These antibodies can destroy the baby's red blood cells. If this happens, the baby must receive a blood transfusion before or right after birth. At 28 weeks of pregnancy and immediately after the birth, an Rh− mother can receive an injection that blocks the production of antibodies to the Rh+ factor. These injections prevent this life-threatening situation. To prevent deadly results, blood groups and Rh factor are checked before transfusions and during pregnancies.

✔ **Reading Check** *Why is it important to check Rh factor?*

## Applying Science

### Will there be enough blood donors?

Successful human blood transfusions began during World War II. This practice is much safer today due to extensive testing of the donated blood prior to transfusion. Health care professionals have determined that each blood type can receive certain other blood types as illustrated in **Table 2.**

| Blood Type Distribution | | |
|---|---|---|
| | Rh+(%) | Rh−(%) |
| O | 37 | 7 |
| A | 36 | 6 |
| B | 9 | 1 |
| AB | 3 | 1 |

### Identifying the Problem

The table on the right lists the average distribution of blood types in the United States. The data are recorded as percents, or a sample of 100 people. By examining these data and the data in **Table 2,** can you determine safe donors for each blood type? Recall that people with Rh− blood cannot receive a transfusion from an Rh+ donor.

### Solving the Problem

1. If a Type B, Rh+ person needs a blood transfusion, how many possible donors are there?
2. Frequently, the supply of donated blood runs low. Which blood type and Rh factor would be most affected in such a shortage? Explain your answer.

# Diseases of Blood

Because blood circulates to all parts of your body and performs so many important functions, any disease of the blood is a cause for concern. One common disease of the blood is anemia (uh NEE mee uh). In this disease of red blood cells, body tissues can't get enough oxygen and are unable to carry on their usual activities. Anemia has many causes. Sometimes, anemia is caused by the loss of large amounts of blood. A diet lacking iron or certain vitamins also might cause anemia. In addition, anemia can be the result of another disease or a side effect of treatment for a disease. Still other types of anemia are inherited problems related to the structure of the red blood cells. Cells from one such type of anemia, sickle-cell anemia, are shown in **Figure 13.**

Leukemia (lew KEE mee uh) is a disease in which one or more types of white blood cells are made in excessive numbers. These cells are immature and do not fight infections well. They fill the bone marrow and crowd out the normal cells. Then not enough red blood cells, normal white blood cells, and platelets can be made. Types of leukemia affect children or adults. Medicines, blood transfusions, and bone marrow transplants are used to treat this disease. If the treatments are not successful, the person eventually will die from related complications.

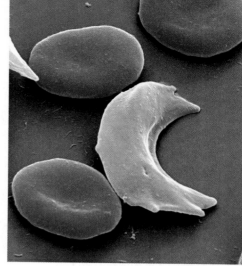

Color-enhanced TEM Magnification: 7400×

**Figure 13** Persons with sickle-cell anemia have misshapened red blood cells. The sickle-shaped cells clog the capillaries of a person with this disease. Oxygen cannot reach tissues served by the capillaries, and wastes cannot be removed. **Describe** *how this damages the affected tissues.*

## section 2 review

### Summary

**Parts of Blood**

- Plasma is made mostly of water, with nutrients, minerals, and oxygen dissolved in it.
- Red blood cells contain hemoglobin, which carries oxygen and carbon dioxide.
- White blood cells control infections and viruses.
- Blood clotting factors and platelets help blood to clot.

**Blood Types**

- People can inherit one of four types of blood and an Rh factor.
- Type A, B, and AB blood all have antigens. Type O blood has no antigens.

**Diseases of Blood**

- Anemia is a disease of red blood cells.
- Leukemia is a disease that produces immature white blood cells that don't fight infections.

### Self Check

1. **List** the four functions of blood in the body.
2. **Infer** why blood type and Rh factor are checked before a transfusion.
3. **Interpret Data** Look at the data in **Table 2** about blood group interactions. To which group(s) can blood type AB donate blood, and which blood type(s) can AB receive blood from?
4. **Think Critically** Think about the main job of your red blood cells. If red blood cells couldn't deliver oxygen to your cells, what would be the condition of your body tissues?

*Hot Words Hot Topics*: Bk 2 (5) pp. 142–143

#### Applying Math

5. **Use Percentages** Find the total number of red blood cells, white blood cells, and platelets in 1 mm³ of blood. Calculate what percentage of the total each type is.

# section 3

# The Lymphatic System

## as you read

### *What* You'll Learn

- **Describe** functions of the lymphatic system.
- **Identify** where lymph comes from.
- **Explain** how lymph organs help fight infections.

### *Why* It's Important

The lymphatic system helps protect you from infections and diseases.

### 🔍 Review Vocabulary

**smooth muscles:** muscles found in your internal organs and digestive track

### New Vocabulary

- lymph
- lymphatic system
- lymphocyte
- lymph node

---

### Living Environment

**LE 1.2b, 1.2f, 1.2j  Analyze** the functions of the lymphatic system and its importance to homeostasis.

## Functions of the Lymphatic System

You're thirsty so you turn on the water faucet and fill a glass with water. The excess water runs down the drain. In a similiar way, your body's excess tissue fluid is removed by the lymphatic (lihm FA tihk) system. The nutrient, water, and oxygen molecules in blood diffuse through capillary walls to nearby cells. Water and other substances become part of the tissue fluid that is found between cells. This fluid is collected and returned to the blood by the lymphatic system.

After tissue fluid diffuses into the lymphatic capillaries it is called **lymph** (LIHMF). Your **lymphatic system,** as shown in **Figure 14,** carries lymph through a network of lymph capillaries and larger lymph vessels. Then, the lymph drains into large veins near the heart. No heartlike structure pumps the lymph through the lymphatic system. The movement of lymph depends on the contraction of smooth muscles in lymph vessels and skeletal muscles. Lymphatic vessels, like veins, have valves that keep lymph from flowing backward. If the lymphatic system is not working properly, severe swelling occurs because the tissue fluid cannot get back to the blood.

In addition to water and dissolved substances, lymph also contains **lymphocytes** (LIHM fuh sites), a type of white blood cell. Lymphocytes help your body defend itself against disease-causing organisms.

✔ **Reading Check**  *What are the differences and similarities between lymph and blood?*

## Lymphatic Organs

Before lymph enters the blood, it passes through lymph nodes, which are bean-shaped organs of varying sizes found throughout the body. **Lymph nodes** filter out microorganisms and foreign materials that have been taken up by lymphocytes. When your body fights an infection, lymphocytes fill the lymph nodes. The lymph nodes become warm, reddened, and tender to the touch. After the invaders are destroyed, the redness, warmth, and tenderness in the lymph nodes goes away.

Besides lymph nodes, the tonsils, the thymus, and the spleen are important lymphatic organs. Tonsils are in the back of your throat and protect you from harmful microorganisms that enter through your mouth and nose. Your thymus is a soft mass of tissue located behind the sternum. It makes lymphocytes that travel to other lymph organs. The spleen is the largest lymphatic organ. It is located behind the upper-left part of the stomach and filters the blood by removing worn out and damaged red blood cells. Cells in the spleen take up and destroy bacteria and other substances that invade your body.

## A Disease of the Lymphatic System

HIV is a deadly virus. When HIV enters a person's body, it attacks and destroys lymphocytes called helper T cells that help make antibodies to fight infections. This affects a person's immunity to some diseases. Usually, the person dies from these dieseases, not from the HIV infection.

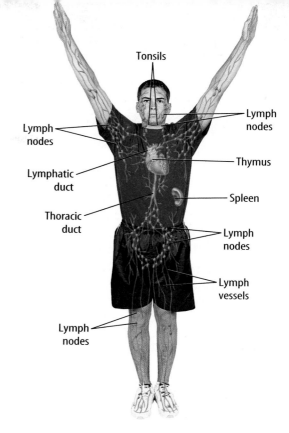

**Figure 14** The lymphatic system is connected by a network of vessels. **Describe** *how muscles help move lymph.*

## section 3 review

### Summary

**Functions of the Lymphatic System**

- Fluid is collected and returned from the body tissues to the blood by the lymphatic system.
- After fluid from tissues diffuses into the lymphatic capillaries it is called lymph.
- Lymphocytes are a type of white blood cell that helps your body defend itself against disease.

**Lymphatic Organs**

- Lymph nodes filter out microorganisms and foreign materials taken up by lymphocytes.
- The tonsils, thymus, and spleen also protect your body from harmful microorganisms that enter through your mouth and nose.

**A Disease of the Lymphatic System**

- HIV destroys helper T cells that help make antibodies to fight infections.

### Self Check

1. **Describe** where lymph comes from and how it gets into the lymphatic capillaries.
2. **Explain** how lymphatic organs fight infection.
3. **Sequence** the events that occur when HIV enters the body.
4. **Think Critically** When the amount of fluid in the spaces between cells increases, so does the pressure in these spaces. What do you infer will happen?

#### Applying Skills

5. **Concept Map** The circulatory system and the lymphatic system work together in several ways. Make a concept map comparing the two systems.
6. **Communicate** An infectious microorganism enters your body. In your Science Journal, describe how the lymphatic system protects the body against the microorganism.

## Design Your Own

# Blood Type Reactions

## Real-World Question

Human blood can be classified into four main blood types—A, B, AB, and O. These types are determined by the presence or absence of antigens on the red blood cells. After blood is collected into a transfusion bag, it is tested to determine the blood type. The type is labeled clearly on the bag. Blood is refrigerated to keep it fresh and available for transfusion. What happens when two different blood types are mixed?

### Goals

■ **Design** an experiment that simulates the reactions between different blood types.

■ **Identify** which blood types can donate to which other blood types.

### Possible Materials

simulated blood (10 mL low-fat milk and 10 mL water plus red food coloring)

lemon juice as antigen A (for blood types B and O)

water as antigen A (for blood types A and AB)

droppers

small paper cups

marking pen

10-mL graduated cylinder

### Safety Precautions

**WARNING:** *Do not taste, eat, or drink any materials used in the lab.*

## Form a Hypothesis

Based on your reading and observations, state a hypothesis about how different blood types will react to each other.

## Test Your Hypothesis

**Make a Plan**

1. As a group, agree upon the hypothesis and decide how you will test it. Identify the results that will confirm the hypothesis.

2. **List** the steps you must take and the materials you will need to test your hypothesis. Be specific. Describe exactly what you will do in each step.

3. **Prepare** a data table like the one at the right in your Science Journal to record your observations.

4. Reread the entire experiment to make sure all steps are in logical order.

5. **Identify** constants and variables. Blood type O will be the control.

| Blood Type Reactions | |
|---|---|
| Blood Type | Clumping (Yes or No) |
| A | Do not write in this book. |
| B | |
| AB | |
| O | |

**Follow Your Plan**

1. While doing the experiment, record your observations and complete the data table in your Science Journal.

## Analyze Your Data

1. **Compare** the reactions of each blood type (A, B, AB, and O) when antigen A was added to the blood.

2. **Observe** where clumping took place.

3. **Compare** your results with those of other groups.

4. What was the control factor in this experiment?

5. What were your variables?

## Conclude and Apply

1. Did the results support your hypothesis? Explain.

2. **Predict** what might happen to a person if other antigens are not matched properly.

3. What would happen in an investigation with antigen B added to each blood type?

### Communicating Your Data

**Write** a brief report on how blood is tested to determine blood type. **Describe** why this is important to know before receiving a blood transfusion. **For more help, refer to the** Science Skill Handbook.

# Have a Heart

**Dr. Daniel Hale Williams was a pioneer in open-heart surgery.**

## People didn't always know where blood came from or how it moved through the body

"Ouch!" You prick your finger, and when blood starts to flow out of the cut, you put on a bandage. But if you were a scientist living long ago, you might have also asked yourself some questions: How did your blood get to the tip of your finger? And why and how does it flow through (and sometimes out of!) your body?

As early as the 1500s, a Spanish scientist named Miguel Serveto (mee GEL • ser VE toh) asked that question. His studies led him to the theory that blood circulated throughout the human body, but he didn't know how or why.

About 100 years later, William Harvey, an English doctor, explored Serveto's idea. Harvey studied animals to develop a theory about how the heart and the circulatory system work.

Harvey hypothesized, from his observations of animals, that blood was pumped from the heart throughout the body, and that it returned to the heart and recirculated. He published his ideas in 1628 in his famous book, *On the Motion of the Heart and Blood in Animals.* His theories were correct, but many of Harvey's patients left him. His patients thought his ideas were ridiculous. His theories were correct, and over time, Harvey's book became the basis for all modern research on heart and blood vessels.

## Medical Pioneer

More than two centuries later, another pioneer stepped forward and used Harvey's ideas to change the science frontier again. His name was Dr. Daniel Hale Williams. In 1893, Williams used what he knew about heart and blood circulation to become a new medical pioneer. He performed the first open-heart surgery by removing a knife from the heart of a stabbing victim. He stitched the wound to the fluid-filled sac surrounding the heart, and the patient lived several more years. In 1970, the U.S. recognized Williams by issuing a stamp in his honor.

**Report** Identify a pioneer in science or medicine who has changed our lives for the better. Find out how this person started in the field, and how they came to make an important discovery. Give a presentation to the class.

Science online

**For more information, visit glencoe.com**

## Reviewing Main Ideas

### Section 1 The Circulatory System

1. Arteries carry blood away from the heart. Capillaries allow the exchange of nutrients, oxygen, and wastes in cells. Veins return blood to the heart.

2. Carbon-dioxide-rich blood enters the right atrium, moves to the right ventricle, and then goes to the lungs through the pulmonary artery. Oxygen-rich blood returns to the left atrium, moves to the left ventricle, and then leaves through the aorta.

3. Pulmonary circulation is the path of blood between the heart and lungs. Circulation through the rest of the body is called systemic circulation. Coronary circulation is the flow of blood to tissues of the heart.

### Section 2 Blood

1. Plasma carries nutrients, blood cells, and other substances.

2. Red blood cells carry oxygen and carbon dioxide, platelets form clots, and white blood cells fight infection.

3. A, B, AB, and O blood types are determined by the presence or absence of antigens on red blood cells.

4. Anemia is a disease of red blood cells, in which not enough oxygen is carried to the body's cells.

5. Leukemia is a disease where one or more types of white blood cells are present in excessive numbers. These cells are immature and do not fight infection well.

### Section 3 The Lymphatic System

1. Lymph structures filter blood, produce white blood cells that destroy bacteria and viruses, and destroy worn out blood cells.

2. HIV attacks helper T cells, which are a type of lymphocyte. The person is unable to fight infections well.

## Visualizing Main Ideas

*Copy and complete this concept map on the functions of the parts of the blood.*

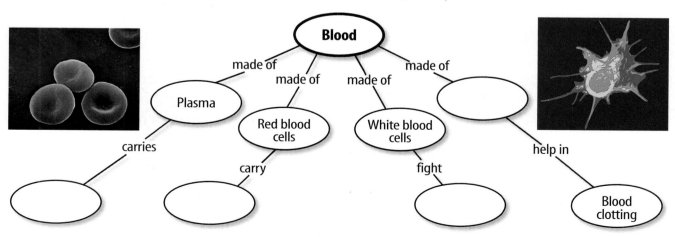

## Using Vocabulary

| | |
|---|---|
| artery p. 422 | lymphocyte p. 434 |
| atrium p. 419 | plasma p. 428 |
| capillary p. 423 | platelet p. 429 |
| coronary circulation p. 419 | pulmonary circulation |
| hemoglobin p. 429 | p. 420 |
| lymph p. 434 | systemic circulation p. 421 |
| lymph node p. 434 | vein p. 422 |
| lymphatic system p. 434 | ventricle p. 419 |

*Fill in the blanks with the correct vocabulary word(s).*

1. The _____ carries blood to the heart.

2. The _____ transports tissue fluid through a network of vessels.

3. _____ is the chemical in red blood cells.

4. _____ are cell fragments.

5. The smallest blood vessels are called the _____.

6. The flow of blood to and from the lungs is called _____.

7. _____ helps protect your body against infections.

8. The largest section of the circulatory system is the _____.

9. _____ are blood vessels that carry blood away from the heart.

10. The two lower chambers of the heart are called the right and left _____.

## Checking Concepts

*Choose the word or phrase that best answers the question.*

11. Where does the exchange of food, oxygen, and wastes occur?
    A) arteries        C) veins
    B) capillaries     D) lymph vessels

12. What is circulation to all body organs called?
    A) coronary        C) systemic
    B) pulmonary       D) organic

13. Where is blood under greatest pressure?
    A) arteries        C) veins
    B) capillaries     D) lymph vessels

14. Which cells fight off infection?
    A) red blood       C) white blood
    B) bone            D) nerve

15. Of the following, which carries oxygen in blood?
    A) red blood cells  C) white blood cells
    B) platelets        D) lymph

16. What is required to clot blood?
    A) plasma          C) platelets
    B) oxygen          D) carbon dioxide

17. What kind of antigen does type O blood have?
    A) A               C) A and B
    B) B               D) no antigen

**Use the figure below to answer question 18.**

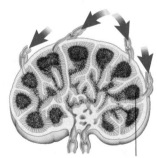

Lymphocytes

18. What is the bean-shaped organ above that filters out microorganisms and foreign materials taken up by lymphocytes?
    A) kidney          C) lung
    B) lymph           D) lymph node

19. What is the largest filtering lymph organ?
    A) spleen          C) tonsil
    B) thymus          D) node

## Thinking Critically

**20. Identify** the following as having oxygen-rich or carbon dioxide-filled blood: *aorta, coronary arteries, coronary veins, inferior vena cava, left atrium, left ventricle, right atrium, right ventricle,* and *superior vena cava.*

**21. Compare and contrast** the three types of blood vessels.

**22. Compare and contrast** the life spans of the red blood cells, white blood cells, and platelets.

**23. Describe** the sequence of blood clotting from the wound to forming a scab.

**24. Compare and contrast** the functions of arteries, veins, and capillaries.

**25. Concept Map** Copy and complete the events-chain concept map showing how lymph moves in your body.

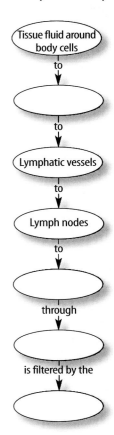

```
Tissue fluid around
    body cells
        | to
        ↓
     (        )
        | to
        ↓
  Lymphatic vessels
        | to
        ↓
    Lymph nodes
        | to
        ↓
     (        )
        | through
        ↓
     (        )
        | is filtered by the
        ↓
     (        )
```

**26. Explain** how the lymphatic system works with the cardiovascular system.

**27. Infer** why cancer of the blood cells or lymph nodes is hard to control.

**28. Explain** why a pulse is usually taken at the neck or wrist, when arteries are distributed throughout the body.

## Performance Activities

**29. Poster** Prepare a poster illustrating heart transplants. Include an explanation of why the patient is given drugs that suppress the immune system and describe the patient's life after the operation.

**30. Scientific Illustrations** Prepare a drawing of the human heart and label its parts.

*Hot Words Hot Topics:* Bk 2 (31) pp. 194, 210; (32) pp. 92, 142–143

## Applying Math

Use the table below to answer question 31.

| Gender and Heart Rate | |
|---|---|
| **Sex** | **Pulse/Minute** |
| Male 1 | 72 |
| Male 2 | 64 |
| Male 3 | 65 |
| Female 1 | 67 |
| Female 2 | 84 |
| Female 3 | 74 |

**31. Heart Rates** Using the table above, find the average heart rate of the three males and the three females. Compare the two averages.

**32. Blood Mass** Calculate how many kilograms of blood is moving through your body, if blood makes up about eight percent of your body's total mass and you weigh 38 kg.

Part I

*Record your answers on the answer sheet provided by your teacher or on a sheet of paper.*

**1** Which of the following is a function of blood?
(1) carry saliva to the mouth
(2) excrete salts from the body
(3) transport nutrients and other substances to cells
(4) remove lymph from around cells

**Use the table below to answer questions 2 and 3.**

| Results from Ashley's Activities | | | |
|---|---|---|---|
| Activity | Pulse Rate (beats/min) | Body Temperature | Degree of Sweating |
| 1 | 80 | 98.6°F | None |
| 2 | 90 | 98.8°F | Minimal |
| 3 | 100 | 98.9°F | Little |
| 4 | 120 | 99.1°F | Moderate |
| 5 | 150 | 99.5°F | Considerable |

**2** Which of the following activities caused Ashley's pulse to be less than 100 beats per minute?
(1) Activity 2     (3) Activity 4
(2) Activity 3     (4) Activity 5

**3** A reasonable hypothesis based on these data, is that during Activity 2, Ashley was probably
(1) sprinting     (3) sitting down
(2) marching     (4) walking slowly

**4** Which of the following activities contributes to cardiovascular disease?
(1) smoking     (3) sleeping
(2) jogging     (4) balanced diet

**5** Where does blood low in oxygen enter first?
(1) right atrium     (3) left ventricle
(2) left atrium     (4) right ventricle

**6** Which of the following is an artery?
(1) left ventricle
(2) aorta
(3) superior vena cava
(4) inferior vena cava

**7.** Which of the following is NOT a part of the lymphatic system?
(1) lymph nodes
(2) valves
(3) heartlike structure
(4) lymph capillaries

**Use the table below to answer questions 8 and 9.**

| Blood Cell Counts (per 1 mm³) | | | |
|---|---|---|---|
| Patient | Red Blood Cells | White Blood Cells | Platelets |
| Normal | 3.58–4.99 million | 3,400–9,600 | 162,000–380,000 |
| Mrs. Stein | 3 million | 8,000 | 400,000 |
| Mr. Chavez | 5 million | 7,500 | 50,000 |

**8** What problem might Mrs. Stein have?
(1) low oxygen levels in tissues
(2) inability to fight disease
(3) poor blood clotting
(4) irregular heart beat

**9** If Mr. Chavez cut himself, what might happen?
(1) minimal bleeding
(2) prolonged bleeding
(3) infection
(4) quick healing

**10** Which lymphatic organ protects your body from harmful microorganisms that enter through your mouth?
(1) spleen
(2) thymus
(3) node
(4) tonsils

( Part II )

*Record your answers on the answer sheet provided by your teacher or on a sheet of paper.*

**11** If red blood cells are made at the rate of 2 million per second in the center of long bones, how many red blood cells are made in one hour?

**12** What would happen if type A blood was given to a person with type O blood?

**Use the illustration below to answer questions 13 and 14.**

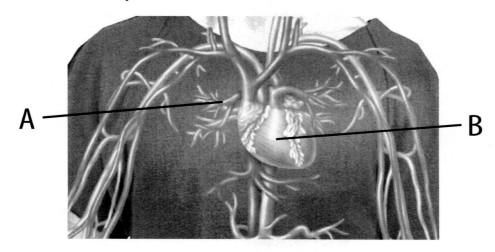

A                                                                 B

**13** What might happen if there was a blood clot blocking vessel "A"?

**14** What might happen if there was a blood clot blocking vessel "B"?

**15** Why don't capillaries have thick, elastic walls?

**16** Why would a cut be dangerous for a person with hemophilia?

**17** Why would a person with leukemia have low numbers of red blood cells, normal white blood cells, and platelets in the blood?

**18** What are some ways to prevent cardiovascular disease?

**19** Compare and contrast diffusion and active transport.

**20** Describe the role of the brain in blood pressure homeostasis. Why is this important?

LE **1.2a:** Each system is composed of organs and tissues which perform specific functions and interact with each other. **1.2b:** Tissues, organs, and organ systems help to provide all cells with nutrients, oxygen, and waste removal. **Also Covered:** LE 1.2c, 1.2d, 1.2e, 1.2j, 5.2a, 5.2b, 5.2e

# Digestion, Respiration, and Excretion

## Playing soccer is hard work.

If you're like most people, when you play an active game like soccer you probably breathe hard and perspire. You need a constant supply of oxygen and energy to keep your body cells functioning. Your body is adapted to meet that need.

**Science Journal**   Write a paragraph describing what you do to help your body recover after an active game.

# Start-Up Activities

## Breathing Rate

Your body can store food and water, but it cannot store much oxygen. Breathing brings oxygen into your body. In the following lab, find out about one factor that can change your breathing rate.

1. Put your hand on the side of your rib cage. Using a watch or clock with a second hand, count the number of breaths you take for 15 s. Multiply this number by four to calculate your normal breathing rate for one minute.

2. Repeat step 1 two more times, then calculate your average breathing rate.

3. Do a physical activity described by your teacher for one minute and repeat step 1 to determine your breathing rate now.

4. Time how long it takes for your breathing rate to return to normal.

5. **Think Critically** In your Science Journal, write a paragraph explaining how breathing rate appears to be related to physical activity.

**FOLDABLES™ Study Organizer**

**Respiration** Make the following Foldable to help identify what you already know, what you want to know, and what you learn about respiration.

**STEP 1** Fold a vertical sheet of paper from side to side. Make the front edge about 1.25 cm shorter than the back edge.

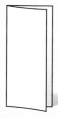

**STEP 2** Turn lengthwise and fold into thirds.

**STEP 3** Unfold and cut only the top layer along both folds to make three tabs. Label each tab.

Know | Want | Learn

**Identify Questions** Before you read the chapter, write *I breathe* under the left tab, and write *Why do I breathe?* under the center tab. As you read the chapter, write the answer you learn under the right tab.

Preview this chapter's content and activities at glencoe.com

# section

# 1

# The Digestive System

## as you read

### *What* You'll Learn

- **Distinguish** the differences between mechanical digestion and chemical digestion.
- **Identify** the organs of the digestive system and what takes place in each.
- **Explain** how homeostasis is maintained in digestion.

### *Why* It's Important

The processes of the digestive system make the food you eat available to your cells.

### ⊙ Review Vocabulary
**bacteria:** one-celled organisms without membrane-bound organelles

### New Vocabulary
- nutrient
- enzyme
- peristalsis
- chyme
- villi

## Functions of the Digestive System

Food is processed in your body in four stages—ingestion, digestion, absorption, and elimination. Whether it is a piece of fruit or an entire meal, all the food you eat is treated to the same processes in your body. As soon as food enters your mouth, or is ingested, digestion begins. Digestion breaks down food so that nutrients (NEW tree unts) can be absorbed and moved into the blood. **Nutrients** are substances in food that provide energy and materials for cell development, growth, and repair. From the blood, these nutrients are transported across the cell membrane to be used by the cell. Unused substances pass out of your body as wastes.

Digestion is mechanical and chemical. Mechanical digestion takes place when food is chewed, mixed, and churned. Chemical digestion occurs when chemical reactions break down food.

## Enzymes

Chemical digestion is possible only because of enzymes (EN zimez). An **enzyme** is a type of protein that speeds up the rate of a chemical reaction in your body. One way enzymes speed up reactions is by reducing the amount of energy necessary for a chemical reaction to begin. If enzymes weren't there to help, the rate of chemical reactions would be too slow. Some reactions might not even happen at all. As shown in **Figure 1,** enzymes work without being changed or used up.

**Figure 1** Enzymes speed up the rate of certain body reactions.
**Explain** *what happens to the enzyme after it separates from the new molecule.*

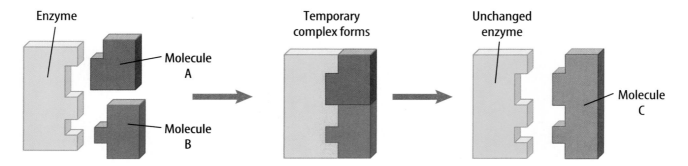

**Enzymes in Digestion** Many enzymes help you digest carbohydrates, proteins, and fats. These enzymes are produced in the salivary glands, stomach, small intestine, and pancreas.

**Reading Check** *What is the role of enzymes in the chemical digestion of food?*

**Other Enzyme Actions** Enzyme-aided reactions are not limited to the digestive process. Enzymes also help speed up chemical reactions responsible for building your body. They are involved in the energy-releasing activities of your muscle and nerve cells. Enzymes also aid in the blood-clotting process. Without enzymes, the chemical reactions in your body would happen too slowly for you to exist.

## Organs of the Digestive System

Your digestive system has two parts—the digestive tract and the accessory organs. The major organs of your digestive tract—mouth, esophagus (ih SAH fuh gus), stomach, small intestine, large intestine, rectum, and anus—are shown in **Figure 2.** Food passes through all of these organs. The tongue, teeth, salivary glands, liver, gallbladder, and pancreas, also shown in **Figure 2,** are the accessory organs. Although food doesn't pass through them, they are important in mechanical and chemical digestion. Your liver, gallbladder, and pancreas produce or store enzymes and other chemicals that help break down food as it passes through the digestive tract.

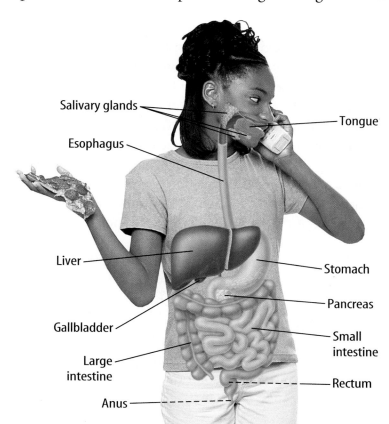

Salivary glands

Tongue

Esophagus

Liver

Stomach

Pancreas

Gallbladder

Small intestine

Large intestine

Rectum

Anus

**Figure 2** The human digestive system can be described as a tube divided into several specialized sections. If stretched out, an adult's digestive system is 6 m to 9 m long.

**Figure 3** About 1.5 L of saliva are produced each day by salivary glands in your mouth. **Describe** *what happens in your mouth when you think about a food you like.*

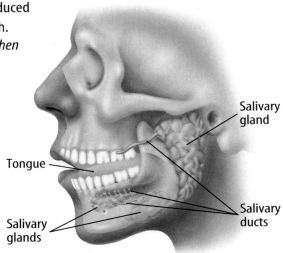

Salivary gland

Tongue

Salivary ducts

Salivary glands

**The Mouth** Mechanical and chemical digestion begin in your mouth. Mechanical digestion happens when you chew your food with your teeth and mix it with your tongue. Chemical digestion begins with the addition of a watery substance called saliva (suh LI vuh), which contains water, mucus, and an enzyme that aids in the breakdown of starch into sugar. Saliva is produced by three sets of glands near your mouth, shown in **Figure 3.** Food mixed with saliva becomes a soft mass and is moved to the back of your mouth by your tongue. It is swallowed and passes into your esophagus. Now ingestion is complete, but the process of digestion continues.

**The Esophagus** Food moving into the esophagus passes over a flap of tissue called the epiglottis (eh puh GLAH tus). This structure automatically covers the opening to the windpipe to prevent food from entering it, otherwise you would choke. Your esophagus is a muscular tube about 25 cm long. No digestion takes place in the esophagus. Smooth muscles in the wall of the esophagus move food downward with a squeezing action. These waves of muscle contractions, called **peristalsis** (per uh STAHL sus), move food through the entire digestive tract. Secretions from the mucous glands in the wall of the esophagus keep food moist.

**The Stomach** The stomach is a muscular bag. When empty, it is somewhat sausage shaped with folds on the inside. As food enters from the esophagus, the stomach expands and the folds smooth out. Mechanical and chemical digestion take place here. Mechanically, food is mixed in the stomach by peristalsis. Chemically, food is mixed with enzymes and strong digestive solutions, such as hydrochloric acid solution, to help break it down.

Specialized cells in the stomach's walls release about two liters of hydrochloric acid solution each day. This solution works with the enzyme pepsin to digest protein and destroys bacteria that are present in food. The stomach also produces mucus, which makes food more slippery and protects the stomach from the strong, digestive solutions. Food is changed in the stomach into a thin, watery liquid called **chyme** (KIME). Slowly, chyme moves out of your stomach and into your small intestine.

> **✔ Reading Check** *Why isn't your stomach digested by the acidic digestive solution?*

**The Small Intestine** Your small intestine, shown in **Figure 4,** is small in diameter, but it measures 4 m to 7 m in length. As chyme leaves your stomach, it enters the first part of your small intestine, called the duodenum (doo AH duh num). Most digestion takes place in your duodenum. Here, bile—a greenish fluid from the liver—is added. The acidic solution from the stomach makes large fat particles float to the top of the chyme. Bile breaks up the large fat particles, similar to the way detergent breaks up grease.

Chemical digestion of carbohydrates, proteins, and fats occurs when a digestive solution from the pancreas is mixed in. This solution contains bicarbonate ions and enzymes. The bicarbonate ions help neutralize the stomach acid that is mixed with chyme. Your pancreas also makes insulin, a hormone that allows glucose to pass from the bloodstream into your cells.

Absorption of broken down food takes place in the small intestine. The wall of the small intestine, shown in **Figure 4,** has many ridges and folds. These folds are covered with fingerlike projections called **villi** (VIH li). Villi increase the surface area of the small intestine, which allows more places for nutrients to be absorbed. Nutrients move into blood vessels within the villi. From here, blood transports the nutrients to all cells of your body. Peristalsis continues to force the remaining undigested and unabsorbed materials slowly into the large intestine.

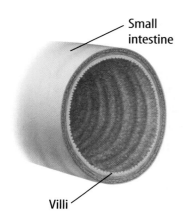

Small intestine

Villi

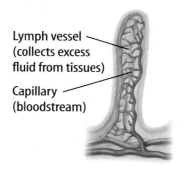

Lymph vessel (collects excess fluid from tissues)

Capillary (bloodstream)

**Figure 4** Hundreds of thousands of densely packed villi give the impression of a velvet cloth surface. If the surface area of your villi could be stretched out, it would cover an area the size of a tennis court.

**Infer** *what would happen to a person's weight if the number of villi were drastically reduced. Why?*

**INTEGRATE Health**

**Large Intestine Bacteria**
The species of bacteria that live in your large intestine are adapted to their habitat. What do you think would happen to the bacteria if their environment were to change? How would this affect your large intestine? Discuss your ideas with a classmate and write your answers in your Science Journal.

**The Large Intestine** When the chyme enters the large intestine, it is still a thin, watery mixture. The large intestine absorbs water from the undigested mass, which helps maintain homeostasis (hoh mee oh STAY sus). Peristalsis usually slows down in the large intestine. After the excess water is absorbed, the remaining undigested materials become more solid. Muscles in the rectum, which is the last section of the large intestine, and the anus control the release of semisolid wastes from the body in the form of feces (FEE seez).

# Bacteria Are Important

Many types of bacteria live in your body. Some bacteria live in many of the organs of your digestive tract including your mouth and large intestine. Some of these bacteria live in a relationship that is beneficial to the bacteria and to your body. The bacteria in your large intestine feed on undigested material like cellulose and make vitamins you need—vitamin K and two B vitamins. Vitamin K is needed for blood clotting. The two B vitamins, niacin and thiamine, are important for your nervous system and for other body functions. Bacterial action also converts bile pigments into new compounds. The breakdown of intestinal materials by bacteria produces gas.

## section 1 review

### Summary

**Functions of the Digestive System**
- Food is processed in four stages—ingestion, digestion, absorption, and elimination.

**Enzymes**
- Enzymes make chemical digestion possible.
- Enzymes are used in other chemical reactions, including blood clotting.

**Organs of the Digestive System**
- In the digestive system, food passes through the mouth, esophagus, stomach, small intestine, large intestine, rectum, and anus.
- Accessory digestive organs help in mechanical and chemical digestion.

**Bacteria Are Important**
- Some bacteria that live in the organs of the digestive tract are helpful to your body.

### Self Check

1. **Compare and contrast** mechanical digestion and chemical digestion.
2. **Describe** the function of each organ through which food passes as it moves through the digestive tract.
3. **Explain** how activities in the large intestine help maintain homeostasis.
4. **Describe** how the accessory organs aid digestion.
5. **Think Critically** Crackers contain starch. Explain why a cracker begins to taste sweet after it is in your mouth for five minutes without being chewed.

#### Applying Skills

6. **Recognize Cause and Effect** What would happen to some of the nutrients in chyme if the pancreas did not secrete its solution into the small intestine?
7. **Communicate** Write a paragraph in your Science Journal explaining what would happen to the mechanical and chemical digestion in a person missing a large portion of his or her stomach.

**LE 5.2b:** Foods contain a variety of substances, which include carbohydrates, fats, vitamins, proteins, minerals, and water. **5.2e:** In order to maintain a balanced state, all organisms have a minimum daily intake of each type of nutrient based on species, size, age, sex, activity, etc. **Also Covered:** LE 5.2a, 5.2d

# Nutrition

## Why do you eat?

You might choose a food because of its taste, because it's readily available, or quickly prepared. However, as much as you don't want to admit it, the nutritional value of and Calories in foods are more important. A Calorie is a measurement of the amount of energy available in food. The amount of food energy a person requires varies with activity level, body weight, age, sex, and natural body efficiency. A chocolate donut might be tasty, quick to eat, and provide plenty of Calories, but it has only some of the nutrients that your body needs.

## Classes of Nutrients

Six kinds of nutrients are available in food—proteins, carbohydrates, fats, vitamins, minerals, and water. Proteins, carbohydrates, vitamins, and fats all contain carbon and are called organic nutrients. Inorganic nutrients, such as water and minerals, do not contain carbon. Foods containing carbohydrates, fats, and proteins need to be digested or broken down before your body can use them. Water, vitamins, and minerals don't require digestion and are absorbed directly into your bloodstream.

**Proteins** Your body uses proteins for replacement and repair of body cells and for growth. Proteins are large molecules that contain carbon, hydrogen, oxygen, nitrogen, and sometimes sulfur. A molecule of protein is made up of a large number of smaller units, or building blocks, called **amino acids.** You can see some sources of proteins in **Figure 5.**

**as you read**

***What* You'll Learn**

- **Distinguish** among the six classes of nutrients.
- **Identify** the importance of each type of nutrient.
- **Explain** the relationship between diet and health.

***Why* It's Important**

You can make healthful food choices if you know what nutrients your body uses daily.

**Review Vocabulary**

**molecule:** the smallest particle of a substance that retains the properties of the substance and is composed of one or more atoms

**New Vocabulary**
- amino acid
- carbohydrate
- vitamin
- mineral

**Figure 5** Meats, poultry, eggs, fish, peas, beans, and nuts are all rich in protein.

**Science Online**

**Topic: Fiber**

Visit glencoe.com for Web links to recent news or magazine articles about the importance of fiber in your diet.

**Activity** In your Science Journal, classify your favorite foods into two groups—*Good source of fiber* and *Little or no fiber.*

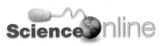

**Protein Building Blocks** Your body needs only 20 amino acids in various combinations to make the thousands of proteins used in your cells. Most of these amino acids can be made in your body's cells, but eight of them cannot. These eight are called essential amino acids. They have to be supplied by the foods you eat. Complete proteins provide all of the essential amino acids. Eggs, milk, cheese, and meat contain complete proteins. Incomplete proteins are missing one or more of the essential amino acids. If you are a vegetarian, you can get all of the essential amino acids by eating a wide variety of protein-rich vegetables, fruits, and grains.

**Carbohydrates** Study the nutrition label on several boxes of cereal. You'll notice that the number of grams of carbohydrates found in a typical serving of cereal is higher than the amounts of the other nutrients. **Carbohydrates** (kar boh HI drayts) usually are the main sources of energy for your body.

Three types of carbohydrates are sugar, starch, and fiber, shown in **Figure 6.** Sugars are called simple carbohydrates. You're probably most familiar with table sugar. However, fruits, honey, and milk also contain forms of sugar. Your cells break down glucose, a simple sugar.

The other two types of carbohydrates—starch and fiber—are called complex carbohydrates. Starch is found in potatoes and foods made from grains such as pasta. Starches are made up of many simple sugars. Fiber, such as cellulose, is found in the cell walls of plant cells. Foods like whole-grain breads and cereals, beans, peas, and other vegetables and fruits are good sources of fiber. Because different types of fiber are found in foods, you should eat a variety of fiber-rich plant foods. You cannot digest fiber, but it is needed to keep your digestive system running smoothly.

**Fats** The term *fat* has developed a negative meaning for some people. However, fats, also called lipids, are necessary because they provide energy and help your body absorb vitamins. Fat tissue cushions your internal organs. A major part of every cell membrane is made up of a type of fat.

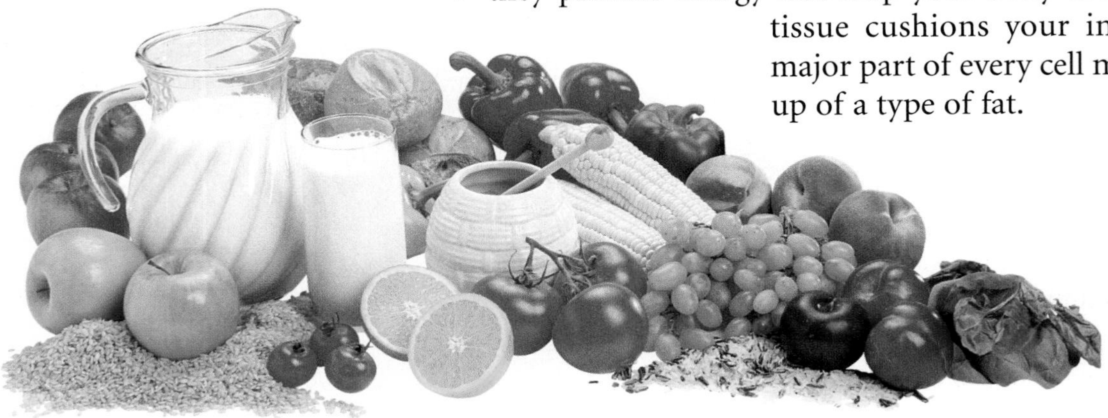

**Figure 6** These foods contain carbohydrates that provide energy for all the things that you do. **Describe** *the role of carbohydrates in your body.*

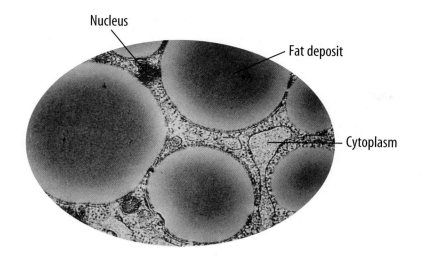

Nucleus

Fat deposit

Cytoplasm

**Figure 7** Fat is stored in certain cells in your body. Fat deposits push the cytoplasm and nucleus to the edge of the cell.

A gram of fat can release more than twice as much energy as a gram of carbohydrate can. Because fat is a good storage unit for energy, excess energy from the foods you eat is converted to fat and stored for later use, as shown in **Figure 7.**

**Reading Check** *Why is fat a good storage unit for energy?*

Fats are classified as unsaturated or saturated based on their chemical structure. Unsaturated fats are usually liquid at room temperature. Vegetable oils as well as fats found in seeds are unsaturated fats. Saturated fats are found in meats, animal products, and some plants and are usually solid at room temperature. Saturated fats have been associated with high levels of blood cholesterol. Your body makes cholesterol in your liver. Cholesterol is part of the cell membrane in all of your cells. However, a diet high in cholesterol may result in deposits forming on the inside walls of blood vessels. These deposits can block the blood supply to organs and increase blood pressure. This can lead to heart disease and strokes.

**Vitamins** Your bone cells need vitamin D to use calcium, and your blood needs vitamin K in order to clot. **Vitamins** are organic nutrients needed in small quantities for growth, regulating body functions, and preventing some diseases.

Vitamins are classified into two groups. Some vitamins dissolve easily in water and are called water-soluble vitamins. They are not stored by your body so you have to consume them daily. Other vitamins dissolve only in fat and are called fat-soluble vitamins. These vitamins are stored by your body. Although you eat or drink most vitamins, some are made by your body. Vitamin D is made when your skin is exposed to sunlight. Recall that vitamin K and two of the B vitamins are made in your large intestine with the help of bacteria that live there.

## Mini LAB

### Comparing the Fat Content of Foods

**Procedure**

1. Collect three pieces of each of the following foods: **potato chips; pretzels; peanuts;** and **small cubes of fruits, cheese, vegetables,** and **meat.**
2. Place the food items on a piece of **brown grocery bag.** Label the paper with the name of each food. Do not taste the foods.
3. Allow foods to sit for 30 min.
4. Remove the items, properly dispose of them, and observe the paper.

**Analysis**

1. Which items left a translucent (greasy) mark? Which left a wet mark?
2. How are the foods that left a greasy mark on the paper alike?
3. Use this test to determine which other foods contain fats. A greasy mark means the food contains fat. A wet mark means the food contains a lot of water.

## Table 1  Minerals

| Mineral | Health Effect | Food Sources |
|---|---|---|
| Calcium | strong bones and teeth, blood clotting, muscle and nerve activity | dairy products, eggs, green leafy vegetables, soy |
| Phosphorus | strong bones and teeth, muscle contraction, stores energy | cheese, meat, cereal |
| Potassium | balance of water in cells, nerve impulse conduction, muscle contraction | bananas, potatoes, nuts, meat, oranges |
| Sodium | fluid balance in tissues, nerve impulse conduction | meat, milk, cheese, salt, beets, carrots, nearly all foods |
| Iron | oxygen is transported in hemoglobin by red blood cells | red meat, raisins, beans, spinach, eggs |
| Iodine (trace) | thyroid activity, metabolic stimulation | seafood, iodized salt |

**INTEGRATE Social Studies**

**Salt Mines** The mineral halite is processed to make table salt. In the United States, most salt comes from underground mines. Research to find the location of these mines, then label them on a map.

**Living Environment**

**5.2b Classify** each of the six kinds of nutrients available in food as organic or inorganic. Support your reasoning with an example of each.

**Minerals** Inorganic nutrients—nutrients that lack carbon and regulate many chemical reactions in your body—are called **minerals.** Of about 14 minerals that your body uses, calcium and phosphorus are used in the largest amounts for a variety of body functions. One of these functions is the formation and maintenance of bone. Some minerals, called trace minerals, are required only in small amounts. Copper and iodine usually are listed as trace minerals. Minerals are not used by the body as a source of energy. However, they do serve many different functions. Several minerals, their health effects, and some food sources for them are listed in **Table 1.**

**Reading Check** *Why is copper considered a trace mineral?*

**Water** Next to oxygen, water is the most important factor for survival. Different organisms need different amounts of water to survive. You could live for a few weeks without food but for only a few days without water because your cells need water to carry out their work. Most of the nutrients you have studied in this chapter can't be used by your body unless they are carried in a solution. This means that they have to be dissolved in water. In cells, chemical reactions take place in solutions.

The human body is about 60 percent water by mass. About two-thirds of your body water is located in your body cells. Water also is found around cells and in body fluids such as blood. **Table 2** shows how your body loses water every day. To replace water lost each day, you need to drink about 2 L of liquids. However, drinking liquids isn't the only way to supply cells with water. Most foods have more water than you realize. An apple is about 80 percent water, and many meats are 90 percent water.

**Why do you get thirsty?** Your body is made up of systems that operate together. When your body needs to replace lost water, messages are sent to your brain that result in a feeling of thirst. Drinking water satisfies your thirst and usually restores the body's homeostasis. When homeostasis is restored, the signal to the brain stops and you no longer feel thirsty.

| Table 2  Water Loss | |
|---|---|
| **Method of Loss** | **Amount (mL/day)** |
| Exhaled air | 350 |
| Feces | 150 |
| Skin (mostly as sweat) | 500 |
| Urine | 1,500 |

## Food Groups

Because no naturally occurring food has every nutrient, you need to eat a variety of foods. Nutritionists have developed a simple system, called the food pyramid, shown in **Figure 8,** to help people select foods that supply all the nutrients needed for energy and growth. The recommended daily amount for each food group will supply your body with the nutrients it needs for good health.

**Figure 8** The pyramid shape reminds you that you should consume more servings from the bread and cereal group than from other groups.
**Analyze** *Where should the least number of servings come from?*

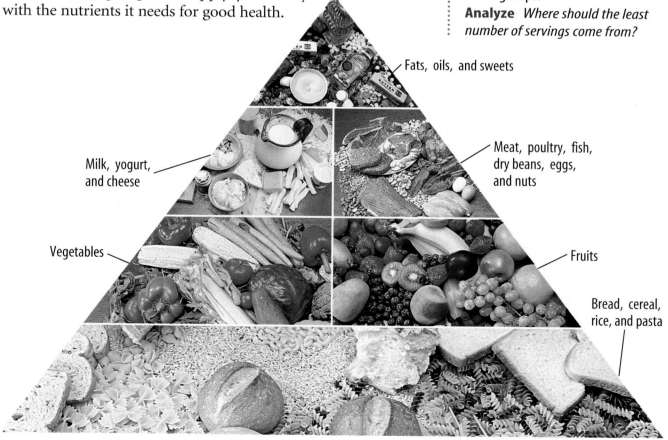

Fats, oils, and sweets

Milk, yogurt, and cheese

Meat, poultry, fish, dry beans, eggs, and nuts

Vegetables

Fruits

Bread, cereal, rice, and pasta

**Figure 9** The information on a food label can help you decide what to eat.

**Nutrition Facts**
Serving Size 1 Meal

| Amount Per Serving | | |
|---|---|---|
| **Calories** 330 | Calories from Fat 60 | |
| | | **% Daily Value*** |
| **Total Fat** 7g | | **10%** |
| Saturated Fat 3.5g | | **17%** |
| Polyunsaturated Fat 1g | | |
| Monounsaturated Fat 2.5g | | |
| **Cholesterol** 35mg | | **12%** |
| **Sodium** 460mg | | **19%** |
| **Total Carbohydrate** 52g | | **18%** |
| Dietary Fiber 6g | | **24%** |
| Sugars 17g | | |
| **Protein** 15g | | |

| Vitamin A 15% | • | Vitamin C 70% |
|---|---|---|
| Calcium 4% | • | Iron 10% |

*	Percent Daily Values are based on a 2,000 calorie diet. Your daily values may be higher or lower depending on your calorie needs.

| | Calories | 2,000 | 2,500 |
|---|---|---|---|
| Total Fat | Less than | 65g | 80g |
| Sat Fat | Less than | 20g | 25g |
| Cholesterol | Less than | 300mg | 300mg |
| Sodium | Less than | 2,400mg | 2,400mg |
| Total Carbohydrate | | 300g | 375g |
| Dietary Fiber | | 25g | 30g |

**Daily Servings** Each day you should eat six to eleven servings from the bread and cereal group, three to five servings from the vegetable group, two to four servings from the fruit group, two to three servings from the milk group, and two to three servings from the meat and beans group. Only small amounts of fats, oils, and sweets should be consumed.

The size of a serving is different for different foods. For example, a slice of bread or one ounce of ready-to-eat cereal is a bread and cereal group serving. One cup of raw leafy vegetables or one-half cup of cooked or chopped raw vegetables make a serving from the vegetable group. One medium apple, banana, or orange, one-half cup of canned fruit, or three-quarter cup of fruit juice is a fruit serving. A serving from the milk group can be one cup of milk or yogurt. Two ounces of cooked lean meat, one-half cup of cooked dry beans, one egg, or two tablespoons of peanut butter counts as a serving from the meat and beans group.

**Food Labels** The nutritional facts found on all packaged foods make it easier to make healthful food choices. These labels, as shown in **Figure 9,** can help you plan meals that supply the daily recommended amounts of nutrients and meet special dietary requirements (for example, a low-fat diet).

## section 2 review

### Summary

**Why do you eat?**
- Nutrients in food provide energy and materials for cell development, growth, and repair.

**Classes of Nutrients**
- Six kinds of nutrients are found in food—proteins, carbohydrates, fats, vitamins, minerals, and water.
- Proteins are used for growth and repair, carbohydrates provide energy, and fats store energy and cushion organs.
- Vitamins and minerals regulate body functions.
- Next to oxygen, water is the most important factor for your survival.

**Food Groups**
- The food pyramid and nutritional labels can help you choose foods that supply all the nutrients you need for energy and growth.

### Self Check

1. **List** one example of a food source for each of the six classes of nutrients.
2. **Explain** how your body uses each class of nutrients.
3. **Discuss** how food choices can positively and negatively affect your health.
4. **Explain** the importance of water in the body.
5. **Think Critically** What foods from each food group would provide a balanced breakfast? Explain.

#### Applying Skills

6. **Interpret Data** Nutritional information can be found on the labels of most foods. Interpret the labels found on three different types of food products.
7. **Use a Spreadsheet** Make a spreadsheet of the minerals listed in **Table 1.** Use reference books to gather information about minerals and add these to the table: *sulfur, magnesium, copper, manganese, cobalt,* and *zinc.*

# Identifying Vitamin C C⊕ntent

Vitamin C is found in many fruits and vegetables. Oranges have a high vitamin C content. Try this lab to test the vitamin C content in different orange juices.

## ● Real-World Question

Which orange juice contains the most vitamin C?

### Goals

■ **Observe** the vitamin C content of different orange juices.

### Materials

test tube (4)  2% tincture of iodine
*paper cups*  dropper
test-tube rack  cornstarch
masking tape  triple-beam balance
wooden stirrer (13)  weighing paper
graduated cylinder  water (50 mL)
*graduated container*  glass-marking pencil
dropper bottles (4) containing orange juice that is:
    (1) freshly squeezed  (3) canned
    (2) from frozen concentrate  (4) in a carton

* Alternate materials

### Safety Precautions

**WARNING:** *Do not taste any of the juices. Iodine is poisonous and can stain skin and clothing. It is an irritant and can cause damage if it comes in contact with your eyes. Notify your teacher if a spill occurs.*

## ● Procedure

1. Make a data table like the example shown to record your observations.

2. Label four test tubes 1 through 4 and place them in the test-tube rack.

| Drops of Iodine Needed to Change Color | | | | |
|---|---|---|---|---|
| Juice | Trial | | | Average |
| | 1 | 2 | 3 | |
| 1 Fresh juice | | | | |
| 2 Frozen juice | *Do not write in this book.* | | | |
| 3 Canned juice | | | | |
| 4 Carton juice | | | | |

3. Measure and pour 5 mL of juice from bottle 1 into test tube 1, 5 mL from bottle 2 into test tube 2, 5 mL from bottle 3 into test tube 3, and 5 mL from bottle 4 into test tube 4.

4. Measure 0.3 g of cornstarch, then put it in a container. Slowly mix in 50 mL of water until the cornstarch completely dissolves.

5. Add 5 mL of the cornstarch solution to each of the four test tubes. Stir well.

6. Add iodine to test tube 1, one drop at a time. Stir after each drop. Record the number of drops it takes for the juice to change to a purple color. The more vitamin C that is present, the more drops it takes to change color.

7. Repeat step 6 with test tubes 2, 3, and 4.

8. Empty and clean the test tubes. Repeat steps 3 through 7 two more times, then average your results.

9. Dispose of all materials as directed by your teacher. Wash your hands thoroughly.

## ● Conclude and Apply

1. **Compare and contrast** the amount of vitamin C in the orange juices tested.

2. **Infer** why the amount of vitamin C varies in the orange juices.

LE 1.2d: During respiration, cells use oxygen to release the energy stored in food. The respiratory system supplies oxygen and removes carbon dioxide (gas exchange). **Also Covered:** LE 1.2a, 1.2j

# section 3

# The Respiratory System

## as you read

### *What* You'll Learn

- **Describe** the functions of the respiratory system.
- **Explain** how oxygen and carbon dioxide are exchanged in the lungs and in tissues.
- **Identify** the pathway of air in and out of the lungs.
- **Explain** the effects of smoking on the respiratory system.

### *Why* It's Important

Your body's cells depend on your respiratory system to supply oxygen and remove carbon dioxide.

### ⚙ Review Vocabulary

**diaphragm:** muscle beneath the lungs that contracts and relaxes to move gases in and out of the body

### New Vocabulary

- larynx
- bronchi
- trachea
- alveoli

## Functions of the Respiratory System

Can you imagine an astronaut walking on the Moon without a space suit or a diver exploring the ocean without scuba gear? Of course not. They couldn't survive in either location under those conditions because humans need to breathe air.

People often confuse the terms *breathing* and *respiration.* Breathing is the movement of the chest that brings air into the lungs and removes waste gases. The air entering the lungs contains oxygen. It passes from the lungs into the circulatory system because there is less oxygen in blood when it enters the lungs than in cells of the lungs.

Blood carries oxygen and glucose from digested food to individual cells. In cells, they are raw materials for a series of chemical reactions called cellular respiration. Without oxygen, cellular respiration cannot occur. Cellular respiration results in the release of energy from glucose. Water and carbon dioxide are waste products of cellular respiration. Blood carries them back to the lungs. As shown in **Figure 10,** exhaling, or breathing out, eliminates waste carbon dioxide and some water molecules.

✓ **Reading Check** *What is cellular respiration?*

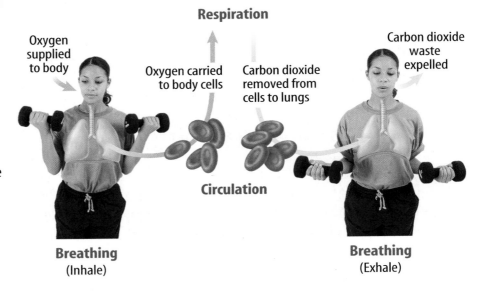

**Figure 10** Several processes are involved in how the body obtains, transports, and uses oxygen.

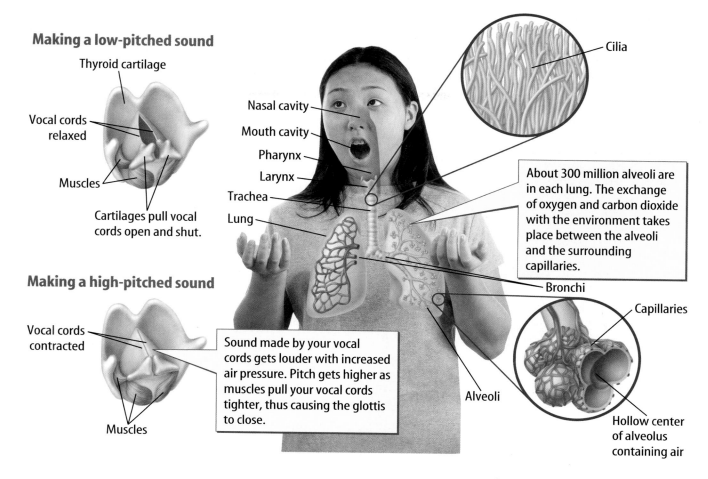

**Making a low-pitched sound**

Thyroid cartilage

Vocal cords relaxed

Muscles

Cartilages pull vocal cords open and shut.

**Making a high-pitched sound**

Vocal cords contracted

Muscles

Sound made by your vocal cords gets louder with increased air pressure. Pitch gets higher as muscles pull your vocal cords tighter, thus causing the glottis to close.

Nasal cavity

Mouth cavity

Pharynx

Larynx

Trachea

Lung

Cilia

About 300 million alveoli are in each lung. The exchange of oxygen and carbon dioxide with the environment takes place between the alveoli and the surrounding capillaries.

Bronchi

Capillaries

Alveoli

Hollow center of alveolus containing air

**Figure 11** Air can enter the body through the nostrils and the mouth.

**Explain** *an advantage of having air enter through the nostrils.*

# Organs of the Respiratory System

The respiratory system, shown in **Figure 11,** is made up of structures and organs that help move oxygen into the body and waste gases out of the body. Air enters your body through two openings in your nose called nostrils or through the mouth. Fine hairs inside the nostrils trap particles from the air. Air then passes through the nasal cavity, where it gets moistened and warmed by the body's heat. Glands that produce sticky mucus line the nasal cavity. The mucus traps particles that were not trapped by nasal hairs. This process helps filter and clean the air you breathe. Tiny, hairlike structures, called cilia (SIH lee uh), sweep mucus and trapped material to the back of the throat where it can be swallowed.

**Pharynx** Warmed, moist air then enters the pharynx (FER ingks), which is a tubelike passageway for food, liquids, and air. At the lower end of the pharynx is the epiglottis. When you swallow, your epiglottis folds down, which allows food or liquids to enter your esophagus instead of your airway. What do you think has happened if you begin to choke?

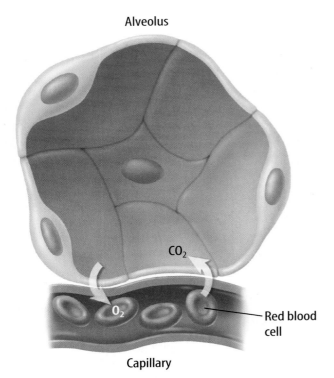

Alveolus

CO₂

O₂

Red blood cell

Capillary

**Figure 12** The thin capillary walls allow gases to be exchanged easily between the alveoli and the capillaries.
**Name** *the two gases that are exchanged by the capillaries and alveoli.*

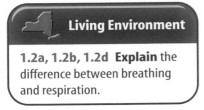

**Living Environment**

**1.2a, 1.2b, 1.2d Explain** the difference between breathing and respiration.

**Larynx and Trachea** Next, the air moves into your larynx (LER ingks). The **larynx** is the airway to which two pairs of horizontal folds of tissue, called vocal cords, are attached, as shown in **Figure 11** on the previous page. Forcing air between the cords causes them to vibrate and produce sounds. When you speak, muscles tighten or loosen your vocal cords, resulting in different sounds. Your brain coordinates the movement of the muscles in your throat, tongue, cheeks, and lips when you talk, sing, or just make noise. Your teeth also are involved in forming letter sounds and words.

From the larynx, air moves into the **trachea** (TRAY kee uh). Strong, C-shaped rings of cartilage prevent the trachea from collapsing. It is lined with mucous membranes and cilia, also shown in **Figure 11** on the previous page. The mucous membranes trap dust, bacteria, and pollen. The cilia move the mucus upward, where it is either swallowed or expelled from the nose or mouth. Why must the trachea stay open all the time?

**Bronchi and the Lungs** Air is carried into your lungs by two short tubes called **bronchi** (BRAHN ki) (singular, *bronchus*) at the lower end of the trachea. Within the lungs, the bronchi branch into smaller and smaller tubes. The smallest tubes are called bronchioles (BRAHN kee ohlz). At the end of each bronchiole are clusters of tiny, thin-walled sacs called **alveoli** (al VEE uh li) (singular, *alveolus*). Air passes into the bronchi, then into the bronchioles, and finally into the alveoli. Lungs are masses of alveoli, like the one shown in **Figure 12**, arranged in grapelike clusters. The capillaries surround the alveoli like a net.

The exchange of oxygen and carbon dioxide takes place between the alveoli and capillaries. The walls of the alveoli and capillaries are only one cell thick, as shown in **Figure 12.** Oxygen moves through the cell membranes of alveoli and through cell membranes of the capillaries into the blood. In blood, oxygen is picked up by hemoglobin (HEE muh gloh bun), a molecule in red blood cells, and carried to all body cells. At the same time, carbon dioxide and other cellular wastes leave the body cells and move into capillaries. Then they are carried by the blood to the lungs. In the lungs, waste gases move through cell membranes from capillaries into alveoli. Then waste gases leave the body when you exhale.

# Why do you breathe?

Signals from your brain tell the muscles in your chest and abdomen to contract and relax. You don't have to think about breathing to breathe, just like your heart beats without you telling it to beat. Your brain can change your breathing rate depending on the amount of carbon dioxide present in your blood. If a lot of carbon dioxide is present, your breathing rate increases. It decreases if less carbon dioxide is in your blood. You do have some control over your breathing—you can hold your breath if you want to. Eventually, your brain will respond to the buildup of carbon dioxide in your blood and signal your chest and abdomen muscles to work automatically. You will breathe whether you want to or not.

**Inhaling and Exhaling** Breathing is partly the result of changes in volume and resulting air pressure. Under normal conditions, a gas moves from an area of higher pressure to an area of lower pressure. When you squeeze an empty, soft-plastic bottle, air is pushed out. This happens because air pressure outside the top of the bottle is less than the pressure you create inside the bottle when you changed its volume. As you release your grip on the bottle, the air pressure inside the bottle becomes less than it is outside the bottle because the bottle's volume changed. Air rushes back in, and the bottle returns to its original shape.

Your lungs work in a way similar to the squeezed bottle. Your diaphragm (DI uh fram) contracts and relaxes, changing the volume of the chest, which helps move gases into and out of your lungs. **Figure 13** illustrates breathing.

**✓ Reading Check** *How does your diaphragm help you breathe?*

When a person's airway is blocked, a rescuer can use abdominal thrusts, as shown in **Figure 14,** to save the life of the choking victim.

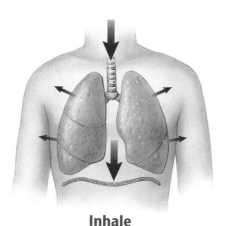
**Inhale**

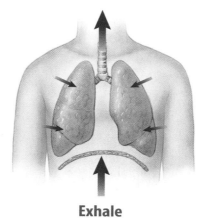
**Exhale**

## Mini LAB

### Comparing Surface Area

**Procedure** 🖳
1. Stand a **bathroom-tissue cardboard tube** in an **empty bowl.**
2. Drop **marbles** into the tube, filling it to the top.
3. Count the number of marbles used.
4. Repeat steps 2 and 3 two more times. Calculate the average number of marbles needed to fill the tube.
5. The tube's inside surface area is approximately 161.29 cm². Each marble has a surface area of approximately 8.06 cm². Calculate the surface area of the average number of marbles.

**Analysis**
1. Compare the inside surface area of the tube with the surface area of the average number of marbles needed to fill the tube.
2. If the tube represents a bronchus, what do the marbles represent?
3. Using this model, explain what makes gas exchange in the lungs efficient.

*Try at Home*

**Figure 13** Your lungs inhale and exhale about 500 mL of air with an average breath. This can increase to 2,000 mL of air per breath when you do strenuous activity.

## Figure 14

When food or other objects become lodged in the trachea, airflow between the lungs and the mouth and nasal cavity is blocked. Death can occur in minutes. However, prompt action by someone can save the life of a choking victim. The rescuer uses abdominal thrusts to force the victim's diaphragm up. This decreases the volume of the chest cavity and forces air up in the trachea. The result is a rush of air that dislodges and expels the food or other object. The victim can breathe again. This technique is shown at right and should only be performed in emergency situations.

Food is lodged in the victim's trachea.

The rescuer places her fist against the victim's stomach.

The rescuer's second hand adds force to the fist.

**A** The rescuer stands behind the choking victim and wraps her arms around the victim's upper abdomen. She places a fist (thumb side in) against the victim's stomach. The fist should be below the ribs and above the navel.

An upward thrust dislodges the food from victim's trachea.

**B** With a violent, sharp movement, the rescuer thrusts her fist up into the area below the ribs. This action should be repeated as many times as necessary.

# Diseases and Disorders of the Respiratory System

 If you were asked to make a list of some things that can harm your respiratory system, you probably would put smoking at the top. As you can see in **Table 3,** many serious diseases are related to smoking. The chemical substances in tobacco—nicotine and tars—are poisons and can destroy cells. The high temperatures, smoke, and carbon monoxide produced when tobacco burns also can injure a smoker's cells. Even if you are a nonsmoker, inhaling smoke from tobacco products—called secondhand smoke—is unhealthy and has the potential to harm your respiratory system. Smoking, polluted air, coal dust, and asbestos (as BES tus) have been related to respiratory problems such as asthma (AZ muh), bronchitis (brahn KI tus), emphysema (em fuh SEE muh), and cancer.

**Respiratory Infections** Bacteria, viruses, and other microorganisms can cause infections that affect any of the organs of the respiratory system. The common cold usually affects the upper part of the respiratory system—from the nose to the pharynx. The cold virus also can cause irritation and swelling in the larynx, trachea, and bronchi. The cilia that line the trachea and bronchi can be damaged. However, cilia usually heal rapidly.

**Chronic Bronchitis** When bronchial tubes are irritated and swell and too much mucus is produced, a disease called bronchitis develops. Many cases of bronchitis clear up within a few weeks, but the disease sometimes lasts for a long time. When this happens, it is called chronic (KRAH nihk) bronchitis.

**Emphysema** A disease in which the alveoli in the lungs enlarge is called emphysema. When cells in the alveoli are reddened and swollen, an enzyme is released that causes the walls of the alveoli to break down. As a result, alveoli can't push air out of the lungs, so less oxygen moves into the bloodstream from the alveoli. When blood becomes low in oxygen and high in carbon dioxide, shortness of breath occurs.

| Table 3 Smokers' Risk of Death from Disease | |
|---|---|
| **Disease** | **Smokers' Risk Compared to Nonsmokers' Risk** |
| Lung cancer | 23 times higher for males; 11 times higher for females |
| Chronic bronchitis and emphysema | 5 times higher |
| Heart disease | 2 times higher |

**Topic: Secondhand Smoke**
Visit glencoe.com for Web links to information about the health aspects of secondhand smoke.

**Activity** Write a paragraph in your Science Journal summarizing the possible effects of secondhand smoke on your health.

## Living Environment

**1.2j** *Disease breaks down the structures of functions of an organism. Some diseases are the result of failures of the system. Other diseases are the result of damage by infection from other organisms.* **List** *some of the diseases and disorders of the respiratory system. Briefly discuss how to avoid harm to your respiratory system from these diseases and disorders.*

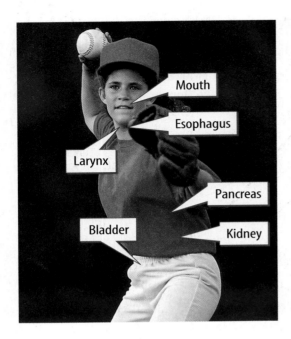

**Figure 15** More than 85 percent of all lung cancer is related to smoking. Smoking also can play a part in the development of cancer in other body organs indicated above.

**Lung Cancer** The third leading cause of death in men and women in the United States is lung cancer. Inhaling the tar in cigarette smoke is the greatest contributing factor to lung cancer. In the body, tar and other ingredients found in smoke act as carcinogens (kar SIH nuh junz). Carcinogens are substances that can cause an uncontrolled growth of cells. In the lungs, this is called lung cancer. Lung cancer is not easy to detect in its early stages. Smoking also has been linked to the development of cancers of the mouth, esophagus, larynx, pancreas, kidney, and bladder. See **Figure 15.**

**Asthma** Shortness of breath, wheezing, or coughing can occur in a lung disorder called asthma. When a person has an asthma attack, the bronchial tubes contract quickly. Inhaling medicine that relaxes the bronchial tubes is the usual treatment for an asthma attack. Asthma can be an allergic reaction. An allergic reaction occurs when the body overreacts to a foreign substance. An asthma attack can result from breathing certain substances such as cigarette smoke or certain plant pollen, eating certain foods, or stress in a person's life.

## section 3 review

### Summary

**Functions of the Respiratory System**

- Breathing moves the chest to bring air into and remove wastes from the lungs.
- Cellular respiration uses oxygen to release energy from glucose.

**Organs of the Respiratory System**

- Air flows from your nostrils or mouth through the pharynx, larynx, trachea, bronchi, and into the alveoli of your lungs.
- Alveoli and capillaries exchange oxygen and carbon dioxide.

**Why do you breathe?**

- Your brain sends signals to your chest and abdominal muscles to contract and relax, which controls breathing rate.

**Diseases of the Respiratory System**

- Problems of the respiratory system include chronic bronchitis, emphysema, and lung cancer.

### Self Check

1. **State** the main function of the respiratory system.
2. **Describe** the exchange of oxygen, carbon dioxide, and other waste gases in the lungs and body tissues.
3. **Explain** how air moves into and out of the lungs.
4. **Describe** the effects of smoking on the respiratory and circulatory systems.
5. **Think Critically** How is the work of the digestive and circulatory systems related to the respiratory system?

#### Applying Skills

6. **Research Information** Nicotine in tobacco is a poison. Using library references, find out how nicotine affects the body.
7. **Communicate** Use references to find out about lung disease common among coal miners, stonecutters, and sandblasters. Find out what safety measures are required now for these trades. In your Science Journal, write a paragraph about these safety measures.

**section**

**4**

**LE 1.2e:** The excretory system functions in the disposal of dissolved waste molecules, the elimination of liquid and gaseous wastes, and the removal of excess heat energy. **Also Covered:** 1.2a

# The Excretory System

## Functions of the Excretory System

It's your turn to take out the trash. You carry the bag outside and put it in the trash can. The next day, you bring out another bag of trash, but the trash can is full. When trash isn't collected, it piles up. Just as trash needs to be removed from your home to keep it livable, your body must eliminate wastes to remain healthy. Undigested material is eliminated by your large intestine. Waste gases are eliminated through the combined efforts of your circulatory and respiratory systems. Some salts are eliminated when you sweat. These systems function together as parts of your excretory system. If wastes aren't eliminated, toxic substances build up and damage organs. If not corrected, serious illness or death occurs.

## The Urinary System

**Figure 16** shows how the urinary system functions as a part of the excretory system. The urinary system rids the blood of wastes produced by the cells. It controls blood volume by removing excess water produced by body cells during cellular respiration. The urinary system also balances the amounts of certain salts and water that must be present for all cellular activities.

### as you read

*What* **You'll Learn**

- **Distinguish** between the excretory and urinary systems.
- **Describe** how the kidneys work.
- **Explain** what happens when urinary organs don't work.

*Why* **It's Important**

The urinary system helps clean your blood of cellular wastes.

⊙ **Review Vocabulary**
**capillary:** blood vessel that connects arteries and veins

**New Vocabulary**
- ● nephron      ● bladder
- ● ureter

**Figure 16** The urinary, digestive, and respiratory systems, and the skin, make up the excretory system.

| **Digestive System** Food and liquid in | **Respiratory System** Oxygen in | **Skin** | **Urinary System** Water and salts in |
|---|---|---|---|

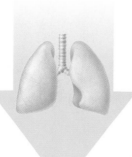

| Water and undigested food out | Carbon dioxide and water out | Salt and some organic substances out | Excess water, metabolic wastes, and salts out |
|---|---|---|---|

**Excretion**

**Regulating Fluid Levels** To stay in good health, the fluid levels within the body must be balanced and normal blood pressure must be maintained. An area in the brain, the hypothalamus (hi poh THA luh mus), constantly monitors the amount of water in the blood. When the brain detects too much water in the blood, the hypothalamus releases a lesser amount of a specific hormone. This signals the kidneys to return less water to the blood and increase the amount of urine that is excreted.

**✔ Reading Check** *How does the urinary system control the volume of water in the blood?*

**Organs of the Urinary System** Excretory organs is another name for the organs of the urinary system. The main organs of the urinary system are two bean-shaped kidneys. Kidneys are located on the back wall of the abdomen at about waist level. The kidneys filter blood that contains wastes collected from cells. In approximately 5 min, all of the blood in your body passes through the kidneys. The red-brown color of the kidneys is due to their enormous blood supply. In **Figure 17,** you can see that blood enters the kidneys through a large artery and leaves through a large vein.

**Figure 17** The urinary system removes wastes from the blood. The urinary system includes the kidneys, the bladder, and the connecting tubes.
**Explain** *how the kidneys help the body balance its fluid levels.*

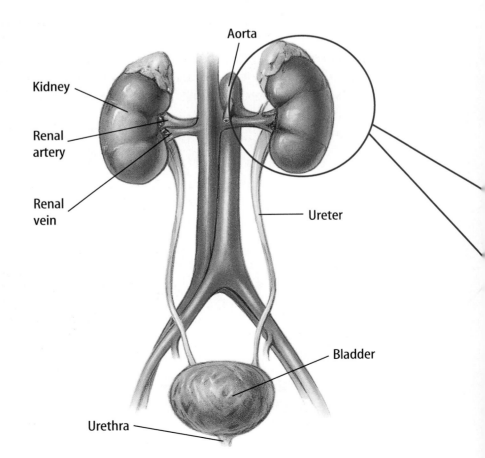

Aorta

Kidney

Renal artery

Renal vein

Ureter

Bladder

Urethra

**Filtration in the Kidney** A two-stage filtration system is an accurate description of a kidney, shown in **Figure 18.** It is made up of about one million tiny filtering units called **nephrons** (NE frahnz), also shown in **Figure 18.** Each nephron has a cuplike structure and a tubelike structure called a duct. Blood moves from a renal artery to capillaries in the cuplike structure. The first filtration occurs when water, sugar, salt, and wastes from the blood pass into the cuplike structure. Left behind in the blood are the red blood cells and proteins. Next, liquid in the cuplike structure is squeezed into a narrow tubule.

Capillaries that surround the tubule perform the second filtration. Most of the water, sugar, and salt are reabsorbed and returned to the blood. These collection capillaries merge to form small veins, which merge to form a renal vein in each kidney. Purified blood is returned to the main circulatory system. The liquid left behind flows into collecting tubules in each kidney. This wastewater, or urine, contains excess water, salts, and other wastes that are not reabsorbed by the body. An average-sized person produces about 1 L of urine per day.

**Urine Collection and Release** The urine in each collecting tubule drains into a funnel-shaped area of each kidney that leads to the **ureter** (YOO ruh tur). Ureters are tubes that lead from each kidney to the bladder. The **bladder** is an elastic, muscular organ that holds urine until it leaves the body. The elastic walls of the bladder can stretch to hold up to 0.5 L of urine. When empty, the bladder looks wrinkled and the cells lining the bladder are thick. When full, the bladder looks like an inflated balloon and the cells lining the bladder are stretched and thin. A tube called the urethra (yoo REE thruh) carries urine from the bladder to the outside of the body.

**Living Environment**

**1.2e List** the four body systems that make up the excretory system. Give an example of how each system helps to eliminate waste.

**Figure 18** A single nephron is a complex structure.
**Describe** *the main function of a nephron.*

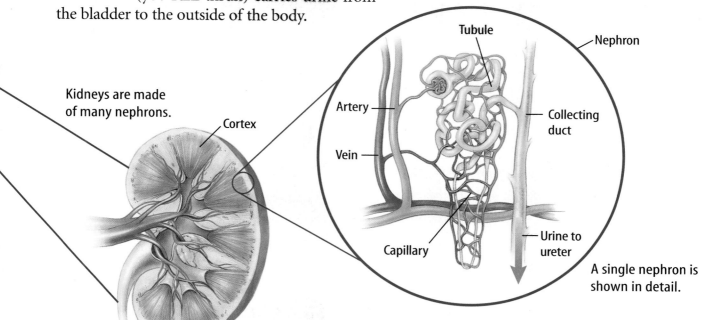

Kidneys are made of many nephrons.

Cortex

Tubule

Nephron

Artery

Vein

Collecting duct

Capillary

Urine to ureter

A single nephron is shown in detail.

# Urinary Diseases and Disorders

What happens when someone's kidneys don't work properly or stop working? Waste products that are not removed build up and act as poisons in body cells. Without excretion, an imbalance of salts occurs. The body responds by trying to restore this balance. If the balance isn't restored, the kidneys and other organs can be damaged. Kidney failure occurs when the kidneys don't work as they should. This is always a serious problem because the kidneys' job is so important to the rest of the body.

## Applying Science

### How does your body gain and lose water?

Your body depends on water. Without water, your cells could not carry out their activities and body systems could not function. Water is so important to your body that your brain and other body systems are involved in balancing water gain and water loss.

#### Identifying the Problem

**Table A** shows the major sources by which your body gains water. Oxidation of nutrients occurs when energy is released from nutrients by your body's cells. Water is a waste product of these reactions. **Table B** lists the major sources by which your body loses water. The data show you how daily gain and loss of water are related.

#### Solving the Problem

1. What is the greatest source of water gained by your body? What is the greatest source of water lost by your body?
2. How would the percentages of water gained and lost change in a person who was working in extremely warm temperatures? In this case, what organ of the body would be the greatest contributor to water loss?

| Table A  Major Sources by Which Body Water Is Gained | | |
|---|---|---|
| **Source** | **Amount (mL)** | **Percent** |
| Oxidation of nutrients | 250 | 10 |
| Foods | 750 | 30 |
| Liquids | 1,500 | 60 |
| **Total** | **2,500** | **100** |

| Table B  Major Sources by Which Body Water Is Lost | | |
|---|---|---|
| **Source** | **Amount (mL)** | **Percent** |
| Urine | 1,500 | 60 |
| Skin | 500 | 20 |
| Lungs | 350 | 14 |
| Feces | 150 | 6 |
| **Total** | **2,500** | **100** |

Because the ureters and urethra are narrow tubes, they can be blocked easily in some disorders. A blockage can cause serious problems because urine cannot flow out of the body properly. If the blockage is not corrected, the kidneys can be damaged.

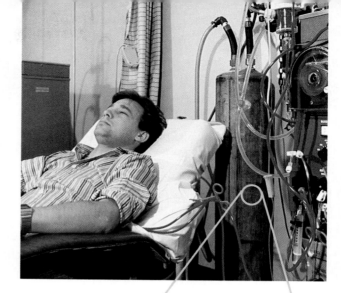

**Reading Check** *Why is a blocked ureter or urethra a serious problem?*

**Dialysis** A person who has only one kidney still can live normally. The remaining kidney increases in size and works harder to make up for the loss of the other kidney. However, if both kidneys fail, the person will need to have his or her blood filtered by an artificial kidney machine in a process called dialysis (di AH luh sus), as shown in **Figure 19**.

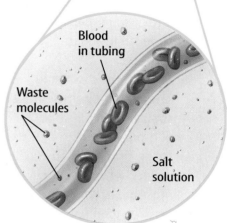

**Figure 19** A dialysis machine can replace or help with some of the activities of the kidneys in a person with kidney failure. Like the kidney, the dialysis machine removes wastes from the blood.

## section 4 review

### Summary

**Functions of the Excretory System**

- The excretory system removes wastes from your body.
- The digestive, respiratory, and urinary systems and skin make up your excretory system.

**The Urinary System**

- The kidneys, which filter wastes from the blood, are the major organs of the urinary system.
- Urine moves from the kidneys through the ureters, into the bladder, then leaves the body through the urethra.

**Urinary Diseases and Disorders**

- Kidney failure can lead to a buildup of waste products in the body.
- An artificial kidney can be used to filter the blood in a process called dialysis.

### Self Check

1. **List** the functions of a person's urinary system.
2. **Explain** how the kidneys remove wastes and keep fluids and salts in balance.
3. **Describe** what happens when the urinary system does not function properly.
4. **Compare** the excretory system and urinary system.
5. **Think Critically** Explain why reabsorption of certain materials in the kidneys is important to your health.

*Hot Words Hot Topics*: Bk 2 (6) pp. 196–197; (7) p. 216

### Applying Math

6. **Make and Use Graphs** Make a circle graph of major sources by which body water is gained. Use the data in **Table A** of the Applying Science activity.
7. **Concept Map** Using a network-tree concept map, compare the excretory functions of the kidneys and the lungs.

# LAB

# Particle Size and Absorption

## ⊙ Real-World Question

Before food reaches the small intestine, it is digested mechanically in the mouth and the stomach. The food mass is reduced to small particles. You can chew an apple into small pieces, but you would feed applesauce to a small child who didn't have teeth. What is the advantage of reducing the size of the food material? Does reducing the size of food particles aid the process of digestion?

## Goals
- **Compare and contrast** the dissolving rates of different sized particles.
- **Predict** the dissolving rate of sugar particles larger than sugar cubes.
- **Predict** the dissolving rate of sugar particles smaller than particles of ground sugar.
- **Infer,** using the lab results, why the body must break down and dissolve food particles.

## Materials
beakers or jars (3)
thermometers (3)
sugar granules
mortar and pestle
triple-beam balance
stirring rod
sugar cubes
weighing paper
warm water
stopwatch

## Safety Precautions

**WARNING:** *Never taste, eat, or drink any materials used in the lab.*

## ⊙ Procedure

1. Copy the data table below into your Science Journal.

### Dissolving Times of Sugar Particles

| Size of Sugar Particles | Mass | Time Until Dissolved |
|---|---|---|
| Sugar cube | | |
| Sugar granules | Do not write in this book. | |
| Ground sugar particles | | |

2. Place a sugar cube into your mortar and grind up the cube with the pestle until the sugar becomes powder.

3. Using the triple-beam balance and weighing paper, measure the mass of the powdered sugar from your mortar. Using separate sheets of weighing paper, measure the mass of a sugar cube and the mass of a sample of the granular sugar. The masses of the powdered sugar, sugar cube, and granular sugar should be approximately equal to each other. Record the three masses in your data table.

4. Place warm water into the three beakers. Use the thermometers to be certain the water in each beaker is the same temperature.

5. Place the sugar cube in a beaker, the powdered sugar in a second beaker, and the granular sugar in a third beaker. Place all the sugar samples in the beakers at the same time and start the stopwatch when you put the sugar samples in the beaker.

6. Stir each sample equally.

7. Measure the time it takes each sugar sample to dissolve and record the times in your data table.

## ▶ *Analyze Your Data*

1. **Identify** the experiment's constants and variables.

2. **Compare** the rates at which the sugar samples dissolved. What type of sugar dissolved most rapidly? Which was the slowest to dissolve?

## ▶ *Conclude and Apply*

1. **Predict** how long it would take sugar particles larger than the sugar cubes to dissolve. Predict how long it would take sugar particles smaller than the powdered sugar to dissolve.

2. **Infer** and explain the reason why small particles dissolve more rapidly than large particles.

3. **Infer** why you should thoroughly chew your food.

4. **Explain** how reducing the size of food particles aids the process of digestion.

### *Communicating Your Data*

Write a news column for a health magazine explaining to health-conscious people what they can do to digest their food better.

## Does the same diet work for everyone?

**G**rowing up in India in the first half of the twentieth century, R. Rajalakshmi (RAH jah lok shmee) saw many people around her who did not get enough food. Breakfast for a poor child might have been a cup of tea. Lunch might have consisted of a slice of bread. For dinner, a child might have eaten a serving of rice with a small piece of fish. This type of diet, low in calories and nutrients, produced children who were often sick and died young.

In the 1960s, R. Rajalakshmi was asked to help manage a program to improve nutrition in her country. North American and European nutritionists suggested foods that were common and worked well for people who lived in these nations. But Rajalakshmi knew this advice was useless in a country such as India.

### The Proper Diet for India

Rajalakshmi knew that for a nutrition program to work, it had to fit Indian culture. First, she found out what healthy middle-class people in India ate. She took note of the nutrients available in those foods. Then she looked for cheap, easy-to-find foods that would provide the same nutrients. Rajalakshmi created a balanced diet of locally grown fruits, vegetables, and grains.

Rajalakshmi's ideas were thought unusual in the 1960s. For example, she insisted that a diet without meat could provide all major nutrients. It took persistence to get others to accept her ideas. Because of Rajalakshmi's program, Indian children almost doubled their food intake. Many children who would have been hungry and ill, grew healthy and strong.

**Thanks to R. Rajalakshmi and other nutritionists, many children in India are eating well and staying healthy.**

**Report** Choose a continent and research what foods are native to that area. As a class, compile a list of the foods and where they originated. Using the class list, create a world map on a bulletin board that shows the origins of the different foods.

Science online

For more information, visit glencoe.com

## Reviewing Main Ideas

### Section 1 The Digestive System

1. Mechanical digestion breaks down food through chewing and churning. Enzymes and other chemicals aid chemical digestion.

2. Food passes through the mouth, esophagus, stomach, small intestine, large intestine, and rectum and then out the anus.

3. The large intestine absorbs water, which helps the body maintain homeostasis.

### Section 2 Nutrition

1. Proteins, carbohydrates, fats, vitamins, minerals, and water are the six nutrients found in foods.

2. Health is affected by the combination of foods that make up a diet.

### Section 3 The Respiratory System

1. The respiratory system brings oxygen into the body and removes carbon dioxide.

2. Breathing is the movement of the chest that allows air to move into the lungs and waste gases to leave the lungs.

3. The chemical reaction in cells that needs oxygen to release energy and produces carbon dioxide and water as wastes is called cellular respiration.

4. Smoking causes many respiratory problems, including chronic bronchitis, emphysema, and lung cancer.

### Section 4 The Excretory System

1. The urinary system is part of the excretory system. The skin, lungs, liver, and large intestine are also excretory organs.

2. The kidneys are the major organs of the urinary system and have a two-stage filtration system that removes wastes.

3. When kidneys fail to work, an artificial kidney can be used to filter the blood in a process called dialysis.

## Visualizing Main Ideas

*Copy and complete the following table on the respiratory and excretory systems.*

| Human Body Systems | | |
|---|---|---|
| | Respiratory System | Excretory System |
| Major Organs | | |
| Wastes Eliminated | Do not write in this book. | |
| Disorders | | |

## Using Vocabulary

| | |
|---|---|
| alveoli p. 460 | mineral p. 454 |
| amino acid p. 451 | nephron p. 467 |
| bladder p. 467 | nutrient p. 446 |
| bronchi p. 460 | peristalsis p. 448 |
| carbohydrate p. 452 | trachea p. 460 |
| chyme p. 449 | ureter p. 467 |
| enzyme p. 446 | villi p. 449 |
| larynx p. 460 | vitamin p. 453 |

*Fill in the blanks with the correct vocabulary word or words.*

1. _____ is the muscular contractions of the esophagus.

2. The building blocks of proteins are _____.

3. The liquid product of digestion is called _____.

4. _____ are inorganic nutrients.

5. _____ are the filtering units of the kidney.

6. _____ are thin-walled sacs in the lungs.

7. The _____ is an elastic muscular organ that holds urine.

## Checking Concepts

*Choose the word or phrase that best answers the question.*

8. Where in humans does most chemical digestion occur?
   **A)** duodenum   **C)** liver
   **B)** stomach   **D)** large intestine

9. In which organ is water absorbed?
   **A)** liver   **C)** small intestine
   **B)** esophagus   **D)** large intestine

10. Which of these organs is an accessory organ?
    **A)** mouth   **C)** small intestine
    **B)** stomach   **D)** liver

11. What beneficial substances are produced by bacteria in the large intestine?
    **A)** fats   **C)** vitamins
    **B)** minerals   **D)** proteins

12. Which food group contains yogurt and cheese?
    **A)** dairy   **C)** meat
    **B)** grain   **D)** fruit

13. When you inhale, which of the following contracts and moves down?
    **A)** bronchioles   **C)** nephrons
    **B)** diaphragm   **D)** kidneys

14. Exchange of gases occurs between capillaries and which of the following structures?
    **A)** alveoli   **C)** bronchioles
    **B)** bronchi   **D)** trachea

15. Which of the following conditions does smoking worsen?
    **A)** arthritis   **C)** excretion
    **B)** respiration   **D)** emphysema

16. Urine is held temporarily in which of the following structures?

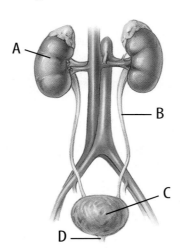

17. Which of the following substances is not reabsorbed by blood after it passes through the kidneys?
    **A)** salt   **C)** wastes
    **B)** sugar   **D)** water

**Vocabulary Puzzlemaker** glencoe.com

## Thinking Critically

18. **Make and use a table** to sequence the order of organs in the digestive system through which food passes. Indicate whether ingestion, digestion, absorption, or elimination takes place in each.

19. **Compare and contrast** the three types of carbohydrates—sugar, starch, and fiber.

20. **Classify** the parts of your favorite sandwich into three of the nutrient categories—carbohydrates, proteins, and fats.

21. **Recognize cause and effect** by discussing how lack of oxygen is related to lack of energy.

22. **Form a hypothesis** about the number of breaths a person might take per minute in each of these situations: asleep, exercising, and on top of Mount Everest. Give a reason for each hypothesis.

23. **Concept Map** Make an events-chain concept map showing how urine forms in the kidneys. Begin with, "In the nephron …"

**Use the table below to answer question 24.**

### Materials Filtered by the Kidneys

| Substance Filtered in Urine | Amount Moving Through Kidney | Amount Excreted |
|---|---|---|
| Water | 125 L | 1 L |
| Salt | 350 g | 10 g |
| Urea | 1 g | 1 g |
| Glucose | 50 g | 0 g |

24. **Interpret Data** Study the data above. How much of each substance is reabsorbed into the blood in the kidneys? What substance is excreted completely in the urine?

25. **Describe** how bile aids the diegestive process.

26. **Explain** how the bacteria that live in your large intestine help your body.

## Performance Activities

27. **Questionnaire and Interview** Prepare a questionnaire that can be used to interview a health specialist who works with lung cancer patients. Include questions on reasons for choosing the career, new methods of treatment, and the most encouraging or discouraging part of the job.

*Hot Words Hot Topics:* Bk 2 28: p. 308; 29: pp. 196–19797

## Applying Math

28. **Kidney Blood Flow** In approximately 5 min, all 5 L of blood in the body pass through the kidneys. Calculate the average rate of flow through the kidneys in liters per minute.

**Use the graph below to answer question 29.**

### Total Lung Capacity

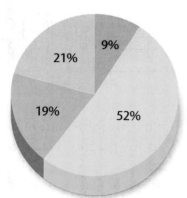

9%
21%
19%
52%

**Total Lung Capacity = 5800 mL**

- Volume of air normally inhaled or exhaled
- Volume of additional air that can be inhaled forcefully
- Volume of additional air that can be exhaled forcefully
- Volume of air left in lungs after forcefully exhaling

29. **Total Lung Capacity** What volume of air (mL) is left in the lungs after forcefully exhaling?

**Part I**

*Record your answers on the answer sheet
provided by your teacher or on a sheet of paper.*

**Use the table below to answer questions 1 and 2.**

| Nutrition Facts of Vanilla Ice Cream | | |
|---|---|---|
| Item | Amount | DV (Daily Values) |
| Serving Size | 112 g | 0 |
| Calories | 208 | 0 |
| Total Fat | 19 g | 29% |
| Saturated Fat | 11 g | 55% |
| Cholesterol | 0.125 g | 42% |
| Sodium | 0.90 g | 4% |
| Total Carbohydrates | 22 g | 7% |
| Fiber | 0 g | 0% |
| Sugars | 22 g | n/a |
| Protein | 5 g | n/a |
| Calcium | 0.117 g | 15% |
| Iron | n/a | 0% |

**1** According to this information, which
mineral has the greatest Daily Value (DV)
percentage?
(1) sodium
(2) cholesterol
(3) iron
(4) calcium

**2** How many grams of saturated fat and
Daily Value (DV) percentage in two servings of this ice cream?
(1) 11 g, 110%
(2) 22 g, 110%
(3) 21 g, 55%
(4) 5.5 g, 110%

**Use the illustration below to answer question 3.**

**3** What is the structure shown above and to
what body system does it belong?
(1) capillary—circulatory
(2) alveolus—respiratory
(3) nephron—urinary
(4) ureter—excretory

**4** If all of the blood in your body passes
through the kidneys in 5 minutes, how
many times does all of your blood pass
through the kidneys in one hour?
(1) 12 times        (3) 5 times
(2) 6 times         (4) 20 times

**5** Which of the following is the correct
sequence of the organs of the digestive tract?
(1) mouth, stomach, esophagus, small
    intestine, large intestine
(2) esophagus, mouth, stomach, small
    intestine, large intestine
(3) mouth, small intestine, stomach, large
    intestine
(4) mouth, esophagus, stomach, small
    intestine, large intestine

**6** Which of the following diseases may be
caused by smoking?
(1) lung cancer      (3) influenza
(2) diabetes         (4) bladder infection

*Record your answers on the answer sheet provided by your teacher or on a sheet of paper.*

**7** Explain the difference between organic and inorganic nutrients. Name a class of nutrients for each.

**8** Enzymes play an important role in the digestive process. But enzyme-aided reactions are also involved in other body systems. Give an example of how enzymes are used by the body in a way that does not involve the digestive system.

**Use the table and paragraph below to answer questions 9–12.**

For one week, research scientists collected and accurately measured the amount of body water lost and gained per day for four different patients. The following table lists results from their investigation.

| Body Water Gained (+) and Lost (−) | | | | |
|---|---|---|---|---|
| Patient | Day 1 (L) | Day 2 (L) | Day 3 (L) | Day 4 (L) |
| Mr. Stoler | +0.15 | +0.15 | −0.35 | +0.12 |
| Mr. Jemma | −0.01 | 0.00 | −0.20 | −0.01 |
| Mr. Lowe | 0.00 | +0.20 | −0.28 | +0.01 |
| Mr. Cheng | −0.50 | −0.50 | −0.55 | −0.32 |

**9** What was Mr. Cheng's average daily body water loss for the 4 days shown in the table?

**10** Which patient had the greatest amount of body water gained on days 1 and 2?

**11** According to the data in the table, on which day was the temperature in each patient's hospital room probably the hottest?

**12** Which patient had the highest total gain in body water over the 4-day period?

**13** Explain the role of cilia in the respiratory system. In chronic bronchitis, cilia are damaged. What effects does this damage have on the respiratory system?

**14** Antibiotics may be given to help a person fight off a bacterial infection. If a person is taking antibiotics, what might happen to the normal bacteria living in the large intestine? How would this affect the body?

**15** Sometimes the esophagus can be affected by a disease in which the smooth muscle in the wall of the esophagus does not work properly. What do you think would happen to food that the person swallowed? Why?

**16** Compare and contrast the roles of mucus in the digestive and respiratory systems.

**17** Urine can be tested for any signs of a urinary tract disease. Mrs. Chavez had a urine test that showed protein in the urine. What might the results of this urine test mean?

# How Are Plants & Medicine Cabinets Connected?

These willow trees are members of the genus *Salix*. More than 2,000 years ago, people discovered that the bark of certain willow species could be used to relieve pain and reduce fever. In the 1820s, a French scientist isolated the willow's pain-killing ingredient, which was named salicin. Unfortunately, medicines made from salicin had an unpleasant side effect—they caused severe stomach irritation. In the late 1800s, a German scientist looked for a way to relieve pain without upsetting patients' stomachs. The scientist synthesized a compound called acetylsalicylic acid (uh SEE tul SA luh SI lihk • A sihd), which is related to salicin but has fewer side effects. A drug company came up with a catchier name for this compound—aspirin. Before long, aspirin had become the most widely used drug in the world. Other medicines in a typical medicine cabinet also are derived from plants or are based on compounds originally found in plants.

NATIONAL
GEOGRAPHIC

### unit ⚡ projects

Visit **glencoe.com** to find project ideas and resources.
Projects include:

- **History** Design a slide show to present information on medicines derived from plants and where these plants grow.
- **Technology** Make your own giant jigsaw puzzle illustrating the five systems of a seed plant, including labels and functions of each plant part.
- **Model** Construct a review game demonstrating knowledge of nitrogen and oxygen cycles. The game and instructions should be assembled in an eco-friendly box.

**WebQuest** Investigate *Origins of Birds* to learn about the theory that birds descended from theropod dinosaurs. Compare and contrast bird characteristics with other animals.

**chapter**

**17**

**LE 1.1e:** Cells are organized for more effective functioning in multicellular organisms. Levels of organization for structure and function of a multicellular organism include cells, tissues, organs, and organ systems. **1.1g:** Multicellular animals often have similar organs and specialized systems for carrying out major life activities. **Also Covered:** 1.1h, 1.2c, 1.2g, 4.3d, 5.1a, 5.1b, 5.1c, 5.1d, 5.1e, 5.1f, 5.1g

# Invertebrate Animals

## chapter preview

### sections

1 **What is an animal?**

2 **Sponges, Cnidarians, Flatworms, and Roundworms**

3 **Mollusks and Segmented Worms**

4 **Arthropods and Echinoderms**

*Lab Observing Complete Metamorphosis*

*Lab Garbage-Eating Worms*

*Virtual Lab How are mollusks, worms, arthropods, and echinoderms classified?*

## Underwater Rhythmic Dancers

Corals and anemones sway with ocean currents. Other animals, like the lemon-peel nudibranch, move in ways that animals that have internal skeletons cannot move. They belong to a group of animals called invertebrates—animals without backbones.

**Science Journal** Describe similarities and differences between you and the nudibranch.

# Start-Up Activities

## How are animals organized?

Scientists have identified at least 1.5 million different kinds of animals. In the following lab, you will learn about organizing animals by building a bulletin board display.

1. Write the names of different groups of animals on large envelopes and attach them to a bulletin board.

2. Choose an animal group to study. Make an information card about each animal with its picture on one side and characteristics on the other side.

3. Place your finished cards inside the appropriate envelope.

4. Select an envelope from the bulletin board for a different group of animals. Using the information on the cards, sort the animals into groups.

5. **Think Critically** What common characteristics do these animals have? What characteristics did you use to classify them into smaller groups? Record your answers in your Science Journal.

 **Preview this chapter's content and activities at glencoe.com**

 **Invertebrates** Make the following Foldable to compare and contrast the characteristics of water and land invertebrates.

**STEP 1** **Fold** one sheet of paper lengthwise.

**STEP 2** **Fold** into thirds.

**STEP 3**  **Unfold and draw** overlapping ovals. **Cut** the top sheet along the folds.

**STEP 4** 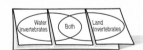 **Label** the ovals as shown.

**Construct a Venn Diagram** As you read this chapter, list the characteristics unique to water invertebrates under the left tab, those unique to land invertebrates under the right tab, and those characteristics common to both under the middle tab.

LE 1.1h: Living things are classified by shared characteristics on the cellular and organism level. In classifying organisms, biologists consider details of internal and external structures. Biological classification systems are arranged from general (kingdom) to specific (species). **Also Covered:** LE 1.1e, 1.1g, 1.2c, 1.2g, 5.1a, 5.1c, 5.1d, 5.1e, 5.1f, 5.1g

# section 1

# What is an animal?

## as you read

### *What* You'll Learn

- **Identify** the characteristics of animals.
- **Differentiate** between vertebrates and invertebrates.
- **Explain** how the symmetry of animals differs.

### *Why* It's Important

All animals have characteristics in common.

### ⊙ Review Vocabulary

**organelle:** structure in the cytoplasm of a eukaryotic cell that can act as a storage site, process energy, move materials, or manufacture substances

### New Vocabulary

- symmetry
- invertebrate

## Animal Characteristics

If you asked ten people for a characteristic common to all animals, you might get ten different answers or a few repeated answers. Look at the animals in **Figure 1.** What are their common characteristics? What makes an animal an animal?

1. Animals are many-celled organisms that are made of different kinds of cells. These cells might digest food, get rid of wastes, help in reproduction, or be part of systems that have these functions.

2. Most animal cells have a nucleus and organelles. The nucleus and many organelles are surrounded by a membrane. This type of cell is called a eukaryotic (yew ker ee AH tihk) cell.

3. Animals cannot make their own food. Some animals eat plants to supply their energy needs. Some animals eat other animals, and some eat both plants and animals.

4. Animals digest their food. Large food particles are broken down into smaller substances that their cells can use.

5. Most animals can move from place to place. They move to find food, shelter, and mates, and to escape from predators.

**Figure 1** Animals come in a variety of shapes and sizes.

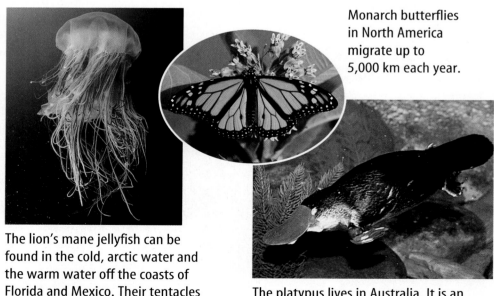

Monarch butterflies in North America migrate up to 5,000 km each year.

The lion's mane jellyfish can be found in the cold, arctic water and the warm water off the coasts of Florida and Mexico. Their tentacles can be up to 30 m long.

The platypus lives in Australia. It is an egg-laying mammal.

**Figure 2** Most animals have radial or bilateral symmetry. Only a few animals are asymmetrical.

Sea anemones have radial symmetry.

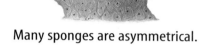

Lobsters have bilateral symmetry.

Many sponges are asymmetrical.

**Symmetry** As you study the different groups of animals, you will look at their symmetry (SIH muh tree). **Symmetry** refers to the arrangement of the individual parts of an object that can be divided into similar halves.

Most animals have either radial symmetry or bilateral symmetry. Animals with body parts arranged in a circle around a central point have radial symmetry. Can you imagine being able to locate food and gather information from all directions? Aquatic animals with radial symmetry, such as jellyfish, sea urchins, and the sea anemone, shown in **Figure 2,** can do that. On the other hand, animals with bilateral symmetry have parts that are nearly mirror images of each other. A line can be drawn down the center of their bodies to divide them into two similar parts. Grasshoppers, lobsters, like the one in **Figure 2,** and humans are bilaterally symmetrical.

Some animals have an irregular shape. They are called asymmetrical (AY suh meh trih kul). They have bodies that cannot be divided into similar halves. Many sponges, like those also in **Figure 2,** are asymmetrical. As you learn more about invertebrates, notice how their body symmetry is related to how they gather food and do other things.

 **Reading Check** *What is symmetry?*

# Animal Classification

Deciding whether an organism is an animal is only the first step in classifying it. Scientists place all animals into smaller, related groups. They can begin by separating animals into two distinct groups—vertebrates and invertebrates. Vertebrates (VUR tuh bruts) are animals that have a backbone. **Invertebrates** (ihn VUR tuh bruts) are animals that do not have a backbone. About 97 percent of all animals are invertebrates.

Scientists classify the invertebrates into smaller groups, as shown in **Figure 3.** The animals within each group share similar characteristics. These characteristics indicate that the animals within the group may have had a common ancestor.

**Living Environment**

**1.1h Summarize** how scientists classify living things.

**Figure 3** This diagram shows the relationships among different groups in the animal kingdom. **Estimate** *the percentage of animals that are vertebrates.*

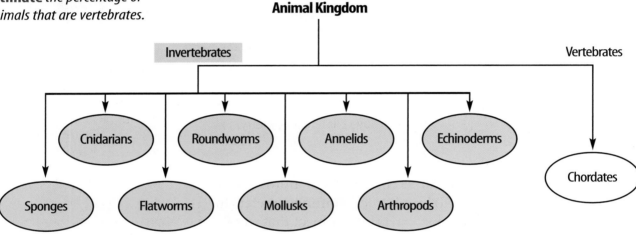

---

## section 1 review

### Summary

**Animal Characteristics**

- Animals are made up of many different kinds of cells.
- Most animal cells have a nucleus and organelles.
- Animals cannot make their own food.
- Animals digest their food.
- Most animals can move from place to place.

**Animal Classification**

- Scientists place all animals into smaller, related groups.
- Two distinct groups of animals are the invertebrates and vertebrates.

### Self Check

1. **Compare and contrast** invertebrate and vertebrate animals.
2. **Describe** the different types of symmetry. Name an animal that has bilateral symmetry.
3. **Think Critically** Most animals do not have a backbone. They are called invertebrates. What are some advantages that invertebrate animals might have over vertebrate animals?

#### Applying Skills

4. **Concept Map** Using the information in this section, make a concept map showing the steps a scientist might use to classify a newly discovered animal.

**More Section Review** glencoe.com

# section 2

# Sponges, Cnidarians, Flatworms, and Roundworms

## Sponges

Can you tell the difference between an animal and a plant? Sounds easy, doesn't it? But for a long time, even scientists didn't know how to classify sponges. Originally they thought sponges were plants because they don't move to search for food. Sponges, however, can't make their own food as most plants do. Sponges are animals. Adult sponges are sessile (SE sul), meaning they remain attached to one place. Approximately 15,000 species of sponges have been identified.

**Filter Feeders** Most species of sponges live in the ocean, but some live in freshwater. Sponge bodies, shown in **Figure 4,** are made of two layers of cells. All sponges are filter feeders. They filter food out of the water that flows through their bodies. Microscopic organisms and oxygen are carried with water into the central cavity through pores of the sponge. The inner surface of the central cavity is lined with collar cells. Thin, whiplike structures, called flagella (flah JEH luh), extend from the collar cells and keep the water moving through the sponge. Other specialized cells digest the food, carry nutrients to all parts of the sponge, and remove wastes.

**Body Support and Defense** Not many animals eat sponges. The soft bodies of many sponges are supported by sharp, glass-like structures called spicules (SPIHK yewlz). Other sponges have a material called spongin. Spongin is similar to foam rubber because it makes sponges soft and elastic. Some sponges have both spicules and spongin to protect their soft bodies.

### as you read

*What* You'll Learn
- **Describe** the structures that make up sponges and cnidarians.
- **Compare** how sponges and cnidarians get food and reproduce.
- **Differentiate** between flatworms and roundworms.

*Why* It's Important
Studying the body plans in sponges, cnidarians, flatworms, and roundworms helps you understand the complex organ systems in other organisms.

🔎 **Review Vocabulary**
**species:** group of organisms that share similar characteristics and can reproduce among themselves

**New Vocabulary**
- cnidarian
- medusa
- polyp

**Figure 4** Red beard sponges grow where the tide moves in and out quickly.

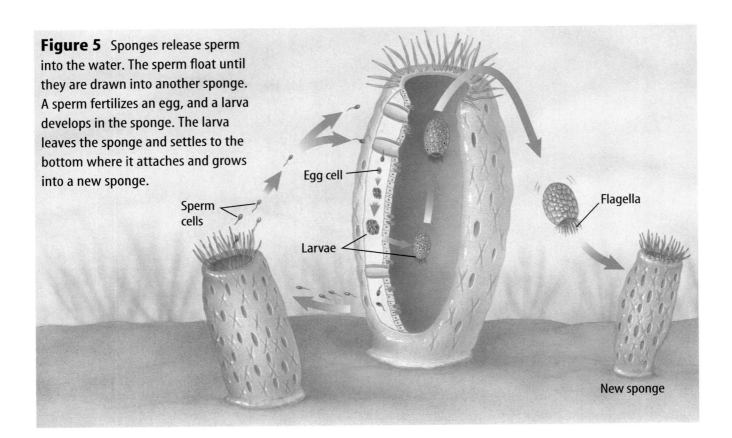

**Figure 5** Sponges release sperm into the water. The sperm float until they are drawn into another sponge. A sperm fertilizes an egg, and a larva develops in the sponge. The larva leaves the sponge and settles to the bottom where it attaches and grows into a new sponge.

Sperm cells

Egg cell

Larvae

Flagella

New sponge

**INTEGRATE Chemistry**

**Spicules** Sponge spicules of "glass" sponges are composed of silica. Other sponges have spicules made of calcium carbonate. Where do organisms get the silica and calcium carbonate that these spicules are made of? Write your prediction in your Science Journal.

**Sponge Reproduction** Sponges can reproduce asexually and sexually. Asexual reproduction occurs when a bud on the side of the parent sponge develops into a small sponge. The small sponge breaks off, floats away, and attaches itself to a new surface. New sponges also may grow from pieces of a sponge. Each piece grows into a new, identical sponge.

Most sponges that reproduce sexually are hermaphrodites (hur MA fruh dites). This means that one sponge produces both eggs and sperm, as shown in **Figure 5.**

## Cnidarians

Cnidarians (nih DAR ee uns), such as jellyfish, sea anemones, hydra, and corals, have tentacles surrounding their mouth. The tentacles shoot out stinging cells called nematocysts (NE ma toh sihsts) to capture prey, similar to casting a fishing line into the water to catch a fish. Because they have radial symmetry, they can locate food that floats by from any direction.

**Cnidarians** are hollow-bodied animals with two cell layers that are organized into tissues. The inner layer forms a digestive cavity where food is broken down. Oxygen moves into the cells from the surrounding water, and carbon dioxide waste moves out of the cells. Nerve cells work together as a nerve net throughout the whole body.

**Body Forms** Cnidarians have two different body forms. The vase-shaped body of the sea anemone and the hydra is called a **polyp** (PAH lup). Although hydras are usually sessile, they can twist to capture prey. They also can somersault to a new location.

Jellyfish have a free-swimming, bell-shaped body that is called a **medusa** (mih DEW suh). Jellyfish are not strong swimmers. Instead, they drift with the ocean currents. Some cnidarians go through both a polyp and a medusa stage during their life cycles.

**Cnidarian Reproduction** Cnidarians reproduce asexually and sexually. Polyp forms of cnidarians, such as hydras, reproduce asexually by budding, as shown in **Figure 6**. The bud eventually falls off of the parent organism and develops into a new polyp. Some polyps also can reproduce sexually by releasing eggs or sperm into the water. The eggs are fertilized by sperm and develop into new polyps. Medusa forms of cnidarians, such as jellyfish, have a two-stage life cycle as shown in **Figure 7**. A medusa reproduces sexually to produce polyps. Then each of these polyps reproduces asexually to form new medusae.

**Figure 6** Polyps, like these hydras, reproduce asexually by budding.
**Compare** *the genetic makeups of the parent organism and the bud.*

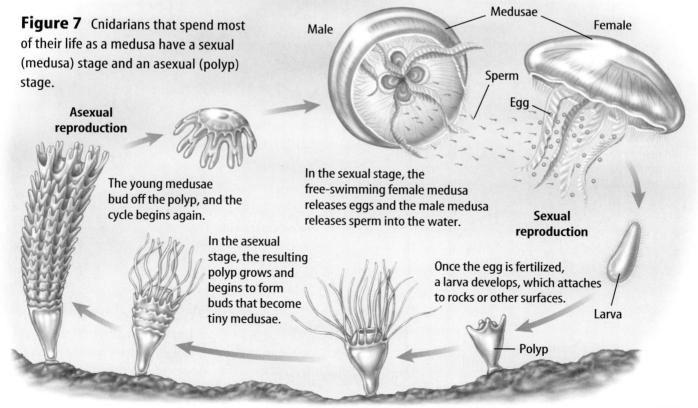

**Figure 7** Cnidarians that spend most of their life as a medusa have a sexual (medusa) stage and an asexual (polyp) stage.

**Asexual reproduction**

The young medusae bud off the polyp, and the cycle begins again.

In the asexual stage, the resulting polyp grows and begins to form buds that become tiny medusae.

Male

Medusae

Female

Sperm

Egg

In the sexual stage, the free-swimming female medusa releases eggs and the male medusa releases sperm into the water.

**Sexual reproduction**

Once the egg is fertilized, a larva develops, which attaches to rocks or other surfaces.

Larva

Polyp

**Figure 8** Tapeworms are intestinal parasites that attach to a host's intestines with hooks and suckers. Their life cycle is shown here.

# Flatworms

Unlike sponges and cnidarians, flatworms search for food. Flatworms are invertebrates with long, flattened bodies and bilateral symmetry. Their soft bodies have three layers of tissue organized into organs and organ systems. Planarians are free-living flatworms that have a digestive system with one opening. They don't depend on one particular organism for food or a place to live. However, most flatworms are parasites that live in or on their hosts. A parasite depends on its host for food and shelter.

**Tapeworms** One type of parasitic flatworm is the tapeworm. To survive, it lives in the intestines of its host, including human hosts. The tapeworm lacks a digestive system so it absorbs nutrients from digested material in the host's intestine. In **Figure 8,** you can see the hooks and suckers on a tapeworm's head that attach it to the host's intestine.

A tapeworm grows by adding sections directly behind its head. Each body segment has both male and female reproductive organs. The eggs and sperm are released into the segment. After it is filled with fertilized eggs, the segment breaks off.

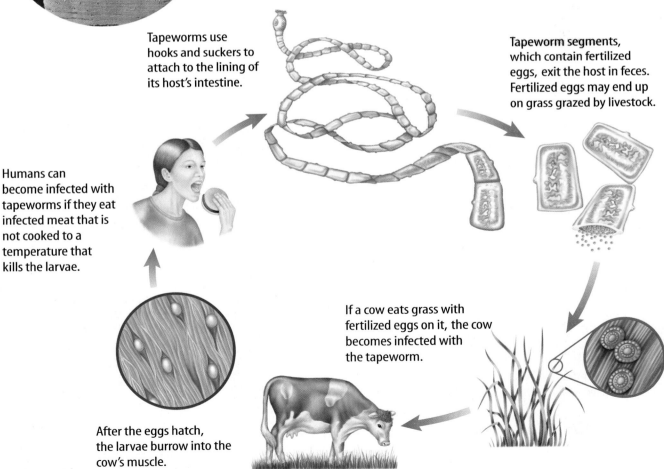

Tapeworms use hooks and suckers to attach to the lining of its host's intestine.

Tapeworm segments, which contain fertilized eggs, exit the host in feces. Fertilized eggs may end up on grass grazed by livestock.

Humans can become infected with tapeworms if they eat infected meat that is not cooked to a temperature that kills the larvae.

If a cow eats grass with fertilized eggs on it, the cow becomes infected with the tapeworm.

After the eggs hatch, the larvae burrow into the cow's muscle.

The segment passes with wastes out of the host's body. If another host eats a fertilized egg, it hatches and develops into a tapeworm. Tapeworm segments aren't ingested directly by humans. Most flatworms have an intermediate or middle host. For example, **Figure 8** shows how cattle are the intermediate host for tapeworms that infect humans.

✔ **Reading Check** *How can flatworms get into humans?*

# Roundworms

If you have a dog, you may know already that heartworm disease, shown in **Figure 9,** can be fatal to dogs. In most areas of the United States, it's necessary to give dogs a monthly medicine to prevent heartworm disease. Heartworms are just one kind of the many thousands of roundworms that exist. Roundworms are the most widespread animal on Earth. Billions can live in an acre of soil. Many people confuse earthworms and roundworms. You will study earthworms in the next section.

A roundworm's body is described as a tube within a tube, with a fluid-filled cavity in between the two tubes. The cavity separates the digestive tract from the body wall. Roundworms are more complex than flatworms because their digestive tract has two openings. Food enters through the mouth, is digested in a digestive tract, and wastes exit through the anus.

Roundworms are a diverse group. Some roundworms are decomposers, others are predators, and some, like the heartworm, are animal parasites. Other roundworms are plant parasites.

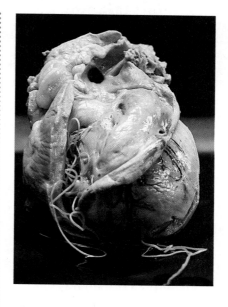

**Figure 9** This dog heart is infested with heartworms. Heartworms are carried by mosquitoes. A heartworm infection can clog a dog's heart and cause death.

## section 2 review

### Summary

**Sponges and Cnidarians**
- Sponges are animals that remain attached to one place and can reproduce both sexually and asexually.
- Cnidarians are hollow-bodied animals with two cell layers that are organized into tissues.

**Flatworms and Roundworms**
- Flatworms have three layers of soft tissue organized into organs and organ systems.
- Most flatworms are parasitic.
- Roundworms are decomposers, predators, or parasites of plants and animals and are the most widespread animal on Earth.

### Self Check

1. **Explain** how sponges and cnidarians get food.
2. **Compare and contrast** the body plan of flatworms to the body plan of roundworms.
3. **Infer** how spongin and spicules discourage predators from eating sponges.
4. **Think Critically** Some types of sponges and cnidarians reproduce asexually. Why is this beneficial to them?

*Hot Words Hot Topics*: Bk 2 (5) pp. 308, 368

### Applying Math

5. **Solve an Equation** A sponge is 1 cm in diameter and 10 cm tall. It can move 22.5 L of water through its body in a day. Calculate the volume of water it pumps through its body in 1 min.

# section
## 3

# Mollusks and Segmented Worms

**as you read**

## *What* You'll Learn

- **Identify** the characteristics of mollusks.
- **Compare** the similarities and differences between an open and a closed circulatory system.
- **Describe** the characteristics of segmented worms.
- **Explain** the digestive process of an earthworm.

## *Why* It's Important

Organ systems and specialized structures allow mollusks and segmented worms to live in varied environments.

### Review Vocabulary

**organ:** structure, such as the heart, made up of different types of tissue that work together

### New Vocabulary

- mollusk
- mantle
- gill
- radula
- open circulatory system
- closed circulatory system

## Mollusks

Imagine yourself walking along an ocean beach at low tide. On the rocks, you see small snails with conelike shells. In a small tidal pool, one arm of a shy octopus can be seen at the opening of its den. The blue-black shells of mussels are exposed along the shore as shown in **Figure 10.** How are these different animals related? What do they have in common?

**Common Characteristics** In many places snails, mussels, and octopuses—all mollusks (MAH lusks)—are eaten by humans. **Mollusks** are soft-bodied invertebrates that usually have a shell. They also have a mantle and a large, muscular foot. The **mantle** is a thin layer of tissue that covers the mollusk's soft body. If the mollusk has a shell, it is secreted by the mantle. The foot is used for moving or for anchoring the animal.

Between the mantle and the soft body is a space called the mantle cavity. Water-dwelling mollusks have gills in the mantle cavity. **Gills** are organs in which carbon dioxide from the animal is exchanged for oxygen in the water. In contrast, land-dwelling mollusks have lungs in which carbon dioxide from the animal is exchanged for oxygen in the air.

**Figure 10** At low tide, many mollusks can be found along a rocky seashore.

Many species of conchs are on the verge of becoming threatened species because they are overharvested for food.

Scallops are used to measure an ecosystem's health because they're sensitive to water quality.

**Figure 11** Many kinds of mollusks are a prized source of food for humans.
**Name** *another mollusk, besides a conch or scallop, that is a source of food for humans.*

**Body Systems** Mollusks have a digestive system with two openings. Many mollusks also have a scratchy, tonguelike organ called the **radula.** The radula (RA juh luh) has rows of fine, teethlike projections that the mollusk uses to scrape off small bits of food.

Some mollusks have an **open circulatory system,** which means they do not have vessels to contain their blood. Instead, the blood washes over the organs, which are grouped together in a fluid-filled body cavity.

## Types of Mollusks

Does the animal have a shell or not? This is the first characteristic that scientists use to classify mollusks. Then they look at the kind of shell or they look at the type of foot. In this section, you will learn about three kinds of mollusks.

**Gastropods** The photo on the left in **Figure 11** shows a gastropod. Gastropods are the largest group of mollusks. Most gastropods, such as the snails and conchs, have one shell. Slugs also are gastropods, but they don't have a shell. Gastropods live in water or on land. All move about on a large, muscular foot. A secretion of mucus allows them to glide across objects.

**Bivalves** How many shells do you think a bivalve has? Think of other words that start with *bi-*. The scallop shown on the right in **Figure 11** is a bivalve. It is an organism with two shell halves joined by a hinge. Large, powerful muscles open and close the shell halves. Bivalves are water animals that also are filter feeders. Food is removed from water that is brought into and filtered through the gills.

**INTEGRATE Social Studies**

**Toxins** Shellfish and crabs accumulate toxins during red tides when they feed on algae containing toxins. These toxins are dangerous to people. The threat of red tides has resulted in closures of both commercial and recreational shellfish harvesting. This causes substantial economic loss. In your Science Journal, write about what is being done to determine when it is safe to harvest shellfish.

**Topic: Red Tides**
Visit glencoe.com for Web links to information about red tides.

**Activity** Explain what red tides are and why it is important to learn more about them. What is being done to try and predict when red tides will occur?

**Figure 12** Living species of *Nautilus* are found in the western Pacific Ocean. The chambered nautilus, squid, and other cephalopods are able to move quickly using a water-propulsion system as shown to the right.

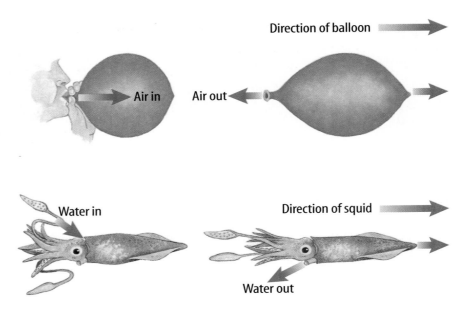

Direction of balloon

Air in    Air out

Water in    Direction of squid

Water out

## Mini LAB

**Modeling Cephalopod Propulsion**

**Procedure**
1. Blow up a **balloon.** Hold the end closed, but don't tie it.
2. Let go of the balloon.
3. Repeat steps 1 and 2 three more times.

**Analysis**
1. In your **Science Journal,** describe how the balloon moved when you let go.
2. If the balloon models an octopus or a squid as it swims through the water, infer how cephalopods can escape from danger.

**Try at Home**

**Cephalopods** The most complex type of mollusks are cephalopods (SE fah lah pawdz). The chambered nautilus, shown in **Figure 12,** octopuses, squid, and cuttlefish are cephalopods. Most cephalopods have an internal plate instead of a shell. They have a well-developed head and a "foot" that is divided into tentacles with strong suckers. At the base of the tentacles is the mouth. They have a **closed circulatory system** in which blood is carried through blood vessels instead of surrounding the organs.

Cephalopods are adapted for quick movement in the ocean. They have a muscular envelope, called the mantle, surrounding their internal organs. Water enters the space between the mantle and the other body organs. When the mantle closes around the collar of the cephalopod, the water is squeezed rapidly through a funnel-like structure called a siphon. The rapid expulsion of water from the siphon creates a force that causes the animal to move in the opposite direction of the stream of water, as illustrated in **Figure 12.**

## Segmented Worms

When you hear the word *worm,* you probably think of an earthworm. Earthworms, leeches, and marine worms are segmented worms, or annelids (A nul idz). Their body is made of repeating segments or rings that make these worms flexible. Each segment has nerve cells, blood vessels, part of the digestive tract, and the coelom (SEE lum). The coelom, or internal body cavity, separates the internal organs from the body wall. Annelids have a closed circulatory system and a complete digestive system with two body openings.

**Earthworms** When did you first encounter earthworms? Maybe it was on a wet sidewalk or in a garden, as shown in **Figure 13.** Earthworms have more than 100 body segments. Each segment has external bristlelike structures called setae (SEE tee). Earthworms use the setae to grip the soil while two sets of muscles move them through the soil. As earthworms move, they take soil into their mouths. Earthworms get the energy they need to live from organic matter found in the soil. From the mouth the soil moves to the crop, where it is stored. Behind the crop is a muscular structure called the gizzard. Here, the soil and food are ground. In the intestine, the food is broken down and absorbed by the blood. Undigested soil and wastes leave the worm through the anus.

**Reading Check** *What is the function of setae?*

Examine the earthworm shown in **Figure 14.** Notice the lack of gills and lungs. Carbon dioxide passes out and oxygen passes in through its mucous-covered skin. It's important not to pick up earthworms with dry hands because if this thin film of mucus is removed, the earthworm may suffocate.

**Figure 13** Earthworms are covered with a thin layer of mucus, which keeps them moist. Setae help them move through the soil.

**Figure 14** Earthworms and other segmented worms have many organ systems including circulatory, reproductive, excretory, digestive, and muscular systems.

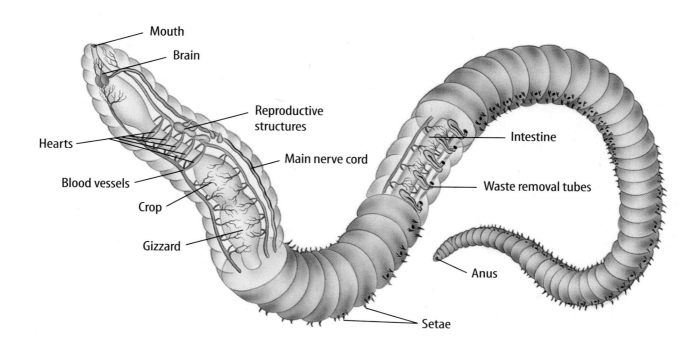

Mouth

Brain

Reproductive structures

Hearts

Main nerve cord

Blood vessels

Crop

Gizzard

Intestine

Waste removal tubes

Anus

Setae

**Figure 15** Leeches attach to fish, turtles, snails, and mammals and remove blood and other body fluids.

**Leeches** They can be found in freshwater, marine waters, and on land in mild and tropical regions. These segmented worms have flat bodies from 5 mm to 460 mm long with sucking disks on both ends. They use these disks to attach themselves to an animal, as shown in **Figure 15,** and remove blood. Some leeches can store as much as ten times their own weight in blood. It can be stored for months and released a little at a time into the digestive system. Although leeches prefer a diet of blood, most of them can survive indefinitely on small aquatic animals.

**✔ Reading Check** *How do leeches attach themselves to an animal?*

**Marine Worms** The animals in **Figure 16** are polychaetes (PAH lee keets), the largest and most diverse group of annelids. Of the 10,000 named species of annelids, more than 8,000 of them are marine worms. The word *polychaete* means "many bristles." Most marine worms have bristles, or setae, along the sides of their body. Because of these bristles, marine worms are sometimes called bristle worms. Bristles are used for walking, swimming, or digging, depending on the type of marine worm.

## Applying Science

### How does soil management affect earthworms?

Some earthworms tunnel through the soil about 30 cm below the soil surface. Earthworms called night crawlers dig deep, permanent tunnels that are up to 1.8 m long. Earthworms' tunnels loosen the soil, which allows better root growth by plants. It also increases air and water movement in the soil. As they tunnel, earthworms take in soil that contains organic matter such as plant material, microorganisms, and animal remains. This is their source of food. Microorganisms break down earthworms' wastes, which adds nutrients to the soil. Earthworms are a food source for frogs, snakes, birds, and other animals.

**Identifying the Problem**

As earthworms tunnel through the soil, they also take in other substances found there. High levels of pesticides and heavy metals can build up in the bodies of earthworms.

**Solving the Problem**
1. One soil management technique is to place municipal sludge on farmland as fertilizer. The sludge might contain heavy metals and harmful organic substances. Predict how this could affect birds.
2. Is the use of sludge as a fertilizer a wise choice? Explain your answer.

**Figure 16** More than 8,000 species of marine worms exist.

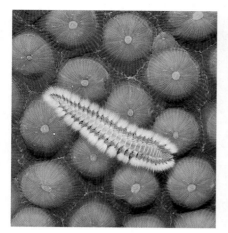

Some polychaetes, like this fire-worm, move around in search of food.

Polychaetes, like this sea mouse, have long bristles that look like hair.

Some polychaetes, like this tube-worm, cannot move around in search of food. Instead, they use their featherlike bristles to filter food from the water.

**Body Types** Some marine worms are filter feeders. They either burrow into the mud or build their own tube cases and use their featherlike bristles to filter food from the water. Some marine worms move around eating plants or decaying material. Other marine worms are predators or parasites. The many different lifestyles of marine worms explain why there are so many different body types.

Although annelids do not look complex, they are more complex than sponges and cnidarians. In the next section, you will learn how they compare to the most complex invertebrates.

> **Living Environment**
>
> **5.1b Discuss** how methods of obtaining food vary among animals depending on their body plan and environment. Support your response with specific examples.

## section 3 review

### Summary

**Mollusks**

- Mollusks are soft-bodied invertebrates that have a mantle, a large, muscular foot, and usually have a shell.

**Types of Mollusks**

- Mollusks are separated into three groups—gastropods, bivalves, and cephalopods.

**Segmented Worms**

- Repeating body segments give segmented worms flexibility.
- Segmented worms have a coelom, or internal body cavity, that separates the internal organs from the body wall.

### Self Check

1. **Explain** what gills are used for.
2. **Describe** how an earthworm feeds and digests its food.
3. **Identify** which type of circulatory system that a cephalopod develops.
4. **Think Critically** Why would it be beneficial to a leech to be able to store blood for months and release it slowly?

### Applying Skills

5. **Communicate** Choose a mollusk or annelid and write about it in your Science Journal. Describe its appearance, how it gets food, where it lives, and other interesting facts.

# section 4

# Arthropods and Echinoderms

**Figure 17** About 8,000 species of ants are found in the world. Ants are social insects that live cooperatively in colonies.

## Arthropods

More than a million species of arthropods (AR thruh pahdz) have been discovered. They are the largest and most diverse group of animals. The term *arthropod* comes from *arthros,* meaning "jointed," and *poda,* meaning "foot." **Arthropods** are animals that have jointed appendages (uh PEN dih juz). **Appendages** are structures such as claws, legs, and antennae that grow from the body.

Arthropods have a rigid body covering called an **exoskeleton.** It protects and supports the body and reduces water loss. The weight of the outer covering increases as the size of the animal increases. As the animal grows, the exoskeleton must be shed because it doesn't grow with the animal. This process is called molting. Weight and hardness of the exoskeleton could make it difficult to move, but the jointed appendages solve part of this problem.

**✓ Reading Check** *What is the function of the exoskeleton?*

Arthropods have bilateral symmetry and segmented bodies similar to annelids. In most cases, arthropods have fewer, more specialized segments. Instead of setae, they have appendages.

**Insects** If asked to name an insect, you might say bee, fly, beetle, or butterfly. Insects make up the largest group of arthropods. More than 700,000 species of insects have been classified, and scientists discover and describe more of them each year.

Insects, like the ant in **Figure 17,** have three body regions—head, thorax, and abdomen. Well-developed sensory organs, including the eyes and antennae, are located on the head. The thorax has three pairs of jointed legs and usually one or two pairs of wings. The wings and legs of insects are highly specialized. The abdomen is divided into segments and has neither wings nor legs attached, but reproductive organs are located there.

Abdomen  Thorax  Head

**Circulatory System** Insects have an open circulatory system. Oxygen is not transported by blood in the system, but food and waste materials are. Oxygen is brought directly to the insect's tissues through small branching tubes. These tubes connect to openings called spiracles (SPIHR ih kulz) located along the sides of the thorax and abdomen.

**Metamorphosis** The young of many insects don't look anything like the adults. This is because many insects completely change their body form as they mature. This change in body form is called **metamorphosis** (met uh MOR fuh sus). The two kinds of insect metamorphosis, complete and incomplete, are shown in **Figure 18.**

Butterflies, ants, bees, and beetles are examples of insects that undergo complete metamorphosis. Complete metamorphosis has four stages—egg, larva, pupa (PYEW puh), and adult. Notice how different each stage is from the others. Some insects, such as grasshoppers, cockroaches, termites, aphids, and dragonflies, undergo incomplete metamorphosis. They have only three stages—egg, nymph, and adult. A nymph looks similar to its parents, only smaller. A nymph molts as it grows until it reaches the adult stage. All the arthropods shown in **Figure 19** on the next two pages molt many times during their life.

**Living Environment**

**4.3d, 5.1a, 5.1b Sequence** the steps of complete metamorphosis and incomplete metamorphosis to compare the patterns of insect development.

**Topic: Butterflies**
Visit glencoe.com for Web links to information about butterflies.

**Activity** What are some of the characteristics that are used to identify butterflies? Make a diagram of the life cycle of a butterfly.

**Figure 18** Insect metamorphosis occurs in two ways.
**State** *the name given a moth larva.*

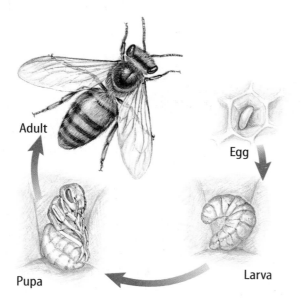

Bees and many other insects undergo the four stages of complete metamorphosis.

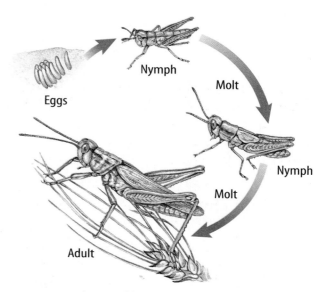

Insects like the grasshopper undergo incomplete metamorphosis.

### Figure 19

**A**rthropods are the most successful group of animals on Earth. Research the traits of each arthropod pictured. Compare and contrast those traits that enhance their survival and reproduction.

◄ **KRILL** Living in the icy waters of the arctic and the antarctic, krill are an important component in the ocean food web. They range in length from 8 to 60 mm. Baleen whales can eat 1,000 kg of krill in one feeding.

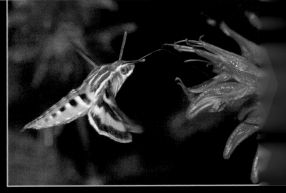

▲ **HUMMINGBIRD MOTH** When hovering near flowers, these moths produce the buzzing sound of hummingbirds. The wingspan of these moths can reach 6 cm.

◄ **GOOSENECK BARNACLES** These arthropods usually live on objects such as buoys and logs, which float in the ocean. They also live on other animals, including sea turtles and snails.

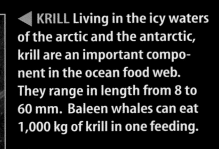

◄ **DIVING BEETLE** These predators feed on other invertebrates as well as small fish. They can grow to more than 40 mm in length.

◄ **ALASKAN KING CRAB** These crabs live in the cold waters of the north Pacific. Here, a gauge of about 18 cm measures a crab too small to keep; Alaskan king crabs can stretch 1.8 m from tip to tip.

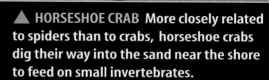

▲ **HORSESHOE CRAB** More closely related to spiders than to crabs, horseshoe crabs dig their way into the sand near the shore to feed on small invertebrates.

◀ **BUMBLEBEE** A thick coat of hair and the ability to shiver their flight muscles to produce heat allow bumblebees to fly in cold weather.

▶ **PILL BUG** Many people think that pill bugs—also known as sow bugs, rolypolies, or wood lice—are insects. Actually, they are crustaceans that live on land.

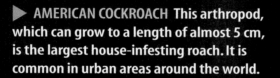

▶ **AMERICAN COCKROACH** This arthropod, which can grow to a length of almost 5 cm, is the largest house-infesting roach. It is common in urban areas around the world.

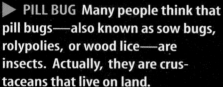

▲ **SPIDER MITE** These web-spinning arachnids are serious pests because they suck the juices out of plants. They damage houseplants, landscape plants, and crops. The spider mite above is magnified 14 times its normal size.

▲ **DADDY LONGLEGS** Moving on legs that can be as much as 20 times longer than their bodies, these arachnids feed on small insects, dead animals, and plant juices. Although they look like spiders, they belong to a different order of arachnids.

Orb weaver spider

Jumping spider

Scorpion

**Figure 20** This orb weaver spider uses its web to catch prey. Then it wraps the prey in silk to eat later. Jumping spiders have four large eyes on their face and four smaller eyes on the top of their head. Scorpions usually hide during the day and hunt for their prey at night.
**Identify** *an advantage that jumping spiders have because of all their eyes.*

**Arachnids** Spiders, ticks, mites, and scorpions belong to a group of arthropods known as arachnids (uh RAK nudz). Arachnids have only two body regions—a cephalothorax (sef uh luh THOR aks) and an abdomen—instead of three. The cephalothorax is made of the fused head and thorax regions. All arachnids have four pairs of legs attached to the cephalothorax.

Spiders are predators. A spider uses a pair of fanglike appendages near its mouth to inject paralyzing venom into its prey. Then it releases substances into its prey that digest the victim, turning it into a liquid, and the spider drinks it. Some spiders, like the one in **Figure 20,** weave webs to trap their prey. Other spiders, like the jumping spider, chase and catch their prey. Other arachnids, like the scorpion, paralyze their prey with venom from their stinger.

✔ **Reading Check** *How do spiders catch their prey?*

**Centipedes and Millipedes** As shown in **Figure 21,** centipedes and millipedes are long, thin, segmented animals. These arthropods have pairs of jointed legs attached to each segment. Centipedes have one pair of jointed legs per segment, and millipedes have two pairs. Centipedes are predators that use poisonous venom to capture their prey. Millipedes eat plants. Besides the number of legs, how else is the centipede different from the millipede?

**Figure 21** Centipedes can have more than 100 segments. When a millipede feels threatened, it will curl itself into a spiral.

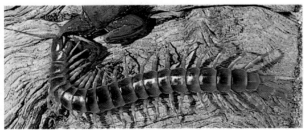

Centipede

Millipede

**Crustaceans** Think about where you can lift the most weight—is it on land or in water? An object seems to weigh less in water because water pushes up against the pull of gravity. Therefore, a large, heavy exoskeleton is less limiting in water than on land. The group of arthropods called crustaceans includes some of the largest arthropods. However, most crustaceans are small marine animals that make up the majority of zooplankton. Zooplankton refers to the tiny, free-floating animals that are food for other marine animals.

Examples of crustaceans include crabs, crayfish, lobsters, shrimp, barnacles, water fleas, and sow bugs. Their body structures vary greatly. Crustaceans usually have two pairs of antennae attached to the head, three types of chewing appendages, and five pairs of legs. Many water-living crustaceans also have appendages called swimmerets on their abdomen. Swimmerets force water over the feathery gills where carbon dioxide from the crustacean is exchanged for oxygen in the water.

## Echinoderms

Most people know what a starfish is. However, today they also are known as sea stars. Sea stars belong to a varied group of animals called echinoderms (ih KI nuh durmz) that have radial symmetry. Sea stars, brittle stars, sea urchins, sand dollars, and sea cucumbers are echinoderms. The name *echinoderm* means "spiny skin." As shown in **Figure 22,** echinoderms have spines of various lengths that cover the outside of their bodies. Most echinoderms are supported and protected by an internal skeleton made up of bonelike plates. Echinoderms have a simple nervous system but don't have heads or brains. Some echinoderms are predators, some are filter feeders, and others feed on decaying matter.

### Mini LAB

**Observing Sow Bugs**

**Procedure**

1. Place six **sow bugs** in a clean, **flat container.**
2. Put a damp **sponge** at one end of the container.
3. Cover the container for 60 s. Remove the cover and observe where the sow bugs are. Record your observations in your **Science Journal.**

**Analysis**

1. What type of habitat do the sow bugs seem to prefer?
2. Where do you think you could find sow bugs near your home?

**Figure 22** Sun stars have up to twelve arms instead of five like many other sea stars. Sea urchins are covered with protective spines. Sand dollars have tube feet on their undersides.

Sun star

Sea urchin

Sand dollar

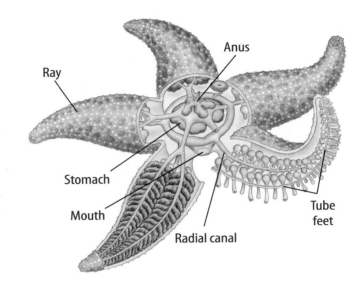

Ray

Anus

Stomach

Mouth

Radial canal

Tube feet

**Figure 23** Echinoderms use their tube feet to move. Sea stars also use their tube feet to capture prey and pull apart the shells. Tube feet are connected to an internal system of canals and are able to act like suction cups.

**Water-Vascular System** All echinoderms have a water-vascular system. It is a network of water-filled canals and thousands of tube feet. The tube feet work like suction cups to help the sea star move and capture prey. **Figure 23** shows how these tube feet are used to pull open prey. Sea stars have a unique way of eating. The sea star pushes its stomach out of its mouth and into the opened shell of its prey. After the prey's body is digested and absorbed, the sea star pulls in its stomach.

Like some invertebrates, sea stars can regenerate lost or damaged parts. In an attempt to reduce the population of sea stars that ate their oysters, oyster farmers once captured sea stars, cut them into pieces, and threw them back into the bay. Within a short time, the sea star population was five times larger. The oyster beds were destroyed—not saved.

## section 4 review

### Summary

**Arthropods**

- Arthropods are the largest and most diverse group of animals.
- Arthropods have bilateral symmetry and segmented bodies.
- Many insect species go through metamorphosis as they mature.

**Echinoderms**

- Echinoderms have radial symmetry and a water-vascular system.
- Like some other invertebrates, sea stars can regenerate damaged parts.

### Self Check

1. **List** the advantages and disadvantages of having an exoskeleton.
2. **Explain** why spiders and ticks aren't insects.
3. **Compare and contrast** centipedes and millipedes.
4. **Think Critically** What might happen to the sea star population after oyster beds are destroyed? Explain.

*Hot Words Hot Topics*: Bk 2 (5) pp. 292–294

#### Applying Math

5. **Use Proportions** A flea that is 4 mm in length can jump 25 cm from a resting position. If this flea were as tall as you are, how far could it jump?

# Observing Complete Metamorphosis

Many insects go through complete metamorphosis during their life cycles. Chemicals that are secreted by the body of the animal control the changes. How different are the body forms of the four stages of metamorphosis?

## ● Real-World Question

What do the stages of metamorphosis look like for a mealworm?

### Goals

■ **Observe** metamorphosis of mealworms.
■ **Compare** the physical appearance of the mealworms at each stage of metamorphosis.

### Materials

large-mouth jar or old fish bowl
bran or oatmeal
dried bread or cookie crumbs mixed with flour
slice of apple or carrot
paper towel
cheesecloth
mealworms
rubber band

### Safety Precautions

**WARNING:** *Be careful when working with animals. Never touch your face during the lab. Wash your hands thoroughly after completing the lab.*

## ● Procedure

1. Set up a habitat for the mealworms by placing a 1-cm layer of bran or oatmeal on the bottom of the jar. Add a 1-cm layer of dried bread or cookie crumbs mixed with flour. Then add another layer of bran or oatmeal.

2. Add a slice of apple or carrot as a source of moisture. Replace the apple or carrot daily.

3. Place 20 to 30 mealworms in the jar. Add a piece of crumpled paper towel.

4. Cover the jar with a piece of cheesecloth. Use the rubber band to secure the cloth to the jar.

5. **Observe** the mealworms daily for two to three weeks. Record daily observations in your Science Journal.

## ● Conclude and Apply

1. **Draw and describe** the mealworms' metamorphosis to adults in your Science Journal.

2. **Describe** some of the advantages of an insect's young being different from the adults.

3. **Infer** where you might find mealworms or adult darkling beetles in your house.

### Communicating Your Data

Draw a cartoon showing the different stages of metamorphosis from mealworm to adult darkling beetle. **For more help, refer to the** Science Skill Handbook.

## Design Your Own

# Garbage-Eating Worms

## Goals

■ **Design** an experiment that compares the condition of soil in two environments—one with earthworms and one without.

■ **Observe** the change in soil conditions for two weeks.

## Possible Materials

worms (red wigglers)
4-L plastic containers with drainage holes (2)
soil (7 L)
shredded newspaper
spray bottle
chopped food scraps including fruit and vegetable peels, pulverized eggshells, tea bags, and coffee grounds (Avoid meat and fat scraps.)

## Safety Precautions

**WARNING:** *Be careful when working with live animals. Always keep your hands wet when handling earthworms. Don't touch your face during the lab. Wash your hands thoroughly after the lab.*

### ⊙ Real-World Question

Susan knows that soil conditions can influence the growth of plants. She is trying to decide what factors might improve the soil in her backyard garden. A friend suggests that earthworms improve the quality of the soil. How could Susan find out if the presence of earthworms has any value in improving soil conditions? How does the presence of earthworms change the condition of the soil?

### ⊙ Form a Hypothesis

Based on your reading and observations, state a hypothesis about how earthworms might improve the conditions of soil.

## Test Your Hypothesis

**Make a Plan**

1. As a group, agree upon a hypothesis and decide how you will test it. Identify what results will support the hypothesis.

2. List the steps you will need to take to test your hypothesis. Be specific. Describe exactly what you will do in each step. List your materials.

3. Prepare a data table in your Science Journal to record your observations.

4. Read over the entire experiment to make sure that all the steps are in a logical order.

5. **Identify** all constants, variables, and controls of the experiment.

**Follow Your Plan**

1. Make sure your teacher approves your plan before you start.

2. Carry out the experiment according to the approved plan.

3. While doing the experiment, record your observations and complete the data table in your Science Journal.

## Analyze Your Data

1. **Compare** the changes in the two sets of soil samples.

2. **Compare** your results with those of other groups.

3. **Identify** the control in this experiment.

4. What were your variables?

## Conclude and Apply

1. **Explain** whether the results support your hypothesis.

2. **Describe** what effect you think rain would have on the soil and worms.

### Communicating Your Data

**Write** an informational pamphlet on how to use worms to improve garden soil. Include diagrams and a step-by-step procedure.

# SCIENCE Stats

## Squid Power

### Did you know...

**... Squid can light up like a multi-colored neon sign** because of chemical reactions inside their bodies. They do this to lure prey into their grasp or to communicate with other squid. These brilliantly-colored creatures, often called fire squid, can produce blue-, red-, yellow-, and white-colored flashes in 0.3-s bursts every 5 s.

**... The scariest-looking squid is the vampire squid.** It can wrap its webbed, spiked arms around itself like a cloak. Its fins look like pointed ears and its body is covered with light-producing organs that blink on and off. Imagine seeing that eerie sight in the dark depths of the ocean, nearly 1 km below the surface of the sea.

*Hot Words Hot Topics*: Bk 2 (Stats) p. 396

**Applying Math** Scientists estimate that the adult vampire squid, which grows to about 15 cm in length, can swim at the rate of two body lengths per second. How fast is that in kilometers per hour?

**... Squid have blue blood** because their oxygen is transported by a blue copper compound not by bright-red hemoglobin like in human blood.

**... Females of many species of squid die just after they lay eggs.** In 1984, a giant squid washed ashore in Scotland, carrying more than 3,000 eggs.

### Find Out About It

Scientists have never seen a living giant squid. Where would you look? At what depth? What kind of equipment would you use? To research these questions, visit glencoe.com .

## Reviewing Main Ideas

### Section 1 What is an animal?

1. Animals are many-celled organisms that must find and digest their own food.

2. Invertebrates are animals without backbones, and vertebrates have backbones.

3. Symmetry is the way that animal body parts are arranged. The three types of symmetry are bilateral, radial, and asymmetrical.

### Section 2 Sponges, Cnidarians, Flatworms, and Roundworms

1. Sponges have no tissues.

2. Adult sponges are sessile and obtain food and oxygen by filtering water.

3. Cnidarians are radially symmetrical, and most have tentacles with stinging cells to get food.

4. Flatworms and roundworms have bilateral symmetry. They have parasitic and free-living members.

### Section 3 Mollusks and Segmented Worms

1. Mollusks are soft-bodied animals that usually have a shell and an open circulatory system.

2. Gastropods, bivalves, and cephalopods are types of mollusks.

3. Annelids have segmented bodies. A body cavity separates internal organs from the body wall.

### Section 4 Arthropods and Echinoderms

1. Arthropods have exoskeletons that cover, protect, and support their bodies.

2. Arthropods develop either by complete metamorphosis or by incomplete metamorphosis.

3. Echinoderms are spiny-skinned invertebrates and have a water-vascular system.

## Visualizing Main Ideas

*Copy and complete the following concept map.*

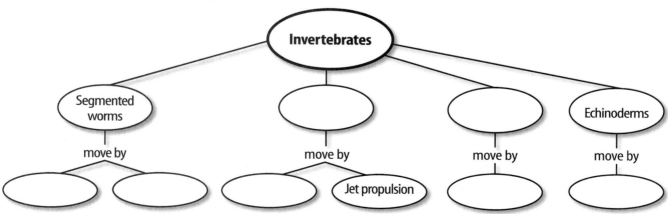

## Using Vocabulary

appendage p. 496
arthropod p. 496
closed circulatory
    system p. 492
cnidarian p. 486
exoskeleton p. 496
gill p. 490
invertebrate p. 484
mantle p. 490

medusa p. 487
metamorphosis p. 497
mollusk p. 490
open circulatory
    system p. 491
polyp p. 487
radula p. 491
symmetry p. 483

*For each set of vocabulary words below, explain the relationship that exists.*

1. medusa—polyp

2. closed circulatory system—open circulatory system

3. vertebrate—invertebrate

4. arthropod—mollusk

5. exoskeleton—mantle

6. arthropod—appendage

7. cnidarian—invertebrate

8. mollusk—mantle

9. medusa—cnidarian

## Checking Concepts

*Choose the word or phrase that best answers the question.*

10. Marine worms can live in all but which of the following?
    **A)** mud burrows    **C)** soil
    **B)** tube cases      **D)** salt water

11. Butterflies, ants, bees, and beetles are examples of insects that undergo
    **A)** incomplete metamorphosis.
    **B)** complete metamorphosis.
    **C)** no metamorphosis.
    **D)** a molt from nymph to adult.

12. The body plans of cnidarians are polyp and which of the following?
    **A)** larva    **C)** pupa
    **B)** medusa   **D)** bud

13. Which of the following is a parasite?
    **A)** sponge    **C)** tapeworm
    **B)** planarian  **D)** jellyfish

14. Which of the following groups of animals molt?
    **A)** crustaceans  **C)** sea stars
    **B)** earthworms   **D)** flatworms

15. Which of these organisms has a closed circulatory system?
    **A)** octopus  **C)** oyster
    **B)** snail    **D)** sponge

16. Radial symmetry is common in which group of invertebrates?
    **A)** annelids  **C)** echinoderms
    **B)** mollusks  **D)** arthropods

17. Which of the following organisms has two body regions?
    **A)** insect   **C)** arachnid
    **B)** mollusk  **D)** annelid

**Use the photo below to answer question 18.**

18. What symmetry does the animal in the illustration above have?
    **A)** asymmetry  **C)** radial
    **B)** bilateral  **D)** anterior

19. Which of the following do not belong to the same group?
    **A)** snails   **C)** octopuses
    **B)** oysters  **D)** sea stars

## Thinking Critically

**20. Infer** Which aspect of sponge reproduction would be evidence that they are more like animals than plants?

**21. Explain** why it is an advantage for organisms to have more than one means of reproduction.

**22. Compare and contrast** the tentacles of cnidarians and cephalopods.

**23. Explain** the main differences between budding and regeneration.

**24. Infer** Centipedes and millipedes have segments. Why are they not classified as worms?

**25. Compare and contrast** the feeding habits of sponges and cnidarians.

**26. Draw Conclusions** Observe the conch in **Figure 11.** Infer why gastropods are sometimes called univalves? Use examples in your answer.

**27. Concept Map** Copy and complete the concept map below about cnidarian classification.

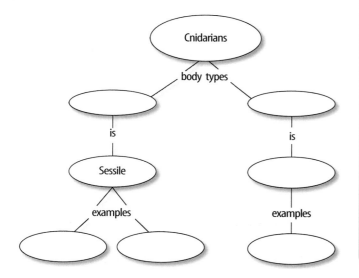

## Performance Activities

**28. Diary** Pretend you are an earthworm. Write a diary with at least ten entries describing your daily life. Include how you move, how you get food, and where you live.

*Hot Words Hot Topics*: Bk 2 (29) p. 106; (30) pp. 92, 201–202; (31) pp. 92; (32) pp. 142–143

## Applying Math

**29. Giant Squid Size** The largest giant squid recorded was 18 m long and weighed 900 kg. The best-preserved specimen is at the American Museum of Natural History. It is about 8 m long and has a mass of 114 kg. This is only a fraction of the largest specimen ever found. What is the fraction?

**Use the following illustration to answer question 30.**

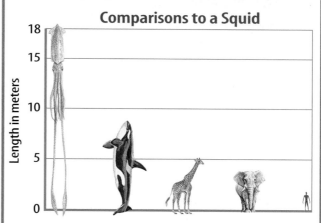

**30. Squid Comparisons** Approximately how many times longer is a giant squid compared to a killer whale? A giraffe? An elephant? A human?

**31. Earthworm Feeding** If you have an apple that weighs 141 g and an earthworm that weighs 11 g, how many days would it take the earthworm to eat the apple? Assume the earthworm can eat its own weight each day.

**32. Insect Species** Approximately 91,000 species of beetles have been identified in the United States. Approximately what percentage of the identified insect species are beetles?

**Part I**

*Record your answers on the answer sheet provided by your teacher or on a sheet of paper.*

**1** Which of the following is NOT a characteristic of animals?
(1) All animals have a definite shape.
(2) All animals are many-celled.
(3) All animals use energy.
(4) The cells of all animals have nuclei and organelles.

**Use the illustrations below to answer questions 2 and 3.**

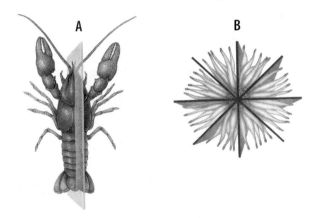

A          B

**2** What type of symmetry is represented by A?
(1) radial symmetry
(2) biradial symmetry
(3) bilateral symmetry
(4) asymmetry

**3** Which of the following animals has the type of symmetry shown in B?
(1) earthworm          (3) cow
(2) clam               (4) sea urchin

**4** Which of the following is NOT an invertebrate animal group?
(1) arthropod
(2) chordate
(3) sponge
(4) cnidarian

**5** Which of the following is a characteristic of cnidarians?
(1) spicules
(2) mantle
(3) nematocysts
(4) coelom

**6** Annelids, or segmented worms, include animals such as
(1) tapeworms.          (3) planaria.
(2) heartworms.         (4) leeches.

**7** Which of the following is a characteristic of echinoderms?
(1) They have two pairs of antennae.
(2) They have a "spiny skin."
(3) They have many setae along the sides of their body.
(4) They move through water by jet propulsion.

**Use the photo below to answer questions 8 and 9.**

**8** What kind of invertebrate is the animal shown above?
(1) mollusk          (3) sponge
(2) arthropod        (4) echinoderm

**9** Which of the following animals is a member of the same invertebrate group as the animals shown above?
(1) hydra          (3) spider
(2) leech          (4) sponge

**Part II**

*Record your answers on the answer sheet provided by your teacher or on a sheet of paper.*

**10** Give three examples of invertebrates: one that has radial symmetry, one that has bilateral symmetry, and one that is asymmetrical.

**Use the illustration below to answer questions 11 and 12.**

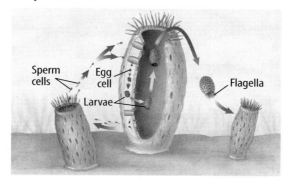

**11** The reproduction of which invertebrates is shown in the diagram above? What type of reproduction is shown?

**12** What other type of reproduction is characteristic of this animal? Explain.

**13** What does the term hermaphrodite mean? Give one example of an invertebrate that is hermaphroditic.

**14** Compare the number of body regions, jointed legs, and pairs of wings in insects and arachnids.

**15** Describe the process of molting. Which invertebrate group exhibits this characteristic?

**16** Draw a flowchart to represent how food matter moves through an earthworm's digestive system.

**17** Compare and contrast a closed circulatory system and an open circulatory system.

**Use the illustration below to answer questions 18 and 19.**

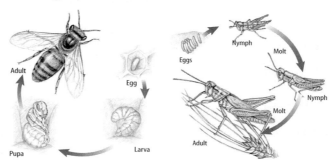

**18** Which of the diagrams above represents complete metamorphosis and which represents incomplete metamorphosis? How can you tell the difference?

**19** Compare and contrast the nymph and larva stages of metamorphosis.

**chapter**

**18**

**LE 4.1d:** Fertilization and/or development in organisms may be internal or external.
**4.3d:** Patterns of development vary among animals. In some species the young resemble the adult, while in others they do not. Some insects and amphibians undergo metamorphosis as they mature.
**Also Covered:** 4.3f, 5.1a, 5.1b, 5.1d, 5.1e, 5.1f, 5.1g

# Vertebrate Animals

## Traits We Share With Animals

An eagle flies through the sky, a salmon swims through a stream, a snake slithers along the ground, and a grizzly bear walks along a river's edge. Each of these animals appears different, but these animals, as well as humans, share a common trait—an internal skeleton.

**Science Journal**   What other traits do these animals and humans share?

# Start-Up Activities

## Animals with a Backbone

An internal skeleton is common to many animals. Skeletons are made of bones or cartilage. They give your body its overall shape and work with your muscles to help move your body. **WARNING:** *Do not eat or drink anything in the lab.*

1. Use pasta wheels, soft-candy circles, and long pipe cleaners to make a model of a backbone.

2. On a pipe cleaner, string in an alternating pattern the pasta wheels and the soft-candy circles until the string is about 10 cm long.

3. Fold over each end of the pipe cleaner so the pasta and candy do not slide off.

4. **Think Critically** Slowly bend the model. Does it move easily? How far can you bend it? What do you think makes up your backbone? Write your observations and answers in your Science Journal.

**FOLDABLES™**
**Study Organizer**

**Vertebrates** Make the following Foldable to help you organize your thoughts about vertebrate animals before you begin reading.

**STEP 1** Collect three sheets of paper and layer them about 1.25 cm apart vertically. Keep the edges level.

**STEP 2** Fold up the bottom edges of the paper to form 6 equal tabs.

**STEP 3** Fold the papers and crease well to hold the tabs in place. Staple along the fold. **Label** the flaps *Vertebrates, Fish, Amphibians, Reptiles, Birds,* and *Mammals,* as shown.

| Vertebrates |
| Fish |
| Amphibians |
| Reptiles |
| Birds |
| Mammals |

**Sequence** Before you read the chapter, write what you know about each group under the tabs. As you read the chapter, add to or change the information you wrote under the tabs.

Preview this chapter's content and activities at glencoe.com

# section
## 1
# Chordate Animals

## What is a chordate?

Suppose you asked your classmates to list their pets. Dogs, cats, birds, snakes, and fish probably would appear on the list. Animals that are familiar to most people are animals with a backbone. These animals belong to a larger group of animals called chordates (KOR dayts). Three characteristics of all **chordates** are a notochord, a nerve cord, and pharyngeal pouches at some time during their development. The notochord, shown in **Figure 1,** is a flexible rod that extends along the length of the developing organism. Pharyngeal pouches are slitlike openings between the body cavity and the outside of the body. They are present only during the early stages of the organism's development. In most chordates, one end of the nerve cord develops into the organism's brain.

**Vertebrates** Scientists classify the 42,500 species of chordates into smaller groups, as shown in **Figure 2.** The animals within each group share similar characteristics, which may indicate that they have a common ancestor. Vertebrates, which include humans, are the largest group of chordates.

Vertebrates have an internal system of bones called an endoskeleton. *Endo-* means "within." The vertebrae, skull, and other bones of the endoskeleton support and protect internal organs. For example, vertebrae surround and protect the nerve cord. Many muscles attach to the skeleton and make movement possible.

**Figure 1** Lancelets are filter feeders that grow to 7 cm in length and live in the ocean. Its pharyngeal pouches develop into gill slits.

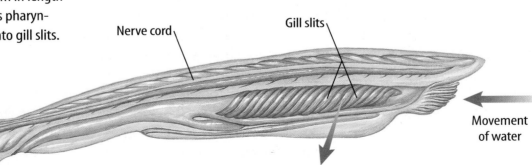

Notochord

Nerve cord

Gill slits

Movement of water

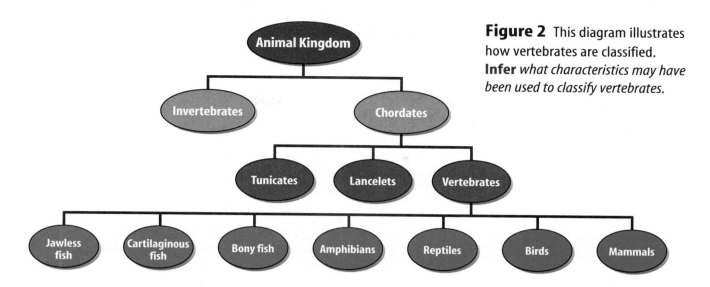

**Figure 2** This diagram illustrates how vertebrates are classified. **Infer** *what characteristics may have been used to classify vertebrates.*

**Body Temperature** Most vertebrate body temperatures change as the surrounding temperature changes. These animals are **ectotherms** (EK tuh thurmz), or cold-blooded animals. Fish are examples of ectotherms.

Humans and many other vertebrates are **endotherms** (EN duh thurmz), or warm-blooded animals. Their body temperature doesn't change with the surrounding temperature. Your body temperature is usually about 37°C, but it can vary by about 1°C, depending on the time of day. Changes of more than a degree or two usually indicate an infection or overexposure to extreme environmental temperatures.

✔ **Reading Check** *Are humans endotherms or ectotherms?*

## Fish

The largest group of vertebrates—fish—lives in water. Fish are ectotherms that can be found in warm desert pools and the subfreezing Arctic Ocean. Some species are adapted to swim in shallow freshwater streams and others in salty ocean depths.

Fish have fleshy filaments called gills, shown in **Figure 3,** where carbon dioxide and oxygen are exchanged. Water, containing oxygen, flows over the gills. When blood is pumped into the gills, the oxygen in the water moves into the blood. At the same time, carbon dioxide moves out of the blood in the gills and into the water.

Most fish have pairs of fanlike fins. The top and the bottom fins stabilize the fish. Those on the sides steer and move the fish. The tail fin propels the fish through the water.

Most fish have scales. Scales are thin structures made of a bony material that overlap like shingles on a house to cover the skin.

**Living Environment**

**5.1a, 1.1h List** five animals and a specific characteristic that scientists use to classify each of the animals into a different category.

**Figure 3** Gas exchange occurs in the gill filaments.

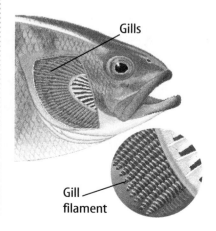

Gills

Gill filament

**Changing Mass** Submarines pump water into and out of special chambers, which causes the submarine to sink or rise. In a similar way, gases move into and out of a fish's swim bladder. This allows the fish to sink or rise in the water. How do fish without swim bladders move up and down in the water? Write your answer in your Science Journal.

# Types of Fish

Scientists classify fish into three groups—bony, jawless, and cartilaginous (kar tuh LA juh nuhs)—which are illustrated in **Figure 4** on the opposite page. Bony fish have skeletons made of bone, while jawless fish and cartilaginous fish have endoskeletons made of cartilage. **Cartilage** (KAR tuh lihj) is a tough, flexible tissue that is similar to bone but is not as hard or brittle. Your external ears and the tip of your nose are made of cartilage.

**Bony Fish** About 95 percent of all fish have skeletons made of bone. Goldfish, trout, bass, and marlins are examples of bony fish. The body structure of a typical bony fish is shown in **Figure 5.** As a bony fish swims, water easily flows over its body because its scales are covered with slimy mucus.

If you've ever watched fish in a tank, you know that they rise and sink to different levels in the water. An important adaptation in most bony fish is the swim bladder. This air sac helps control the depth at which the fish swims. The swim bladder inflates and deflates as gases—mostly oxygen in deep-water fish and nitrogen in shallow-water fish—move between the swim bladder and the blood. As the swim bladder fills with gas, the fish rises in the water. When the gas leaves the bladder, it deflates and the fish sinks lower in the water.

Most bony fish use external fertilization (fur tuh luh ZAY shun) to reproduce. External fertilization means that the eggs are fertilized outside the female's body. Females release large numbers of eggs into the water. Then, a male swims over the eggs, releases the sperm into the water, and many eggs are fertilized.

**Figure 5** The many types of bony fish range in size from a few millimeters to many meters in length.
**Infer** why all bony fish might have the same basic body plan.

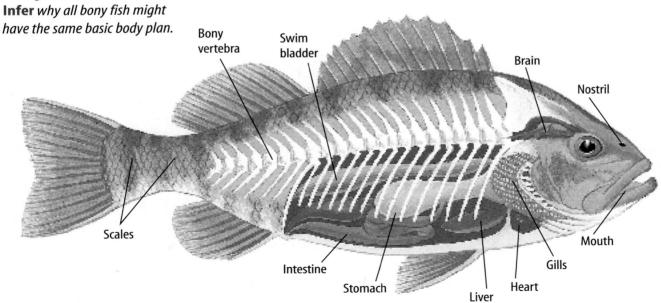

Bony vertebra · Swim bladder · Brain · Nostril · Scales · Intestine · Stomach · Liver · Heart · Gills · Mouth

# NATIONAL GEOGRAPHIC VISUALIZING FISH DIVERSITY

## Figure 4

**F**ish are the most numerous and varied of all vertebrates, with more than 20,000 living species. These species can be organized into three groups—jawless, cartilaginous, and bony. Jawless fish are the most primitive and form the smallest group. Cartilaginous fish include more than 600 species, nearly all of them predators. Bony fish are the most numerous and diverse group. This page features photos of fish from each group.

**Sturgeon**

**Whale Shark**

**Wolf Eel**

**BONY FISH** The bodies of bony fish vary. The fins of the coelacanth below have jointed bones, like the legs of many land animals. Amphibians may have evolved from ancestors of coelacanths.

**Ratfish**

**CARTILAGINOUS FISH** The cartilage that gives these fish their shape is a lightweight material that is softer than bone. The hammerhead shark below has been known to use the cartilage in its hammer-shaped head to pin down stingrays, one of its favorite meals, before it devours them.

**Angelfish**

**Coelacanth**

**Electric Ray**

**JAWLESS FISH** Only about 70 species make up the jawless group of fish. Jawless fish are often parasitic. The hagfish, right, often crawls into fish trapped in nets and eats them from the inside out.

**Hagfish**

**Hammerhead shark**

The inside of a lamprey's mouth contains structures that are used to attach to larger fish.

**Figure 6** Lampreys are specialized predators. In places such as the Great Lakes, lampreys have caused a decrease in some fish populations.

**Jawless and Cartilaginous Fish** Only a few species of fish are classified as jawless fish, like the one in **Figure 6.** Jawless fish have scaleless, long, tubelike bodies; an endoskeleton made of cartilage; and a round, muscular mouth without a jaw. But the mouth contains sharp, toothlike structures. One type of jawless fish, the lamprey, attaches itself to a larger host fish using its strong mouth and toothlike structures. Its tongue has sharp ridges that scrape through the host fish's skin. The lamprey obtains nutrients by feeding on the host fish's blood.

Sharks, skates, and rays are cartilaginous fish. They have skeletons made of cartilage just like the jawless fish. However, cartilaginous fish have rough, sandpaperlike scales and movable jaws. Many sharks have sharp teeth made from modified scales. Most cartilaginous fish are predators.

## section 1 review

### Summary

**Chordate**

- All chordates have a notochord, a nerve cord, and pharyngeal pouches at some time during their development.
- A vertebrate is a chordate with an internal system of bones called an endoskeleton.
- Most vertebrates are ectotherms (cold-blooded animals), but humans and many other vertebrates are endotherms (warm-blooded animals).

**Fish**

- Fish are ectotherms that live in the water and belong to the largest group of vertebrates.

**Types of Fish**

- About 95 percent of all fish have bony skeletons.
- Lampreys, sharks, skates, and rays are fish with a skeleton made of cartilage.

### Self Check

1. **List** the three groups of fish. What are some of the differences that separate these groups?

2. **Compare and contrast** ectothermic and endothermic animals.

3. **Form a Hypothesis** Sharks don't have swim bladders and must move constantly or they sink. Hypothesize about the amount of food that a shark must eat compared to the amount eaten by a bony fish of the same size.

4. **Think Critically** In one lake, millions of fish eggs are laid and fertilized annually. Why doesn't the lake become overcrowded with fish?

*Hot Words Hot Topics*: Bk 2 (5) pp. 142–143, 196–197

#### Applying Math

5. **Make and Use Graphs** Make a circle graph of the number of fish species currently classified: *jawless fish*—70; *cartilaginous fish*—820; and *bony fish*—23,500.

LE 4.3d: Patterns of development vary among animals. In some species the young resemble the adult, while in others they do not. Some insects and amphibians undergo metamorphosis as they mature.
**Also Covered:** LE 4.3f, 5.1a, 5.1b

section 2

# Amphibians and Reptiles

## Amphibians

A spy might lead a double life, but what about an animal? Amphibians (am FIH bee unz) are animals that spend part of their lives in water and part on land. In fact, the term *amphibian* comes from the Greek word *amphibios,* which means "double life." Frogs, toads, newts, and salamanders, such as the red-spotted salamander pictured in **Figure 7,** are examples of amphibians.

**Amphibian Adaptations** Living on land is different from living in water. Think about some of the things an amphibian must deal with in its environment. Temperature changes more quickly and more often in air than in water. More oxygen is available in air than in water. However, air doesn't support body weight as well as water does. Amphibians are adapted for survival in these different environments.

Amphibians are ectotherms. They adjust to changes in the temperature of their environment. In northern climates where the winters are cold, amphibians bury themselves in mud or leaves and remain inactive until the warmer temperatures of spring and summer arrive. This period of cold-weather inactivity is called **hibernation.** Amphibians that live in hot, dry environments move to cooler, more humid conditions underground and become inactive until the temperature cools down. This period of inactivity during hot, dry summer months is called **estivation** (es tuh VAY shun).

as you read

### What You'll Learn

- **Describe** how amphibians have adapted to live in water and on land.
- **Explain** what happens during frog metamorphosis.
- **Identify** the adaptations that allow reptiles to live on land.

### Why It's Important

Amphibians are sensitive to environmental changes, which may help identify problems that could affect humans.

**Review Vocabulary**
**metamorphosis:** change of body form that can be complete (egg, larva, pupa, adult) or incomplete (egg, nymph, adult)

**New Vocabulary**
- hibernation
- estivation
- amniotic egg

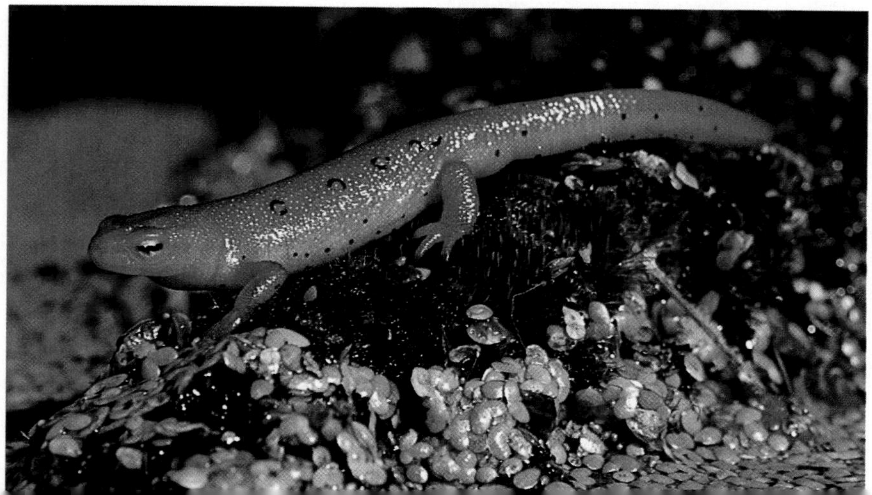

**Figure 7** Amphibians have many adaptations that allow for life both on land and in the water. This red-spotted salamander spends most of its life on land. **Explain** *why they must return to the water.*

**Amphibian Characteristics** Amphibians are vertebrates with a strong endoskeleton made of bones. The skeleton helps support their body while on land. Adult frogs and toads have strong hind legs that are used for swimming and jumping.

Adult amphibians use lungs instead of gills to exchange oxygen and carbon dioxide. This is an important adaptation for survival on land. However, because amphibians have three-chambered hearts, the blood carrying oxygen mixes with the blood carrying carbon dioxide. This mixing makes less oxygen available to the amphibian. Adult amphibians also exchange oxygen and carbon dioxide through their skin, which increases their oxygen supply. Amphibians can live on land, but they must stay moist so this exchange can occur.

Amphibian hearing and vision also are adapted to life on land. The tympanum (TIHM puh nuhm), or eardrum, vibrates in response to sound waves and is used for hearing. Large eyes assist some amphibians in capturing their prey.

**Reading Check** *What amphibian senses are adapted for life on land?*

Land environments offer a great variety of insects as food for adult amphibians. A long, sticky tongue extends quickly to capture an insect and bring it into the waiting mouth.

**Figure 8** Most young amphibians, like these tadpoles, look nothing like their parents when they hatch. The larvae go through metamorphosis in the water and eventually develop into adult frogs that live on land.

Tadpoles hatch from eggs that are laid in or near water.

Tadpoles use their gills for gas exchange.

**Amphibian Metamorphosis** Young animals such as kittens and calves are almost miniature versions of their parents, but young amphibians do not look like their parents. A series of body changes called metamorphosis (me tuh MOR fuh sus) occurs during the life cycle of an amphibian. Most amphibians go through a metamorphosis, as illustrated in **Figure 8.** Eggs are laid most often in water and hatch into larvae. Most adult amphibians live mainly on land.

The young larval forms of amphibians are dependent on water. They have no legs and breathe through gills. Over time, they develop body structures needed for life on land, including legs and lungs. The rate at which metamorphosis occurs depends on the species, the water temperature, and the amount of available food. If food is scarce and the water temperature is cool, then metamorphosis will take longer.

Like fish, most amphibians have external fertilization and require water for reproduction. Although most amphibians reproduce in ponds and lakes, some take advantage of other sources of water. For example, some species of rain forest tree frogs lay their eggs in rainwater that collects in leaves. Even more unusual is the Surinam toad shown in **Figure 9.** The fertilized eggs are placed on the mother's back. Her skin swells and covers the eggs to keep them moist. After metamorphosis occurs, fully formed toads emerge from under her skin.

**Figure 9** Surinam toads live along the Amazon River. A female carries 60 to 100 fertilized eggs on her back. Complete metamorphosis takes 12 to 20 weeks.
**Explain** *how this would be an advantage for young Surinam toads.*

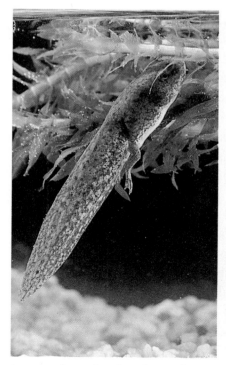

Legs begin to develop. Soon, the tail will disappear.

An adult frog uses lungs and skin for gas exchange.

**Figure 10** Reptiles have different body plans.

The rubber boa is one of only two species of boas in North America. Rubber boas have flexible jaws that enable them to eat prey that is larger than their head.

Crocodiles and American alligators like this one build their nests on land near a body of water. They protect their eggs while they wait for them to hatch.

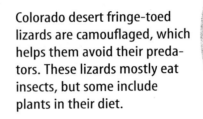

Sea turtles, like this loggerhead turtle, are threatened around the world because of pollution, loss of nesting habitat, drowning in nets, and lighted beaches.

Colorado desert fringe-toed lizards are camouflaged, which helps them avoid their predators. These lizards mostly eat insects, but some include plants in their diet.

**INTEGRATE**
*Career*

**Herpetologist** Most people are familiar with herpetologists, who are responsible for naming and classifying reptiles and amphibians. They often work in museums or universities. Their work usually involves field trips and gathering information for publication. What methods do taxonomists use to determine relationships between organisms? Write your answer in your Science Journal.

## Reptiles

Reptiles come in many shapes, sizes, and colors. Snakes, lizards, turtles, and crocodiles are reptiles. Reptiles are ectothermic vertebrates with dry, scaly skin. Because reptiles do not depend on water for reproduction, most are able to live their entire lives on land. They also have several other adaptations for life on land.

**Types of Reptiles** As shown in **Figure 10,** reptilian body plans vary. Turtles are covered with a hard shell, into which they withdraw for protection. Turtles eat insects, worms, fish, and plants.

Alligators and crocodiles are predators that live in and near water. These large reptiles live in warmer climates such as those found in the southern United States.

Lizards and snakes make up the largest group of reptiles. They have a highly developed sense of smell. An organ in the roof of the mouth senses molecules collected by the tongue. The constant in-and-out motion of the tongue allows a snake or lizard to smell its surroundings. Lizards have movable eyelids and external ears, and most lizards have legs with clawed toes. Snakes don't have eyelids, ears, or legs. Instead of hearing sounds, they feel vibrations in the ground.

**Reptile Adaptations** A thick, dry, waterproof skin is an adaptation that reptiles have for life on land. The skin is covered with scales that reduce water loss and help prevent injury.

**✓ Reading Check** *What are two functions of a reptile's skin?*

All reptiles have lungs for exchanging oxygen and carbon dioxide. Even sea snakes and sea turtles, which can stay submerged for long periods of time, must eventually come to the surface to breathe. Reptiles also have a neck that allows them to scan the horizon.

Two adaptations enable reptiles to reproduce successfully on land—internal fertilization and laying shell-covered, amniotic (am nee AH tihk) eggs. During internal fertilization, sperm are deposited directly into the female's body. Water isn't necessary for reptilian reproduction.

The embryo develops within the moist protective environment of the **amniotic egg,** as shown in **Figure 11.** The yolk supplies food for the developing embryo, and the leathery shell protects the embryo and yolk. When eggs hatch, young reptiles are fully developed. In some snake species, the female does not lay eggs. Instead, the eggs are kept within her body, where they incubate and hatch. The young snakes leave her body soon after they hatch.

**Figure 11** Young reptiles hatch from amniotic eggs. **Describe** *the advantages of this.*

**Living Environment**

**4.1d, 4.3c, 4.3d, 4.3f, 5.1b**
**Sequence** the steps of amphibian metamorphosis and reptilian development to compare the processes of growth and development from egg to adult.

## section 2 review

### Summary

**Amphibians**

- Amphibians are animals that spend part of their lives in water and part on land.
- Although they have a strong endoskeleton to support their body while on land, amphibians depend on water for external fertilization.
- Amphibians go through a series of bodily changes called metamorphosis.

**Reptiles**

- Reptiles are ectothermic vertebrates with dry, scaly skin.
- Lizards and snakes make up the largest group of reptiles.
- Two adaptations enable reptiles to reproduce successfully on land: internal fertilization and laying shell-covered, amniotic eggs.

### Self Check

1. **Infer** how a thick, dry, waterproof skin helps a reptile to live on land.
2. **Sequence** the steps of a frog's two-stage metamorphosis.
3. **Infer** why internal fertilization is efficient.
4. **Explain** how amphibians use adaptations to deal with cold winter months and hot, dry summer months.
5. **Think Critically** Some nonpoisonous snakes' patterns are similar to those of poisonous snakes. How is this coloring an advantage for a nonpoisonous snake?

### Applying Skills

6. **Compare and contrast** the exchange of oxygen and carbon dioxide in adult amphibians and reptiles.
7. **Communicate** Write an explanation about why amphibians must live in wet or moist environments.

# Frog Metamorphosis

Frogs and other amphibians use external fertilization to reproduce. Female frogs lay hundreds of jellylike eggs in water. Male frogs then fertilize these eggs. Once larvae hatch, the process of metamorphosis begins.

## ● Real-World Question

What changes occur as a tadpole goes through metamorphosis?

### Goals

- **Observe** how body structures change as a tadpole develops into an adult frog.
- **Determine** how long metamorphosis takes.

### Materials

4-L aquarium or jar          aquatic plants
frog egg mass                washed gravel
lake or pond water           lettuce
stereoscopic microscope          (previously
watch glass                      boiled)
small fishnet                large rock

### Safety Precautions

**WARNING:** *Handle the eggs with care.*

## ● Procedure

1. Copy the data table in your Science Journal.

| Frog Metamorphosis | |
|---|---|
| **Date** | **Observations** |
| | Do not write in this book. |
| | |

2. As a class, use the aquarium, pond water, gravel, rock, and plants to prepare a water habitat for the frog eggs.

3. Place the egg mass in the aquarium's water. Use the fishnet to separate a few eggs from the mass and place them on the watch glass. Observe the eggs using the microscope. Record all observations in your data table. Return the eggs to the aquarium.

4. **Observe** the eggs twice a week until hatching begins. Then observe the tadpoles twice weekly. Identify the mouth, eyes, gill cover, gills, nostrils, back fin, and legs.

5. In your Science Journal, write a description of how tadpoles eat cooled, boiled lettuce.

## ● Conclude and Apply

1. **Explain** why the jellylike coating around the eggs is important.

2. **Compare** the eyes of young tadpoles with the eyes of older tadpoles.

3. **Calculate** how long it takes for eggs to hatch, legs to develop, and to become a frog.

### ○ommunicating
#### Your Data

Draw the changes you observe as the egg hatches and the tadpole goes through metamorphosis. **For more help, refer to the Science Skill Handbook.**

# Birds

## Characteristics of Birds

Ostriches have strong legs for running, and pelicans have specialized bills for scooping fish. Penguins can't fly but are excellent swimmers, and house wrens and hummingbirds are able to perch on branches. These birds are different, but they, and all birds, have common characteristics. Birds are endothermic vertebrates that have two wings, two legs, and a bill or beak. Birders, or bird-watchers, can tell where a bird lives and what it eats by looking at the type of wings, feet, and beak or bill it has. Birds are covered mostly with feathers—a feature unique to birds. They lay hard-shelled eggs and sit on these eggs to keep them warm until they hatch. Besides fish, birds are the most numerous vertebrates on Earth. **Figure 12** illustrates some of the more than 8,600 species of birds and their adaptations.

**as you read**

*What* **You'll Learn**

- **Identify** the characteristics of birds.
- **Describe** the adaptations birds have for flight.
- **Explain** the function of feathers.

*Why* **It's Important**

Humans modeled airplanes after the flight of birds.

**Review Vocabulary**

**appendage:** structure such as a claw, leg, or antenna that grows from the body

**New Vocabulary**

- contour feather
- down feather

**Figure 12** Emus can't fly but they have strong legs and feet that are adapted for running.

Horned puffins can fly and their sleek bodies and small, pointed wings also enable them to "fly" underwater.

An albatross glides in the air.

Birds of prey, like this osprey, have sharp, strong talons that enable them to grab their prey.

**Figure 13** Wings provide an upward force called lift in both birds and airplanes.

Bald eagles are able to soar for long periods of time because their wings have a large surface area to provide lift.

The glider gets lift from its wings the same way a bald eagle gets lift.

**Science nline**

**Topic: Wing Designs**

Visit glencoe.com for Web links to information about wing designs of different aircraft.

**Activity** Draw as many wing designs as you can find and explain how they are different.

# Adaptations for Flight

The bodies of most birds are designed for flight. They are streamlined and have light yet strong skeletons. The inside of a bird's bone is almost hollow. Internal crisscrossing structures strengthen the bones without making them as heavy as mammal bones are. Because flying requires a rigid body, a bird's tail vertebrae are joined together to provide the needed rigidity, strength, and stability. Birds use their tail to help them steer through the air. While a bird can still fly without a tail, their flight is usually shorter and not as smooth.

> ✔ **Reading Check** *What advantage do birds' bones give them for flight?*

Flight requires a lot of energy and oxygen. Birds eat insects, nectar, fish, meats, or other high-energy foods. They also have a large, efficient heart and a specialized respiratory system. A bird's lungs connect to air sacs that provide a constant supply of oxygen to the blood and make the bird more lightweight.

Slow-motion video shows that birds beat their wings up and down as well as forward and back. A combination of wing shape, surface area, air speed, and angle of the wing to the moving air, along with wing movements, provide an upward push that is needed for the flight of a bald eagle, as shown in **Figure 13.** Inventors of the first flying machines, such as gliders, used the body plan of birds as a model for flight. As wind passes above and below the wing, it creates lift. Lift is what allows birds, as well as planes, to stay in flight.

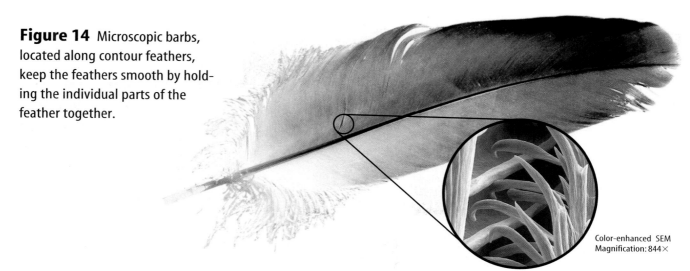

**Figure 14** Microscopic barbs, located along contour feathers, keep the feathers smooth by holding the individual parts of the feather together.

Color-enhanced SEM
Magnification: 844×

# Functions of Feathers

Birds are the only animals with feathers. They have two main types of feathers—contour feathers and down feathers. Strong, lightweight **contour feathers** give adult birds their stream-lined shape and coloring. A close look at the contour feather in **Figure 14** shows the parallel strands, called barbs, that branch off the main shaft. Outer contour feathers help a bird move through the air or water. It is these long feathers on the wings and tail that help the bird steer and keep it from spinning out of control. Feather colors and patterns can help identify species. They also are useful in attracting mates and protecting birds from predators because they can be a form of camouflage.

Have you ever noticed that the hair on your arm stands up on a cold day? This response is one way your body works to trap and keep warm air close to your skin. Birds have **down feathers** that trap and keep warm air next to their bodies. These fluffy feathers, as shown in **Figure 15,** provide an insulating layer under the contour feathers of adult birds and cover the bodies of some young birds.

**Reading Check** *What are two ways feathers protect birds?*

**Figure 15**
Some species of birds, like chickens and these pheasants, are covered with feathers when they hatch. **Explain** *how this might be an advantage.*

## Mini LAB

### Modeling Feather Function

**Procedure**
1. Wrap **polyester fiber** or **cotton** around the bulb of an **alcohol thermometer.** Place it into a **plastic bag.** Record the temperature in your **Science Journal.**
2. Place a second **alcohol thermometer** into a **plastic bag** and record the temperature.
3. Simultaneously submerge the thermometers into a **container** of **cold water,** keeping the top of each bag above the water's surface.
4. After 2 min, record the temperature of each thermometer.

**Analysis**
1. Which thermometer had the greater change in temperature?
2. Infer the type of feather that the fiber or cotton models.

**Try at Home**

**Figure 16** Cormorants' feathers get wet when they go underwater to catch fish. When they return to their roost, they have to hold their wings out to dry.

**Care of Feathers** Clothes keep you warm only if they are dry and in good condition. In a similar way, well-maintained feathers keep birds dry, warm, and able to fly. Birds preen to clean and reorganize their feathers. During preening, many birds also spread oil over their bodies and feathers. This oil comes from a gland found on the bird's back at the base of its tail. The oil helps keep the skin soft, and feathers and scales from becoming brittle. The oil does not waterproof the feathers as once thought. It is the arrangement of a feather's microscopic structures that repels water more than the oil does. Cormorants, like the one in **Figure 16,** have wettable outer feathers that must be air-dried after diving for food.

**Living Environment**

**5.1a, 5.1b, 5.1g Discuss** five characteristics that help birds maintain homeostasis and survive.

## section 3 review

### Summary

**Characteristics of Birds**

- Birds are endothermic vertebrates, have two wings, two legs, and a bill or beak, and are covered mostly with feathers.

**Adaptations for Flight**

- Birds are streamlined and have light, yet strong, skeletons.
- The inside of a bird's bone is almost hollow.
- Wings provide an upward force called lift.

**Functions of Feathers**

- Birds have contour feathers that help them move through the air or water.
- Down feathers trap and keep warm air next to birds' bodies.

### Self Check

1. **List** several reasons why birds preen their feathers.
2. **Describe** how a bird's skeletal system, respiratory system, and circulatory system all work together to enable it to fly.
3. **Think Critically** Explain why birds can reproduce in Antarctica when temperatures are below 0°C.

*Hot Words Hot Topics*: Bk 2 (4) pp. 292–294, 436–441

### Applying Math

4. **Use an Electronic Spreadsheet** During every 10 seconds of flight, a crow beats its wings 20 times, a robin 23 times, a chickadee 270 times, and a hummingbird 700 times. Use a spreadsheet to find out how many times the wings of each bird beat during a 5-minute flight.

LE 5.1b: An organism's overall body plan and its environment determine the way that the organism carries out the life processes. **Also Covered:** LE 4.1d, 5.1a, 5.1d, 5.1f.

# Mammals

## Mammal Characteristics

How many different kinds of mammals can you name? Moles, dogs, bats, dolphins, horses, and people are all mammals. They live in water and in many different climates on land. They burrow through the ground and fly through the air.

Mammals are endothermic vertebrates. They have mammary glands in their skin. In females, mammary glands produce milk that nourishes the young. A mammal's skin usually is covered with hair that insulates its body from cold and heat. It also protects the animal from wind and water. Some mammals, such as bears, are covered with thick fur. Others, like humans, have only patches of thick hair while the rest of their body is sparsely covered with hair. Still others, like the dolphins shown in **Figure 17,** have little hair. Wool, spines, quills, and certain horns are modified hair. What function do you think quills and spines serve?

**Mammary Glands** Mammals put a great deal of time and energy into the care of their young, even before birth. When female mammals are pregnant, the mammary glands increase in size. After birth, milk is produced and released from these glands. For the first weeks or months of a young mammal's life, the milk provides all of the nutrition the young mammal needs.

### as you read

*What* **You'll Learn**

- **Identify** the characteristics common to all mammals.
- **Explain** how mammals are adapted to the different environments on Earth.
- **Distinguish** among monotremes, marsupials, and placentals.

*Why* **It's Important**

All mammals have similar body structures.

⚲ **Review Vocabulary**

**symmetry:** refers to the arrangement of the individual parts of an object that can be divided into matching halves

**New Vocabulary**
- herbivore
- carnivore
- omnivore
- monotremes
- marsupial
- placental

Porcupines have fur next to their skin but sharp quills on the outside. Quills are modified hairs.

Dolphins do not have much hair on their bodies. A layer of fat under the skin acts as insulation.

**Figure 17** The type of hair mammals have varies from species to species.
**Explain** *the advantages and disadvantages of having hair.*

**Figure 18** Mountain lions are carnivores. They have sharp canines that are used to rip and tear flesh.

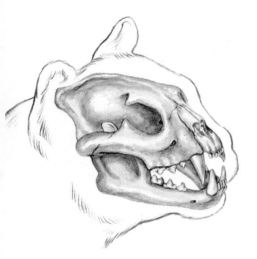

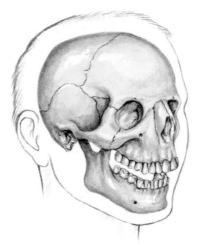

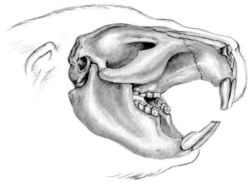

Herbivores, like this beaver, have incisors that cut vegetation and large, flat molars that grind it.

Humans are omnivores. They have incisors that cut vegetables, premolars that are sharp enough to chew meat, and molars that grind food.

## Mini LAB

### Inferring How Blubber Insulates

**Procedure**

1. Fill a **self-sealing plastic bag** about one-third full with solid **vegetable shortening.**
2. Turn another **self-sealing plastic bag** inside out. Place it inside the first bag so you are able to zip one bag to the other. This is a blubber mitten.
3. Put your hand in the blubber mitten. Place your mittened hand in **ice water** for 5 s. Remove the blubber mitten when finished.
4. Put your other bare hand in the same bowl of ice water for 5 s.

**Analysis**

1. Which hand seemed colder?
2. Infer the advantage a layer of blubber would give in the cold.

**Different Teeth** Mammals have teeth that are specialized for the type of food they eat. Plant-eating animals are called **herbivores.** Animals that eat meat are called **carnivores,** and animals that eat plants and animals are called **omnivores.** As shown in **Figure 18,** you usually can tell from the kind of teeth a mammal has whether it eats plants, other animals, or both. The four types of teeth are incisors, canines, premolars, and molars.

**Reading Check** *How are herbivores, carnivores, and omnivores different?*

**Body Systems** Mammals live active lives. They run, swim, climb, hop, and fly. Their body systems must interact and be able to support all of these activities.

Mammals have well-developed lungs made of millions of microscopic sacs called alveoli, which enable the exchange of carbon dioxide and oxygen during breathing. They also have a complex nervous system and are able to learn and remember more than many other animals. The brain of a mammal is usually larger than the brain of other animals of the same size.

All mammals have internal fertilization. After an egg is fertilized, the developing mammal is called an embryo. Most mammal embryos develop inside a female organ called the uterus. Mammals can be divided into three groups based on how their embryos develop. The three groups of mammals are monotremes, marsupials, and placentals.

## Mammal Types

The duck-billed platypus, shown in **Figure 19,** along with two species of echidnas (ih KID nuhs)—spiny anteaters—belong to the smallest group of mammals called the monotremes. They are different from other mammals because **monotremes** lay eggs with tough, leathery shells instead of having live births. The female incubates the eggs for about ten days. Monotremes also differ from other mammals because their mammary glands lack nipples. Instead, the milk seeps through the skin onto their fur. The young monotremes then nurse by licking the milk from the fur surrounding the mammary glands. Duck-billed platypuses and spiny anteaters are found in New Guinea and Australia.

**Figure 19** Duck-billed platypuses and spiny anteaters are the only species of mammals that lay eggs.

*Hot Words Hot Topics*: Bk 2 (1) pp. 132–134, 406

## Applying Math     Working with Percentages

**HOW MUCH TIME?** It is estimated that during the four months elephant seals spend at sea, 90 percent of their time is spent underwater. On a typical day, how much of the time between the hours of 10:00 A.M. and 3:00 P.M. does the elephant seal stay at the surface?

### Solution

**1** *This is what you know:*
- Total time: From 10:00 A.M. to 3:00 P.M. is 5 h.
  1 h = 60 min, so 5 × 60 = 300 min
- % of time on surface = 100% − 90% = 10% = 0.10

**2** *This is what you need to know:*
How much time is spent on the surface?

**3** *This is the procedure you need to use:*
- Use this equation:
  surface time = (total time)(% of time on surface)
- Substitute the known values:
  surface time = (300 min)(0.10) = 30 min

**4** *Check your answer:*
Divide your answer by the total time. Is the answer equal to 10 percent?

### Practice Problems

1. On a typical day during those four months, how much time do elephant seals stay at the surface from 11:00 P.M. until 6:00 A.M.?

2. On a typical day during those four months, how much time do elephant seals spend underwater from 9:00 A.M. until 6:00 P.M.?

Science Online | **For more practice, visit** glencoe.com

**Figure 20** Marsupials, such as opposums, are born before they are completely developed. Newborn marsupials make the journey to a nipple that is usually in the mother's pouch where they will finish developing.

**Living Environment**

LE 4.3a, 4.3c, 4.3d **Compare** the birth and development of monotremes and marsupials.

**Figure 21** Placental embryos rely on the umbilical cord to bring nutrients and to remove wastes. Your navel is where your umbilical cord was connected to you.

**Marsupials** Most **marsupials** carry their young in a pouch. Their embryos develop for only a few weeks within the uterus. When the young are born, they are without hair, blind, and not fully formed. Using their sense of smell, the young crawl toward a nipple and attach themselves to it. Here they feed and complete their development. Most marsupials—such as kangaroos, koalas, Tasmanian devils, and wallabies—live in Australia, Tasmania, and New Guinea. The opossum, shown in **Figure 20,** is the only marsupial that lives in North America.

✔ **Reading Check** *Why do most marsupials have a pouch?*

**Placentals** The largest number of mammals belongs to a group called placentals. **Placentals** are named for the placenta, which is a saclike organ that develops from tissues of the embryo and uterus. In the placenta, food, oxygen, and wastes are exchanged between the mother's blood and the embryo's blood, but their bloods do not mix. An umbilical cord, as seen in **Figure 21,** connects the embryo to the placenta. Food and oxygen are absorbed from the mother's blood for the developing young. Blood vessels in the umbilical cord carry food and oxygen to the developing young, then take away wastes. In the placenta, the mother's blood absorbs wastes from the developing young. This time of development, from fertilization to birth, is called the gestation period. Mice and rats have a gestation period of about 21 days. Human gestation lasts about 280 days. The gestation period for elephants is about 616 days, or almost two years.

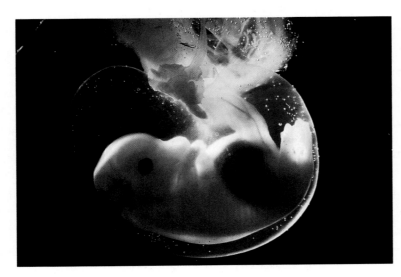

# Mammals Today

More than 4,000 species of mammals exist on Earth today. Mammals can be found on every continent, from cold arctic regions to hot deserts. Each kind of mammal has certain adaptations that enable it to live successfully within its environment.

Mammals, like all other groups of animals, have an important role in maintaining a balance in the environment. Large carnivores, such as wolves, help control populations of herbivores, such as deer and elk, thus preventing overgrazing. Bats and other small mammals such as honey possums help pollinate flowers. Other mammals unknowingly pick up plant seeds in their fur and distribute them. However, mammals and other animals are in trouble today because their habitats are being destroyed. They are left without enough food, shelter, and space to survive as millions of acres of wildlife habitat are damaged by pollution or developed for human needs. The grizzly bear, pictured in **Figure 22,** lives in North America and Europe and is an endangered species—a species in danger of becoming extinct—in most of its range because of habitat destruction.

**Figure 22** Grizzly bears, sometimes called brown bears, used to range all over the western half of the United States. Now, because of human settlement, habitat loss, and overhunting, grizzly bears are found only in Alaska, Montana, Wyoming, Idaho, and Washington.

## section 4 review

### Summary

**Mammal Characteristics**

- Mammals have mammary glands that produce milk for their young.
- Mammals have teeth that are specialized for the type of food they eat.
- The body systems of mammals are designed to support activities such as running, swimming, climbing, hopping, and flying.

**Mammal Types**

- The smallest group of mammals, called monotremes, lay eggs with leathery shells.
- Marsupials are born before they are completely developed, and most marsupials carry their young in a pouch.
- The placentals are the largest group of mammals.

**Mammals Today**

- More than 4,000 species of mammals exist on Earth today.

### Self Check

1. **Infer** why the brain of a mammal usually is larger than the brain of other animals of the same size.
2. **Explain** why animals are in trouble today.
3. **List** examples of how the teeth of mammals are specialized.
4. **Research Information** The monotremes are the smallest group of mammals. Using the library and online resources, explain where monotremes likely originated from and what continents monotreme fossils have been found on.
5. **Think Critically** Compare and contrast the development of embryos in placentals and marsupials.

*Hot Words Hot Topics*: Bk 2 (6) pp. 135–136

### Applying Math

6. **Solve One-Step Equations** The tallest mammal is the giraffe at 5.6 m. Calculate your height in meters and determine how many of you it would take to be as tall as a giraffe.

# LAB

## Model and Invent

# H🐾MES FOR ENDANGERED ANIMALS

### Goals
- **Research** the natural habitat and basic needs of one endangered vertebrate species.
- **Research and model** an appropriate zoo, animal park, or aquarium environment for this animal. Working cooperatively with your classmates, design an entire zoo or animal park.

### Possible Materials
poster board
markers or colored pencils
materials with which to
    make a scale model

### ▶ *Real-World Question*

Zoos, animal parks, and aquariums are safe places for endangered animals. Years ago, captive animals were kept in small cages or behind glass windows. The animals were on display like artwork in a museum. Now, some captive animals are kept in exhibit areas that closely resemble their natural habitats. These areas provide suitable environments for the animals so that they can reproduce, raise young, and have healthier and longer lives. What types of environments are best suited for raising animals in captivity? How can endangered animals be rescued?

## ◉ Make a Model

1. **Choose** an endangered animal to research. Find out where this animal is found in nature. What does it eat? Who are its natural predators? Does it exhibit unique territorial, courtship, or other types of social behavior? How is this animal adapted to its natural environment?

2. Why is this animal considered to be endangered?

3. **Design** a model of your proposed habitat in which this animal can live successfully.

4. **Research** how a zoo, animal park, or aquarium provides a habitat for this animal. This information can be obtained by contacting a zoo, animal park, or aquarium.

5. **Present** your design plan to your class in the form of a poster, slide show, or video. Compare your proposed habitat with that of the animal's natural environment. Make sure you include a picture of your animal in its natural environment.

## ◉ Test the Model

1. Using all of the information you have gathered, create a model exhibit area for your animal.

2. List other plants and animals that might be present in the exhibit area.

## ◉ Analyze Your Data

1. **Decide** whether all of the endangered animals studied in this activity could exist in the same zoo or wildlife preserve.

2. **Predict** which animals could be grouped together in exhibit areas.

## ◉ Conclude and Apply

1. **Determine** how much land your zoo or wildlife preservation needs. Which animals require the largest habitat?

2. Using the information provided by all your classmates, design a zoo or wildlife preserve for the majority of endangered animals you've studied.

3. **Analyze** which type of problems might exist in your design.

### Communicating Your Data

Give an oral presentation on endangered animals and wildlife conservation to another class of students using your model. Use materials from zoos to supplement your presentation.

# Cosmic Dust and Dinosaurs

## What killed the dinosaurs? Here is one theory.

Tiny bits of dust from comets and asteroids constantly sprinkle down on Earth. This cosmic dust led scientists Luis and Walter Alvarez to a hypothesis about one of science's most intriguing mysteries: What caused the extinction of dinosaurs?

It began some 65 million years ago when mass extinction wiped out 60 percent of all species alive on Earth, including the dinosaurs. Walter Alvarez and his father Luis Alvarez were working together on a geology expedition in Italy analyzing a layer of sedimentary rock. Using dating techniques, they were able to determine that this layer was deposited at roughly the same time that the dinosaurs became extinct. The younger Alvarez hypothesized that the rock might hold some clue to the mass extinction.

The Alvarezes proposed that the sedimentary rock be analyzed for the presence of the element iridium. Iridium is a dense and rare metal found in very low concentrations in Earth's core. The scientists expected to find a small amount of iridium. To their surprise, the sedimentary rock contained unusually high levels of iridium.

High concentrations of iridium are believed to be common in comets and asteroids.

**Did asteroids kill the dinosaurs? An artist drew this picture to show how Earth might have looked.**

If a huge asteroid collided with Earth, its impact would send tons of dust, debris, and iridium high into the atmosphere. The dust would block the Sun, causing global temperatures to decrease, plants to die, and animals to starve, resulting in a mass extinction. When the dust settled, iridium would fall to the ground as evidence of the catastrophe.

The Alvarez hypothesis, published in 1980, is still debated. However, it has since been supported by other research, including the discovery of a huge, ancient crater in Mexico. Scientists theorize that this crater was formed by the impact of an asteroid as big as Mount Everest.

**Write** Imagine that an asteroid has collided with Earth. You are one of the few human survivors. Write a five-day journal describing the events that take place.

**Science Online**
For more information, visit glencoe.com

## Reviewing Main Ideas

### Section 1 Chordate Animals

1. All chordates, at some time in their development, have a notochord and gill slits.

2. Endothermic animals maintain an internal body temperature. Ectothermic animals have body temperatures that change with the temperature of their surroundings.

3. The three classes of fish are jawless, cartilaginous, and bony. All fish are ectotherms.

### Section 2 Amphibians and Reptiles

1. Amphibians are ectothermic vertebrates that spend part of their lives in water and part on land. Most amphibians go through a metamorphosis, which includes water-living larva and land-living adult stages.

2. Reptiles are ectothermic land animals that have dry, scaly skin.

3. Most reptiles lay eggs with a leathery shell.

### Section 3 Birds

1. Birds are endotherms with feathers, and they lay eggs enclosed in hard shells.

2. Wings, feathers, and a light, strong skeleton are adaptations that allow birds to fly.

### Section 4 Mammals

1. Mammals are endotherms that have mammary glands. All mammals have some hair.

2. Mammals have specialized teeth that mostly determine what foods they eat.

3. There are three groups of mammals. Monotremes lay eggs. Most marsupials have pouches in which embryos develop. Placentals have a placenta, and the embryos develop within the female's uterus.

4. Mammals have a variety of adaptations that allow them to live in different types of environments.

## Visualizing Main Ideas

*Copy and complete the following table comparing the characteristics of fish, amphibians, and reptiles.*

| Vertebrate Characteristics | | | |
|---|---|---|---|
| Characteristic | Fish | Amphibians | Reptiles |
| Body temperature | ectotherm | | |
| Body covering | | | |
| Respiratory organs | Do not write in this book. | | |
| Method of movement | | legs | |
| Fertilization | | | internal |
| Kind of egg | lacks shell | | |

## Using Vocabulary

amniotic egg  p. 523
carnivore  p. 530
cartilage  p. 516
chordate  p. 514
contour feather  p. 527
down feather  p. 527
ectotherm  p. 515
endotherm  p. 515

estivation  p. 519
herbivore  p. 530
hibernation  p. 519
marsupial  p. 532
monotreme  p. 531
omnivore  p. 530
placental  p. 532

*Using complete sentences, explain how the vocabulary words in each pair listed below are alike and how they are different.*

1. contour feather—down feather

2. ectotherm—endotherm

3. chordate—cartilage

4. estivation—hibernation

5. carnivore—herbivore

6. marsupial—monotreme

7. amniotic egg—monotreme

8. down feather—endotherm

9. omnivore—carnivore

10. placental—marsupial

## Checking Concepts

*Choose the word or phrase that best answers the question.*

11. Which of the following animals have fins, scales, and gills?
    **A)** amphibians        **C)** reptiles
    **B)** crocodiles        **D)** fish

12. Which of these is an example of a cartilaginous fish?
    **A)** trout        **C)** shark
    **B)** bass        **D)** goldfish

13. Which of the following fish has a swim bladder?
    **A)** shark        **C)** trout
    **B)** lamprey        **D)** skate

14. Which of the following is an adaptation that helps a bird fly?
    **A)** lightweight bones
    **B)** webbed feet
    **C)** hard-shelled eggs
    **D)** large beaks

15. Which of the following animals has skin without scales?
    **A)** dolphin        **C)** lizard
    **B)** snake        **D)** fish

16. Lungs and moist skin are characteristics of which of the following vertebrates?
    **A)** amphibians        **C)** reptiles
    **B)** fish        **D)** lizards

17. Which of these are mammals that lay eggs?
    **A)** carnivores        **C)** monotremes
    **B)** marsupials        **D)** placentals

18. Which of the following animals eat only plant materials?
    **A)** carnivores        **C)** omnivores
    **B)** herbivores        **D)** endotherms

**Use the illustration below to answer question 19.**

19. What is the primary function of the feather in the illustration above?
    **A)** flight        **C)** attracting mates
    **B)** insulation        **D)** repelling water

## Thinking Critically

**20. Discuss** why there are fewer species of amphibians on Earth than any other type of vertebrate.

**21. List** the important adaptation that allows a reptile to live and reproduce on land while an amphibian must return to water to reproduce and complete its life cycle.

**22. Draw a Conclusion** You observe a mammal in a field catching and eating a rabbit. What kind of teeth does this animal probably have? Explain how it uses its teeth.

**23. Explain** how the development of the amniotic egg led to the early success of reptiles on land.

**24. Compare and contrast** the teeth of herbivores, carnivores, and omnivores. How is each type of tooth tooth adapted to the animal's diet?

**25. Draw a Conclusion** How can a bird like the arctic tern stand on ice and not lose too much body heat?

**26. Concept Map** Copy and complete this concept map that describes groups of mammals.

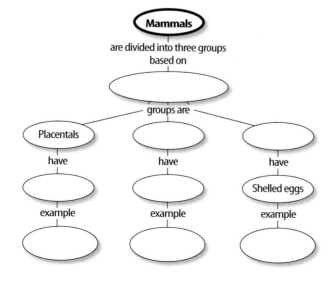

## Performance Activities

**27. Identify and Manipulate Variables and Controls** Design an experiment to find out the effect of water temperature on frog egg development.

**28. Debate** Reptiles are often portrayed as dangerous and evil in fairy tales, folktales, and other fictional stories. Nonfiction information about reptiles presents another view. What is your opinion? Use the library or online resources to find evidence to support your position. Debate this issue with a classmate who has an opposing opinion.

*Hot Words Hot Topics*: Bk 2 (29) pp. 199; (30) pp. 276–278; (31) p. 91

## Applying Math

**Use the following table to answer questions 29 and 30.**

| Bull Trout Population | |
|---|---|
| Year | Number per 100-m$^2$ Section |
| 1996 | 4 |
| 1997 | 7 |
| 1998 | 5 |
| 1999 | 3 |
| 2000 | 4 |

**29. Population Changes** Make a line graph from the data in the table above.

**30. Fish Population Density** Calculate the average number of bull trout per 100-m$^2$ section of stream for all years combined. Which years had a larger population than the average?

**31. Egg Development** A salamander egg in water at 15–16°C will hatch after 60–70 days. A salamander egg in water at 17°C will hatch after 69–92 days. What are the minimum and maximum differences in hatching times?

**Part I**

*Record your answers on the answer sheet provided by your teacher or on a sheet of paper.*

**1** Which of the following is NOT an ectotherm?
(1) amphibian     (3) reptile
(2) mammal     (4) fish

**2** Three of the following are made of cartilage. Which is made of bone?
(1) goldfish
(2) ears
(3) tip of your nose
(4) jawless fish

**3** Which of the following is NOT a group of fish?
(1) cartilaginous     (3) bony
(2) jawless     (4) angelfish

**Use the photo below to answer questions 4 and 5.**

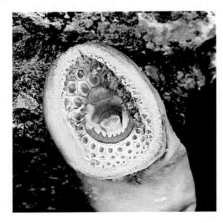

**4** The fish in the illustration is an example of
(1) jawless fish     (3) bony fish
(2) ratfish     (4) cartilaginous fish

**5** Which of the following is NOT one of its traits?
(1) scaleless, long, tubelike body
(2) rough, sandpaperlike scales
(3) round, muscular mouth without a jaw
(4) sharp, toothlike structures

**6** Which of the following spend part of their life on land and part in the water?
(1) reptiles
(2) fish
(3) amphibians
(4) mammals

**Use the photo below to answer questions 7 and 8.**

**7** This animal becomes inactive in cold weather using which of the following?
(1) hibernation
(2) estivation
(3) hydration
(4) hyperthermia

**8** This animal has three of the following characteristics. Which one doesn't it possess?
(1) three-chambered heart
(2) vibrating tympanum
(3) exchange of oxygen and carbon dioxide through skin
(4) lays shell-covered, amniotic eggs

**9** Which of the following is a monotreme?
(1) kangaroo
(2) koala
(3) wallaby
(4) platypus

Part II

*Record your answers on the answer sheet provided by your teacher or on a sheet of paper.*

**Use the illustration below to answer questions 10 and 11.**

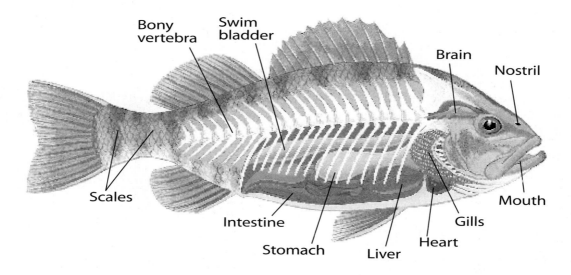

**10** This animal has a particular method of swimming to different levels. Explain how they do this.

**11** How do most of these animals reproduce?

**12** Animals need to get oxygen and dispose of carbon dioxide. How do adult amphibians get enough oxygen and get rid of carbon dioxide?

**13** Birds use a special method to keep their feathers in good shape. What is this process called and how do they do it?

**14** What characteristics do all mammals have in common?

**15** Name two ways that monotremes are different from other animals.

**16** Animals may have to compete with one another for survival. Explain how some animals compete for the same food and how predators can help in this process.

**LE 1.1c:** Most cells have cell membranes, genetic material, and cytoplasm. Some cells have a cell wall and/or chloroplasts. Many cells have a nucleus. **1.1f:** Many plants have roots, stems, leaves, and reproductive structures. These organized groups of tissues are responsible for a plant's life activities. **Also Covered:** LE 1.1h, 3.1b, 4.1a, 4.1b, 4.3e, 5.1a, 5.1b, 5.1d, 5.1g, 5.2e, 6.2c

# Plants

## How are all plants alike?

Plants are found nearly everywhere on Earth. A tropical rain forest like this one is crowded with lush, green plants. When you look at a plant, what do you expect to see? Do all plants have green leaves? Do all plants produce flowers and seeds?

**Science Journal**   Write three characteristics that you think all plants have in common.

# Start-Up Activities

## How do you use plants?

Plants are just about everywhere—in parks and gardens, by streams, on rocks, in houses, and even on dinner plates. Do you use plants for things other than food?

1. Brainstorm with two other classmates and make a list of everything that you use in a day that comes from plants.
2. Compare your list with those of other groups in your class.
3. Search through old magazines for images of the items on your list.
4. As a class, build a bulletin board display of the magazine images.
5. **Think Critically** In your Science Journal, list things that were made from plants 100 years or more ago but today are made from plastics, steel, or some other material.

| Preview this chapter's content and activities at glencoe.com |

**Plants** Make the following Foldable to help identify what you already know, what you want to know, and what you learned about plants.

**STEP 1** **Fold** a vertical sheet of paper from side to side. Make the front edge 1.25 cm shorter than the back edge.

**STEP 2** **Turn** lengthwise and fold into thirds.

**STEP 3** **Unfold and cut** only the top layer along both folds to make three tabs.

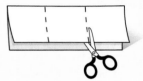

**STEP 4** **Label** each tab as shown.

**Identify Questions** Before you read the chapter, write what you already know about plants under the left tab of your Foldable, and write questions about what you'd like to know under the center tab. After you read the chapter, list what you learned under the right tab.

# section 1

# An Overview of Plants

### as you read

*What* You'll Learn

- **Identify** characteristics common to all plants.
- **Explain** which plant adaptations make it possible for plants to survive on land.
- **Compare and contrast** vascular and nonvascular plants.

*Why* It's Important

Plants produce food and oxygen, which are required for life by most organisms on Earth.

🔍 **Review Vocabulary**

**species:** closely related organisms that share similar characteristics and can reproduce among themselves

**New Vocabulary**
- cuticle
- cellulose
- vascular plant
- nonvascular plant

## What is a plant?

What is the most common sight you see when you walk along nature trails in parks like the one shown in **Figure 1?** Maybe you've taken off your shoes and walked barefoot on soft, cool grass. Perhaps you've climbed a tree to see what things look like from high in its branches. In each instance, plants surrounded you.

If you named all the plants that you know, you probably would include trees, flowers, vegetables, fruits, and field crops like wheat, rice, or corn. Between 260,000 and 300,000 plant species have been discovered and identified. Scientists think many more species are still to be found, mainly in tropical rain forests. Plants are important food sources to humans and other consumers. Without plants, most life on Earth as we know it would not be possible.

**Plant Characteristics** Plants range in size from microscopic water ferns to giant sequoia trees that are sometimes more than 100 m in height. Most have roots or rootlike structures that hold them in the ground or onto some other object like a rock or another plant. Plants are adapted to nearly every environment on Earth. Some grow in frigid, ice-bound polar regions and others grow in hot, dry deserts. All plants need water, but some plants cannot live unless they are submerged in either freshwater or salt water.

**Figure 1** All plants are many-celled and nearly all contain chlorophyll. Grasses, trees, shrubs, mosses, and ferns are all plants.

**Plant Cells** Like other living things, plants are made of cells. A plant cell has a cell membrane, a nucleus, and other cellular structures. In addition, plant cells have cell walls that provide structure and protection. Animal cells do not have cell walls.

Many plant cells contain the green pigment chlorophyll (KLOR uh fihl) so most plants are green. Plants need chlorophyll to make food using a process called photosynthesis. Chlorophyll is found in a cell structure called a chloroplast. Plant cells from green parts of the plant usually contain many chloroplasts.

Most plant cells have a large, membrane-bound structure called the central vacuole that takes up most of the space inside of the cell. This structure plays an important role in regulating the water content of the cell. Many substances are stored in the vacuole, including the pigments that make some flowers red, blue, or purple.

**Living Environment**

**1.1c, 1.1h, 5.1a, 5.1d, 5.2a, 6.2a Summarize** three important structures of most plants that help scientists classify an organism as a plant.

## Origin and Evolution of Plants

Have plants always existed on land? The first plants that lived on land probably could survive only in damp areas. Their ancestors were probably ancient green algae that lived in the sea. Green algae are one-celled or many-celled organisms that use photosynthesis to make food. Today, plants and green algae have the same types of chlorophyll and carotenoids (kuh RAH tun oydz) in their cells. Carotenoids are red, yellow, or orange pigments that also are used for photosynthesis. These facts lead scientists to think that plants and green algae have a common ancestor.

**Reading Check** *How are plants and green algae alike?*

**Fossil Record** The fossil record for plants is not like that for animals. Most animals have bones or other hard parts that can fossilize. Plants usually decay before they become fossilized. The oldest fossil plants are about 420 million years old. **Figure 2** shows *Cooksonia,* a fossil of one of these plants. Other fossils of early plants are similar to the ancient green algae. Scientists hypothesize that some of these early plants evolved into the plants that exist today.

Cone-bearing plants, such as pines, probably evolved from a group of plants that grew about 350 million years ago. Fossils of these plants have been dated to about 300 million years ago. It is estimated that flowering plants did not exist until about 120 million years ago. However, the exact origin of flowering plants is not known.

**Figure 2** This is a fossil of a plant named *Cooksonia.* These plants grew about 420 million years ago and were about 2.5 cm tall.

**Cellulose** Plant cell walls are made mostly of cellulose. Anselme Payen, a French scientist, first isolated and identified the chemical composition of cellulose in 1838, while analyzing the chemical makeup of wood. Choose a type of wood and research to learn the uses of that wood. Make a classroom display of research results.

**Figure 3** The alga *Spirogyra*, like all algae, must have water to survive. If the pool where it lives dries up, it will die.

LM Magnification: 22×

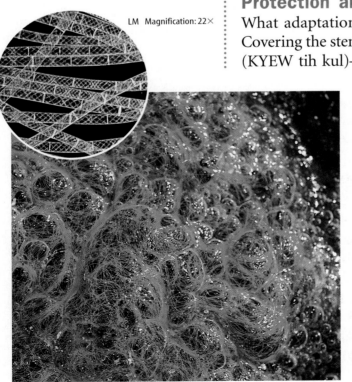

# Life on Land

Life on land has some advantages for plants. More sunlight and carbon dioxide—needed for photosynthesis—are available on land than in water. During photosynthesis, plants give off oxygen. Long ago, as more and more plants adapted to life on land, the amount of oxygen in Earth's atmosphere increased. This was the beginning for organisms that depend on oxygen.

# Adaptations to Land

What is life like for green algae, shown in **Figure 3,** as they float in a shallow pool? The water in the pool surrounds and supports them as the algae make their own food through the process of photosynthesis. Because materials can enter and leave through their cell membranes and cell walls, the algae cells have everything they need to survive as long as they have water.

If the pool begins to dry up, the algae are on damp mud and are no longer supported by water. As the soil becomes drier and drier, the algae will lose water too because water moves through their cell membranes and cell walls from where there is more water to where there is less water. Without enough water in their environment, the algae will die. Plants that live on land have adaptations that allow them to conserve water, as well as other differences that make it possible for survival.

**Protection and Support** Water is important for plants. What adaptations would help a plant conserve water on land? Covering the stems, leaves, and flowers of many plants is a **cuticle** (KYEW tih kul)—a waxy, protective layer secreted by cells onto the surface of the plant. The cuticle slows the loss of water. The cuticle and other adaptations shown in **Figure 4** enable plants to survive on land.

 **Reading Check** *What is the function of a plant's cuticle?*

Supporting itself is another problem for a plant on land. Like all cells, plant cells have cell membranes, but they also have rigid cell walls outside the membrane. Cell walls contain **cellulose** (SEL yuh lohs), which is a chemical compound that plants can make out of sugar. Long chains of cellulose molecules form tangled fibers in plant cell walls. These fibers provide structure and support.

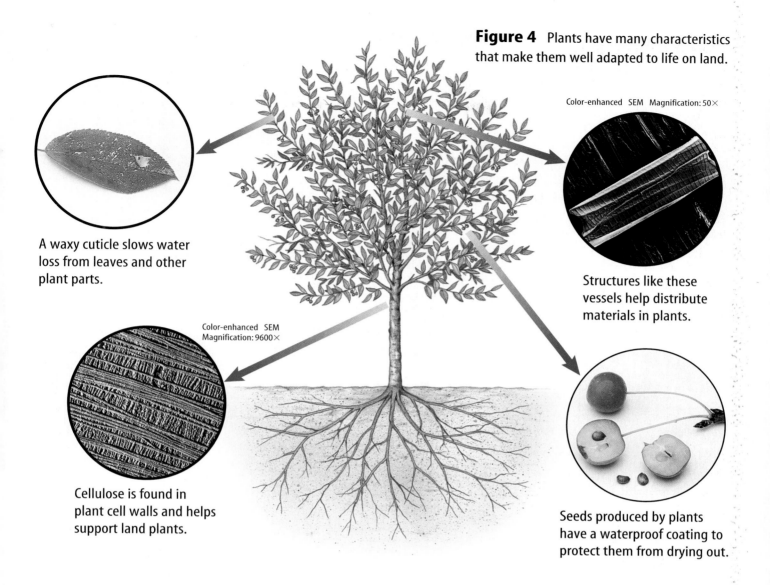

**Figure 4** Plants have many characteristics that make them well adapted to life on land.

A waxy cuticle slows water loss from leaves and other plant parts.

Color-enhanced SEM Magnification: 50×

Structures like these vessels help distribute materials in plants.

Color-enhanced SEM Magnification: 9600×

Cellulose is found in plant cell walls and helps support land plants.

Seeds produced by plants have a waterproof coating to protect them from drying out.

**Other Cell Wall Substances** Cells of some plants secrete other substances into the cellulose that make the cell wall even stronger. Trees, such as oaks and pines, could not grow without these strong cell walls. Wood from trees can be used for construction mostly because of strong cell walls.

Life on land means that each plant cell is not surrounded by water and dissolved nutrients that can move into the cell. Through adaptations, structures developed in many plants that distribute water, nutrients, and food to all plant cells. These structures also help provide support for the plant.

**Reproduction** Changes in reproduction were necessary if plants were to survive on land. The presence of water-resistant spores helped some plants reproduce successfully. Other plants adapted by producing water-resistant seeds in cones or in flowers that developed into fruits.

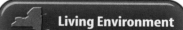

**Living Environment**

**1.1f, 5.1b Analyze** the importance of the four major adaptations of plants that determine the survival of plants on land.

# NATIONAL GEOGRAPHIC VISUALIZING PLANT CLASSIFICATION

## Figure 5

Scientists group plants as either vascular—those with water- and food-conducting cells in their stems—or nonvascular. Vascular plants are further divided into those that produce spores and those that make seeds.

Vascular

Nonvascular

Seed vascular

Seedless vascular

Flowering

Joint firs

Cycads

Conifers

Ginkgoes

Mosses

Liverworts

Hornworts

Horsetails

Ferns

Club mosses

Sunflower

Joint fir

Cycad

Douglas fir

Ginkgo

Horsetail

Hornwort

Moss

Liverwort

Fern

Club moss

# Classification of Plants

The plant kingdom is classified into major groups called divisions. A division is the same as a phylum in other kingdoms. Another way to group plants is as vascular (VAS kyuh lur) or nonvascular plants, as illustrated in **Figure 5. Vascular plants** have tubelike structures that carry water, nutrients, and other substances throughout the plant. **Nonvascular plants** do not have these tubelike structures and use other ways to move water and substances.

**Naming Plants** Why do biologists call a pecan tree *Carya illinoiensis* and a white oak *Quercus alba*? They are using words that accurately name the plant. In the third century B.C., most plants were grouped as trees, shrubs, or herbs and placed into smaller groups by leaf characteristics. This simple system survived until late in the eighteenth century when a Swedish botanist, Carolus Linnaeus, developed a new system. His new system used many characteristics to classify a plant. He also developed a way to name plants called binomial nomenclature (bi NOH mee ul • NOH mun klay chur). Under this system, every plant species is given a unique two-word name like the names above for the pecan tree and white oak and for the two daisies in **Figure 6.**

Shasta daisy,
*Chrysanthemum maximum*

African daisy,
*Dimorphotheca aurantiaca*

**Figure 6** Although these two plants are both called daisies, they are not the same species of plant. Using their binomial names helps eliminate the confusion that might come from using their common names.

---

## section 1 review

### Summary

**What is a plant?**
- All plant cells are surrounded by a cell wall.
- Many plant cells contain chlorophyll.

**Origin and Evolution of Plants**
- Ancestors of land plants were probably ancient green algae.

**Adaptations to Land**
- A waxy cuticle helps conserve water.
- Cellulose strengthens cell walls.

**Classification of Plants**
- The plant kingdom is divided into two groups—nonvascular plants and vascular plants.
- Vascular tissues transport nutrients.

### Self Check

1. **List** the characteristics of plants.
2. **Compare and contrast** the characteristics of vascular and nonvascular plants.
3. **Identify** three adaptations that allow plants to survive on land.
4. **Explain** why binomial nomenclature is used to name plants.
5. **Thinking Critically** If you left a board lying on the grass for a few days, what would happen to the grass underneath the board? Why?

**Applying Skills**

6. **Form a hypothesis** about adaptations a land plant might undergo if it lived submerged in water.

---

# section

## 2

# Seedless Plants

**as you read**

## *What* You'll Learn

- **Distinguish** between characteristics of seedless nonvascular plants and seedless vascular plants.
- **Identify** the importance of some nonvascular and vascular plants.

## *Why* It's Important

Seedless plants are among the first to grow in damaged or disturbed environments and help build soil for the growth of other plants.

### ◉ Review Vocabulary
**spore:** waterproof reproductive cell

### New Vocabulary
- rhizoid
- pioneer species

**Figure 7** The seedless nonvascular plants include mosses, liverworts, and hornworts.

## Seedless Nonvascular Plants

If you were asked to name the parts of a plant, you probably would list roots, stems, leaves, and flowers. You also might know that many plants grow from seeds. However, some plants, called nonvascular plants, don't grow from seeds and they do not have all of these parts. **Figure 7** shows some common types of nonvascular plants.

Nonvascular plants are usually just a few cells thick and only 2 cm to 5 cm in height. Most have stalks that look like stems and green, leaflike growths. Instead of roots, threadlike structures called **rhizoids** (RI zoydz) anchor them where they grow. Most nonvascular plants grow in places that are damp. Water is absorbed and distributed directly through their cell membranes and cell walls. Nonvascular plants also do not have flowers or cones that produce seeds. They reproduce by spores. Mosses, liverworts, and hornworts are examples of nonvascular plants.

**Mosses** Most nonvascular plants are classified as mosses, like the ones in **Figure 7.** They have green, leaflike growths arranged around a central stalk. Their rhizoids are made of many cells. Sometimes stalks with caps grow from moss plants. Reproductive cells called spores are produced in the caps of these stalks. Mosses often grow on tree trunks and rocks or the ground. Although they commonly are found in damp areas, some are adapted to living in deserts.

Close-up of moss plants   Close-up of a liverwort   Close-up of a hornwort

 **Figure 8** Mosses can grow in the thin layer of soil that covers these rocks.

**Liverworts** In the ninth century, liverworts were thought to be useful in treating diseases of the liver. The suffix *-wort* means "herb," so the word *liverwort* means "herb for the liver." Liverworts are rootless plants with flattened, leaflike bodies, as shown in **Figure 7.** They usually have one-celled rhizoids.

**Hornworts** Most hornworts are less than 2.5 cm in diameter and have a flattened body like liverworts, as shown in **Figure 7.** Unlike other nonvascular plants, almost all hornworts have only one chloroplast in each of their cells. Hornworts get their name from their spore-producing structures, which look like tiny horns of cattle.

 **Nonvascular Plants and the Environment** Mosses and liverworts are important in the ecology of many areas. Although they require moist conditions to grow and reproduce, many of them can withstand long, dry periods. They can grow in thin soil and in soils where other plants could not grow, as shown in **Figure 8.**

Spores of mosses and liverworts are carried by the wind. They will grow into plants if growing conditions are right. Mosses often are among the first plants to grow in new or disturbed environments, such as lava fields or after a forest fire. Organisms that are the first to grow in new or disturbed areas are called **pioneer species.** As pioneer plants grow and die, decaying material builds up. This, along with the slow breakdown of rocks, builds soil. When enough soil has formed, other organisms can move into the area.

 *Why are pioneer plant species important in disturbed environments?*

**Measuring Water Absorption by a Moss**

**Procedure** 🥽 👕 ☣ 🧤
1. Place a few teaspoons of *Sphagnum* moss on a piece of **cheesecloth.** Gather the corners of the cloth and twist, then tie them securely to form a ball.
2. Weigh the ball.
3. Put 200 mL of **water** in a **container** and add the ball.
4. After 15 min, remove the ball and drain the excess water into the container.
5. Weigh the ball and measure the amount of water left in the container.
6. Wash your hands after handling the moss.

**Analysis**
In your **Science Journal,** calculate how much water was absorbed by the *Sphagnum* moss.

# Seedless Vascular Plants

The fern in **Figure 9** is growing next to some moss plants. Ferns and mosses are alike in one way. Both reproduce by spores instead of seeds. However, ferns are different from mosses because they have vascular tissue. The vascular tissue in seedless vascular plants, like ferns, is made up of long, tubelike cells. These cells carry water, minerals, and food to cells throughout the plant. Why is vascular tissue an advantage to a plant? Nonvascular plants like the moss are usually only a few cells thick. Each cell absorbs water directly from its environment. As a result, these plants cannot grow large. Vascular plants, on the other hand, can grow bigger and thicker because the vascular tissue distributes water and nutrients to all plant cells.

## Applying Science

### What is the value of rain forests?

Throughout history, cultures have used plants for medicines. Some cultures used willow bark to cure headaches. Willow bark contains salicylates (suh LIH suh layts), the main ingredient in aspirin. Heart problems were treated with foxglove, which is the main source of digitalis (dih juh TAH lus), a drug prescribed for heart problems. Have all medicinal plants been identified?

### Identifying the Problem

Tropical rain forests have the largest variety of organisms on Earth. Many plant species are still unknown. These forests are being destroyed rapidly. The map below shows the rate of destruction of the rain forests.

Some scientists estimate that most tropical rain forests will be destroyed in 30 years.

### Solving the Problem

1. What country has the most rain forest destroyed each year?
2. Where can scientists go to study rain forest plants before the plants are destroyed?
3. Predict how the destruction of rain forests might affect research on new drugs from plants.

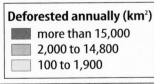

**Deforested annually (km²)**
- more than 15,000
- 2,000 to 14,800
- 100 to 1,900

## Types of Seedless Vascular Plants

Besides ferns, seedless vascular plants include ground pines, spike mosses, and horsetails. About 1,000 species of ground pines, spike mosses, and horsetails are known to exist. Ferns are more abundant, with at least 12,000 known species. Many species of seedless vascular plants are known only from fossils. They flourished during the warm, moist period 360 million to 286 million years ago. Fossil records show that some horsetails grew 15 m tall, unlike modern species, which grow only 1 m to 2 m tall.

**Ferns** The largest group of seedless vascular plants is the ferns. They include many different forms, as shown in **Figure 10.** They have stems, leaves, and roots. Fern leaves are called fronds. Ferns produce spores in structures that usually are found on the underside of their fronds. Thousands of species of ferns now grow on Earth, but many more existed long ago. From clues left in rock layers, scientists infer that about 360 million years ago much of Earth was tropical. Steamy swamps covered large areas. The tallest plants were species of ferns. The ancient ferns grew as tall as 25 m—as tall as the tallest fern species alive today. Most modern tree ferns are about 3 m to 5 m in height and grow in tropical regions of the world.

**Figure 9** The mosses and ferns pictured here are seedless plants. **Explain** *why the fern can grow taller than the moss.*

**Figure 10** Ferns come in many different shapes and sizes.

The sword fern has a typical fern shape. Spores are produced in structures on the back of the frond.

This fern grows on other plants, not in the soil.
**Infer** *why it's called the staghorn fern.*

Tree ferns, like this one in Hawaii, grow in tropical areas.

**Club Mosses** Ground pines and spike mosses are groups of plants that often are called club mosses. They are related more closely to ferns than to mosses. These seedless vascular plants have needle-like leaves. Spores are produced at the end of the stems in structures that look like tiny pine cones. Ground pines, shown in **Figure 11,** are found from arctic regions to the tropics, but rarely in large numbers. In some areas, they are endangered because they have been over collected to make wreaths and other decorations.

**✔ Reading Check** *Where are spores in club mosses produced?*

**Figure 11** Photographers once used the dry, flammable spores of club mosses as flash powder. It burned rapidly and produced the light that was needed to take photographs.

Spike mosses resemble ground pines. One species of spike moss, the resurrection plant, is adapted to desert conditions. When water is scarce, the plant curls up and seems dead. When water becomes available, the resurrection plant unfurls its green leaves and begins making food again. The plant can repeat this process whenever necessary.

**Horsetails** The stem structure of horsetails is unique among the vascular plants. The stem is jointed and has a hollow center surrounded by a ring of vascular tissue. At each joint, leaves grow out from around the stem. In **Figure 12,** you can see these joints. If you pull on a horsetail stem, it will pop apart in sections. Like the club mosses, spores from horsetails are produced in a conelike structure at the tips of some stems. The stems of the horsetails contain silica, a gritty substance found in sand. For centuries, horsetails have been used for polishing objects, sharpening tools, and scouring cooking utensils. Another common name for horsetails is scouring rush.

**Figure 12** Most horsetails grow in damp areas and are less than 1 m tall.
**Identify** *where spores would be produced on this plant.*

## Importance of Seedless Plants

When many ancient seedless plants died, they became submerged in water and mud before they decomposed. As this plant material built up, it became compacted and compressed and eventually turned into coal—a process that took millions of years.

Today, a similar process is taking place in bogs, which are poorly drained areas of land that contain decaying plants. The plants in bogs are mostly seedless plants like mosses and ferns.

**Peat** When bog plants die, the waterlogged soil slows the decay process. Over time, these decaying plants are compressed into a substance called peat. Peat, which forms from the remains of sphagnum moss, is mined from bogs to use as a low-cost fuel in places such as Ireland and Russia, as shown in **Figure 13.** Peat supplies about one-third of Ireland's energy requirements. Scientists hypothesize that over time, if additional layers of soil bury, compact, and compress the peat, it will become coal.

**Uses of Seedless Vascular Plants** Many people keep ferns as houseplants. Ferns also are sold widely as landscape plants for shady areas. Peat and sphagnum mosses also are used for gardening. Peat is an excellent soil conditioner, and sphagnum moss often is used to line hanging baskets. Ferns also are used as weaving material for basketry.

Although most mosses are not used for food, parts of many other seedless vascular plants can be eaten. The rhizomes and young fronds of some ferns are edible. The dried stems of one type of horsetail can be ground into flour. Seedless plants have been used as folk medicines for hundreds of years. For example, ferns have been used to treat bee stings, burns, fevers, and even dandruff.

**Figure 13** Peat is cut from bogs and used for a fuel in some parts of Europe.

## section 2 review

### Summary

**Seedless Nonvascular Plants**
- Seedless nonvascular plants include mosses, liverworts, and hornworts.
- They are usually only a few cells thick and no more than a few centimeters tall.
- They produce spores rather than seeds.

**Seedless Vascular Plants**
- Seedless vascular plants include ferns, club mosses, and horsetails.
- Vascular plants grow taller and can live farther from water than nonvascular plants.

**Importance of Seedless Plants**
- Nonvascular plants help build new soil.
- Coal deposits formed from ancient seedless plants that were buried in water and mud before they began to decay.

### Self Check

1. **Compare and contrast** the characteristics of mosses and ferns.
2. **Explain** what fossil records tell about seedless plants that lived on Earth long ago.
3. **Identify** growing conditions in which you would expect to find pioneer plants such as mosses and liverworts.
4. **Summarize** the functions of vascular tissues.
5. **Think Critically** The electricity that you use every day might be produced by burning coal. What is the connection between electricity production and seedless vascular plants?

*Hot Words Hot Topics*: Bk 2 (6) p. 110

### Applying Math

6. **Use Fractions** Approximately 8,000 species of liverworts and 9,000 species of mosses exist today. Estimate what fraction of these seedless nonvascular plants are mosses.

# section 3

# Seed Plants

## as you read

### *What* You'll Learn

- **Identify** the characteristics of seed plants.
- **Explain** the structures and functions of roots, stems, and leaves.
- **Describe** the main characteristics and importance of gymnosperms and angiosperms.
- **Compare** similarities and differences between monocots and dicots.

### *Why* It's Important

Humans depend on seed plants for food, clothing, and shelter.

### ⊙ Review Vocabulary
**seed:** plant embryo and food supply in a protective coating

### New Vocabulary

- stomata
- guard cell
- xylem
- phloem
- cambium
- gymnosperm
- angiosperm
- monocot
- dicot

## Characteristics of Seed Plants

What foods from plants have you eaten today? Apples? Potatoes? Carrots? Peanut butter and jelly sandwiches? All of these foods and more come from seed plants.

Most of the plants you are familiar with are seed plants. Most seed plants have leaves, stems, roots, and vascular tissue. They also produce seeds, which usually contain an embryo and stored food. The stored food is the source of energy for the embryo's early growth as it develops into a plant. Most of the plant species that have been identified in the world today are seed plants. The seed plants generally are classified into two major groups—gymnosperms (JIHM nuh spurmz) and angiosperms (AN jee uh spurmz).

**Leaves** Most seed plants have leaves. Leaves are the organs of the plant where the food-making process—photosynthesis—usually occurs. Leaves come in many shapes, sizes, and colors. Examine the structure of a typical leaf, shown in **Figure 14.**

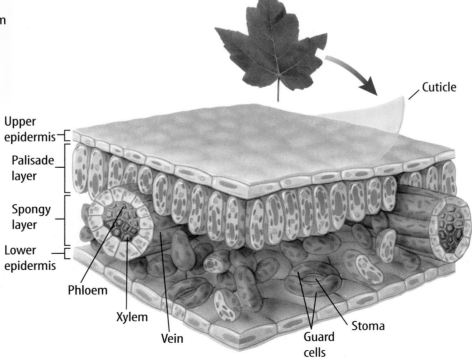

**Figure 14** The structure of a typical leaf is adapted for photosynthesis.
**Explain** *why cells in the palisade layer have more chloroplasts than cells in the spongy layer.*

Upper epidermis
Palisade layer
Spongy layer
Lower epidermis
Phloem
Xylem
Vein
Cuticle
Guard cells
Stoma

**Leaf Cell Layers** A typical leaf is made of several different layers of cells. On the upper and lower surfaces of a leaf is a thin layer of cells called the epidermis, which covers and protects the leaf. A waxy cuticle coats the epidermis of some leaves. Most leaves have small openings in the epidermis called **stomata** (STOH muh tuh) (singular, *stoma*). Stomata allow carbon dioxide, water, and oxygen to enter into and exit from a leaf. Each stoma is surrounded by two **guard cells** that open and close it.

Just below the upper epidermis is the palisade layer. It consists of closely packed, long, narrow cells that usually contain many chloroplasts. Most of the food produced by plants is made in the palisade cells. Between the palisade layer and the lower epidermis is the spongy layer. It is a layer of loosely arranged cells separated by air spaces. In a leaf, veins containing vascular tissue are found in the spongy layer.

**Stems** The trunk of a tree is really the stem of the tree. Stems usually are located above ground and support the branches, leaves, and reproductive structures. Materials move between leaves and roots through the vascular tissue in the stem. Stems also can have other functions, as shown in **Figure 15.**

Plant stems are either herbaceous (hur BAY shus) or woody. Herbaceous stems usually are soft and green, like the stems of a tulip, while trees and shrubs have hard, rigid, woody stems. Lumber comes from woody stems.

**Figure 15** Some plants have stems with special functions.

These potatoes are stems that grow underground and store food for the plant.

The stems of this cactus store water and can carry on photosynthesis.

Some stems of this grape plant help it climb on other plants.

**Figure 16** The root system of a tree can be as long as the tree can be tall.

**Infer** *why the root system of a tree would need to be so large.*

**Roots** Imagine a lone tree growing on top of a hill. What is the largest part of this plant? Maybe you guessed the trunk or the branches. Did you consider the roots, like those shown in **Figure 16?** The root systems of most plants are as large or larger than the aboveground stems and leaves.

Roots are important to plants. Water and other substances enter a plant through its roots. Roots have vascular tissue in which water and dissolved substances move from the soil through the stems to the leaves. Roots also act as anchors, preventing plants from being blown away by wind or washed away by moving water. Underground root systems support other plant parts that are aboveground—the stem, branches, and leaves of a tree. Sometimes, part of or all of the roots are aboveground, too.

Roots can store food. When you eat carrots or beets, you eat roots that contain stored food. Plants that continue growing from one year to the next use this stored food to begin new growth in the spring. Plants that grow in dry areas often have roots that store water.

Root tissues also can perform functions such as absorbing oxygen that is used in the process of respiration. Because water does not contain as much oxygen as air does, plants that grow with their roots in water might not be able to absorb enough oxygen. Some swamp plants have roots that grow partially out of the water and take in oxygen from the air. In order to perform all these functions, the root systems of plants must be large.

**Reading Check** *What are several functions of roots in plants?*

**Vascular Tissue** Three tissues usually make up the vascular system in a seed plant. **Xylem** (ZI lum) tissue is made up of hollow, tubular cells that are stacked one on top of the other to form a structure called a vessel. These vessels transport water and dissolved substances from the roots throughout the plant. The thick cell walls of xylem are also important because they help support the plant.

**Phloem** (FLOH em) is a plant tissue also made up of tubular cells that are stacked to form structures called tubes. Tubes are different from vessels. Phloem tubes move food from where it is made to other parts of the plant where it is used or stored.

In some plants, a cambium is between xylem and phloem. **Cambium** (KAM bee um) is a tissue that produces most of the new xylem and phloem cells. The growth of this new xylem and phloem increases the thickness of stems and roots. All three tissues are illustrated in **Figure 17.**

**INTEGRATE Health**

**Vascular Systems** Plants have vascular tissue, and you have a vascular system. Your vascular system transports oxygen, food, and wastes through blood vessels. Instead of xylem and phloem, your blood vessels include veins and arteries. In your Science Journal write a paragraph describing the difference between veins and arteries.

**Figure 17** The vascular tissue of some seed plants includes xylem, phloem, and cambium. **Identify** *which of these tissues transports food throughout the plant.*

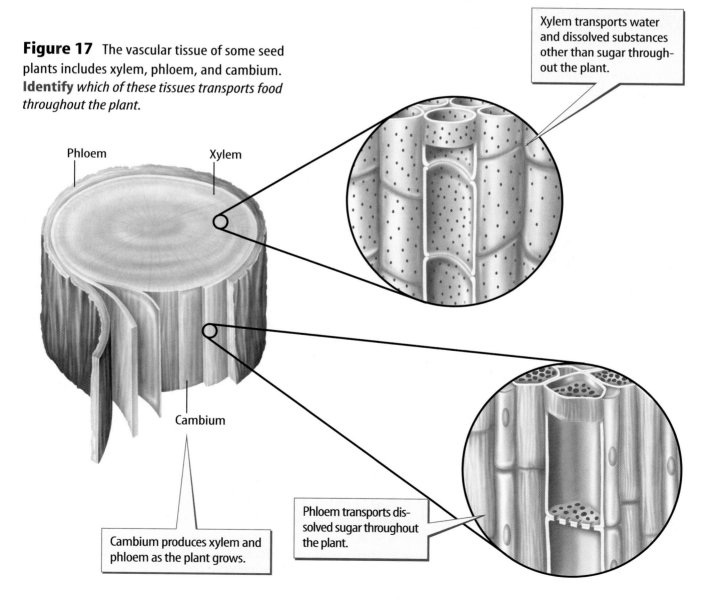

Xylem transports water and dissolved substances other than sugar throughout the plant.

Phloem transports dissolved sugar throughout the plant.

Cambium produces xylem and phloem as the plant grows.

Phloem  Xylem

Cambium

**Figure 18** The gymnosperms include four divisions of plants.

Conifers are the largest, most diverse division. Most conifers are evergreen plants, such as this ponderosa pine (above).

About 100 species of cycads exist today. Only one genus is native to the United States.

More than half of the 70 species of gnetophytes, such as this joint fir, are in one genus.

The ginkgoes are represented by one living species. Ginkgoes lose their leaves in the fall.
**Explain** *how this is different from most gymnosperms.*

**Living Environment**

1.1f, 1.1h, 4.3c, 4.3e Use a Venn diagram to compare and contrast gymnosperms and angiosperms.

# Gymnosperms

The oldest trees alive are gymnosperms. A bristlecone pine tree in the White Mountains of eastern California is estimated to be 4,900 years old. **Gymnosperms** are vascular plants that produce seeds that are not protected by fruit. The word *gymnosperm* comes from the Greek language and means "naked seed." Another characteristic of gymnosperms is that they do not have flowers. Leaves of most gymnosperms are needlelike or scalelike. Many gymnosperms are called evergreens because some green leaves always remain on their branches.

Four divisions of plants—conifers, cycads, ginkgoes, and gnetophytes (NE tuh fites)—are classified as gymnosperms. **Figure 18** shows examples of the four divisions. You are probably most familiar with the division Coniferophyta (kuh NIH fur uh fi tuh), the conifers. Pines, firs, spruces, redwoods, and junipers belong to this division. It contains the greatest number of gymnosperm species. All conifers produce two types of cones—male and female. Both types usually are found on the same plant. Cones are the reproductive structures of conifers. Seeds develop on the female cone but not on the male cone.

 **Reading Check** *What is the importance of cones to gymnosperms?*

# Angiosperms

When people are asked to name a plant, most name an angiosperm. An **angiosperm** is a vascular plant that flowers and produces fruits with one or more seeds, such as the peaches shown in **Figure 19.** The fruit develops from a part or parts of one or more flowers. Angiosperms are familiar plants no matter where you live. They grow in parks, fields, forests, jungles, deserts, freshwater, salt water, and in the cracks of sidewalks. You might see them dangling from wires or other plants, and one species of orchid even grows underground. Angiosperms make up the plant division Anthophyta (AN thoh fi tuh). More than half of the known plant species belong to this division.

**Flowers** The flowers of angiosperms vary in size, shape, and color. Duckweed, an aquatic plant, has a flower that is only 0.1 mm long. A plant in Indonesia has a flower that is nearly 1 m in diameter and can weigh 9 kg. Nearly every color can be found in some flower, although some people would not include black. Multicolored flowers are common. Some plants have flowers that are not recognized easily as flowers, such as the flowers of ash trees, shown below.

Some flower parts develop into a fruit. Most fruits contain seeds, like an apple, or have seeds on their surface, like a strawberry. If you think all fruits are juicy and sweet, there are some that are not. The fruit of the vanilla orchid, as shown to the right, contains seeds and is dry.

Angiosperms are divided into two groups—the monocots and the dicots—shortened forms of the words *monocotyledon* (mah nuh kah tuh LEE dun) and *dicotyledon* (di kah tuh LEE dun).

**Figure 19** Angiosperms have a wide variety of flowers and fruits.

The fruit of the vanilla orchid is the source of vanilla flavoring.

The flowers and fruit of a peach tree are typical of many angiosperms.

Ash flowers are not large and colorful. Their fruits are small and dry.

**Monocots and Dicots** A cotyledon is part of a seed often used for food storage. The prefix *mono* means "one," and *di* means "two." Therefore, **monocots** have one cotyledon inside their seeds and **dicots** have two. The flowers, leaves, and stems of monocots and dicots are shown in **Figure 20.**

Many important foods come from monocots, including corn, rice, wheat, and barley. If you eat bananas, pineapple, or dates, you are eating fruit from monocots. Lilies and orchids also are monocots.

Dicots also produce familiar foods such as peanuts, green beans, peas, apples, and oranges. You might have rested in the shade of a dicot tree. Most shade trees, such as maple, oak, and elm, are dicots.

**Figure 20** By observing a monocot and a dicot, you can determine their plant characteristics.

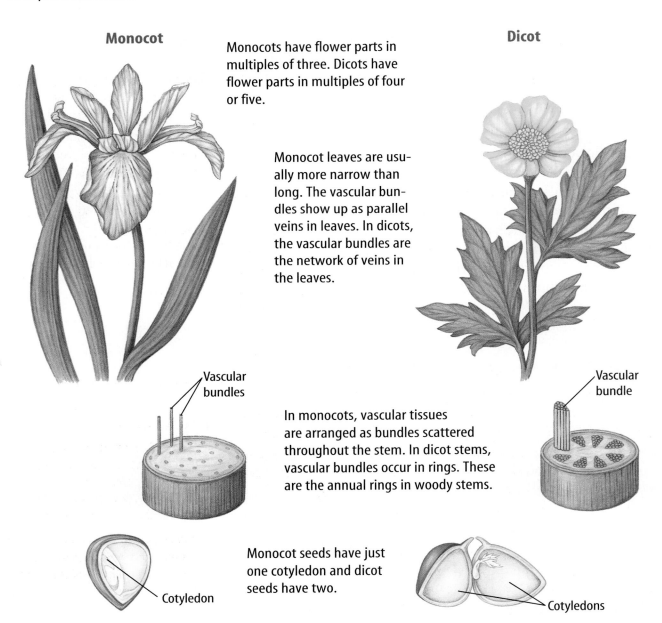

**Monocot**

**Dicot**

Monocots have flower parts in multiples of three. Dicots have flower parts in multiples of four or five.

Monocot leaves are usually more narrow than long. The vascular bundles show up as parallel veins in leaves. In dicots, the vascular bundles are the network of veins in the leaves.

Vascular bundles

Vascular bundle

In monocots, vascular tissues are arranged as bundles scattered throughout the stem. In dicot stems, vascular bundles occur in rings. These are the annual rings in woody stems.

Cotyledon

Monocot seeds have just one cotyledon and dicot seeds have two.

Cotyledons

Petunias

Parsley

Pecan tree

**Life Cycles of Angiosperms** Flowering plants vary greatly in appearance. Their life cycles are as varied as the kinds of plants, as shown in **Figure 21.** Some angiosperms grow from seeds to mature plants with their own seeds in less than a month. The life cycles of other plants can take as long as a century. If a plant's life cycle is completed within one year, it is called an annual. These plants must be grown from seeds each year.

Plants called biennials (bi EH nee ulz) complete their life cycles within two years. Biennials such as parsley store a large amount of food in an underground root or stem for growth in the second year. Biennials produce flowers and seeds only during the second year of growth. Angiosperms that take more than two years to grow to maturity are called perennials. Herbaceous perennials such as peonies appear to die each winter but grow and produce flowers each spring. Woody perennials such as fruit trees produce flowers and fruits on stems that survive for many years.

## Importance of Seed Plants

What would a day at school be like without seed plants? One of the first things you'd notice is the lack of paper and books. Paper is made from wood pulp that comes from trees, which are seed plants. Are the desks and chairs at your school made of wood? They would need to be made of something else if no seed plants existed. Clothing that is made from cotton would not exist because cotton comes from seed plants. At lunchtime, you would have trouble finding something to eat. Bread, fruits, and potato chips all come from seed plants. Milk, hamburgers, and hot dogs all come from animals that eat seed plants. Unless you like to eat plants such as mosses and ferns, you'd go hungry. Without seed plants, your day at school would be different.

**Figure 21** Life cycles of angiosperms include annuals, biennials, and perennials. Petunias, which are annuals, complete their life cycle in one year. Parsley plants, which are biennials, do not produce flowers and seeds the first year. Perennials, such as the pecan tree, flower and produce fruits year after year.

**Topic: Renewable Resources**
Visit glencoe.com for Web links to information and recent news or magazine articles about the timber industry's efforts to replant trees.

**Activity** List in your Science Journal the species of trees that are planted and some of their uses.

| Table 1  Some Products of Seed Plants | | |
|---|---|---|
| **From Gymnosperms** | | **From Angiosperms** |
| lumber, paper, soap, varnish, paints, waxes, perfumes, edible pine nuts, medicines |  | foods, sugar, chocolate, cotton cloth, linen, rubber, vegetable oils, perfumes, medicines, cinnamon, flavorings, dyes, lumber  |

**Products of Seed Plants** Conifers are the most economically important gymnosperms. Most wood used for construction and for paper production comes from conifers. Resin, a waxy substance secreted by conifers, is used to make chemicals found in soap, paint, varnish, and some medicines.

The most economically important plants on Earth are the angiosperms. They form the basis of the diets of most animals. Angiosperms were the first plants that humans grew. They included grains, such as barley and wheat, and legumes, such as peas and lentils. Angiosperms are also the source of many of the fibers used in clothing. Besides cotton, linen fabrics come from plant fibers. **Table 1** shows just a few of the products of angiosperms and gymnosperms.

## section 3 review

### Summary

**Characteristics of Seed Plants**

- Leaves are organs in which photosynthesis takes place.
- Stems support leaves and branches and contain vascular tissues.
- Roots absorb water and nutrients from soil.

**Gymnosperms**

- Gymnosperms do not have flowers and produce seeds that are not protected by a fruit.

**Angiosperms**

- Angiosperms produce flowers that develop into a fruit with seeds.

**Importance of Seed Plants**

- The diets of most animals are based on angiosperms.

### Self Check

1. **List** four characteristics common to all seed plants.
2. **Compare and contrast** the characteristics of gymnosperms and angiosperms.
3. **Classify** a flower with five petals as a monocot or a dicot.
4. **Explain** why the root system might be the largest part of a plant.
5. **Think Critically** The cuticle and epidermis of leaves are transparent. If they weren't, what might be the result?

**Applying Skills**

6. **Form a hypothesis** about what substance or substances are produced in palisade cells but not in xylem cells.

# Identifying Conifers

How can you tell a pine from a spruce or a cedar from a juniper? One way is to observe their leaves. The leaves of most conifers are either needlelike—shaped like needles—or scalelike—shaped like the scales on a fish. Examine and identify some conifer branches using the key to the right.

## ⊙ Real-World Question

How can leaves be used to classify conifers?

### Goals
- **Identify** the difference between needlelike and scalelike leaves.
- **Classify** conifers according to their leaves.

### Materials

short branches of the following conifers:

| | | |
|---|---|---|
| pine | Douglas fir | redwood |
| cedar | hemlock | arborvitae |
| spruce | fir | juniper |

*illustrations of the conifers above
*Alternate materials

### Safety Precautions 🥽 👕 🧤
Wash your hands after handling leaves.

## ⊙ Procedure

1. **Observe** the leaves or illustrations of each conifer, then use the key to identify it.
2. **Write** the number and name of each conifer you identify in your Science Journal.

## ⊙ Conclude and Apply

1. **Name** two traits of hemlock leaves.
2. **Compare and contrast** pine and cedar leaves.

### Key to Classifying Conifer Leaves

1. All leaves are needlelike.
   a. yes, go to 2
   b. no, go to 8

2. Needles are in clusters.
   a. yes, go to 3
   b. no, go to 4

3. Clusters contain two, three, or five needles.
   a. yes, pine
   b. no, cedar

4. Needles grow on all sides of the stem.
   a. yes, go to 5
   b. no, go to 7

5. Needles grow from a woody peg.
   a. yes, spruce
   b. no, go to 6

6. Needles appear to grow from the branch.
   a. yes, Douglas fir
   b. no, hemlock

7. Most of the needles grow upward.
   a. yes, fir
   b. no, redwood

8. All the leaves are scalelike but not prickly.
   a. yes, arborvitae
   b. no, juniper

## Communicating Your Data

Use the key above to identify conifers growing on your school grounds. Draw and label a map that locates these conifers. Post the map in your school. **For more help, refer to the** Science Skill Handbook.

# Use the Internet

# Planⓣs as Medicine

## Goals

- **Identify** two plants that can be used as a treatment for illness or as a supplement to support good health.
- **Research** the cultural and historical use of each of the two selected plants as medical treatments.
- **Review** multiple sources to understand the effectiveness of each of the two selected plants as a medical treatment.
- **Compare and contrast** the research and form a hypothesis about the medicinal effectiveness of each of the two plants.

### Data Source

Science▬nline

Visit **glencoe.com** for more information about plants that can be used for maintaining good health and for data collected by other students.

## ▶ *Real-World Question*

You may have read about using peppermint to relieve an upset stomach, or taking *Echinacea* to boost your immune system and fight off illness. But did you know that pioneers brewed a cough medicine from lemon mint? In this lab, you will explore plants and their historical use in treating illness, and the benefits and risks associated with using plants as medicine. How are plants used in maintaining good health?

*Echinacea*

## ▶ *Make a Plan*

1. **Search** for information about plants that are used as medicine and identify two plants to investigate.

2. **Research** how these plants are currently recommended for use as medicine or to promote good health. Find out how each has been used historically.

3. **Explore** how other cultures used these plants as a medicine.

*Mentha*

### ◉ Follow Your Plan

1. Make sure your teacher approves your plan before you start.
2. **Record** data you collect about each plant in your Science Journal.

### ◉ Analyze Your Data

1. **Write** a description of how different cultures have used each plant as medicine.
2. How have the plants you investigated been used as medicine historically?
3. **Record** all the uses suggested by different sources for each plant.
4. **Record** the side effects of using each plant as a treatment.

### ◉ Conclude and Apply

1. After conducting your research, what do you think are the benefits and draw-backs of using these plants as alternative medicines?
2. **Describe** any conflicting information about using each of these plants as medicine.
3. Based on your analysis, would you recommend the use of each of these two plants to treat illness or promote good health? Why or why not?
4. What would you say to someone who was thinking about using any plant-based, over-the-counter, herbal supplement?

### 𝒞ommunicating Your Data

Find this lab using the link below. Post your data for the two plants you investigated in the tables provided. **Compare** your data to those of other students. Review data that other students have entered about other plants that can be used as medicine.

*Monarda*

# A LOOPY Idea Inspires a "Fastenating" Invention

**A wild cocklebur plant inspired the hook-and-loop fastener.**

Scientists often spend countless hours in the laboratory dreaming up useful inventions. Sometimes, however, the best ideas hit them in unexpected places at unexpected times. That's why scientists are constantly on the lookout for things that spark their curiosity.

One day in 1948, a Swiss inventor named George deMestral strolled through a field with his dog. When they returned home, deMestral discovered that the dog's fur was covered with cockleburs, parts of a prickly plant. These burs were also stuck to deMestral's jacket and pants. Curious about what made the burs so sticky, the inventor examined one under a microscope.

DeMestral noticed that the cocklebur was covered with lots of tiny hooks. By clinging to animal fur and fabric, this plant is carried to other places. While studying these burs, he got the idea to invent a new kind of fastener that could do the work of buttons, snaps, zippers, and laces—but better!

After years of experimentation, deMestral came up with a strong, durable hook-and-loop fastener made of two strips of nylon fabric. One strip has thousands of small, stiff hooks; the other strip is covered with soft, tiny loops. Today, this hook-and-loop fastening tape is used on shoes and sneakers, watchbands, hospital equipment, space suits, clothing, book bags, and more. You may have one of those hook-and-loop fasteners somewhere on you right now. They're the ones that go rrrrrrrip when you open them.

So, if you ever get a fresh idea that clings to your mind like a hook to a loop, stick with it and experiment! Who knows? It may lead to a fabulous invention that changes the world!

**This photo provides a close-up view of a hook-and-loop fastener.**

**List** Make a list of ten ways hook-and-loop tape is used today. Think of three new uses for it. Since you can buy strips of hook-and-loop fastening tape in most hardware and fabric stores, try out some of your favorite ideas.

Science Online
**For more information, visit glencoe.com**

## Reviewing Main Ideas

### Section 1  An Overview of Plants

1. Plants are made up of eukaryotic cells and vary greatly in size and shape.

2. Plants usually have some form of leaves, stems, and roots.

3. As plants evolved from aquatic to land environments, changes occurred in how they reproduced, supported themselves, and moved substances from one part of the plant to another.

4. The plant kingdom is classified into groups called divisions.

### Section 2  Seedless Plants

1. Seedless plants include nonvascular and vascular types.

2. Most seedless nonvascular plants have no true leaves, stems, or roots. Reproduction usually is by spores.

3. Seedless vascular plants have vascular tissues that move substances throughout the plant. These plants may reproduce by spores.

4. Many ancient forms of these plants underwent a process that resulted in the formation of coal.

### Section 3  Seed Plants

1. Seed plants are adapted to survive in nearly every environment on Earth.

2. Seed plants produce seeds and have vascular tissue, stems, roots, and leaves.

3. The two major groups of seed plants are gymnosperms and angiosperms. Gymnosperms generally have needlelike leaves and some type of cone. Angiosperms are plants that flower and are classified as monocots or dicots.

4. Seed plants are the most economically important plants on Earth.

## Visualizing Main Ideas

*Copy and complete the following concept map about the seed plants.*

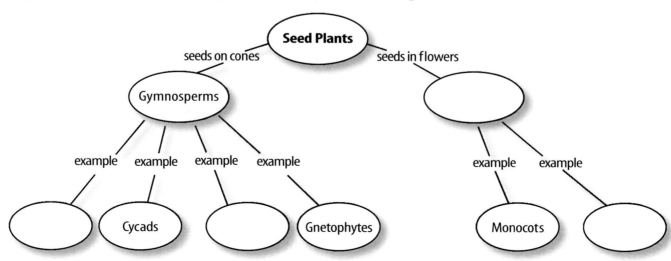

## Using Vocabulary

| | |
|---|---|
| angiosperm p. 561 | nonvascular plant p. 549 |
| cambium p. 559 | phloem p. 559 |
| cellulose p. 546 | pioneer species p. 551 |
| cuticle p. 546 | rhizoid p. 550 |
| dicot p. 562 | stomata p. 557 |
| guard cell p. 557 | vascular plant p. 549 |
| gymnosperm p. 560 | xylem p. 559 |
| monocot p. 562 | |

*Complete each analogy by providing the missing vocabulary word.*

1. Angiosperm is to flower as _____ is to cone.

2. Dicot is to two seed leaves as _____ is to one seed leaf.

3. Root is to fern as _____ is to moss.

4. Phloem is to food transport as _____ is to water transport.

5. Vascular plant is to horsetail as _____ is to liverwort.

6. Cellulose is to support as _____ is to protect.

7. Fuel is to ferns as _____ is to bryophytes.

8. Cuticle is to wax as _____ is to fibers.

## Checking Concepts

*Choose the word or phrase that best answers the question.*

9. Which of the following is a seedless vascular plant?
   A) moss         C) horsetail
   B) liverwort    D) pine

10. What are the small openings in the surface of a leaf surrounded by guard cells called?
    A) stomata      C) rhizoids
    B) cuticles     D) angiosperms

11. What are the plant structures that anchor the plant called?
    A) stems        C) roots
    B) leaves       D) guard cells

12. Where is most of a plant's new xylem and phloem produced?
    A) guard cell   C) stomata
    B) cambium      D) cuticle

13. What group has plants that are only a few cells thick?
    A) gymnosperms  C) ferns
    B) cycads       D) mosses

14. The oval plant parts shown to the right are found only in which plant group?

    A) nonvascular  C) gymnosperms
    B) seedless     D) angiosperms

15. What kinds of plants have structures that move water and other substances?
    A) vascular     C) nonvascular
    B) protist      D) bacterial

16. In what part of a leaf does most photosynthesis occur?
    A) epidermis    C) stomata
    B) cuticle      D) palisade layer

17. Which one of the following do ferns have?
    A) cones        C) spores
    B) rhizoids     D) seeds

18. Which of these is an advantage to life on land for plants?
    A) more direct sunlight
    B) less carbon dioxide
    C) greater space to grow
    D) less competition for food

## Thinking Critically

19. **Predict** what might happen if a land plant's waxy cuticle was destroyed.

20. **Draw Conclusions** On a walk through the woods with a friend, you find a plant neither of you has seen before. The plant has green leaves and yellow flowers. Your friend says it is a vascular plant. How does your friend know this?

21. **Infer** Plants called succulents store large amounts of water in their leaves, stems, and roots. In what environments would you expect to find succulents growing naturally?

22. **Explain** why mosses usually are found in moist areas.

23. **Recognize Cause and Effect** How do pioneer species change environments so that other plants can grow there?

24. **Concept Map** Copy and complete this map for the seedless plants of the plant kingdom.

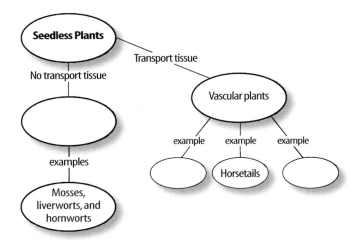

25. **Interpret Scientific Illustrations** Using **Figure 20** in this chapter, compare and contrast the number of cotyledons, bundle arrangement in the stem, veins in leaves, and number of flower parts for monocots and dicots.

26. **Sequence** Put the following events in order to show how coal is formed from plants: *living seedless plants, coal is formed, dead seedless plants decay,* and *peat is formed.*

27. **Predict** what would happen if a ring of bark and camium layer were removed from around the trunk of a tree.

## Performance Activities

28. **Poem** Choose a topic in this chapter that interests you. Look it up in a reference book, in an encyclopedia, or on a CD-ROM. Write a poem to share what you learn.

29. **Display** Use dried plant material, photos, drawings, or other materials to make a poster describing the form and function of roots, stems, and leaves.

*Hot Words Hot Topics*: Bk 2 (30) p. 194; (31) pp. 142-143, 196-197; (32) p. 194

## Applying Math

**Use the table below to answer questions 30–32.**

| Number of Stomata (per mm$^2$) | | |
|---|---|---|
| **Plant** | **Upper Surface** | **Lower Surface** |
| Pine | 50 | 71 |
| Bean | 40 | 281 |
| Fir | 0 | 228 |
| Tomato | 12 | 13 |

30. **Gas Exchange** What do the data in this table tell you about where gas exchange occurs in the leaf of each plant species?

31. **Compare Leaf Surfaces** Make two circle graphs—upper surface and lower surface—using the table above.

32. **Guard Cells** On average, how many guard cells are found on the lower surface of a bean leaf?

*Record your answers on the answer sheet provided by your teacher or on a sheet of paper.*

**1** Which of the following do plants use to photosynthesize?
(1) blood
(2) iron
(3) chlorophyll
(4) cellulose

**2** Which of the following describes the function of the central vacuole in plant cells?
(1) It helps in reproduction.
(2) It helps regulate water content.
(3) It plays a key role in photosynthesis.
(4) It stores food.

**Use the illustration below to answer questions 3 and 4.**

**Leaf Cross Section**

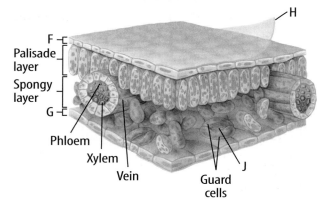

**3** In the leaf cross section, what is indicated by H?
(1) upper epidermis
(2) cuticle
(3) stoma
(4) lower epidermis

**4** What flows through the structure indicated by J?
(1) water only
(2) carbon dioxide and water only
(3) oxygen and carbon dioxide only
(4) water, carbon dioxide, and oxygen

**5** In seed plants, vascular tissue refers to which of the following?
(1) xylem and phloem only
(2) xylem only
(3) phloem only
(4) xylem, phloem, and cambium

**Use the illustration below to answer questions 6 and 7.**

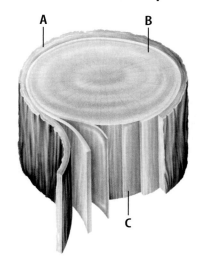

**6** What is the function of the structure labeled C?
(1) It transports nutrients throughout the plant.
(2) It produces new xylem and phloem.
(3) It transports water from the roots to other parts of the plant.
(4) It absorbs water from outside the plant.

**7** What type of vascular tissue is indicated by B?
(1) xylem
(2) cambium
(3) phloem
(4) cellulose

*Record your answers on the answer sheet provided by your teacher or on a sheet of paper.*

**Use the two illustrations below to answer question 8.**

A          B

**8** Identify the flowers shown above as a monocot or a dicot. Explain the differences between the flowers of monocots and dicots.

**9** How are plants that live on land able to conserve water?

**10** Explain why reproductive adaptations were necessary in order for plants to survive on land.

**Use the two diagrams below to answer questions 11–12.**

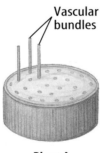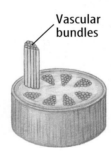

Plant A          Plant B

**11** Two plants, A and B, have stem cross sections as shown in the diagrams above. What does the different vascular bundle arrangement tell you about each plant?

**12** Draw what the seed from each plant would look like.

**13** Compare and contrast vascular and nonvascular plants. Include examples of each type of plant.

**14** Explain what peat is and how it is formed. How is peat used today?

LE 5.1a: Animals and plants have a great variety of body plans and internal structures that contribute to their ability to maintain a balanced condition. **5.1b:** An organism's overall body plan and its environment determine the way that the organism carries out the life processes.
**Also Covered:** 5.1c, 5.1g, 6.2a, 6.2b, 6.2c

# Plant Processes

## chapter preview

### sections

**1** **Photosynthesis and Respiration**
  *Lab* *Stomata in Leaves*

**2** **Plant Responses**
  *Lab* *Tropism in Plants*

 *Virtual Lab* *Which colors of the light spectrum are most important for plant growth?*

## How did it get so big?

From crabgrass to giant sequoias, many plants start as small seeds. Some trees may grow to be more than 20 m tall. One tree can produce enough lumber to build a house. Where does all that wood come from? Did you know that plants are essential to the survival of all animals on Earth?

**Science Journal**  Describe what would happen to life on Earth if all the green plants disappeared.

# Start-Up Activities

## Do plants lose water?

Plants, like all other living organisms, are made of cells, reproduce, and need water to live. What would happen if you forgot to water a houseplant? From your own experiences, you probably know that the houseplant would wilt. Do the following lab to discover one way plants lose water.

1. Obtain a self-sealing plastic bag, some aluminum foil, and a small potted plant from your teacher.

2. Using the foil, carefully cover the soil around the plant in the pot. Place the potted plant in the plastic bag.

3. Seal the bag and place it in a sunny window. Wash your hands.

4. Observe the plant at the same time every day for a few days.

5. **Think Critically** Write a paragraph that describes what happened in the bag. If enough water is lost by a plant and not replaced, predict what will happen to the plant.

**Photosynthesis and Respiration** Make the following Foldable to help you distinguish between photosynthesis and respiration.

**STEP 1** **Fold** a vertical sheet of paper in half from top to bottom.

**STEP 2** **Fold** in half from side to side with the fold at the top.

**STEP 3** **Unfold** the paper once. **Cut** only the fold of the top flap to make two tabs.

**STEP 4** **Turn** the paper vertically and **label** the front tabs as shown.

Photosynthesis

Respiration

**Compare and Contrast** As you read the chapter, write the characteristics of respiration and photosynthesis under the appropriate tab.

Preview this chapter's content and activities at glencoe.com

**section**

**1**

# Photosynthesis and Respiration

**as you read**

*What* **You'll Learn**

- **Explain** how plants take in and give off gases.
- **Compare and contrast** photosynthesis and respiration.
- **Discuss** why photosynthesis and respiration are important.

*Why* **It's Important**

Understanding photosynthesis and respiration in plants will help you understand how life exists on Earth.

🔍 **Review Vocabulary**
**cellulose:** chemical compound made of sugar; forms tangled fibers in plant cell walls and provides structure and support

**New Vocabulary**
- stomata
- photosynthesis
- chlorophyll
- respiration

## Taking in Raw Materials

Sitting in the cool shade under a tree, you eat lunch. Food is one of the raw materials you need to grow. Oxygen is another. It enters your lungs and eventually reaches every cell in your body. Your cells use oxygen to help release energy from the food that you eat. The process that uses oxygen to release energy from food produces carbon dioxide and water as wastes. These wastes move in your blood to your lungs, where they are removed as gases when you exhale. You look up at the tree and wonder, "Does a tree need to eat? Does it use oxygen? How does it get rid of wastes?"

**Movement of Materials in Plants** Trees and other plants don't take in foods the way you do. Plants make their own foods using the raw materials water, carbon dioxide, and inorganic chemicals in the soil. Just like you, plants also produce waste products.

Most of the water used by plants is taken in through roots, as shown in **Figure 1.** Water moves into root cells and then up through the plant to where it is used. When you pull up a plant, its roots are damaged and some are lost. If you replant it, the plant will need extra water until new roots grow to replace those that were lost.

Leaves, instead of lungs, are where most gas exchange occurs in plants. Most of the water taken in through the roots exits through the leaves of a plant. Carbon dioxide, oxygen, and water vapor exit and enter the plant through openings in the leaf. The leaf's structure helps explain how it functions in gas exchange.

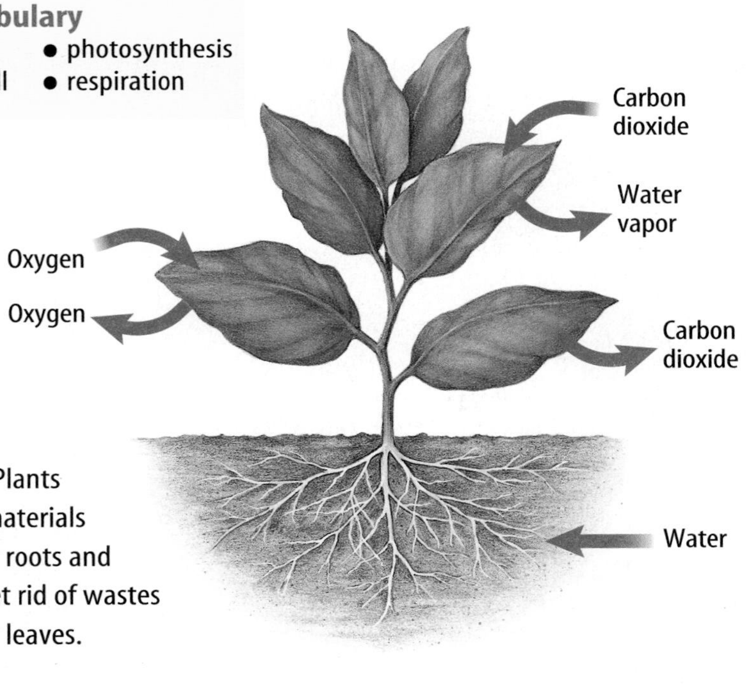

Carbon dioxide

Water vapor

Oxygen

Oxygen

Carbon dioxide

Water

**Figure 1** Plants take in raw materials through their roots and leaves and get rid of wastes through their leaves.

**Figure 2** A leaf's structure determines its function. Food is made in the inner layers. Most stomata are found on the lower epidermis.

**Identify** *the layer that contains most of the cells with chloroplasts.*

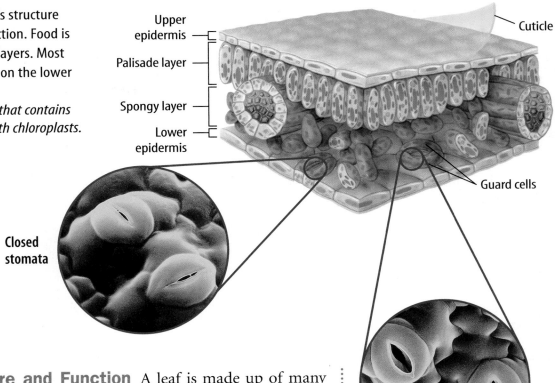

Upper epidermis

Palisade layer

Spongy layer

Lower epidermis

Cuticle

Guard cells

Closed stomata

Open stomata

**Leaf Structure and Function** A leaf is made up of many different layers, as shown in **Figure 2.** The outer cell layer of the leaf is the epidermis. A waxy cuticle that helps keep the leaf from drying out covers the epidermis. Because the epidermis is nearly transparent, sunlight—which is used to make food—reaches the cells inside the leaf. If you examine the epidermis under a microscope, you will see that it contains many small openings. These openings, called **stomata** (stoh MAH tuh) (singular, *stoma*), act as doorways for raw materials such as carbon dioxide, water vapor, and waste gases to enter and exit the leaf. Stomata also are found on the stems of many plants. More than 90 percent of the water plants take in through their roots is lost through the stomata. In one day, a growing tomato plant can lose up to 1 L of water.

Two cells called guard cells surround each stoma and control its size. As water moves into the guard cells, they swell and bend apart, opening a stoma. When guard cells lose water, they deflate and close the stoma. **Figure 2** shows closed and open stomata.

Stomata usually are open during the day, when most plants need to take in raw materials to make food. They usually are closed at night when food making slows down. Stomata also close when a plant is losing too much water. This adaptation conserves water, because less water vapor escapes from the leaf.

Inside the leaf are two layers of cells, the spongy layer and the palisade layer. Carbon dioxide and water vapor, which are needed in the food-making process, fill the spaces of the spongy layer. Most of the plant's food is made in the palisade layer.

**INTEGRATE**
**Career**

**Nutritionist** Vitamins are substances needed for good health. Nutritionists promote healthy eating habits. Research to learn about other roles that nutritionists fulfill. Create a pamphlet to promote the career of nutritionist.

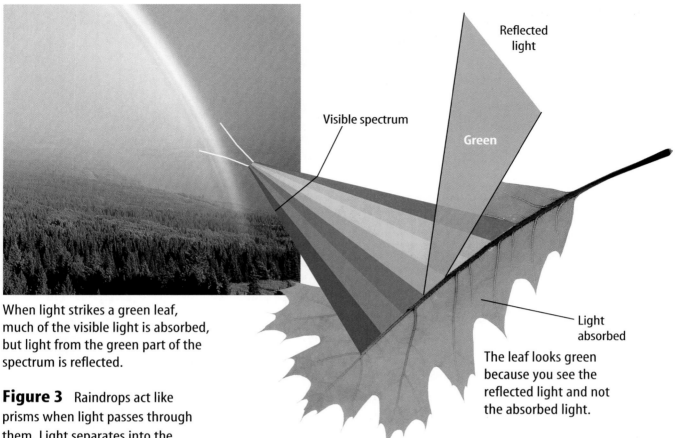

When light strikes a green leaf, much of the visible light is absorbed, but light from the green part of the spectrum is reflected.

**Reflected light**

**Visible spectrum**

**Green**

**Light absorbed**

The leaf looks green because you see the reflected light and not the absorbed light.

**Figure 3** Raindrops act like prisms when light passes through them. Light separates into the colors of the visible spectrum. You see a rainbow when this happens.

**Chloroplasts and Plant Pigments** If you look closely at the leaf in **Figure 2,** you'll see that some of the cells contain small, green structures called chloroplasts. Most leaves look green because some of their cells contain so many chloroplasts. Chloroplasts are green because they contain a green pigment called **chlorophyll** (KLOR uh fihl).

**✔ Reading Check** *Why are chloroplasts green?*

As shown in **Figure 3,** light from the Sun contains all colors of the visible spectrum. A pigment is a substance that reflects a particular part of the visible spectrum and absorbs the rest. When you see a green leaf, you are seeing green light energy reflected from chlorophyll. Most of the other colors of the spectrum, especially red and blue, are absorbed by chlorophyll. In the spring and summer, most leaves have so much chlorophyll that it hides all other pigments. In fall, the chlorophyll in some leaves breaks down and the leaves change color as other pigments become visible. Pigments, especially chlorophyll, are important to plants because the light energy that they absorb is used to make food. For plants, this food-making process—photosynthesis—happens in the chloroplasts.

# The Food-Making Process

**Photosynthesis** (foh toh SIHN thuh suhs) is the process during which a plant's chlorophyll traps light energy and sugars are produced. In plants, photosynthesis occurs only in cells with chloroplasts. For example, photosynthesis occurs only in a carrot plant's lacy green leaves, shown in **Figure 4.** Because a carrot's root cells lack chlorophyll and normally do not receive light, they can't perform photosynthesis. But excess sugar produced in the leaves is stored in the familiar orange root that you and many animals eat.

Besides light, plants also need the raw materials carbon dioxide and water for photosynthesis. The overall chemical equation for photosynthesis is shown below. What happens to each of the raw materials in the process?

$$6CO_2 + 6H_2O + \text{light energy} \xrightarrow{\text{chlorophyll}} C_6H_{12}O_6 + 6O_2$$

carbon dioxide  water                           glucose  oxygen

**Light-Dependent Reactions** Some of the chemical reactions that take place during photosynthesis require light, but others do not. Those that need light can be called the light-dependent reactions of photosynthesis. During light-dependent reactions, chlorophyll and other pigments trap light energy that eventually will be stored in sugar molecules. Light energy causes water molecules, which were taken up by the roots, to split into oxygen and hydrogen. The oxygen leaves the plant through the stomata. This is the oxygen that you breathe. Hydrogen produced when water is split is used in photosynthesis reactions that occur when there is no light.

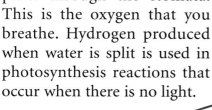

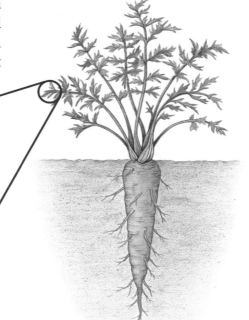

## Mini LAB

**Inferring What Plants Need to Produce Chlorophyll**

**Procedure**
1. Cut two pieces of **black construction paper** large enough so that each one completely covers one leaf on a **plant**.
2. Cut a square out of the center of each piece of paper.
3. Sandwich the leaf between the two paper pieces and **tape** the pieces together along their edges.
4. Place the plant in a sunny area. Wash your hands.
5. After seven days, carefully remove the paper and observe the leaf.

**Analysis**
In your **Science Journal,** describe how the color of the areas covered by paper compare to the areas not covered. Infer why this happened.

Try at Home

**Figure 4** Because they contain chloroplasts, cells in the leaf of the carrot plant are the sites for photosynthesis.

**Light-Independent Reactions** Reactions that don't need light are called the light-independent reactions of photosynthesis. Carbon dioxide, the raw material from the air, is used in these reactions. The light energy trapped during the light-dependent reactions is used to combine carbon dioxide and hydrogen to make sugars. One important sugar that is made is glucose. The chemical bonds that hold glucose and other sugars together are stored energy. **Figure 5** compares what happens during each stage of photosynthesis.

What happens to the oxygen and glucose that were made during photosynthesis? Most of the oxygen from photosynthesis is a waste product and is released through stomata. Glucose is the main form of food for plant cells. A plant usually produces more glucose than it can use. Excess glucose is stored in plants as other sugars and starches. When you eat carrots, as well as beets, potatoes, or onions, you are eating the stored product of photosynthesis.

Glucose also is the basis of a plant's structure. You don't grow larger by breathing in and using carbon dioxide. However, that's exactly what plants do as they take in carbon dioxide gas and convert it into glucose. Cellulose, an important part of plant cell walls, is made from glucose. Leaves, stems, and roots are made of cellulose and other substances produced using glucose. The products of photosynthesis are used for plant growth.

**Figure 5** Photosynthesis includes two sets of reactions, the light-dependent reactions and the light-independent reactions.
**Describe** what happens to the glucose produced during photosynthesis.

Standard plant cell

Chloroplast

Light

$H_2O$        $O_2$

$CO_2$

$C_6H_{12}O_6$

During light-dependent reactions, light energy is trapped and water is split into hydrogen and oxygen. Oxygen leaves the plant.

During light-independent reactions, energy is used to combine carbon dioxide and hydrogen to make glucose and other sugars.

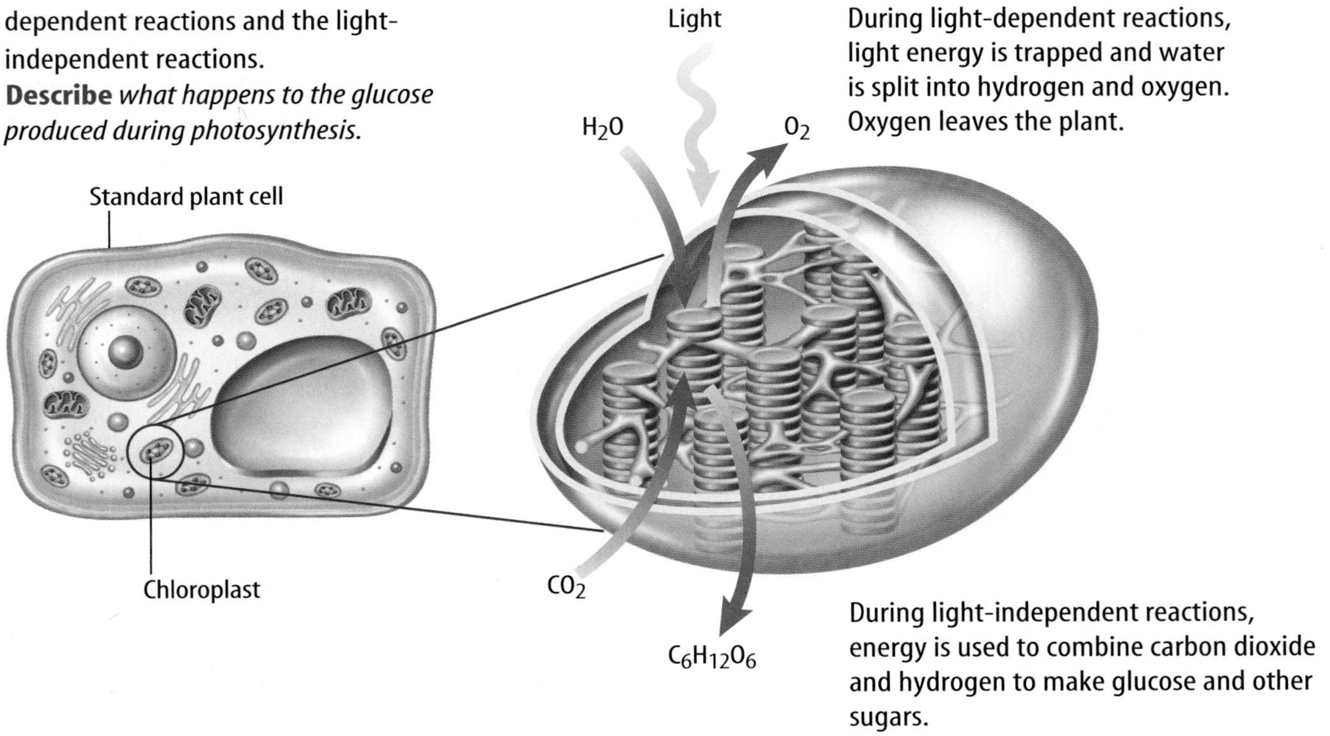

Figure 6 Tropical rain forests contain large numbers of photosynthetic plants.

**Infer** *why tropical forests are considered an important source of oxygen.*

**Importance of Photosynthesis** Why is photosynthesis important to living things? First, photosynthesis produces food. Organisms that carry on photosynthesis provide food directly or indirectly for nearly all the other organisms on Earth. Second, photosynthetic organisms, like the plants in **Figure 6,** use carbon dioxide and release oxygen. This removes carbon dioxide from the atmosphere and adds oxygen to it. Most organisms, including humans, need oxygen to stay alive. As much as 90 percent of the oxygen entering the atmosphere today is a result of photosynthesis.

**Living Environment**

**5.1c, 5.2a, 6.2a, 6.2b  Analyze** the importance of chloroplasts to plants. Explain the importance of chloroplasts in plants to humans.

# The Breakdown of Food

Look at the photograph in **Figure 7.** Do the fox and the plants in the photograph have anything in common? They don't look alike, but the fox and the plants are made of cells that break down food and release energy in a process called respiration. How does this happen?

**Respiration** is a series of chemical reactions that breaks down food molecules and releases energy. Respiration occurs in cells of most organisms. The breakdown of food might or might not require oxygen. Respiration that uses oxygen to break down food chemically is called aerobic respiration. In plants and many organisms that have one or more cells, a nucleus, and other organelles, aerobic respiration occurs in the mitochondria (singular, *mitochondrion*). The overall chemical equation for aerobic respiration is shown below.

Figure 7 You know that animals such as this red fox carry on respiration, but so do all the plants that surround the fox.

$$C_6H_{12}O_6 + 6O_2 \longrightarrow 6CO_2 + 6H_2O + energy$$

glucose    oxygen    carbon    water
                     dioxide

**Figure 8** Aerobic respiration takes place in the mitochondria of plant cells. **Describe** *what happens to a molecule before it enters a mitochondrion.*

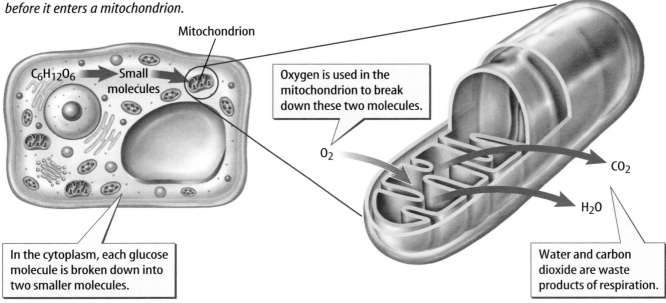

Mitochondrion

$C_6H_{12}O_6$ → Small molecules

Oxygen is used in the mitochondrion to break down these two molecules.

$O_2$

$CO_2$

$H_2O$

In the cytoplasm, each glucose molecule is broken down into two smaller molecules.

Water and carbon dioxide are waste products of respiration.

**Figure 9** Plants use the energy released during respiration to carry out many functions.

Plant structure and function

Production of chlorophyll

Sprouting of seeds

**Aerobic Respiration** Before aerobic respiration begins, glucose molecules are broken down into two smaller molecules. This happens in the cytoplasm. The smaller molecules then enter a mitochondrion, where aerobic respiration takes place. Oxygen is used in the chemical reactions that break down the small molecules into water and carbon dioxide. The reactions also release energy. Every cell in the organism needs this energy. **Figure 8** shows aerobic respiration in a plant cell.

**Importance of Respiration** Although food contains energy, it is not in a form that can be used by cells. Respiration changes food energy into a form all cells can use. This energy drives the life processes of almost all organisms on Earth.

✔ **Reading Check** *What organisms use respiration?*

Plants use energy produced by respiration to transport sugars and to open and close stomata. Some of the energy is used to produce substances needed for photosynthesis, such as chlorophyll. When seeds sprout, they use energy from the respiration of stored food in the seed. **Figure 9** shows some uses of energy in plants.

The waste product carbon dioxide is also important. Aerobic respiration returns carbon dioxide to the atmosphere, where it can be used again by plants and some other organisms for photosynthesis.

## Table 1  Comparing Photosynthesis and Aerobic Respiration

|  | Energy | Raw Materials | End Products | Where |
|---|---|---|---|---|
| **Photosynthesis** | stored | water and carbon dioxide | glucose and oxygen | cells with chlorophyll |
| **Aerobic respiration** | released | glucose and oxygen | water and carbon dioxide | cells with mitochondria |

# Comparison of Photosynthesis and Respiration

Look back in the section to find the equations for photosynthesis and aerobic respiration. You can see that aerobic respiration is almost the reverse of photosynthesis. Photosynthesis combines carbon dioxide and water by using light energy. The end products are glucose (food) and oxygen. During photosynthesis, energy is stored in food. Photosynthesis occurs only in cells that contain chlorophyll, such as those in the leaves of plants. Aerobic respiration combines oxygen and food to release the energy in the chemical bonds of the food. The end products of aerobic respiration are energy, carbon dioxide, and water. All plant cells contain mitochondria. Any cell with mitochondria can use the process of aerobic respiration. **Table 1** compares photosynthesis and aerobic respiration.

### Living Environment

**5.1c, 5.2a, 6.2a, 6.2b**
**Summarize** the products taken in and given off during photosynthesis and aerobic respiration.

## section 1 review

### Summary

**Taking in Raw Materials**

- Leaves take in carbon dioxide that is used in photosynthesis.
- Oxygen and carbon dioxide are waste products of photosynthesis and respiration.

**The Food-Making Process**

- Photosynthesis takes place in chloroplasts.
- Photosynthesis is a series of chemical reactions that transforms energy from light into energy stored in the chemical bonds of sugar molecules.

**The Breakdown of Food**

- Aerobic respiration uses oxygen to release energy from food.
- Aerobic respiration takes place in mitochondria.

### Self Check

1. **Describe** how gases enter and exit a leaf.
2. **Explain** why photosynthesis and respiration are important.
3. **Identify** what must happen to glucose molecules before respiration begins.
4. **Compare and contrast** the number of organisms that respire and the number that photosynthesize.
5. **Think Critically** Humidity is water vapor in the air. Infer how plants contribute to humidity.

*Hot Words Hot Topics*: Bk 2 (6) pp. 282–286

### Applying Math

6. **Solve One-Step Equations** How many $CO_2$ molecules result from the respiration of a glucose molecule $(C_6H_{12}O_6)$? Refer to the equation in this section.

# Stomata in Leaves

Stomata open and close, which allows gases into and out of a leaf. These openings are usually invisible without the use of a microscope. Do this lab to see some stomata.

## ⊙ Real-World Question

Where are stomata in lettuce leaves?

### Goals
- **Describe** guard cells and stomata.
- **Infer** the conditions that make stomata open and close.

### Materials
lettuce in dish of water    microscope slide
coverslip    salt solution
microscope    forceps

### Safety Precautions

🥽 👓 🧼 🚫 ✋

**WARNING:** *Never eat or taste any materials used in the laboratory.*

## ⊙ Procedure

1. Copy the Stomata Data table into your Science Journal.

2. From a head of lettuce, tear off a piece of an outer, crisp, green leaf.

3. Bend the piece of leaf in half and carefully use a pair of forceps to peel off some of the epidermis, the transparent tissue that covers a leaf. Prepare a wet mount of this tissue.

4. Examine your prepared slide under low and high power on the microscope.

5. Count the total number of stomata in your field of view and then count the number of

| Stomata Data (Sample data only) | | |
|---|---|---|
| | **Wet Mount** | **Salt-Solution Mount** |
| Total Number of Stomata | | |
| Number of Open Stomata | Do not write in this book. | |
| Percent Open | | |

open stomata. Enter these numbers in the data table.

6. Make a second slide of the lettuce leaf epidermis. This time place a few drops of salt solution on the leaf instead of water.

7. Wait a few minutes. Repeat steps 4 and 5.

8. **Calculate** the percent of open stomata using the following equation:

$$\frac{\text{number of open stomata}}{\text{total number of stomata}} \times 100 = \text{percent open}$$

## ⊙ Conclude and Apply

1. **Determine** which slide preparation had a greater percentage of open stomata.

2. **Infer** why fewer stomata were open in the salt-solution mount.

3. What can you infer about the function of stomata in a leaf?

### 𝒞ommunicating Your Data

Collect data from your classmates and compare it to your data. Discuss any differences you find and why they occurred. **For more help, refer to the** Science Skill Handbook.

# section 2

# Plant Responses

## What are plant responses?

It's dark. You're alone in a room watching a horror film on television. Suddenly, the telephone near you rings. You jump, and your heart begins to beat faster. You've just responded to a stimulus. A stimulus is anything in the environment that causes a response in an organism. The response often involves movement either toward the stimulus or away from the stimulus. A stimulus may come from outside (external) or inside (internal) the organism. The ringing telephone is an example of an external stimulus. It caused you to jump, which is a response. Your beating heart is a response to an internal stimulus. Internal stimuli are usually chemicals produced by organisms. Many of these chemicals are hormones. Hormones are substances made in one part of an organism for use somewhere else in the organism.

All living organisms, including plants, respond to stimuli. Many different chemicals are known to act as hormones in plants. These internal stimuli have a variety of effects on plant growth and function. Plants respond to external stimuli such as touch, light, and gravity. Some responses, such as the response of the Venus's-flytrap plant in **Figure 10,** are rapid. Other plant responses are slower because they involve changes in growth.

## as you read

### *What* You'll Learn
- **Identify** the relationship between a stimulus and a tropism in plants.
- **Compare and contrast** long-day and short-day plants.
- **Explain** how plant hormones and responses are related.

### *Why* It's Important
You will be able to grow healthier plants if you understand how they respond to certain stimuli.

### ⊙ Review Vocabulary
**behavior:** the way in which an organism interacts with other organisms and its environment

### New Vocabulary
- tropism
- auxin
- photoperiodism
- long-day plant
- short-day plant
- day-neutral plant

**Figure 10** A Venus's-flytrap has three small trigger hairs on the surface of its toothed leaves. When two hairs are touched at the same time, the plant responds by closing its trap in less than 1 second.

**Figure 11** Tropisms are responses to external stimuli.
**Identify** *the part of a plant that shows negative gravitropism.*

The pea plant's tendrils respond to touch by coiling around things.

This plant is growing toward the light, an example of positive phototropism.

This plant was turned on its side. With the roots visible, you can see that they are showing positive gravitropism.

## Tropisms

Some responses of a plant to an external stimuli are called tropisms. A **tropism** (TROH pih zum) can be seen as movement caused by a change in growth and can be positive or negative. For example, plants might grow toward a stimulus—a positive tropism—or away from a stimulus—a negative tropism.

**Touch** One stimulus that can result in a change in a plant's growth is touch. When the pea plant, as shown in **Figure 11,** touches a solid object, it responds by growing faster on one side of its stem than on the other side. As a result the stem bends and twists around any object it touches.

**Light** Did you ever see a plant leaning toward a window? Light is an important stimulus to plants. When a plant responds to light, the cells on the side of the plant opposite the light get longer than the cells facing the light. Because of this uneven growth, the plant bends toward the light. This response causes the leaves to turn in such a way that they can absorb more light. When a plant grows toward light it is called a positive response to light, or positive phototropism, shown in **Figure 11.**

**Gravity** Plants respond to gravity. The downward growth of plant roots, as shown in **Figure 11,** is a positive response to gravity. A stem growing upward is a negative response to gravity. Plants also may respond to electricity, temperature, and darkness.

# Plant Hormones

Hormones control the changes in growth that result from tropisms and affect other plant growth. Plants often need only millionths of a gram of a hormone to stimulate a response.

**Ethylene** Many plants produce the hormone ethylene (EH thuh leen) gas and release it into the air around them. Ethylene is produced in cells of ripening fruit, which stimulates the ripening process. Commercially, fruits such as oranges and bananas are picked when they are unripe and the green fruits are exposed to ethylene during shipping so they will ripen. Another plant response to ethylene causes a layer of cells to form between a leaf and the stem. The cell layer causes the leaf to fall from the stem.

*Hot Words Hot Topics*: Bk 2 (1) pp. 201–202, 210; (2) p. 210

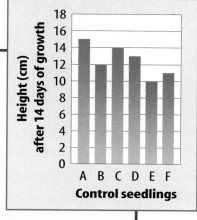
**Control seedlings**

## Applying Math    Calculate Averages

**GROWTH HORMONES** Gibberellins are plant hormones that increase growth rate. The graphs on the right show data from an experiment to determine how gibberellins affect the growth of bean seedlings. What is the average height of control bean seedlings after 14 days?

### Solution

**1** *This is what you know:*
- height of control seedlings after 14 days
- number of control seedlings

**2** *This is what you need to find out:*

What is the average height of control seedlings after 14 days?

**3** *This is the procedure you need to use:*
- Find the total of the seedling heights. $15 + 12 + 14 + 13 + 10 + 11 = 75$ cm
- Divide the height total by the number of control seedlings to find the average height. 75 cm/6 = 12.5 cm

**4** *Check your answer:*

Multiply 12.5 cm by 6 and you should get 75 cm.

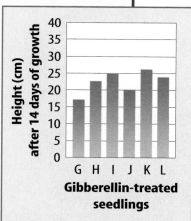
**Gibberellin-treated seedlings**

### Practice Problems

1. Calculate the average height of seedlings treated with gibberellin.

2. In an experiment, the heights of gibberellin-treated rose stems were 20, 26, 23, 24, 23, 25, and 26 cm. The average height of the controls was 23 cm. Did gibberellin have an effect?

**For more practice, visit glencoe.com**

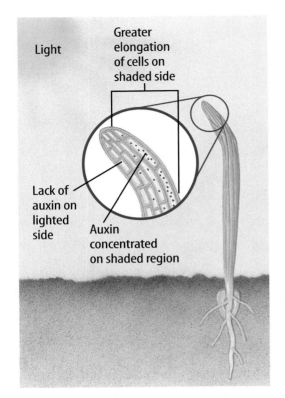

Light

Greater elongation of cells on shaded side

Lack of auxin on lighted side

Auxin concentrated on shaded region

**Figure 12** The concentration of auxin on the shaded side of a plant causes cells on that side to lengthen.

## Mini LAB

### Observing Ripening

**Procedure**

1. Place a **green banana** in a **paper bag**. Roll the top shut and place it on a table or counter.
2. Place another green banana near the paper bag.
3. After two days check the bananas to see how they have ripened. **WARNING:** *Do not eat the materials used in the lab.*

**Analysis**

Which banana ripened more quickly? Why?

Try at Home

**Auxin** Scientists identified the plant hormone, **auxin** (AWK sun) more than 100 years ago. Auxin is a type of plant hormone that causes plant stems and leaves to exhibit positive response to light. When light shines on a plant from one side, the auxin moves to the shaded side of the stem where it causes a change in growth, as shown in **Figure 12.** Auxins also control the production of other plant hormones, including ethylene.

✓ **Reading Check** *How are auxins and positive response to light related?*

Development of many parts of the plant, including flowers, roots, and fruit, is stimulated by auxins. Because auxins are so important in plant development, synthetic auxins have been developed for use in agriculture. Some of these synthetic auxins are used in orchards so that all plants produce flowers and fruit at the same time. Other synthetic auxins damage plants when they are applied in high doses and are used as weed killers.

**Gibberellins and Cytokinins** Two other groups of plant hormones that also cause changes in plant growth are gibberellins and cytokinins. Gibberellins (jih buh REH lunz) are chemical substances that were isolated first from a fungus. The fungus caused a disease in rice plants called "foolish seedling" disease. The fungus infects the stems of plants and causes them to grow too tall. Gibberellins can be mixed with water and sprayed on plants and seeds to stimulate plant stems to grow and seeds to germinate.

Like gibberellins, cytokinins (si tuh KI nunz) also cause rapid growth. Cytokinins promote growth by causing faster cell divisions. Like ethylene, the effect of cytokinins on the plant also is controlled by auxin. Interestingly, cytokinins can be sprayed on stored vegetables to keep them fresh longer.

**Abscisic Acid** Because hormones that cause growth in plants were known to exist, biologists suspected that substances that have the reverse effect also must exist. Abscisic (ab SIH zihk) acid is one such substance. Many plants grow in areas that have cold winters. Normally, if seeds germinate or buds develop on plants during the winter, they will die. Abscisic acid is the substance that keeps seeds from sprouting and buds from developing during the winter. This plant hormone also causes stomata to close and helps plants respond to water loss on hot summer days. **Figure 13** summarizes how plant hormones affect plants and how hormones are used.

## Figure 13

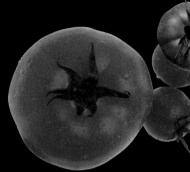

Chemical compounds called plant hormones help determine how a plant grows. There are five main types of hormones. They coordinate a plant's growth and development, as well as its responses to environmental stimuli, such as light, gravity, and changing seasons. Most changes in plant growth are a result of plant hormones working together, but exactly how hormones cause these changes is not completely understood.

▲ **ETHYLENE** By controlling the exposure of these tomatoes to ethylene, a hormone that stimulates fruit ripening, farmers are able to harvest unripe fruit and make it ripen just before it arrives at the supermarket.

◄ **GIBBERELLINS** The larger mustard plant in the photo at left was sprayed with gibberellins, plant hormones that stimulate stem elongation and fruit development.

Lateral buds

Lateral branches

◄ **CYTOKININS** Lateral buds do not usually develop into branches. However, if a plant's main stem is cut, as in this bean plant, naturally occurring cytokinins will stimulate the growth of lateral branches, causing the plant to grow "bushy."

▼ **AUXINS** Powerful growth hormones called auxins regulate responses to light and gravity, stem elongation, and root growth. The root growth on the plant cuttings, center and right, is the result of auxin treatment.

Bag
Leaf
0    IPA

Bag
Leaf
0.3%    IPA

Bag
Leaf
0.8%    IPA

▶ **ABA (ABSCISIC ACID)** In plants such as the American basswood, right, abscisic acid causes buds to remain dormant for the winter. When spring arrives, ABA stops working and the buds sprout.

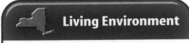
# Photoperiods

**INTEGRATE Earth Science**

Sunflowers bloom in the summer, and cherry trees flower in the spring. Some plant species produce flowers at specific times during the year. A plant's response to the number of hours of daylight and darkness it receives daily is **photoperiodism** (foh toh PIHR ee uh dih zum).

Earth revolves around the Sun once each year. As Earth moves in its orbit, it also rotates. One rotation takes about 24 h. Because Earth is tilted about 23.5° from a line perpendicular to its orbit, the hours of daylight and darkness vary with the seasons. As you probably have noticed, the Sun sets later in summer than in winter. These changes in lengths of daylight and darkness affect plant growth.

**Darkness and Flowers** Many plants require a specific length of darkness to begin the flowering process. Generally, plants that require less than 10 h to 12 h of darkness to flower are called **long-day plants.** You may be familiar with some long-day plants such as spinach, lettuce, and beets. Plants that need 12 or more hours of darkness to flower are called **short-day plants.** Some short-day plants are poinsettias, strawberries, and ragweed. **Figure 14** shows what happens when a short-day plant receives less darkness than it needs to flower.

✓ **Reading Check** *What is needed to begin the flowering process?*

**Day-Neutral Plants** Plants like dandelions and roses are **day-neutral plants.** They have no specific photoperiod, and the flowering process can begin within a range of hours of darkness.

In nature, photoperiodism affects where flowering plants can grow and produce flowers and fruit. Even if a particular environment has the proper temperature and other growing conditions for a plant, it will not flower and produce fruit without the correct photoperiod. **Table 2** shows how day length affects flowering in all three types of plants.

Sometimes the photoperiod of a plant has a narrow range. For example, some soybeans will flower with 9.5 h of darkness but will not flower with 10 h of darkness. Farmers must choose the variety of soybeans with a photoperiod that matches the hours of darkness in the section of the country where they plant their crop.

**Figure 14** When short-day plants receive less darkness than required to produce flowers, they produce larger leaves instead.

## Table 2 Photoperiodism

| | Long-Day Plants | Short-Day Plants | Day-Neutral Plants |
|---|---|---|---|
| **Early Summer**<br>Noon / 6 AM / 6 PM / Midnight | | | |
| **Late Fall**<br>Noon / 6 AM / 6 PM / Midnight | | | |
| | An iris is a long-day plant that is stimulated by short nights to flower in the early summer. | Goldenrod is a short-day plant that is stimulated by long nights to flower in the fall. | Roses are day-neutral plants and have no specific photoperiod. |

Today, greenhouse growers are able to provide any length of artificial daylight or darkness. This means that you can buy short-day flowering plants during the summer and long-day flowering plants during the winter.

## section 2 review

### Summary

**What are plant responses?**
- Plants respond to both internal and external stimuli.

**Tropisms**
- Tropisms are plant responses to external stimuli, including touch, light, and gravity.

**Plant Hormones**
- Hormones control changes in plant growth, including changes that result from tropisms.

**Photoperiods**
- Long-day plants flower in late spring or summer.
- Short-day plants flower in late fall or winter.

### Self Check

1. **List** one example of an internal stimulus and one example of an external stimulus in plants.
2. **Compare and contrast** photoperiodism and phototropism.
3. **Identify** the term that describes the photoperiod of red raspberries that produce fruit in late spring and in the fall.
4. **Distinguish** between abscisic acid and gibberellins.
5. **Think Critically** Describe the relationship between hormones and tropisms.

#### Applying Skills

6. **Compare and contrast** the responses of roots and stems to gravity.

# Tropism in Plants

## ◉ Real-World Question

Grapevines can climb on trees, fences, or other nearby structures. This growth is a response to the stimulus of touch. Tropisms are specific plant responses to stimuli outside of the plant. One part of a plant can respond positively while another part of the same plant can respond negatively to the same stimulus. Gravitropism is a response to gravity. Why might it be important for some plant parts to have a positive response to gravity while other plant parts have a negative response? Do stems and roots respond to gravity in the same way? You can design an experiment to test how some plant parts respond to the stimulus of gravity.

### Goals
- **Describe** how roots and stems respond to gravity.
- **Observe** how changing the stimulus changes the growth of plants.

### Materials
paper towel
30-cm × 30-cm sheet of aluminum foil
water
mustard seeds
marking pen
1-L clear-glass or plastic jar

### Safety Precautions

**WARNING:** *Some kinds of seeds are poisonous. Do not put any seed in your mouth.*

## Procedure

1. Copy the data table on the right in your Science Journal.

2. Moisten the paper towel with water so that it's damp but not dripping. Fold it in half twice.

3. Place the folded paper towel in the center of the foil and sprinkle mustard seeds in a line across the center of the towel.

| Response to Gravity | | |
|---|---|---|
| Position of Arrow on Foil Package | Observations of Seedling Roots | Observations of Seedling Stems |
| Arrow up | | |
| Arrow down | Do not write in this book. | |

4. Fold the foil around the towel and seal each end by folding the foil over. Make sure the paper towel is completely covered by the foil.

5. Use a marking pen to draw an arrow on the foil, and place the foil package in the jar with the arrow pointing upward.

6. After five days, carefully open the package and record your observations in the data table. (Note: *If no stems or roots are growing yet, reseal the package and place it back in the jar, making sure that the arrow points upward. Reopen the package in two days.*)

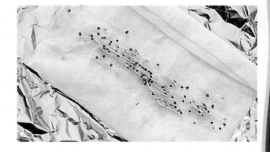

7. Reseal the foil package, being careful not to disturb the seedlings. Place it in the jar so that the arrow points downward instead of upward.

8. After five more days, reopen the package and observe any new growth of the seedlings' roots and stems. Record your observations in your data table.

## Analyze Your Data

1. **Classify** the responses you observed as positive or negative tropisms.

2. **Explain** why the plants' growth changed when you placed them upside down.

## Conclude and Apply

1. **Infer** why it was important that no light reach the seedlings during your experiment.

2. **Describe** some other ways you could have changed the position of the foil package to test the seedlings' response.

**Communicating Your Data**

**Compare** drawings you make of the growth of the seedlings before and after you turned the package. **Compare** your drawings with those of other students in your class. **For more help, refer to the** Science Skill Handbook.

# Science and Language Arts

## "Sunkissed: An Indian Legend"
### as told by Alberto and Patricia De La Fuente

*A long time ago, deep down in the very heart of the old Mexican forests, so far away from the sea that not even the largest birds ever had time to fly that far, there was a small, beautiful valley. A long chain of snow-covered mountains stood between the valley and the sea. . . . Each day the mountains were the first ones to tell everybody that Tonatiuh, the King of Light, was coming to the valley. . . .*

"Good morning, Tonatiuh!" cried a little meadow. . . .

The wild flowers always started their fresh new day with a kiss of golden sunlight from Tonatiuh, but it was necessary to first wash their sleepy baby faces with the dew that Metztli, the Moon, sprinkled for them out of her bucket onto the nearby leaves during the night. . . .

. . . All night long, then, Metztli Moon would walk her night-field making sure that by sun-up all flowers had the magic dew that made them feel beautiful all day long.

However, much as flowers love to be beautiful as long as possible, they want to be happy too. So every morning Tonatiuh himself would give each one a single golden kiss of such power that it was possible to be happy all day long after it. As you can see, then, a flower needs to feel beautiful in the first place, but if she does not feel beautiful, she will not be ready for her morning sun-kiss. If she cannot wash her little face with the magic dew, the whole day is lost.

## Understanding Literature

**Legends and Oral Traditions** A legend is a traditional story often told orally and believed to be based on actual people and events. Legends are believed to be true even if they cannot be proved. "Sunkissed: An Indian Legend" is a legend about a little flower that is changed forever by the Sun. This legend also is an example of an oral tradition. Oral traditions are stories or skills that are handed down by word of mouth. What in this story indicates that it is a legend?

### Respond to the Reading

1. What does this passage tell you about the relationship between the Sun and plants?
2. What does this passage tell you about the relationship between water and the growth of flowers?
3. **Linking Science and Writing** Create an idea for a fictional story that explains why the sky becomes so colorful during a sunset. Then retell your story to your classmates.

The passage from "Sunkissed: An Indian Legend" does not teach us the details about photosynthesis or respiration. However, it does show how sunshine and water are important to plant life. The difference between the legend and the information contained in your textbook is this—photosynthesis and respiration can be proved scientifically, and the legend, although fun to read, cannot.

## Reviewing Main Ideas

### Section 1 — Photosynthesis and Respiration

1. Carbon dioxide and water vapor enter and leave a plant through openings in the epidermis called stomata. Guard cells cause a stoma to open and close.

2. Photosynthesis takes place in the chloroplasts of plant cells. Light energy is used to produce glucose and oxygen from carbon dioxide and water.

3. Photosynthesis provides the food for most organisms on Earth.

4. All organisms use respiration to release the energy stored in food molecules. Oxygen is used in the mitochondria to complete respiration in plant cells and many other types of cells. Energy is released and carbon dioxide and water are produced.

5. The energy released by respiration is used for the life processes of most living organisms, including plants.

6. Photosynthesis and respiration are almost the reverse of each other. The end products of photosynthesis are the raw materials needed for aerobic respiration. The end products of aerobic respiration are the raw materials needed for photosynthesis.

### Section 2 — Plant Responses

1. Plants respond positively and negatively to stimuli. The response may be a movement, a change in growth, or the beginning of some process such as flowering.

2. A stimulus from outside the plant is called a tropism. Outside stimuli include light, gravity, and touch.

3. The length of darkness each day can affect flowering times of plants.

4. Plant hormones cause responses in plants. Some hormones cause plants to exhibit tropisms. Other hormones cause changes in plant growth rates.

## Visualizing Main Ideas

*Copy and complete the following concept map on photosynthesis and respiration.*

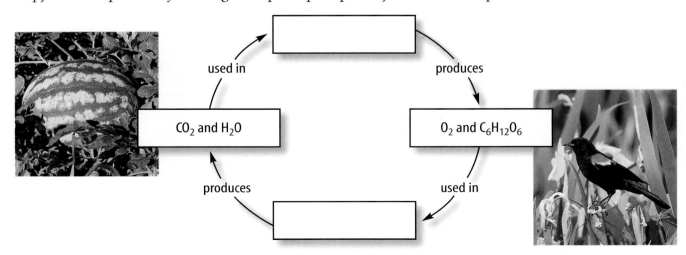

used in    produces

$CO_2$ and $H_2O$    $O_2$ and $C_6H_{12}O_6$

produces    used in

## Using Vocabulary

| | |
|---|---|
| auxin p. 588 | photosynthesis p. 579 |
| chlorophyll p. 578 | respiration p. 581 |
| day-neutral plant p. 590 | short-day plant p. 586 |
| long-day plant p. 590 | stomata p. 577 |
| photoperiodism p. 590 | tropism p. 586 |

*Fill in the blanks with the correct vocabulary word(s) from the list above.*

1. _____ is a hormone that causes plant stems and leaves to exhibit positive phototropism.

2. _____ is a light-dependent process conducted by green plants but not by animals.

3. _____ is required for photosynthesis.

4. A poinsettia, often seen flowering during December holidays, is a(n) _____.

5. In most living things, energy is released from food by _____.

6. Spinach requires only ten hours of darkness to flower, which makes it a(n) _____.

7. A(n) _____ can cause a plant to bend toward light.

8. Plants usually take in carbon dioxide through _____.

9. _____ controls a plant's response to day length.

10. Plants that flower without regard to day length are _____.

## Checking Concepts

*Choose the word or phrase that best answers the question.*

11. What raw material needed by plants enters through open stomata?
    A) sugar
    B) chlorophyll
    C) carbon dioxide
    D) cellulose

12. What is a function of stomata?
    A) photosynthesis
    B) to guard the interior cells
    C) to allow sugar to escape
    D) to permit the release of oxygen

13. What plant process produces water, carbon dioxide, and energy?
    A) cell division
    B) photosynthesis
    C) growth
    D) respiration

14. What are the products of photosynthesis?
    A) glucose and oxygen
    B) carbon dioxide and water
    C) chlorophyll and glucose
    D) carbon dioxide and oxygen

15. What are plant substances that affect plant growth called?
    A) tropisms
    B) glucose
    C) germination
    D) hormones

16. Leaves change colors because what substance breaks down?
    A) hormone
    B) carotenoid
    C) chlorophyll
    D) cytoplasm

17. Which of these is a product of respiration?
    A) $CO_2$
    B) $O_2$
    C) $C_2H_4$
    D) $H_2$

**Use the photo below to answer question 18.**

18. What stimulus is this plant responding to?
    A) light
    B) gravity
    C) touch
    D) water

*Vocabulary Puzzlemaker* glencoe.com

## Thinking Critically

**19. Predict** You buy pears at the store that are not completely ripe. What could you do to help them ripen more rapidly?

**20. Name** each tropism and state whether it is positive or negative.
 **a.** Stem grows up.
 **b.** Roots grow down.
 **c.** Plant grows toward light.
 **d.** A vine grows around a pole.

**21. Infer** Scientists who study sedimentary rocks and fossils suggest that oxygen was not in Earth's atmosphere until plantlike, one-celled organisms appeared. Why?

**22. Explain** why apple trees bloom in the spring but not in the summer.

**23. Discuss** why day-neutral and long-day plants grow best in countries near the equator.

**24. Form a hypothesis** about when guard cells open and close in desert plants.

**25. Concept Map** Copy and complete the following concept map about photoperiodism using the following information: flower year-round—*corn, dandelion, tomato*; flower in the spring, fall, or winter—*chrysanthemum, rice, poinsettia*; flower in summer—*spinach, lettuce, petunia*.

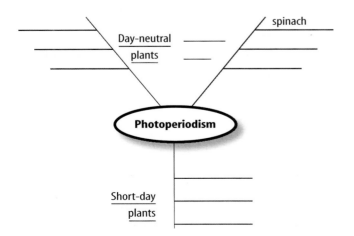

**26. Compare and contrast** the action of auxin and the action of ethylene on a plant.

## Performance Activities

**27. Coloring Book** Create a coloring book of day-neutral plants, long-day plants, and short-day plants. Use pictures from magazines and seed catalogs to get your ideas. Label the drawings with the plant's name and how it responds to darkness. Let a younger student color the flowers in your book.

*Hot Words Hot Topics*: Bk 2 (28) pp. 142–143; (29) p. 199

## Applying Math

**28. Stomata** A houseplant leaf has 1,573 stomata. During daylight hours, when the plant is well watered, about 90 percent of the stomata were open. During daylight hours when the soil was dry, about 25 percent of the stomata remained open. How many stomata were open (a) when the soil was wet and (b) when it was dry?

**Use the graph below to answer question 29.**

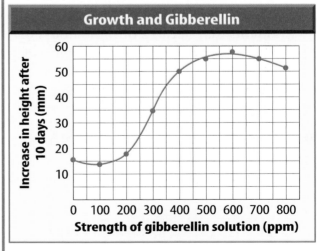

**29. Gibberellins** The graph above shows the results of applying different amounts of gibberellin to the roots of bean plants. What effect did a 100-ppm solution of gibberellin have on bean plant growth? Which gibberellin solution resulted in the tallest plants?

**Part I**

*Record your answers on the answer sheet provided by your teacher or on a sheet of paper.*

1 Which statement correctly describes the leaf epidermis?
   (1) This is an inner cell layer of the leaf.
   (2) This layer is nearly transparent.
   (3) Food is made in this layer.
   (4) Sunlight cannot penetrate this layer.

2 What happens when a plant is losing too much water?
   (1) stomata close
   (2) guard cells swell
   (3) stomata open
   (4) respiration increases

3 Which statement is TRUE?
   (1) Changes in length of daylight and darkness have no effect on plant growth.
   (2) Plants that need less than 10 to 12 hours of darkness to flower are called short-day plants.
   (3) Plants that need 12 or more hours of darkness to flower are called short-day plants.
   (4) Very few plants rely on a specific length of darkness to flower.

**Use the illustration below to answer question 4.**

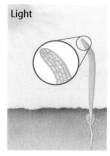

Light

4 The plant above is showing a growth response that is controlled by
   (1) auxin               (3) abscisic acid.
   (2) gravity             (4) length of darkness.

**Use the illustration below to answer questions 5 and 6.**

5 What type of response is displayed by this plant?
   (1) negative phototropism
   (2) positive gravitropism
   (3) positive phototropism
   (4) negative gravitropism

6 What plant hormone is responsible for the response shown here?
   (1) abscisic acid        (3) a gibberellin
   (2) auxin                (4) a cytokinin

7 In which plant cell structure does respiration take place?
   (1) nucleus              (3) vacuole
   (2) mitochondrion        (4) cell wall

8 Which of these is NOT produced through aerobic respiration?
   (1) glucose              (3) water
   (2) energy               (4) carbon dioxide

9 Which plant hormone prevents the development of buds during the winter?
   (1) abscisic acid        (3) gibberellin
   (2) auxin                (4) cytokinin

10 What chemical absorbs light energy which plants use in photosynthesis?
   (1) oxygen               (3) chlorophyll
   (2) hydrogen             (4) glucose

**Part II**

*Record your answers on the answer sheet provided by your teacher or on a sheet of paper.*

**Use the illustration below to answer questions 11 and 12.**

$$6CO_2 + 6H_2O + \text{light energy} \xrightarrow{\text{chlorophyll}} C_6H_{12}O_6 + 6O_2$$

**11** Identify this process. How would this process change if the amount of available water was limited?

**12** Based on this equation, what is the main food source for plant cells? How do animals use this food source?

**13** Why is respiration necessary for plants? Describe some plant processes which require energy.

**14** Many people who save poinsettia plants from Christmas cannot get them to flower the following Christmas. Why?

**15** Describe the relationship between chlorophyll and the color of leaves in spring and summer.

**16** Organisms which make their own food generate most of the oxygen in Earth's atmosphere. Trace the path of this element from a component of water in the soil to a gas in the air.

**17** What advantages might thigmotropism provide for some plants?

**18** The destruction of large areas of rain forest concerns scientists on many levels. Describe the relationship between environmental conditions for plant growth in rainforest regions, their relative rate of photosynthesis, and the amount of oxygen this process adds to the atmosphere.

**LE 1.1c:** Most cells have cell membranes, genetic material, and cytoplasm. Some cells have a cell wall and/or chloroplasts. Many cells have a nucleus. **1.1d:** Some organisms are single cells; others, including humans, are multicellular. **Also Covered:** 1.2j, 4.1a, 5.1b, 5.1d, 5.1e, 6.1a, 6.2c

# Bacteria, Protists, and Fungi

## Teeming with Life

The pond water appears crystal clear as the scientist uses a dropper to extract a sample for examination. However, in the lab when he examines some of the water under a microscope, he discovers that it contains hundreds of organisms. Some are only one cell, others appear to be groups of cells, and some are many-celled.

**Science Journal**    List possible functions of these organisms in a pond environment.

# Start-Up Activities

## Investigate Bacterial Growth

Did you know that millions of microorganisms are living on and inside of you at this moment? What are these organisms? Bacteria. They live nearly everywhere. What affects their growth? Find out by doing this lab.

1. Label six 200-mL beakers 1 through 6. Dissolve two beef bouillon cubes in 600 mL of hot water. Measure then pour 100 mL of this solution into each beaker.

2. Add a teaspoon of salt to 1 and 2, a teaspoon of vinegar to 3 and 4, and add nothing to 5 and 6.

3. Place 1, 3, and 5 in a warm place and 2, 4, and 6 in a refrigerator.

4. Observe the beakers after 48 hours.

5. **Think Critically** A cloudy solution is an indication of bacterial growth. Write a paragraph in your Science Journal comparing the bacterial growth in the six beakers. Infer from your results the growing conditions that favor bacterial growth.

**Positive and Negative Effects** Make the following Foldable to help you see how some organisms are similar and different.

**STEP 1** Fold a sheet of paper lengthwise. Make the front edge 1.25 cm shorter than the back edge.

**STEP 2** Fold into thirds.

**STEP 3** Unfold and cut only the top layer along both folds to make three tabs. **Label** each tab as shown.

**Identify Questions** Before you read the chapter, skim through it and write examples of each type of organism on the front of the tabs. As you read the chapter, list positive effects on the back of the tabs and negative effects under the tabs.

Preview this chapter's content and activities at glencoe.com

# section 1

# Bacteria

## as you read

### *What* You'll Learn

- **Identify** the characteristics of bacterial cells.
- **Name** the two major groups of bacteria.
- **Discuss** the overall importance of bacteria.

### *Why* It's Important

Bacteria are found in all environments and affect all living things.

### 🔍 Review Vocabulary

**disease:** a condition with symptoms that interferes with body functions

### New Vocabulary

- aerobe
- anaerobe
- endospore
- antibiotic
- pathogen
- vaccine
- pasteurization
- saprophyte

## What are bacteria?

They are found almost everywhere—in the air you breathe, in the food you eat, in the water you drink, and even deep in the ocean. They are on your clothes, on your shoes, and on the family dog or cat. A shovelful of soil contains billions of them. It might be hard to imagine, but you have huge populations of them living in and on your body that are beneficial to you.

For thousands of years, people did not know about bacteria. In the latter half of the seventeenth century, Antonie van Leeuwenhoek, a Dutch merchant, used his simple microscope to look at scrapings from his teeth. Leeuwenhoek did not know that the tiny organisms he observed were bacteria, as shown in **Figure 1.** His drawings were made about 200 years before it was proved that bacteria are living cells.

## Characteristics of Bacteria

All bacteria are one-celled organisms. Their cells are considered to be prokaryotic (proh kar ee AH tihk) because they do not have their genetic material in a nucleus. Some bacteria are found as individual cells. Others grow in groups or in long chains of cells.

**Producers and Consumers** Bacteria obtain their food in a variety of ways. Some bacteria use energy from sunlight to make their own food. Other bacteria use energy from inorganic chemicals to make food. Any organism that can make its own food is called a producer. Organisms that can't make their own food are called consumers. Consumer bacteria obtain food in many ways. Some break down dead organisms to obtain energy, and others live as parasites, absorbing nutrients from living organisms.

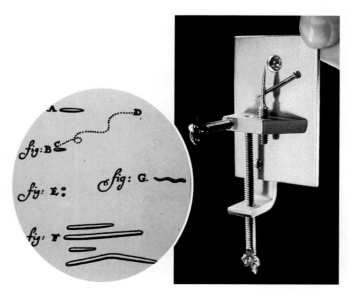

**Figure 1** Leeuwenhoek used a simple microscope like this to examine scrapings from his teeth. This drawing shows different types of bacteria that he observed.

**Aerobes and Anaerobes** Most bacteria live in places that have a supply of oxygen. An organism that uses oxygen for respiration is called an **aerobe** (AR ohb). You are an aerobic organism. Some bacteria are called **anaerobes** (A nuh rohbz) and they can live without oxygen.

**Structure and Function** Bacteria cells are usually much smaller than plant and animal cells and do not contain as many internal structures. The general structure of a bacterium can be seen in **Figure 2.** A bacterium contains cytoplasm surrounded by a cell membrane and a cell wall. Bacterial hereditary material is found in the cytoplasm. Some bacteria have a thick, gel-like capsule around the cell wall. The capsule helps protect the bacterium. Many bacteria that live in moist conditions have whiplike tails called flagella that help them move.

Some bacteria are able to produce a thick wall around themselves when environmental conditions are unfavorable. Inside this thick-walled structure, the bacterium produces a dormant form called an **endospore**. It can survive for hundreds of years this way.

**☑ Reading Check** *What conditions might cause bacteria to form endospores?*

The bacteria that normally inhabit your home and body have three basic shapes—spheres, rods, and spirals—as shown in **Figure 3.** Sphere-shaped bacteria are called cocci (KAW ki) (singular, *coccus*), rod-shaped bacteria are called bacilli (buh SIH li) (singular, *bacillus*), and spiral-shaped bacteria are called spirilla (spi RIH luh) (singular, *spirillum*).

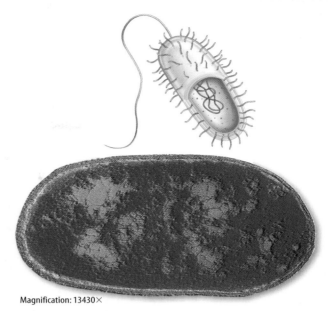

Magnification: 13430×

**Figure 2** Even though their cellular structure is simple, bacteria may be considered the most successful organisms living on Earth.

**Figure 3** Most bacteria can be identified as having one of these three shapes.
**Determine** *what shape you think a bacterium called* Streptococcus *would have.*

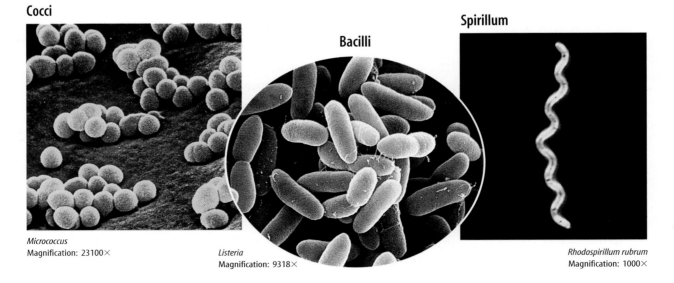

**Cocci**

*Micrococcus*
Magnification: 23100×

**Bacilli**

*Listeria*
Magnification: 9318×

**Spirillum**

*Rhodospirillum rubrum*
Magnification: 1000×

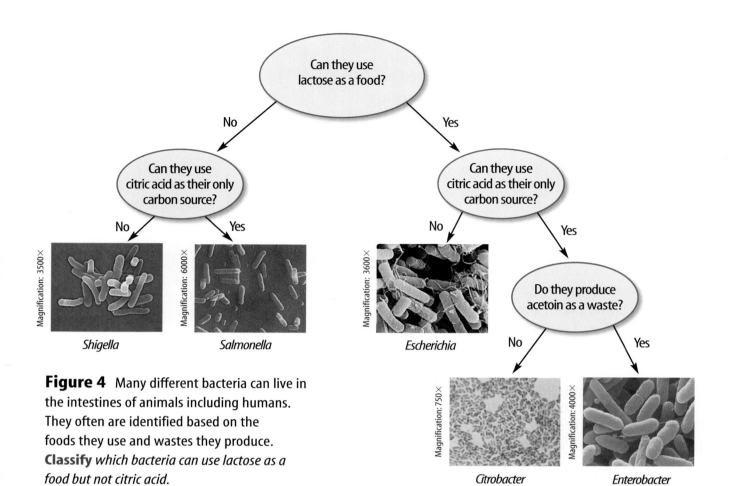

**Figure 4** Many different bacteria can live in the intestines of animals including humans. They often are identified based on the foods they use and wastes they produce. **Classify** which bacteria can use lactose as a food but not citric acid.

## Types of Bacteria

Two main groups of bacteria are archaebacteria (ar kee bak TIHR ee uh) and eubacteria (YOO bak tihr ee uh). Most known archaebacteria live in harsh environments where few kinds of other organisms can live. Eubacteria usually live in less harsh environments. Archaebacteria and eubacteria are thought to have existed for billions of years.

**Eubacteria** The larger of the two groups of bacteria is eubacteria. Eubacteria include many diverse groups. Although most eubacteria are consumers, some are producers. Some are aerobes and others are anaerobes. Most bacteria are beneficial. All bacteria that cause known diseases are eubacteria.

Most eubacteria have been classified and identified based upon conditions under which they grow and other chemical characteristics, such as composition of their cell walls, how they obtain food, and which waste products they produce. **Figure 4** shows one way to identify some bacteria that grow in the intestinal tracts of animals.

**Figure 5** Salt-loving bacteria can grow in evaporation ponds used for salt production. These bacteria contain a purple pigment.

Some bacteria grow in hot and acidic environments such as this hot spring in Yellowstone National Park and near deep ocean vents.

Some anaerobic archaebacteria live in the digestive tracts of animals and produce methane gas as a waste.

**INTEGRATE Earth Science**   **Archaebacteria** The archaebacteria usually are grouped according to the extreme environment in which they live, as shown and described in **Figure 5.**

*Hot Words Hot Topics*: Bk 2 (1) p. 397; (2) p. 397

## Applying Math    Solve a One-Step Equation

**BACTERIA POPULATION** One *E. coli* bacterium has a length of 0.002 mm. How many *E. coli* would fit across the top of an eraser that has a diameter of 10 mm?

### Solution

**1** *This is what you know:*
- length of *E. coli* = 0.002 mm
- diameter of eraser = 10 mm

**2** *This is what you need to find out:*    The number of *E. coli* that would fit across eraser.

**3** *This is the procedure you need to use:*    Divide the diameter of the eraser by the length of *E. coli*.

10 mm/0.002 mm = 5,000 *E. coli* would fit across the eraser

**4** *Check your answer:*    Multiplying your answer by the length of the *E. coli*. You should get 10 mm.

### Practice Problems

1. How many *E. coli* would fit end to end on a paper clip that is 4 cm long? (*Hint: Convert centimeters to millimeters.*)

2. There are 12,000 *E. coli* cells end to end on a pin. How long is the pin?

 **Science** Online   For more practice, visit glencoe.com

# Bacteria and Your Health

You probably know that some bacteria can cause you to get sick. However, do you know that bacteria can keep you healthy? You cannot survive without some bacteria living in or on your body.

**Helpful Bacteria** Some bacteria produce chemicals called **antibiotics** that limit the growth of or kill other bacteria. For example, one type of bacteria that is commonly found living in soil produces the antibiotic streptomycin. Many diseases in humans and animals can be treated with antibiotics.

Millions of bacteria live on your skin and all other parts of your body that are exposed to the outside world and some parts that are not. Certain types of these bacteria are usually harmless. Because they grow on or in your body, they limit the growth of other harmful bacteria. Most of the bacteria found in your large intestine are harmless to you and help you stay healthy. Some bacteria in your intestine produce vitamin K, which is needed for your blood to clot.

**Harmful Bacteria** Some bacteria are pathogens. A **pathogen** is any organism that causes disease. Bacteria that normally grow in your mouth can cause a common disease—tooth decay. As shown in **Figure 6,** these bacteria grow on the surface of your teeth and use sugar as a food. As they break down sugar, an acid is produced that can damage the enamel of your teeth. Bacteria then decay the softer parts of teeth.

You probably have been vaccinated against the bacterial diseases diphtheria, whooping cough, and tetanus. A **vaccine** is made from particles taken from damaged bacterial cell walls or from killed bacteria. Immunization with certain vaccines can prevent other bacterial diseases.

**Figure 6** One important bacteria that has been found to cause tooth decay is *Streptococcus mutans.*

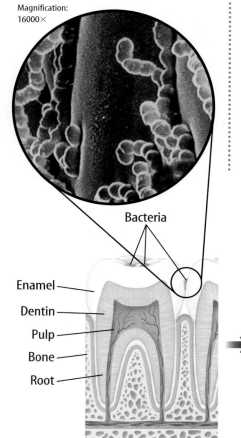

Magnification: 16000×

Bacteria

Enamel

Dentin

Pulp

Bone

Root

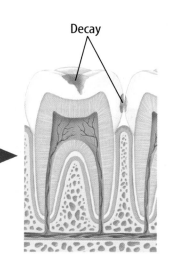

Decay

**Toxins** Many bacteria and other pathogens produce poisons called toxins as they grow in your body or as they grow in food that you might eat. Botulism, a type of food poisoning, is the result of a toxin produced by anaerobic bacteria whose endospores can survive in canned food. Most endospores and other bacteria are destroyed by the long-term heat treatment known as sterilization. Most canned food that you can buy has been sterilized.

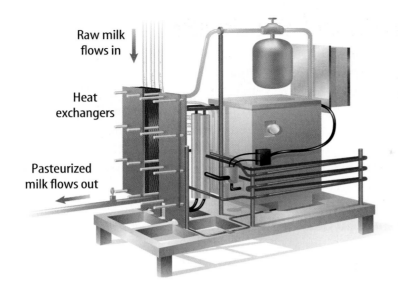

Raw milk flows in

Heat exchangers

Pasteurized milk flows out

**Figure 7** Most milk is pasteurized by heating it to at least 71.6°C for only 15 s. In the process, milk flows continuously past a heat exchanger.

# Bacteria and Industry

Would you want to eat food that contained bacteria and their wastes? Usually not, but many foods that you probably enjoy are produced using bacteria. Even before people understood that bacteria were involved, they used bacteria in the production of foods. One of the first uses of bacteria was in making yogurt, a food that has been eaten in Europe and Asia for hundreds of years. Cheeses, buttermilk, chocolate, vinegar, and sauerkraut all are produced with the aid of bacteria.

Unless it is sterilized, all food contains some bacteria. But heating food to sterilization temperature can change the taste of food. **Pasteurization** is a process that is used to kill most harmful bacteria with a minimum effect on the flavor of the product, as shown in **Figure 7.** Pasteurization also increases the length of time foods can be stored without spoiling. You are probably most familiar with pasteurized milk, but fruit juices and other foods also are pasteurized.

**Reading Check** *Why are some foods pasteurized?*

Many industries rely on bacteria. Today, bacteria and their by-products are cultivated in bioreactors. Bioreactors are used to make medicines, vitamins, alcohol, cleansers, adhesives, food thickeners, and other substances. Some landfills are bioreactors.

Some bacteria break down industrial, agricultural, or sewage wastes into simpler, harmless compounds. Sewage-treatment plants and septic systems use bacteria to process waste. The ability of certain bacteria to digest petroleum has been extremely important in helping clean up extensive oil spills in Alaska, California, and Texas.

**INTEGRATE Environment**

**Bioremediation** Bacteria exist that can feed on almost any chemical that contains carbon. Using bacteria to break down wastes and clean up spills is called bioremediation. To use this process properly requires matching the correct bacteria with the waste or contaminant to be "eaten." Find out some wastes that are treated in this way and list them in your Science Journal.

**Living Environment**

1.2j, 5.1e, 5.2f, 6.1c, 7.1d
**Create** a chart to compare the helpful bacteria to harmful bacteria.

# Bacteria and the Environment

Some consumer bacteria are called saprophytes (SAP ruh fites). A **saprophyte** is any organism that uses dead material as a food and energy source. When saprophytic bacteria digest dead organisms, the nutrients that they contain are made available for use by other organisms. When you compost kitchen, yard, and garden wastes, you put these bacteria to work for you. Without saprophytic bacteria, layers of dead material would be deeper than you are tall all over Earth's surface.

**Figure 8** Nitrogen-fixing bacteria live in the nodules on the roots of this peanut plant. They convert atmospheric nitrogen to a form usable by the plant and animals that eat the plant.

**Reading Check** *What is a saprophyte?*

**Nitrogen Fixation** All living things need nitrogen for making proteins and nucleic acids, but the nitrogen in Earth's atmosphere isn't in a form that can be used by most organisms. Certain bacteria called nitrogen-fixing bacteria are the only organisms that can combine nitrogen with other chemicals so it can be used by plants. Nitrogen-fixing bacteria live in growths on the roots of plants such as peas, soybeans, and peanuts, as shown in **Figure 8.** Some organisms obtain nitrogen by eating plants that contain the fixed nitrogen. These organisms then might be eaten by other organisms. In this way, nitrogen-fixing bacteria are an essential part of many food chains.

## section 1 review

### Summary

**Bacteria**
- Bacteria can be producers or consumers.
- Most bacteria are aerobic, others are anaerobic.
- Eubacteria are the largest group of bacteria.
- Archaebacteria are adapted to extreme environments.

**Bacteria and Your Health**
- Some bacteria can produce antibiotics, others can produce vitamin K in your intestine.
- Bacteria can cause disease or produce toxins.

**Bacteria and Industry**
- Many foods are made using bacteria.
- Some bacteria break down wastes.

**Bacteria and the Environment**
- Saprophytic bacteria digest dead organisms.
- Some bacteria fix nitrogen.

### Self Check

1. **List** the characteristics of bacteria.
2. **Identify** two reasons why bacteria are important in the environment.
3. **Explain** how some types of bacteria can help you stay healthy and other kinds of bacteria can make you sick.
4. **Describe** the types of environments in which archaebacteria are found.
5. **Think Critically** Why is botulism associated with canned foods and not with fresh foods?

*Hot Words Hot Topics*: Bk 2 (6) pp. 282–286

### Applying Math

6. **Solve One-Step Equations** Air may have more than 3,500 bacteria per cubic meter. Use this number to estimate the number of bacteria in the air in your classroom.

**LE 5.1b:** An organism's overall body plan and its environment determine the way that the organism carries out the life processes. **Also Covered:** LE 1.1d, 4.1a, 5.1d, 5.1e

# section 2 Protists

## What is a protist?

A **protist** is a one- or many-celled organism that lives in moist or wet surroundings. Unlike bacteria, protists' cells are eukaryotic. These organisms have a membrane-bound nucleus and other membrane-bound structures in their cytoplasm.

Protists are a diverse group that includes organisms with funguslike, animallike, or plantlike characteristics. To add to the confusion, many protists have characteristics similar to plants and animals. Protists get their food in a variety of ways. Some are producers, and others are predators, parasites, or saprophytes. **Table 1** lists the characteristics of each group. In which group would you place the protist pictured below?

**Funguslike Protists** Many funguslike protists spend part of their lives as one-celled organisms and part of their lives as many-celled organisms. Although many are called molds, they are not the same as the molds you will read about in the next section of this chapter. Slime molds, water molds, and downy mildews are examples of funguslike protists. The funguslike protists are consumers. They are either saprophytes or parasites.

| Table 1 Characteristics of Protist Groups | | |
|---|---|---|
| **Funguslike** | **Animal-like** | **Plantlike** |
| Consumers; most saprophytes or parasites | Consumers; obtain food in many ways | Producers that contain chlorophyll |
| Most reproduce using spores, like fungi. | Like animals, most do not have cell walls. | Many have cell walls like plants. |
| | Most can move from place to place using cilia, flagella, or pseudopods. | Many-celled forms remain attached to surfaces with rootlike structures. |

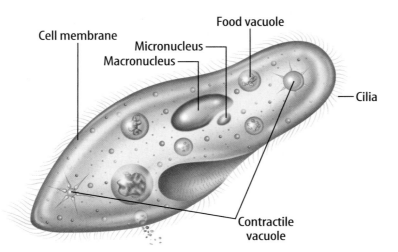

Cell membrane

Micronucleus
Macronucleus

Food vacuole

Cilia

Contractile vacuole

**Figure 9** The contractile vacuoles seen in this *Paramecium* act like pumps. As they contract, the vacuoles push water out.

## Identifying Protists

### Procedure

1. Fill a **wide-mouthed jar** with **pond water.** Add a **pond rock.**
2. Place the jar in direct sunlight for two weeks. Add new pond water to replace the water that evaporates.
3. Using a **dropper,** place a drop of water on a **slide.** Cover the drop with a **coverslip** and view the drop under a **microscope.**
4. Explore your pond zoo for protists. Identify organisms using a **guide to pond life.**

### Analysis

1. What protists could you identify in your pond zoo?
2. What did you observe about the pond water during the two-week time period?

**Animal-like Protists** One-celled, animal-like protists are known as **protozoans.** These complex organisms live in water, soil, and living and dead organisms. Many protozoans contain special structures for getting rid of excess water, as shown in **Figure 9.**

Protozoans often are separated into groups by how they move from place to place. Many protozoans move using one or more whiplike flagella. Others are covered with cilia (SIHL ee uh), which are short, threadlike structures that extend from the cell membrane. The cilia move like tiny oars to propel the protozoan through its watery environment. Another way some protozoans move is by using temporary extensions of their cytoplasm called **pseudopods** (SEW duh pahdz).

**Reading Check** *What are cilia and flagella and how do protozoans use them to move?*

All protozoans are consumers, and many have interesting ways of taking in food. Some, like *Paramecium,* use cilia to sweep food into mouthlike openings. Others, like amoebas, surround and trap food particles, such as a bacterium, with pseudopods. The food is then enclosed in a sphere called a vesicle. Some protozoans are saprophytes, and others are parasites that cause disease in animals and humans.

**Plantlike Protists** Plantlike protists are known as **algae** (AL jee). Some species of algae are one-celled and others are many-celled, as shown in **Figure 10.** One-celled algae have structures that are visible only under the microscope. Many small algae have flagella and can move from place to place. If you visit a beach, you are likely to find many-celled algae, sometimes called seaweed, washed up on the shore. Many-celled algae provide food and shelter for a large number of organisms.

Algae usually are grouped based on their structure and the pigments they contain. There are algae that are red, brown, golden, or different shades of green. All algae can make their own food and produce oxygen because they contain a green pigment called chlorophyll. However, so much of another pigment can be present in some algae that the chlorophyll cannot be observed.

**Figure 10**

The protist kingdom is so diverse that many scientists propose reorganizing it into several smaller kingdoms. In general, the traits of protists are used to group them as either funguslike, animal-like, or plantlike. Examples of each group are shown on this page.

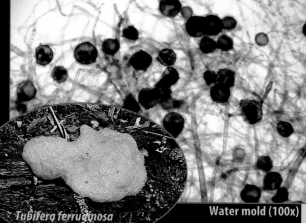

Water mold (100x)

*Tubifera ferruginosa*

**▲ FUNGUSLIKE PROTISTS** Water molds (shown actual size at top) secrete enzymes that digest other organisms. Slime molds (shown actual size in inset) go through a stage in which individual cells come together to form a slimy mass.

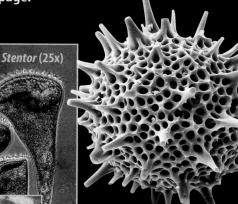

Stentor (25x)

Giardia (250x)

Radiolarian shell (300x)

**◄ ANIMAL-LIKE PROTISTS** These are one-celled predators, such as radiolarians and *Stentor*, or parasites, such as *Giardia*.

**▼ PLANTLIKE PROTISTS** Diatoms and algae—including giant kelp, which can grow to nearly nine meters—are considered plantlike protists because they have chloroplasts and make their own food.

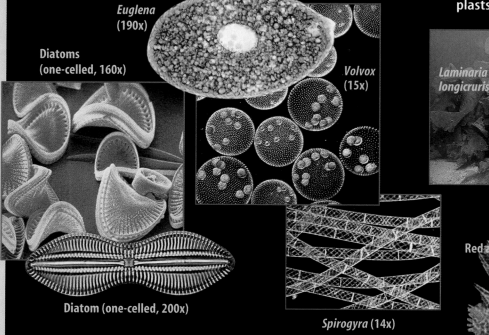

*Euglena* (190x)

Diatoms (one-celled, 160x)

*Volvox* (15x)

*Laminaria longicruris*

Diatom (one-celled, 200x)

*Spirogyra* (14x)

Red algae, *Antithamnion* (75x)

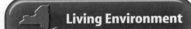
**Living Environment**

**1.2j, 5.2f Identify** several harmful effects of protists or their products.

**Figure 11** *Plasmodium,* a protozoan, causes the disease malaria. It spends part of its life cycle in mosquitoes and part in humans.

## The Importance of Protists

Are these organisms, most of which you can't see without a microscope, important to you or to the environment? The answer is yes. Many animals depend on these organisms for food, some of them cause disease, and many of them or their products are used in industry.

**Protists and Humans** You might use a protist or its product every day and not realize it. Algae or their products are ingredients in toothpaste, pudding, and ice cream. People in many parts of the world eat some algae. Other algae are used to make fertilizers, and some produce the sparkle that makes road lines visible at night.

Many protozoans are parasites that cause disease. One protozoan spends part of its life in an insect called a tsetse fly. People bitten by the fly can get a disease called African sleeping sickness.

Probably the most important disease caused by a protozoan is malaria. **Figure 11** shows how the parasite is carried by mosquitoes and transferred to humans. Malaria kills more than one million people each year.

A water mold caused the Irish potato famine in the 1840s. In a short time, most of the potato crop became diseased and the mold either killed the plants or made the potatoes inedible. More than a million people died in Ireland from the resulting famine. Potato blight continues to be a problem for potato growers, including in the United States.

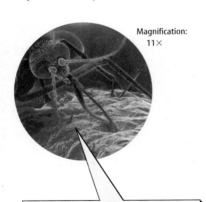

Magnification: 11×

*Plasmodium* lives in the salivary glands of certain female mosquitoes. The parasite can be transferred to the blood of people if an infected mosquito bites them.

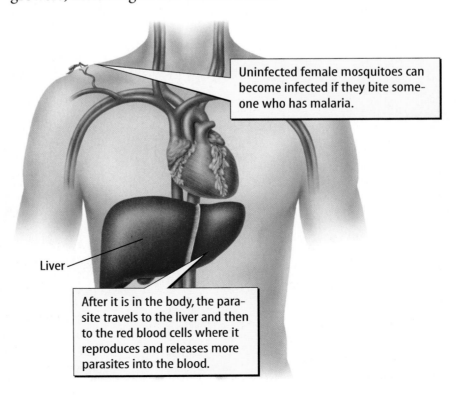

Uninfected female mosquitoes can become infected if they bite someone who has malaria.

Liver

After it is in the body, the parasite travels to the liver and then to the red blood cells where it reproduces and releases more parasites into the blood.

**Protists in the Environment** Algae are important as food for animals that live in lakes, rivers, oceans, and other bodies of water. Diatoms and one-celled green algae are eaten by protozoans and other small animals. Just like you, animals that live in the water need oxygen. Much of the oxygen dissolved in Earth's water is produced by algae.

However, algae can cause problems in water environments. Sometimes so much algal growth is present that the water becomes the color of the algae. This is called an algal bloom. Blooms in oceans of one type of algae can cause the water to turn red. Algal wastes are produced in such large amounts that fish and other organisms can die, as shown in **Figure 12.** Humans who drink or swim in the water might also get sick.

Have you ever tried to eat wood? If you were a termite, that would be your food source. Protozoans live in a termite's digestive system. The protozoan have bacteria on their surface and inside of them, which produce substances that help the termite digest wood.

✔ **Reading Check** *Why are protozoans important to termites?*

Many of the slime molds are important decomposers. Other funguslike protists cause disease in plants and animals. If you have an aquarium, you might have seen water molds attack a fish and cause its death.

Magnification: 7800×

**Figure 12** Blooms of the algae known as dinoflagellates can produce toxins that kill fish and cause clams and mussels to be poisonous when eaten.

---

## section 2 review

### Summary

**What is a protist?**
- Protists are funguslike, animal-like, or plantlike.

**The Importance of Protists**
- Most protists are microscopic.
- Humans use protists or their products everyday.
- Some protists have caused famines or economic disasters.
- Algae are an important food source for many organisms.
- Some protists form relationships with other organisms such as termites.
- Many protists are decomposers.

### Self Check

1. **List** the main characteristics shared by all protists.
2. **Compare and contrast** three groups of protists.
3. **Identify** some human or plant diseases caused by protozoans.
4. **Define** an algal bloom.
5. **Think Critically** Why might it be a problem for fish and other small organisms in a pond if all the algae die?

**Applying Skills**

6. **Use a spreadsheet** to compare protozoans. Include group, example species, method of transportation, and other characteristics.

# Comparing Algae and Protozoans

Algae and protozoans share enough characteristics that they usually are placed in the same kingdom. However, protists vary greatly in form. In this lab, you can observe many of the differences that make protists so diverse.

## ◉ Real-World Question

What are some of the differences between algae and protozoans?

### Goals
■ **Draw and label** the organisms you examine.
■ **Observe** the differences among algae, protozoans, and slime molds.

### Materials
cultures of *Paramecium, Amoeba, Euglena,* and *Spirogyra*
*prepared slides of above organisms*
prepared slide of slime mold
coverslips (4)            dropper
microscope                microscope slides (4)
stereomicroscope          petri dish
*Alternate materials*

### Safety Precautions
🚫 🧤 🥽 ✋ 🧼 ☣ ✋

## ◉ Procedure

1. **Design** a data table in your Science Journal for your drawings and observations.

2. Make a wet mount of the *Paramecium* culture. If you need help doing this, refer to the **Reference Handbooks.**

3. **Observe** the wet mount under low power and then under high power. In your Science Journal, make a labeled drawing of the organism.

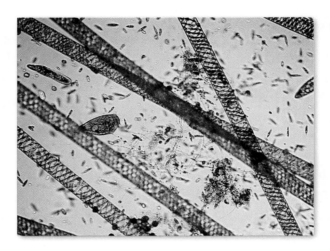

4. Repeat Steps 2 and 3 with the other cultures. Return all preparations to your teacher and wash your hands.

5. **Observe** the slide of slime mold under low and high power. Record your observations.

## ◉ Conclude and Apply

1. **Label** the structure that enabled the movement of each organism that could move.

2. **Infer** which protists make their own food. List facts that support your inference.

3. **Determine** which protist had animal-like and plantlike characteristics. Explain.

## 𝒞ommunicating
### Your Data

Make a set of cards with drawings of each organism that you examined. On the back of each card, write the organism's name and characteristics. See whether other students in your class can identify your drawings. **For more help, refer to the** Science Skill Handbook.

# section 3 Fungi

## What are fungi?

Do you like fungi on your pizza? You do if you like mushrooms. Mushrooms are a type of fungi. You might be surprised to know that a mushroom is only a small part of the organism that produces it. Most of the fungus grows below the mushroom underground, as shown in **Figure 13,** or beneath the surface of the organic material on which it is growing.

**Characteristics of Fungi** Most species of fungi are many-celled. Their cells are eukaryotic and contain membrane-bound cell structures including a nucleus. Some fungi cells contain more than one nucleus.

Fungi once were considered plants. Like plants, their cells have cell walls, and some fungi grow anchored in soil. Unlike plants, fungi do not have specialized tissues and organs such as leaves and roots. Fungi cells don't contain chlorophyll and cannot make their own food. They are not producers. Most fungi are saprophytes, but some are parasites.

Through the production of small, waterproof structures called spores, fungi reproduce. Spores can spread from place to place and grow into a new fungus under the right conditions.

Fungi grow best in warm, humid areas, such as tropical forests or the spaces between your toes. Mildew, a type of fungus, might be growing on the shower curtain in your bathroom.

### as you read

**What You'll Learn**
- **Identify** the characteristics shared by all fungi.
- **Classify** fungi into groups based on their methods of reproduction.
- **Differentiate** among the imperfect fungi and all other fungi.

**Why It's Important**
Fungi are important sources of food and medicines, and they recycle Earth's wastes.

**Review Vocabulary**
**producer:** an organism that can make its own food; usually through photosynthesis

**New Vocabulary**
- hyphae
- sporangia
- lichen
- mycorrhizae

**Figure 13** Often the visible part of a fungus is not the largest part of the organism.
**Identify** *the hyphae in this figure.*

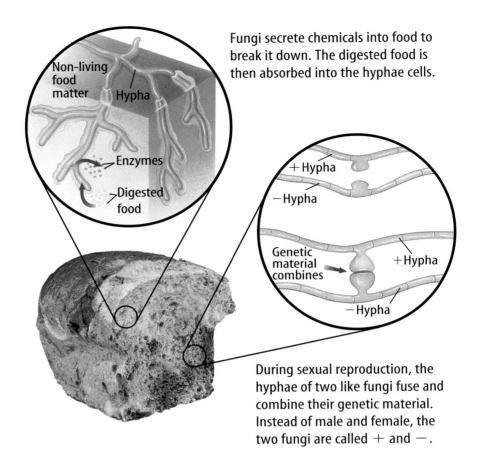

**Figure 14** Hyphae grow throughout the fungi's food source.

Fungi secrete chemicals into food to break it down. The digested food is then absorbed into the hyphae cells.

Non-living food matter
Hypha
Enzymes
Digested food

+Hypha
−Hypha
Genetic material combines
+Hypha
−Hypha

During sexual reproduction, the hyphae of two like fungi fuse and combine their genetic material. Instead of male and female, the two fungi are called + and −.

## Mini LAB

### Creating Fungus Art

**Procedure**

1. Find or grow some **blue-green mold** on **a piece of fruit, old bread, or a biscuit.**
2. Tear a slice of **fresh bread** in half.
3. Using a **toothpick** as your brush, lightly touch the mold, which is your paint, and draw a line, a circle, or your initials on each half slice of bread.
4. Wrap each half slice in **plastic wrap** or in separate **plastic bags.**
5. Set one of the wrapped pieces on the counter. Place one wrapped piece in a drawer or other dark place. Wash your hands thoroughly.
6. Examine the bread pieces each day over the next week to see how your fungus art develops.

**Analysis**

1. Describe your artwork on both pieces of the bread.
2. How did the amount of light affect the fungal growth?

Try at Home

**Structure and Function** The body of a fungus is usually a mass of many-celled, threadlike tubes called **hyphae** (HI fee) (singular, *hypha*), as shown in **Figure 14.** Filaments of hyphae form a mat in most fungi. The appearance of a mat of fungal hyphae can be a clue to the kind of fungus you see. Mats of hyphae can be fuzzy like those produced by mold growing on bread.

The hyphae grow throughout the fungus's food source. Enzymes from the fungus help break down the food. The fungal cells in the mat of hyphae then absorb the digested food.

Hyphae are also important in sexual reproduction in fungi. When fungi reproduce sexually, they do not produce sex cells. Instead, the hyphae of two different organisms of the same type of fungus grow close together and fuse, as shown in **Figure 14.** A special reproductive structure grows where the two hyphae join, and spores are produced in it. The type of structure that is produced depends on the type of fungus it is.

## Types of Fungi

Today, fungi are classified by several methods. Comparison of hereditary material provides some answers. However, their structure and the type of reproductive structures produced are still useful in identifying types of fungi.

**Figure 15** Club fungi are identified by their reproductive structures.

Most club fungi are mushrooms. Although many mushrooms are edible, some are poisonous.

Puffball mushrooms break open to release their spores.

You might have seen shelf fungi growing on trees or on rotting wood.

**Club Fungi** Mushrooms, shelf fungi, puffballs, and toadstools are all examples of club fungi, as shown in **Figure 15.** The spores of these fungi are produced in a club-shaped part found on the reproductive structure. On the bottom of the cap of a mushroom, you will see structures called gills. If you use a microscope to look at a gill, you will see spores hanging from these club-shaped parts.

✓ **Reading Check** *Where are spores produced in mushrooms?*

**Sac Fungi** Yeasts, molds, morels, and truffles are all examples of sac fungi. The spores of these fungi are produced in little sac-like parts of the reproductive structure. This group also includes examples of one-celled fungi, the yeasts. **Figure 16** shows some examples of the sac fungi.

**Living Environment**

**1.1h, 4.1a, 4.1c, 5.1a, 5.1b**
**Describe** the characteristics scientists use to classify fungi.

**Figure 16** Sac fungi produce eight spores in each sac.

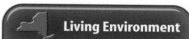

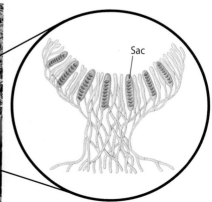
Sac

Many morels are edible and appear in early spring. Spore sacs are located in the many folds.

Spore sacs are produced inside the cup-shaped area of the cup fungus.

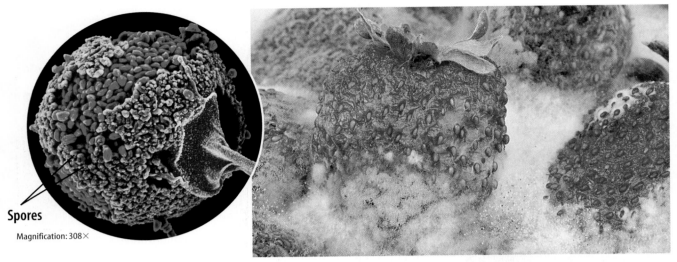

**Figure 17** The mold growing on these strawberries is a zygospore fungi. If you look at the fungus with a microscope, you will see large round sporangia where spores are produced.

Spores

Magnification: 308×

**Zygospore Fungi** The fuzzy, black mold that you sometimes find growing on old bread or a piece of fruit is a type of zygospore fungus. When two hyphae fuse in this group, a cell called a zygospore forms. **Sporangia** (spuh RAN jee uh) (singular, *sporangium*) are reproductive structures that grow from the zygospore and form on the tips of upright hyphae. Spores are produced in sporangia, as shown in **Figure 17.** As each sporangium splits open, hundreds of spores are released into the air. Each spore will grow into more fungi if it lands where enough moisture, warmth, and food are available.

**Other Fungi** Some fungi never have been observed undergoing sexual reproduction, or they never undergo sexual reproduction. Fungi that do not undergo sexual reproduction are referred to as imperfect because they have an imperfect life cycle. If one of these fungi is observed producing reproductive structures as a result of sexual reproduction, it immediately is classified as one of the other three types of fungi. Several diseases in humans, including athlete's foot, are caused by fungi in this group.

## Fungi in the Environment

Fungi are important in the environment because they break down organic materials. Food scraps, clothing, and dead plants and animals are made of organic material. When fungi decompose, or break down, these materials, energy is released and chemicals are returned to the soil. The chemicals returned to the soil are used by plants. Fungi, along with bacteria, are nature's recyclers.

Fungi can cause diseases in plants and animals. Dutch elm disease and chestnut blight are caused by sac fungi. These diseases killed hundreds of millions of American elm and American chestnut trees in the twentieth century.

**Lichens** Some fungi live in close associations with other organisms. The fungi and the other organism benefit from the association. A **lichen** (LI kun) is formed when a fungus and either a green alga or a cyanobacterium live together. The alga or the cyanobacterium gets a moist, protected place to live, and the fungus gets food made by the green alga or cyanobacterium. The colorful organisms in **Figure 18** are lichens.

Lichens that grow in the surface cracks of a rock play an important role in the formation of soil. As lichens grow, they release acids as part of their metabolism. The acids help break down the rock. As bits of rock accumulate and lichens die and decay, soil is formed.

 **Living Environment**

**7.1e, 7.2a, 7.2d Infer** how scientists might use lichens to help monitor the pollutants in rain or air.

**Reading Check** *How do lichens help form soil?*

Lichens can be used to help monitor pollution levels in an area because they are sensitive to pollutants present in rain and air. The disappearance of lichens from an area can indicate environmental problems.

**Crusty lichen**

**Figure 18** Lichens can grow upright, appear leafy, or look like a crust on bare rock.
**Classify** *How might lichens be classified?*

**Fruticose lichen**

**Foliose lichen**

**Figure 19** Mycorrhizae greatly increase the growth of plants. These two groups of plants are the same species. They were planted at the same time and grown under the same conditions.

These plants do not have mycorrhizae associated with their roots.

These plants have mycorrhizae associated with their roots.

**Mycorrhizae** An association similar to that in lichens exists between certain plants and fungi. The fungi form an intricate web called **mycorrhizae** (mi kuh RI zee) (singular *mycorrhiza*) around the roots of the plants. The plants provide the fungi with food and the fungi help the plant roots absorb water and nutrients, as shown in **Figure 19.** Scientists have found mychorrhizae around the roots of 90 percent of the plants they have studied. Some plants cannot grow unless the mycorrhizae are present.

## Fungi and Humans

You already know that many people eat mushrooms, but fungi are important in producing other foods, too. The bread in your sandwich probably was produced using yeast, as shown in **Figure 20.** Yeasts and other fungi also are used in the production of some cheeses.

Fungi can spoil food as well. You might find mold, a type of fungus, growing on an old loaf of bread or leftover food in the back of the refrigerator.

**Figure 20** Fungi are economically important to humans. Yeasts are used in the production of bread. As yeast cells feed on carbohydrates in the bread dough, they produce the waste gas carbon dioxide that causes the bread to rise.

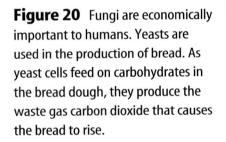

Unrisen bread dough

Risen bread dough

Smuts, like this one growing on corn, cause damage to crops worldwide.

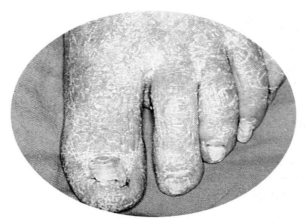

The fungus that causes athlete's foot grows best in warm, damp places.

**Figure 21** Some types of fungi cause disease in plants and animals.

**Helpful and Harmful Fungi** Many fungi naturally produce antibiotics to prevent bacteria from growing near them. These antibiotics can be produced in bioreactors and used to fight infections. Penicillin is an important antibiotic produced by fungi.

Rust and smuts, shown in **Figure 21,** are types of club fungi that cause billions of dollars worth of damage to corn, wheat, and other major food crops each year. Fungi can grow on or in your body and sometimes they cause disease. For example, athlete's foot and ring-worm are caused by fungus.

## section 3 review

### Summary

**What are fungi?**

- Fungi have eukaryotic cells, most reproduce through spores, and are many-celled.
- Hereditary material and reproductive structures are used to classify fungi.

**Fungi in the Environment**

- Fungi break down organic materials and can cause disease.
- Lichens can be environmental indicators for pollution.
- Many plants depend on mycorrhizae.

**Fungi and Humans**

- Some fungi are used to produce food. Others cause food to spoil.
- Many fungi produce antibiotics and others harm plants and animals.

### Self Check

1. **Explain** why a particular fungi would be classified as imperfect.
2. **Describe** how their method of sexual reproduction is used to place fungi into groups.
3. **Identify** one way that fungi and plants are alike and two ways that fungi are different from plants.
4. **List** three ways fungi are important to the environment and three ways they are important to humans.
5. **Think Critically** If an imperfect fungus under some circumstances were found to produce spores on clublike structures, how would the fungus be reclassified?

### Applying Skills

6. **Make and Use a Graph** Approximately 30,000 species of sac fungi, 25,000 species each of club and imperfect fungi, 22,000 species of lichens, 5,000 species of mycorrhizae, and 600 species of zygospore fungi exist. Construct a circle graph using this information.

# LAB

## Making Yogurt

### Goals

- **Make** your own yogurt.
- **Describe** the role of bacteria in the process of making yogurt.

### Materials

hot plate
saucepan
plastic spoon
thermometer
   (nonmercury)
plastic container with lid
insulated picnic cooler
milk (about 0.5 L)
live-culture yogurt
   (about 25 g)
*yogurt culture
   (1 package)
*Alternate materials

### Safety Precautions

**WARNING:** *Use care near heat sources and when handling hot objects. Do not eat anything in the lab unless you are instructed to by your teacher.*

### ▶ *Real-World Question*

You probably have eaten yogurt at some point. Do you know how yogurt is made? Live bacteria are combined with milk to produce yogurt. How long does the process of changing milk into yogurt take? Is it healthy to eat food that you know contains bacteria? How can you make yogurt in the lab?

### ▶ *Procedure*

1. Use the hot plate to heat milk to 85°C. When you check the temperature, be sure that the thermometer is not touching the bottom of the saucepan. Stir the milk continuously with the spoon to avoid scorching.

2. When the milk reaches 85°C, keep it at that temperature for 30 min.

3. After 30 min. have passed, cool the milk to 45°C. One way to do this is to set the saucepan into a sink partially filled with cold water. Change the water if it becomes warm.

4. Add yogurt or yogurt culture to the cooled milk and stir well.

5. Put the mixture into a plastic container and cover it. Then, place the container in the insulated picnic cooler so that the yogurt will stay warm.

6. Yogurt should be made in 3–7 h. Try not to disturb the equipment while the yogurt is growing.

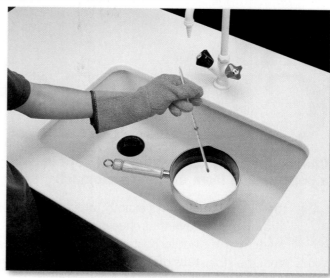

## ● Analyze Your Data

1. **Explain** why it is important not to allow the milk to boil.

2. **Determine** why it is important to keep the mixture warm during the yogurt-making process.

## ● Conclude and Apply

1. **Infer** what was in the yogurt or yogurt culture that helped to change the milk to yogurt. Describe the role of bacteria in making yogurt.

2. **Draw Conclusions** Suppose the milk that is used to make yogurt contains antibiotics. How would that affect the yogurt-making process?

**Communicating Your Data**

The next time you see a family member or friend eating yogurt, describe the process of making yogurt and the role that bacteria play in that process.

# SAY CHEESE

**Cheese probably came from milk kept in a pouch made from a sheep's stomach**

Although no one knows exactly, most authorities believe that cheese was first made in the Middle East, about 4,000 years ago. One story tells of an Arabian traveler carrying milk with him in a pouch made from a sheep's stomach. During his journey across the desert, he opened the pouch and discovered that the milk had separated into thick solids and a watery fluid. The Arabian traveler had accidentally invented cheese.

How did the milk become cheese? First, the Sun warmed the bag of milk. Second, the dried digestive juice in the sheep-stomach pouch caused the milk to coagulate (koh A gyuh layt), separating it into curds and a thin liquid called whey (WAY). The digestive juice contained rennet, an enzyme that still is used to make cheese today. People soon realized that cheese was a good way to preserve milk. Once milk was made into cheese, it could be kept for a longer period of time.

**These test tubes contain Penicillium roqueforti that is used to make a French cheese.**

## Bacteria Help

The basis of cheese is milk that has been curdled by the by-products of bacteria. Today, milk is first pasteurized to kill harmful bacteria. Then useful bacteria cultures are added to the milk. The bacteria feed on lactose (sugar) in the milk and produce lactic acid wastes that help curdle or thicken the milk into curd. The major protein in milk, casein, forms the thickened curd.

The curd is then cut to release the whey, leaving the solid mass of curd behind. The curd can become different types of cheese, depending on how cheese makers treat it.

## Types of Cheese

There are more than 2,000 varieties of cheese, with different textures, tastes, and appearances. Cheese can be made from the milk of many animals including cows, goats, sheep, buffalo, and reindeer.

To make cottage cheese, the curd is broken up, rinsed with water, then mixed with cream and salt. Hard cheeses, such as cheddar or Parmesan, are packed into molds and pressed to remove additional whey. Some cheeses are then aged.

**Write** Prepare a report on cheese making in your state. What types are made? Where does your state rank in cheese production? Compare your report with those of your classmates.

## Reviewing Main Ideas

**Section 1** **Bacteria**

1. Bacteria are prokaryotic cells. They contain DNA and cytoplasm but lack membrane-bound organelles.

2. Bacteria have been found living in nearly every environment on Earth and are grouped as either eubacteria or archaebacteria.

3. Some bacteria are harmful because they can cause disease when they infect organisms.

4. Most bacteria are helpful. They help in recycling nutrients, fixing nitrogen, and food production. They even can be used to break down harmful pollutants.

**Section 2** **Protists**

1. Protists are one- or many-celled organisms that live in moist or wet environments.

2. The protists are plantlike, animal-like, or funguslike.

3. Algae are important in freshwater and salt-water environments as food and oxygen producers. They also are used by humans to make many different products.

4. Some protists cause diseases in humans and in plants, such as malaria and potato blight.

**Section 3** **Fungi**

1. Fungi are composed of eukaryotic cells that grow in long chains called hyphae. They absorb food through the hyphae and are either saprophytes or parasites.

2. Most fungi reproduce sexually by producing spores.

3. Four classifications of fungi exist—club fungi, sac fungi, zygospore fungi, and imperfect fungi.

4. One of the most important roles of fungi is to decompose organic material and return nutrients to the soil. They also live in associations with algae and plants, produce antibiotics, and can cause diseases.

## Visualizing Main Ideas

*Copy and complete the following spider map to show the importance of bacteria.*

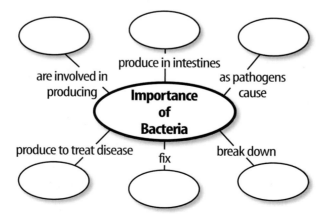

are involved in producing

produce in intestines

as pathogens cause

**Importance of Bacteria**

produce to treat disease

fix

break down

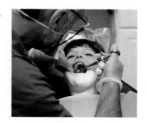

## Using Vocabulary

| | |
|---|---|
| aerobe p.603 | pasteurization p.607 |
| algae p.610 | pathogen p.606 |
| anaerobe p.603 | protist p.609 |
| antibiotic p.606 | protozoan p.610 |
| endospore p.603 | pseudopod p.610 |
| hyphae p.616 | saprophyte p.610 |
| lichen p.619 | sporangia p.618 |
| mycorrhizae p.620 | vaccine p.606 |

*Fill in the blanks with the correct vocabulary word or words.*

1. A(n) _____ is an organism that gets nutrition from dead materials.

2. A(n) _____ can survive without oxygen.

3. A(n) _____ is a protective structure formed by bacteria.

4. _____ can prevent some bacterial diseases.

5. A one-celled plantlike, animal-like, or funguslike organism is a(n) _____.

6. An organism composed of an alga and a fungus is a(n) _____.

7. Fungi grow as a mass of many-celled, threadlike tubes called _____.

## Checking Concepts

*Choose the word or phrase that best answers the question.*

8. Which organisms usually are grouped according to the extreme environment in which they live?
   **A)** archaebacteria   **C)** protists
   **B)** eubacteria   **D)** fungi

9. What are the threadlike tubes by which fungi grow called?
   **A)** spores   **C)** imperfect fungi
   **B)** lichens   **D)** hyphae

10. What type of consumers use dead material as an energy source?
    **A)** producers   **C)** saprophytes
    **B)** flagella   **D)** parasites

11. What gas found in Earth's atmosphere is combined with other chemicals by bacteria so that plants can use it?
    **A)** oxygen   **C)** carbon dioxide
    **B)** hydrogen   **D)** nitrogen

12. Which protist group produces food and the greatest amount of oxygen in water environments?
    **A)** algae   **C)** protozoans
    **B)** lichens   **D)** eubacteria

13. Decomposition of organic materials is an important role of which organisms?
    **A)** protozoans   **C)** plants
    **B)** algae   **D)** fungi

14. What name is given to rod-shaped bacteria?
    **A)** bacilli   **C)** spirilla
    **B)** cocci   **D)** colonies

15. Which group of fungi has not been observed undergoing sexual reproduction?
    **A)** club fungi   **C)** zygospore fungi
    **B)** sac fungi   **D)** imperfect fungi

**Use the figure below to answer question 16.**

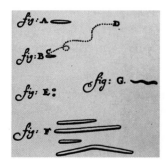

16. What name would be given to the bacteria Antonie van Leeuwenhoek drew and labeled *Fig. G*?
    **A)** bacilli   **C)** spirilla
    **B)** cocci   **D)** colonies

Hot Words Hot Topics: Bk 2 (25) p. 194; (26) pp. 91, 199

## Thinking Critically

17. **Explain** Yeast can use sugar in bread dough as a source of food. As they use the sugar, they produce waste carbon dioxide gas and the dough rises. If yeast are added to dough in very hot or very cold water, why might the dough not rise?

18. **List** some precautions that can be taken to prevent food poisoning.

19. **Compare and contrast** lichens and mycorrhizae.

20. **Infer** why brushing and flossing your teeth help prevent tooth decay.

21. **Interpret Scientific Illustrations** Use **Figure 11** to answer the following question. When the malaria parasite is transferred to the blood from a mosquito bite, what organ does the parasite first infect?

22. **Concept Map** Copy and complete the following concept map that compares the three groups of protists.

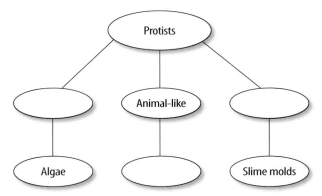

23. **Compare and Contrast** Make a chart comparing and contrasting club fungi, sac fungi, zygospore fungi, and imperfect fungi.

## Performance Activities

24. **Make a Poster** Find or draw pictures on a poster to show the importance of bacteria, protists, or fungi to life on Earth. Be sure to include helpful and harmful examples.

## Applying Math

**Use the table below to answer question 25.**

| Bacterial Reproduction Rates | |
|---|---|
| Temperature (°C) | Doubling Rate per Hour |
| 20.5 | 2.0 |
| 30.5 | 3.0 |
| 36.0 | 2.5 |
| 39.2 | 1.2 |

25. **Temperature and Growth Rates** What is the effect of temperature on the bacterial growth rates shown in the table above?

**Use the graph below to answer question 26.**

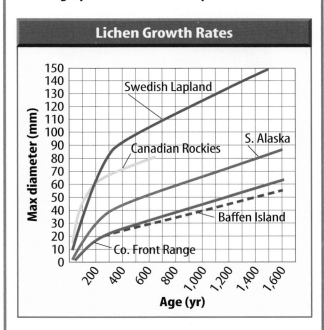

26. **Growth and Climate** The graph above illustrates that lichens grow at different rates depending on the climate. According to the graph, which climate is the most favorable for lichen growth? What is the difference between the diameter of a 200-year-old colony in the Swedish Lapland compared to a 200-year-old colony on Baffen Island?

**Part I**

*Record your answers on the answer sheet provided by your teacher or on a sheet of paper.*

**1** Which type of bacterium uses light energy to make food?
(1) consumer
(2) pathogen
(3) producer
(4) saprophyte

**2** What are the two main groups of bacteria?
(1) archaebacteria and eubacteria
(2) pathogens and saprophytes
(3) prokaryotes and eukaryotes
(4) salt-loving and acid-loving

**Use the illustration below to answer question 3.**

**3** What type of fungi is this?
(1) club
(2) imperfect
(3) sac
(4) zygospore

**4** What is used to classify fungi?
(1) hyphae
(2) reproductive strategy
(3) vegetative structures
(4) zygospore

**5** What do some bacteria produce that limits the growth of other bacteria?
(1) algae
(2) antibiotics
(3) antiseptics
(4) lichens

**Use the illustration below to answer questions 6 and 7.**

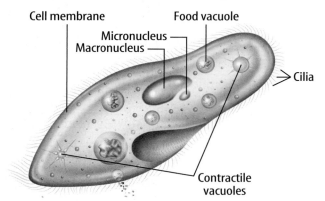

**6** What type of protist is this?
(1) algal-like
(2) animal-like
(3) funguslike
(4) plantlike

**7** What structures would the protist in the illustration above use for motility?
(1) cell membrane
(2) cilia
(3) contractile vacuole
(4) micronucleus

**8** Which disease is caused by a protozoan carried by mosquitoes?
(1) African sleeping sickness
(2) botulism
(3) malaria
(4) potato blight

**Part II**

**Use the illustration below to answer question 10.**

**10** How are the round structures on these roots critical to the environment?

**11** Compare and contrast a one-celled protist and a bacterium.

**12** What two organisms can form a lichen? How do lichens help form soil?

**13** Discuss the ways that bacteria, protists, and fungi can be helpful to humans.

**14** How are saprophytes different from parasites?

**15** What environmental conditions in a refrigerator would slow fungal growth on food?

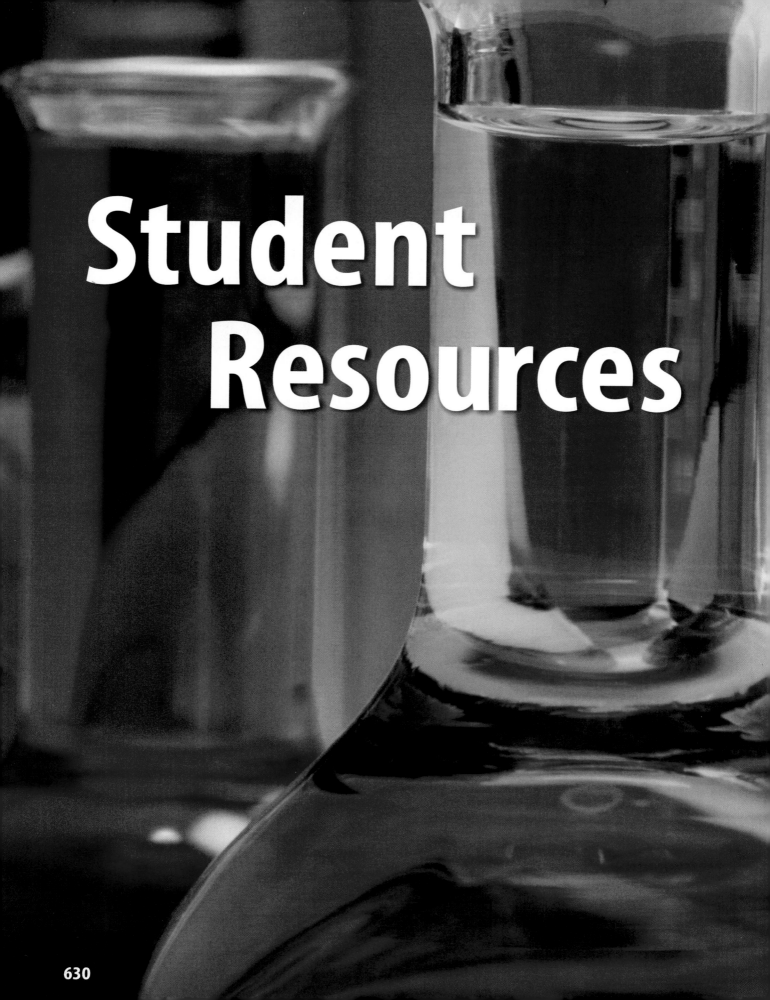

# Student Resources

## CONTENTS

# Scientific Methods

Scientists use an orderly approach called the scientific method to solve problems. This includes organizing and recording data so others can understand them. Scientists use many variations in this method when they solve problems.

## Identify a Question

The first step in a scientific investigation or experiment is to identify a question to be answered or a problem to be solved. For example, you might ask which gasoline is the most efficient.

## Gather and Organize Information

After you have identified your question, begin gathering and organizing information. There are many ways to gather information, such as researching in a library, interviewing those knowledgeable about the subject, testing and working in the laboratory and field. Fieldwork is investigations and observations done outside of a laboratory.

**Researching Information** Before moving in a new direction, it is important to gather the information that already is known about the subject. Start by asking yourself questions to determine exactly what you need to know. Then you will look for the information in various reference sources, like the student is doing in **Figure 1.** Some sources may include textbooks, encyclopedias, government documents, professional journals, science magazines, and the Internet. Always list the sources of your information.

**Figure 1** The Internet can be a valuable research tool.

**Evaluate Sources of Information** Not all sources of information are reliable. You should evaluate all of your sources of information, and use only those you know to be dependable. For example, if you are researching ways to make homes more energy efficient, a site written by the U.S. Department of Energy would be more reliable than a site written by a company that is trying to sell a new type of weatherproofing material. Also, remember that research always is changing. Consult the most current resources available to you. For example, a 1985 resource about saving energy would not reflect the most recent findings.

Sometimes scientists use data that they did not collect themselves, or conclusions drawn by other researchers. This data must be evaluated carefully. Ask questions about how the data were obtained, if the investigation was carried out properly, and if it has been duplicated exactly with the same results. Would you reach the same conclusion from the data? Only when you have confidence in the data can you believe it is true and feel comfortable using it.

**Interpret Scientific Illustrations** As you research a topic in science, you will see drawings, diagrams, and photographs to help you understand what you read. Some illustrations are included to help you understand an idea that you can't see easily by yourself, like the tiny particles in an atom in **Figure 2.** A drawing helps many people to remember details more easily and provides examples that clarify difficult concepts or give additional information about the topic you are studying. Most illustrations have labels or a caption to identify or to provide more information.

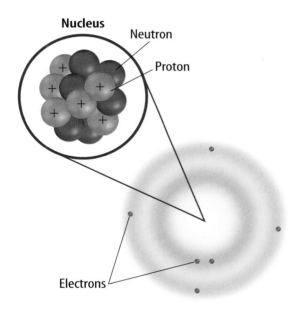

**Figure 2** This drawing shows an atom of carbon with its six protons, six neutrons, and six electrons.

**Concept Maps** One way to organize data is to draw a diagram that shows relationships among ideas (or concepts). A concept map can help make the meanings of ideas and terms more clear, and help you understand and remember what you are studying. Concept maps are useful for breaking large concepts down into smaller parts, making learning easier.

**Network Tree** A type of concept map that not only shows a relationship, but how the concepts are related is a network tree, shown in **Figure 3.** In a network tree, the words are written in the ovals, while the description of the type of relationship is written across the connecting lines.

When constructing a network tree, write down the topic and all major topics on separate pieces of paper or notecards. Then arrange them in order from general to specific. Branch the related concepts from the major concept and describe the relationship on the connecting line. Continue to more specific concepts until finished.

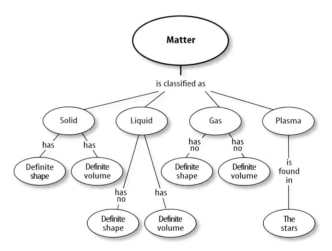

**Figure 3** A network tree shows how concepts or objects are related.

**Events Chain** Another type of concept map is an events chain. Sometimes called a flow chart, it models the order or sequence of items. An events chain can be used to describe a sequence of events, the steps in a procedure, or the stages of a process.

When making an events chain, first find the one event that starts the chain. This event is called the initiating event. Then, find the next event and continue until the outcome is reached, as shown in **Figure 4.**

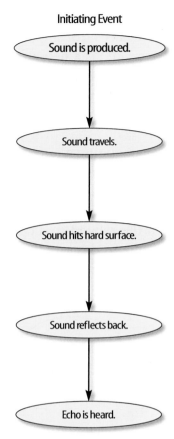

**Figure 4** Events-chain concept maps show the order of steps in a process or event. This concept map shows how a sound makes an echo.

**Cycle Map** A specific type of events chain is a cycle map. It is used when the series of events do not produce a final outcome, but instead relate back to the beginning event, such as in **Figure 5.** Therefore, the cycle repeats itself.

To make a cycle map, first decide what event is the beginning event. This is also called the initiating event. Then list the next events in the order that they occur, with the last event relating back to the initiating event. Words can be written between the events that describe what happens from one event to the next. The number of events in a cycle map can vary, but usually contain three or more events.

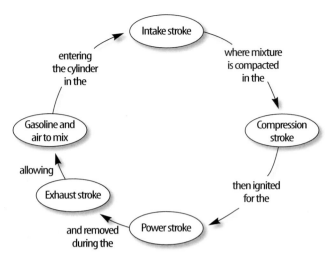

**Figure 5** A cycle map shows events that occur in a cycle.

**Spider Map** A type of concept map that you can use for brainstorming is the spider map. When you have a central idea, you might find that you have a jumble of ideas that relate to it but are not necessarily clearly related to each other. The spider map on sound in **Figure 6** shows that if you write these ideas outside the main concept, then you can begin to separate and group unrelated terms so they become more useful.

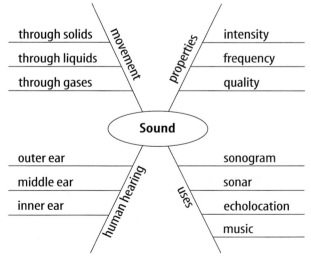

**Figure 6** A spider map allows you to list ideas that relate to a central topic but not necessarily to one another.

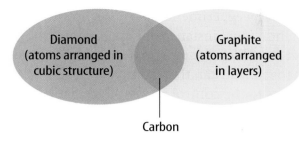

**Figure 7** This Venn diagram compares and contrasts two substances made from carbon.

**Venn Diagram** To illustrate how two subjects compare and contrast you can use a Venn diagram. You can see the characteristics that the subjects have in common and those that they do not, shown in **Figure 7.**

To create a Venn diagram, draw two overlapping ovals that that are big enough to write in. List the characteristics unique to one subject in one oval, and the characteristics of the other subject in the other oval. The characteristics in common are listed in the overlapping section.

**Make and Use Tables** One way to organize information so it is easier to understand is to use a table. Tables can contain numbers, words, or both.

To make a table, list the items to be compared in the first column and the characteristics to be compared in the first row. The title should clearly indicate the content of the table, and the column or row heads should be clear. Notice that in **Table 1** the units are included.

| Table 1 Recyclables Collected During Week | | | |
|---|---|---|---|
| **Day of Week** | **Paper (kg)** | **Aluminum (kg)** | **Glass (kg)** |
| Monday | 5.0 | 4.0 | 12.0 |
| Wednesday | 4.0 | 1.0 | 10.0 |
| Friday | 2.5 | 2.0 | 10.0 |

**Make a Model** One way to help you better understand the parts of a structure, the way a process works, or to show things too large or small for viewing is to make a model. For example, an atomic model made of a plastic-ball nucleus and pipe-cleaner electron shells can help you visualize how the parts of an atom relate to each other. Other types of models can by devised on a computer or represented by equations.

## Form a Hypothesis

A possible explanation based on previous knowledge and observations is called a hypothesis. After researching gasoline types and recalling previous experiences in your family's car you form a hypothesis—our car runs more efficiently because we use premium gasoline. To be valid, a hypothesis has to be something you can test by using an investigation.

**Predict** When you apply a hypothesis to a specific situation, you predict something about that situation. A prediction makes a statement in advance, based on prior observation, experience, or scientific reasoning. People use predictions to make everyday decisions. Scientists test predictions by performing investigations. Based on previous observations and experiences, you might form a prediction that cars are more efficient with premium gasoline. The prediction can be tested in an investigation.

**Design an Experiment** A scientist needs to make many decisions before beginning an investigation. Some of these include: how to carry out the investigation, what steps to follow, how to record the data, and how the investigation will answer the question. It also is important to address any safety concerns.

## Test the Hypothesis

Now that you have formed your hypothesis, you need to test it. Using an investigation, you will make observations and collect data, or information. This data might either support or not support your hypothesis. Scientists collect and organize data as numbers and descriptions.

**Follow a Procedure** In order to know what materials to use, as well as how and in what order to use them, you must follow a procedure. **Figure 8** shows a procedure you might follow to test your hypothesis.

### Procedure
1. Use regular gasoline for two weeks.
2. Record the number of kilometers between fill-ups and the amount of gasoline used.
3. Switch to premium gasoline for two weeks.
4. Record the number of kilometers between fill-ups and the amount of gasoline used.

**Figure 8** A procedure tells you what to do step by step.

**Identify and Manipulate Variables and Controls** In any experiment, it is important to keep everything the same except for the item you are testing. The one factor you change is called the independent variable. The change that results is the dependent variable. Make sure you have only one independent variable, to assure yourself of the cause of the changes you observe in the dependent variable. For example, in your gasoline experiment the type of fuel is the independent variable. The dependent variable is the efficiency.

Many experiments also have a control—an individual instance or experimental subject for which the independent variable is not changed. You can then compare the test results to the control results. To design a control you can have two cars of the same type. The control car uses regular gasoline for four weeks. After you are done with the test, you can compare the experimental results to the control results.

## Collect Data

Whether you are carrying out an investigation or a short observational experiment, you will collect data, as shown in **Figure 9.** Scientists collect data as numbers and descriptions and organize it in specific ways.

**Observe** Scientists observe items and events, then record what they see. When they use only words to describe an observation, it is called qualitative data. Scientists' observations also can describe how much there is of something. These observations use numbers, as well as words, in the description and are called quantitative data. For example, if a sample of the element gold is described as being "shiny and very dense" the data are qualitative. Quantitative data on this sample of gold might include "a mass of 30 g and a density of 19.3 g/cm$^3$."

**Figure 9** Collecting data is one way to gather information directly.

**Figure 10** Record data neatly and clearly so it is easy to understand.

When you make observations you should examine the entire object or situation first, and then look carefully for details. It is important to record observations accurately and completely. Always record your notes immediately as you make them, so you do not miss details or make a mistake when recording results from memory. Never put unidentified observations on scraps of paper. Instead they should be recorded in a note-book, like the one in **Figure 10.** Write your data neatly so you can easily read it later. At each point in the experiment, record your observations and label them. That way, you will not have to determine what the figures mean when you look at your notes later. Set up any tables that you will need to use ahead of time, so you can record any observations right away. Remember to avoid bias when collecting data by not including personal thoughts when you record observations. Record only what you observe.

**Estimate** Scientific work also involves esti-mating. To estimate is to make a judgment about the size or the number of something without measuring or counting. This is important when the number or size of an object or population is too large or too dif-ficult to accurately count or measure.

**Sample** Scientists may use a sample or a portion of the total number as a type of estimation. To sample is to take a small, rep-resentative portion of the objects or organ-isms of a population for research. By making careful observations or manipulat-ing variables within that portion of the group, information is discovered and con-clusions are drawn that might apply to the whole population. A poorly chosen sample can be unrepresentative of the whole. If you were trying to determine the rainfall in an area, it would not be best to take a rainfall sample from under a tree.

**Measure** You use measurements everyday. Scientists also take measurements when col-lecting data. When taking measurements, it is important to know how to use measuring tools properly. Accuracy also is important.

**Length** To measure length, the distance between two points, scientists use meters. Smaller measurements might be measured in centimeters or millimeters.

Length is measured using a metric ruler or meter stick. When using a metric ruler, line up the 0-cm mark with the end of the object being measured and read the number of the unit where the object ends. Look at the metric ruler shown in **Figure 11.** The cen-timeter lines are the long, numbered lines, and the shorter lines are millimeter lines. In this instance, the length would be 4.50 cm.

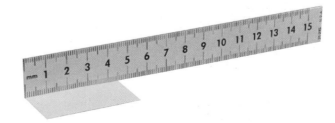

**Figure 11** This metric ruler has centimeter and millimeter divisions.

**Mass** The SI unit for mass is the kilogram (kg). Scientists can measure mass using units formed by adding metric prefixes to the unit gram (g), such as milligram (mg). To measure mass, you might use a triple-beam balance similar to the one shown in **Figure 12.** The balance has a pan on one side and a set of beams on the other side. Each beam has a rider that slides on the beam.

When using a triple-beam balance, place an object on the pan. Slide the largest rider along its beam until the pointer drops below zero. Then move it back one notch. Repeat the process for each rider proceeding from the larger to smaller until the pointer swings an equal distance above and below the zero point. Sum the masses on each beam to find the mass of the object. Move all riders back to zero when finished.

Instead of putting materials directly on the balance, scientists often take a tare of a container. A tare is the mass of a container into which objects or substances are placed for measuring their masses. To mass objects or substances, find the mass of a clean container. Remove the container from the pan, and place the object or substances in the container. Find the mass of the container with the materials in it. Subtract the mass of the empty container from the mass of the filled container to find the mass of the materials you are using.

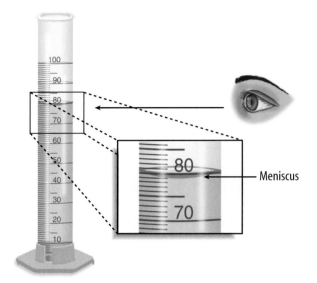

**Figure 13** Graduated cylinders measure liquid volume.

**Liquid Volume** To measure liquids, the unit used is the liter. When a smaller unit is needed, scientists might use a milliliter. Because a milliliter takes up the volume of a cube measuring 1 cm on each side it also can be called a cubic centimeter ($cm^3$ = cm × cm × cm).

You can use beakers and graduated cylinders to measure liquid volume. A graduated cylinder, shown in **Figure 13,** is marked from bottom to top in milliliters. In lab, you might use a 10-mL graduated cylinder or a 100-mL graduated cylinder. When measuring liquids, notice that the liquid has a curved surface. Look at the surface at eye level, and measure the bottom of the curve. This is called the meniscus. The graduated cylinder in **Figure 13** contains 79.0 mL, or 79.0 $cm^3$, of a liquid.

**Temperature** Scientists often measure temperature using the Celsius scale. Pure water has a freezing point of 0°C and boiling point of 100°C. The unit of measurement is degrees Celsius. Two other scales often used are the Fahrenheit and Kelvin scales.

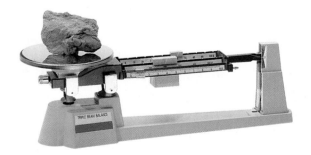

**Figure 12** A triple-beam balance is used to determine the mass of an object.

**Figure 14** A thermometer measures the temperature of an object.

Scientists use a thermometer to measure temperature. Most thermometers in a laboratory are glass tubes with a bulb at the bottom end containing a liquid such as colored alcohol. The liquid rises or falls with a change in temperature. To read a glass thermometer like the thermometer in **Figure 14,** rotate it slowly until a red line appears. Read the temperature where the red line ends.

**Form Operational Definitions** An operational definition defines an object by how it functions, works, or behaves. For example, when you are playing hide and seek and a tree is home base, you have created an operational definition for a tree.

Objects can have more than one operational definition. For example, a ruler can be defined as a tool that measures the length of an object (how it is used). It can also be a tool with a series of marks used as a standard when measuring (how it works).

## Analyze the Data

To determine the meaning of your observations and investigation results, you will need to look for patterns in the data. Then you must think critically to determine what the data mean. Scientists use several approaches when they analyze the data they have collected and recorded. Each approach is useful for identifying specific patterns.

**Interpret Data** The word *interpret* means "to explain the meaning of something." When analyzing data from an experiment, try to find out what the data show. Identify the control group and the test group to see whether or not changes in the independent variable have had an effect. Look for differences in the dependent variable between the control and test groups.

**Classify** Sorting objects or events into groups based on common features is called classifying. When classifying, first observe the objects or events to be classified. Then select one feature that is shared by some members in the group, but not by all. Place those members that share that feature in a subgroup. You can classify members into smaller and smaller subgroups based on characteristics. Remember that when you classify, you are grouping objects or events for a purpose. Keep your purpose in mind as you select the features to form groups and subgroups.

**Compare and Contrast** Observations can be analyzed by noting the similarities and differences between two more objects or events that you observe. When you look at objects or events to see how they are similar, you are comparing them. Contrasting is looking for differences in objects or events.

**Recognize Cause and Effect** A cause is a reason for an action or condition. The effect is that action or condition. When two events happen together, it is not necessarily true that one event caused the other. Scientists must design a controlled investigation to recognize the exact cause and effect.

## Draw Conclusions

When scientists have analyzed the data they collected, they proceed to draw conclusions about the data. These conclusions are sometimes stated in words similar to the hypothesis that you formed earlier. They may confirm a hypothesis, or lead you to a new hypothesis.

**Infer** Scientists often make inferences based on their observations. An inference is an attempt to explain observations or to indicate a cause. An inference is not a fact, but a logical conclusion that needs further investigation. For example, you may infer that a fire has caused smoke. Until you investigate, however, you do not know for sure.

**Apply** When you draw a conclusion, you must apply those conclusions to determine whether the data supports the hypothesis. If your data do not support your hypothesis, it does not mean that the hypothesis is wrong. It means only that the result of the investigation did not support the hypothesis. Maybe the experiment needs to be redesigned, or some of the initial observations on which the hypothesis was based were incomplete or biased. Perhaps more observation or research is needed to refine your hypothesis. A successful investigation does not always come out the way you originally predicted.

**Avoid Bias** Sometimes a scientific investigation involves making judgments. When you make a judgment, you form an opinion. It is important to be honest and not to allow any expectations of results to bias your judgments. This is important throughout the entire investigation, from researching to collecting data to drawing conclusions.

## Communicate

The communication of ideas is an important part of the work of scientists. A discovery that is not reported will not advance the scientific community's understanding or knowledge. Communication among scientists also is important as a way of improving their investigations.

Scientists communicate in many ways, from writing articles in journals and magazines that explain their investigations and experiments, to announcing important discoveries on television and radio. Scientists also share ideas with colleagues on the Internet or present them as lectures, like the student is doing in **Figure 15.**

**Figure 15** A student communicates to his peers about his investigation.

# SAFETY SYMBOLS

| SAFETY SYMBOLS | HAZARD | EXAMPLES | PRECAUTION | REMEDY |
|---|---|---|---|---|
| **DISPOSAL** | Special disposal procedures need to be followed. | certain chemicals, living organisms | Do not dispose of these materials in the sink or trash can. | Dispose of wastes as directed by your teacher. |
| **BIOLOGICAL** | Organisms or other biological materials that might be harmful to humans | bacteria, fungi, blood, unpreserved tissues, plant materials | Avoid skin contact with these materials. Wear mask or gloves. | Notify your teacher if you suspect contact with material. Wash hands thoroughly. |
| **EXTREME TEMPERATURE** | Objects that can burn skin by being too cold or too hot | boiling liquids, hot plates, dry ice, liquid nitrogen | Use proper protection when handling. | Go to your teacher for first aid. |
| **SHARP OBJECT** | Use of tools or glassware that can easily puncture or slice skin | razor blades, pins, scalpels, pointed tools, dissecting probes, broken glass | Practice common-sense behavior and follow guidelines for use of the tool. | Go to your teacher for first aid. |
| **FUME** | Possible danger to respiratory tract from fumes | ammonia, acetone, nail polish remover, heated sulfur, moth balls | Make sure there is good ventilation. Never smell fumes directly. Wear a mask. | Leave foul area and notify your teacher immediately. |
| **ELECTRICAL** | Possible danger from electrical shock or burn | improper grounding, liquid spills, short circuits, exposed wires | Double-check setup with teacher. Check condition of wires and apparatus. | Do not attempt to fix electrical problems. Notify your teacher immediately. |
| **IRRITANT** | Substances that can irritate the skin or mucous membranes of the respiratory tract | pollen, moth balls, steel wool, fiberglass, potassium permanganate | Wear dust mask and gloves. Practice extra care when handling these materials. | Go to your teacher for first aid. |
| **CHEMICAL** | Chemicals can react with and destroy tissue and other materials | bleaches such as hydrogen peroxide; acids such as sulfuric acid, hydrochloric acid; bases such as ammonia, sodium hydroxide | Wear goggles, gloves, and an apron. | Immediately flush the affected area with water and notify your teacher. |
| **TOXIC** | Substance may be poisonous if touched, inhaled, or swallowed. | mercury, many metal compounds, iodine, poinsettia plant parts | Follow your teacher's instructions. | Always wash hands thoroughly after use. Go to your teacher for first aid. |
| **FLAMMABLE** | Flammable chemicals may be ignited by open flame, spark, or exposed heat. | alcohol, kerosene, potassium permanganate | Avoid open flames and heat when using flammable chemicals. | Notify your teacher immediately. Use fire safety equipment if applicable. |
| **OPEN FLAME** | Open flame in use, may cause fire. | hair, clothing, paper, synthetic materials | Tie back hair and loose clothing. Follow teacher's instruction on lighting and extinguishing flames. | Notify your teacher immediately. Use fire safety equipment if applicable. |

 **Eye Safety** Proper eye protection should be worn at all times by anyone performing or observing science activities.

 **Clothing Protection** This symbol appears when substances could stain or burn clothing.

 **Animal Safety** This symbol appears when safety of animals and students must be ensured.

 **Handwashing** After the lab, wash hands with soap and water before removing goggles.

# Safety in the Science Laboratory

The science laboratory is a safe place to work if you follow standard safety procedures. Being responsible for your own safety helps to make the entire laboratory a safer place for everyone. When performing any lab, read and apply the caution statements and safety symbol listed at the beginning of the lab.

## General Safety Rules

1. Obtain your teacher's permission to begin all investigations and use laboratory equipment.

2. Study the procedure. Ask your teacher any questions. Be sure you understand safety symbols shown on the page.

3. Notify your teacher about allergies or other health conditions which can affect your participation in a lab.

4. Learn and follow use and safety procedures for your equipment. If unsure, ask your teacher.

5. Never eat, drink, chew gum, apply cosmetics, or do any personal grooming in the lab. Never use lab glassware as food or drink containers. Keep your hands away from your face and mouth.

6. Know the location and proper use of the safety shower, eye wash, fire blanket, and fire alarm.

## Prevent Accidents

1. Use the safety equipment provided to you. Goggles and a safety apron should be worn during investigations.

2. Do NOT use hair spray, mousse, or other flammable hair products. Tie back long hair and tie down loose clothing.

3. Do NOT wear sandals or other open-toed shoes in the lab.

4. Remove jewelry on hands and wrists. Loose jewelry, such as chains and long necklaces, should be removed to prevent them from getting caught in equipment.

5. Do not taste any substances or draw any material into a tube with your mouth.

6. Proper behavior is expected in the lab. Practical jokes and fooling around can lead to accidents and injury.

7. Keep your work area uncluttered.

## Laboratory Work

1. Collect and carry all equipment and materials to your work area before beginning a lab.

2. Remain in your own work area unless given permission by your teacher to leave it.

3. Always slant test tubes away from your-self and others when heating them, adding substances to them, or rinsing them.

4. If instructed to smell a substance in a container, hold the container a short distance away and fan vapors towards your nose.

5. Do NOT substitute other chemicals/substances for those in the materials list unless instructed to do so by your teacher.

6. Do NOT take any materials or chemicals outside of the laboratory.

7. Stay out of storage areas unless instructed to be there and supervised by your teacher.

## Laboratory Cleanup

1. Turn off all burners, water, and gas, and disconnect all electrical devices.

2. Clean all pieces of equipment and return all materials to their proper places.

3. Dispose of chemicals and other materials as directed by your teacher. Place broken glass and solid substances in the proper containers. Never discard materials in the sink.

4. Clean your work area.

5. Wash your hands with soap and water thoroughly BEFORE removing your goggles.

## Emergencies

1. Report any fire, electrical shock, glass-ware breakage, spill, or injury, no matter how small, to your teacher immediately. Follow his or her instructions.

2. If your clothing should catch fire, STOP, DROP, and ROLL. If possible, smother it with the fire blanket or get under a safety shower. NEVER RUN.

3. If a fire should occur, turn off all gas and leave the room according to established procedures.

4. In most instances, your teacher will clean up spills. Do NOT attempt to clean up spills unless you are given permission and instructions to do so.

5. If chemicals come into contact with your eyes or skin, notify your teacher immediately. Use the eyewash or flush your skin or eyes with large quantities of water.

6. The fire extinguisher and first-aid kit should only be used by your teacher unless it is an extreme emergency and you have been given permission.

7. If someone is injured or becomes ill, only a professional medical provider or some-one certified in first aid should perform first-aid procedures.

# EXTRA  Labs

### From Your Kitchen, Junk Drawer, or Yard

## 1 The Strongest Bag

**⯈ Real-World Question**

How can you test the strength of self-sealing bags?

**Possible Materials** 🖾
- several self-sealing bags of different brand names
- several generic-brand self-sealing bags
- marbles or round stones
- plastic basin

**⯈ Procedure**

1. Place a handful of marbles or stones in one of the self-sealing bags and seal the bag tight.
2. Invert the bag and hold it upside down over a plastic basin for 5 s.
3. If the seal does not break, open the bag, and add more stones or marbles. Reseal the bag, and invert it for 5 s over the plastic basin.
4. Continue adding weights to the bag until the seal can no longer hold them, and they spill into the basin. Record the maximum number of marbles or stones the bag held in your science journal.
5. Repeat steps 1–4 for the other self-sealing bags to test their strengths.

**⯈ Conclude and Apply**

1. Identify the strongest brand of self-sealing bag. Identify the weakest bag.
2. Infer whether or not brand-name bags are worth the extra cost.

## 2 3-D Maps

**⯈ Real-World Question**

How can you make a topographical map of your room?

**Possible Materials**
- meterstick
- metric ruler
- metric tape measure
- poster board
- black marker
- construction paper
- transparent tape

**⯈ Procedure**

1. Measure the length and width of your room in meters. Include the measurements of any odd shapes or angles in the room.
2. Decide upon a scale for your map.
3. Using your scale, draw the outline of your room on the poster board.
4. Measure the length, width, and height of a piece of furniture.
5. Using your scale, measure and cut out the sides for a model of the furniture piece from construction paper. Tape the pieces of the model together.
6. Place your furniture model on your map to match the actual piece's location in your room.
7. Construct two or three other models of furniture for your map.

**⯈ Conclude and Apply**

1. What scale did you use for your map?
2. Infer how a biologist might use a topographical map.

**Adult supervision required for all labs.**

## 3 Scratch Tests

### Real-World Question

What is the relative hardness of various minerals?

**Possible Materials**

- chalk
- sharpened pencil (use the graphite portion)
- penny
- iron nail
- Science Journal

### Procedure

1. Copy the data table in your Science Journal. Label the top *Scratcher*, and label the left side *Scratched.*
2. Try to scratch each material with each other material. If a material can scratch another, put a check in that box.
3. Try other materials from around the house. Add those to your data table.

|        | chalk | graphite | penny | iron nail |
|--------|-------|----------|-------|-----------|
| chalk  | ■     |          |       |           |
| graphite |     | ■        |       |           |
| penny  |       |          | ■     |           |
| iron nail |    |          |       | ■         |

### Conclude and Apply

1. Use your chart to make a hardness scale of these materials. Put the material that will scratch all other things at the top, and the material that is scratched by all other things, at the bottom.
2. A gemstone such as a diamond, emerald, or ruby, would scratch all of the materials in this lab. Explain why gemstones are so valuable.

## 4 Soil Creatures

### Real-World Question

What types of organisms live in the soil near your home or school?

**Possible Materials**

- garden shovel
- garden trowel
- gloves
- window screen
- collecting jars
- bucket
- cotton
- tweezers
- magnifying lens
- invertebrate field guide

### Procedure

1. Go to a wooded area near your home or school, clear away a patch of leaf litter and debris, and dig a hole 30 cm wide and 15 cm deep.
2. As you remove soil from the hole, place it on a window screen. Have a partner sift the soil through the screen into the bucket.
3. Collect any organisms you find and place them in a collecting jar.
4. Use a field guide to identify the types of organisms you find in the soil.
5. Search the soil of two other sites and compare the types of organisms you find in all three locations.

### Conclude and Apply

1. List the types of soil organisms you discovered.
2. Infer why organisms are important for soil.

## 5 Making Burrows

▶ *Real-World Question*

How does burrowing affect sediment layers?

**Possible Materials**
- clear-glass bowl
- white flour
- colored gelatin powder (3 packages)
- paintbrush
- pencil

▶ *Procedure*

1. Add 3 cm of white flour to the bowl. Flatten the top of the flour layer.
2. Carefully sprinkle gelatin powder over the flour to form a colored layer about 1/4 cm thick.
3. The two layers represent two different layers of sediment.
4. Use a paintbrush or pencil to make "burrows" in the "sediment."
5. Make sure to make some of the burrows at the edge of the bowl so that you can see how it affects the sediment.
6. Continue to make more burrows and observe the effect on the two layers.

▶ *Conclude and Apply*

1. How did the two layers of powder change as you continued to make burrows?
2. Were the "trace fossils" easy to recognize at first? How about after a lot of burrowing?
3. How do you think burrowing animals affect layers of sediment on the ocean floor? How could this burrowing be recognized in rock?

## 6 Measuring Movement

▶ *Real-World Question*

How can we model continental drift?

**Possible Materials**
- flashlight, nail, rubber band or tape, thick circle of paper
- protractor
- mirror
- stick-on notepad paper
- marker
- metric ruler
- calculator

▶ *Procedure*

1. Cut a circle of paper to fit around the lens of the flashlight. Use a nail to make a hole in the paper. Fasten the paper with the rubber band or tape. You should now have a flashlight that shines a focused beam of light.
2. Direct the light beam of the flashlight on a protractor held horizontally so that the beam lines up to the 90° mark.
3. Darken a room and aim the light beam at a mirror from an angle. Measure the angle. Observe where the reflected beam hits the wall.
4. Have a partner place a stick on the wall and mark the location of the beam with a marker.
5. Move the flashlight to a 100° angle and mark the beam's location on the wall with a second note.
6. Measure the distance between the two points on the wall and divide by 10 to determine the distance per degree.

▶ *Conclude and Apply*

1. What was the distance per degree of your measurements?
2. Calculate what the distance would be between the first spot and a third spot marking the location of the flashlight at a 40° angle.
3. Explain how this lab models measuring continental drift.

**Adult supervision required for all labs.**

## 7 Earth's Layers

### ▶ Real-World Question
What is the relative thickness of Earth's different layers?

**Possible Materials**
- meterstick
- masking tape

### ▶ Procedure
1. Use a piece of masking tape to mark a spot on the floor. This spot represents the center of Earth.
2. Measure a distance of 1.22 m from the first tape mark and place a second piece of tape.
3. From the second piece of tape, measure a distance of 2.27 m and place a third piece of tape.
4. From the third piece of tape, measure a distance of 2.89 m and place a fourth piece of tape.
5. From the fourth piece of tape, make two measurements. Measure a distance of 0.005 m and a distance of 0.06 m. Place two more pieces of tape to mark these two distances.

### ▶ Conclude and Apply
1. Identify the name of each of the levels you drew.
2. Calculate the scale you used for the thickness of your earth layers.

## 8 Disappearing Dots

### ▶ Real-World Question
Do your eyes have a blind spot?

**Possible Materials**
- white paper
- metric ruler
- colored pencils

### ▶ Procedure
1. Hold a sheet of white paper horizontally. Near the left edge of the paper, draw a black dot about 0.5 cm in diameter.
2. Draw a red dot 5 cm to the right of the black dot.
3. Hold the paper out in front of you, close your left eye, and look at the black dot with your right eye. Slowly move the paper toward you and observe what happens to the red dot.
4. Draw a blue dot 10 cm to the right of the black dot and a green dot 15 cm from the black dot.
5. Hold the paper out at arm's length, close your left eye, and look at the black dot with your right eye. Slowly move the paper toward you and observe what happens to the dots.

### ▶ Conclude and Apply
1. Describe what happened to the red, blue, and green dots as you moved the paper toward you.
2. The optic nerve carries visual images to the brain, and it is attached to the retina in your eye. Infer why the dots disappeared.

## 9 Materials Matter

### ▶ Real-World Question
Which materials will react together? How can materials change?

**Possible Materials**
- hotplate
- rusty nail
- shiny new nail
- baking soda
- vinegar
- flour
- water
- salt
- chalk
- aluminum foil

### ▶ Procedure
1. Experiment and record as many physical and chemical changes as possible in 45 min. Prepare your data charts in advance. Try to be efficient rather than speedy. Accurate observations are important.

2. Use at least three words to describe the physical properties of each material. If you know any chemical properties of the materials, add those to your chart.
3. Make physical changes to as many materials as you can. Combine materials to make chemical changes.
4. Describe your observations in the chart.

### ▶ Conclude and Apply
1. How is knowledge about physical and chemical properties used in building and manufacturing in the real world? Give examples.
2. Were you satisfied with your lab method? What would you do to make your work better next time?

## 10 Comparing Atom Sizes

### ▶ Real-World Question
How do the sizes of different types of atoms compare?

**Possible Materials**
- metric ruler or meterstick
- 1-m length of white paper
- transparent or masking tape
- colored pencils

### ▶ Procedure
1. Tape a 1-m sheet of paper on the floor.
2. Use a scale of 1 mm: 1 picometer for measuring and drawing the relative diameters of all the atoms.
3. Study the chart of atomic sizes.
4. Use your scale to measure the relative size of a hydrogen atom on the sheet of paper. Use a red pencil to draw the relative diameter of a hydrogen atom on your paper.
5. Use your scale to measure the relative sizes of an oxygen atom, iron atom, gold atom, and francium atom. Use four other colored pencils to draw the relative diameters of these atoms on the paper.
6. Compare the relative sizes of these different atoms.

| Atomic Sizes (picometers) | |
|---|---|
| **Element** | **Diameter** |
| Hydrogen | 50 |
| Oxygen | 146 |
| Iron | 248 |
| Gold | 288 |
| Francium | 540 |

### ▶ Conclude and Apply
1. Research the length of a picometer.
2. Using your scale, list the diameters of the atoms that you drew on your paper.

**Adult supervision required for all labs.**

## 11 A Good Mix?

### ▶ Real-World Question
What liquids will dissolve in water?

**Possible Materials** 🌊 ⚗️ 🧪
- cooking oil
- water
- apple or grape juice
- rubbing alcohol
- spoon
- glass
- measuring cup

### ▶ Procedure
1. Pour 100 mL of water into a large glass.
2. Pour 100 mL of apple juice into the glass and stir the water and juice together. Observe your mixture to determine whether juice is soluble in water.
3. Empty and rinse out your glass.
4. Pour 100 mL of water and 100 mL of cooking oil into the glass and stir them together. Observe your mixture to determine whether oil is soluble in water.
5. Empty and rinse out your glass.
6. Pour 100 mL of water and 100 mL of rubbing alcohol into the glass and stir them together. Observe your mixture to determine whether alcohol is soluble in water.

### ▶ Conclude and Apply
1. List the liquid(s) that are soluble in water.
2. List the liquid(s) that are not soluble in water.
3. Infer why some liquids are soluble in water and others are not.

## 12 Mini Fireworks

### ▶ Real-World Question
Where do the colors in fireworks come from?

**Possible Materials** 🔥 💧 🌊 ⚗️ 🧪
- candle
- lighter
- wooden chopsticks (or a fork or tongs)
- penny
- water in an old cup
- steel wool

### ▶ Procedure
1. Light the candle.
2. Use the chopsticks to get a firm grip on the penny.
3. Hold the penny in the flame until you observe a change. *(Hint: this experiment is more fun in the bathroom with the lights off!)*
4. Drop the penny in the water when you are finished and plunge the burning end of the chopsticks or hot part of the fork into the water as well.
5. Repeat the procedure using steel wool.

### ▶ Conclude and Apply
1. What color did you see?
2. Infer why copper and iron are used in fireworks.
3. Research what other elements are used in fireworks.

**Adult supervision required for all labs.**

## 13 Expanding Eggs

### ▶ Real-World Question
How can you observe liquids passing through a cell membrane?

**Possible Materials** 🔬 🥽 🧪 🧤
- glass jar with lid
- white vinegar
- medium chicken egg
- tape measure or string and ruler
- tongs
- measuring cup

### ▶ Procedure
1. Obtain a glass jar with a lid and a medium sized egg.
2. Make certain your egg easily fits into your jar.
3. Measure the circumference of your egg.
4. Pour 250 mL of white vinegar into the jar.
5. Carefully place your egg in the jar so that it is submerged in the vinegar. Be careful not to crack or break the egg.
6. Observe your egg each day for three days. Measure the circumference of the egg after three days.

### ▶ Conclude and Apply
1. Describe the changes that happened to your egg.
2. Infer why the egg's circumference changed. *HINT: A hen's egg is a single cell.*

## 14 Spinning Like a Top

### ▶ Real-World Question
How can you observe your inner ear restoring your body's balance?

**Possible Materials** 🥽
- large pillows
- stopwatch or watch

### ▶ Procedure
1. Choose a carpeted location several meters away from any furniture.
2. Lay large pillows on the floor around you.
3. Spin around in a circle once, stare straight ahead, and observe what the room looks like. Have a friend spot you to prevent you from falling.
4. Spin around in circles continuously for 5 s, stare straight ahead, and observe what the room looks like. Have a friend spot you.
5. After you stop, use a stopwatch to time how long it takes for the room to stop spinning.
6. With a friend spotting you, spin for 10 s and time how long it takes for the room to stop spinning.

### ▶ Conclude and Apply
1. How long did it take for the room to stop spinning after you spun in circles for 5 s and for 10 s?
2. Infer why the room appeared to spin even after you stopped spinning.

## 15 What's in blood?

**Real-World Question**

What are the proportions of the components of your blood?

Possible Materials
- bag of brown rice
- white rice
- small bag of wild rice
- measuring cup
- large bowl or large cooking tray

**Procedure**

1. Measure 1.25 liters of brown rice and pour the rice into a large bowl or on a cooking tray.
2. Measure 100 mL of wild rice and pour it into the bowl or on the tray.
3. Count out 50 grains of white rice and place them in the bowl or on the tray.
4. Mix the three types of rice thoroughly and observe the proportions of the three major components of your blood.

**Conclude and Apply**

1. Infer what type of rice represents red blood cells.
2. Infer what type of rice represents white blood cells.
3. Infer what type of rice represents platelets.

## 16 Vitamin Search

**Real-World Question**

How many vitamins and minerals are in the foods you eat?

Possible Materials
- labels from packaged foods and drinks
- nutrition guidebook or cookbook

**Procedure**

1. Create a data table to record the "% Daily Value" of important vitamins and minerals for a variety of foods.
2. Collect packages from a variety of packaged foods and check the Nutrition Facts chart for the "% Daily Value" of all the vitamins and minerals it contains. These values are listed at the bottom of the chart.
3. Use cookbooks or nutrition guidebooks to research the "% Daily Value" of vitamins and minerals found in several fresh fruits and vegetables such as strawberries, spinach, oranges, and lentils.

**Conclude and Apply**

1. Infer why a healthy diet includes fresh fruits and vegetables.
2. Infer why a healthy diet includes a wide variety of nutritious foods.

**Nutrition Facts**

Serving Size 1 Meal

**Amount Per Serving**

| Calories 330 | Calories from Fat 60 |
|---|---|
| | **% Daily Value*** |
| **Total Fat** 7g | **10%** |
| Saturated Fat 3.5g | **17%** |
| Polyunsaturated Fat 1g | |
| Monounsaturated Fat 2.5g | |
| **Cholesterol** 35mg | **12%** |
| **Sodium** 460mg | **19%** |
| **Total Carbohydrate** 52g | **18%** |
| Dietary Fiber 6g | **24%** |
| Sugars 17g | |
| **Protein** 15g | |

| Vitamin A 15% | • | Vitamin C 70% |
|---|---|---|
| Calcium 4% | • | Iron 10% |

* Percent Daily Values are based on a 2,000 calorie diet. Your daily values may be higher or lower depending on your calorie needs.

| | Calories | 2,000 | 2,500 |
|---|---|---|---|
| Total Fat | Less than | 65g | 80g |
| Sat Fat | Less than | 20g | 25g |
| Cholesterol | Less than | 300mg | 300mg |
| Sodium | Less than | 2,400mg | 2,400mg |
| Total Carbohydrate | | 300g | 375g |
| Dietary Fiber | | 25g | 30g |

**Adult supervision required for all labs.**

# Extra Try at Home Labs

## 17 Aquatic Worm Search

### Real-World Question
What types of worms live in freshwater?

**Possible Materials**
- ice cube tray
- bucket
- collecting jar
- aquatic net
- field guide to pond life
- magnifying lens
- microscope slide
- eyedropper
- waterproof boots

### Procedure
1. Search for aquatic worms underneath rocks and leaves in a creek. Worms live beneath flat rocks and decaying leaves in slow, shallow water.
2. Carefully place the worms you find in different compartments of your ice cube tray and examine them closely under a microscope or magnifying lens.
3. Collect a sample of stream or pond water.
4. Place a drop of pond water on a microscope slide and search for microscopic aquatic worms living in the water.
5. Use your field guide to pond life to identify the organisms you find.

### Conclude and Apply
1. List the aquatic worms you found.
2. Research the classification of the worms you discovered under the rocks and leaves of the stream.

## 18 Bare Bones

### Real-World Question
What do the bones of a chicken wing look like?

**Possible Materials**
- stove or hot plate
- pot
- water
- fork or kitchen knife
- toothpick
- tongs
- paper towels
- plate
- chicken wing

### Procedure
1. Boil water and cook a chicken wing in the pot.
2. Use the tongs to remove the wing from the water. Wait until the wing cools and use a kitchen knife or fork to remove all the meat.
3. Identify the following bones of your chicken wing: humerus, radius, ulna, carpal, metacarpal, first digit, second digit, and third digit.
4. Snap either the radius or ulna in half and remove the bone marrow inside with a toothpick.

### Conclude and Apply
1. Explain how bones help vertebrates.
2. Describe what the inside of the bird's bone is like. Infer why it is like this.

**Adult supervision required for all labs.**

## 19 Prickly Plants

### Real-World Question
Why does a cactus have needles?

**Possible Materials**
- toilet paper roll or paper towel roll (cut in half)
- transparent tape
- toothpicks (15)
- metric ruler
- oven mitt
- self-sealing bag
- water
- measuring cup

### Procedure
1. Pour 50 mL of water into a small self-sealing bag.
2. Stuff the bag of water into the toilet paper roll so that the bag is just inside the roll's rim.
3. Stand the roll on a table and hold it firmly with one hand. Place the oven mitt on your other hand and try to take the bag out of the roll.
4. If needed, place the bag back into the roll.
5. Securely tape toothpicks around the lip of the roll about 1 cm apart. About 4 cm of each toothpick should stick up above the rim.
6. Hold the roll on the table, put the oven mitt on, and try to take the bag out of the roll without breaking the toothpicks.

### Conclude and Apply
1. Compare how easy it was to remove the water bag from the toilet paper roll with and without the toothpicks protecting the water.
2. Infer why desert cacti have needles.

## 20 Breathing Plants

### Real-World Question
How do plants breathe?

**Possible Materials**
- houseplant
- petroleum jelly
- paper towel
- soap
- water

### Procedure
1. Scoop some petroleum jelly out of the jar with your fingertips and coat the top of three or four leaves of the houseplant with jelly. Cover the entire top surface of the leaves only.
2. Coat the bottom of three or four different leaves with a layer of jelly.
3. Choose two or three stems not connected to the leaves you have covered with jelly. Coat these stems from top to bottom with a layer of jelly. Cover the entire stems but not their leaves.
4. Wash your hands with soap and water.
5. Observe the houseplant for three days.

### Conclude and Apply
1. Describe what happened to the leaves and stems covered with jelly.
2. Infer how plants breathe.

## 21 Fungi Hunt

### Real-World Question
What types of fungi grow near your home?

**Possible Materials**
- camera
- film
- sketch pad
- colored pencils and markers
- poster board
- field guide to fungi

### Procedure
1. Take an adult with you to a nearby forest, stand of trees, or other shady spot.
2. Search for different types of fungi on dead logs, large trees, broken limbs, and in moist soil.
3. Take photographs or draw sketches of all the different types of fungi you discover.
4. Create a fungi poster board display with your photographs or sketches and a list of the places where you found them.
5. Use a fungi field guide to identify as many species as possible. Write the common and scientific names of the fungi you identify next to the matching picture or photograph on your poster.

### Conclude and Apply
1. List the types of fungi you discovered.
2. Infer why fungi grow rapidly in wet conditions.

**Adult supervision required for all labs.**

# Computer Skills

People who study science rely on computer technology to do research, record experimental data, analyze results from investigations, and communicate with other scientists. Whether you work in a laboratory or just need to write a lab report, good computer skills are necessary.

**Figure 16** Students and scientists rely on computers to gather data and communicate ideas.

## Hardware Basics

Your personal computer is a system consisting of many components. The parts you can see and touch are called hardware.

**Figure 17** Most desktop computers consist of the components shown above. Notebook computers have the same components in a compact unit.

Desktop systems, like the one shown in **Figure 17,** typically have most of these components. Notebook and tablet computers have most of the same components as a desktop computer, but the components are integrated into a single, book-sized portable unit.

## Storing Your Data

When you save documents created on computers at your school, they probably are stored in a directory on your school's network. However, if you want to take the documents you have created home, you need to save them on something portable. Removable media, like those shown in **Figure 18,** are disks and drives that are designed to be moved from one computer to another.

**Figure 18** Removable data storage is a convenient way to carry your documents from place to place.

Removable media vary from floppy disks and recordable CDs and DVDs to small solid-state storage. Tiny USB "keychain" drives have become popular because they can store large amounts of data and plug into any computer with a USB port. Each of these types of media stores different amounts of data. Be sure that you save your data to a medium that is compatible with your computer.

## Getting Started with Word Processing Programs

A word processor is used for the composition, editing, and formatting of written material. Word processors vary from program to program, but most have the basic functions shown in **Figure 19.** Most word processors also can be used to make simple tables and graphics.

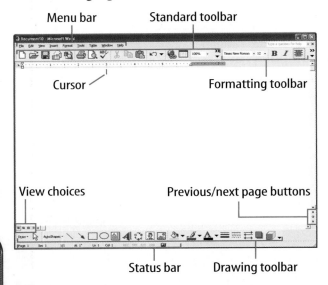

**Figure 19** Word processors have functions that easily allow you to edit, format, view, and save text, tables, and images, making them useful for writing lab reports and research papers.

### Word Processor Tips

- As you type, text will automatically wrap to the next line. Press *Enter* on your keyboard if you wish to start a new paragraph.
- You can move multiple lines of text around by using the *cut* and *paste* functions on the toolbar.
- If you make a typing or formatting error, use the *undo* function on the toolbar.
- Be sure to save your document early and often. This will prevent you from losing your work if your computer turns off unexpectedly.

- Use the *spell-check* function to check your spelling and grammar. Remember that *spell-check* will not catch words that are misspelled to look like other words, such as *cold* instead of *gold*. Reread your document to look for spelling and grammar mistakes.
- Graphics and spreadsheets can be added to your document by copying them from other programs and pasting them into your document.
- If you have questions about using your word processor, ask your teacher or use the program's *help* menu.

## Getting Started with Spreadsheet Programs

A spreadsheet, like the one shown in **Figure 20,** helps you organize information into columns and rows. Spreadsheets are particularly useful for making data tables. Spreadsheets also can be used to perform mathematical calculations with your data. Then, you can use the spreadsheet to generate graphs and charts displaying your results.

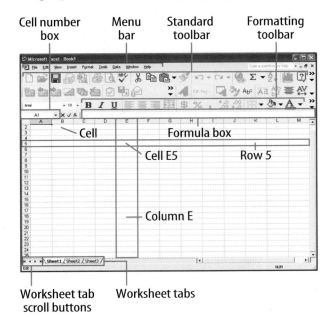

**Figure 20** With formulas and graphs, spreadsheets help you organize and analyze your data.

## Spreadsheet Tips

- Think about how to organize your data before you begin entering data.

- Each column (vertical) is assigned a letter and each row (horizontal) is assigned a number. Each point where a row and column intersect is called a cell, and is labeled according to where it is located. For example: column A, row 1 is cell A1.

- To edit the information in a cell, you must first activate the cell by clicking on it.

- When using a spreadsheet to generate a graph, make sure you use the type of graph that best represents the data. Review the *Science Skill Handbook* in this book for help with graphs.

- To learn more about using your spreadsheet program ask your teacher or use the program's Help menu.

## Getting Started with Presentation Programs

There are many programs that help you orally communicate results of your research in an organized and interesting way. Many of these are slideshow programs, which allow you to organize text, graphs, digital photographs, sound, animations, and digital video into one multimedia presentation. Presentations can be printed onto paper or displayed on-screen. Slideshow programs are particularly effective when used with video projectors and interactive whiteboards, like the one shown in **Figure 21.** Although presentation programs are not the only way to communicate information publicly, they are an effective way to organize your presentation and remind your audience of major points.

**Figure 21** Video projectors and interactive whiteboards allow you to present information stored on a computer to an entire classroom. They are becoming increasingly common in the classrooms.

## Presentation Program Tips

- Often, color and strong images will convey a point better than words alone. But, be sure to organize your presentation clearly. Don't let the graphics confuse the message.

- Most presentation programs will let you copy and paste text, spreadsheets, art and graphs from other programs.

- Most presentation programs have built-in templates that help you organize text and graphics.

- As with any kind of presentation, familiarize yourself with the equipment and practice your presentation before you present it to an audience.

- Most presentation programs will allow you to save your document in html format so that you can publish your document on a Web site.

- If you have questions about using your presentation software or hardware, ask your teacher or use the program's Help menu.

## Doing Research with the World Wide Web

The Internet is a global network of computers where information can be stored and shared by anyone with an internet connection. One of the easiest ways to find information on the internet is by using the World Wide Web, a vast graphical system of documents written in the computer language, html (hypertext markup language). Web pages are arranged in collections of related material called "Web sites." The content on a Web site is viewed using a program called a Web browser. Web browsers, like the one shown in **Figure 22,** allow you to browse or surf the Web by clicking on highlighted hyperlinks, which move you from Web page to Web page. Web content can be searched by topic using a search engine. Search engines are located on Web sites which catalog key words on Web pages all over the World Wide Web.

Navigation buttons    Address bar    Loading indicator

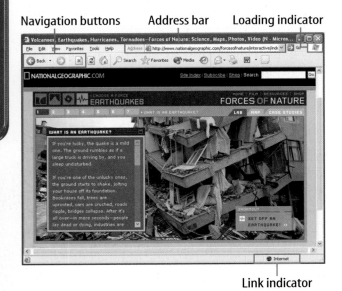

Link indicator

**Figure 22** Web browsers have all the tools you need to navigate and view information on the Web.

### World Wide Web Tips

- Search the Web using specific keywords. For example, if you want to research the element gold don't type *elements* into the search engine.
- When performing a Web search, enclose multiple keywords with quotes to narrow your results to the most relevant pages.
- The first hit your Web search results in is not always the best. Search results are arranged by popularity, not by relevance to your topic. Be patient and look at many links in your search results to find the best information.
- Think critically when you do science research on the Web. Compared to a traditional library, finding accurate information on the Web is not always easy because anyone can create a Web site. Some of the best places to start your research are websites for major newspapers and magazines, as well as U.S. government (*.gov*) and university (*.edu*) Web sites.
- Security is a major concern when browsing the Web. Your computer can be exposed to advertising software and computer viruses, which can hurt your computer's data and performance. *Do not download software at your school unless your teacher tells you to do so.*
- Cite information you find on the Web just as you would books and journals. An example of proper Web citation is the following:
  Menk, Amy J. (2004). *Urban Ecology*. Retrieved January 21, 2005, from McGraw-Hill Web site: http://www.mcgraw-hill.com/papers/urban.html
- The World Wide Web is a great resource for information, but don't forget to utilize local libraries, including your school library.

# Math Review

## Use Fractions

A fraction compares a part to a whole. In the fraction $\frac{2}{3}$, the 2 represents the part and is the numerator. The 3 represents the whole and is the denominator.

**Reduce Fractions**  To reduce a fraction, you must find the largest factor that is common to both the numerator and the denominator, the greatest common factor (GCF). Divide both numbers by the GCF. The fraction has then been reduced, or it is in its simplest form.

**Example**  Twelve of the 20 chemicals in the science lab are in powder form. What fraction of the chemicals used in the lab are in powder form?

**Step 1**  Write the fraction.
$$\frac{\text{part}}{\text{whole}} = \frac{12}{20}$$

**Step 2**  To find the GCF of the numerator and denominator, list all of the factors of each number.
Factors of 12: 1, 2, 3, 4, 6, 12 (the numbers that divide evenly into 12)
Factors of 20: 1, 2, 4, 5, 10, 20 (the numbers that divide evenly into 20)

**Step 3**  List the common factors.
1, 2, 4

**Step 4**  Choose the greatest factor in the list.
The GCF of 12 and 20 is 4.

**Step 5**  Divide the numerator and denominator by the GCF.
$$\frac{12 \div 4}{20 \div 4} = \frac{3}{5}$$

In the lab, $\frac{3}{5}$ of the chemicals are in powder form.

**Practice Problem**  At an amusement park, 66 of 90 rides have a height restriction. What fraction of the rides, in its simplest form, has a height restriction?

**Add and Subtract Fractions**  To add or subtract fractions with the same denominator, add or subtract the numerators and write the sum or difference over the denominator. After finding the sum or difference, find the simplest form for your fraction.

**Example 1**  In the forest outside your house, $\frac{1}{8}$ of the animals are rabbits, $\frac{3}{8}$ are squirrels, and the remainder are birds and insects. How many are mammals?

**Step 1**  Add the numerators.
$$\frac{1}{8} + \frac{3}{8} = \frac{(1 + 3)}{8} = \frac{4}{8}$$

**Step 2**  Find the GCF.
$$\frac{4}{8} \quad (\text{GCF, 4})$$

**Step 3**  Divide the numerator and denominator by the GCF.
$$\frac{4 \div 4}{8 \div 4} = \frac{1}{2}$$

$\frac{1}{2}$ of the animals are mammals.

**Example 2**  If $\frac{7}{16}$ of the Earth is covered by freshwater, and $\frac{1}{16}$ of that is in glaciers, how much freshwater is not frozen?

**Step 1**  Subtract the numerators.
$$\frac{7}{16} - \frac{1}{16} = \frac{(7 - 1)}{16} = \frac{6}{16}$$

**Step 2**  Find the GCF.
$$\frac{6}{16} \quad (\text{GCF, 2})$$

**Step 3**  Divide the numerator and denominator by the GCF.
$$\frac{6 \div 2}{16 \div 2} = \frac{3}{8}$$

$\frac{3}{8}$ of the freshwater is not frozen.

**Practice Problem**  A bicycle rider is riding at a rate of 15 km/h for $\frac{4}{9}$ of his ride, 10 km/h for $\frac{2}{9}$ of his ride, and 8 km/h for the remainder of the ride. How much of his ride is he riding at a rate greater than 8 km/h?

# Math Skill Handbook

**Unlike Denominators** To add or subtract fractions with unlike denominators, first find the least common denominator (LCD). This is the smallest number that is a common multiple of both denominators. Rename each fraction with the LCD, and then add or subtract. Find the simplest form if necessary.

**Example 1** A chemist makes a paste that is $\frac{1}{2}$ table salt (NaCl), $\frac{1}{3}$ sugar ($C_6H_{12}O_6$), and the remainder is water ($H_2O$). How much of the paste is a solid?

**Step 1** Find the LCD of the fractions.

$$\frac{1}{2} + \frac{1}{3} \quad (\text{LCD, 6})$$

**Step 2** Rename each numerator and each denominator with the LCD.

**Step 3** Add the numerators.

$$\frac{3}{6} + \frac{2}{6} = \frac{(3 + 2)}{6} = \frac{5}{6}$$

$\frac{5}{6}$ of the paste is a solid.

**Example 2** The average precipitation in Grand Junction, CO, is $\frac{7}{10}$ inch in November, and $\frac{3}{5}$ inch in December. What is the total average precipitation?

**Step 1** Find the LCD of the fractions.

$$\frac{7}{10} + \frac{3}{5} \quad (\text{LCD, 10})$$

**Step 2** Rename each numerator and each denominator with the LCD.

**Step 3** Add the numerators.

$$\frac{7}{10} + \frac{6}{10} = \frac{(7 + 6)}{10} = \frac{13}{10}$$

$\frac{13}{10}$ inches total precipitation, or $1\frac{3}{10}$ inches.

**Practice Problem** On an electric bill, about $\frac{1}{8}$ of the energy is from solar energy and about $\frac{1}{10}$ is from wind power. How much of the total bill is from solar energy and wind power combined?

**Example 3** In your body, $\frac{7}{10}$ of your muscle contractions are involuntary (cardiac and smooth muscle tissue). Smooth muscle makes $\frac{3}{15}$ of your muscle contractions. How many of your muscle contractions are made by cardiac muscle?

**Step 1** Find the LCD of the fractions.

$$\frac{7}{10} - \frac{3}{15} \quad (\text{LCD, 30})$$

**Step 2** Rename each numerator and each denominator with the LCD.

$$\frac{7 \times 3}{10 \times 3} = \frac{21}{30}$$

$$\frac{3 \times 2}{15 \times 2} = \frac{6}{30}$$

**Step 3** Subtract the numerators.

$$\frac{21}{30} - \frac{6}{30} = \frac{(21 - 6)}{30} = \frac{15}{30}$$

**Step 4** Find the GCF.

$$\frac{15}{30} \quad (\text{GCF, 15})$$

$$\frac{1}{2}$$

$\frac{1}{2}$ of all muscle contractions are cardiac muscle.

**Example 4** Tony wants to make cookies that call for $\frac{3}{4}$ of a cup of flour, but he only has $\frac{1}{3}$ of a cup. How much more flour does he need?

**Step 1** Find the LCD of the fractions.

$$\frac{3}{4} - \frac{1}{3} \quad (\text{LCD, 12})$$

**Step 2** Rename each numerator and each denominator with the LCD.

$$\frac{3 \times 3}{4 \times 3} = \frac{9}{12}$$

$$\frac{1 \times 4}{3 \times 4} = \frac{4}{12}$$

**Step 3** Subtract the numerators.

$$\frac{9}{12} - \frac{4}{12} = \frac{(9 - 4)}{12} = \frac{5}{12}$$

$\frac{5}{12}$ of a cup of flour

**Practice Problem** Using the information provided to you in Example 3 above, determine how many muscle contractions are voluntary (skeletal muscle).

**Multiply Fractions** To multiply with fractions, multiply the numerators and multiply the denominators. Find the simplest form if necessary.

**Example**   Multiply $\frac{3}{5}$ by $\frac{1}{3}$.

**Step 1**  Multiply the numerators and denominators.

$$\frac{3}{5} \times \frac{1}{3} = \frac{(3 \times 1)}{(5 \times 3)} = \frac{3}{15}$$

**Step 2**  Find the GCF.

$$\frac{3}{15} \quad (\text{GCF, 3})$$

**Step 3**  Divide the numerator and denominator by the GCF.

$$\frac{3 \div 3}{15 \div 3} = \frac{1}{5}$$

$\frac{3}{5}$ multiplied by $\frac{1}{3}$ is $\frac{1}{5}$.

**Practice Problem**   Multiply $\frac{3}{14}$ by $\frac{5}{16}$.

**Find a Reciprocal** Two numbers whose product is 1 are called multiplicative inverses, or reciprocals.

**Example**   Find the reciprocal of $\frac{3}{8}$.

**Step 1**  Inverse the fraction by putting the denominator on top and the numerator on the bottom.

$$\frac{8}{3}$$

The reciprocal of $\frac{3}{8}$ is $\frac{8}{3}$.

**Practice Problem**   Find the reciprocal of $\frac{4}{9}$.

**Divide Fractions** To divide one fraction by another fraction, multiply the dividend by the reciprocal of the divisor. Find the simplest form if necessary.

**Example 1**   Divide $\frac{1}{9}$ by $\frac{1}{3}$.

**Step 1**  Find the reciprocal of the divisor.

The reciprocal of $\frac{1}{3}$ is $\frac{3}{1}$.

**Step 2**  Multiply the dividend by the reciprocal of the divisor.

$$\frac{\frac{1}{9}}{\frac{1}{3}} = \frac{1}{9} \times \frac{3}{1} = \frac{(1 \times 3)}{(9 \times 1)} = \frac{3}{9}$$

**Step 3**  Find the GCF.

$$\frac{3}{9} \quad (\text{GCF, 3})$$

**Step 4**  Divide the numerator and denominator by the GCF.

$$\frac{3 \div 3}{9 \div 3} = \frac{1}{3}$$

$\frac{1}{9}$ divided by $\frac{1}{3}$ is $\frac{1}{3}$.

**Example 2**   Divide $\frac{3}{5}$ by $\frac{1}{4}$.

**Step 1**  Find the reciprocal of the divisor.

The reciprocal of $\frac{1}{4}$ is $\frac{4}{1}$.

**Step 2**  Multiply the dividend by the reciprocal of the divisor.

$$\frac{\frac{3}{5}}{\frac{1}{4}} = \frac{3}{5} \times \frac{4}{1} = \frac{(3 \times 4)}{(5 \times 1)} = \frac{12}{5}$$

$\frac{3}{5}$ divided by $\frac{1}{4}$ is $\frac{12}{5}$ or $2\frac{2}{5}$.

**Practice Problem**   Divide $\frac{3}{11}$ by $\frac{7}{10}$.

## Use Ratios

When you compare two numbers by division, you are using a ratio. Ratios can be written 3 to 5, 3:5, or $\frac{3}{5}$. Ratios, like fractions, also can be written in simplest form.

Ratios can represent one type of probability, called odds. This is a ratio that compares the number of ways a certain outcome occurs to the number of possible outcomes. For example, if you flip a coin 100 times, what are the odds that it will come up heads? There are two possible outcomes, heads or tails, so the odds of coming up heads are 50:100. Another way to say this is that 50 out of 100 times the coin will come up heads. In its simplest form, the ratio is 1:2.

**Example 1**  A chemical solution contains 40 g of salt and 64 g of baking soda. What is the ratio of salt to baking soda as a fraction in simplest form?

**Step 1**  Write the ratio as a fraction.
$$\frac{salt}{baking\ soda} = \frac{40}{64}$$

**Step 2**  Express the fraction in simplest form.
The GCF of 40 and 64 is 8.
$$\frac{40}{64} = \frac{40 \div 8}{64 \div 8} = \frac{5}{8}$$

The ratio of salt to baking soda in the sample is 5:8.

**Example 2**  Sean rolls a 6-sided die 6 times. What are the odds that the side with a 3 will show?

**Step 1**  Write the ratio as a fraction.
$$\frac{number\ of\ sides\ with\ a\ 3}{number\ of\ possible\ sides} = \frac{1}{6}$$

**Step 2**  Multiply by the number of attempts.
$$\frac{1}{6} \times 6\ attempts = \frac{6}{6}\ attempts = 1\ attempt$$

1 attempt out of 6 will show a 3.

**Practice Problem**  Two metal rods measure 100 cm and 144 cm in length. What is the ratio of their lengths in simplest form?

## Use Decimals

A fraction with a denominator that is a power of ten can be written as a decimal. For example, 0.27 means $\frac{27}{100}$. The decimal point separates the ones place from the tenths place.

Any fraction can be written as a decimal using division. For example, the fraction $\frac{5}{8}$ can be written as a decimal by dividing 5 by 8. Written as a decimal, it is 0.625.

**Add or Subtract Decimals**  When adding and subtracting decimals, line up the decimal points before carrying out the operation.

**Example 1**  Find the sum of 47.68 and 7.80.

**Step 1**  Line up the decimal places when you write the numbers.
$$\begin{array}{r} 47.68 \\ + \ 7.80 \\ \end{array}$$

**Step 2**  Add the decimals.
$$\begin{array}{r} {\scriptstyle 1\ 1} \\ 47.68 \\ + \ 7.80 \\ \hline 55.48 \\ \end{array}$$

The sum of 47.68 and 7.80 is 55.48.

**Example 2**  Find the difference of 42.17 and 15.85.

**Step 1**  Line up the decimal places when you write the number.
$$\begin{array}{r} 42.17 \\ - 15.85 \\ \end{array}$$

**Step 2**  Subtract the decimals.
$$\begin{array}{r} {\scriptstyle 3\ 11} \\ 4\cancel{2}.\cancel{1}7 \\ - 15.85 \\ \hline 26.32 \\ \end{array}$$

The difference of 42.17 and 15.85 is 26.32.

**Practice Problem**  Find the sum of 1.245 and 3.842.

**Multiply Decimals** To multiply decimals, multiply the numbers like numbers without decimal points. Count the decimal places in each factor. The product will have the same number of decimal places as the sum of the decimal places in the factors.

**Example** Multiply 2.4 by 5.9.

**Step 1** Multiply the factors like two whole numbers.
$24 \times 59 = 1416$

**Step 2** Find the sum of the number of decimal places in the factors. Each factor has one decimal place, for a sum of two decimal places.

**Step 3** The product will have two decimal places.
14.16

The product of 2.4 and 5.9 is 14.16.

**Practice Problem** Multiply 4.6 by 2.2.

**Divide Decimals** When dividing decimals, change the divisor to a whole number. To do this, multiply both the divisor and the dividend by the same power of ten. Then place the decimal point in the quotient directly above the decimal point in the dividend. Then divide as you do with whole numbers.

**Example** Divide 8.84 by 3.4.

**Step 1** Multiply both factors by 10.
$3.4 \times 10 = 34$, $8.84 \times 10 = 88.4$

**Step 2** Divide 88.4 by 34.

$$
\begin{array}{r}
2.6 \\
34\overline{)88.4} \\
-68\phantom{.4} \\
\hline
204 \\
-204 \\
\hline
0
\end{array}
$$

8.84 divided by 3.4 is 2.6.

**Practice Problem** Divide 75.6 by 3.6.

## Use Proportions

An equation that shows that two ratios are equivalent is a proportion. The ratios $\frac{2}{4}$ and $\frac{5}{10}$ are equivalent, so they can be written as $\frac{2}{4} = \frac{5}{10}$. This equation is a proportion.

When two ratios form a proportion, the cross products are equal. To find the cross products in the proportion $\frac{2}{4} = \frac{5}{10}$, multiply the 2 and the 10, and the 4 and the 5. Therefore $2 \times 10 = 4 \times 5$, or $20 = 20$.

Because you know that both ratios are equal, you can use cross products to find a missing term in a proportion. This is known as solving the proportion.

**Example** The heights of a tree and a pole are proportional to the lengths of their shadows. The tree casts a shadow of 24 m when a 6-m pole casts a shadow of 4 m. What is the height of the tree?

**Step 1** Write a proportion.
$$\frac{\text{height of tree}}{\text{height of pole}} = \frac{\text{length of tree's shadow}}{\text{length of pole's shadow}}$$

**Step 2** Substitute the known values into the proportion. Let $h$ represent the unknown value, the height of the tree.
$$\frac{h}{6} = \frac{24}{4}$$

**Step 3** Find the cross products.
$$h \times 4 = 6 \times 24$$

**Step 4** Simplify the equation.
$$4h = 144$$

**Step 5** Divide each side by 4.
$$\frac{4h}{4} = \frac{144}{4}$$
$$h = 36$$

The height of the tree is 36 m.

**Practice Problem** The ratios of the weights of two objects on the Moon and on Earth are in proportion. A rock weighing 3 N on the Moon weighs 18 N on Earth. How much would a rock that weighs 5 N on the Moon weigh on Earth?

## Use Percentages

The word *percent* means "out of one hundred." It is a ratio that compares a number to 100. Suppose you read that 77 percent of the Earth's surface is covered by water. That is the same as reading that the fraction of the Earth's surface covered by water is $\frac{77}{100}$. To express a fraction as a percent, first find the equivalent decimal for the fraction. Then, multiply the decimal by 100 and add the percent symbol.

**Example** Express $\frac{13}{20}$ as a percent.

**Step 1** Find the equivalent decimal for the fraction.

$$
\begin{array}{r}
0.65 \\
20\overline{)13.00} \\
\underline{12\,0}\phantom{0} \\
1\,00 \\
\underline{1\,00} \\
0
\end{array}
$$

**Step 2** Rewrite the fraction $\frac{13}{20}$ as 0.65.

**Step 3** Multiply 0.65 by 100 and add the % symbol.
$$0.65 \times 100 = 65 = 65\%$$

So, $\frac{13}{20} = 65\%$.

This also can be solved as a proportion.

**Example** Express $\frac{13}{20}$ as a percent.

**Step 1** Write a proportion.
$$\frac{13}{20} = \frac{x}{100}$$

**Step 2** Find the cross products.
$$1300 = 20x$$

**Step 3** Divide each side by 20.
$$\frac{1300}{20} = \frac{20x}{20}$$
$$65\% = x$$

**Practice Problem** In one year, 73 of 365 days were rainy in one city. What percent of the days in that city were rainy?

## Solve One-Step Equations

A statement that two expressions are equal is an equation. For example, $A = B$ is an equation that states that $A$ is equal to $B$.

An equation is solved when a variable is replaced with a value that makes both sides of the equation equal. To make both sides equal the inverse operation is used. Addition and subtraction are inverses, and multiplication and division are inverses.

**Example 1** Solve the equation $x - 10 = 35$.

**Step 1** Find the solution by adding 10 to each side of the equation.
$$x - 10 = 35$$
$$x - 10 + 10 = 35 + 10$$
$$x = 45$$

**Step 2** Check the solution.
$$x - 10 = 35$$
$$45 - 10 = 35$$
$$35 = 35$$

Both sides of the equation are equal, so $x = 45$.

**Example 2** In the formula $a = bc$, find the value of $c$ if $a = 20$ and $b = 2$.

**Step 1** Rearrange the formula so the unknown value is by itself on one side of the equation by dividing both sides by $b$.
$$a = bc$$
$$\frac{a}{b} = \frac{bc}{b}$$
$$\frac{a}{b} = c$$

**Step 2** Replace the variables $a$ and $b$ with the values that are given.
$$\frac{a}{b} = c$$
$$\frac{20}{2} = c$$
$$10 = c$$

**Step 3** Check the solution.
$$a = bc$$
$$20 = 2 \times 10$$
$$20 = 20$$

Both sides of the equation are equal, so $c = 10$ is the solution when $a = 20$ and $b = 2$.

**Practice Problem** In the formula $h = gd$, find the value of $d$ if $g = 12.3$ and $h = 17.4$.

## Use Statistics

The branch of mathematics that deals with collecting, analyzing, and presenting data is statistics. In statistics, there are three common ways to summarize data with a single number—the mean, the median, and the mode.

The **mean** of a set of data is the arithmetic average. It is found by adding the numbers in the data set and dividing by the number of items in the set.

The **median** is the middle number in a set of data when the data are arranged in numerical order. If there were an even number of data points, the median would be the mean of the two middle numbers.

The **mode** of a set of data is the number or item that appears most often.

Another number that often is used to describe a set of data is the range. The **range** is the difference between the largest number and the smallest number in a set of data.

A **frequency table** shows how many times each piece of data occurs, usually in a survey. **Table 2** below shows the results of a student survey on favorite color.

| Table 2 Student Color Choice | | |
|---|---|---|
| **Color** | **Tally** | **Frequency** |
| red | \|\|\|\| | 4 |
| blue | \|\|\|\| | 5 |
| black | \|\| | 2 |
| green | \|\|\| | 3 |
| purple | \|\|\|\| \|\| | 7 |
| yellow | \|\|\|\| \| | 6 |

Based on the frequency table data, which color is the favorite?

**Example** The speeds (in m/s) for a race car during five different time trials are 39, 37, 44, 36, and 44.

**To find the mean:**

**Step 1** Find the sum of the numbers.
$$39 + 37 + 44 + 36 + 44 = 200$$

**Step 2** Divide the sum by the number of items, which is 5.
$$200 \div 5 = 40$$

The mean is 40 m/s.

**To find the median:**

**Step 1** Arrange the measures from least to greatest.
36, 37, 39, 44, 44

**Step 2** Determine the middle measure.
36, 37, <u>39</u>, 44, 44

The median is 39 m/s.

**To find the mode:**

**Step 1** Group the numbers that are the same together.
44, 44, 36, 37, 39

**Step 2** Determine the number that occurs most in the set.
<u>44, 44</u>, 36, 37, 39

The mode is 44 m/s.

**To find the range:**

**Step 1** Arrange the measures from greatest to least.
44, 44, 39, 37, 36

**Step 2** Determine the greatest and least measures in the set.
<u>44</u>, 44, 39, 37, <u>36</u>

**Step 3** Find the difference between the greatest and least measures.
$$44 - 36 = 8$$

The range is 8 m/s.

**Practice Problem** Find the mean, median, mode, and range for the data set 8, 4, 12, 8, 11, 14, 16.

## Use Geometry

The branch of mathematics that deals with the measurement, properties, and relationships of points, lines, angles, surfaces, and solids is called geometry.

**Perimeter**  The **perimeter** ($P$) is the distance around a geometric figure. To find the perimeter of a rectangle, add the length and width and multiply that sum by two, or $2(l + w)$. To find perimeters of irregular figures, add the length of the sides.

**Example 1**  Find the perimeter of a rectangle that is 3 m long and 5 m wide.

**Step 1**  You know that the perimeter is 2 times the sum of the width and length.
$$P = 2(3 \text{ m} + 5 \text{ m})$$

**Step 2**  Find the sum of the width and length.
$$P = 2(8 \text{ m})$$

**Step 3**  Multiply by 2.
$$P = 16 \text{ m}$$

The perimeter is 16 m.

**Example 2**  Find the perimeter of a shape with sides measuring 2 cm, 5 cm, 6 cm, 3 cm.

**Step 1**  You know that the perimeter is the sum of all the sides.
$$P = 2 + 5 + 6 + 3$$

**Step 2**  Find the sum of the sides.
$$P = 2 + 5 + 6 + 3$$
$$P = 16$$

The perimeter is 16 cm.

**Practice Problem**  Find the perimeter of a rectangle with a length of 18 m and a width of 7 m.

**Practice Problem**  Find the perimeter of a triangle measuring 1.6 cm by 2.4 cm by 2.4 cm.

**Area of a Rectangle**  The **area** ($A$) is the number of square units needed to cover a surface. To find the area of a rectangle, multiply the length times the width, or $l \times w$. When finding area, the units also are multiplied. Area is given in square units.

**Example**  Find the area of a rectangle with a length of 1 cm and a width of 10 cm.

**Step 1**  You know that the area is the length multiplied by the width.
$$A = (1 \text{ cm} \times 10 \text{ cm})$$

**Step 2**  Multiply the length by the width. Also multiply the units.
$$A = 10 \text{ cm}^2$$

The area is 10 cm$^2$.

**Practice Problem**  Find the area of a square whose sides measure 4 m.

**Area of a Triangle**  To find the area of a triangle, use the formula:

$$A = \frac{1}{2}(\text{base} \times \text{height})$$

The base of a triangle can be any of its sides. The height is the perpendicular distance from a base to the opposite endpoint, or vertex.

**Example**  Find the area of a triangle with a base of 18 m and a height of 7 m.

**Step 1**  You know that the area is $\frac{1}{2}$ the base times the height.
$$A = \frac{1}{2}(18 \text{ m} \times 7 \text{ m})$$

**Step 2**  Multiply $\frac{1}{2}$ by the product of $18 \times 7$. Multiply the units.
$$A = \frac{1}{2}(126 \text{ m}^2)$$
$$A = 63 \text{ m}^2$$

The area is 63 m$^2$.

**Practice Problem**  Find the area of a triangle with a base of 27 cm and a height of 17 cm.

**Circumference of a Circle** The **diameter** ($d$) of a circle is the distance across the circle through its center, and the **radius** ($r$) is the distance from the center to any point on the circle. The radius is half of the diameter. The distance around the circle is called the **circumference** ($C$). The formula for finding the circumference is:

$$C = 2\pi r \ \text{ or } \ C = \pi d$$

The circumference divided by the diameter is always equal to 3.1415926... This nonterminating and nonrepeating number is represented by the Greek letter $\pi$ (pi). An approximation often used for $\pi$ is 3.14.

**Example 1** Find the circumference of a circle with a radius of 3 m.

**Step 1** You know the formula for the circumference is 2 times the radius times $\pi$.
$$C = 2\pi(3)$$

**Step 2** Multiply 2 times the radius.
$$C = 6\pi$$

**Step 3** Multiply by $\pi$.
$$C \approx 19 \text{ m}$$

The circumference is about 19 m.

**Example 2** Find the circumference of a circle with a diameter of 24.0 cm.

**Step 1** You know the formula for the circumference is the diameter times $\pi$.
$$C = \pi(24.0)$$

**Step 2** Multiply the diameter by $\pi$.
$$C \approx 75.4 \text{ cm}$$

The circumference is about 75.4 cm.

**Practice Problem** Find the circumference of a circle with a radius of 19 cm.

**Area of a Circle** The formula for the area of a circle is:
$$A = \pi r^2$$

**Example 1** Find the area of a circle with a radius of 4.0 cm.

**Step 1** $A = \pi(4.0)^2$

**Step 2** Find the square of the radius.
$$A = 16\pi$$

**Step 3** Multiply the square of the radius by $\pi$.
$$A \approx 50 \text{ cm}^2$$

The area of the circle is about 50 cm$^2$.

**Example 2** Find the area of a circle with a radius of 225 m.

**Step 1** $A = \pi(225)^2$

**Step 2** Find the square of the radius.
$$A = 50625\pi$$

**Step 3** Multiply the square of the radius by $\pi$.
$$A \approx 159043.1$$

The area of the circle is about 159043.1 m$^2$.

**Example 3** Find the area of a circle whose diameter is 20.0 mm.

**Step 1** You know the formula for the area of a circle is the square of the radius times $\pi$, and that the radius is half of the diameter.
$$A = \pi\left(\frac{20.0}{2}\right)^2$$

**Step 2** Find the radius.
$$A = \pi(10.0)^2$$

**Step 3** Find the square of the radius.
$$A = 100\pi$$

**Step 4** Multiply the square of the radius by $\pi$.
$$A \approx 314 \text{ mm}^2$$

The area is about 314 mm$^2$.

**Practice Problem** Find the area of a circle with a radius of 16 m.

**Volume** The measure of space occupied by a solid is the **volume** (*V*). To find the volume of a rectangular solid multiply the length times width times height, or $V = l \times w \times h$. It is measured in cubic units, such as cubic centimeters ($cm^3$).

**Example** Find the volume of a rectangular solid with a length of 2.0 m, a width of 4.0 m, and a height of 3.0 m.

**Step 1** You know the formula for volume is the length times the width times the height.

$$V = 2.0\,m \times 4.0\,m \times 3.0\,m$$

**Step 2** Multiply the length times the width times the height.

$$V = 24\,m^3$$

The volume is 24 m³.

**Practice Problem** Find the volume of a rectangular solid that is 8 m long, 4 m wide, and 4 m high.

To find the volume of other solids, multiply the area of the base times the height.

**Example 1** Find the volume of a solid that has a triangular base with a length of 8.0 m and a height of 7.0 m. The height of the entire solid is 15.0 m.

**Step 1** You know that the base is a triangle, and the area of a triangle is $\frac{1}{2}$ the base times the height, and the volume is the area of the base times the height.

$$V = \left[\frac{1}{2}(b \times h)\right] \times 15$$

**Step 2** Find the area of the base.

$$V = \left[\frac{1}{2}(8 \times 7)\right] \times 15$$
$$V = \left(\frac{1}{2} \times 56\right) \times 15$$

**Step 3** Multiply the area of the base by the height of the solid.

$$V = 28 \times 15$$
$$V = 420\,m^3$$

The volume is 420 m³.

**Example 2** Find the volume of a cylinder that has a base with a radius of 12.0 cm, and a height of 21.0 cm.

**Step 1** You know that the base is a circle, and the area of a circle is the square of the radius times $\pi$, and the volume is the area of the base times the height.

$$V = (\pi r^2) \times 21$$
$$V = (\pi 12^2) \times 21$$

**Step 2** Find the area of the base.

$$V = 144\pi \times 21$$
$$V = 452 \times 21$$

**Step 3** Multiply the area of the base by the height of the solid.

$$V \approx 9{,}500\,cm^3$$

The volume is about 9,500 cm³.

**Example 3** Find the volume of a cylinder that has a diameter of 15 mm and a height of 4.8 mm.

**Step 1** You know that the base is a circle with an area equal to the square of the radius times $\pi$. The radius is one-half the diameter. The volume is the area of the base times the height.

$$V = (\pi r^2) \times 4.8$$
$$V = \left[\pi\left(\frac{1}{2} \times 15\right)^2\right] \times 4.8$$
$$V = (\pi 7.5^2) \times 4.8$$

**Step 2** Find the area of the base.

$$V = 56.25\pi \times 4.8$$
$$V \approx 176.71 \times 4.8$$

**Step 3** Multiply the area of the base by the height of the solid.

$$V \approx 848.2$$

The volume is about 848.2 mm³.

**Practice Problem** Find the volume of a cylinder with a diameter of 7 cm in the base and a height of 16 cm.

# Science Applications

## Measure in SI

The metric system of measurement was developed in 1795. A modern form of the metric system, called the International System (SI), was adopted in 1960 and provides the standard measurements that all scientists around the world can understand.

The SI system is convenient because unit sizes vary by powers of 10. Prefixes are used to name units. Look at **Table 3** for some common SI prefixes and their meanings.

| Table 3 Common SI Prefixes | | | |
|---|---|---|---|
| **Prefix** | **Symbol** | **Meaning** | |
| *kilo-* | k | 1,000 | thousand |
| *hecto-* | h | 100 | hundred |
| *deka-* | da | 10 | ten |
| *deci-* | d | 0.1 | tenth |
| *centi-* | c | 0.01 | hundredth |
| *milli-* | m | 0.001 | thousandth |

**Example** How many grams equal one kilogram?

**Step 1** Find the prefix *kilo-* in **Table 3.**

**Step 2** Using **Table 3,** determine the meaning of *kilo-*. According to the table, it means 1,000. When the prefix *kilo-* is added to a unit, it means that there are 1,000 of the units in a "kilounit."

**Step 3** Apply the prefix to the units in the question. The units in the question are grams. There are 1,000 grams in a kilogram.

**Practice Problem** Is a milligram larger or smaller than a gram? How many of the smaller units equal one larger unit? What fraction of the larger unit does one smaller unit represent?

## Dimensional Analysis

**Convert SI Units** In science, quantities such as length, mass, and time sometimes are measured using different units. A process called dimensional analysis can be used to change one unit of measure to another. This process involves multiplying your starting quantity and units by one or more conversion factors. A conversion factor is a ratio equal to one and can be made from any two equal quantities with different units. If 1,000 mL equal 1 L then two ratios can be made.

$$\frac{1,000 \text{ mL}}{1 \text{ L}} = \frac{1 \text{ L}}{1,000 \text{ mL}} = 1$$

One can convert between units in the SI system by using the equivalents in **Table 3** to make conversion factors.

**Example 1** How many cm are in 4 m?

**Step 1** Write conversion factors for the units given. From **Table 3,** you know that 100 cm = 1 m. The conversion factors are

$$\frac{100 \text{ cm}}{1 \text{ m}} \quad and \quad \frac{1 \text{ m}}{100 \text{ cm}}$$

**Step 2** Decide which conversion factor to use. Select the factor that has the units you are converting from (m) in the denominator and the units you are converting to (cm) in the numerator.

$$\frac{100 \text{ cm}}{1 \text{ m}}$$

**Step 3** Multiply the starting quantity and units by the conversion factor. Cancel the starting units with the units in the denominator. There are 400 cm in 4 m.

$$4 \text{ m} \times \frac{100 \text{ cm}}{1 \text{ m}} = 400 \text{ cm}$$

**Practice Problem** How many milligrams are in one kilogram? (Hint: You will need to use two conversion factors from **Table 3.**)

# Math Skill Handbook

## Table 4 Unit System Equivalents

| Type of Measurement | Equivalent |
|---|---|
| Length | 1 in = 2.54 cm |
| | 1 yd = 0.91 m |
| | 1 mi = 1.61 km |
| Mass and Weight* | 1 oz = 28.35 g |
| | 1 lb = 0.45 kg |
| | 1 ton (short) = 0.91 tonnes (metric tons) |
| | 1 lb = 4.45 N |
| Volume | $1\ in^3 = 16.39\ cm^3$ |
| | 1 qt = 0.95 L |
| | 1 gal = 3.78 L |
| Area | $1\ in^2 = 6.45\ cm^2$ |
| | $1\ yd^2 = 0.83\ m^2$ |
| | $1\ mi^2 = 2.59\ km^2$ |
| | 1 acre = 0.40 hectares |
| Temperature | $°C = \dfrac{(°F - 32)}{1.8}$ |
| | $K = °C + 273$ |

*Weight is measured in standard Earth gravity.

**Convert Between Unit Systems  Table 4** gives a list of equivalents that can be used to convert between English and SI units.

**Example**  If a meterstick has a length of 100 cm, how long is the meterstick in inches?

**Step 1**  Write the conversion factors for the units given. From **Table 4,** 1 in = 2.54 cm.

$$\frac{1\ in}{2.54\ cm} \quad and \quad \frac{2.54\ cm}{1\ in}$$

**Step 2**  Determine which conversion factor to use. You are converting from cm to in. Use the conversion factor with cm on the bottom.

$$\frac{1\ in}{2.54\ cm}$$

**Step 3**  Multiply the starting quantity and units by the conversion factor. Cancel the starting units with the units in the denominator. Round your answer to the nearest tenth.

$$100\ \cancel{cm} \times \frac{1\ in}{2.54\ \cancel{cm}} = 39.37\ in$$

The meterstick is about 39.4 in long.

**Practice Problem**  A book has a mass of 5 lbs. What is the mass of the book in kg?

**Practice Problem**  Use the equivalent for in and cm (1 in = 2.54 cm) to show how $1\ in^3 = 16.39\ cm^3$.

## Precision and Significant Digits

When you make a measurement, the value you record depends on the precision of the measuring instrument. This precision is represented by the number of significant digits recorded in the measurement. When counting the number of significant digits, all digits are counted except zeros at the end of a number with no decimal point such as 2,050, and zeros at the beginning of a decimal such as 0.03020. When adding or subtracting numbers with different precision, round the answer to the smallest number of decimal places of any number in the sum or difference. When multiplying or dividing, the answer is rounded to the smallest number of significant digits of any number being multiplied or divided.

**Example** The lengths 5.28 and 5.2 are measured in meters. Find the sum of these lengths and record your answer using the correct number of significant digits.

**Step 1** Find the sum.

| 5.28 m | 2 digits after the decimal |
|---|---|
| + 5.2 m | 1 digit after the decimal |
| 10.48 m | |

**Step 2** Round to one digit after the decimal because the least number of digits after the decimal of the numbers being added is 1.

The sum is 10.5 m.

**Practice Problem** How many significant digits are in the measurement 7,071,301 m? How many significant digits are in the measurement 0.003010 g?

**Practice Problem** Multiply 5.28 and 5.2 using the rule for multiplying and dividing. Record the answer using the correct number of significant digits.

## Scientific Notation

Many times numbers used in science are very small or very large. Because these numbers are difficult to work with scientists use scientific notation. To write numbers in scientific notation, move the decimal point until only one non-zero digit remains on the left. Then count the number of places you moved the decimal point and use that number as a power of ten. For example, the average distance from the Sun to Mars is 227,800,000,000 m. In scientific notation, this distance is $2.278 \times 10^{11}$ m. Because you moved the decimal point to the left, the number is a positive power of ten.

The mass of an electron is about 0.000 000 000 000 000 000 000 000 000 000 911 kg. Expressed in scientific notation, this mass is $9.11 \times 10^{-31}$ kg. Because the decimal point was moved to the right, the number is a negative power of ten.

**Example** Earth is 149,600,000 km from the Sun. Express this in scientific notation.

**Step 1** Move the decimal point until one non-zero digit remains on the left.
1.496 000 00

**Step 2** Count the number of decimal places you have moved. In this case, eight.

**Step 3** Show that number as a power of ten, $10^8$.

Earth is $1.496 \times 10^8$ km from the Sun.

**Practice Problem** How many significant digits are in 149,600,000 km? How many significant digits are in $1.496 \times 10^8$ km?

**Practice Problem** Parts used in a high performance car must be measured to $7 \times 10^{-6}$ m. Express this number as a decimal.

**Practice Problem** A CD is spinning at 539 revolutions per minute. Express this number in scientific notation.

### Make and Use Graphs

Data in tables can be displayed in a graph—a visual representation of data. Common graph types include line graphs, bar graphs, and circle graphs.

**Line Graph** A line graph shows a relationship between two variables that change continuously. The independent variable is changed and is plotted on the *x*-axis. The dependent variable is observed, and is plotted on the *y*-axis.

**Example** Draw a line graph of the data below from a cyclist in a long-distance race.

| Table 5  Bicycle Race Data | |
|---|---|
| **Time (h)** | **Distance (km)** |
| 0 | 0 |
| 1 | 8 |
| 2 | 16 |
| 3 | 24 |
| 4 | 32 |
| 5 | 40 |

**Step 1** Determine the *x*-axis and *y*-axis variables. Time varies independently of distance and is plotted on the *x*-axis. Distance is dependent on time and is plotted on the *y*-axis.

**Step 2** Determine the scale of each axis. The *x*-axis data ranges from 0 to 5. The *y*-axis data ranges from 0 to 50.

**Step 3** Using graph paper, draw and label the axes. Include units in the labels.

**Step 4** Draw a point at the intersection of the time value on the *x*-axis and corresponding distance value on the *y*-axis. Connect the points and label the graph with a title, as shown in **Figure 20.**

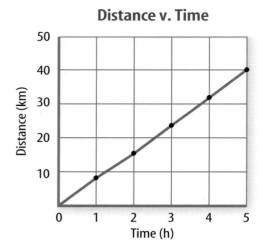

**Distance v. Time**

**Figure 23** This line graph shows the relationship between distance and time during a bicycle ride.

**Practice Problem** A puppy's shoulder height is measured during the first year of her life. The following measurements were collected: (3 mo, 52 cm), (6 mo, 72 cm), (9 mo, 83 cm), (12 mo, 86 cm). Graph this data.

**Find a Slope** The slope of a straight line is the ratio of the vertical change, rise, to the horizontal change, run.

$$\text{Slope} = \frac{\text{vertical change (rise)}}{\text{horizontal change (run)}} = \frac{\text{change in } y}{\text{change in } x}$$

**Example** Find the slope of the graph in **Figure 23.**

**Step 1** You know that the slope is the change in *y* divided by the change in *x*.
$$\text{Slope} = \frac{\text{change in } y}{\text{change in } x}$$

**Step 2** Determine the data points you will be using. For a straight line, choose the two sets of points that are the farthest apart.
$$\text{Slope} = \frac{(40-0) \text{ km}}{(5-0) \text{ h}}$$

**Step 3** Find the change in *y* and *x*.
$$\text{Slope} = \frac{40 \text{ km}}{5 \text{ h}}$$

**Step 4** Divide the change in *y* by the change in *x*.
$$\text{Slope} = \frac{8 \text{ km}}{\text{h}}$$

The slope of the graph is 8 km/h.

**Bar Graph** To compare data that does not change continuously you might choose a bar graph. A bar graph uses bars to show the relationships between variables. The *x*-axis variable is divided into parts. The parts can be numbers such as years, or a category such as a type of animal. The *y*-axis is a number and increases continuously along the axis.

**Example** A recycling center collects 4.0 kg of aluminum on Monday, 1.0 kg on Wednesday, and 2.0 kg on Friday. Create a bar graph of this data.

**Step 1** Select the *x*-axis and *y*-axis variables. The measured numbers (the masses of aluminum) should be placed on the *y*-axis. The variable divided into parts (collection days) is placed on the *x*-axis.

**Step 2** Create a graph grid like you would for a line graph. Include labels and units.

**Step 3** For each measured number, draw a vertical bar above the *x*-axis value up to the *y*-axis value. For the first data point, draw a vertical bar above Monday up to 4.0 kg.

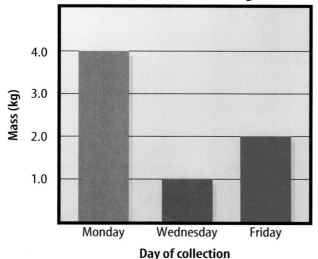

**Aluminum Collected During Week**

Mass (kg) / Day of collection

**Practice Problem** Draw a bar graph of the gases in air: 78% nitrogen, 21% oxygen, 1% other gases.

**Circle Graph** To display data as parts of a whole, you might use a circle graph. A circle graph is a circle divided into sections that represent the relative size of each piece of data. The entire circle represents 100%, half represents 50%, and so on.

**Example** Air is made up of 78% nitrogen, 21% oxygen, and 1% other gases. Display the composition of air in a circle graph.

**Step 1** Multiply each percent by 360° and divide by 100 to find the angle of each section in the circle.

$$78\% \times \frac{360°}{100} = 280.8°$$

$$21\% \times \frac{360°}{100} = 75.6°$$

$$1\% \times \frac{360°}{100} = 3.6°$$

**Step 2** Use a compass to draw a circle and to mark the center of the circle. Draw a straight line from the center to the edge of the circle.

**Step 3** Use a protractor and the angles you calculated to divide the circle into parts. Place the center of the protractor over the center of the circle and line the base of the protractor over the straight line.

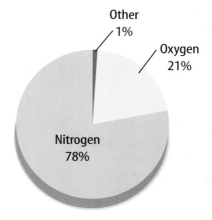

Other 1%
Oxygen 21%
Nitrogen 78%

**Practice Problem** Draw a circle graph to represent the amount of aluminum collected during the week shown in the bar graph to the left.

# Minerals

| Minerals | | | | | |
|---|---|---|---|---|---|
| Mineral (formula) | Color | Streak | Hardness | Breakage Pattern | Uses and Other Properties |
| **Graphite** (C) | black to gray | black to gray | 1–1.5 | basal cleavage (scales) | pencil lead, lubricants for locks, rods to control some small nuclear reactions, battery poles |
| **Galena** (PbS) | gray | gray to black | 2.5 | cubic cleavage perfect | source of lead, used for pipes, shields for X rays, fishing equipment sinkers |
| **Hematite** ($Fe_2O_3$) | black or reddish-brown | reddish-brown | 5.5–6.5 | irregular fracture | source of iron; converted to pig iron, made into steel |
| **Magnetite** ($Fe_3O_4$) | black | black | 6 | conchoidal fracture | source of iron, attracts a magnet |
| **Pyrite** ($FeS_2$) | light, brassy, yellow | greenish-black | 6–6.5 | uneven fracture | fool's gold |
| **Talc** ($Mg_3 Si_4 O_{10} (OH)_2$) | white, greenish | white | 1 | cleavage in one direction | used for talcum powder, sculptures, paper, and tabletops |
| **Gypsum** ($CaSO_4 \cdot 2H_2O$) | colorless, gray, white, brown | white | 2 | basal cleavage | used in plaster of paris and dry wall for building construction |
| **Sphalerite** (ZnS) | brown, reddish-brown, greenish | light to dark brown | 3.5–4 | cleavage in six directions | main ore of zinc; used in paints, dyes, and medicine |
| **Muscovite** ($KAl_3Si_3 O_{10}(OH)_2$) | white, light gray, yellow, rose, green | colorless | 2–2.5 | basal cleavage | occurs in large, flexible plates; used as an insulator in electrical equipment, lubricant |
| **Biotite** ($K(Mg,Fe)_3 (AlSi_3O_{10}) (OH)_2$) | black to dark brown | colorless | 2.5–3 | basal cleavage | occurs in large, flexible plates |
| **Halite** (NaCl) | colorless, red, white, blue | colorless | 2.5 | cubic cleavage | salt; soluble in water; a preservative |

# Minerals

| Minerals | | | | | |
|---|---|---|---|---|---|
| Mineral (formula) | Color | Streak | Hardness | Breakage Pattern | Uses and Other Properties |
| **Calcite** ($CaCO_3$) | colorless, white, pale blue | colorless, white | 3 | cleavage in three directions | fizzes when HCl is added; used in cements and other building materials |
| **Dolomite** ($CaMg(CO_3)_2$) | colorless, white, pink, green, gray, black | white | 3.5–4 | cleavage in three directions | concrete and cement; used as an ornamental building stone |
| **Fluorite** ($CaF_2$) | colorless, white, blue, green, red, yellow, purple | colorless | 4 | cleavage in four directions | used in the manufacture of optical equipment; glows under ultraviolet light |
| **Hornblende** ($(CaNa)_{2-3}(Mg,Al,Fe)_5-(Al,Si)_2 Si_6O_{22}(OH)_2$) | green to black | gray to white | 5–6 | cleavage in two directions | will transmit light on thin edges; 6-sided cross section |
| **Feldspar** ($KAlSi_3O_8$) ($NaAl Si_3O_8$), ($CaAl_2Si_2 O_8$) | colorless, white to gray, green | colorless | 6 | two cleavage planes meet at 90° angle | used in the manufacture of ceramics |
| **Augite** ($(Ca,Na)(Mg,Fe,Al)(Al,Si)_2 O_6$) | black | colorless | 6 | cleavage in two directions | square or 8-sided cross section |
| **Olivine** ($(Mg,Fe)_2 SiO_4$) | olive, green | none | 6.5–7 | conchoidal fracture | gemstones, refractory sand |
| **Quartz** ($SiO_2$) | colorless, various colors | none | 7 | conchoidal fracture | used in glass manufacture, electronic equipment, radios, computers, watches, gemstones |

# Rocks

| Rocks | | |
|---|---|---|
| **Rock Type** | **Rock Name** | **Characteristics** |
| **Igneous** (intrusive) | Granite | Large mineral grains of quartz, feldspar, hornblende, and mica. Usually light in color. |
| | Diorite | Large mineral grains of feldspar, hornblende, and mica. Less quartz than granite. Intermediate in color. |
| | Gabbro | Large mineral grains of feldspar, augite, and olivine. No quartz. Dark in color. |
| **Igneous** (extrusive) | Rhyolite | Small mineral grains of quartz, feldspar, hornblende, and mica, or no visible grains. Light in color. |
| | Andesite | Small mineral grains of feldspar, hornblende, and mica or no visible grains. Intermediate in color. |
| | Basalt | Small mineral grains of feldspar, augite, and possibly olivine or no visible grains. No quartz. Dark in color. |
| | Obsidian | Glassy texture. No visible grains. Volcanic glass. Fracture looks like broken glass. |
| | Pumice | Frothy texture. Floats in water. Usually light in color. |
| **Sedimentary** (detrital) | Conglomerate | Coarse grained. Gravel or pebble-size grains. |
| | Sandstone | Sand-sized grains 1/16 to 2 mm. |
| | Siltstone | Grains are smaller than sand but larger than clay. |
| | Shale | Smallest grains. Often dark in color. Usually platy. |
| **Sedimentary** (chemical or organic) | Limestone | Major mineral is calcite. Usually forms in oceans and lakes. Often contains fossils. |
| | Coal | Forms in swampy areas. Compacted layers of organic material, mainly plant remains. |
| **Sedimentary** (chemical) | Rock Salt | Commonly forms by the evaporation of seawater. |
| **Metamorphic** (foliated) | Gneiss | Banding due to alternate layers of different minerals, of different colors. Parent rock often is granite. |
| | Schist | Parallel arrangement of sheetlike minerals, mainly micas. Forms from different parent rocks. |
| | Phyllite | Shiny or silky appearance. May look wrinkled. Common parent rocks are shale and slate. |
| | Slate | Harder, denser, and shinier than shale. Common parent rock is shale. |
| **Metamorphic** (nonfoliated) | Marble | Calcite or dolomite. Common parent rock is limestone. |
| | Soapstone | Mainly of talc. Soft with greasy feel. |
| | Quartzite | Hard with interlocking quartz crystals. Common parent rock is sandstone. |

# Topographic Map Symbols

## Topographic Map Symbols

| | | | |
|---|---|---|---|
| Primary highway, hard surface | | Index contour |
| Secondary highway, hard surface | | Supplementary contour |
| Light-duty road, hard or improved surface | | Intermediate contour |
| Unimproved road | | Depression contours |
| Railroad: single track | | |
| Railroad: multiple track | | Boundaries: national |
| Railroads in juxtaposition | | State |
| | | County, parish, municipal |
| Buildings | | Civil township, precinct, town, barrio |
| Schools, church, and cemetery | | Incorporated city, village, town, hamlet |
| Buildings (barn, warehouse, etc.) | | Reservation, national or state |
| Wells other than water (labeled as to type) | | Small park, cemetery, airport, etc. |
| Tanks: oil, water, etc. (labeled only if water) | | Land grant |
| Located or landmark object; windmill | | Township or range line, U.S. land survey |
| Open pit, mine, or quarry; prospect | | Township or range line, approximate location |
| Marsh (swamp) | | |
| Wooded marsh | | Perennial streams |
| Woods or brushwood | | Elevated aqueduct |
| Vineyard | | Water well and spring |
| Land subject to controlled inundation | | Small rapids |
| Submerged marsh | | Large rapids |
| Mangrove | | Intermittent lake |
| Orchard | | Intermittent stream |
| Scrub | | Aqueduct tunnel |
| Urban area | | Glacier |
| | | Small falls |
| x7369 Spot elevation | | Large falls |
| 670 Water elevation | | Dry lake bed |

# Weather Map Symbols

## Sample Station Model

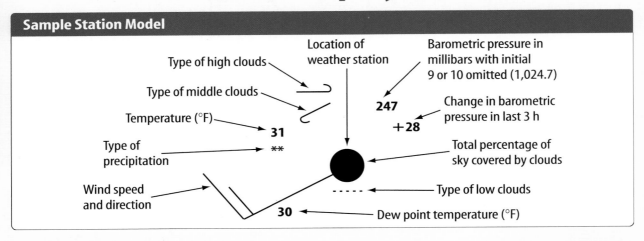

Type of high clouds

Type of middle clouds

Temperature (°F)  31

Type of precipitation  **

Wind speed and direction

Location of weather station

Barometric pressure in millibars with initial 9 or 10 omitted (1,024.7)

247

+28  Change in barometric pressure in last 3 h

Total percentage of sky covered by clouds

- - - - -  Type of low clouds

30  Dew point temperature (°F)

## Sample Plotted Report at Each Station

| Precipitation | | Wind Speed and Direction | | Sky Coverage | | Some Types of High Clouds | |
|---|---|---|---|---|---|---|---|
| ☰ | Fog | ○ | 0 calm | ○ | No cover | ⌐⌐ | Scattered cirrus |
| ★ | Snow | / | 1–2 knots | ◐ | 1/10 or less | ⌐⌐ | Dense cirrus in patches |
| ● | Rain | ⌐ | 3–7 knots | ◓ | 2/10 to 3/10 | ⌐⌐ | Veil of cirrus covering entire sky |
| ⊼ | Thunderstorm | ⌐ | 8–12 knots | ◑ | 4/10 | ⌐⌐ | Cirrus not covering entire sky |
| , | Drizzle | ⌐ | 13–17 knots | ◑ | — | | |
| ▽ | Showers | ⌐ | 18–22 knots | ◕ | 6/10 | | |
| | | ⌐ | 23–27 knots | ◕ | 7/10 | | |
| | | ⌐ | 48–52 knots | ◑ | Overcast with openings | | |
| | | 1 knot = 1.852 km/h | | ● | Completely overcast | | |

| Some Types of Middle Clouds | | Some Types of Low Clouds | | Fronts and Pressure Systems | |
|---|---|---|---|---|---|
| ∠ | Thin altostratus layer | ◠ | Cumulus of fair weather | (H) or High (L) or Low | Center of high- or low-pressure system |
| ⫽ | Thick altostratus layer | ◡ | Stratocumulus | ▲▲▲▲ | Cold front |
| ⌒ | Thin altostratus in patches | - - - - - | Fractocumulus of bad weather | ●●●● | Warm front |
| ⌒ | Thin altostratus in bands | — | Stratus of fair weather | ▲●▲▲ | Occluded front |
| | | | | ●▲●▲ | Stationary front |

# Use and Care of a Microscope

**Eyepiece** Contains magnifying lenses you look through.

**Arm** Supports the body tube.

**Low-power objective** Contains the lens with the lowest power magnification.

**Stage clips** Hold the microscope slide in place.

**Coarse adjustment** Focuses the image under low power.

**Fine adjustment** Sharpens the image under high magnification.

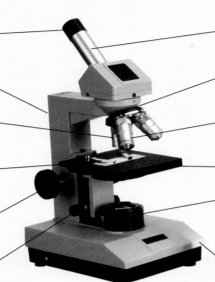

**Body tube** Connects the eyepiece to the revolving nosepiece.

**Revolving nosepiece** Holds and turns the objectives into viewing position.

**High-power objective** Contains the lens with the highest magnification.

**Stage** Supports the microscope slide.

**Light source** Provides light that passes upward through the diaphragm, the specimen, and the lenses.

**Base** Provides support for the microscope.

## Caring for a Microscope

1. Always carry the microscope holding the arm with one hand and supporting the base with the other hand.

2. Don't touch the lenses with your fingers.

3. The coarse adjustment knob is used only when looking through the lowest-power objective lens. The fine adjustment knob is used when the high-power objective is in place.

4. Cover the microscope when you store it.

## Using a Microscope

1. Place the microscope on a flat surface that is clear of objects. The arm should be toward you.

2. Look through the eyepiece. Adjust the diaphragm so light comes through the opening in the stage.

3. Place a slide on the stage so the specimen is in the field of view. Hold it firmly in place by using the stage clips.

4. Always focus with the coarse adjustment and the low-power objective lens first. After the object is in focus on low power, turn the nosepiece until the high-power objective is in place. Use ONLY the fine adjustment to focus with the high-power objective lens.

## Making a Wet-Mount Slide

1. Carefully place the item you want to look at in the center of a clean, glass slide. Make sure the sample is thin enough for light to pass through.

2. Use a dropper to place one or two drops of water on the sample.

3. Hold a clean coverslip by the edges and place it at one edge of the water. Slowly lower the coverslip onto the water until it lies flat.

4. If you have too much water or a lot of air bubbles, touch the edge of a paper towel to the edge of the coverslip to draw off extra water and draw out unwanted air.

# PERIODIC TABLE OF THE ELEMENTS

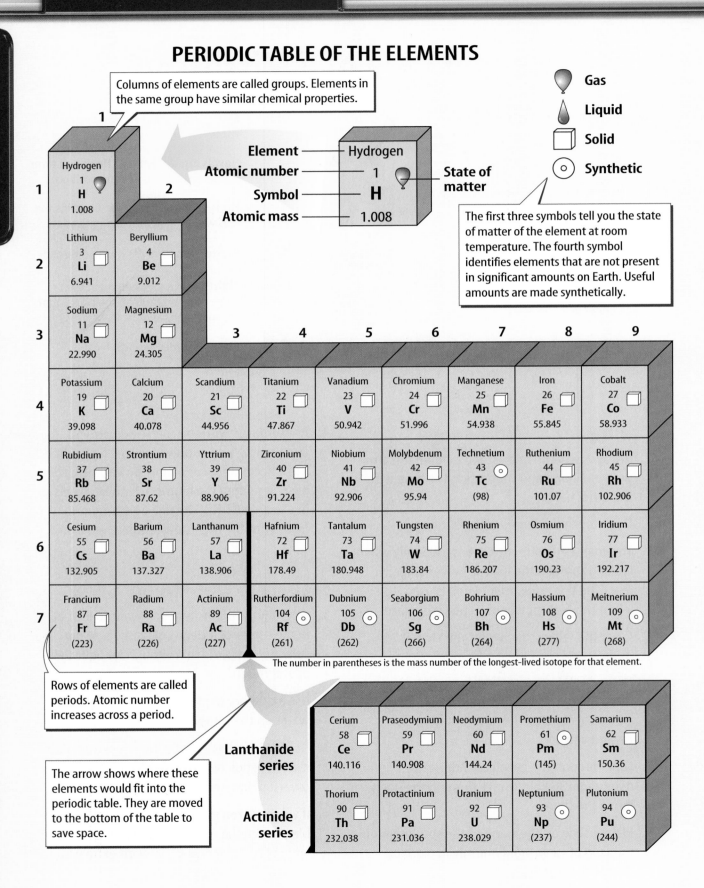

Columns of elements are called groups. Elements in the same group have similar chemical properties.

| | | | Gas |
|---|---|---|---|
| Element | Hydrogen | | Liquid |
| Atomic number | 1 | State of matter | Solid |
| Symbol | **H** | | Synthetic |
| Atomic mass | 1.008 | | |

The first three symbols tell you the state of matter of the element at room temperature. The fourth symbol identifies elements that are not present in significant amounts on Earth. Useful amounts are made synthetically.

Rows of elements are called periods. Atomic number increases across a period.

The arrow shows where these elements would fit into the periodic table. They are moved to the bottom of the table to save space.

The number in parentheses is the mass number of the longest-lived isotope for that element.

**Group 1**

| 1 | Hydrogen 1 **H** 1.008 |
| 2 | Lithium 3 **Li** 6.941 |
| 3 | Sodium 11 **Na** 22.990 |
| 4 | Potassium 19 **K** 39.098 |
| 5 | Rubidium 37 **Rb** 85.468 |
| 6 | Cesium 55 **Cs** 132.905 |
| 7 | Francium 87 **Fr** (223) |

**Group 2**

| Beryllium 4 **Be** 9.012 |
| Magnesium 12 **Mg** 24.305 |
| Calcium 20 **Ca** 40.078 |
| Strontium 38 **Sr** 87.62 |
| Barium 56 **Ba** 137.327 |
| Radium 88 **Ra** (226) |

| Group 3 | Group 4 | Group 5 | Group 6 | Group 7 | Group 8 | Group 9 |
|---|---|---|---|---|---|---|
| Scandium 21 **Sc** 44.956 | Titanium 22 **Ti** 47.867 | Vanadium 23 **V** 50.942 | Chromium 24 **Cr** 51.996 | Manganese 25 **Mn** 54.938 | Iron 26 **Fe** 55.845 | Cobalt 27 **Co** 58.933 |
| Yttrium 39 **Y** 88.906 | Zirconium 40 **Zr** 91.224 | Niobium 41 **Nb** 92.906 | Molybdenum 42 **Mo** 95.94 | Technetium 43 **Tc** (98) | Ruthenium 44 **Ru** 101.07 | Rhodium 45 **Rh** 102.906 |
| Lanthanum 57 **La** 138.906 | Hafnium 72 **Hf** 178.49 | Tantalum 73 **Ta** 180.948 | Tungsten 74 **W** 183.84 | Rhenium 75 **Re** 186.207 | Osmium 76 **Os** 190.23 | Iridium 77 **Ir** 192.217 |
| Actinium 89 **Ac** (227) | Rutherfordium 104 **Rf** (261) | Dubnium 105 **Db** (262) | Seaborgium 106 **Sg** (266) | Bohrium 107 **Bh** (264) | Hassium 108 **Hs** (277) | Meitnerium 109 **Mt** (268) |

**Lanthanide series**

| Cerium 58 **Ce** 140.116 | Praseodymium 59 **Pr** 140.908 | Neodymium 60 **Nd** 144.24 | Promethium 61 **Pm** (145) | Samarium 62 **Sm** 150.36 |

**Actinide series**

| Thorium 90 **Th** 232.038 | Protactinium 91 **Pa** 231.036 | Uranium 92 **U** 238.029 | Neptunium 93 **Np** (237) | Plutonium 94 **Pu** (244) |

Metal
Metalloid
Nonmetal

The color of an element's block tells you if the element is a metal, nonmetal, or metalloid.

**Science Online**
Visit glencoe.com for updates to the periodic table.

| 13 | 14 | 15 | 16 | 17 | 18 |
|---|---|---|---|---|---|
| | | | | | Helium 2 He 4.003 |
| Boron 5 B 10.811 | Carbon 6 C 12.011 | Nitrogen 7 N 14.007 | Oxygen 8 O 15.999 | Fluorine 9 F 18.998 | Neon 10 Ne 20.180 |
| Aluminum 13 Al 26.982 | Silicon 14 Si 28.086 | Phosphorus 15 P 30.974 | Sulfur 16 S 32.065 | Chlorine 17 Cl 35.453 | Argon 18 Ar 39.948 |

| 10 | 11 | 12 | | | | | | |
|---|---|---|---|---|---|---|---|---|
| Nickel 28 Ni 58.693 | Copper 29 Cu 63.546 | Zinc 30 Zn 65.409 | Gallium 31 Ga 69.723 | Germanium 32 Ge 72.64 | Arsenic 33 As 74.922 | Selenium 34 Se 78.96 | Bromine 35 Br 79.904 | Krypton 36 Kr 83.798 |
| Palladium 46 Pd 106.42 | Silver 47 Ag 107.868 | Cadmium 48 Cd 112.411 | Indium 49 In 114.818 | Tin 50 Sn 118.710 | Antimony 51 Sb 121.760 | Tellurium 52 Te 127.60 | Iodine 53 I 126.904 | Xenon 54 Xe 131.293 |
| Platinum 78 Pt 195.078 | Gold 79 Au 196.967 | Mercury 80 Hg 200.59 | Thallium 81 Tl 204.383 | Lead 82 Pb 207.2 | Bismuth 83 Bi 208.980 | Polonium 84 Po (209) | Astatine 85 At (210) | Radon 86 Rn (222) |
| Darmstadtium 110 Ds (281) | Roentgenium 111 Rg (272) | Ununbium * 112 Uub (285) | | Ununquadium * 114 Uuq (289) | | | | |

* The names and symbols for elements 112 and 114 are temporary. Final names will be selected when the elements' discoveries are verified.

| Europium 63 Eu 151.964 | Gadolinium 64 Gd 157.25 | Terbium 65 Tb 158.925 | Dysprosium 66 Dy 162.500 | Holmium 67 Ho 164.930 | Erbium 68 Er 167.259 | Thulium 69 Tm 168.934 | Ytterbium 70 Yb 173.04 | Lutetium 71 Lu 174.967 |
|---|---|---|---|---|---|---|---|---|
| Americium 95 Am (243) | Curium 96 Cm (247) | Berkelium 97 Bk (247) | Californium 98 Cf (251) | Einsteinium 99 Es (252) | Fermium 100 Fm (257) | Mendelevium 101 Md (258) | Nobelium 102 No (259) | Lawrencium 103 Lr (262) |

# Physical Science Reference Tables

## Standard Units

| Symbol | Name | Quantity |
|--------|------|----------|
| m | meter | length |
| kg | kilogram | mass |
| Pa | pascal | pressure |
| K | kelvin | temperature |
| mol | mole | amount of a substance |
| J | joule | energy, work, quantity of heat |
| s | second | time |
| C | coulomb | electric charge |
| V | volt | electric potential |
| A | ampere | electric current |
| $\Omega$ | ohm | resistance |

## Wavelengths of Light in a Vacuum

| | |
|--|--|
| Violet | $4.0 - 4.2 \times 10^{-7}$ m |
| Blue | $4.2 - 4.9 \times 10^{-7}$ m |
| Green | $4.9 - 5.7 \times 10^{-7}$ m |
| Yellow | $5.7 - 5.9 \times 10^{-7}$ m |
| Orange | $5.9 - 6.5 \times 10^{-7}$ m |
| Red | $6.5 - 7.0 \times 10^{-7}$ m |

## Physical Constants and Conversion Factors

| | | |
|--|--|--|
| Acceleration due to gravity | g | 9.8 m/s/s or m/s$^2$ |
| Avogadro's Number | $N_A$ | $6.02 \times 10^{23}$ particles per mole |
| Electron charge | e | $1.6 \times 10^{-19}$ C |
| Electron rest mass | $m_e$ | $9.11 \times 10^{-31}$ kg |
| Gravitation constant | G | $6.67 \times 10^{-11}$ N $\times$ m$^2$/kg$^2$ |
| Mass-energy relationship | | 1 u (amu) $= 9.3 \times 10^2$ MeV |
| Speed of light in a vacuum | c | $3.00 \times 10^8$ m/s |
| Speed of sound at STP | | 331 m/s |
| Standard Pressure | | 1 atmosphere |
| | | 101.3 kPa |
| | | 760 Torr or mmHg |
| | | 14.7 lb/in.$^2$ |

## The Index of Refraction for Common Substances
### ($\lambda = 5.9 \times 10^{-7}$ m)

| | |
|--|--|
| Air | 1.00 |
| Alcohol | 1.36 |
| Canada Balsam | 1.53 |
| Corn Oil | 1.47 |
| Diamond | 2.42 |
| Glass, Crown | 1.52 |
| Glass, Flint | 1.61 |
| Glycerol | 1.47 |
| Lucite | 1.50 |
| Quartz, Fused | 1.46 |
| Water | 1.33 |

## Heat Constants

| | Specific Heat (average) (kJ/kg $\times$ °C) (J/g $\times$ °C) | Melting Point (°C) | Boiling Point (°C) | Heat of Fusion (kJ/kg) (J/g) | Heat of Vaporization (kJ/kg) (J/g) |
|--|--|--|--|--|--|
| Alcohol (ethyl) | 2.43 (liq.) | $-117$ | 79 | 109 | 855 |
| Aluminum | 0.90 (sol.) | 660 | 2467 | 396 | 10500 |
| Ammonia | 4.71 (liq.) | $-78$ | $-33$ | 332 | 1370 |
| Copper | 0.39 (sol.) | 1083 | 2567 | 205 | 4790 |
| Iron | 0.45 (sol.) | 1535 | 2750 | 267 | 6290 |
| Lead | 0.13 (sol.) | 328 | 1740 | 25 | 866 |
| Mercury | 0.14 (liq.) | $-39$ | 357 | 11 | 295 |
| Platinum | 0.13 (sol.) | 1772 | 3827 | 101 | 229 |
| Silver | 0.24 (sol.) | 962 | 2212 | 105 | 2370 |
| Tungsten | 0.13 (sol.) | 3410 | 5660 | 192 | 4350 |
| Water (solid) | 2.05 (sol.) | 0 | – | 334 | – |
| Water (liquid) | 4.18 (liq.) | – | 100 | – | – |
| Water (vapor) | 2.01 (gas) | – | – | – | 2260 |
| Zinc | 0.39 (sol.) | 420 | 907 | 113 | 1770 |

## Standard Units

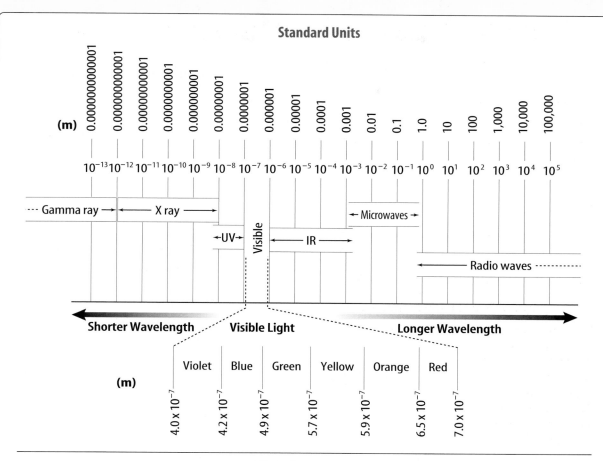

## Heat Constants

### Atomic number and chemical symbol

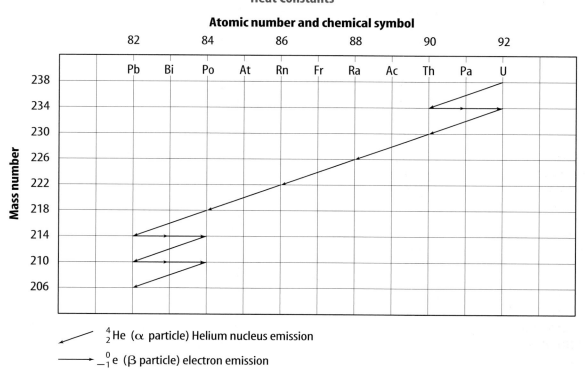

$^{4}_{2}$He ($\alpha$ particle) Helium nucleus emission

$^{0}_{-1}$e ($\beta$ particle) electron emission

# Diversity of Life: Classification of Living Organisms

**A** six-kingdom system of classification of organisms is used today. Two kingdoms—Kingdom Archaebacteria and Kingdom Eubacteria—contain organisms that do not have a nucleus and that lack membrane-bound structures in the cytoplasm of their cells. The members of the other four kingdoms have a cell or cells that contain a nucleus and structures in the cytoplasm, some of which are surrounded by membranes. These kingdoms are Kingdom Protista, Kingdom Fungi, Kingdom Plantae, and Kingdom Animalia.

## Kingdom Archaebacteria

one-celled; some absorb food from their surroundings; some are photosynthetic; some are chemosynthetic; many are found in extremely harsh environments including salt ponds, hot springs, swamps, and deep-sea hydrothermal vents

## Kingdom Eubacteria

one-celled; most absorb food from their surroundings; some are photosynthetic; some are chemosynthetic; many are parasites; many are round, spiral, or rod-shaped; some form colonies

## Kingdom Protista

**Phylum Euglenophyta** one-celled; photosynthetic or take in food; most have one flagellum; euglenoids

**Phylum Bacillariophyta** one-celled; photosynthetic; have unique double shells made of silica; diatoms

**Phylum Dinoflagellata** one-celled; photosynthetic; contain red pigments; have two flagella; dinoflagellates

**Phylum Chlorophyta** one-celled, many-celled, or colonies; photosynthetic; contain chlorophyll; live on land, in freshwater, or salt water; green algae

**Phylum Rhodophyta** most are many-celled; photosynthetic; contain red pigments; most live in deep, saltwater environments; red algae

**Phylum Phaeophyta** most are many-celled; photosynthetic; contain brown pigments; most live in saltwater environments; brown algae

**Phylum Rhizopoda** one-celled; take in food; are free-living or parasitic; move by means of pseudopods; amoebas

**Kingdom Eubacteria**
*Bacillus anthracis*

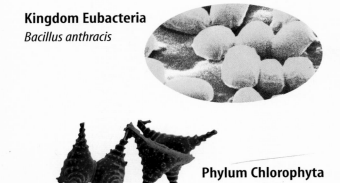

**Phylum Chlorophyta**
*Desmids*

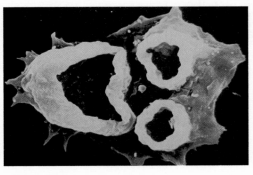

**Amoeba**

**Phylum Zoomastigina** one-celled; take in food; free-living or parasitic; have one or more flagella; zoomastigotes

**Phylum Ciliophora** one-celled; take in food; have large numbers of cilia; ciliates

**Phylum Sporozoa** one-celled; take in food; have no means of movement; are parasites in animals; sporozoans

**Phylum Myxomycota**
Slime mold

**Phylum Oomycota**
*Phytophthora infestans*

**Phyla Myxomycota and Acrasiomycota** one- or many-celled; absorb food; change form during life cycle; cellular and plasmodial slime molds

**Phylum Oomycota** many-celled; are either parasites or decomposers; live in freshwater or salt water; water molds, rusts and downy mildews

## Kingdom Fungi

**Phylum Zygomycota** many-celled; absorb food; spores are produced in sporangia; zygote fungi; bread mold

**Phylum Ascomycota** one- and many-celled; absorb food; spores produced in asci; sac fungi; yeast

**Phylum Basidiomycota** many-celled; absorb food; spores produced in basidia; club fungi; mushrooms

**Phylum Deuteromycota** members with unknown reproductive structures; imperfect fungi; *Penicillium*

**Phylum Mycophycota** organisms formed by symbiotic relationship between an ascomycote or a basidiomycote and green alga or cyanobacterium; lichens

**Lichens**

## Kingdom Plantae

**Divisions Bryophyta** (mosses), **Anthocerophyta** (hornworts), **Hepaticophyta** (liverworts), **Psilophyta** (whisk ferns) many-celled nonvascular plants; reproduce by spores produced in capsules; green; grow in moist, land environments

**Division Lycophyta** many-celled vascular plants; spores are produced in conelike structures; live on land; are photosynthetic; club mosses

**Division Arthrophyta** vascular plants; ribbed and jointed stems; scalelike leaves; spores produced in conelike structures; horsetails

**Division Pterophyta** vascular plants; leaves called fronds; spores produced in clusters of sporangia called sori; live on land or in water; ferns

**Division Ginkgophyta** deciduous trees; only one living species; have fan-shaped leaves with branching veins and fleshy cones with seeds; ginkgoes

**Division Cycadophyta** palmlike plants; have large, featherlike leaves; produces seeds in cones; cycads

**Division Coniferophyta** deciduous or evergreen; trees or shrubs; have needlelike or scalelike leaves; seeds produced in cones; conifers

**Division Anthophyta**
Tomato plant

**Phylum Platyhelminthes**
Flatworm

**Division Gnetophyta** shrubs or woody vines; seeds are produced in cones; division contains only three genera; gnetum

**Division Anthophyta** dominant group of plants; flowering plants; have fruits with seeds

## Kingdom Animalia

**Phylum Porifera** aquatic organisms that lack true tissues and organs; are asymmetrical and sessile; sponges

**Phylum Cnidaria** radially symmetrical organisms; have a digestive cavity with one opening; most have tentacles armed with stinging cells; live in aquatic environments singly or in colonies; includes jellyfish, corals, hydra, and sea anemones

**Phylum Platyhelminthes** bilaterally symmetrical worms; have flattened bodies; digestive system has one opening; parasitic and free-living species; flatworms

**Division Bryophyta**
Liverwort

**Phylum Chordata**

**Phylum Nematoda** round, bilaterally symmetrical body; have digestive system with two openings; free-living forms and parasitic forms; roundworms

**Phylum Mollusca** soft-bodied animals, many with a hard shell and soft foot or footlike appendage; a mantle covers the soft body; aquatic and terrestrial species; includes clams, snails, squid, and octopuses

**Phylum Annelida** bilaterally symmetrical worms; have round, segmented bodies; terrestrial and aquatic species; includes earthworms, leeches, and marine polychaetes

**Phylum Arthropoda** largest animal group; have hard exoskeletons, segmented bodies, and pairs of jointed appendages; land and aquatic species; includes insects, crustaceans, and spiders

**Phylum Echinodermata** marine organisms; have spiny or leathery skin and a water-vascular system with tube feet; are radially symmetrical; includes sea stars, sand dollars, and sea urchins

**Phylum Chordata** organisms with internal skeletons and specialized body systems; most have paired appendages; all at some time have a notochord, nerve cord, gill slits, and a post-anal tail; include fish, amphibians, reptiles, birds, and mammals

# Glossary/Glosario

**Cómo usar el glosario en español:**
1. Busca el término en inglés que desees encontrar.
2. El término en español, junto con la definición, se encuentran en la columna de la derecha.

## Pronunciation Key

Use the following key to help you sound out words in the glossary.

| | | | |
|---|---|---|---|
| a | back (BAK) | ew | food (FEWD) |
| ay | day (DAY) | yoo | pure (PYOOR) |
| ah | father (FAH thur) | yew | few (FYEW) |
| ow | flower (FLOW ur) | uh | comma (CAH muh) |
| ar | car (CAR) | u (+ con) | rub (RUB) |
| e | less (LES) | sh | shelf (SHELF) |
| ee | leaf (LEEF) | ch | nature (NAY chur) |
| ih | trip (TRIHP) | g | gift (GIHFT) |
| i (i + con + e) | idea (i DEE uh) | j | gem (JEM) |
| oh | go (GOH) | ing | sing (SING) |
| aw | soft (SAWFT) | zh | vision (VIH zhun) |
| or | orbit (OR buht) | k | cake (KAYK) |
| oy | coin (COYN) | s | seed, cent (SEED, SENT) |
| oo | foot (FOOT) | z | zone, raise (ZOHN, RAYZ) |

## English — A — Español

**abrasion:** a form of erosion that occurs when wind blows sediments into rocks, makes pits in the rocks, and produces smooth, polished surfaces. (p. 106)

**absolute age:** age, in years, of a rock or other object; can be determined by using properties of the atoms that make up materials. (p. 135)

**acid:** substance that releases $H^+$ ions and produces hydronium ions when dissolved in water. (p. 314)

**activation energy:** minimum amount of energy needed to start a chemical reaction. (p. 343)

**aerobe (AR ohb):** organism that uses oxygen for respiration. (p. 603)

**algae (AL jee):** one- or many-celled plantlike protists that usually are grouped based on their structure and the pigments they contain. (p. 610)

**alveoli (al VEE uh li):** tiny, thin-walled, grapelike clusters at the end of each bronchiole that are surrounded by capillaries; carbon dioxide and oxygen exchange takes place. (p. 460)

**abrasión:** forma de erosión que ocurre cuando la acción del viento causa que los sedimentos penetren en las rocas, hace huecos en ellas y produce superficies lisas y pulidas. (p. 106)

**edad absoluta:** edad, en años, de una roca u otro objeto; puede determinarse utilizando las propiedades de los átomos de los materiales. (p. 135)

**ácido:** sustancia que libera iones $H^+$ y produce iones de hidronio al ser disuelta en agua. (p. 314)

**energía de activación:** cantidad mínima de energía necesaria para iniciar una reacción química. (p. 343)

**aerobio:** organismo que utiliza oxígeno para respirar. (p. 603)

**algas:** protistas unicelulares o multicelulares similares a las plantas; se agrupan con base en su estructura y los pigmentos que contienen. (p. 610)

**alvéolos:** racimos parecidos a las uvas, pequeños y de paredes finas encontrados en el extremo de cada bronquiolo, los cuales están rodeados de capilares y en donde se realiza el intercambio de dióxido de carbono y oxígeno. (p. 460)

**amino acid:** building block of protein. (p. 451)

**amniotic egg:** adaptation of reptiles that allows them to reproduce on land; encloses the embryo within a moist environment, protected by a leathery shell, and has a yolk that supplies the embryo with food. (p. 523)

**amplitude:** for a transverse wave, one half the distance between a crest and a trough. (p. 215)

**anaerobe (A nuh rohb):** organism that can live without oxygen. (p. 603)

**angiosperms:** flowering vascular plants that produce fruits containing one or more seeds; monocots and dicots. (p. 561)

**antibiotic:** chemical produced by a bacterium or fungus that limits or stops the growth of bacteria. (p. 606)

**appendage:** structure such as a claw, leg, or antenna that grows from the body. (p. 496)

**aqueous (A kwee us):** solution in which water is the solvent. (p. 306)

**artery:** blood vessel that carries blood away from the heart, and has thick, elastic walls made of connective tissue and smooth muscle tissue. (p. 423)

**arthropod:** bilaterally symmetrical animal with jointed appendages, a protective endoskeleton, and a segmented body. (p. 496)

**asthenosphere (as THE nuh sfihr):** plasticlike layer of Earth on which the lithospheric plates float and move around. (p. 158)

**atom:** a very small particle that makes up most kinds of matter and consists of smaller parts called protons, neutrons, and electrons. (p. 271)

**atomic mass:** average mass of an atom of an element; its unit of measure is the atomic mass unit (u), which is 1/12 the mass of a carbon-12 atom. (p. 282)

**atomic number:** number of protons in the nucleus of each atom of a given element; is the top number in the periodic table. (p. 281)

**atriums (AY tree umz):** two upper chambers of the heart that contract at the same time during a heartbeat. (p. 419)

**auxin (AWK sun):** plant hormone that causes plant leaves and stems to exhibit positive phototropisms. (p. 588)

**aminoácido:** bloque formador de las proteínas. (p. 451)

**huevo amniótico:** adaptación de los reptiles que les permite reproducirse en la tierra; envuelve al embrión en un medio húmedo protegido por un caparazón correoso y tiene una yema que proporciona alimentos al embrión. (p. 523)

**amplitud:** para una onda transversal, es la mitad de la distancia entre la cresta y la depresión. (p. 215)

**anaerobio:** organismo que puede vivir sin oxígeno. (p. 603)

**angiospermas:** plantas vasculares que producen flores y frutos que contienen una o más semillas; pueden ser monocotiledóneas o dicotiledóneas. (p. 561)

**antibiótico:** sustancia química producida por una bacteria u hongo que limita o detiene el crecimiento de bacterias. (p. 606)

**apéndice:** estructura en forma de pinza, pata o antena que se proyecta del cuerpo. (p. 496)

**acuoso:** solución en la cual el agua es el solvente. (p. 306)

**arteria:** vaso sanguíneo que transporta sangre desde el corazón y tiene paredes gruesas y elásticas hechas de tejido conectivo y tejido muscular liso. (p. 423)

**artrópodo:** animal simétrico bilateralmente con apéndices articulados, endoesqueleto protector y cuerpo segmentado. (p. 496)

**astenosfera:** capa flexible de la Tierra en la que las placas litosféricas flotan y se mueven de un lugar a otro. (p. 158)

**átomo:** partícula muy pequeña que constituye la mayoría de los tipos de materia y que está formada por partes más pequeñas llamadas protones, neutrones y electrones. (p. 271)

**masa atómica:** masa promedio de un átomo de un elemento; su unidad de medida es la unidad de masa atómica (u), la cual es 1/12 de la masa de un átomo de carbono-12. (p. 282)

**número atómico:** número de protones en el núcleo de un átomo de determinado elemento; es el número superior en la tabla periódica. (p. 281)

**aurículas:** las dos cámaras superiores del corazón que se contraen al mismo tiempo durante el latido cardiaco. (p. 419)

**auxina:** hormona vegetal que causa que las hojas y tallos de las plantas desarrollen un fototropismo positivo. (p. 588)

# Glossary/Glosario

## B

**bacteria:** smallest organisms on Earth, each of which is made up of only one cell. (p. 363)

**base:** substance that accepts H$^+$ ions and produces hydroxide ions when dissolved in water. (p. 317)

**bias:** personal opinion. (p. 21)

**bladder:** elastic, muscular organ that holds urine until it leaves the body through the urethra. (p. 467)

**boiling point:** temperature at which a substance in a liquid state becomes a gas. (p. 247)

**bronchi (BRAHN ki):** two short tubes that branch off the lower end of the trachea and carry air into the lungs. (p. 460)

**bacteria:** los organismos más pequeños en la Tierra, cada uno de los cuales está formado por una sola célula. (p. 363)

**base:** sustancia que acepta los iones H$^+$ y produce iones de hidróxido al ser disuelta en agua. (p. 317)

**sesgo:** opinión personal. (p. 21)

**vejiga:** órgano muscular elástico que retiene la orina hasta que ésta sale del cuerpo a través de la uretra. (p. 467)

**punto de ebullición:** temperatura a la cual una sustancia en estado líquido se convierte en gas. (p. 247)

**bronquios:** dos tubos cortos que salen del extremo inferior de la tráquea y llevan el aire a los pulmones. (p. 460)

## C

**cambium (KAM bee um):** vascular tissue that produces xylem and phloem cells as a plant grows. (p. 559)

**capillary:** microscopic blood vessel that connects arteries and veins; has walls one cell thick, through which nutrients and oxygen diffuse into body cells, and waste materials and carbon dioxide diffuse out of body cells. (p. 424)

**carbohydrate (kar boh HI drayt):** nutrient that usually is the body's main source of energy. (p. 452)

**carbon film:** thin film of carbon residue preserved as a fossil. (p. 122)

**carnivore:** meat-eating animal with sharp canine teeth specialized to rip and tear flesh. (p. 530)

**cartilage:** thick, smooth, flexible and slippery tissue layer that covers the ends of bones, makes movement easier by reducing friction, and absorbing shocks. (p. 395)

**cartilage (KART uh lihj):** tough, flexible tissue similar to bone but is softer and less brittle. (p. 516)

**cast:** a type of body fossil that forms when crystals fill a mold or sediments wash into a mold and harden into rock. (p. 123)

**cámbium:** tejido vascular que produce las células del xilema y floema conforme crece la planta. (p. 559)

**capilar:** vaso sanguíneo microscópico que conecta las arterias con las venas; su pared tiene el grosor de una célula y los nutrientes y el oxígeno se difunden a través de ella hacia las células del cuerpo y los materiales de desecho y el dióxido de carbono hacia afuera de éstas. (p. 424)

**carbohidrato:** nutriente que por lo general es la principal fuente de energía del cuerpo. (p. 452)

**película de carbono:** capa delgada de residuos de carbono preservada como un fósil. (p. 122)

**carnívoro:** animal que se alimenta de carne y posee dientes caninos afilados especializados en desgarrar y arrancar carne. (p. 530)

**cartílago:** capa de tejido delgado, liso, flexible y resbaladizo que cubre los extremos de los huesos, facilita el movimiento al reducir la fricción y absorbe los golpes. (p. 395)

**cartílago:** tejido fuerte y flexible similar al hueso pero más suave y menos quebradizo que éste. (p. 516)

**vaciado:** tipo de cuerpo fósil que se forma cuando los cristales llenan un molde o los sedimentos son lavados hacia un molde y se endurecen convirtiéndose en roca. (p. 123)

**catalyst/cinder cone volcano**

**catalyst:** substance that speeds up a chemical reaction but is not used up itself or permanently changed. (p. 347)

**cell membrane:** flexible structure that holds a cell together, forms a boundary between the cell and its environment, and helps control what enters and leaves the cell. (p. 365)

**cell wall:** structure of plants, algae, fungi, and many types of bacteria that supports and protects the cell membrane. (p. 365)

**cellulose (SEL yuh lohs):** chemical compound made out of sugar; forms tangled fibers in the cell walls of many plants and provides structure and support. (p. 546)

**central nervous system:** division of the nervous system, made up of the brain and spinal cord. (p. 401)

**chemical change:** change in which the identity of a substance changes due to its chemical properties and forms a new substance or substances. (p. 253)

**chemical equation:** shorthand form for writing what reactants are used and what products are formed in a chemical reaction; sometimes shows whether energy is produced or absorbed. (p. 334)

**chemical property:** any characteristic, such as the ability to burn, that allows a substance to undergo a change that results in a new substance. (p. 252)

**chemical reaction:** process that produces chemical change, resulting in new substances that have properties different from those of the original substances. (p. 332)

**chemical weathering:** process in which the chemical composition of rocks is changed by agents such as natural acids and oxygen. (p. 96)

**chlorophyll (KLOR uh fihl):** green, light-trapping pigment in plant chloroplasts that is important in photosynthesis. (p. 578)

**chloroplast (KLOR uh plast):** green organelle in a plant's leaf cells where most photosynthesis takes place. (p. 367)

**chordate:** animal that at some time in its development has a notochord, nerve cord, and pharyngeal pouches. (p. 514)

**chyme (KIME):** liquid product of digestion. (p. 449)

**cinder cone volcano:** relatively small volcano formed by moderate to explosive eruptions of tephra. (p. 190)

**catalizador/volcán de cono de cenizas**

**catalizador:** sustancia que acelera una reacción química pero que ella misma ni se agota ni sufre cambios permanentes. (p. 347)

**membrana celular:** estructura flexible que mantiene unida a la célula, constituye un límite entre la célula y su entorno y ayuda a controlar todo aquello que entre o salga de ésta. (p. 365)

**pared celular:** estructura de las plantas, algas, hongos y varios tipos de bacterias, la cual sostiene y protege a la membrana celular. (p. 365)

**celulosa:** compuesto químico formado por azúcares y que forma fibras intrincadas en la pared celular de muchas plantas proporcionando estructura y soporte. (p. 546)

**sistema nervioso central:** división del sistema nervioso compuesto por el cerebro y la médula espinal. (p. 401)

**cambio químico:** cambio producido en la identidad de una sustancia debido a sus propiedades químicas para formar una nueva sustancia o sustancias. (p. 253)

**ecuación química:** forma breve para representar los reactivos utilizados y los productos que se forman en una reacción química; algunas veces muestra si se produce o absorbe energía. (p. 334)

**propiedad química:** cualquier característica, como la capacidad para quemarse, que permite a una sustancia sufrir un cambio que da como resultado una nueva sustancia. (p. 252)

**reacción química:** proceso que produce cambios químicos que dan como resultado nuevas sustancias cuyas propiedades son diferentes a aquellas de las sustancias originales. (p. 332)

**desgaste químico:** proceso en el que agentes tales como ácidos naturales y oxígeno cambian la composición química de las rocas. (p. 96)

**clorofila:** pigmento verde que absorbe luz y que se encuentra en los cloroplastos de las plantas; es importante para la fotosíntesis. (p. 578)

**cloroplasto:** organelo verde de la célula de las hojas de las plantas en donde tiene lugar la mayor parte de la fotosíntesis. (p. 367)

**cordado:** animal que en algún momento de su desarrollo tiene un notocordio, cordón nervioso, y pequeñas bolsas faríngeas. (p. 514)

**quimo:** líquido producido durante la digestión. (p. 449)

**volcán de cono de cenizas:** volcán relativamente pequeño formado por erupciones moderadas o explosivas de tefra. (p. 190)

# Glossary/Glosario

**closed circulatory system:** a type of blood-circulation system in which blood is transported through blood vessels rather than washing over the organs. (p. 492)

**cnidarian (NIH dar ee un):** radially symmetrical, hollow-bodied animal with two cell layers organized into tissues. (p. 486)

**composite volcano:** steep-sided volcano formed from alternating layers of violent eruptions of tephra and quieter eruptions of lava. (p. 191)

**compound:** a substance produced when elements combine and whose properties are different from each of the elements in it. (p. 285)

**compressional wave:** mechanical wave that causes particles in matter to move back and forth along the direction the wave travels. (p. 213)

**concentration:** describes how much solute is present in a solution compared to the amount of solvent. (p. 311)

**concentration:** describes how much solute is present in a solution compared to the amount of solvent. (p. 345)

**conic projection:** map made by projecting points and lines from a globe onto a cone. (p. 45)

**constant:** variable that does not change in an experiment. (p. 10)

**continental drift:** Wegener's hypothesis that all continents were once connected in a single large landmass that broke apart about 200 million years ago and drifted slowly to their current positions. (p. 150)

**contour feather:** strong, lightweight feather that gives a bird its shape and coloring and can help the bird steer, attract a mate, and avoid predators. (p. 527)

**contour line:** line on a map that connects points of equal elevation. (p. 46)

**control:** standard for comparison in an experiment. (p. 10)

**convection current:** current in Earth's mantle that transfers heat in Earth's interior and is the driving force for plate tectonics. (p. 163)

**coronary (KOR uh ner ee) circulation:** flow of blood to and from the tissues of the heart. (p. 419)

**creep:** a process in which sediments move slowly downhill. (p. 103)

**sistema circulatorio cerrado:** tipo de sistema circulatorio en el cual la sangre es transportada a través de vasos sanguíneos en lugar de bañar los órganos. (p. 492)

**cnidario:** animal de cuerpo hueco simétrico radial con dos capas de células organizadas en tejidos. (p. 486)

**volcán compuesto:** volcán de costados inclinados formado por capas alternas producto de erupciones violentas de tefra y erupciones silenciosas de lava. (p. 191)

**compuesto:** sustancia resultante de la combinación de elementos cuyas propiedades son diferentes de los elementos que la componen. (p. 285)

**onda de compresión:** onda mecánica que hace que las partículas de materia se muevan hacia adelante y hacia atrás en la dirección en que viaja la onda. (p. 213)

**concentración:** describe la cantidad de soluto presente en una solución, comparada con la cantidad de solvente. (p. 311)

**concentración:** describe la cantidad de soluto presente en una solución en relación con la cantidad de solvente. (p. 345)

**proyección cónica:** mapa hecho por la proyección de puntos y líneas desde un globo a un cono. (p. 45)

**constante:** variable que no cambia en un experimento. (p. 10)

**deriva continental:** hipótesis de Wegener respecto a que todos los continentes estuvieron alguna vez conectados en una gran masa terrestre única que se fraccionó cerca de 200 millones de años atrás y sus trozos se han movilizado lentamente a la deriva hasta sus posiciones actuales. (p. 150)

**pluma de contorno:** pluma fuerte y liviana que da a las aves su forma y color y les ayuda a dirigirse, atraer a una pareja y evadir a los depredadores. (p. 527)

**curva de nivel:** línea en un mapa que conecta puntos de la misma elevación. (p. 46)

**control:** modelo de comparación en un experimento. (p. 10)

**corriente de convección:** corriente en el manto de la Tierra que transfiere calor en el interior de la Tierra y es la causa de la tectónica de placas. (p. 163)

**circulación coronaria:** flujo sanguíneo desde y hacia los tejidos del corazón. (p. 419)

**escurrimiento:** proceso en el cual los sedimentos se mueven lentamente cuesta abajo. (p. 103)

**crystal:** solid material with atoms arranged in a repeating pattern. (p. 64)

**cuticle (KYEWT ih kul):** waxy, protective layer that covers the stems, leaves, and flowers of many plants and helps prevent water loss. (p. 546)

**cytoplasm (SI tuh pla zum):** gelatinlike substance inside the cell membrane that contains water, chemicals, and cell parts. (p. 365)

**cristal:** material sólido con átomos distribuidos en un patrón repetido. (p. 64)

**cutícula:** capa cerosa protectora que recubre el tronco, hojas y flores de muchas plantas y ayuda a prevenir la pérdida de agua. (p. 546)

**citoplasma:** sustancia gelatinosa en el interior de la membrana celular, la cual contiene agua, químicos y partes de la célula. (p. 365)

## D

**day-neutral plant:** plant that doesn't require a specific photoperiod and can begin the flowering process over a range of night lengths. (p. 590)

**deflation:** erosion of land that occurs when wind blows across loose sediments and carries them away, often leaving behind particles too heavy to move. (p. 106)

**density:** measurable physical property that can be found by dividing the mass of an object by its volume. (p. 244)

**dependent variable:** factor being measured in an experiment. (p. 10)

**dermis:** skin layer below the epidermis that contains blood vessels, nerves, oil, and sweat glands, and other structures. (p. 384)

**dicot:** angiosperm with two cotyledons inside its seed, flower parts in multiples of four or five, and vascular bundles in rings. (p. 562)

**diffraction:** bending of waves around an object. (p. 218)

**down feather:** fluffy feather that traps and keeps air warm against a bird's body. (p. 527)

**planta de día neutro:** planta que no requiere de un fotoperiodo específico y que puede comenzar su periodo de floración basándose en un rango de duración de las noches. (p. 590)

**deflación:** erosión del terreno que ocurre cuando el viento sopla sobre sedimentos sueltos y se los lleva, con frecuencia dejando atrás las partículas muy pesadas. (p. 106)

**densidad:** propiedad física que se puede medir dividiendo la masa de un objeto por su volumen. (p. 244)

**variable dependiente:** factor que se mide en un experimento. (p. 10)

**dermis:** capa de piel debajo de la epidermis que contiene vasos sanguíneos, nervios, grasa y glándulas sudoríparas, además de otra estructuras. (p. 384)

**dicotiledónea:** angiosperma con dos cotiledones dentro de su semilla, partes florales en múltiplos de cuatro o cinco y haces vasculares distribuidos en anillos. (p. 562)

**difracción:** curvatura de las ondas alrededor de un objeto. (p. 218)

**plumón:** pluma esponjosa que atrapa y mantiene el aire caliente cerca del cuerpo de las aves. (p. 527)

## E

**Earth science:** study of Earth and space, including rocks, fossils, climate, volcanoes, land use, ocean water, earthquakes, and objects in space. (p. 9)

**ciencia de la Tierra:** estudio de la Tierra y el espacio, incluyendo rocas, fósiles, clima, volcanes, uso del suelo, aguas oceánicas, terremotos y objetos en el espacio. (p. 9)

**earthquake:** movement of the ground that occurs when rocks inside Earth pass their elastic limit, break suddenly, and experience elastic rebound. (p. 178)

**ectotherm (EK tuh thurm):** cold-blooded animal whose body temperature changes with the temperature of its surrounding environment. (p. 515)

**electromagnetic spectrum:** complete range of electromagnetic wave frequencies and wavelengths. (p. 226)

**electromagnetic waves:** waves that can travel through matter or empty space, include radio waves, infrared waves, visible light waves, ultraviolet waves, X rays and gamma rays. (p. 225)

**electron:** invisible, negatively charged particle located in a cloudlike formation that surrounds the nucleus of an atom. (p. 274)

**element:** natural or synthetic material that cannot be broken down into simpler materials by ordinary means; has unique properties and is generally classified as a metal, metalloid, or nonmetal. (p. 278)

**endospore:** a dormant form of a bacterium surrounded by a thick wall; formed when environmental conditions are unfavorable. (p. 603)

**endotherm (EN duh thurm):** warm-blooded animal whose body temperature does not change with its surrounding environment. (p. 515)

**endothermic (en duh THUR mihk) reaction:** chemical reaction in which heat energy is absorbed. (p. 339)

**enzyme:** a type of protein that speeds up chemical reactions in the body without being changed or used up itself. (pp. 348, 446)

**epicenter:** point on Earth's surface directly above an earthquake's focus. (p. 180)

**epidermis:** outer, thinnest skin layer, that constantly produces new cells to replace the dead cells that are rubbed off its surface. (p. 384)

**equator:** imaginary line that wraps around Earth at 0° latitude, halfway between the north and south poles. (p. 40)

**erosion:** wearing away and removal of rock material that occurs by agents such as gravity, ice, wind, and water. (p. 101)

**terremoto:** movimiento del suelo que ocurre cuando las rocas del interior de la Tierra sobrepasan su límite de elasticidad, se rompen súbitamente y experimentan rebotes elásticos. (p. 178)

**ectotérmico:** animal de sangre fría cuya temperatura corporal cambia con la temperatura del medio ambiente circundante. (p. 515)

**espectro electromagnético:** rango total de las frecuencias y longitudes de onda de las ondas electromagnéticas. (p. 226)

**ondas electromagnéticas:** ondas que pueden viajar a través de la materia o del espacio vacío; incluyen las ondas de radio, las infrarrojas, las de luz visible, las ultravioleta y los rayos X y gama. (p. 225)

**electrón:** partícula invisible con carga negativa, localizada en una formación parecida a una nube que rodea el núcleo de un átomo. (p. 274)

**elemento:** material natural o sintético que no puede ser descompuesto fácilmente en materiales más simples por medios ordinarios; tiene propiedades únicas y generalmente es clasificado como metal, metaloide o no metal. (p. 278)

**endospora:** forma durmiente de una bacteria rodeada por una pared gruesa; se forma cuando las condiciones ambientales son desfavorables. (p. 603)

**endotérmico:** animal de sangre caliente cuya temperatura corporal no cambia con la temperatura del medio ambiente circundante. (p. 515)

**reacción endotérmica:** reacción química en la cual se absorbe energía calórica. (p. 339)

**enzima:** tipo de proteína que acelera las reacciones químicas en el cuerpo sin que ésta sufra modificaciones o se agote. (pp. 348, 446)

**epicentro:** punto de la superficie terrestre directamente encima del foco del terremoto. (p. 180)

**epidermis:** la capa más delgada y externa de la piel que constantemente produce células nuevas para reemplazar a las células muertas que han sido eliminadas de la superficie. (p. 384)

**ecuador:** línea imaginaria que rodea a la Tierra en el punto de latitud 0°, a la mitad de la distancia entre el polo norte y el polo sur. (p. 40)

**erosión:** desgaste y eliminación de material rocoso causado por agentes tales como la gravedad, el hielo, el viento y el agua. (p. 101)

**estivation (es tuh VAY shun):** period of inactivity during hot, dry weather; in amphibians, involves moving to cooler, more humid areas underground. (p. 519)

**ethics:** study of moral values about what is good or bad. (p. 20)

**exoskeleton:** rigid, protective body covering of an arthropod that supports the body and reduces water loss. (p. 496)

**exothermic (ek soh THUR mihk) reaction:** chemical reaction in which heat energy is released. (p. 339)

**extrusive (ehk STREW sihv):** describes igneous rocks that have small or no crystals and form when melted rock cools quickly on Earth's surface. (p. 71)

**estivación:** período de inactividad durante clima caliente y seco; en los anfibios implica la emigración a áreas más frías debajo de la tierra. (p. 519)

**ética:** estudio de los valores morales sobre lo que es bueno o malo. (p. 20)

**exoesqueleto:** capa rígida protectora del cuerpo de los artrópodos que sostiene el cuerpo y reduce la pérdida de agua. (p. 496)

**reacción exotérmica:** reacción química en la cual se libera energía calórica. (p. 339)

**extrusiva:** describe a las rocas volcánicas que tienen cristales pequeños o que carecen de ellos y que se forman cuando las rocas fundidas se enfrían rápidamente en la superficie terrestre. (p. 71)

## F

**fault:** fracture that occurs when rocks break and that results in relative movement of opposing sides; can form as a result of compression (reverse fault), being pulled apart (normal fault), or shear (strike-slip fault). (p. 179)

**fault-block mountains:** mountains formed from huge, tilted blocks of rock that are separated from surrounding rocks by faults. (p. 38)

**focus:** point deep inside Earth where energy is released, causing an earthquake. (p. 180)

**folded mountains:** mountains formed when horizontal rock layers are squeezed from opposite sides, causing them to buckle and fold. (p. 37)

**foliated:** describes metamorphic rocks with visible layers of minerals. (p. 80)

**fossils:** remains, imprints, or traces of prehistoric organisms that can tell when and where organisms once lived and how they lived. (p. 121)

**frequency:** number of wavelengths that pass a given point in one second, measured in hertz (Hz). (p. 214)

**falla:** fractura que ocurre cuando al romperse una roca se presentan relativos movimientos de los lados opuestos; se pueden formar como resultado de una compresión (falla reversa), al separarse (falla normal) o al deslizarse (falla por desplazamiento). (p. 179)

**montañas de fallas:** montañas formadas por bloques rocosos grandes e inclinados separados de las rocas circundantes por fracturas. (p. 38)

**foco:** punto profundo de la Tierra donde se genera energía causando un terremoto. (p. 180)

**montañas de plegamiento:** montañas formadas cuando las capas rocosas horizontales son comprimidas desde lados opuestos, causando que se colapsen y plieguen. (p. 37)

**foliado:** describe a las rocas metamórficas con capas visibles de minerales. (p. 80)

**fósiles:** restos, huellas o trazas de organismos prehistóricos que pueden informar cuándo, dónde y cómo vivieron tales organismos. (p. 121)

**frecuencia:** número de longitudes de onda que pasan un punto determinado en un segundo; se mide en hertz (Hz). (p. 214)

## G

**gem:** rare, valuable mineral that can be cut and polished. (p. 68)

**gill:** organ that allows a water-dwelling animal to exchange carbon dioxide for dissolved oxygen in the water. (p. 490)

**guard cells:** pairs of cells that surround stomata and control their opening and closing. (p. 557)

**gymnosperms:** vascular plants that do not flower, generally have needlelike or scalelike leaves, and produce seeds that are not protected by fruit; conifers, cycads, ginkgoes, and gnetophytes. (p. 560)

**gema:** mineral escaso y valioso que puede ser cortado y pulido. (p. 68)

**branquia:** órgano que permite a los animales que viven en el agua intercambiar dióxido de carbono por oxígeno disuelto en el agua. (p. 490)

**células oclusoras:** pares de células que rodean al estoma y que controlan su cierre y apertura. (p. 557)

**gimnospermas:** plantas vasculares que no florecen, generalmente tienen hojas en forma de aguja o de escama y producen semillas que no están protegidas por el fruto; se clasifican en coníferas, cicadáceas, ginkgoales y gnetofitas. (p. 560)

## H

**half-life:** time it takes for half the atoms of an isotope to decay. (p. 18)

**hemoglobin (HEE muh gloh bun):** chemical in red blood cells that carries oxygen from the lungs to body cells, and carries some carbon dioxide from body cells back to the lungs. (p. 429)

**herbivore:** plant-eating mammal with incisors specialized to cut vegetation and large, flat molars to grind it. (p. 530)

**heterogeneous mixture:** type of mixture where the substances are not evenly mixed. (p. 301)

**hibernation:** period of inactivity during cold weather; in amphibians, involves burying themselves in mud or leaves. (p. 519)

**homogeneous mixture:** type of mixture where two or more substances are evenly mixed on a molecular level but are not bonded together. (p. 302)

**hot spot:** hot, molten rock material that has been forced upward from deep inside Earth, which may cause magma to break through Earth's mantle and crust and may form volcanoes. (p. 196)

**hydronium ion:** hydrogen ion combines with a water molecule to form a hydronium ion, $H_3O^+$. (p. 314)

**vida media:** tiempo que le toma a la mitad de los átomos de un isótopo para desintegrarse. (p. 18)

**hemoglobina:** sustancia química de los glóbulos rojos que transporta oxígeno de los pulmones a las células del cuerpo y parte del dióxido de carbono de las células del cuerpo a los pulmones. (p. 429)

**herbívoro:** mamífero que se alimenta de plantas y que posee incisivos especializados en cortar vegetación y molares grandes y planos para molerla. (p. 530)

**mezcla heterogénea:** tipo de mezcla en la cual las sustancias no están mezcladas de manera uniforme. (p. 301)

**hibernación:** período de inactividad durante el tiempo frío; en los anfibios implica enterrarse en el barro o entre las hojas. (p. 519)

**mezcla homogénea:** tipo de mezcla en la cual dos o más sustancias están mezcladas en de manera uniforme a nivel molecular pero no están enlazadas. (p. 302)

**punto caliente:** material de roca fundida, caliente, que ha sido lanzado hacia arriba desde lo más profundo de la Tierra y que puede producir que el magma se rompa a través del manto y la corteza pudiendo formar volcanes. (p. 196)

**ion de hidronio:** ion de hidrógeno combinado con una molécula de agua para formar un ion de hidronio, $H_3O^+$. (p. 314)

**hyphae (HI fee):** mass of many-celled, threadlike tubes that makes up the body of most fungi. (p. 616)

**hypothesis:** an educated guess. (p. 7)

**hifas:** masa de tubos entretejidos conformados por numerosas células que componen el cuerpo de la mayoría de hongos. (p. 616)

**hipótesis:** una suposición fundamentada. (p. 7)

---

**I**

---

**igneous (IHG nee us) rock:** intrusive or extrusive rock that is produced when melted rock from inside Earth cools and hardens. (p. 71)

**independent variable:** factor that changes in an experiment. (p. 10)

**index fossils:** remains of species that existed on Earth for a relatively short period of time, were abundant and widespread geographically, and can be used by geologists to assign the ages of rock layers. (p. 125)

**indicator:** compound that changes color at different pH values when it reacts with acidic or basic solutions. (p. 320)

**infrared waves:** electromagnetic waves with wavelengths between about one thousandth of a meter and 700 billionths of a meter (p. 227)

**inhibitor:** substance that slows down a chemical reaction, making the formation of a certain amount of product take longer. (p. 346)

**intensity:** amount of energy a wave carries past a certain area each second. (p. 220)

**intrusive (ihn trew sihv):** describes a type of igneous rock that generally contains large crystals and forms when magma cools slowly beneath Earth's surface. (p. 71)

**invertebrate (ihn VURT uh brayt):** an animal without a backbone. (p. 484)

**involuntary muscle:** muscle, such as heart muscle, that cannot be consciously controlled. (p. 389)

**isotopes (I suh tohps):** two or more atoms of the same element that have different numbers of neutrons in their nuclei. (p. 281)

**roca ígnea:** roca intrusiva o extrusiva producida cuando la roca fundida proveniente del interior de la Tierra se enfría y endurece. (p. 71)

**variable independiente:** factor que cambia en un experimento. (p. 10)

**fósiles índice:** restos de especies que existieron sobre la Tierra durante un periodo de tiempo relativamente corto y que fueron abundantes y ampliamente diseminadas geográficamente; los geólogos pueden usarlos para inferir las edades de las capas rocosas. (p. 125)

**indicador:** compuesto que cambia de color con diferentes valores de pH al reaccionar con soluciones ácidas o básicas. (p. 320)

**ondas infrarrojas:** ondas electromagnéticas con longitudes de onda entre aproximadamente una milésima y 700 billonésimas de metro. (p. 227)

**inhibidor:** sustancia que reduce la velocidad de una reacción química, haciendo que la formación de una determinada cantidad de producto tarde más tiempo. (p. 346)

**intensidad:** cantidad de energía que transporta una onda al pasar por un área determinada en un segundo. (p. 220)

**intrusiva:** describe un tipo de roca volcánica que por lo general contiene grandes cristales y que se forma cuando el magma se enfría lentamente debajo de la superficie terrestre. (p. 71)

**invertebrado:** animal que carece de columna vertebral. (p. 484)

**músculo involuntario:** músculo, como el músculo cardíaco, que no puede ser controlado voluntariamente. (p. 389)

**isótopos:** dos o más átomos del mismo elemento que tienen diferente número de neutrones en su núcleo. (p. 281)

**J**

**joint:** any place where two or more bones come together; can be movable or immovable. (p. 396)

**articulación:** todo lugar en donde dos o más huesos se unen y la cual puede ser móvil o inmóvil. (p. 396)

**L**

**larynx:** airway to which the vocal cords are attached. (p. 460)

**latitude:** distance in degrees north or south of the equator. (p. 40)

**lava:** molten rock flowing onto Earth's surface. (p. 187)

**law of conservation of mass:** states that the mass of the products of a chemical change is always the same as the mass of what you started with. (p. 257)

**law of conservation of matter:** states that matter is not created or destroyed but only changes its form. (p. 272)

**law of reflection:** states that the angle the incoming wave makes with the normal to the reflecting surface equals the angle the reflected wave makes with the surface. (p. 217)

**lichen (LI kun):** forms when a fungus and either a green alga or cyanobacterium live together in a close, beneficial association. (p. 619)

**ligament:** tough band of tissue that holds bones together at joints. (p. 396)

**lithosphere (LIH thuh sfihr):** rigid layer of Earth about 100 km thick, made of the crust and a part of the upper mantle. (p. 158)

**long-day plant:** plant that generally requires short nights—less than ten to 12 hours of darkness—to begin the flowering process. (p. 590)

**longitude:** distance in degrees east or west of the prime meridian. (p. 41)

**lymph (LIHMF):** tissue fluid that has diffused into lymphatic capillaries. (p. 434)

**lymph nodes:** bean-shaped organs found throughout the body that filters out microorganisms and foreign materials taken up by the lymphocytes. (p. 434)

**laringe:** pasaje aéreo al cual están adheridas las cuerdas vocales. (p. 460)

**latitud:** distancia en grados al norte o sur del ecuador. (p. 40)

**lava:** roca fundida que fluye en la superficie terrestre. (p. 187)

**ley de la conservación de la masa:** establece que la masa de los productos de un cambio químico siempre es igual a la masa inicial. (p. 257)

**ley de la conservación de la materia:** establece que la materia no se crea ni se destruye, solamente cambia de forma. (p. 272)

**ley de reflexión:** establece que el ángulo que forman la onda que llega y la normal hacia la superficie reflejante es igual al ángulo que la onda reflejada forma con la superficie. (p. 217)

**liquen:** se forma cuando un hongo y un alga verde o una cianobacteria viven juntos en una asociación estrecha y benéfica para ambos. (p. 619)

**ligamento:** banda dura de tejido que mantiene los huesos unidos a las articulaciones. (p. 396)

**litosfera:** capa rígida de la Tierra de unos 100 kilómetros de profundidad, comprende la corteza y una parte del manto superior. (p. 158)

**planta de día largo:** planta que generalmente requiere de noches cortas—menos de 12 horas de oscuridad—para comenzar su proceso de floración. (p. 590)

**longitud:** distancia en grados al este u oeste del meridiano inicial. (p. 41)

**linfa:** fluido tisular que se ha difundido hacia los capilares linfáticos. (p. 434)

**ganglio linfático:** órganos en forma de fríjol que se encuentran en todo el cuerpo; filtran y extraen microorganismos y materiales extraños captados por los linfocitos. (p. 434)

**lymphatic system:** carries lymph through a network of lymph capillaries and vessels, and drains it into large veins near the heart; helps fight infections and diseases. (p. 434)

**lymphocyte (LIHM fuh site):** a type of white blood cell that fights infection. (p. 434)

**sistema linfático:** sistema que transporta la linfa a través de una red de vasos y capilares linfáticos y la vierte en venas grandes cerca del corazón; ayuda a combatir enfermedades e infecciones. (p. 434)

**linfocito:** tipo de glóbulo blanco que combate las infecciones. (p. 434)

## M

**magnitude:** a measure of the energy released by an earthquake. (p. 181)

**mantle:** thin layer of tissue that covers a mollusk's body and that can secrete a shell. (p. 490)

**map legend:** explains the meaning of symbols used on a map. (p. 48)

**map scale:** relationship between distances on a map and distances on Earth's surface that can be represented as a ratio or as a small bar divided into sections. (p. 48)

**marsupial:** mammal that gives birth to incompletely developed young that finish developing in their mother's pouch. (p. 532)

**mass movement:** occurs when gravity alone causes rock or sediment to move down a slope. (p. 101)

**mass number:** sum of the number of protons and neutrons in the nucleus of an atom. (p. 281)

**matter:** anything that has mass and takes up space and is made up of different kinds of atoms; includes all things that can be seen, tasted, smelled, or touched but does not include heat, sound, or light. (pp. 243, 270)

**mechanical weathering:** process that breaks rocks down into smaller pieces without changing them chemically. (p. 94)

**medusa (mih DEW suh):** free-swimming, bell-shaped body form in the life cycle of a cnidarian. (p. 487)

**melanin:** pigment produced by the epidermis, that protects skin and gives skin and eyes their color. (p. 385)

**melting point:** temperature at which a solid becomes a liquid. (p. 247)

**metal:** element that is malleable, ductile, a good conductor of electricity, and generally has a shiny or metallic luster. (p. 282)

**magnitud:** medida de la energía generada por un terremoto. (p. 181)

**manto:** capa delgada de tejido que cubre el cuerpo de los moluscos y que puede producir/secretar una concha. (p. 490)

**leyenda del mapa:** explica el significado de los símbolos utilizados en un mapa. (p. 48)

**escala del mapa:** relación entre las distancias en un mapa y las distancias sobre la superficie terrestre, que puede representarse como una relación o como una barra pequeña dividida en secciones. (p. 48)

**marsupial:** mamífero que da a luz crías con un desarrollo incompleto que terminan su desarrollo en la bolsa de su madre. (p. 532)

**movimiento de masa:** ocurre cuando las rocas o sedimentos se mueven sobre una pendiente sólo por acción de la gravedad. (p. 101)

**número de masa:** suma del número de protones y neutrones en el núcleo de un átomo. (p. 281)

**materia:** todo lo que tenga masa, ocupe espacio y esté hecho de diferentes tipos de átomos; incluye todo lo que se puede ver, saborear, oler o tocar, pero no incluye el calor, el sonido o la luz. (pp. 243, 270)

**desgaste mecánico:** proceso mediante el cual las rocas se rompen en pedazos más pequeños sin cambiar químicamente. (p. 94)

**medusa:** cuerpo en forma de campana durante el ciclo de vida de un cnidario. (p. 487)

**melanina:** pigmento producido por la epidermis que protege la piel y da el color a los ojos y a la piel. (p. 385)

**punto de fusión:** temperatura a la cual un sólido se convierte en líquido. (p. 247)

**metal:** elemento maleable, dúctil y buen conductor de electricidad que generalmente tiene un lustre brillante o metálico. (p. 282)

# Glossary/Glosario

**metalloid:** element that has characteristics of both metals and nonmetals and is a solid at room temperature. (p. 283)

**metamorphic (met uh MOR fihk) rock:** new rock that forms when existing rock is heated or squeezed. (p. 79)

**metamorphosis (met uh MOR fuh sus):** change of body form that can be complete (egg, larva, pupa, adult) or incomplete (egg, nymph, adult). (p. 497)

**mineral:** in Earth science, inorganic, solid material found in nature that always has the same chemical makeup, atoms arranged in an orderly pattern, and properties such as cleavage and fracture, color, hardness, and streak and luster (p. 62); in life science, inorganic nutrient that regulates many chemical reactions in the body. (p. 454).

**mitochondria (mi tuh KAHN dree uh):** cell organelles where cellular respiration takes place. (p. 366)

**mixture:** a combination of compounds and elements that has not formed a new substance and whose proportions can be changed without changing the mixture's identity. (p. 287)

**mold:** a type of body fossil that forms in rock when an organism with hard parts is buried, decays or dissolves, and leaves a cavity in the rock. (p. 123)

**mollusk:** soft-bodied, bilaterally symmetrical invertebrate with a large, muscular foot, a mantle, and an open circulatory system; usually has a shell. (p. 490)

**monocot:** angiosperm with one cotyledon inside its seed, flower parts in multiples of three, and vascular tissues in bundles scattered throughout the stem. (p. 562)

**monotreme:** mammal that lays eggs with tough, leathery shells instead of giving birth to live young. (p. 531)

**mycorrhizae (mi kuh RI zee):** formed when an intricate web of fungi grows around the roots of a plant. (p. 620)

**metaloide:** elemento que comparte características de los metales y de los no metales y es sólido a temperatura ambiente. (p. 283)

**roca metamórfica:** roca nueva que se forma cuando la roca existente se calienta o comprime. (p. 79)

**metamorfosis:** cambio de forma del cuerpo que puede ser completo (huevo, larva, ninfa, adulto) o incompleto (huevo, ninfa, adulto). (p. 497)

**mineral:** en la ciencia de la Tierra, material inorgánico, sólido, que se encuentra en la naturaleza y que siempre tiene la misma composición química, átomos dispuestos en un patrón ordenado y propiedades tales como fisuras y fracturas, color, dureza, vetas pequeñas y brillo (p. 62); en las ciencias biológicas, nutriente inorgánico que regula muchas reacciones químicas en el cuerpo. (p. 454).

**mitocondria:** organelo celular en donde se lleva a cabo la respiración celular. (p. 366)

**mezcla:** combinación de compuestos y elementos que no han formado una nueva sustancia y cuyas proporciones pueden ser cambiadas sin que se pierda la identidad de la mezcla. (p. 287)

**moldura:** tipo de cuerpo fósil que se formó en la roca cuando un organismo con partes duras fue enterrado, descompuesto o disuelto, dejando una cavidad en la roca. (p. 123)

**molusco:** invertebrado de cuerpo blando simétricamente bilateral que posee una pata grande muscular, un manto y un sistema circulatorio abierto, y que por lo general tiene concha. (p. 490)

**monocotiledóneas:** angiospermas con un solo cotiledón dentro de la semilla, partes florales dispuestas en múltiplos de tres y tejidos vasculares distribuidos en haces diseminados por todo el tallo. (p. 562)

**monotrema:** mamífero que pone huevos con cascarones fuertes y correosos en lugar de dar a luz a una cría. (p. 531)

**micorriza:** se forma cuando una intrincada red de hongos crece alrededor de las raíces de una planta. (p. 620)

**N**

**nephron (NEF rahn):** tiny filtering unit of the kidney. (p. 467)

**nefrona:** pequeña unidad de filtración en el riñón. (p. 467)

**neuron (NOO rahn):** basic functioning unit of the nervous system, made up of a cell body, dendrites, and axons. (p. 400)

**neutralization (new truh luh ZAY shun):** reaction in which an acid reacts with a base and forms water and a salt. (p. 320)

**neutron:** an uncharged particle located in the nucleus of an atom. (p. 276)

**nonfoliated:** describes metamorphic rocks that lack distinct layers or bands. (p. 80)

**nonmetals:** elements that are usually gases or brittle solids and poor conductors of electricity and heat; are the basis of the chemicals of life. (p. 283)

**nonvascular plant:** plant that absorbs water and other substances directly through its cell walls instead of through tubelike structures. (p. 549)

**nucleus (NEW klee us):** in physical science, positively charged, central part of an atom (p. 275); in life science, cell organelle that contains the hereditary material (p. 366).

**nutrients (NEW tree unts):** substances in foods —proteins, carbohydrates, fats, vitamins, minerals, and water—that provide energy and materials for cell development, growth, and repair. (p. 446)

**neurona:** unidad básica funcional del sistema nervioso compuesta por un cuerpo celular, dendritas y axones. (p. 400)

**neutralización:** reacción en la cual un ácido reacciona con una base para formar agua y una sal. (p. 320)

**neutrón:** partícula sin carga localizada en el núcleo de un átomo (p. 276)

**no foliado:** describe a las rocas metamórficas que carecen de capas o bandas definidas. (p. 80)

**no metales:** elementos que por lo general son gases o sólidos frágiles y malos conductores de electricidad y calor; son la base de los compuestos químicos biológicos. (p. 283)

**planta no vascular:** planta que absorbe agua y otras sustancias directamente a través de sus paredes celulares en vez de utilizar estructuras tubulares. (p. 549)

**núcleo:** en la ciencia física, parte central con carga positiva del átomo. (p. 275); en las ciencias biológicas, organelo celular que contiene material genético (p. 366).

**nutrientes:** sustancias en los alimentos (proteínas, carbohidratos, grasas, vitaminas, minerales y agua) que suministran energía y materiales para el desarrollo, crecimiento y reparación de las células. (p. 446)

## O

**omnivore:** plant- and meat-eating animal with incisors that cut vegetables, sharp premolars that chew meat, and molars that grind food. (p. 530)

**open circulatory system:** a type of blood-circulation system that lacks blood vessels and in which blood washes over the organs. (p. 491)

**ore:** material that contains enough of a useful metal that it can be mined and sold at a profit. (p. 69)

**organ:** structure made of two or more different tissue types that work together to do a certain job. (p. 373)

**organ system:** group of organs that work together to perform a certain task. (p. 373)

**omnívoro:** animal que se alimenta de plantas y animales y que posee incisivos para cortar vegetales, premolares afilados para masticar carne y molares para triturar la comida. (p. 530)

**sistema circulatorio abierto:** tipo de sistema circulatorio que carece de vasos sanguíneos y en el cual la sangre baña los órganos. (p. 491)

**mena:** material que contiene el metal útil suficiente para ser extraído y vendido para obtener utilidades. (p. 69)

**órgano:** estructura formada por dos o más tipos de tejidos que trabajan juntos para realizar una función determinada. (p. 373)

**sistema de órganos:** grupo de órganos que trabajan en conjunto para realizar una función determinada. (p. 373)

# Glossary/Glosario

**organelles (or guh NELZ):** specialized cell parts that perform a cell's activities. (p. 365)

**organelos:** partes especializadas de las células que realizan las funciones celulares. (p. 365)

---

**P**

**Pangaea (pan JEE uh):** large, ancient landmass that was composed of all the continents joined together. (p. 150)

**Pangea:** masa terrestre extensa y antigua que estaba compuesta por todos los continentes unidos. (p. 150)

**pasteurization:** process used to kill most harmful bacteria in food; increases the length of time foods can be stored without spoiling. (p. 607)

**pasteurización:** proceso usado para matar a la mayoría de las bacterias dañinas en los alimentos; aumenta el periodo de tiempo durante el cual se pueden almacenar los alimentos sin que se echen a perder. (p. 607)

**pathogen:** any organism that causes disease. (p. 606)

**patógeno:** cualquier organismo que cause una enfermedad. (p. 606)

**periosteum (pur ee AHS tee um):** tough, tight-fitting membrane, that covers a bone's surface and contains blood vessels that transport nutrients into the bone. (p. 395)

**periostio:** membrana fuerte y ajustada que cubre la superficie de los huesos y contiene vasos sanguíneos que transportan nutrientes a los huesos. (p. 395)

**peripheral nervous system:** division of the nervous system; includes of all the nerves outside the CNS; connects the brain and spinal cord to other body parts. (p. 401)

**sistema nervioso periférico:** parte del sistema nervioso compuesta por todos los nervios que no pertenecen al sistema nervioso central y que conecta el cerebro y la médula espinal con otras partes del cuerpo. (p. 401)

**peristalsis (per uh STAHL sus):** waves of muscular contractions that move food through the digestive tract. (p. 448)

**peristalsis:** ondas de contracciones musculares que mueven al alimento a través del sistema digestivo. (p. 448)

**permineralized remains:** fossils in which the spaces inside are filled with minerals from groundwater. (p. 122)

**restos permineralizados:** fósiles en los que los espacios interiores son llenados con minerales de aguas subterráneas. (p. 122)

**pH:** measure of how acidic or basic a solution is, ranging in a scale from 0 to 14. (p. 318)

**pH:** medida para saber qué tan básica o ácida es una solución, en una escala de 0 a 14. (p. 318)

**phloem (FLOH em):** vascular tissue that forms tubes that transport dissolved sugar throughout a plant. (p. 559)

**floema:** tejido vascular que forma tubos que transportan azúcares disueltos a toda la planta. (p. 559)

**photoperiodism:** a plant's response to the lengths of daylight and darkness each day. (p. 590)

**fotoperiodicidad:** la respuesta de una planta a la duración de la luz y de la oscuridad cada día. (p. 590)

**photosynthesis (foh toh SIHN thuh suhs):** process by which plants, algae, and many types of bacteria use light energy to produce a simple sugar from carbon dioxide and water and give off oxygen. (pp. 367, 579)

**fotosíntesis:** proceso mediante el cual las plantas, las algas, y muchos tipos de bacterias utilizan la energía luminosa para producir azúcares simples a partir de dióxido de carbono y agua y desprender oxígeno. (pp. 367, 579)

**physical change:** change in which the properties of a substance change but the identity of the substance always remains the same. (p. 243)

**cambio físico:** cambio en el cual las propiedades de una sustancia cambian pero la identidad de la sustancia sigue siendo la misma. (p. 243)

**physical property:** any characteristic of a material, such as state, color, and volume, that can be observed or measured without changing or attempting to change the material. (p. 242)

**pioneer species:** first organisms to grow in new or disturbed areas; break down rock and build up decaying plant material so that other plants can grow. (p. 551)

**pitch:** human perception of the frequency of sound (p. 221)

**placental:** mammal whose offspring develops inside the female's uterus; has a placenta—a saclike organ—which supplies the embryo with food and oxygen and removes wastes. (p. 532)

**plain:** large, flat landform that often has thick, fertile soil and is usually found in the interior region of a continent. (p. 34)

**plasma:** liquid part of blood, made mostly of water, in which oxygen, nutrients, and minerals are dissolved. (p. 428)

**plate:** a large section of Earth's oceanic or continental crust and rigid upper mantle that moves around on the asthenosphere. (p. 158)

**plate tectonics:** theory that Earth's crust and upper mantle are broken into plates that float and move around on a plasticlike layer of the mantle. (p. 158)

**plateau (pla TOH):** flat, raised landform made up of nearly horizontal rocks that have been uplifted. (p. 36)

**platelet:** irregularly shaped cell fragment that helps clot blood and releases chemicals, that help form fibrin. (p. 429)

**polyp (PAHL up):** vase-shaped, usually sessile body form in the life cycle of a cnidarian. (p. 487)

**precipitate:** solid that comes back out of its solution because of a chemical reaction or physical change. (p. 302)

**prime meridian:** imaginary line that represents 0° longitude and runs from the north pole through Greenwich, England, to the south pole. (p. 41)

**principle of superposition:** states that in undisturbed rock layers, the oldest rocks are on the bottom and the rocks become progressively younger toward the top. (p. 128)

**propiedad física:** cualquier característica de un material, tal como estado, color y volumen, que pueden ser observados o medidos sin cambiar o tratar de cambiar el material. (p. 242)

**especies pioneras:** los primeros organismos que crecen en áreas nuevas o alteradas; descomponen la roca y acumulan material vegetal en descomposición para que otras plantas puedan crecer. (p. 551)

**tono:** percepción humana de la frecuencia del sonido. (p. 221)

**placentario:** mamífero cuyas crías se desarrollan en el útero femenino; tiene una placenta, órgano parecido a un saco, el cual suministra al embrión alimento y oxígeno y elimina los desechos. (p. 532)

**planicie:** formación de terreno extenso y plano que a menudo tiene suelos gruesos y fértiles; generalmente se encuentra en la región interior de un continente. (p. 34)

**plasma:** parte líquida de la sangre compuesta principalmente por agua y en la que se encuentran disueltos oxígeno, nutrientes y minerales. (p. 428)

**placa:** gran sección de la corteza terrestre u oceánica y del manto rígido superior que se mueve sobre la astenosfera. (p. 158)

**tectónica de placas:** teoría respecto a que la corteza terrestre y el manto superior están fraccionados en placas que flotan y se mueven sobre una capa plástica del manto. (p. 158)

**meseta:** formación de terreno plano y elevado constituida por rocas casi horizontales que han sido levantadas. (p. 36)

**plaqueta:** fragmento celular de forma irregular que ayuda a coagular la sangre y libera químicos que ayudan a formar fibrina. (p. 429)

**pólipo:** cuerpo en forma de jarrón generalmente sésil en el ciclo de vida de un cnidario. (p. 487)

**precipitado:** sólido que se aísla de su solución mediante una reacción química o un cambio físico. (p. 302)

**meridiano inicial:** línea imaginaria que representa los cero grados de longitud y va desde el polo norte pasando por Greenwich, Inglaterra, hasta el polo sur. (p. 41)

**principio de superposición:** establece que en las capas rocosas no perturbadas, las rocas más antiguas están en la parte inferior y las rocas son más jóvenes conforme están más cerca de la superficie. (p. 128)

# Glossary/Glosario

**product:** substance that forms as a result of a chemical reaction. (p. 334)

**protist:** one- or many-celled eukaryotic organism that lives in moist or wet surroundings; can be plantlike, animal-like, or funguslike. (p. 609)

**proton:** positively charged particle located in the nucleus of an atom and that is counted to identify the atomic number. (p. 275)

**protozoan:** one-celled, animal-like protist that lives in water, soil, and living and dead organisms, and can move by using flagella, cilia, or pseudopods. (p. 610)

**pseudopod (SEWD uh pahd):** temporary extension of cytoplasm by which some protozoans move. (p. 610)

**pulmonary circulation:** flow of blood through the heart to the lungs and back to the heart. (p. 420)

**producto:** sustancia que se forma como resultado de una reacción química. (p. 334)

**protista:** organismo eucariota unicelular o multicelular que vive en ambientes húmedos o acuáticos; puede ser similar a una planta, animal u hongo. (p. 609)

**protón:** partícula cargada positivamente, localizada en el núcleo de un átomo y que se cuenta para identificar el número atómico. (p. 275)

**protozoario:** protista unicelular parecido a un animal, el cual vive en el agua, en el suelo o en organismos vivos o muertos y que se puede desplazar mediante flagelos, cilios o seudópodos. (p. 610)

**seudópodo:** extensión temporal de citoplasma que permite a algunos protozoarios desplazarse. (p. 610)

**circulación pulmonar:** flujo sanguíneo del corazón hacia los pulmones y de regreso al corazón. (p. 420)

## R

**radioactive decay:** process in which some isotopes break down into other isotopes and particles. (p. 135)

**radiometric dating:** process used to calculate the absolute age of rock by measuring the ratio of parent isotope to daughter product in a mineral and knowing the half-life of the parent. (p. 137)

**radula:** scratchy, tonguelike organ in many mollusks that has rows of teethlike projections used to scrape and grate food. (p. 491)

**rate of reaction:** measure of how fast a chemical reaction occurs. (p. 344)

**reactant:** substance that exists before a chemical reaction begins. (p. 334)

**refraction:** change in direction of a wave when it changes speed as it travels from one material into another. (p. 217)

**relative age:** the age of something compared with other things. (p. 139)

**respiration:** series of chemical reactions used to release energy stored in food molecules. (p. 581)

**reverberation:** repeated echoes of sound waves. (p. 223)

**radioactive decay/desintegración radiactiva:** proceso en el que algunos isótopos se desintegran en otros isótopos y partículas. (p. 135)

**fechado radiométrico:** proceso utilizado para calcular la edad absoluta de las rocas midiendo la relación isótopo parental a producto derivado en un mineral y conociendo la vida media del parental. (p. 137)

**rádula:** órgano punzante en forma de lengua en muchos moluscos, la cual presenta filas de proyecciones similares a los dientes usadas para raspar y rallar alimentos. (p. 491)

**velocidad de reacción:** medida de la rapidez con que se produce una reacción química. (p. 344)

**reactivo:** sustancia que existe antes de que comience una reacción química. (p. 334)

**refracción:** cambio de dirección de una onda al cambiar su velocidad cuando pasa de un material a otro. (p. 217)

**edad relativa:** la edad de algo comparado con otras cosas. (p. 139)

**respiración:** serie de reacciones químicas usadas para liberar la energía almacenada en las moléculas de los alimentos. (p. 581)

**reverberación:** ecos repetidos de ondas sonoras. (p. 223)

**rhizoids (RI zoydz):** threadlike structures that anchor nonvascular plants to the ground. (p. 550)

**rift:** long crack, fissure, or trough that forms between tectonic plates moving apart at plate boundaries. (p. 195)

**rock:** solid inorganic material that is usually made of two or more minerals and can be metamorphic, sedimentary, or igneous. (p. 62)

**rock cycle:** diagram that shows the slow, continuous process of rocks changing from one type to another. (p. 81)

**runoff:** water that flows over Earth's surface. (p. 107)

**rizoides:** estructuras en forma de hilos que anclan las plantas no vasculares al suelo. (p. 550)

**ruptura:** grieta larga, fisura o hueco que se forma entre placas tectónicas que se separan en los límites de las placas. (p. 195)

**roca:** material sólido inorgánico generalmente compuesto por dos o más minerales y que puede ser metamórfico, sedimentario o volcánico. (p. 62)

**ciclo de una roca:** diagrama que muestra el proceso lento y continuo de las rocas al cambiar de un tipo a otro. (p. 81)

**afluencia:** agua que fluye sobre la superficie terrestre. (p. 107)

**S**

**saprophyte:** any organism that uses dead material as a food source. (p. 608)

**saturated:** describes a solution that holds the total amount of solute that it can hold under given conditions. (p. 310)

**science:** process of looking at and studying things in the world in order to gain knowledge. (p. 8)

**scientific law:** rule that describes the behavior of something in nature; usually describes what will happen in a situation but not why it happens. (p. 19)

**scientific methods:** problem-solving procedures that can include identifying the problem or question, gathering information, developing a hypothesis, testing the hypothesis, analyzing the results, and drawing conclusions. (p. 8)

**scientific theory:** explanation that is supported by results from repeated experimentation or testing. (p. 18)

**seafloor spreading:** Hess's theory that new seafloor is formed when magma is forced upward toward the surface at a mid-ocean ridge. (p. 155)

**sedimentary rock:** a type of rock made from pieces of other rocks, dissolved minerals, or plant and animal matter that collect to form rock layers. (p. 75)

**saprofito:** cualquier organismo que utilice material muerto como fuente alimenticia. (p. 608)

**saturado:** describe a una solución que retiene toda la cantidad de soluto que puede retener bajo determinadas condiciones. (p. 310)

**ciencia:** proceso de observación y estudio de las cosas en el mundo con el propósito de adquirir conocimientos. (p. 8)

**ley científica:** regla que describe el comportamiento de algo en la naturaleza; usualmente describe qué sucederá en una situación pero no el porqué sucedería. (p. 19)

**métodos científicos:** procedimientos para solucionar problemas que pueden incluir la identificación del problema o pregunta, la recopilación de información, el desarrollo de una hipótesis, la prueba de la hipótesis, el análisis de los resultados y la extracción de conclusiones. (p. 8)

**teoría científica:** explicación apoyada por los resultados de la experimentación o de pruebas repetidas. (p. 18)

**expansión del suelo oceánico:** teoría de Hess respecto a que se forma un nuevo suelo oceánico cuando el magma es empujado hacia la superficie a través de un surco en la mitad del océano. (p. 155)

**roca sedimentaria:** tipo de roca formada por fracciones de otras rocas, minerales disueltos o materiales de plantas y animales que se unen para formar capas de rocas. (p. 75)

# Glossary/Glosario

**seismic safe:** describes the ability of structures to stand up against the vibrations caused by an earthquake. (p. 185)

**seismic waves:** earthquake waves, including primary waves, secondary waves, and surface waves. (p. 180)

**seismograph:** instrument used to record seismic waves. (p. 181)

**shield volcano:** large, broad volcano with gently sloping sides that is formed by the buildup of basaltic layers. (p. 190)

**short-day plant:** plant that generally requires long nights—12 or more hours of darkness—to begin the flowering process. (p. 590)

**slump:** occurs when a mass of rock or sediment moves downhill along a curved surface. (p. 103)

**soil:** mixture of weathered rock, organic matter, water, and air that evolves over time and supports the growth of plant life. (p. 98)

**solubility (sahl yuh BIH luh tee):** measure of how much solute can be dissolved in a certain amount of solvent. (p. 309)

**solute:** substance that dissolves and seems to disappear into another substance. (p. 302)

**solution:** homogeneous mixture whose elements and/or compounds are evenly mixed at the molecular level but are not bonded together. (p. 302)

**solvent:** substance that dissolves the solute. (p. 302)

**state of matter:** physical property that is dependent on both temperature and pressure and occurs in four forms—solid, liquid, gas, or plasma. (p. 245)

**stomata (STOH muh tuh):** tiny openings in a plant's epidermis through which carbon dioxide, water vapor, and oxygen enter and exit. (pp. 557, 577)

**substance:** matter that has the same composition and properties throughout. (pp. 285, 300)

**symmetry:** arrangement of individual body parts; can be radial (arranged around a central point) or bilateral (mirror-image parts). (p. 483)

**synapse (SIHN aps):** small space across, which an impulse moves from an axon to the dendrites or cell body of another neuron. (p. 400)

**seguridad antisísmica:** describe la capacidad de las estructuras de resistir las vibraciones producidas por los terremotos. (p. 185)

**ondas sísmicas:** ondas producidas durante los terremotos, las cuales pu ser primarias, secundarias y superficiales. (p. 180)

**sismógrafo:** instrumento usado para registrar las ondas sísmicas. (p. 181)

**volcán escudo:** volcán grande y ancho con lados ligeramente inclinados que se forma por la aparición de capas basálticas. (p. 190)

**planta de día corto:** planta que generalmente requiere de noches largas—12 horas o más de oscuridad—para comenzar su proceso de floración. (p. 590)

**hundimiento:** ocurre cuando una masa rocosa o sedimento se desliza sobre una superficie curva. (p. 103)

**suelo:** mezcla de roca desgastada por la acción atmosférica, materia orgánica, agua y aire que evoluciona con el tiempo y ayuda al desarrollo de la vida vegetal. (p. 98)

**solubilidad:** medida de la cantidad de soluto que puede disolverse en cierta cantidad de solvente. (p. 309)

**soluto:** sustancia que se disuelve y parece desaparecer en otra sustancia. (p. 302)

**solución:** mezcla homogénea cuyos elementos o compuestos están mezclados de manera uniforme a nivel molecular pero no se enlazan. (p. 302)

**solvente:** sustancia que disuelve al soluto. (p. 302)

**estado de la materia:** propiedad física que depende de la temperatura y la presión, y que ocurre en cuatro formas: sólido, líquido, gas, o plasma. (p. 245)

**estomas:** aperturas pequeñas en la epidermis de las plantas a través de las cuales entra y sale dióxido de carbono, vapor de agua y oxígeno. (p. 557, 577)

**sustancia:** materia que siempre tiene la misma composición y las mismas propiedades. (pp. 285, 300)

**simetría:** distribución de las partes individuales del cuerpo; puede ser radial (distribuidas alrededor de un punto central) o bilateral. (partes que se reflejan a sí mismas). (p. 483)

**sinapsis:** pequeño espacio a través del cual un impulso se mueve desde el axón hasta las dendritas o los cuerpos celulares de otra neurona. (p. 400)

**systemic circulation:** largest part of the circulatory system, in which oxygen-rich blood flows to all the organs and body tissues, except the heart and lungs, and oxygen-poor blood is returned to the heart. (p. 421)

**circulación sistémica:** la parte más grande del sistema circulatorio en la que la sangre rica en oxígeno fluye hacia todos los órganos y tejidos corporales excepto el corazón y los pulmones, y la sangre pobre en oxígeno regresa al corazón. (p. 421)

### T

**technology:** use of scientific discoveries for practical purposes, making people's lives easier and better. (p. 12)

**tecnología:** uso de descubrimientos científicos para propósitos prácticos, haciendo que la vida de las personas sea mejor y más fácil. (p. 12)

**tendon:** thick band of tissue that attaches bones to muscles. (p. 390)

**tendón:** banda de tejido grueso que une los huesos y los músculos. (p. 390)

**tissue:** group of similar cells that all do the same work. (p. 373)

**tejido:** grupo de células similares que desempeñan la misma función. (p. 373)

**topographic map:** map that shows the changes in elevation of Earth's surface and indicates such features as roads and cities. (p. 46)

**mapa topográfico:** mapa que muestra los cambios en la elevación de la superficie terrestre que puede ser representado como una relación e indica características como carreteras y ciudades. (p. 46)

**topography:** configuration of surface features, including position and slope; also influences the types of soils that develop. (p. 98)

**topografía:** configuración de características de la superficie, incluyendo posición e inclinación, y que también influye en los tipos de suelos que se desarrollan. (p. 98)

**trachea (TRAY kee uh):** air-conducting tube that connects the larynx with the bronchi, is lined with mucous membranes and cilia, and contains strong cartilage rings. (p. 460)

**tráquea:** tubo conductor de aire que conecta a la laringe con los bronquios, está forrada con membranas mucosas y cilios y contiene fuertes anillos de cartílagos. (p. 460)

**transverse wave:** mechanical wave that causes particles in matter to move at right angles to the direction the wave travels. (p. 213)

**onda transversal:** onda mecánica que hace que las partículas de materia se muevan en ángulos rectos respecto a la dirección en que viaja la onda. (p. 213)

**tropism:** positive or negative plant response to an external stimulus such as touch, light, or gravity. (p. 586)

**tropismo:** respuesta positiva o negativa de una planta a un estímulo externo como el rozamiento, la luz o la gravedad. (p. 586)

**tsunami:** powerful seismic sea wave that begins over an ocean-floor earthquake, can reach 30 m in height when approaching land, and can cause destruction in coastal areas. (p. 183)

**tsunami:** poderosa onda sísmica marina que comienza en un terremoto en el lecho oceánico, pudiendo alcanzar 30 metros de altura al acercarse a la tierra y causar gran destrucción en las áreas costeras. (p. 183)

### U

**ultraviolet waves:** electromagnetic waves with wavelengths between about 400 billionths and 10 billionths of a meter. (p. 228)

**ondas ultravioleta:** ondas electromagnéticas con longitudes de onda entre aproximadamente 10 y 400 billonésimas de metro. (p. 228)

**unconformity (un kun FOR mih tee):** gap in the rock layer that is due to erosion or periods without any deposition. (p. 140)

**uniformitarianism:** principle stating that Earth processes occurring today are similar to those that occurred in the past. (p. 139)

**upwarped mountains:** mountains formed when blocks of Earth's crust are pushed up by forces inside Earth. (p. 38)

**ureter:** tube that carries urine from each kidney to the bladder. (p. 467)

**discordancia:** brecha en la capa rocosa que es debida a la erosión o a periodos sin deposición. (p. 140)

**uniformitarianismo:** principio que establece que los procesos de la Tierra que ocurren actualmente son similares a los que ocurrieron en el pasado. (p. 139)

**montañas de levantamiento:** montañas que se forman cuando los bloques de la corteza terrestre son empujados hacia arriba por fuerzas del interior de la Tierra. (p. 38)

**uréter:** tubo que transporta la orina desde cada uno de los riñones hasta la vejiga. (p. 467)

**vaccine:** provides immunity from some bacterial and viral diseases such as tetanus and influenza, and is made from particles taken from damaged bacterial cells, killed bacteria, or killed or damaged viruses. (p. 606)

**vacuole (VAK yew ohl):** balloonlike cell organelle in the cytoplasm that can store food, water, and other substances. (p. 366)

**variables:** different factors that can be changed in an experiment. (p. 10)

**vascular plant:** plant with tubelike structures that move minerals, water, and other substances throughout the plant. (p. 549)

**vein:** blood vessel that carries blood back to the heart, and has one-way valves that keep blood moving toward the heart. (p. 422)

**ventricles (VEN trih kulz):** two lower chambers of the heart, that contract at the same time, during a heartbeat. (p. 419)

**villi (VIHL I):** fingerlike projections covering the wall of the small intestine that increase the surface area for food absorption. (p. 449)

**vitamin:** water-soluble or fat-soluble organic nutrient needed in small quantities for growth, for preventing some diseases, and for regulating body functions. (p. 443)

**vacuna:** suministra inmunidad contra algunas enfermedades bacterianas o virales tales como el tétano y la influenza, y está hecha de partículas tomadas de células bacterianas dañadas, bacterias muertas, o virus muertos o dañados. (p. 606)

**vacuola:** organelo celular en forma de balón que se encuentra en el citoplasma y que puede almacenar alimentos, agua y otras sustancias. (p. 366)

**variables:** diferentes factores que pueden cambiarse en un experimento. (p. 10)

**planta vascular:** planta con estructuras semejantes a tubos, las cuales sirven para movilizar minerales, agua y otras sustancias a toda la planta. (p. 549)

**vena:** vaso sanguíneo que lleva sangre de regreso al corazón y tiene válvulas unidireccionales que mantienen a la sangre en movimiento hacia el corazón. (p. 422)

**ventrículos:** las dos cámaras inferiores del corazón que se contraen al mismo tiempo durante el latido cardiaco. (p. 419)

**vellosidades:** proyecciones en forma de dedo que cubren las paredes del intestino delgado y aumentan el área de superficie para la absorción de los alimentos. (p. 449)

**vitamina:** nutriente orgánico soluble en agua o en grasa, necesario en pequeñas cantidades para el crecimiento, para prevenir algunas enfermedades y para regular las funciones biológicas. (p. 443)

**volcanic mountains:** mountains formed when molten material reaches Earth's surface through a weak crustal area and piles up into a cone-shaped structure. (p. 39)

**volcano:** cone-shaped hill or mountain formed when hot magma, solids, and gas erupt onto Earth's surface through a vent. (p. 187)

**voluntary muscle:** muscle, such as a leg or arm muscle, that can be consciously controlled. (p. 389)

**montañas volcánicas:** montañas formadas cuando material derretido alcanza la superficie a través de un área débil de la corteza terrestre y se acumula formando una estructura en forma de cono. (p. 39)

**volcán:** colina o montaña cónica que se forma cuando el magma caliente, sólidos y gases, hacen erupción en la superficie terrestre a través de una abertura. (p. 187)

**músculo voluntario:** músculo, como el músculo de una pierna o de un brazo, que puede ser controlado voluntariamente. (p. 389)

## W

**wave:** disturbance that moves through matter and space and carries energy. (p. 212)

**wavelength:** distance between one point on a wave and the nearest point moving with the same speed and direction. (p. 214)

**weathering:** natural mechanical or chemical process that causes rocks to change by breaking them down and causing them to crumble. (p. 94)

**xylem (ZI lum):** vascular tissue that forms hollow vessels that transport substances, other than sugar, throughout a plant. (p. 559)

**onda:** perturbación que se mueve a través de la materia y el espacio y que transporta energía. (p. 212)

**longitud de onda:** distancia entre un punto en una onda y el punto más cercano, moviéndose con la misma rapidez y dirección. (p. 214)

**desgaste:** proceso natural, mecánico o químico que produce cambios en las roca, rompiéndolas y haciendo que se desmoronen. (p. 94)

**xilema:** tejido vascular que forma vasos ahuecados que trasportan todo tipo de sustancias, excepto azúcares, en toda la planta. (p. 559)

*Italic numbers = illustration/photo* **Bold numbers = vocabulary term**
*lab = indicates a page on which the entry is used in a lab*
*act = indicates a page on which the entry is used in an activity*

**Index**

Index

# Index

Index

Index

Index

**Index**

Index

**Index**

Index

## Photo Credits

**Cover** (t)Nicholas Reuss/Lonely Planet Images, (bl)Getty Images, (br)Altrendo Nature/Getty Images; **4-5** Dutheil Didier/CORBIS Sygma; **7** (t)Michael Habicht/Earth Scenes, (b)Michael Wilhelm/ENP Images; **8** Richard Cummins/CORBIS; **9** John Heseltine/Science Photo Library/Photo Researchers; **10 11** Aaron Haupt; **12** (t)Michael Dwyer/Stock Boston, (c)Tim Courlas, (b)Mark Segal/Stock Boston; **13** (t)Science Museum/Science & Society Picture Library, (cl)reprinted by permission of Parks Canada and Newfoundland Museum, (c cr)Dorling Kindersley, (b)NASA; **14** Russ Underwood/Lockheed Martin Space Systems; **15** Todd Gustafson/Danita Delimont, Agent; **16** Smithsonian Institution; **18** NASA/MSFC; **19** European Space Agency/Science Photo Library/Photo Researchers; **20** (l)Frans Lanting/Minden Pictures, (c)Ted Levin/Animals Animals, (r)Al & Linda Bristor/Visuals Unlimited; **21** Matt Meadows; **22** Bates Littlehales/National Geographic Image Collection; **23** Aaron Haupt; **24** Mark Burnett; **25** Timothy Fuller; **26** AP/Wide World Photos; **27** (l)CABISCO/Visuals Unlimited, (r)Jan Hinsch/Science Photo Libray/Photo Researchers; **29** Paul Silverman/Fundamental Photographs; **32-33** GSFC/NASA; **35** (tl)Alan Maichrowicz/Peter Arnold, Inc., (tr)Carr Clifton/Minden Pictures; (b)Stephen G. Maka/DRK Photo; **36** Ron Mellot; **38** (t)John Kieffer/Peter Arnold, Inc., (b)Carr Clifton/Minden Pictures; **39** David Muench/CORBIS; **42** Dominic Oldershaw; **47** (t)Rob & Ann Simpson, (b)courtesy Maps a la Carte, Inc. and TopoZone.com; **50** CORBIS; **52** (t)Layne Kennedy/CORBIS, (b)John Evans; **53** John Evans; **54** (tl)Culver Pictures, (tcl b)PhotoDisc, (tcr)William Manning/The Stock Market/CORBIS, (tr)Kunio Owaki/The Stock Market/CORBIS, (c)Pictor; **55** (l)Tom Bean/DRK Photo, (r)Marc Muench; **56** William Weber; **58** Aaron Haupt; **60-61** Steve Vidler/SuperStock; **62** (l)Doug Martin, (r)Mark Burnett; **63** Mark A. Schneider/Visuals Unlimited; **64** (t)Manuel Sanchis Calvete/CORBIS, (bl)Doug Martin, (bc)Jose Manuel Sanchis Calvete/CORBIS, (br)Mark A. Schneider/Visuals Unlimited; **65** (t)Albert J. Copley/Visuals Unlimited, (b)Fundamental Photographs; **66** Tim Courlas; **68** (tl)Ryan McVay/ PhotoDisc, (tr)Lester V. Bergman/CORBIS, (b)Margaret Courtney-Clarke/Photo Researchers; **69** (t)Walter H. Hodge/Peter Arnold, Inc., (b)Craig Aurness/CORBIS; **70** KS Studios; **71** Kyodo/AP/Wide World Photos; **72** (l)Stephen J. Krasemann/DRK Photo, (r)Brent P. Kent/Earth Scenes; **73** (l)Breck P. Kent/Earth Scenes, **73** (r)Brent Turner/BLT Productions; **74** (bkgd) Galen Rowell/Mountain Light, (tl)Martin Miller, (tr)Steve Kaufman/CORBIS, (b)David Muench/CORBIS; **75** (t)John D. Cunningham/Visuals Unlimited, (b)Morrison Photography; **76** Jeff Foott/DRK Photo; **77** (l)Yann Arthus-Bertrand/CORBIS, (r)Alfred Pasieka/Science Photo Library/Photo Researchers; **78** NASA/CORBIS; **79** (tl)Brent Turner/BLT Productions, (tr br)Breck P. Kent/Earth Scenes, (cl)Andrew J. Martinez/Photo Researchers, (cr)Tom Pantages/PhotoTake NYC/PictureQuest, (bl)Runk/Schoenberger from Grant Heilman; **80** (tl)Stephen J. Krasemann/DRK Photo, (tr)Peter Arnold/Peter Arnold, Inc., (bl)M. Angelo/ CORBIS, (br)Christian Sarramon/CORBIS; **81** (l)Doug Martin, (tr)Breck P. Kent/Earth Scenes, (br)Andrew J. Martinez/Photo Researchers; **82** Bernhard Edmaier/Science Photo Library/Photo Researchers; **83** Andrew J. Martinez/Photo Researchers; **84** Matt Meadows; **86** (tl)Arne Hodalic/CORBIS; **86** (tl)Archive Photos, (tr)Stock Montage, (bl)Brown Brothers, (br)Herbert Gehr/Timepix; **87** (l)A.J. Copley/Visuals Unlimited, (c)Barry L. Runk from Grant Heilman, (r)Breck P. Kent/Earth Scenes; **90** Tim Courlas, **92-93** Carmen Redondo/CORBIS; **94** Jonathan Blair/CORBIS; **95** R. & E. Thane/Earth Scenes; **96** Doug Martin; **97** (t)Aaron Haupt, (bl)Layne Kennedy/CORBIS, (br)Richard Cummins/CORBIS; **100** KS Studios; **101** USGS; **102** (tl)DP Schwert/ND State University, (tr)Martin Miller, (b)Roger Ressmeyer/CORBIS, (l)Chris Rainier/CORBIS, (r)Glenn M. Oliver/Visuals Unlimited; **105** (l)John Lemker/Earth Scenes, (r)Francois Gohier/Photo Researchers, (b)Paul A. Souders/CORBIS; **106** (t)Gerald & Buff Corsi/Visuals Unlimited, (b)Dean Conger/CORBIS; **107** (t)KS Studios, (b)Tess & David Young/Tom Stack & Assoc.; **108** (t)Gerard Lacz/Earth Scenes, (b)Vanessa Vick/Photo Researchers; **109** Martin G. Miller/Visuals Unlimited; **110** (t)Matt Meadows, (b)Dominic Oldershaw; **112** (t)Morton Beebe, SF/CORBIS, (b)Will & Deni McIntyre/Photo Researchers; **113** (l)Martin G. Miller/Visuals Unlimited, (r)James P. Rowan/DRK Photo; **116** Jonathan Blair/CORBIS; **117** (t)Owen Franken/CORBIS, (b)David Muench/CORBIS; **118-119** Hugh Sitton /Getty Images; **120** (t)Mark E. Gibson/Visuals Unlimited, (b)D.E. Hurlbert & James DiLoreto/Smithsonian Institution; **121** Jeffrey Rotman/CORBIS; **122** (t)Dr. John A. Long, (b)A.J. Copley/Visuals Unlimited; **124** (t)PhotoTake NYC/PictureQuest, (b)Louie Psihoyos; **126** David M. Dennis; **127** (l)Gary Retherford/Photo Researchers, (r)Lawson Wood/CORBIS; **128** Aaron Haupt; **131** (bkgd)Lyle Rosbotham, (l)IPR/12-18 T. Bain, British Geological Survey/NERC. All rights reserved, (r)Tom Bean/CORBIS; **132** Jim Hughes/PhotoVenture/Visuals Unlimited; **133** (l)Michael T. Sedam/CORBIS, (r)Pat O'Hara/CORBIS; **135** Aaron Haupt; **137** James King-Holmes/Science Photo Library/Photo Researchers; **138** Kenneth Garrett; **139** WildCountry/CORBIS; **140** (t)A.J. Copley/Visuals Unlimited, (b)Lawson Wood/CORBIS; **141** Matt Meadows; **142** Jacques Bredy; **143** (tl)Francois Gohier/Photo Researchers, (tr)Sinclair Stammers/Photo Researchers, (b)Mark E. Gibson/DRK Photo; **146** Tom Bean/CORBIS; **148-149** Bourseiller/Durieux/Photo Researchers; **152** Martin Land/Science Source/Photo Researchers; **155** Ralph White/CORBIS; **161** Davis Meltzer; **162** Craig Aurness/CORBIS; **164** Craig Brown/Index Stock; **165** Ric Ergenbright/CORBIS; **166** Roger Ressmeyer/CORBIS; **168** Burhan Ozbilici/AP/Wide World Photos; **170** L. Lauber/Earth Scenes; **176-177** Reuters NewMedia Inc./CORBIS; **178** KS Studios; **181** (t)Krafft/Explorer/Photo Researchers, (b)Jean Miele/The Stock Market/CORBIS; **184** (bkgd) Galen Rowell/CORBIS, (t b)NOAA; **185** (t)KS Studios, (b)Pacific Seismic Products, Inc.; **186** Roger Ressmeyer/CORBIS; **188** (l)AP/Wide World Photos, (r)Kevin West/AP/Wide World Photos; **190** (t)Breck P. Kent/Earth Scenes, (b)Dewitt Jones/CORBIS; **191** (t)Lynn Gerig/Tom Stack & Associates, (b)Milton Rand/Tom Stack & Associates; **193** Otto Hahn/Peter Arnold, Inc.; **194** Spencer

Grant/PhotoEdit; **196** NASA/GSFC/JPL, MISR Team; **200 201** Aaron Haupt; **202** (t)Ted Streshinky/CORBIS, (b)Underwood & Underwood/CORBIS; **203** (t)James L. Amos/CORBIS, (c)Michael Collier, (b)Phillip Wallick/The Stock Market/CORBIS; **210-211** Mark A. Johnson/CORBIS; **212** (l)David W. Hamilton/Getty Images, (r)Ray Massey/Getty Images; **217 218** Richard Megna/Fundamental Photographs, NYC; **220** (t)AFP/Hector Mata/Getty Images, (b)David Young-Wolff / Photo Edit, Inc.; **221** (tl)Ian O'Leary/Stone/Getty Images, (tr)David Young-Wolff/PhotoEdit, Inc., (bl)Mark A. Schneider/Visuals Unlimited, (bc)Rafael Macia/Photo Researchers, (br)SuperStock; **224** Matt Meadows; **225** James Blank/Getty Images; **230** (t)Nation Wong/CORBIS, (b)Jon Feingersh/CORBIS; **231** Ralph C. Eagle, Jr./Photo Researchers; **232 233** Matt Meadows; **234** (t)Bettmann/CORBIS, (b)image courtesy of NRAO/AUI: **239** (r)David Young-Wolff/PhotoEdit; **240-241** Greg Garay/AFP/Getty Images; **242 243 244** Matt Meadows; **245** Aaron Haupt; **247** (t)David Taylor/Science Photo Library/Photo Researchers, (b)Jeff J. Daly/Visuals Unlimited; **248** (t)SuperStock, (b)Ray Pfortner/Peter Arnold, Inc.; **249** Amanita Pictures; **250** (l)Steve Kaufman/CORBIS, (tr)Tom McHugh/Photo Researchers, (br)Fred Bavendam/Minden Pictures; **251** Don Tremain/PhotoDisc; **252** (l)Richard Megna/Fundamental Photographs, (cl)John Lund/Stone/Getty Images, (cr)Richard Pasley/Stock Boston, (r)T.J. Florian/Rainbow/PictureQuest; **253** (l)Philippe Colombi/PhotoDisc, (c)Michael Newman/PhotoEdit, Inc., (r)Roger K. Burnard; **254** (r)Matt Meadows; **255** (t)Ralph Cowan, (b)Aaron Haupt; **258** Timothy Fuller; **259** John Evans; **260** (t)John A. Rizzo/PhotoDisc, (b)Aaron Haupt; **261** Matt Meadows; **262** (t)Denso/Rex Features, (b)Alexander Tsiaras/Photo Researchers; **263** (l)John Evans, (r)Siede Preis/PhotoDisc; **264** Henry Groskinsky/TimePix; **265** Elaine Shay; **266** Aaron Haupt; **267** (t)Richard Megna/Fundamental Photographs, (bl)John Lund/Stone/Getty Images, (br)T.J. Florian/Rainbow/PictureQuest; **268-269** Russell Dohrman/Index Stock Imagery; **269** Morrison Photography; **270** (l)Gary C. Will/Visuals Unlimited, (c)Mark Burnett/Stock Boston, (r)CORBIS; **272** Mark Burnett; **273** (l)Mark Burnett, (r)NASA; **274** Van Bucher/Photo Researchers; **278** Fermi National Accelerator Laboratory/Science Photo Library/Photo Researchers; **279** Tom Stewart/The Stock Market/CORBIS; **280** (bkgd tr bl)Bettmann/CORBIS, (br)New York Public Library, General Research Division, Astor, Lenox, and Tilden Foundations; **282** Emmanuel Scorcelletti/Liaison Agency/Getty Images; **284** Doug Martin; **285** NASA; **286** Mark Burnett; **287** Klaus Guldbrandsen/Science Photo Library/Photo Researchers; **288** (tl)Mark Thayer, (tr)CORBIS, (bl)Kenneth Mengay/Liaison Agency/Getty Images, (bc)Arthur Hill/Visuals Unlimited, (br)RMIP/Richard Haynes; **288-289** KS Studios; **290** (t)Mark Burnett, (b)Michael Newman/PhotoEdit; **292** (tl)Robert Essel/The Stock Market/CORBIS, (tr)John Eastcott & Yva Momatiuk/DRK Photo., (cr)Diaphor Agency/Index Stock Imagery, (bl)Ame Hodalic/CORBIS, (br)no credit; **298-299** Joseph Sohm/ChromoSohm, Inc./CORBIS; **301** (l)Stephen W. Frisch/Stock Boston, (r)Doug Martin; **302** (t)IRB/IndexStock Imagery, (b)Doug Martin; **303** Richard Hamilton/CORBIS; **304** John Evans; **305** (l)SuperStock, (r)Annie Griffiths/CORBIS; **308** John Evans; **310** Richard Nowitz/Phototake/PictureQuest; **312** Aaron Haupt; **313** KS Studios/Mullenix; **315** John Evans; **316** (tl)Joe Sohm, Chromosohm/Stock Connection/PictureQuest, (tc)Andrew Popper/Phototake/PictureQuest, (tr)A. Wolf/Explorer, Photo Researchers, (b)Stephen R. Wagner; **317** John Evans; **318** (tl tr)Elaine Shay, (tcl)Brent Turner/BLT Productions, (tcr)Matt Meadows, (bl bcl)CORBIS, (bcr)Icon Images, (br)StudiOhio; **322 323** KS Studios; **324 326** CORBIS; **329** Stephen W. Frisch/Stock Boston; **330-331** Simon Fraser/Science Photo Library/Photo Researchers; **332** (l)Aaron Haupt, (r)Doug Martin; **333** (tl)Patricia Lanza, (tc)Jeff J. Daly/Visuals Unlimited, (tr)Susan T. McElhinney, (bl)Craig Fujii/Seattle Times, (br)Sovfoto/Eastfoto/PictureQuest; **334** Amanita Pictures; **337** Sovfoto/Eastfoto/PictureQuest; **339** Christopher Swann/Peter Arnold, Inc.; **340** (tl)Frank Balthis, (tr)Lois Ellen Frank/CORBIS, (b)Matt Meadows; **341** David Young-Wolff/PhotoEdit/PictureQuest; **342** (l)Amanita Pictures, (r)Richard Megna/Fundamental Photographs/Photo Researchers; **343** Victoria Arocho/AP/Wide World Photos; **344** (t)Aaron Haupt, (bl)Kevin Schafer/CORBIS, (br)Icon Images; **345** (l)SuperStock, (r)SuperStock; **346** (tl)Chris Arend/Alaska Stock Images/PictureQuest, (tr)Aaron Haupt, (b)Bryan F. Peterson/ CORBIS; **347** courtesy General Motors; **348 349** Matt Meadows; **350** Amanita Pictures; **351** Bob Daemmrich; **352** (l)Tino Hammid Photography, (r)Joe Richard/UF News & Public Affairs; **353** David Young-Wolff/PhotoEdit; **356** Lester V. Bergman/CORBIS; **360-361** Dave G. Houser/CORBIS; **361** Matt Meadows; **362** The Science Museum, London; **363** (tr)David M. Phillips/Visuals Unlimited, (cr)Richard Shiell/Earth Scenes, (bl)Michael Keller/The Stock Market/CORBIS, (bc)Zig Leszczynski/Animals Animals, (br)Reed/Williams/Animals Animals; **367** Gabe Palmer/The Stock Market; **368** Matt Meadows; **370** (l)R. Kessel/G. Shih/Visuals Unlimited, (tr)Carolina Biological Supply Co./Earth Scenes, (c)Doug Martin, (br)Bruce Iverson; **374** (t)Envision/George Mattei, (b)Doug Martin; **375** Morrison Photography; **376** Custom Medical Stock Photo; **377** (l)Kevin Collins/Visuals Unlimited, (r)David M. Phillips/Visuals Unlimited; **381** Matt Meadows; **382-383** Michael Pasdzior/Getty Images; **383** Matt Meadows; **385** (tl)Clyde H. Smith/Peter Arnold, Inc., (tcl)Erik Sampers/Photo Researchers, (tcr)Dean Conger/CORBIS, (tr)Michael A. Keller/The Stock Market/CORBIS, (bl)Peter Turnley/CORBIS, (bcl)Joe McDonald/Visuals Unlimited, (bcr)Art Stein/Photo Researchers, (br)Ed Bock/The Stock Market; **387** Jim Grace/Photo Researchers; **388** Mark Burnett; **389** (l)Aaron Haupt, (r)Aaron Haupt; **390** (l)Breck P. Kent, (c)Runk/Schoenberger from Grant Heilman, (r)PhotoTake NYC/Carolina Biological Supply Company; **391** (t)C Squared Studios/PhotoDisc, (b)M. McCarron; **397** Geoff Butler; **398** Science Photo Library/Photo Researchers; **399 402** KS Studios; **407** Michael Newman/PhotoEdit; **408** (t)Jeff Greenberg/PhotoEdit, (b)Amanita Pictures; **409** Amanita Pictures; **410** (t)Sara Davis/The Herald-Sun, (b)Sara Davis/The Herald-Sun; **415** Eamonn McNulty/Science Photo Library/Photo Researchers; **416-417** Steve Allen/Getty Images; **418 421** Aaron Haupt; **423** Matt Meadows; **424** (tl)Stephen R. Wagner, (tr cl bl)Martin M. Rotker, (cr br)Stephen R. Wagner;

425 (t)StudiOhio, (b)Matt Meadows; 427 First Image; 429 (l)National Cancer Institute/Science Photo Library/ Photo Researchers, (r)Don W. Fawcett/Visuals Unlimited; 433 Meckes/Ottawa/Photo Researchers; 435 Aaron Haupt; 436 (t)Matt Meadows/Peter Arnold, Inc., (b)Matt Meadows; 438 no credit; 439 (l)Manfred Kage/Peter Arnold, Inc., (r)K.G. Murti/Visuals Unlimited; 444-445 Chris Trotman/NewSport/CORBIS; 447 Geoff Butler; 451 452 KS Studios; 453 Visuals Unlimited; 455 456 KS Studios; 458 Dominic Oldershaw; 459 Bob Daemmrich; 462 Richard T. Nowitz; 464 Renee Lynn/Photo Researchers; 469 (t)KS Studios, (b)Richard Hutchings/Photo Researchers; 471 Matt Meadows; 473 (tl)Ed Beck/The Stock Market/CORBIS, (tr)Tom & DeeAnn McCarthy/The Stock Market/ CORBIS, (b)Goldwater/Network/Saba Press Photos; 480-481 Stuart Westmorland/CORBIS; 482 (l)Fred Bravendam/Minden Pictures, (c)Scott Smith/Animals Animals, (r)Fritz Prenzel/Animals Animals; 487 (t)Carolina Biological Supply/PhotoTake NYC, (b)Runk/Schoenberger from Grant Heilman; 488 Oliver Meckes/Photo Researchers; 489 Renee Stockdale/Animals Animals; 490 Anne Wertheim/Animals Animals; 491 (l)David Hall/PhotoResearchers, (r)Andrew J. Martinez/Photo Researchers; 492 Alex Kerstitch/ KERST/Bruce Coleman, Inc.; 493 Robert Maier/Animals Animals; 494 James M. Robinson/Photo Researchers; 495 (l)Chris McLaughlin/Animals Animals, (c)Nancy Sefton, (r)A. Flowers & L. Newman/Photo Researchers; 496 SuperStock; 498 (tl)Peter Johnson/CORBIS, (tr)Joe McDonald/CORBIS, (cl)Stuart Westmoreland/CORBIS, (cr)Natural History Museum, London, (b)Joseph S. Rychetnik; 499 (tl)John Shaw, (tr)Scott T. Smith/CORBIS, (cl br)Brian Gordon Green, (cr)Richard T. Nowitz/ CORBIS, (bl)PhotoTake NYC; 500 (tl)Jerry Shulman/ SuperStock, (tc)Donald Specker/Animals Animals, (tr)SuperStock, (bl)Tom McHugh/Photo Researchers, (br)John Shaw/Tom Stack & Associates; 501 (l)Alex Kerstitch/Bruce Coleman, Inc., (c)Nancy Sefton, (r)Scott Johnson/Animals Animals; 502 Richard Mariscal/Bruce Coleman, Inc.; 503 Matt Meadows; 504 (t)William Hamilton/SuperStock, (b)Matt Meadows; 505 Matt Meadows; 506 (l)Kim Reisenbichler MBARI, (c)Runk/ Schoenberger from Grant Heilman, (r)Mike Severns/Tom Stack & Associates; 508 Tom McHugh/Photo Researchers; 510 James L. Stanfield/NGS/Getty; 512-513 Tom & Pat Leeson; 513 Amanita Pictures; 517 (l)Stuart Westmoreland/Stone, (t)Gerard Lacz/Animals Animals, (cl)D. Fleetham/OSF/Animals Animals, (cr)Joyce & Frank Burek/Animals Animals, (r)Mickey Gibson/Animals Animals, (bl)Amos Nachoum/CORBIS, (bcl)D. Fox/OSF/Animals Animals, (bcr)Tom McHugh/Photo Researchers, (br)Brandon D. Cole/CORBIS; 518 (l)Science VU/Visuals Unlimited, (r)Runk/Schoenberger from Grant Heilman; 519 S.R. Maglione/Photo Researchers; 520 Runk Schoenberger from Grant Heilman; 521 (t)Visuals Unlimited, (bl)Runk Schoenberger from Grant Heilman, (br)George H. Harrison from Grant Heilman; 522 (tl)Robert J. Erwin/Photo Researchers, (tr)Wendell D. Metzen/Bruce Coleman, Inc., (bl)Photo Researchers, (br)Dan Suzio/Photo Researchers; 524 Stephen Dalton/Photo Researchers; 525 (l)Photo Researchers, (cl)Jane McAlonen/Visuals Unlimited, (cr)Erwin C. Nielson/Visuals Unlimited, (r)Fritz Polking/Visuals

Unlimited; 526 (l)Jeff Lepore/Photo Researchers, (r)Arthur R. Hill/Visuals Unlimited; 527 (tl)Tom & Pat Leeson/Photo Researchers, (tr)Andrew Syred/Science Photo Library/Photo Researchers, (bl)Crown Studios, (br)Marcia Griffen/Animals Animals; 528 Visuals Unlimited; 529 (l)Gerard Fuehrer/Visuals Unlimited, (r)Francois Gohier/Photo Researchers; 531 Dave Watts/ Tom Stack & Associates; 532 (tl)S.R. Maglione/Photo Researchers, (tr)SuperStock, (b)Carolina Biological Supply/PhotoTake NYC; 533 Ted Kerasote/Photo Researchers; 534 (t)Mark Newman/Photo Researchers, (b)Alan Carey; 535 Mella Panzella/Animals Animals; 536 Mark Garlick/Science Photo Library/Photo Researchers; 537 (t)John Cancalosi/DRK Photo, (b)Alvin E. Staffan/Photo Researchers; 538 Buddy Mays/CORBIS; 540 (l)Runk/Schoenberger from Grant Heilman, (r)S.R. Maglione/Photo Researchers; 542-543 Peter Adams /Getty Images; 544 Tom Stack & Assoc.; 545 Laat-Siluur; 546 (t)Kim Taylor/Bruce Coleman, Inc., (b)William E. Ferguson; 547 (tl)Amanita Pictures, (tr)Ken Eward/Photo Researchers, (bl)Photo Researchers, (br)Amanita Pictures; 548 (cw from top)Dan McCoy from Rainbow, David Sieren/Visuals Unlimited, Douglas Peebles/CORBIS, Edward S. Ross, Gerald & Buff Corsi/Visuals Unlimited, Gerald & Buff Corsi/Visuals Unlimited, Kevin & Betty Collins/Visuals Unlimited, Mack Henley/Visuals Unlimited,Martha McBride/Unicorn Stock Photos, Philip Dowell/DK Images, Steve Callaham/Visuals Unlimited; 549 (t)Gail Jankus/Photo Researchers, (b)Michael P. Fogden/Bruce Coleman, Inc.; 550 (l)Larry West/Bruce Coleman, Inc., (c)Scott Camazine/Photo Researchers, (r)Kathy Merrifield/Photo Researchers; 551 Michael P. Gadomski/Photo Researchers; 553 (t)Farrell Grehan/ Photo Researchers, (bl)Steve Solum/Bruce Coleman, Inc., (bc)R. Van Nostrand/Photo Researchers, (br)Inga Spence/ Visuals Unlimited; 554 (t)Joy Spurr/Bruce Coleman, Inc., (b)W.H. Black/Bruce Coleman, Inc.; 555 Farrell Grehan/ Photo Researchers; 556 Amanita Pictures; 557 (l)Nigel Cattlin/Photo Researchers, (c)Doug Sokel/Tom Stack & Assoc., (r)Charles D. Winters/Photo Researchers; 558 Bill Beatty/Visuals Unlimited; 560 (l)Doug Sokell/Tom Stack & Assoc., (tc)Robert C. Hermes/Photo Researchers, (r)Bill Beatty/Visuals Unlimited, (bc)David M. Schleser/Photo Researchers; 561 (cw from top)Tom Stack & Assoc., Dia Lein/Photo Researchers, E. Valentin/Photo Researchers, Eva Wallander, Eva Wallander, Joy Spurr/Photo Researchers; 563 (l)Dwight Kuhn, (c)Joy Spurr/Bruce Coleman, Inc., (r)John D. Cunningham/Visuals Unlimited; 564 (l)J. Lotter/Tom Stack & Assoc., (r)J.C. Carton/Bruce Coleman, Inc.; 566 (t)Inga Spence/ Visuals Unlimited, (b)David Sieren/Visuals Unlimited; 567 Jim Steinberg/Photo Researchers; 568 (t)Michael Rose/Frank Lane Picture Agency/CORBIS, (b)Dr. Jeremy Burgess/Science Photo Library/Photo Researchers; 570 Stephen P. Parker/Photo Researchers; 574-575 Terry Thompson/Panoramic Images; 575 Matt Meadows; 577 Dr. Jeremy Burgess/Science Photo Library/Photo Researchers; 578 (l)John Kieffer/Peter Arnold, Inc., (r)Runk/Schoenberger from Grant Heilman; 579 M. Eichelberger/Visuals Unlimited; 581 (t)Jacques Jangoux/Peter Arnold, Inc., (b)Jeff Lepore/Photo Researchers; 582 Michael P. Gadomski/Photo Researchers; 585 Howard Miller/Photo Researchers; 586 (l)Scott Camazine/Photo Researchers, (c r)Matt Meadows;

**589** (t)Artville, (cl)Runk/Schoenberger from Grant Heilman, (c cr)Prof. Malcolm B. Wilkins/University of Glasgow, (bl)Eric Brennan, (br)John Sohlden/Visuals Unlimited; **590** Jim Metzger; **592** (t)Ed Reschke/Peter Arnold, Inc., (b)Matt Meadows; **593** Matt Meadows; **594** Greg Vaughn/Getty Images; **595** (l)Norm Thomas/Photo Researchers, (r)S.R. Maglione/Photo Researchers; **596** Runk/Schoenberger from Grant Heilman; **598** Matt Meadows; **600-601** John D. Cunningham/Visuals Unlimited; **602** (l)Science VU/Visuals Unlimited, (r)K. Talaro/Visuals Unlimited; **603** (l)David M. Phillips/Visuals Unlimited, (t)CNRI/Phototake NYC, (c)Stone/Getty Images, (r)PDS-3/Visuals Unlimited; **604** (tl)Dr. Dennis Kunkel/PhotoTake NYC, (tc)David M. Phillips/Visuals Unlimited, (tr)R. Kessel/G. Shih/Visuals Unlimited, (bl)Ann Siegleman/Visuals Unlimited, (br)SCIMAT/Photo Researchers; **605** (tl)Yann Arthus-Bertrand/CORBIS, (tc)Fritz Polking/Visuals Unlimited, (tr)David R. Frazier Photolibrary, (br)K.G. Murti/Visuals Unlimited; **606** David M. Phillips/Visuals Unlimited; **608** Breck P. Kent/Earth Scenes; **609** Francois Gohier/Photo Researchers; **611** (l to r, t to b)Professors P.M. Motta & F.M. Magliocca/Science Photo Library/Photo Researchers, Eric Grave/Photo Researchers, Juergen Berger/Max-Planck Institute/Science Photo Library/Photo Researchers, Ray Simons/Photo Researchers, Bruce Iverson, Andrew Syred/Science Photo Library/Photo Researchers, Eric Grave/Photo Researchers, Winston Patnode/Photo Researchers, M.I. Walker/Science Source/Photo Researchers, J. Richardson/Visuals Unlimited, Andrew J. Martinez/Photo Researchers, D.P. Wilson/Eric & David Hosking/Photo Researchers; **612** Lennart Nilsson/Albert Bonniers Forlag AB; **613** (t)Don Brown/Animals Animals, (b)David M. Phillips/Visuals Unlimited; **614** Runk/Schoenberger from Grant Heilman; **616** Mark Steinmetz; **617** (t br)Mark Steinmetz, (tc)Adrian P. Davies/Bruce Coleman, Inc., (bl)Fred Habegger from Grant Heilman; **618** (l)Dr. Dennis Kunkel/PhotoTake NYC, (r)Mark Steinmetz; **619** (l)John Shaw/Bruce Coleman, Inc., (r)Dwight Kuhn; **620** (t)Runk/Schoenberger from Grant Heilman, (c)Ken Eward/Science Source/Photo Researchers, (b)Amanita Pictures; **621** (l)Doug Wechsler/Earth Scenes, (r)Ken Greer/Visuals Unlimited; **622 623** KS Studios; **624** (t)Luis Rosendo/FPG, (b)Adam Woolfit/CORBIS; **625** (tl)Doug Martin, (tr)Eric Anderson/Visuals Unlimited, (bl)KS Studios, (br)David R. Frazier Photolibrary; **627** Science VU/Visuals Unlimited; **628** Fred Habegger from Grant Heilman; **629** Breck P. Kent/Earth Scenes; **630** PhotoDisc; **632** Tom Pantages; **636** Michell D. Bridwell/PhotoEdit; **637** Matt Meadows; **638** StudiOhio; **639** Timothy Fuller; **640** Aaron Haupt; **642** Geoff Butler; **643** Matt Meadows; **655** (l)Brad Armstrong/AP/Wide World Photos, (r)File photo; **657** Stuart Ramson/AP/Wide World Photos; **679** Matt Meadows; **685** (t)Runk/Schoenberger from Grant Heilman, (bl)Andrew Syred/Science Photo Library/Photo Researchers, (br)Rich Brommer; **686** (t)G.R. Roberts, (bl)Ralph Reinhold/Earth Scenes, (br)Scott Johnson/Animals Animals; **687** Martin Harvey/DRK Photo; **737** Rolf Bruderer/The Stock Market/CORBIS; **740** Fred Bravendam/Minden Pictures; **741** (t)SuperStock, (b)Ken Cole/Earth Scenes; **742** Arthur Gloor/Animals Animals; **743** (t)Joe McDonald/CORBIS, (b)Sid & Shirley Rucker/DRK Photo; **744** David M. Phillips/Visuals Unlimited, Inc.; **745** Dr. Jeremy Burgess/Science Photo Library/Photo Researchers; **747** Matt Meadows; **749** (tl)Pat & Tom Leeson/Photo Researchers, (tr)Gregory G. Dimijian/Photo Researchers Inc., (b)George Wilder/Visuals Unlimited; **viii** Pat O'Hara/CORBIS; **ix** (t)R. & E. Thane/Earth Scenes, (b)Doug Martin; **x** (t)Bjorn Backe/Papilio/CORBIS, (b)John S. Shelton; **xi** (t)H. Richard Johnston, (b)Randy Faris/CORBIS; **xii** (t)Meckes/Ottawa/Photo Researchers, (b)Greg Vaughn/Tom Stack & Associates; **xiii** (t)Rod Planck/Photo Researchers, (b)Kjell B. Sandved/Visuals Unlimited; **xiv** (t)Amanita Pictures, (b)Howard Miller/Photo Researchers; **xv** Kevin West/AP/Wide World Photos; **xx** Bob Daemmrich; **xxiii** (t)Roger Ressmeyer/CORBIS.

# Homeostasis

The human body can sense changes outside and inside itself. It responds to these changes by making changes to body functions. These responses keep the body's inside environment about the same at all times. Scientists call this ability of an organism to keep its internal environment about the same at all times **homeostasis.**

## Interdependence of Body Systems

You have probably noticed that your heart rate and breathing are faster after you exercise. These changes are responses to an increased level of activity. During physical activity, your muscle cells use up more and more oxygen and produce lots of carbon dioxide waste. Without you being aware of it, your brain responds to these changes. It directs your heart and lungs to work harder, delivering more oxygen to your muscle cells and carrying away carbon dioxide at a faster rate. This restores homeostasis to your muscles.

Homeostasis is also active when the body overheats, as shown in **Figure 1.** When the brain senses an increased internal temperature, it directs the body to make changes to cool it down. Sweating, for example, is one response to an increased internal temperature. Sweat is mostly water. The evaporation of water from the skin carries away thermal energy and helps cool the body. Another response that cools the body is the opening or dilation of blood vessels in the skin. This means that more blood passes near the surface of the skin, which helps to release excess thermal energy.

**Figure 1** The regulation of body temperature is a familiar example of homeostasis.

**Negative Feedback** Most body systems maintain homeostasis by negative feedback. Negative feedback is all of the body's responses that happen to restore a specific normal condition. When you exercise and become overheated, negative feedback responses remove excess thermal energy from your body. Blood pressure also is controlled by negative feedback. The walls of major arteries have cells that sense changes in blood pressure. If blood pressure increases, a message about this change travels from the arteries to the brain. The brain responds by sending a message to the heart to slow down—an action that decreases blood pressure.

Negative feedback also is important for maintaining a normal chemical balance in the body. Glucose is a type of sugar. It is carried in the blood throughout your body.

The glucose level in the blood usually becomes greater than normal after you eat, as shown in **Figure 2.** When the glucose level in the blood is too high, the pancreas releases the hormone insulin. Cells respond to insulin by taking in more glucose. Also, the liver takes in and stores excess glucose as glycogen. Both of these actions help keep a normal level of glucose in the blood.

If the glucose level in the blood is too low, the pancreas releases the hormone glucagon. Glucagon causes the liver to change glycogen back into glucose and to release it into the blood. This restores the normal glucose level in the blood.

**Figure 2** Negative-feedback systems control many internal body conditions, such as hormone level, blood sugar level, and body temperature.

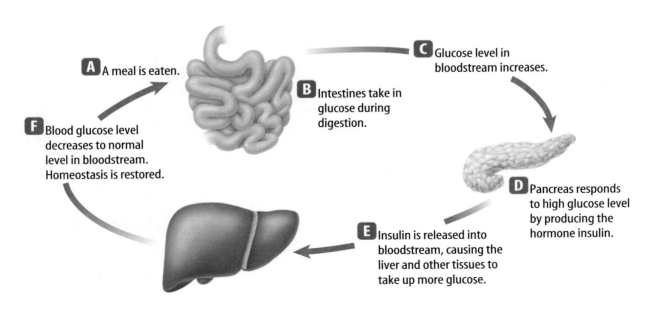

**A** A meal is eaten.

**B** Intestines take in glucose during digestion.

**C** Glucose level in bloodstream increases.

**D** Pancreas responds to high glucose level by producing the hormone insulin.

**E** Insulin is released into bloodstream, causing the liver and other tissues to take up more glucose.

**F** Blood glucose level decreases to normal level in bloodstream. Homeostasis is restored.

**Positive Feedback** Unlike negative feedback, positive feedback does not restore the body back to a normal level. Instead, the body responds by creating even more change. Positive feedback is rare in the healthy body.

Blood clotting, as shown in **Figure 3,** is an example of positive feedback. A cut or tear to the skin and a blood vessel causes the blood vessel to narrow. This limits the amount of blood that can escape. Next chemicals are released that activate platelets in the blood.

Platelets move to and clump at the damaged area of the vessel. This happens because chemical reactions occur in the platelets that make their surfaces sticky. This stickiness increases the release of chemicals that activate additional platelets. Therefore, more platelets become sticky and stick to one another. The process stops when the opening in the vessel is plugged. The clot becomes hard, white blood cells destroy any bacteria that might be present, and skin cells begin to repair the cut or tear.

## Homeostasis in Invertebrates

**Invertebrates** are animals without backbones. They are the most numerous animals on Earth, accounting for more than 95 percent of animal species. They range in size from tiny rotifers, measuring less than 0.001 mm in length, to giant squid, which can be over 13 m long. Invertebrates thrive in forests, deserts, oceans, and even in the air around us. The ability to maintain homeostasis allows invertebrates to function effectively across a large range of environmental conditions.

**Figure 3** When the skin is damaged, a sticky blood clot seals the leaking blood vessel. Eventually a scab forms to protect the wound from further damage and allow it to heal.

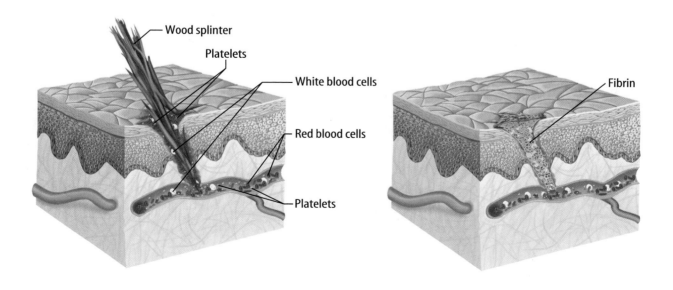

**Figure 4** In the two cell-layer body plan of a cnidarian, such as the lion's mane jellyfish, no cell is ever far from the water. In each cell, oxygen from the water is exchanged for carbon dioxide and other cell wastes.

**Oxygen/Carbon Dioxide Balance** To survive, animals must take in oxygen from the environment and remove waste carbon dioxide. These actions must be balanced to maintain homeostasis. **Cnidarians,** which are simple invertebrates such as jellyfish, sea anemones, and corals, and **annelids,** such as earthworms, accomplish this exchange through direct diffusion. **Direct diffusion** is when oxygen passes from the surrounding environment through cells on the animal's surface and into individual cells inside the organism. As waste carbon dioxide accumulates, it diffuses back across cell surfaces into the surrounding water or air. The lion's mane jellyfish, as shown in **Figure 4,** maintains homeostasis through direct diffusion.

Some invertebrates have specialized body structures for exchanging oxygen and carbon dioxide. Some arachnids, like a spider, have organs called **book lungs,** as shown in **Figure 5.** As air moves over the folded "pages," or plates, making up the book lung, oxygen diffuses into the blood while carbon dioxide diffuses out. Because the book lung is folded, it has a larger surface area over which the exchange of gases can take place.

Many insects have openings, called **spiracles,** along their bodies that allow air to enter and exit. The spiracles connect to a network of tubes, which extends throughout the body. Air moves through successively smaller tubes, eventually reaching specialized cells called tracheoles. The exchange of oxygen and carbon dioxide occurs in **tracheoles.** Many insects have valves that close the spiracles and prevent water loss.

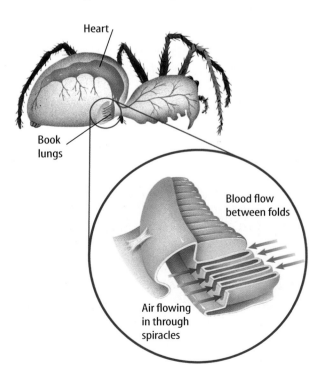

**Figure 5** Air circulates between the moist folds of the book lungs, bringing oxygen to the blood.

**Figure 6** One of the largest types of ants is the carpenter ant. Like all insects, it has a head, thorax, and abdomen. The exoskeleton serves several purposes, one of which is to regulate water loss.

**Water Balance** Insects are members of phylum **Arthropoda.** Insects have three body regions—a head, thorax, and abdomen, as shown in **Figure 6.** A hard outer covering called an **exoskeleton** provides support and protection for internal organs. The exoskeleton is also important in regulating water loss. Because an insect's body has a large surface area to volume ratio, it can dry out easily. The exoskeleton has a waxy, water-repellent component that forms a seal, slowing water loss from the insect's body.

Cold temperatures can present special water-related issues for insects. Freezing temperatures cause ice crystals to form that can destroy cells and tissues and sometimes cause death. As temperatures approach freezing, some insects undergo a process in which water molecules in the cells are replaced with a chemical called glycerol. Glycerol acts as an antifreeze in insect cells, reducing the temperature at which freezing will occur. As temperatures increase, the process is reversed: Glycerol is broken down and replaced with water.

**Temperature Control** Flying insects like bees use specific strategies to maintain homeostasis across temperature extremes. Bumblebees, for example, are covered in a thick layer of furry scales that provide insulation. When the air temperature is cool, a bumblebee may hang from a leaf or flower and warm up in the sunshine. A bee can also increase its body temperature by shivering its flight muscles. Contracting these muscles metabolizes stored energy, releasing heat which is distributed through the bee's body. As shown in **Figure 7,** in honeybee colonies, worker bees huddle together in groups to keep warm during the winter. Bees in the core of the cluster shiver, releasing heat that is shared throughout the colony. Bees near the outside of the cluster insulate the colony against heat loss.

**Figure 7** To survive cold winter temperatures, honeybees in the interior of the hive shiver, producing heat that is shared throughout the colony.

**Figure 8** When animals need to replace water, messages are sent to the brain that result in a feeling of thirst.

## Homeostasis in Vertebrates

Animals with backbones are called **vertebrates.** Vertebrates include mammals, amphibians, reptiles, birds, and fish. They have skulls that enclose and protect a brain, advanced nervous systems, and muscles. These features allow vertebrates to move efficiently and in complex ways. Vertebrates have tremendous advantages when competing for resources in the natural world. Internal processes and external behaviors help vertebrates maintain homeostasis in a variety of environmental conditions.

**Water Balance** Why do mammals, like the animals in **Figure 8,** feel thirsty? Thirst is one strategy for maintaining homeostasis in body chemistry. Normal body function can cause cells to lose water, resulting in dehydration. In dehydrated cells, the balance between sodium and water is disrupted. How does the body respond to this imbalance?

When an animal is dehydrated, receptor cells in the brain detect an increase in the amount of sodium compared to water. These cells trigger another part of the brain to send a signal to the pituitary gland. The pituitary gland releases a substance that causes the kidneys to slow the production of urine. At the same time, a thirst drive is created in the brain. Thirst causes the animal to drink fluid, restoring the balance between sodium and water.

**Hibernation** Many vertebrates live in regions where temperature and food availability vary greatly over time. American red squirrels are ground squirrels that inhabit evergreen forests in North America. They survive the cold winter months by **hibernating.**

Environmental stimuli, including changes in the hours of daylight and a decreasing food supply, trigger specific responses in these squirrels. Before hibernating, a ground squirrel eats more food. It also gathers and stores food in its den. Once the squirrel enters its den for the winter, physical changes occur. Its body temperature lowers until it is slightly above the outside temperature. Breathing and heart rate slow greatly. During hibernation, the squirrel's heart will beat only a few times each minute. Because the amount of energy required to sustain life functions is reduced, the squirrel can maintain homeostasis during extreme environmental conditions.

**Figure 9** Northern Copperheads sometimes go into a dormant state during summer months when ponds dry up.

**Estivation** A process similar to hibernation, **estivation** occurs in some organisms that live in hot, dry regions. Snakes are **ectotherms,** organisms that regulate body temperature by moving to warmer or cooler places as necessary. During long periods of hot, dry weather, a snake might estivate. As shown in **Figure 9,** a snake may seek shelter under a bush or rock. As the snake's body cools, its breathing and heart rate slow down. With greatly reduced energy requirements, the snake can survive long periods with relatively little food or water.

**Thermal Regulation** Vertebrates known as **endotherms** maintain a steady body temperature regardless of the surrounding environment. How does this happen? When an endotherm's body temperature changes, specialized receptors alert the brain, which sends the body into action. When an endotherm loses thermal energy, the brain triggers muscle contractions that cause the animal to shiver. Shivering releases thermal energy that increases the organism's body temperature. When an endotherm's body temperature rises above a certain level, responses may include panting or sweating, actions that cool the animal through evaporation.

**Metabolic Control** What bird beats its wings between 60 and 80 times each second during normal flight? If you guessed the hummingbird, you are right. A hummingbird needs a lot of energy to fly. To maintain an energy balance, the hummingbird must take in at least as many calories in food as it uses through its life functions.

A hummingbird spends much of its life gathering food to meet its energy needs. It may eat up to 50 percent of its weight in sugar each day from nectar, as shown in **Figure 10,** and tree sap. Insects eaten by hummingbirds provide the protein needed for muscle growth. But, how does a hummingbird meet its energy needs when the weather is too cold for feeding? It may enter a sleeplike state called **torpor,** during which both body temperature and heart rate decrease. As the hummingbird comes out of torpor, its heart rate and breathing increase, and it begins vibrating its wings. This vibration uses stored energy and releases thermal energy, warming the hummingbird's body.

**Figure 10** A hummingbird must take in sufficient calories each day to maintain its high metabolism.

# Homeostasis in Plants

As the basis for most food chains on Earth, **plants** are crucial to the survival of Earth's inhabitants. Plants help regulate climates, stabilize soil, and produce oxygen as a by-product of their life processes. From single-celled phytoplankton floating in the ocean, to moss covering a stony slope in Antarctica, to a giant sequoia towering 100 meters above the forest floor, plants display unique adaptations that allow them to thrive nearly everywhere on Earth.

What characteristics do plants share? Most have roots or rootlike structures that help anchor them to a surface. Many plants contain **chlorophyll,** and most are green due to the presence of this chemical in their cells. Chlorophyll absorbs sunlight and is necessary for **photosynthesis.** Plant cells are bound by a **cell wall,** as shown in **Figure 11,** and though their water requirements vary greatly, all plants need water. Like animals, plants must maintain homeostasis to survive.

**Maintaining Water Balance** Have you ever been asked to water a plant? If so, you know that a plant can appear quite different before and after watering. Deprived of sufficient amounts of water, a plant will die. Likewise, a plant can also die if it receives more water than it needs. Because survival depends on a healthy water balance, plant adaptations enable the storage of water and release of water to the air.

**Figure 11** The cell wall provides support and protection for the cell.

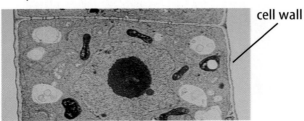

cell wall

## Activity

### Observing Homeostasis in *Elodea*
**Procedure**

1. Using **forceps,** remove **one leaf** from near the tip of the *Elodea* plant.
2. Prepare a wet mount of this leaf using **tap water, a slide,** and **a coverslip.** If you need help, see page 679.
3. Examine your wet-mount slide under the **microscope** on low and then high power. Draw what you observe on high power in your Science Journal. Label the cell wall, cell membrane, and chloroplasts.
4. Remove the slide from the stage of the microscope. Touch the edge of the cover-slip with a **paper towel.** Absorb as much water as possible.
5. Use a **dropper** and place one or two drops of the **salt solution** next to the edge of the coverslip.
6. Wait two minutes, then examine your wet-mount slide under the microscope on low and then high power. Draw what you observe in your Science Journal.
7. Repeat step 4.
8. Place one or two drops of **distilled water** next to the edge of the coverslip.
9. Repeat step 6.

**Analysis**

1. Compare and contrast the positions of the chloroplasts in step 3 with what you observed in step 5.
2. Describe how the distilled water affected the cells.
3. Explain how a plant cell's semi-permeable cell membrane helps maintain homeostasis.

**Vacuoles** are cell organelles that store materials needed for plant growth, including salts, minerals, and nutrients. Under optimal conditions, vacuoles are filled with water and exert pressure against the cell wall. This helps the plant to remain rigid. When water is lost, vacuoles shrink. Because vacuoles can no longer assist the cell wall in its support role, the plant begins to wilt.

How does a plant maintain homeostasis during dry conditions? Water escapes from a plant through **stomata,** microscopic openings in plant leaves through which gases travel into and out of plant cells. Two **guard cells** surround each stoma and regulate its size. As water moves into these guard cells, they swell and bend apart. This opens the stoma and allows carbon dioxide, water vapor, and waste gases to move into and out of the plant. When guard cells lose water, they deflate and the stoma closes. This limits the plant's water loss. **Figure 12** shows closed and open stomata.

**Figure 12** Stomata act as doorways for raw materials, such as carbon dioxide, water vapor, and waste gases to enter and exit the leaf.

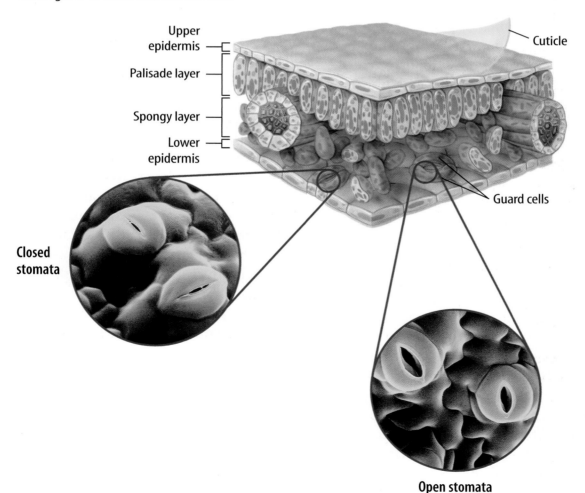

Upper epidermis

Palisade layer

Spongy layer

Lower epidermis

Cuticle

Guard cells

**Closed stomata**

**Open stomata**

**Figure 13** Tropisms are responses to external stimuli.

This plant is growing toward the light, an example of positive phototropism.

This plant was turned on its side. With the roots visible, you can see that they are showing positive gravitropism.

### Responding to Environmental Stimuli

While they may not be able to move in the way animals do, plants can respond to conditions in the environment through movement. Plant movements help them maintain homeostasis related to factors like gravity and the availability of light.

Have you ever seen a plant leaning toward a window? Light is an important stimulus to plants. When a plant responds to light, cells on the side of the plant opposite the light become longer than cells facing the light. This uneven growth causes the plant to bend toward the light. Leaves turn toward the light source. Then, they absorb more light. This response is called **positive phototropism** because the plant's movement is toward the light, as shown in **Figure 13.**

Plants also respond to gravity. The downward growth of plant roots, as shown in **Figure 13,** is a response to gravity called **positive gravitropism.** A stem growing upward demonstrates **negative gravitropism.** These and other **tropisms** result in growth patterns in response to environmental conditions. Plants also respond to temperature and darkness.

**Supplying Energy for Seeds** Plants make sugars using light energy through **photosynthesis.** Photosynthesis is the process through which light energy from the Sun is converted to chemical energy for use by the cell. In this reaction, autotrophs use light energy, carbon dioxide, and water to form glucose and oxygen. The plant's energy requirements are balanced by its ability to produce, store, and break down these sugars.

A plant releases energy for life processes through **cellular respiration,** a process that uses oxygen to break down stored sugars, produce carbon dioxide and water, and release energy.

$$C_6H_{12}O_6 + 6O_2 \rightarrow 6CO_2 + 6H_2O + energy$$

glucose    oxygen    carbon    water
dioxide

**Figure 14** Seed germination results in a new plant.

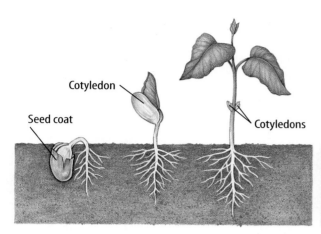

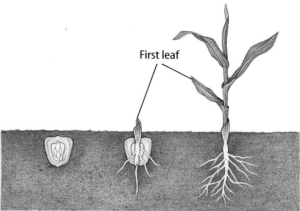

**Dormancy** What about seeds? While seeds perform a critical function in some plants' life cycles, they cannot transform light energy in the same way the parent plant can. Instead, seeds rely on stored energy reserves to survive. After a seed drops from a plant, it usually enters a resting period called **dormancy.** During dormancy, the seed's chemical activities are low. This means the seed uses stored energy reserves slowly and maintains homeostasis. Because seeds and nuts contain large reserves of food, they can survive long periods of dormancy.

**Germination** Specific environmental stimuli, including factors such as the breakdown of the seed coat, changes in soil temperature and moisture, and changes in light, trigger seed **germination.** As a seed emerges from dormancy and begins to germinate, its energy needs greatly increase. Cellular respiration increases to meet these needs. As shown in **Figure 14,** seeds emerging from dormancy respire at a much higher rate, using stored food faster to meet the increased energy demand.

## Homeostasis in Fungi, Bacteria, and Protists

Unlike plants, **fungi** do not have chlorophyll and cannot produce their own food. What is their energy supply? A fungus releases enzymes into the organic matter in its environment. These enzymes break down the material, which is then absorbed into fungal cells.

**Spore Survival** Fungi reproduction usually involves the production of **spores,** which are reproductive cells that can grow into a new fungus. Spores can survive in conditions where the parent might not. The spore cells of some fungi are surrounded by thick, tough cell walls. These cells are waterproof and can survive long periods of unfavorable conditions including freezing, lack of food, and dry conditions.

**Bacteria** Like fungi, **bacteria** are decomposers. **Decomposers** break down chemical elements inside other living or dead organisms. Some bacteria live in the intestinal tracks of animals, helping decompose food particles for digestion. Other bacteria live in soil, recycling elements including carbon, nitrogen, and sulfur as they decompose matter.

**Dormancy in Bacteria** The environmental conditions that a bacterium requires for growth differs with each species. In response to unfavorable environmental conditions, some bacteria can produce thick-walled structures called **endospores.** An endospore, like those shown in **Figure 15,** contains the DNA of the original bacterium. While in dormancy, endospores require no food and are resistant to ultraviolet radiation, drying out, and temperature extremes. Endospores can exist for hundreds of years before they begin growing again. When environmental conditions improve, endospores emerge from dormancy. Metabolism resumes, and these structures develop into bacterial cells.

**Figure 15** Bacterial endospores can survive harsh winters, dry conditions, and heat.

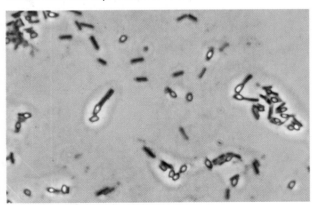

**Figure 16** Most slime molds (right) are found on decaying logs or dead leaves in moist, cool, shady environments. Green algae (left) can often be seen on the surface of ponds in the summer.

**Protists** The **protist** kingdom includes both unicellular and multicellular organisms. Protists have one or more **eukaryotic** cells, which contain a nucleus and other membrane-bound organelles. Organisms in this kingdom can be classified based on how they obtain energy.

Some protists, like the slime mold shown in **Figure 16,** are similar to fungi. They produce spores and cannot make their own food. Plantlike protists, like the green algae shown in **Figure 16,** contain chlorophyll and have the ability to make their own food using light energy.

**Figure 17** Paramecium are found in many freshwater environments. These rapidly swimming protists consume bacteria.

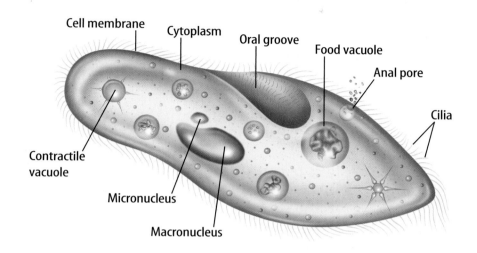

Cell membrane · Cytoplasm · Oral groove · Food vacuole · Anal pore · Cilia · Contractile vacuole · Micronucleus · Macronucleus

### Water Regulation in Protists

Surrounded by a watery environment, a protist must maintain a balance of fluid in its cells. Excess water in an organism could cause the cell to burst, resulting in death. An organelle called the **contractile vacuole** helps some protists maintain homeostasis. The contractile vacuole collects and stores extra water in the cell. When the vacuole contracts, excess water is ejected from the cell into the surrounding environment. The vacuole can then fill again. By pumping water out of the organism as needed, fluid pressure inside the organism remains balanced and homeostasis is maintained.

## Importance of Homeostasis

The survival of every organism, from the simplest protozoan to the most complex vertebrate, depends on its ability to successfully respond to changes in its environment. If an organism cannot maintain stable, balanced internal conditions, it will suffer damage or death. Organisms monitor internal and external environmental factors constantly and make specific adjustments that allow body processes to remain in equilibrium. This dynamic interaction among body systems makes homeostasis, and survival, possible.

# PERIODIC TABLE OF THE ELEMENTS

Columns of elements are called groups. Elements in the same group have similar chemical properties.

**Gas**
**Liquid**
**Solid**
**Synthetic**

Element — Hydrogen
Atomic number — 1
Symbol — H
Atomic mass — 1.008
State of matter

The first three symbols tell you the state of matter of the element at room temperature. The fourth symbol identifies elements that are not present in significant amounts on Earth. Useful amounts are made synthetically.

| 1 | 2 | 3 | 4 | 5 | 6 | 7 | 8 | 9 |
|---|---|---|---|---|---|---|---|---|
| Hydrogen 1 **H** 1.008 | | | | | | | | |
| Lithium 3 **Li** 6.941 | Beryllium 4 **Be** 9.012 | | | | | | | |
| Sodium 11 **Na** 22.990 | Magnesium 12 **Mg** 24.305 | | | | | | | |
| Potassium 19 **K** 39.098 | Calcium 20 **Ca** 40.078 | Scandium 21 **Sc** 44.956 | Titanium 22 **Ti** 47.867 | Vanadium 23 **V** 50.942 | Chromium 24 **Cr** 51.996 | Manganese 25 **Mn** 54.938 | Iron 26 **Fe** 55.845 | Cobalt 27 **Co** 58.933 |
| Rubidium 37 **Rb** 85.468 | Strontium 38 **Sr** 87.62 | Yttrium 39 **Y** 88.906 | Zirconium 40 **Zr** 91.224 | Niobium 41 **Nb** 92.906 | Molybdenum 42 **Mo** 95.94 | Technetium 43 **Tc** (98) | Ruthenium 44 **Ru** 101.07 | Rhodium 45 **Rh** 102.906 |
| Cesium 55 **Cs** 132.905 | Barium 56 **Ba** 137.327 | Lanthanum 57 **La** 138.906 | Hafnium 72 **Hf** 178.49 | Tantalum 73 **Ta** 180.948 | Tungsten 74 **W** 183.84 | Rhenium 75 **Re** 186.207 | Osmium 76 **Os** 190.23 | Iridium 77 **Ir** 192.217 |
| Francium 87 **Fr** (223) | Radium 88 **Ra** (226) | Actinium 89 **Ac** (227) | Rutherfordium 104 **Rf** (261) | Dubnium 105 **Db** (262) | Seaborgium 106 **Sg** (266) | Bohrium 107 **Bh** (264) | Hassium 108 **Hs** (277) | Meitnerium 109 **Mt** (268) |

The number in parentheses is the mass number of the longest-lived isotope for that element.

Rows of elements are called periods. Atomic number increases across a period.

The arrow shows where these elements would fit into the periodic table. They are moved to the bottom of the table to save space.

| **Lanthanide series** | Cerium 58 **Ce** 140.116 | Praseodymium 59 **Pr** 140.908 | Neodymium 60 **Nd** 144.24 | Promethium 61 **Pm** (145) | Samarium 62 **Sm** 150.36 |
|---|---|---|---|---|---|
| **Actinide series** | Thorium 90 **Th** 232.038 | Protactinium 91 **Pa** 231.036 | Uranium 92 **U** 238.029 | Neptunium 93 **Np** (237) | Plutonium 94 **Pu** (244) |